P9-DDE-806

New Perspectives on

Macromedia® Flash™ MX 2004

Comprehensive

Luis A. Lopez
St. Philip's College

THOMSON

COURSE TECHNOLOGY

Australia • Canada • Mexico • Singapore • Spain • United Kingdom • United States

THOMSON

COURSE TECHNOLOGY

New Perspectives on Macromedia® Flash™ MX 2004—Comprehensive

is published by Course Technology.

Managing Editor:
Rachel Goldberg

Senior Product Manager:
Kathy Finnegan

Senior Technology Product Manager:
Amanda Young Shelton

Product Manager:
Karen Stevens, Brianna Germain

Associate Product Manager:
Emilie Perreault

Editorial Assistant:
Shana Rosenthal

Marketing Manager:
Joy Stark

Developmental Editors:
Kim T. M. Crowley

Production Editor:
Brooke Booth

Composition:
GEX Publishing Services

Text Designer:
Steve Deschene

Cover Designer:
Nancy Goulet

Cover Artist:
Ed Carpenter
www.edcarpenter.net

COPYRIGHT © 2004 Course Technology, a division of Thomson Learning, Inc. Thomson Learning™ is a trademark used herein under license.

Printed in the United States of America

1 2 3 4 5 6 7 8 9 GLOB 08 07 06 05 04

For more information, contact Course Technology, 25 Thomson Place, Boston, Massachusetts, 02210.

Or find us on the World Wide Web at: www.course.com

ALL RIGHTS RESERVED. No part of this work covered by the copyright hereon may be reproduced or used in any form or by any means—graphic, electronic, or mechanical, including photocopying, recording, taping, Web distribution, or information storage and retrieval systems—without the written permission of the publisher.

For permission to use material from this text or product, submit a request online at www.thomsonrights.com

Any additional questions about permissions can be submitted by e-mail to thomsonrights@thomson.com

Disclaimer
Course Technology reserves the right to revise this publication and make changes from time to time in its content without notice.

Disclaimer
Any fictional URLs used throughout this book are intended for instructional purposes only. At the time this book was printed, any such URLs were fictional and not belonging to any real persons or companies.

Some of the product names and company names used in this book have been used for identification purposes only and may be trademarks or registered trademarks of their respective manufacturers and sellers.

ISBN 0-619-24346-5

Preface

Real, Thought-Provoking, Engaging, Dynamic, Interactive—these are just a few of the words that are used to describe the New Perspectives Series' approach to learning and building computer skills.

Without our critical-thinking and problem-solving methodology, computer skills could be learned but not retained. By teaching with a case-based approach, the New Perspectives Series challenges students to apply what they've learned to real-life situations.

Our ever-growing community of users understands why they're learning what they're learning. Now you can too!

See what instructors are saying about the best-selling New Perspectives Series:

"First of all, I just have to say that I wish that all of my textbooks were written in the style of the New Perspectives series. I am using these titles for all of the courses that I teach that have a book available."
— Diana Kokoska, University of Maine at Augusta

"The New Perspectives format is a pleasure to use. The Quick Checks and the tutorial Review Assignments help students view this complex topic from a real work perspective."
— Craig Shaw, Central Community College, Hastings

... and about New Perspectives on Macromedia Flash:

"The detail was excellent without being overbearing and the work is practical and useful."
— Tamara Davis, Tulsa Community College — West

www.course.com/NewPerspectives

Why *New Perspectives* will work for you

Context

Each tutorial begins with a problem presented in a "real-world" case that is meaningful to students. The case sets the scene to help students understand what they will do in the tutorial.

Hands-on Approach

Each tutorial is divided into manageable sessions that combine reading and hands-on, step-by-step work. Screenshots help guide students through the steps (see sample below). **Trouble?** tips anticipate common mistakes or problems to help students stay on track and continue with the tutorial.

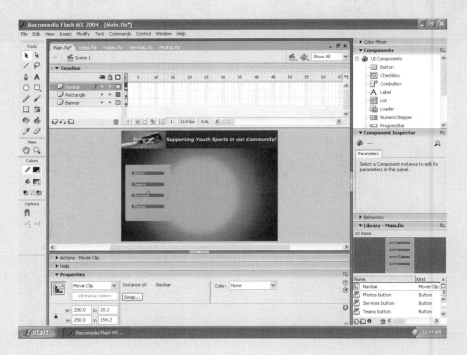

Review

In New Perspectives, retention is a key component to learning. At the end of each session, a series of Quick Check questions helps students test their understanding of the concepts before moving on.

Assessment

Engaging and challenging Review Assignments and Case Problems have always been a hallmark feature of the New Perspectives Series. Students reinforce and apply the skills they learned in the tutorial to new scenarios to demonstrate their mastery.

Reference

While contextual learning is excellent for retention, there are times when students will want a high-level understanding of how to accomplish a task. Within each tutorial, Reference Windows appear before critical sets of steps to provide a succinct summary and preview of how to perform a task. In addition, a complete Task Reference at the back of the book provides quick access to information on how to carry out common tasks.

www.course.com/NewPerspectives

New Perspectives offers an entire system of instruction

The New Perspectives Series is more than just a handful of books. It's a complete system of offerings:

New Perspectives catalog
Our online catalog is never out of date! Go to the catalog link on our Web site to check out our available titles, request a desk copy, download a book preview, or locate online files.

Coverage to meet your needs!
Whether you're looking for just a small amount of coverage or enough to fill a semester-long class, we can provide you with a textbook that meets your needs.

- Brief books typically cover the essential skills in just 2 to 4 tutorials.
- Introductory books build and expand on those skills and contain an average of 5 to 8 tutorials.
- Comprehensive books are great for a full-semester class, and contain 9 to 12+ tutorials.
- Power Users or Advanced books are perfect for a highly accelerated introductory class or a second course in a given topic.

So if the book you're holding does not provide the right amount of coverage for you, there's probably another offering available. Go to our Web site or contact your Course Technology sales representative to find out what else we offer.

Instructor Resources

We offer more than just a book. We have all the tools you need to enhance your lectures, check students' work, and generate exams in a new, easier-to-use and completely revised package. This book's Instructor's Manual, ExamView testbank, data files, solution files, figure files, and a sample syllabus are all available on a single CD-ROM or for downloading at www.course.com.

How will your students master Computer Concepts and Microsoft Office?

Add more muscle and flexibility to your course with SAM (Skills Assessment Manager)! SAM adds the power of skill-based assessment and the award-winning SAM classroom administration system to your course, putting you in control of how you deliver exams and training.

By adding SAM to your curriculum, you can:
- Reinforce your students' knowledge of key computer concepts and application skills with hands-on exercises.
- Allow your students to "learn by listening," with access to rich audio in their training.
- Build hands-on computer concepts exams from a test bank of more than 200 skill-based concepts, windows, and applications tasks.
- Schedule your students' training and testing exercises with powerful administrative tools.
- Track student exam grades and training progress using more than one dozen student and classroom reports.

Teach your introductory course with the simplicity of a single system! You can now administer your entire Computer Concepts and Microsoft Office course through the SAM platform. For more information on the SAM administration system, SAM Computer Concepts, and other SAM products, please visit www.course.com/sam.

Distance Learning

Enhance your course with any of our online learning platforms. Go to www.course.com or speak with your Course Technology sales representative to find the platform or the content that's right for you.

www.course.com/NewPerspectives

About This Book

This book offers a case-based, problem-solving approach to learning Macromedia Flash MX 2004. Students will learn how to create rich interactive experiences for the Web, from banners and interactive menus to a complete Web site, using Flash.

- Covers new features of Flash MX 2004, including new timeline effects and behaviors and the new history panel.
- New! Three new tutorials on creating a Web site using Flash, ActionScript, and incorporating video.
- Focus on planning! Each tutorial opens with a plan of the proposed animation or Web site before starting Flash. Tutorial 7 features planning for an entire Flash-based Web site.
- Includes four running Case Problems in which students use what they have learned to create rich Flash animations for realistic business Web sites.
- As the official provider of academic publications for Macromedia, Course Technology provides you the most accurate, comprehensive look at their applications.

Acknowledgments

I would like to thank all of the people at Course Technology who have made this book possible, including Rachel Goldberg, Senior Editor, for the opportunities she has given me. Thanks also to Brooke Booth, Production Editor; to Danielle Shaw, Alex White, and John Freitas, Quality Assurance Testers, for their careful testing of the tutorials; and to Jennifer Campbell for her help on this book.

Special thanks to Kim Crowley, Developmental Editor, who improved the book with her expert editorial skill and attention to detail, and to Karen Stevens, Product Manager, who kept the project on track.

And finally, this book would not have been possible without the love and support of my wife, Gloria, and our daughter, Alyssandra. This book is dedicated to them.

—Luis A. Lopez

Table of Contents

Tutorial 9   FL 415

Using Video, Flash Components, and Printing .... FL 415

New Perspectives on

MACROMEDIA FLASH MX 2004

Read **This Before You Begin**

To the Student

Data Files

To complete Tutorials 1-6 of this text you will need the starting student Data Files. Your instructor will either provide you with these Data Files or ask you to obtain them yourself. Tutorials 1-6 require the folders shown to complete the Tutorials, Review Assignments, and Case Problems. You will need to copy these folders from a file server, a standalone computer, or the Web to the drive and folder where you will be storing your Data Files. Your instructor will tell you which computer, drive letter, and folder(s) contain the files you need. You can also download the files by going to **www.course.com**; see the inside back or front cover for more information on downloading the files, or ask your instructor or technical support person for assistance.

Flash MX 2004
Tutorial.01
Tutorial.02
Tutorial.03
Tutorial.04
Tutorial.05
Tutorial.06

System Requirements

If you are going to work through this book using your own computer, you need:

■ **System Requirements** This text assumes a default installation of Macromedia Flash MX 2004 and Macromedia Flash Player 7. The screenshots in this book were taken using a computer running Windows XP Professional, and when showing a browser, Internet Explorer 6. If you are using a different operating system or a different browser, your screen might differ from the figures shown in the book.

Macromedia recommends the following Windows system configuration for Flash MX 2004: 600 MHz Intel Pentium III processor or equivalent; Windows 98 SE (4.10.2222 A), Windows 2000, or Windows XP; 128 MB RAM (256 MB recommended); and 275 MB available disk space.

■ **Data Files** You will not be able to complete the tutorials or exercises in this book using your own computer until you have the necessary starting Data Files.

To the Instructor

The Data Files are available on the Instructor Resources CD for this title. Follow the instructions in the Help file on the CD to install the programs to your network or standalone computer. See the "To the Student" section above for information on how to set up the Data Files that accompany this text.

You are granted a license to copy the Data Files to any computer or computer network used by students who have purchased this book.

In this tutorial you will:

- Discover the types of Web media you can create using Flash

- Compare vector graphics and bitmap graphics

- Start Flash and explore its main program window elements

- Display grid lines, guides, and rulers

- Set the document's properties

- Learn about strokes, fills, and colors

- Select and modify objects

- Use Flash Help

INTRODUCTION TO MACROMEDIA FLASH MX 2004

Getting Familiar with the Basic Features of Flash

CASE

Admiral Web Design

Admiral Web Design is a fast growing Web site design and development company that specializes in building Web sites for small to medium-sized businesses and organizations. Since the founding of Admiral Web Design in 2001, the company has established itself as an innovative Web design company meeting the needs of a growing list of clients from various industries, including a national sports equipment company and a local pet store. The company's rapid growth and success has largely been due to its energetic and creative employees and their dedication to the company's clients.

Admiral Web Design is co-owned by Gloria Adamson and Jim Torres, both graduates of a Web design and multimedia program at a local college. There are three other full-time employees at Admiral Web Design: Aly Garcia, Chris Johnson, and Raj Sharma. Each of the partners and employees is responsible for a different aspect of the company's operation. Gloria handles the bulk of the business decisions and also oversees the Web site design and development projects. Jim is responsible for marketing and manages the company's finances. Aly is the graphics designer, and Chris and Raj are the site designers responsible for developing the content for the clients' Web sites.

Recently, Aly has begun exploring Macromedia Flash MX, a Web-authoring tool for developing Web graphics, Web site navigation controls, animations, and even entire Web sites. With this tool the company can enhance its clients' Web sites to include more visually exciting and interactive components, such as animated logos, and online interactive advertising. Gloria and Jim are excited about Flash and they have approved hiring you to help Aly develop Flash graphics and animations.

In this tutorial you will begin your new position at Admiral Web Design by learning the basics of Flash from Aly. In the remaining tutorials in the book, you will work on projects assigned to you. These projects range from planning and creating simple nonanimated logos to creating more complex animations such as ad banners with sounds and buttons for user interaction, videos, and a small Web site.

SESSION 1.1

In this session, you will learn about Flash and the types of Web media you can create using Flash. You will preview a document with a simple animation and you will also learn about the differences between bitmap and vector graphics. This review will prepare you for your tasks at Admiral Web Design incorporating Flash graphics into Web pages.

What is Macromedia Flash MX 2004?

Macromedia Flash MX 2004 is a program developed by Macromedia, Inc. that was initially designed for creating small, fast loading animations that could be used in Web pages. Over the years, it has evolved into a full Web page production tool that allows developers to create interactive Web media ranging from animated logos to Web site navigational controls and even entire Web sites.

Before you begin working with Flash MX, you need an understanding of the different types of Web media.

Types of Web Media

Web pages are made up text, graphics, animations, sounds, and videos. These elements are referred to as **Web media**. The different types of Web media are created by a variety of programs, and then pulled together to work as a cohesive whole on a Web page through HTML, the underlying programming language used in creating Web pages. The most common types of Web media found on Web pages, besides text, are graphics and animations, both of which can be created in Flash.

Bitmap and Vector Graphics

There are essentially two types of graphics: bitmap and vector. Each has its advantages, disadvantages, and appropriate uses in Web page design.

A **bitmap graphic** is a row-by-row list of every pixel in the graphic, along with each pixel's color. A **pixel** is the smallest picture element on the monitor screen that can be controlled by the computer. A 100 × 100-pixel bitmap graphic is simply a grid containing 10,000 colored pixels. As a result, bitmap graphics cannot be resized without unattractive side effects. If you enlarge a bitmap graphic, for example, the edges become ragged as the pixels get redistributed to fit the larger grid. There is also no simple way to take a bitmap graphic apart to modify only one portion of the image. Bitmap graphics, however, provide blending and subtle variations in colors and textures. A common example of a bitmap graphic is a photograph that has been scanned or captured by a digital camera. You can also create bitmap graphics using imaging software such as Macromedia Fireworks or Adobe Photoshop. The two most common file formats for bitmap graphics used in Web pages are JPEG (Joint Photographic Experts Group) and GIF (Graphic Interchange Format). Bitmap graphic files stored in these formats have a file extension of .jpg or .gif, respectively.

A **vector graphic**, on the other hand, is a set of mathematical instructions that describe the color, outline, and position of all the shapes of the image. Each shape is defined by numbers which represent the shape's position in the window in which it is being displayed. Other numbers represent the points that establish the shape's outline. As a result, vector graphics scale well, which means you can resize a vector image proportionally and the quality remains the same. Vector graphics also appear uniform regardless of the size or resolution of the monitor on which they are displayed. Individual shapes within a vector graphic can also be modified independently of the rest. Vector graphics excel at sharp lines, smooth colors, and precise detail. Also, an advantage of vector graphic files over bitmap graphic files is that they are generally smaller. This means that vector files take less time to download than bitmap files. Common examples of vector graphics are images created in drawing programs such as Macromedia Freehand and Adobe Illustrator. Images created in Flash are in the vector format, although bitmap images may also be imported into Flash documents.

Bitmap graphics can be imported and used in Flash. Bitmap images often provide a realistic compliment when combined with vector graphics. For example, bitmap images such as photographs often appear as the background to Flash vector animation sequences. They tend to soften the overall effect, and add a little realism to Flash documents.

Figure 1-1 shows an image of a basketball in the two different formats. The one on the left is a bitmap graphic. The one on the right is a vector graphic. Notice how the enlarged version of the bitmap graphic becomes distorted while the enlarged version of the vector graphic retains its quality.

Figure 1-1	BITMAP GRAPHIC COMPARED TO VECTOR GRAPHIC

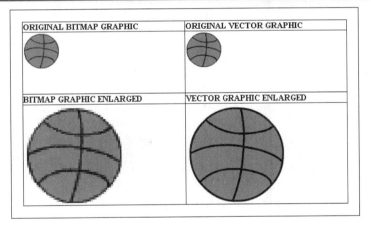

Bitmap and Vector Animation

Animation is accomplished when a series of still images is displayed in sequence giving the illusion of motion. Animation can be accomplished with both bitmap and vector images.

Bitmap animation consists of putting bitmap still images into motion for Web viewing. This can be accomplished by creating a file consisting of a sequence of bitmap frames. The playback of the frames produces a perception of smooth motion as long as the frame frequency is high enough and the changes from frame to frame are gradual enough.

Each change in what the viewer sees on the screen requires changing the colors of pixels in the frame. A significant amount of information is required to keep track of all of the pixel changes even for small images of short duration. The amount of information that must be stored increases dramatically for larger frame sizes, longer sequences, or smoother motion. Because of the importance for rapid transmission over the Internet, bitmap motion graphics are usually limited to small frame sizes and short sequences.

Vector animation consists of a listing of shapes and their transformations. These too are played back in sequence to provide the perception of motion. The amount of information required to describe the modification of shapes in a vector animation is usually less than the amount of information required to describe the pixel changes in a bitmap animation. Also, because vector graphics are resolution independent, meaning that they always appear with the optimum on-screen quality regardless of image size or the screen resolution, increasing the display size of the shapes in a vector animation has no effect on the file size.

Web Media in Flash

Flash allows developers to create media-rich elements that integrate with Web pages and that download quickly. Flash graphics also have streaming capability, which allows animations to start playing even before they download completely. Web media created in Flash are called **documents** and include static images as well as animations. Flash animations are created when you create a series of graphic objects and then sequence them. The graphics that are created in Flash are primarily vector graphics but may also include bitmap graphics. The Flash program also supports a wide variety of import formats so that developers can include media from a broad range of sources without having to convert them to vector graphics first.

A completed Flash document can include anything from silent still imagery to motion graphics with sound and interactivity. Flash enables you to add sound—as sound effects, voiceovers, or music—to any element within your document. You can choose to have sound play all the time, be activated by a mouse click, be turned on and off by the user, or be synchronized with events in your document. You can also set up multiple sounds to play simultaneously if your Flash document requires that. Like any other media file, a Flash file must be referenced in an HTML file in order to be viewed in a Web page. As a Flash developer, you can publish the HTML files and references automatically from within the Flash program. Alternately, although the syntax is a bit more involved than for a simple graphic image, if you are experienced with HTML, you can insert the reference manually, or create your own HTML file to reference and control the Flash file.

While developing content using Flash, you work with a Flash authoring document, referred to as a **FLA** file. That is, Flash documents have a file extension appended to their filename of .fla. When you're ready to deliver that content for viewing by end users, you publish the Flash document as a **SWF** file which has an extension of .swf (small Web file). For example, if your first assignment as Aly's assistant is to create an animation to be used on Admiral Web Design's own Web site, the document you create and develop in Flash might have the name AWDanim.fla. Once you finish the animation and publish it for the Admiral Web Design home page, the filename for the published file would be AWDanim.swf.

The SWF file plays in an HTML file in a Web browser using the **Flash Player plug-in**. The plug-in is free and can be found at *www.macromedia.com/downloads*. All current versions of the major Web browsers come with the Flash Player plug-in already installed. Besides allowing Flash documents to be viewed in your browser, the Flash Player plug-in provides controls for zooming in and out, rewinding, playing individual frames, and other functions. The controls can be accessed by right-clicking the animation to display a **context menu** as shown in Figure 1-2.

| Figure 1-2 | FLASH PLAYER PLUG-IN CONTEXT MENU |

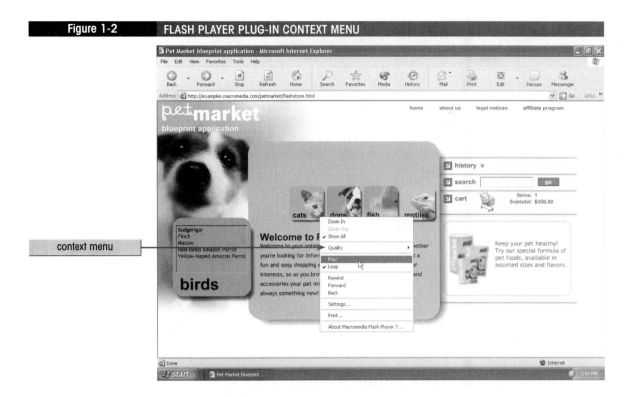

context menu

Finally, another element of Flash is **ActionScript**, a scripting programming language that allows you to add interactivity to buttons and other Web media that a user can click or select to control the Flash graphics or animation they are viewing. You will learn more about ActionScript in a later tutorial.

Viewing Examples of Flash Documents

In order to get a feeling for what you can create with Flash, Aly wants you to look at several examples of Flash documents she has created. She asks you to look at these examples located on the Admiral Web Design Web site.

Opening a Flash Web page is no different than opening any other page in your browser. If you have the Flash Player plug-in installed, the streaming capability of a Flash file allows the player to begin playing the animation as soon as enough of the file has been downloaded.

To view examples of Flash documents in your browser:

1. Make sure that your computer is turned on, and the Windows XP desktop is displayed.

2. Start your Web browser, and then open the **awdflash.htm** file stored in the **Tutorial.01\Tutorial** folder included with your Data Files. The Admiral Web Design sample page displays in the browser window. This page contains several examples of Flash graphics that are available for Actions' clients to review.

3. Right-click one of the animations on the screen. The context menu containing controls for the Flash file opens. See Figure 1-3.

   TROUBLE? If the context menu does not appear as shown in Figure 1-3, right-click a different graphic on the screen.

Figure 1-3   SAMPLE FLASH GRAPHICS

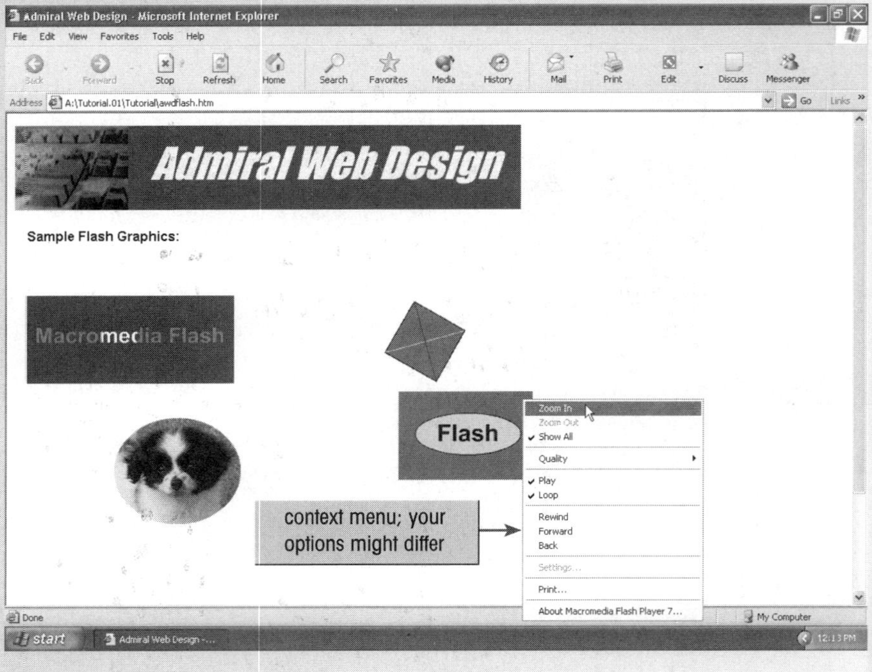

4. Click **Play** on the context menu to remove the check mark from this command and deselect it. The animation stops. Open the context menu again, and click **Zoom In** to increase the graphic's magnification level. Continue to use the context menu controls to rewind, zoom out, and step forward and back through the animation.

5. When you are done reviewing the sample Flash documents, click the **Close** button ⊠ on the browser's title bar to close the browser window.

Now that you have viewed some Flash documents, you are ready to start Flash.

Starting Flash

You start Flash by clicking the Start button on the Windows taskbar, and accessing the Macromedia submenu from the All Programs menu. If the Flash program icon appears on the desktop you can also double-click it to start the program.

When you first start Flash, or when the program is running but no documents are opened, the Start page displays. The Start page provides access to the most commonly used actions such as opening a recently used file, creating a new Flash document, or taking a quick tour of Flash. Once you open a document or create a new one, the Flash program window will consist of several components. The program allows you to organize its various elements to suit your work style and needs. Aly suggests you start the Flash program and set the program window to its default layout so she can help you identify the main program window components you need to become familiar with before you can begin creating Flash documents.

To start Flash and set the program window to its default layout:

1. Click the **Start** button on the taskbar, and then point to **All Programs** to display all the programs installed on your computer.

2. Point to **Macromedia** and then click **Macromedia Flash MX 2004**. The Flash program window opens and displays the Start page.

   TROUBLE? If this is the first time you have started Flash, the Flash Serialization dialog box may open. Enter your name and the serial number provided to you when you purchased Flash, then click the OK button. If you do not know your serial number, ask your instructor for assistance.

   TROUBLE? If a dialog box opens indicating new help content is available, click the No button to choose not to download it at this time.

3. Click **Flash Document** under the Create New section of the Start page, and then, if necessary, click the **Maximize** button 🔲 on the title bar to maximize the Flash program window.

   TROUBLE? If the Start page does not display, click File on the menu bar, click New, and then click Flash Document in the Type list box on the General tab of the New Document dialog box.

   The Flash window is customizable, which means you can easily change the way different elements are arranged in the program window. To ensure your screens match those shown in these steps, you can change the layout of the Flash program window to its default layout.

4. Click **Window** on the menu bar, point to **Panel Sets**, and then click **Default Layout**.

5. Click **Window** on the menu bar, and then point to **Toolbars**. Make sure that the options **Main** and **Controller** do not have check marks next to them. If one of these menu options has a check mark, then click it to deselect it. Make sure that the option **Edit Bar** is selected.

   The Flash program window arranges its various panels to look like that shown in Figure 1-4.

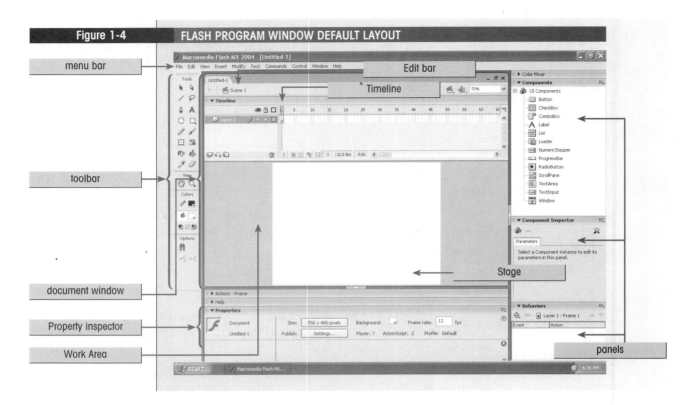

Figure 1-5 briefly describes each of the main components of the Flash program window.

Figure 1-5	MAIN COMPONENTS OF THE FLASH PROGRAM WINDOW
FLASH COMPONENT	**DESCRIPTION**
Menu bar	Lists the menu options such as File, Edit, View, Insert, and Help; these menu options include commands to access most of the features of the Flash program
Edit bar	Displays the current scene number, the Edit Scene button, the Edit Symbol button, and the Zoom control
Toolbar	Contains the Flash tools; the toolbar includes tools for drawing and painting lines and shapes, selecting objects, changing the view of the Stage, and choosing colors
Stage	Located in the document window, the area where you assemble and position all of the objects that are part of a Flash document
Work Area	Located in the document window and used to place objects that are not part of the viewable Stage; also used to position objects that move onto or off the Stage as part of an animation
Timeline	Located in the document window; displays and controls the layers and frames that make up an animation and organizes the objects that are part of the document
Panels	Contain controls for viewing and changing the properties of objects
Property inspector	Provides easy access to the most common attributes of the currently selected tool or object

Later in this session we will discuss in greater detail the five elements of the Flash window you will use most frequently; the Stage, Work Area, Timeline, toolbar, and panels. Next, Aly wants you to preview a simple document she has created.

Previewing Documents

As you are developing a Flash document, you often need to preview it to check the results of your changes. There are several ways to preview your work in Flash. You can preview or play the document's animation within the Flash program window, publish the file to play in a separate Flash Player window, or publish it to play in a Web page in your default Web browser.

Previewing the document in the Flash program window is the quickest method, although some animation effects and interactive functions only work in the published format. You will view Aly's document from the Flash program window. The SimpleKite.fla file is a Flash document consisting of a simple animation and is stored with your Data Files.

To preview the sample document in the Flash program window:

1. Click **File** on the menu bar, and then click **Open**. The Open dialog box is displayed.

2. Navigate to the location where your Data Files are stored, open the **Tutorial.01\Tutorial** folder, click **SimpleKite** in the file list, and then click the **Open** button. The SimpleKite document opens on the Stage.

   Trouble? If the SimpleKite file includes the FLA extension in its filename, your computer's operating system is configured to display file extensions. If this is the case, just click the file named SimpleKite.fla in the file list.

3. To see the entire document, click **View** on the menu bar, point to **Magnification**, and then click **Show All**. The Flash program window changes to look like that shown in Figure 1-6.

Figure 1-6	SIMPLEKITE DOCUMENT

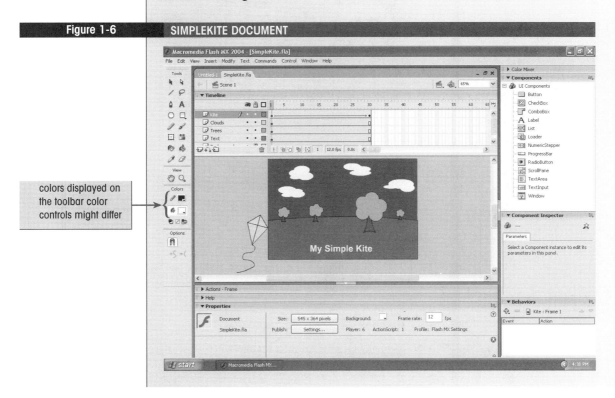

colors displayed on the toolbar color controls might differ

4. Click **Control** on the menu bar, and then click **Play**. As the animation plays, notice that the Timeline tracks the animation's progress. You will learn more about the elements in the Timeline later in this session.

You can also preview the published file in a separate Flash Player window or in a browser window.

To preview the published file in a separate Flash Player window and then in a browser:

1. Click **Control** on the menu bar, and then click **Test Movie**. Flash creates a file in the SWF format, opens it in a separate window, and then plays it with the Flash Player as shown in Figure 1-7.

Figure 1-7	SIMPLEKITE DOCUMENT PLAYING IN FLASH PLAYER WINDOW

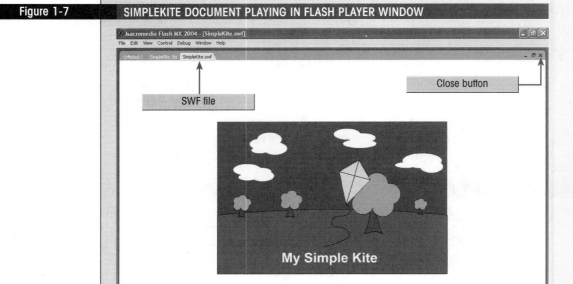

2. Click the **Close** button ⊠ on the Flash Player's window to close it and to return to the Flash document.

TROUBLE? If you accidentally click the Close button on the Flash program window, you will exit Flash. If that is the case, restart Flash and open the SimpleKite document again.

Now you will preview the Flash file in a Web page.

3. Click **File** on the menu bar, point to **Publish Preview**, and then click **HTML**. The default browser on your computer opens and the SWF file plays in a Web page. See Figure 1-8.

Figure 1-8 SIMPLEKITE.SWF FILE PLAYING IN A WEB BROWSER

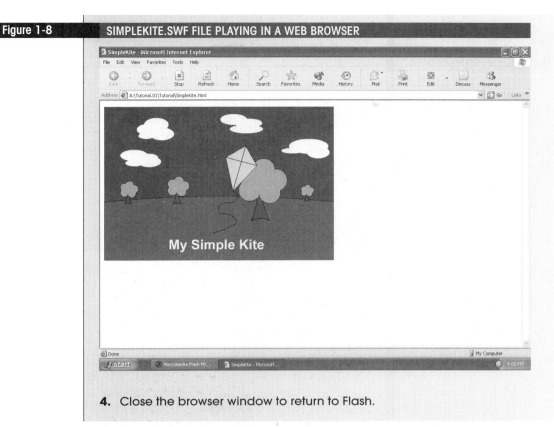

4. Close the browser window to return to Flash.

You have completed the first part of your training by learning about Web media, and by viewing some sample Flash documents. In the next session, you will learn about the main elements of the Flash program window and how to change a document's settings.

Session 1.1 QUICK CHECK

1. Flash creates _____-based images.

2. What file extension will a Flash document have after it has been published for Internet delivery?

3. List three things you might find in a Flash document.

4. Flash allows you to synchronize sound with events in your document. True or False?

5. Bitmap graphics store information as a grid of _____.

6. How does a vector graphic store image data?

7. Does the term "resolution-independent" apply to bitmap graphics, vector graphics, or both?

8. What are two common results of enlarging a bitmap image?

SESSION 1.2

In this session, you will become familiar with the Flash program window components, the tools found on the toolbar, and the panels. You will learn how to customize the panels, how to change the Stage settings and how to change the document properties.

Flash Program Window Elements

The main elements of the Flash window are the Stage, Work Area, Timeline, toolbar, and panels. The Stage, the Work Area, and the Timeline make up the document window.

Stage

The **Stage** is where you create, import, and assemble all of the graphic objects for your document. The Stage is the central area of the document window and is within the Work Area. Any graphic object that is to be displayed in the final document must be on the Stage, whether it is a static object or one that is animated.

It is important, however, to understand that the Stage only shows the objects that are visible at a particular point in an animation. In fact, the Stage in Flash is just like the stage in a dramatic production. As the production progresses, actors appear and disappear, and move around from place to place on the Stage.

Because Flash may be used to create animations, you would expect different objects to be visible at different times during playback. While you are working on a project, therefore, the Stage only displays those objects that are associated with the currently selected frame. Flash documents are divided into frames and each frame may contain different images or different states of the same image. If you select a different frame, different objects may appear or disappear, or objects may be in different positions or be changed in appearance.

Work Area

Surrounding the Stage is a gray area called the **Work Area**. When you complete a Flash document and publish it to view it on a Web page, only the objects and portions of objects that are within the Stage will appear. Objects and portions of objects in the Work Area will not be shown. The Work Area is a convenient place to store elements until you are ready to add them to the Stage, or for storing notes and other information you want to refer to as you develop the document. You can also place a graphic in the Work Area and then animate it to move onto the stage.

Timeline

The **Timeline**, shown in Figure 1-9, is used to control and coordinate the frames and layers that make up a Flash document. **Layers** are used to organize the images, animations, and other objects that are part of a document. A **frame** represents a unit of time. Another key element of the Timeline is the **playhead**. The playhead is a marker that indicates which frame is currently selected on the Timeline. You will learn more about these and many of the other Timeline elements in later tutorials.

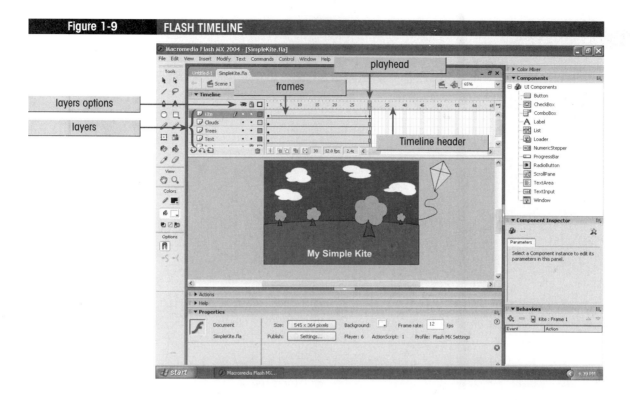

Figure 1-9 **FLASH TIMELINE**

Flash documents are divided into frames similar to a motion picture film. The Timeline is used to coordinate and control the timing of the animation by determining how and when these frames are displayed. Each frame may contain different images or different states of the same image. As the document's animation is played over time, the playhead moves from frame to frame and the contents of each frame are displayed in succession, thus achieving the perception of motion. You can also play the animation manually by dragging the playhead back and forth through the frames with your mouse. This is called **scrubbing** and is useful when testing the animation during development. When you first start a new document in Flash it contains one frame. You add more frames as you build your animation.

In addition to frames, layers are also controlled using the Timeline. The layers are listed in a column on the left side of the Timeline. Each row within the column represents one layer. The frames for that layer are shown to the right of the layer. A new Flash document starts with one layer. As you add more layers, additional rows representing the layers are inserted into the Timeline. You can then place different objects on the different layers. When you draw on a layer or change something on a layer, the objects on the other layers are not affected. Only the contents of the active layer are changed.

To explore the frames, layers, and playhead in the Timeline:

1. If you took a break after the last session, open the **SimpleKite** document stored in the **Tutorial.01\Tutorial** folder included with your Data Files, set the magnification of the Stage to Show All, and set the panels to the default layout.

2. Scrub the playhead back and forth by clicking and dragging it with your pointer to see how the animation on the Stage changes based on the contents of the different frames. The animation changes as you scrub the playhead.

3. Click **Frame 15** in the Timeline header to make it the current frame as shown in Figure 1-10. The Stage displays the contents of Frame 15.

Figure 1-10   SELECTING A FRAME IN THE TIMELINE HEADER

Frame 15 in the
Timeline header

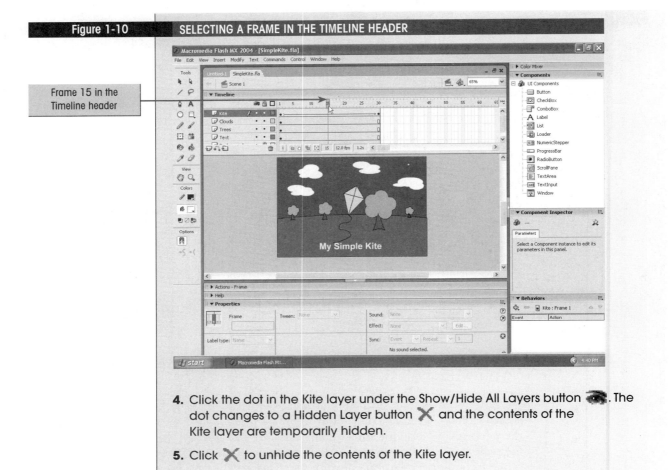

4. Click the dot in the Kite layer under the Show/Hide All Layers button ![icon]. The dot changes to a Hidden Layer button ✕ and the contents of the Kite layer are temporarily hidden.

5. Click ✕ to unhide the contents of the Kite layer.

Now learn about the toolbar.

The Toolbar

The **toolbar** located on the left side of the Flash program window contains the tools that let you draw, paint, select, and modify Flash graphics. The toolbar, as shown in Figure 1-11, is divided into four areas. These areas are tools, view, colors, and options.

Figure 1-11	TOOLBAR TOOLS

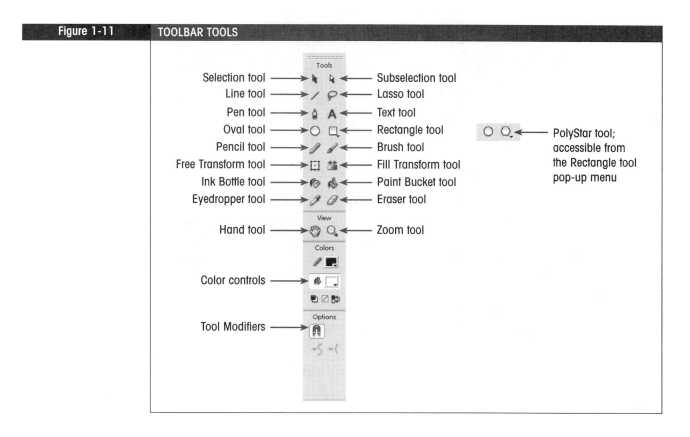

Each of the tools in these areas may be selected by clicking the tool's icon or by pressing the tool's keyboard shortcut. Note that the PolyStar tool is accessed by the Rectangle tool on the toolbar. To select it, click and hold the mouse pointer on the Rectangle tool. Then click the PolyStar tool on the pop-up menu. To get back to the Rectangle tool, click and hold the PolyStar tool and then click the Rectangle tool on the pop-up menu. Both of these tools have the same keyboard shortcut. The function of each of the tools and its corresponding icon and shortcut are described in Figure 1-12.

Figure 1-12	TOOLBAR TOOLS AND THEIR FUNCTIONS		
TOOL NAME	**BUTTON**	**SHORTCUT KEY**	**FUNCTION**
Selection		V	Selects objects in the document window; an object must be selected before it can be modified
Subselection		A	Modifies specific anchor points in a line or curve
Line		N	Draws straight lines (strokes) of varying lengths, widths, and colors
Lasso		L	Selects objects or a group of objects
Pen		P	Draws lines or curves by creating anchor points that connect them; clicking will draw points for straight lines; clicking and dragging will draw points for smooth, curved lines
Text		T	Creates and edits text
Oval		O	Draws ovals of different sizes and colors
Rectangle		R	Draws rectangles of different sizes and colors

Figure 1-12	TOOLBAR TOOLS AND THEIR FUNCTIONS, CONTINUED		
TOOL NAME	**BUTTON**	**SHORTCUT KEY**	**FUNCTION**
PolyStar		R	Accessible from the Rectangle tool pop-up menu; draws polygons and stars of different sizes, colors, and number of sides
Pencil		Y	Draws lines and shapes in a free-form mode
Brush		B	Paints fills with brush strokes
Free Transform		Q	Use to move, scale, rotate, skew, or distort objects
Fill Transform		F	Use to transform a gradient or bitmap fill by adjusting its size, direction, or center point
Ink Bottle		S	Applies color, thickness, and styles to lines
Paint Bucket		K	Fills enclosed areas of a drawing with color
Eyedropper		I	Picks up styles of existing lines, fills, and text and applies them to other objects
Eraser		E	Erases lines and fills
Hand		H	Moves the view of the Stage and Work Area
Zoom		M, Z	Increases or reduces the view of the Stage and Work Area

The first area of the toolbar, **tools**, contains tools that are used to create and modify the lines, shapes, and text that make up the graphic images of a Flash document. For example, you can draw ovals and rectangles, you can draw lines and curves, and you can fill in shapes with color. These tools also allow you to select specific parts of the graphic and then resize, rotate, and distort them to create new shapes.

The **view area** includes the **Hand tool** and the **Zoom tool**. The Hand tool converts the pointer to a hand that can then be dragged to move the view of the Stage. This is especially useful when you want to see a different area of a document that has been magnified. The Zoom tool changes the view of the Stage by reducing or enlarging it. Neither of these tools affects the way the Flash graphic is displayed to the user.

The **colors area**, as shown in Figure 1-13, includes options to specify the colors for strokes and fills. **Strokes** refer to the lines that make up a Flash graphic and **fills** refer to the areas enclosed by the lines. (You will learn more about strokes and fills in the next session.)

Figure 1-13	COLORS AREA OF TOOLBAR

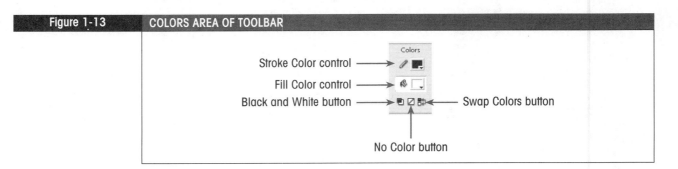

The Stroke Color control is used to set the stroke color. The Fill Color control is used to set the fill color. With either color control you select a color by clicking its color button and then selecting a color from the Color pop-up window. The bottom of this area has three additional icons. The Black and White button is used to change the stroke and fill colors to their default of black and white. The No Color button specifies that no color be used. This may be applied to either the stroke or the fill color. The Swap Colors button swaps the current stroke and fill colors.

The last area of the toolbar is the **options area**. This area displays tool modifiers that change the way a specific tool functions. The modifiers in this area change to reflect the tool that is currently selected. For example, when the Zoom tool is selected, the Enlarge and Reduce buttons are displayed in the options area.

As you create documents in Flash, the tools you use most often will be those found on the toolbar. Always look carefully at which tool is currently selected before you click an object on the Stage. You can tell which tool is selected by seeing that its button is depressed on the toolbar. The mouse pointer also changes to reflect the function of the tool that is currently selected. For example, when the Zoom tool is selected, the pointer appears as a magnifying glass.

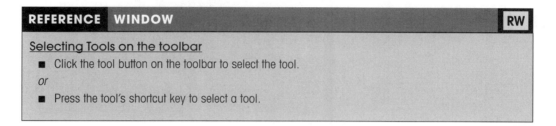

REFERENCE WINDOW   **RW**

Selecting Tools on the toolbar
- Click the tool button on the toolbar to select the tool.

or
- Press the tool's shortcut key to select a tool.

Aly wants you to try using some of the tools on the toolbar to modify the SimpleKite document.

To use tools on the toolbar:

1. Click **Control** on the menu bar, and then click **Rewind** to make Frame 1 of the document the current frame.

2. If necessary, click **View** on the menu bar, point to **Magnification**, and then click **Show All** from the Magnification submenu to display all the document's elements.

3. Click the **Selection** tool ⬚ on the toolbar. Click the **kite** in the Work Area to the left of the Stage to select it. Notice that a light-blue line surrounds the kite to indicate that it has been selected as shown in Figure 1-14. This is called a **selection box** or **selection marquee**. You will learn more about selecting objects and the selection marquee in the next session.

   TROUBLE? If you accidentally double-clicked the kite, the rest of the document will fade and you will be in a different editing mode. Click Scene 1 on the Edit bar and repeat Step 3.

Figure 1-14   KITE SELECTED

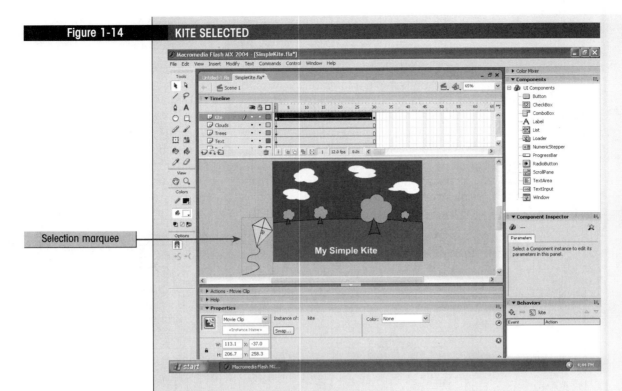

Selection marquee

4. Click and drag the **kite** up towards the top part of the Work Area just to the left of the Stage. This will be the new starting point for the kite animation.

   Now preview the animation to see how moving the kite has changed its path.

5. Click **Control** on the menu bar, and then click **Play**. Notice that the animation has changed based on the different starting point of the kite.

Aly points out that there are many kinds of objects you can create in Flash, and each object has different properties that you can control. Flash puts most of the controls you need into panels that you can keep handy as you work.

Panels

Flash panels contain controls for viewing and changing the properties of objects. There are also panels for aligning objects, transforming objects, and mixing and selecting colors. To display a list of all of the available panels, you can click Window on the menu bar and then point to one of the three panel groups, Design Panels, Development Panels, or Other Panels. Those panels that appear with a check mark next to them are currently displayed in the Flash program window. Panels can be organized according to your needs. You can close panels you do not use often; you can reposition panels according to how you work; if desired, you can also group several panels together to make a **panel set**. Once you customize how you want the panels arranged, you can save the layout. Then next time you start Flash you can select your saved panel layout to arrange the panels according to your customized arrangement. See Figure 1-15.

Figure 1-15   **PANELS IN THEIR DEFAULT LAYOUT**

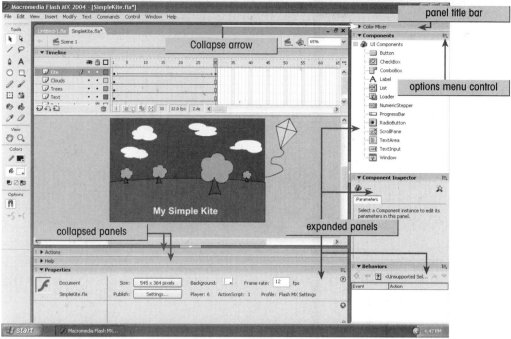

Organizing Panels

Each panel has a title bar with the name of the panel. Most panels also have an options menu that is accessible by clicking the options menu control located on the right side of the title bar. A panel can also be collapsed by clicking the Collapse arrow next to the panel's name in the title bar. When you collapse a panel, only the title bar is visible. When you click the Collapse arrow again, the panel expands. To move a panel, you position the mouse pointer on the left edge of the panel's title bar until the pointer changes to ✛ , and then drag the title bar to the new location. To group panels into a set, you drag one panel into another or into an existing group.

To collapse, expand, group, and reposition a panel:

1. If necessary, click **Window** on the menu bar, point to **Panel Sets**, and then click **Default Layout**. The Color Mixer's title bar displays in the upper-right corner of the program window.

2. To expand the Color Mixer panel, click the **Collapse** arrow ▶. The Color Mixer panel expands as shown in Figure 1-16.

Figure 1-16	COLOR MIXER PANEL

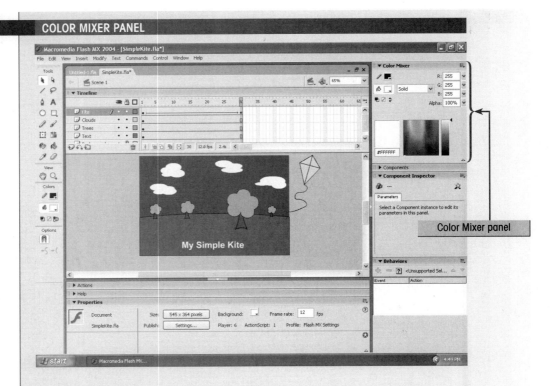

Color Mixer panel

3. Click **Window** on the menu bar, point to **Design Panels**, and click **Color Swatches**. The Color Swatches panel opens in its own window.

   You can also group two or more panels together to make a panel set.

4. Position the pointer on the left border of the Color Mixer title bar until the pointer changes to ⊕. Click and drag the panel to place it inside the window containing the Color Swatches panel. The Color Swatches panel and the Color Mixer panel are now grouped together as shown in Figure 1-17.

Figure 1-17   GROUPED PANELS

5. To move the panels back to their default layout, click **Window** on the menu
bar, point to **Panel Sets**, and then click **Default Layout**. The Color Mixer panel
is again in the upper-right corner of the program window, and the Color
Swatches panel is no longer displayed.

Many of the most frequently used options are located in a special panel called the
Property inspector. You will work with that panel next.

The Property Inspector

The **Property inspector** is a panel located at the bottom of the Flash program window. It
provides easy access to the most common attributes of the currently selected tool or object.
The contents of the Property inspector change to reflect the tool that is selected. For example, if you select the Selection tool, the Property inspector displays information about the
document such as the background color or the frame rate, as shown in Figure 1-18.

Figure 1-18	PROPERTY INSPECTOR WITH THE SELECTION TOOL SELECTED

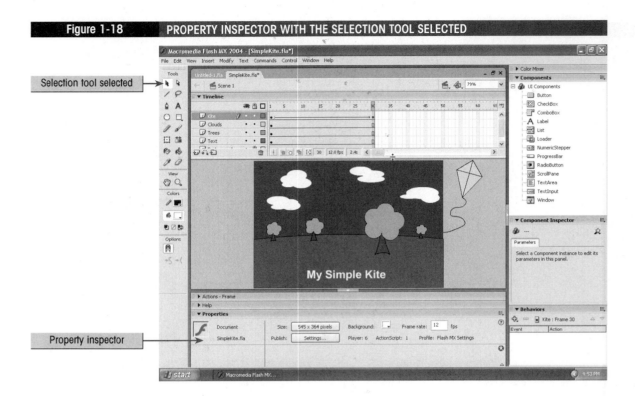

If you select an object on the Stage such as the kite, the contents of the Property inspector will change as shown in Figure 1-19.

Figure 1-19	PROPERTY INSPECTOR WITH AN OBJECT SELECTED

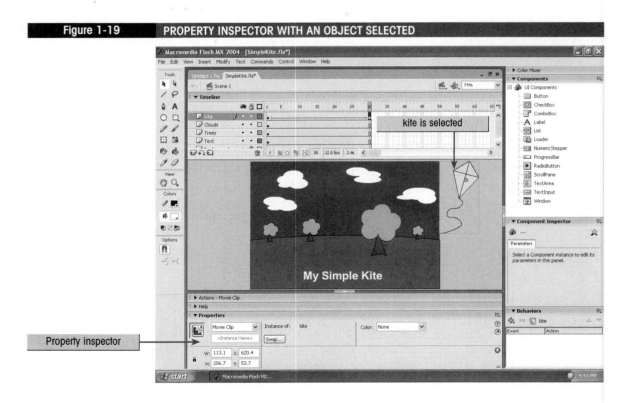

In this case the Property inspector displays properties specific to the object, such as the name of the object, its X and Y coordinates (location on the Stage), and its width and height. You can change these properties within the Property inspector.

To use the Property inspector:

1. Click **Control** on the menu bar, and then click **Rewind** to make Frame 1 the current frame.

2. If necessary, click **View** on the menu bar, point to **Magnification**, and then click **Show All**.

3. If the Properties inspector panel is not visible, click **Window** on the menu bar, and then click **Properties**.

4. Click the **Selection** tool [ ] on the toolbar, and then click the **kite** to select it.

   To change the kite's position, you will change its X and Y coordinates. These values represent the horizontal (X) and vertical (Y) position of the kite relative to the upper-left corner of the Stage.

5. Double-click the value in the **X:** text box in the Property inspector, type **100**, and then press the **Enter** key. The position of the kite changes horizontally. See Figure 1-20. Note that your kite's vertical position may be different from that shown in Figure 1-20.

Figure 1-20	KITE IN NEW POSITION

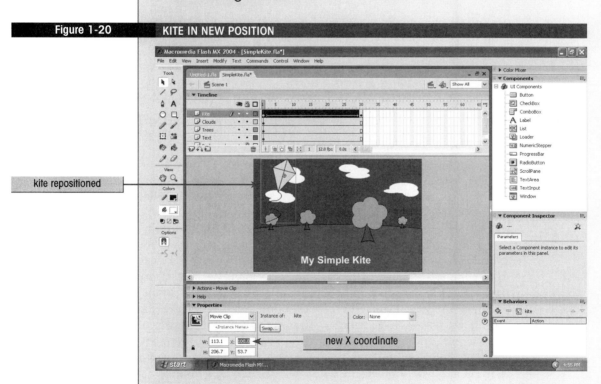

kite repositioned

new X coordinate

6. Double-click the value displayed in the **Y:** text box, type **100**, and then press the **Enter** key. The kite changes position vertically.

   You can also change the kite's dimensions by changing the width (W) value and the height (H) value.

7. Change the value in the **W:** text box to **100** in the Property inspector. The kite gets skinnier.

8. Change the value in the **H:** text box to **100**. The kite now appears shorter.

Now you will play the document's animation to see the effect of the changes you made to the properties of the kite.

9. Click **Control** on the menu bar, and then click **Play**.

The kite starts in its new position and moves to its end position as before. Notice that the kite gradually changes back to its original dimensions. Because you only changed the dimensions of the kite in Frame 1, Flash automatically adjusted the rest of the frames to change the kite to its original dimensions in the last frame. This feature of Flash will be covered in Tutorial 3.

You will no longer use the SimpleKite file so you should close it. Do not save any changes you made.

10. Click **File** on the menu bar, and then click **Close**. Also, close the blank document, Untitled-1.fla. The files close and the Start page displays.

Changing the View of the Stage

As you develop graphics on the Stage, you at times need to change your view of the Stage by adjusting the magnification level. You do this by using the Zoom tool on the toolbar. When you select the Zoom tool, the **Enlarge** and **Reduce** modifiers display in the options area of the toolbar. The Enlarge modifier is selected by default. If you want to use the Zoom tool to reduce the magnification level of the Stage, then click the Reduce modifier. Once you select the Zoom tool, you click the part of the Stage that you want to enlarge or reduce. You can also click and drag the pointer over a certain area of the Stage to draw a rectangular selection marquee around it. This selects the area to enlarge. The concept of selecting objects in Flash is covered in more detail later in this session.

In addition to the Zoom tool, you can also use the **Zoom In** or **Zoom Out** commands on the View menu. The Zoom In and Zoom Out commands change the view of the Stage accordingly. Another command on the View menu is the Magnification command, which has a submenu of percentage levels that can be applied to the view of the Stage, and the commands Show All, and Show Frame. Selecting the **Show All** command changes the view of the Stage to display all of its current contents including objects in the Work Area. Selecting the **Show Frame** command changes the magnification level so that the entire Stage is visible. The commands found on the Magnification submenu are also available from the Zoom control located in the upper-right corner of the Stage window on the Edit bar.

Once you have magnified the view of the Stage, some graphic objects may no longer be visible within the Stage window. To move the view of the Stage without having to change the magnification level you can use the Hand tool. You select the Hand tool from the toolbar and then click and drag the pointer on the Stage to move it so that the graphic objects you need to work on become visible within the Stage window.

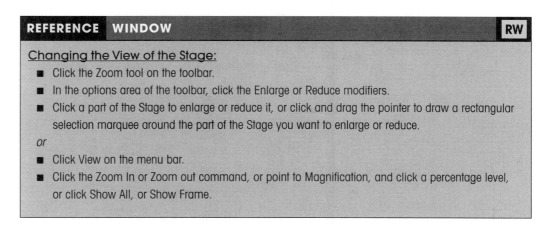

Aly suggests you familiarize yourself with the various ways to change the view of the Stage. You will use a document of Aly's that contains sample objects she has drawn in Flash.

To open the Sample document and change the view of the Stage:

1. Click **File** on the menu bar, and then click **Open**. In the Open dialog box, navigate to the location where your Data Files are stored, open the **Tutorial.01\Tutorial** folder, click **Sample** in the file list, and then click the **Open** button to open the file in the program window.

2. To position the panels to their default layout, click **Window** on the menu bar, point to **Panel Sets**, and then click **Default Layout**. The panels are repositioned to their default positions. See Figure 1-21.

Figure 1-21	SAMPLE FILE IN FLASH

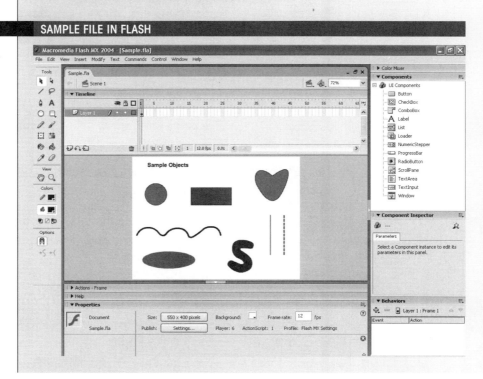

You should collapse the Timeline panel because you will not be using it in this tutorial, and collapsing it will provide more room for your work on the Stage.

3. Click the **Timeline's** title bar to collapse the panel. Now change the view of the Stage.

4. Click the **Zoom control** list arrow on the Edit bar, and then click **50%**. The view of the document on the Stage changes.

Next use the Zoom tool to zoom in on the heart graphic.

5. Click the **Zoom** tool in the view area of the toolbar, and then click the **Enlarge** modifier in the options area of the toolbar. The pointer changes to ⊕.

6. Click the middle of the **heart-shaped object** on the Stage, and then click the **heart** one more time. The magnification level of the view increases each time you click the heart. The heart also appears in the center of the Stage window each time you click it. See Figure 1-22.

| Figure 1-22 | ZOOMING IN ON HEART SHAPE |

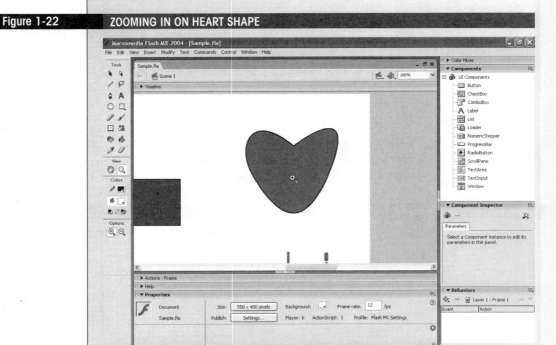

You can also use the Hand tool to adjust the view of the Stage. This tool is useful when you want to focus on a particular portion of the Stage without changing the magnification level. Try that next.

To use the Hand tool to view a different portion of the Stage:

1. Click the **Hand** tool in the view area of the toolbar. The pointer changes to a hand as you move it over the **Stage**.

2. Using the , click and drag the **Stage** to the right until you see the red circle in the middle of the Stage as shown in Figure 1-23.

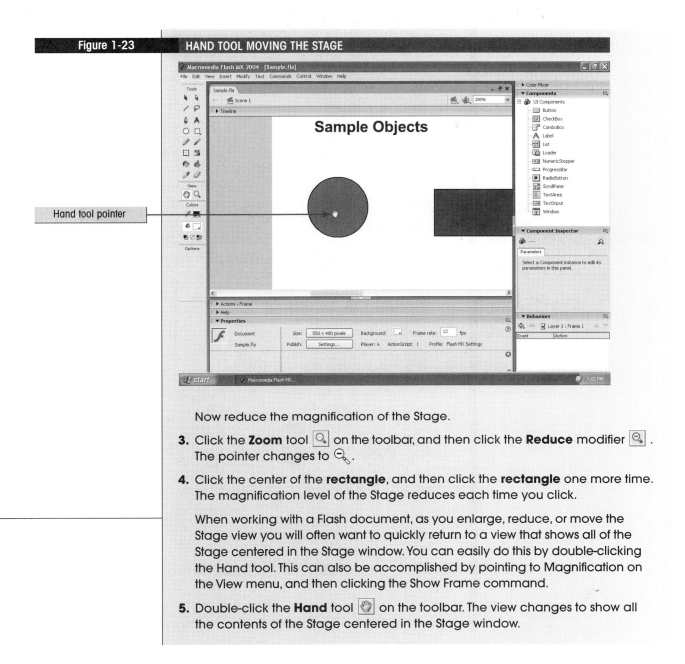

Figure 1-23   HAND TOOL MOVING THE STAGE

Hand tool pointer

Now reduce the magnification of the Stage.

3. Click the **Zoom** tool on the toolbar, and then click the **Reduce** modifier . The pointer changes to .

4. Click the center of the **rectangle**, and then click the **rectangle** one more time. The magnification level of the Stage reduces each time you click.

   When working with a Flash document, as you enlarge, reduce, or move the Stage view you will often want to quickly return to a view that shows all of the Stage centered in the Stage window. You can easily do this by double-clicking the Hand tool. This can also be accomplished by pointing to Magnification on the View menu, and then clicking the Show Frame command.

5. Double-click the **Hand** tool on the toolbar. The view changes to show all the contents of the Stage centered in the Stage window.

The Stage also includes some features designed to aid you as you create your documents. These features are the grid, rulers, and guides.

Displaying the Grid, Rulers, and Guides

When working with Flash you can lay out objects on the Stage more precisely if you display the Grid. The **Grid** appears as a set of lines on the Stage behind all of the objects you place or draw on the Stage. The grid lines do not become part of your document. They are only visible while you are developing your document. The Grid menu offers several commands for controlling the grid, and is located on the View menu. For example, to display the grid on the Stage, you use the Show Grid command. The Grid menu also includes the Edit Grid command which opens the Edit Grid dialog box in which you can change the color of the grid lines and change the spacing between the lines. You can also select the Snap to Grid option if you want objects to snap to the grid lines as you move or draw them on the Stage. This can help you align different objects vertically or horizontally. Changes you make to the grid are saved with the currently active document.

Aly suggests that you practice with the Sample document and explore how to change its settings. You will first display the grid.

To display and edit the grid:

1. Click **View** on the menu bar, point to **Grid**, and then click the **Show Grid** command to place a check mark next to it. The grid lines are displayed on the Stage. See Figure 1-24.

Figure 1-24 | **GRID DISPLAYED ON THE STAGE**

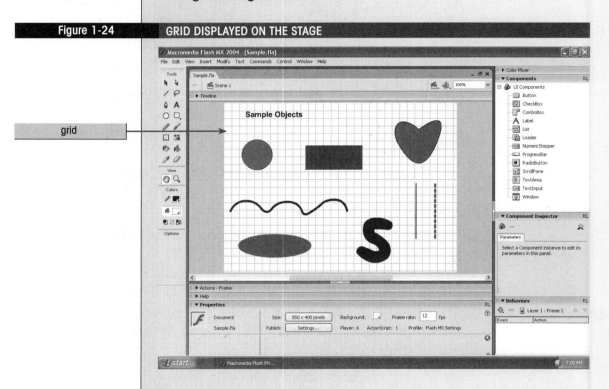

You can modify how the grid is displayed on the Stage to better suit your needs and work habits. To do this you access the different options for the grid from the Edit Grid dialog box.

2. Click **View** on the menu bar, point to **Grid**, and then click **Edit Grid**. The Grid dialog box opens as shown in Figure 1-25.

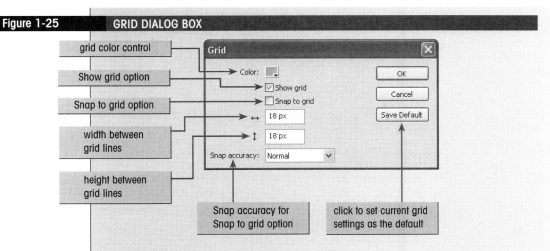

Figure 1-25   GRID DIALOG BOX

grid color control

Show grid option

Snap to grid option

width between grid lines

height between grid lines

Snap accuracy for Snap to grid option

click to set current grid settings as the default

In this dialog box, you can select a specific color for the grid lines. This may be necessary if the background color of the document is similar to the grid lines color, in which case the grid lines may be hard to see.

3. Click the **Color list arrow** to open the color pop-up window. The pointer changes to an eyedropper ⧉.

4. Click the **yellow color swatch** located in the first column, tenth row of the color pop-up window.

Also, you can use the grid lines as you draw or move objects on the Stage. By turning on the Snap to grid option, objects will snap to, or align with, the nearest grid line when you move them or as you draw them.

5. Click the **Snap to grid** check box to select that option.

The width and height values are expressed in pixels. A **pixel** is a unit of measurement that represents the smallest picture element on the monitor screen that can be controlled by the computer. Web graphics and other elements on Web pages are commonly measured in pixels. In the grid settings the width and height represent the distance between the lines.

6. Click **OK** to close the dialog box. The grid lines now reflect the settings you selected in the Grid dialog box.

Another option that can be very helpful when you are developing your graphics is to display the **rulers**. These rulers are vertically displayed on the left edge of the Stage window and horizontally displayed on the top edge. To show the rulers, you select the Rulers command on the View menu. The rulers show the unit of measurement, such as pixels, that is specified in the Document Properties dialog box. The rulers can be very helpful when placing objects on the Stage according to specific coordinates. Also, when the rulers are displayed you can create vertical or horizontal guides. A **guide** is a line used to align objects that can be moved to a specific part of the Stage using the rulers for reference. To create a guide, click a ruler and drag a line onto the Stage. If you drag from the top ruler, a horizontal guide is created. If you drag from the left ruler, a vertical guide is created. You can also edit the guide lines to change their color, to have objects snap to them, and to lock them into place. Just as the grid lines do not become part of your document, the same applies to the guide lines as they are only visible while you are working with your document. Also, guide lines can be created whether the grid is displayed or not.

Aly wants you to practice creating guide lines using the Sample document. You will need to display the rulers first before creating guide lines. You will also practice changing the guide line properties.

To display the rulers and create guides:

1. Click **View** on the menu bar, and then click **Rulers**. The rulers are displayed in the Stage window.

2. Make sure the **Selection** tool is selected on the toolbar.

3. Click the horizontal ruler at the top of the Stage window. The pointer changes to . Click and drag the pointer down to the Stage to create a guide. Use the vertical ruler on the left of the Stage to position the horizontal guide so that it is approximately 55 pixels from the top border of the Stage. It should snap to the closest grid line. See Figure 1-26.

Figure 1-26	HORIZONTAL GUIDE LINE

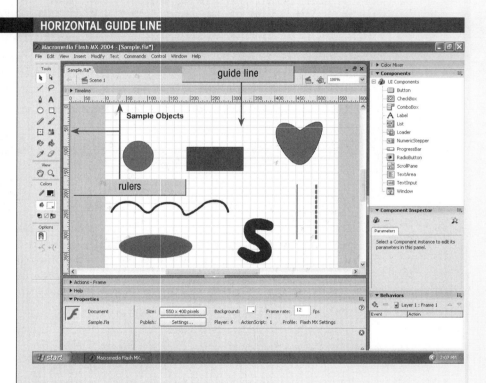

Next you will create a vertical guide.

4. Click the vertical ruler on the left edge of the Stage, and drag the pointer to the Stage to create a vertical guide. Use the horizontal ruler at the top of the Stage to line up the guide so that it is approximately 105 pixels from the left border of the Stage. It should snap to the closest grid line.

5. Click **View** on the menu bar, point to **Guides**, and then click **Edit Guides**. The Guides dialog box opens as shown on Figure 1-27.

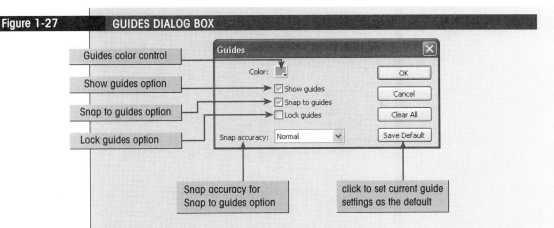

Figure 1-27   GUIDES DIALOG BOX

Guides color control

Show guides option

Snap to guides option

Lock guides option

Snap accuracy for
Snap to guides option

click to set current guide
settings as the default

If necessary, the color of the guide lines can be changed to make them easier to see against the background color.

6. Click the **Color** list arrow to open the color pop-up window. The pointer changes to an eyedropper 🖋.

7. Click the **red** color swatch located in the first column, seventh row of the pop-up window.

8. Click the **OK** button to close the dialog box. The guide lines are now red.

Changing the Document Properties

Every document in Flash has certain properties, such as Stage size, background color, and frame rate. (The frame rate is used when working with animations and specifies how many frames are to be displayed in one second. You will learn about using frames for animations in Tutorial 3.) The document properties are set at default values when you first open a new document in the program. For example, the Stage size has the default dimensions of 550 pixels wide by 400 pixels high. In addition to the default dimensions, the Stage background color is set to white, the frame rate is set to 12 frames per second and the ruler units are set to pixels. The ruler units determine what unit of measurement is displayed on the rulers. A document's default properties can be changed by accessing the Document Properties dialog box. To open the Document Properties dialog box, you select the Document command on the Modify menu. You can also open the Document Properties dialog box by clicking the Size button in the Property inspector. Changes you make in the dialog box are reflected on the Stage.

Aly suggests you practice changing the Sample document's properties by changing its background color.

To change the Sample document's background color:

1. Click **Modify** on the menu bar, and then click **Document**. The Document Properties dialog box opens. See Figure 1-28.

Figure 1-28 | DOCUMENT PROPERTIES DIALOG BOX

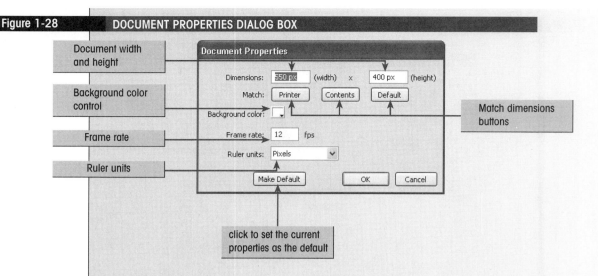

Document width and height

Background color control

Frame rate

Ruler units

Match dimensions buttons

click to set the current properties as the default

You can use the options in this dialog box to change the dimensions and background color of the document. These options are described in Figure 1-29.

Figure 1-29 | OPTIONS IN THE DOCUMENT PROPERTIES DIALOG BOX

OPTION	DESCRIPTION
Dimensions (width and height)	Values for the size of the Stage are entered into the width and height text boxes
Match: Printer	Matches the size of the Stage to be the same as the maximum print area
Match: Contents	Matches the size of the Stage to that of the current contents; an equal amount of space is placed around all sides of the existing contents
Match: Default	Sets the size of the stage to the default values for width and height
Background color	Opens a color palette to select a color for the Stage's background
Frame rate	Determines how many frames of animation are displayed per second; a frame is one particular image in a series of images that create an animation
Ruler units	Determines what unit of measurement is displayed on the rulers
Make Default	Makes the current settings the default properties for all new documents

2. Click the **Background color** list arrow to open its color pop-up window. Using the eyedropper 🖊, click the **gray** color swatch located in the first column, third row.

   The default setting of 12 for the Frame rate is appropriate, as is the Ruler units at pixels. You can close the Document Properties dialog box.

3. Click the **OK** button to close the dialog box. The Stage now appears with the new background color.

   You can also change the document's background color in the Property inspector.

4. Click the **Background color** list arrow in the Property inspector. Select the white color swatch located in the first column, sixth row in the color pop-up window. The Stage now displays a white background.

In this session you learned about the basic elements of the Flash program window. You learned how to open and reposition the panels, how to change the display of the Stage, how to modify the document settings, and how to use the tools on the toolbar. In the next session, you will learn how graphic objects drawn in Flash interact with each other and how to select and group objects.

Session 1.2 QUICK CHECK

1. What is the name of the area in which you position the objects that will appear in your document?

2. What is the name of the area which displays your document's frame and layer information?

3. What is the Hand tool used for?

4. Dragging the playhead back and forth in the Timeline to test a document is called _____.

5. A new Flash document starts with _____ frame and _____ layer.

6. Which special panel changes to display different options depending on which tool or object is selected?

7. What are layers used for?

8. What are the default dimensions for a Flash document?

9. Describe two ways to access the magnification levels to change the view of the Stage.

10. The grid displays lines on the Stage that become part of your document. True or False?

11. How do you get the rulers to display on the Stage window?

12. How do you create a horizontal guide?

SESSION 1.3

In this session, you will learn how objects interact with each other on the Stage. You will learn how to select and group objects and you will also learn about an object's stroke, fill, and colors. Finally, you will learn how to use the Flash help system.

Working with Objects in Flash

The drawing and painting tools available on the toolbar include the Line, Pen, Pencil, Oval, Rectangle, and Brush. These tools allow you to create the lines and shapes that make up the images in a Flash document. Before using these tools, it is important to understand how the objects you draw behave and how you can change their basic characteristics, such as their color. In particular, you need to be aware of how shapes or lines you draw interact with existing shapes or lines.

Also, when drawing objects you can specify the colors for the lines and shapes before or after you draw them. Selecting the colors can be done through the toolbar color controls, the color controls in the Property inspector, or through the Color Mixer panel.

Strokes and Fills

When drawing objects in Flash you create strokes and fills. **Strokes** are the lines that you draw. These lines may be straight or curved and can either be individual line segments or they can connect together to form shapes. The drawing tools in Flash give you a great deal of flexibility and allow you to draw almost any type of line you need for your document. **Fills** are the areas you paint with color. These areas may or may not be enclosed by strokes.

Before you draw a shape, such as an oval or a rectangle, you can specify whether you want the shape to have a stroke, a fill, or both. For example, you can draw a circle that has both a fill and a stroke. You can draw one that has a painted fill but has no stroke. Or you can draw the circle with a stroke but no fill. See the examples in Figure 1-30.

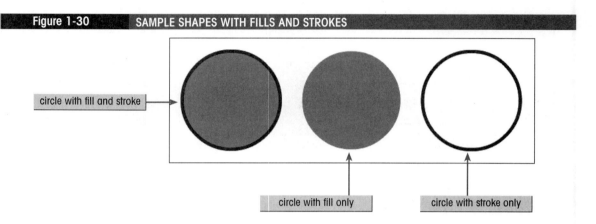

Figure 1-30   SAMPLE SHAPES WITH FILLS AND STROKES

circle with fill and stroke

circle with fill only

circle with stroke only

You can also add a stroke or fill after you draw an object, and you can always modify its stroke or fill properties.

When drawing objects, you need to be aware of how the various objects interact with each other and how you can control their interaction.

Grouping Objects

All objects drawn on the Stage are at the same level unless they reside on different layers. Recall from Session 1.2 that layers allow you to organize the various graphic objects that are part of a document and keep these objects from changing each other when they overlap. Layers are displayed in the document's Timeline. By default, a Flash document starts with one layer, but you can add more layers as needed. (You will work more with layers in a later tutorial.)

Objects on the same layer are not considered to be on top of or below one another. As a result, objects drawn or moved on top of other objects connect with or **segment** the existing objects. For example, when you draw a line through an existing shape such as a circle, the line is split into line segments at the points where it intersects the circle. The circle is also split into separate shapes. These line segments and split shapes can then be moved individually.

Also, if you draw or move a fill on top of another fill of the same color, the two fills connect and become one shape. If you draw a fill of one color on top of another fill of a different color, then the new fill cuts away at the existing fill. See Figure 1-31.

Figure 1-31	HOW OBJECTS INTERACT WITH EACH OTHER

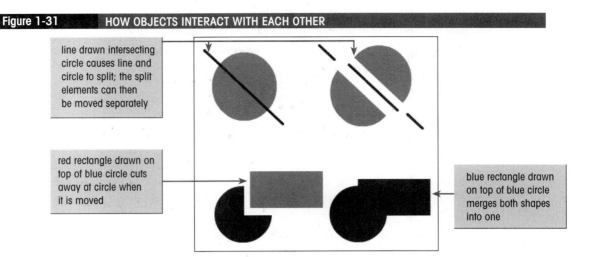

line drawn intersecting circle causes line and circle to split; the split elements can then be moved separately

red rectangle drawn on top of blue circle cuts away at circle when it is moved

blue rectangle drawn on top of blue circle merges both shapes into one

There are several ways to prevent objects from impacting each other. One way is to group objects together. Another way is to place objects on different layers. Placing objects on different layers will be covered in a later tutorial.

If you want to treat two or more objects such as a stroke and a fill as one entity, you can group them. To group the objects you first select them at the same time using the Selection tool. You then click the Group command on the Modify menu. A thin blue rectangular outline appears around the grouped object when it is selected. Grouped objects are on top of nongrouped objects so they do not connect with or segment other objects. To modify a grouped object, you select the object, and then click the Edit Selected command on the Edit menu. You can also double-click the grouped object. You can then edit the individual objects within the group. When editing the objects within a group, the rest of the objects on the Stage are dimmed, indicating they are not accessible as shown in Figure 1-32. Once you are done modifying the individual objects you exit the group editing mode by clicking the Edit All command on the Edit menu or by double-clicking a blank area of the Stage away from the grouped object. You can also click the Scene 1 link on the Edit bar.

Figure 1-32	EDITING A GROUPED OBJECT

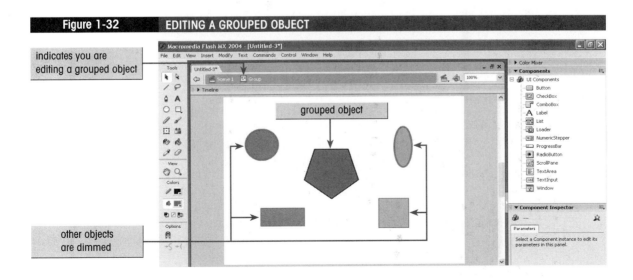

indicates you are editing a grouped object

grouped object

other objects are dimmed

As you draw objects on the Stage, you will want to control the colors of both the strokes and the fills. There are various ways to set the colors before and after you draw an object.

Color Controls and the Color Mixer

All strokes and fills can be drawn with different colors. You can specify the colors before you draw strokes and fills or you can change the colors of existing strokes and fills. Flash provides several methods by which you can specify colors. The first method is by using the color controls found in the colors area of the toolbar. You use the Stroke Color control to specify the color for strokes and you use the Fill Color control to specify the color for fills. Each of these controls has a list arrow that you can click to open a color pop-up window. Figure 1-33 shows the color pop-up window for the Fill Color control.

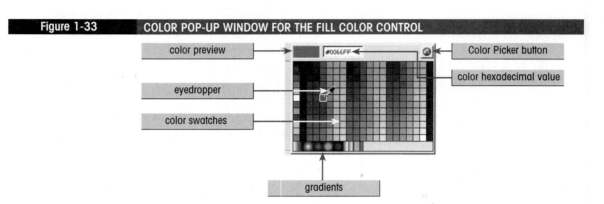

Figure 1-33   COLOR POP-UP WINDOW FOR THE FILL COLOR CONTROL

color preview

eyedropper

color swatches

#0066FF

Color Picker button

color hexadecimal value

gradients

When the color pop-up window opens, the pointer changes to an eyedropper. You use the eyedropper to select a particular color in the pop-up window. A color square in the pop-up window is referred to as a **swatch**. By default, the color swatches displayed in the color pop-up window are the 216 **Web-safe colors**. These are colors that are displayed the same on both Internet Explorer and Netscape Navigator browsers, as well as on both Windows and Macintosh operating systems. If you need to use a color that is not one of the 216 Web-safe colors, you can enter its hexadecimal value into the text box above the color swatches. The hexadecimal value (such as #000000 for black) is based on the three basic colors used on computer monitors, red, green, and blue, or RGB. The first two hexadecimal digits represent the amount of red, the next two digits represent the amount of green, and the last two digits represent the amount of blue. These three color values combine to form the desired color. The color pop-up window for fills also displays a set of preset gradients below the color swatches. A **gradient** is a blend of two or more colors. A **linear gradient** blends the colors from one point to another in a straight line. A **radial gradient** blends the colors in a circular pattern. Also from within the color pop-up window you can click the Color Picker button to open the Color dialog box which you use to create custom colors.

You can also select colors using the Property inspector. When you select a tool used to draw strokes or fills, color controls are displayed in the Property inspector. These controls work the same way as those you access using the Stroke Color and Fill Color controls on the toolbar. These controls are also displayed when you select an existing stroke or fill on the Stage, allowing you to change the color of the selected object.

A third way to select colors is by using the Color Mixer panel shown in Figure 1-34. Using this panel, you can select colors in one of several ways. You can use the panel's color controls to open the color pop-up window, you can enter a color's hexadecimal value, or you can create custom colors.

Figure 1-34	COLOR MIXER

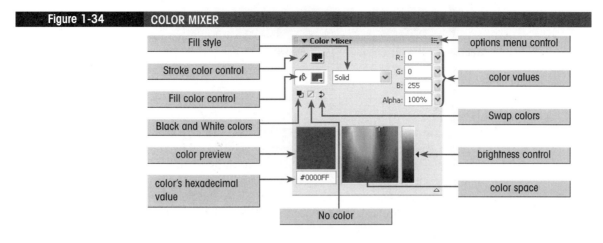

Figure 1-35 gives a description of each of the main elements in the Color Mixer panel.

Figure 1-35	COLOR MIXER ELEMENTS

OPTION	DESCRIPTION
Fill style	Lists the types of fills you can use: solid, gradient, or bitmap
Stroke color control	Displays the color pop-up window to select colors for strokes
Fill color control	Displays the color pop-up window to select colors for fills
Black and White colors	Sets the stroke color to black and the fill color to white
No color	Sets the stroke or fill to have no color
Swap colors	Swaps the stroke and fill color selections
Color preview	Previews the currently selected color
Color's hexadecimal value	Used to enter a color's hexadecimal value
Options menu control	Opens the panel's options menu
Color values	Used to enter specific values for red, green, and blue
Alpha	Specifies the amount of transparency in a color
Brightness control	Adjusts the brightness of the color being previewed
Color space	Shows the range of available colors

The Color Mixer panel allows you to create custom colors in several ways. You can use the RGB color mode, which is the default mode, and enter specific values for red, green, and blue. The RGB values combine to form a particular color. Or you can choose to work with the HSB color mode and enter values for hue, saturation, and brightness. You change modes by using the panel's options menu, which you open by clicking the options menu control located on the panel's title bar. As you enter or change the values, the color sample preview window displays the selected color. Any custom color you create can be added to the color pop-up window by clicking the Add Swatch command from the panel's options menu. This then makes the color available any time you access the color pop-up window for that document.

Now that you have an understanding of the individual elements—strokes, fills, and colors—of graphics created in Flash, you are ready to learn how to select these objects to enhance or modify them.

Selecting Objects

Once you draw a graphic object on the Stage, you can change its characteristics. However, to change an object's characteristics you first need to select the object using the selection tools. The selection tools include the Selection, Subselection, and Lasso. With these tools you are able to select part of an object, the entire object, or several objects at one time. It is important to be familiar with these tools, especially the Selection tool, as you will be using them frequently as you create graphics for Admiral Web Design's clients.

Selection Tool

The **Selection** tool is used to select strokes or fills and can also be used to select a group of objects. You can also use the Selection tool to move objects on the Stage or in the Work Area and to modify objects. You select objects by clicking them or by clicking and dragging the pointer to draw a rectangular selection marquee around the object, which is useful when you need to select more than one object at a time. When you select a graphic object, Flash will cover it with a pattern of dots to indicate it has been selected. Some selected objects, such as text blocks, display a rectangular outline around them instead of a pattern of dots. These objects have special characteristics you will learn about later. Once you have selected an object you are able to move it with the Selection tool by clicking and dragging it to its new position. To modify an object with the Selection tool, deselect the object and then move the Selection pointer ▸▫ to one of the object's edges or corners. If you move the pointer to a corner of a rectangle, for example, the pointer changes to a corner pointer ▸⌐ as shown in Figure 1-36. You can then drag this pointer to change the shape of the object.

Figure 1-36 **MODIFYING AN OBJECT USING THE SELECTION TOOL**

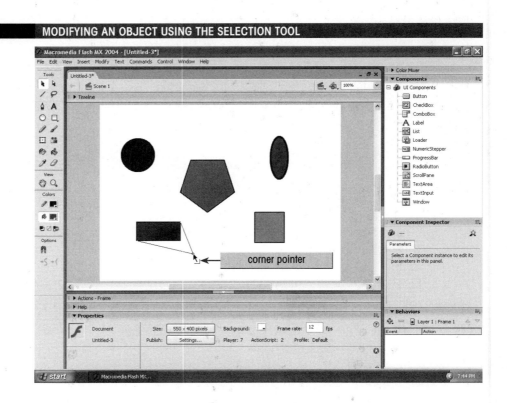

corner pointer

As you learned earlier, many of the tools on the toolbar have modifiers that change the way they work. These modifiers display in the options area of the toolbar when the tool is selected. The Selection tool includes the **Snap to Objects**, **Smooth**, and **Straighten** modifiers which are shown in Figure 1-37.

Figure 1-37	SELECTION TOOL MODIFIERS	
MODIFIER ICON	**MODIFIER**	**DESCRIPTION**
⌂	Snap to Objects	Snaps selected objects to other objects when they are moved close together
↝S	Smooth	Smoothes the selected line or shape outline
↝(	Straighten	Straightens the selected line or shape outline

To continue your training in Flash, Aly wants you to practice using the Selection tool to select and modify objects. You can do this using the graphics in her sample document.

To select and modify objects with the Selection tool:

1. If you took a break after the last session, open the **Sample** document stored in the **Tutorial.01\Tutorial** folder included with your Data Files, set the magnification of the Stage to Show All, and set the panels to the default layout.

2. If necessary, collapse the Timeline, click **View** on the menu bar, and then click **Rulers** to turn off the rulers. Click **View** again, point to **Grid**, and click **Show Grid** to turn off the grid. Click **View** one more time, point to **Guides**, and click **Show Guides** to turn off the guide lines.

3. Click the **Zoom** tool ⊕ on the toolbar, and then click the **Enlarge** modifier button ⊕. Now, you will zoom in and enlarge the red circle.

4. Click the **red circle** to enlarge its view and to bring it to the center of the Stage window.

5. Click the **Selection** tool ▸ on the toolbar to select it.

6. Click the center of the red circle and drag it to the right. Release it just before you get to the rectangle. The circle's fill is now separated from its stroke and has a pattern of dots showing it is still selected. See Figure 1-38.

Figure 1-38 | CIRCLE'S FILL AND STROKE SEPARATED

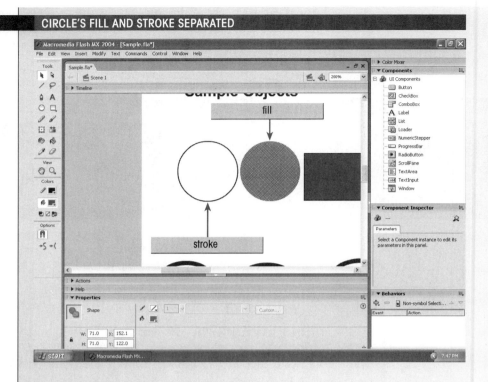

You can easily undo a modification using the Undo command.

7. Click **Edit** on the menu bar, click **Undo Move**, and then click a blank area of the Stage to deselect the circle's fill. You can also use the Selection tool to select both the fill and the stroke of the circle simultaneously. You do this by double-clicking the image.

8. Double-click the **circle** to select both the fill and the stroke, and then drag the selected **circle** to the right. Both the stroke and the fill move together.

9. Click a blank area of the Stage to deselect the circle.

   You can also use the Selection tool to modify a stroke or a fill. For example, you can use it to change the shape of the circle.

10. Move the pointer over the stroke of the circle until the pointer changes to ,
    then click and drag the stroke of the circle away from the center of the circle to change its shape as shown in Figure 1-39. When you release the mouse the fill expands to the new shape.

Figure 1-39	CHANGING THE SHAPE OF THE CIRCLE

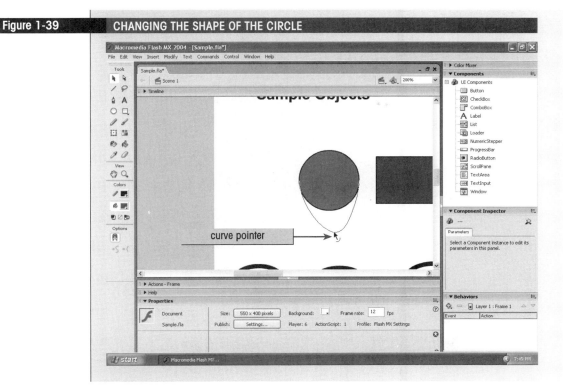

As you have seen, the Selection tool can be used to modify a line or a shape. To more precisely modify an object, you use the Subselection tool. The Subselection tool reveals points on lines or shapes drawn with the Pencil, Brush, Line, Oval, or Rectangle tools. These points can then be adjusted to modify the lines or shapes.

Subselection Tool

The **Subselection** tool is used to display points, referred to as **anchor points**, on strokes and on the outlines of fills that have no stroke. The strokes and fills may then be modified by adjusting these points. To reveal anchor points, select the Subselection tool on the toolbar, and then click a stroke or the outline of a fill. This displays anchor points along the stroke or fill outline. If you click and drag an anchor point on a straight line segment, you can change the angle or the length of the line. If you click an anchor point on a curved line, **tangent handles** are displayed next to the selected point. See Figure 1-40. You can then change the curve by dragging the tangent handles.

Figure 1-40   **CHANGING A CURVE'S ANCHOR POINT**

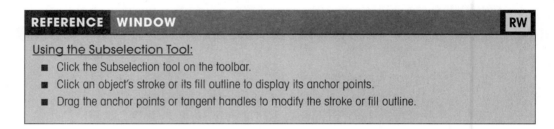

anchor points

tangent handles

REFERENCE   WINDOW   **RW**

Using the Subselection Tool:
- Click the Subselection tool on the toolbar.
- Click an object's stroke or its fill outline to display its anchor points.
- Drag the anchor points or tangent handles to modify the stroke or fill outline.

Aly suggests you practice using the Subselection tool to select and modify objects in the Sample document.

To modify an object using the Subselection tool:

1. Click the **Hand** tool 🖑 on the toolbar to select it, and then use 🖑 to drag the view of the Stage so that the blue rectangle is in the middle of the Stage window.

2. Click the **Subselection** tool 🔍 on the toolbar to select it. You can use this tool to display the rectangle's stroke anchor points.

3. Click the stroke of the blue rectangle. A thin blue outline displays around the rectangle, and square anchor points are displayed on the rectangle's corners. To modify the stroke you can drag an anchor point.

4. Drag the anchor point for the upper-right corner away from the center of the rectangle as shown in Figure 1-41.

Figure 1-41	DRAGGING AN ANCHOR POINT TO CHANGE THE SHAPE

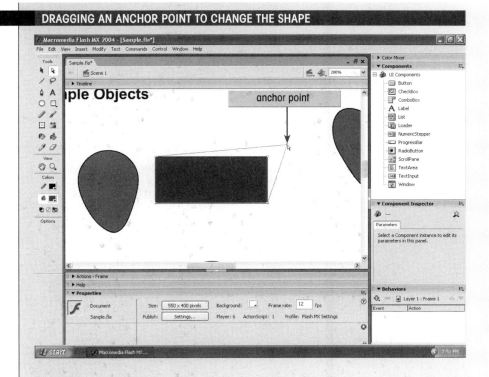

When you release the pointer, the rectangle's fill expands to fill the new shape. Now you will use the Subselection tool to modify the green oval.

5. Use 🖑 to move the view of the Stage so that the green oval is in the center of the Stage window.

6. Click � , and then click the green oval's outline. Anchor points appear along the oval's outline.

7. Click the anchor point at the bottom of the oval's outline once. Because this is a curved outline, tangent handles display. Now you can modify the oval using a tangent handle.

8. Click and drag the tangent handle on the left side of the bottom anchor point to change the shape. The shape's fill expands to fit the new shape as shown In Figure 1-42.

Figure 1-42 | MODIFIED OVAL WITH TANGENT HANDLES

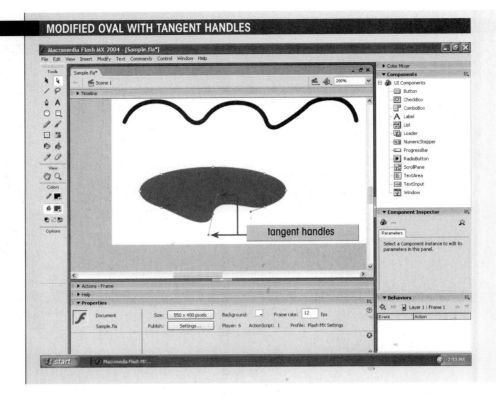

You have used the Selection tool to select and modify objects, and you have used the Subselection tool to select a line's or fill outline's anchor points to modify them. Now you will see how the Lasso tool is used to select an object, several objects at one time, or just part of an object. The Lasso tool is especially useful if you need to select just part of a fill or a stroke, which you cannot do with the Selection or Subselection tools.

Lasso Tool

The **Lasso** tool is used to select several objects at one time or to select an irregularly shaped area of an object by drawing a free-form selection marquee around the area. You click the Lasso tool on the toolbar and then click and drag the Lasso pointer ♀ on the Stage to draw a selection marquee around the area or objects you want to select. Once you have made the selection you can move the selection or apply other effects to it such as changing the color of all the selected fills at one time.

Aly suggests you practice using the Lasso tool with the objects in the Sample document.

To select objects with the Lasso tool:

1. Double-click the **Hand** tool 🖑 to make all of the Stage visible.

2. Click the **Lasso** tool 🔾 on the toolbar to select it. The pointer changes to a lasso ♀ when moved over the Stage. You use this tool to select multiple objects at once.

3. Click and drag the pointer to create a free-form selection marquee that includes part of the blue rectangle, part of the red heart, part of the brown S-shape, and part of the red vertical line. Figure 1-43 shows the marquee around the selected areas before the mouse button is released. After you release the mouse button, all the selected areas appear with a dot pattern to indicate they have been selected.

Figure 1-43	FREE-FORM MARQUEE

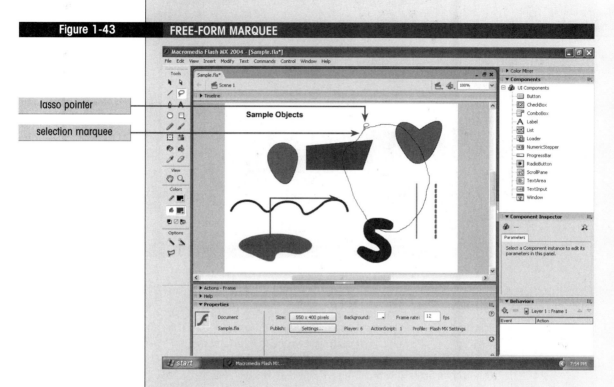

lasso pointer

selection marquee

TROUBLE? If the Polygon Mode modifier 🏴 is selected on the toolbar, you will not be able to create a free-form selection marquee. If this is the case, deselect the modifier, and then repeat Step 3.

Now you will change the color of the fills that have been selected.

4. Click the **Fill Color control** list arrow on the toolbar to open the color pop-up window. Click the **yellow** color swatch (first column, tenth row). The fill color of the areas in the rectangle, heart, and S-shape change to yellow. The line and strokes are not affected because they are not fills. See Figure 1-44.

Figure 1-44 | NEW FILL COLOR FOR SELECTED AREAS

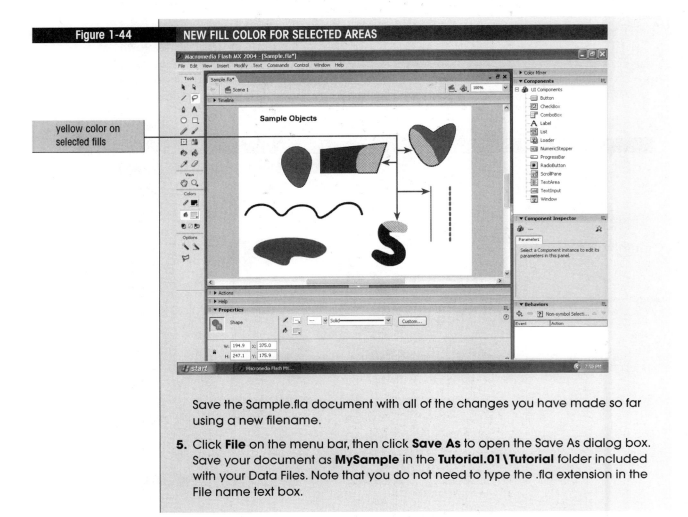

yellow color on selected fills

Save the Sample.fla document with all of the changes you have made so far using a new filename.

5. Click **File** on the menu bar, then click **Save As** to open the Save As dialog box. Save your document as **MySample** in the **Tutorial.01\Tutorial** folder included with your Data Files. Note that you do not need to type the .fla extension in the File name text box.

Another feature of Flash that Aly wants you to become familiar with is its help system. The help system can be very useful for finding information about features in Flash as you work with a document. You will explore the Flash Help system next.

Getting **Help in Flash**

To access the Flash Help system, click the Help panel's title bar or click Help on the menu bar and then select one of the following commands on the Help menu: Help, How Do I, What's New, Using Flash, ActionScript Dictionary, and Using Components. You can also click a panel's options menu control icon and then click Help from the options menu. Using a panel's options menu automatically displays the help information associated with that panel. Flash Help displays in the Help panel which is divided into two panes as shown in Figure 1-45.

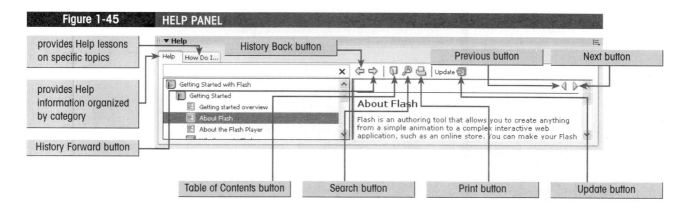

Figure 1-45 — HELP PANEL

The options in the Help panel are described in Figure 1-46.

Figure 1-46 — HELP PANEL BUTTONS

BUTTON	BUTTON NAME	DESCRIPTION
⇦	History Back	A history is maintained in the order topics are viewed; clicking the History Back icon displays a topic viewed previous to the currently displayed topic
⇨	History Forward	After using the History Back icon, click the History Forward icon to display a topic viewed after the currently displayed topic
🗐	Table of Contents	Lists the help categories and topics
🔍	Search	Displays a search text box and button
🖨	Print	Prints the currently displayed topic
📥	Update	Downloads current help content from Macromedia
▷	Next	Displays the next topic based on the table of contents
◁	Previous	Displays the previous topic based on the table of contents

The Help panel also has two tabs labeled Help and How Do I. The Help tab displays information based on specific categories or topics. The How Do I tab displays lessons you can work through to get familiar with Flash. The left pane of the Help panel shows a table of contents with a selection of categories in the form of books. The table of contents for the Help tab includes Getting Started with Flash, Using Flash, ActionScript Reference Guide, ActionScript Dictionary, and Using Components. The table of contents for the How Do I tab includes one book labeled Quick Start which includes lessons. Double-clicking one of the help books displays additional books or help topics. When you click one of the help topics, the right pane displays the associated help information. The information in the right pane also contains links to related topics. Clicking one of these links displays another section of information for that help topic.

Clicking the Search button displays a text box and a Search button in the left pane of the Help panel. When you type a keyword in the text box and then click the Search button, a list of books and topics that contain the keyword displays in the table of contents pane. You can then click a topic to display its help information in the right pane of the Help panel.

To practice using the Flash Help system, Aly wants you to use the Help table of contents to obtain more information about the Property inspector.

To use the Flash Help system to get more information about the Property inspector:

1. Click the Help panel's title bar to expand it. The Help panel expands and displays the Flash Help system.

   TROUBLE? If the Help panel is not big enough to see all of the topic information, you can reduce the size of the document window which contains the Stage. Drag the bottom edge of the document window up, thereby increasing the space available for the Help panel.

2. Double-click **Getting Started with Flash** in the table of contents displayed in the left pane. A list of subcategories displays.

3. Double-click **Getting to Know the Workspace** subcategory to display more subcategories and topics.

4. Scroll down the left pane to locate the **Using panels and Property inspector** subcategory and double-click it to display its topics. Aly wants you to learn more about the Property inspector so you will select the appropriate topic in the list.

5. Scroll down to locate the **About the Property inspector** topic and click it. The help information for this topic displays in the right pane as shown in Figure 1-47.

Figure 1-47   **HELP TOPIC DISPLAYED**

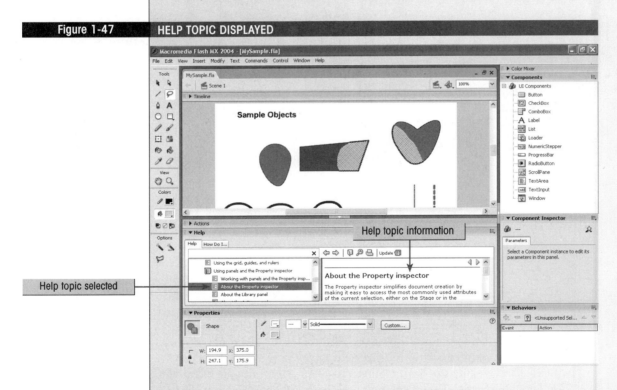

6. Read the help information and then click the Help panel's title bar to collapse the panel.

You have completed your exploration of the Flash program window. Now you will learn how to close a document and exit Flash.

Closing a Document and Exiting Flash

Once you finish working with a document in Flash, you should close it. If necessary, first save the document before you close it. Flash documents are saved in the FLA format.

To close a document and exit Flash:

1. Click **File** on the menu bar, and then click **Close** to close the Sample document. If prompted to save the file, click the **Yes** button. The document closes and the Start page displays.

2. Click **File** on the menu bar, and then click **Exit** to exit Flash.

You have spent some time with Flash, and have begun working with the Flash program and become familiar with the program's main features. Aly has shown you the basic elements of the Flash program window including the tools and panels that you will be using as you create and modify documents. You have examined the various ways in which the view of the Stage can be modified to make your work with Flash easier. You have also learned that when you draw objects they may contain strokes, fills, or both. And you also learned about how objects interact with each other when they are drawn or moved over each other on the Stage. You have learned about colors and how to use the selection tools to select and modify objects or parts of objects. In the next tutorial, you will learn how to use the drawing tools to create the graphics for a banner for the Flounders Pet Shop Web site.

Session 1.3 QUICK CHECK

1. What is the difference between strokes and fills?

2. If you draw a blue oval on top of an ungrouped red rectangle, the rectangle will not be modified. True or False?

3. Grouped objects cannot be edited. True or False?

4. By default, how many colors are shown on the color pop-up window for the Stroke Color control?

5. Which panel can be used to create custom colors?

6. What are two ways you can select both the stroke and the fill of an oval at the same time?

7. How can you select several objects at the same time using the Lasso tool?

8. What will you find in the How Do I tab of the Help panel?

REVIEW ASSIGNMENTS

To review what you have learned with Macromedia Flash, Aly would like you to explore some sample Flash files from the Macromedia Web site. She would also like you to work with some of the tools in Flash and to change the document settings by modifying the SimpleKite document. By practicing these skills, you will be better prepared to use Flash to develop graphics for Admiral Web Design's clients.

If necessary, start Flash, connect to the Internet, and then do the following:

1. Click Help on the menu bar, and then click Flash Support Center. Your default browser opens and displays the Macromedia Flash Support Center Web page. Click the Macromedia Flash Developer Center link. Look for a section listing Flash tutorials and samples on the Macromedia Flash Developer Center page. Within this section look for the link for Sample Files and click this link. A page displays with a list of Flash sample files. To view a sample file, click its link. Read the information provided with the sample and then experiment with the interactive components, if available. To return to the list of sample files, use the browser's Back button.

2. With your browser still open, type **http://www.macromedia.com** in the Address bar, and press the Enter key to open the Macromedia home page. Click the link for Products, and then click the link for Flash MX 2004. On the Flash product page look for a column of links and find a link called Showcase. Click the Showcase link to view a list of Web sites that use Flash. Click a link on the Macromedia Showcase page to view a page with more information about the particular Web site. This page should include a graphic related to the showcased site and a link to the actual Web site. Click this link to open the Web site in a separate browser window.

3. As you navigate to some of the sites showcased, study and compare the animation effects you see. Listen for sound effects, music, and voiceovers. See if you can distinguish between bitmap and vector graphics. To view other showcased Web sites, close your browser window and use the Back button on the browser window with the Macromedia Showcase page to return to the list of showcased links. When you are done exploring the showcased sites, close your browser.

4. Return to Flash and open the SimpleKite file stored in the Tutorial.01\Tutorial folder included with your Data Files. Make sure the magnification level is set to Show All and that the panels are arranged in their default layout. Click Control and then click Rewind to make Frame 1 the current frame, if necessary.

Explore   5. Click Window on the menu bar, and then click Library to open the Library panel. This panel contains the objects that are part of this document.

6. Click the Selection tool on the toolbar to select it, and then click the kite.

Explore   7. Click the Swap button in the Property inspector. In the Swap Symbol dialog box, click balloon to select the balloon symbol, and then click OK. The yellow kite is now replaced by a red balloon.

Explore   8. Click Control on the menu bar, and then click Go To End to move the playhead to the last frame (Frame 30). Select the kite on the Stage, then click the Swap button in the Property inspector, and select the balloon symbol to replace the kite symbol with the balloon, and then click the OK button.

9. Play the animation to test the changes you have made.

Explore   10. Rewind the playhead to Frame 1. Click the Selection tool on the toolbar and click one of the clouds on the Stage. Use the fill color control on the toolbar to change the fill color to a light gray. The color of the selected cloud changes to light gray. Repeat these steps to change the color of the other clouds to light gray.

Explore   11. On the Stage, double-click the text My Simple Kite. Change the word Kite to **Balloon**. When you are done editing the text, click the Selection tool on the toolbar.

12. Use the Save As command to save the revised document. Name the file **SimpleBalloon** and save it in the Tutorial.01\Review folder included with your Data Files.

Case 1. Exploring Flash Media   Sandy's Party Center is a party supplies store that specializes in products for every type of celebration. They sell party decorations such as balloons, ribbons, and banners. They also sell greeting cards, party plates, party favors, tableware, and napkins. They will even assist customers in planning a party. In order to help promote the store, Sandy Rodriguez, the owner, recently hired John Rossini to develop a Web site for the store. The site will include graphics and animation in addition to textual information. John wants to use Flash to develop the elements for the site and he has hired you to help him.

Because John wants to use Flash to develop the Web site, you decide to find Flash resources on the Internet and to explore examples of Web media that may be used for the Web site. You will also explore a sample Flash document to get more familiar with the program.

If necessary, start Flash, start your browser, connect to the Internet, and then do the following:

1. In your browser, open the home page for the Flashkit site at **http://www.flashkit.com**. On the home page for this Web site, look for a list of hyperlinks, usually located at the top of page. In this list of hyperlinks, click the link to "Featured" sites. Follow the links to several of the featured sites to see examples of how Flash is being used. Each site opens in a separate browser window, so to get back to the Flashkit site, be sure to close the window that the site opens in. Record the URL of the two sites you like best. Record what you like best about each site (e.g., colors, sound, pictures, navigation, etc.).

2. At the Flashkit site, look for and click the link for the "Gallery." This leads to a page where you can see different types of Web media. Scroll down and look for a category that you like. Click the category's link. At the category's page, scroll down to see a list of graphic images available for download. Notice that each image has information such as its width, height, size in number of bytes, and its format, such as .jpg or .gif. If an image has a link, click it to see the image displayed in its actual size. Find at least three examples of .jpg images and three examples of .gif images. Record the information provided about each of these images (name, width, height, size, and format). Based on the images you saw, record what you think are the main differences between the .jpg and .gif formats.

3. Close your browser and your Internet connection, if necessary.

4. In Flash open the **Shapes** file stored in the Tutorial.01\Cases folder included with your Data Files. Make sure the magnification level is set to 100% and that the panels are arranged in their default layout.

5. Display the Rulers and display the Grid. Make sure that Snap to Grid is turned off and that Snap to Guide is turned on. Drag a horizontal guide line from the top ruler and place it at the grid line about 145 pixels from the top of the Stage.

Explore   6. Use the Selection tool to move the triangle to the left side of the Stage. The bottom side of the triangle should rest on the guide line. Make sure to move both the triangle's fill and stroke together. Select the entire basketball and use the Group command on the Modify menu to group all of the parts of the basketball together. Then move the basketball so that it too rests on the guide line. It should be to the right of the triangle.

7. Select all of the baseball and group its parts together. Move the baseball to the right of the basketball so that it rests on the guide line. Select the cube. Move the cube to the right of the baseball and on the guide line.

8. Move the text block and place it to the right of the cube and on the guide line. All of the objects should be lined up on the guide line.

9. Save the revised document as **Shapes2** in the Tutorial.01\Cases folder. Close the file.

Case 2. Customizing the Flash Program Window   River City Music, established in 1990, is a musical instruments and supplies store that specializes in meeting the needs of local schools. The store provides many music-related services to its customers, including the sale of band instruments and sheet music for all age and skill levels. River City Music staff also work with private piano teachers by referring potential students to them and by allowing them to use the store's large presentation room for piano recitals.

Alex Smith was recently commissioned by Janet Meyers, store manager, to develop Flash graphics for the River City Music Web site. Alex hires you to help him and asks you to prepare for this by learning how to customize the panels you may use regularly so you can look for information in the Flash Help system.

If necessary, start Flash, and then do the following:

1. If necessary, create a new Flash document. To learn how to organize the panels and to save the customized settings, start by setting the panels to their default layout. Click Window on the menu bar, point to Panel Sets, and then click Default Layout.

2. Click Window on the menu bar, point to Design Panels and then click Align to open the Align panel. The panel opens in its own window. Move this window to the left side of the screen by clicking and dragging the window's title bar. Also open the Info panel and the Transform panel. Note that as you open new panels, they may cover panels that are already opened.

Explore   3. To group these three panels into one window, drag the Transform panel out of its own window and into the Align panel's window. Move your pointer to the left edge of the Transform panel's title bar just to the left of the Collapse arrow. When the pointer changes to a four-headed arrow, drag the panel and drop it inside the Align panel's window. The two panels should now be grouped into one window.

4. Repeat these steps to drag the Info panel into the window with the Transform and Align panels. All three panels should now be grouped together.

Explore   5. Click Window on the menu bar, and click Save Panel Layout. Name the saved layout **My Layout**.

6. Return the panels to their default layout.

7. Click Window on the menu bar, point to Panel Sets, and this time click My Layout, which now appears on the list of panel layouts. The panel arrangement should reflect the changes you made.

Explore   8. To get a printout showing your panel arrangement, first copy the screen image to the Windows clipboard. Do this by pressing the Print Screen key on the keyboard. Start the WordPad program by clicking the Start button, pointing to All Programs, pointing to Accessories, and then clicking WordPad. In the WordPad document window, type your name as the first line in the document. Press the Enter key. Click Edit on the menu bar, and then click Paste to paste the image of the Flash program window below your name. To print this WordPad document, click File on the menu bar, and then click Print. In the Print dialog box, click Print again. Once you have your printout, close WordPad. You do not need to save the document.

9. Close the window with the three grouped panels.

Explore   10. To find out more about the Align panel, expand the Help panel. If necessary, click the Help tab to display the table of contents. Click the Search icon and type Align panel in the search text box, then click the Search button. In the search results in the left pane, click the Aligning objects topic under the Using Flash book. In the right pane, read the information for Aligning objects. Use the scroll bar to move through the page and then at the bottom of the page click the link, To align objects. The steps for aligning objects are displayed. Finally, use the Print icon in the Help panel to print the Aligning objects page. Click the Collapse arrow for the Help panel to collapse the panel.

QUICK CHECK ANSWERS

Session 1.1

1. Flash creates vector-based images.
2. A completed Flash file published for Internet delivery is called a Macromedia Flash Player document and is in the SWF format.
3. Three things you might find in a Flash document include any of the following: still imagery, sound, animation, hyperlinks, buttons, text, and scripted programming.
4. True. Flash allows you to synchronize sound with events in your document.
5. Bitmap graphics store information as a grid of pixels.
6. Vector graphics store image data as a set of mathematical instructions that describe the color, outline, and position of all the shapes of the image.
7. The term "resolution independent" applies to vector graphics.
8. A bitmap image that has been enlarged looks jagged or blurred.

Session 1.2

1. The area in which you position the objects that will appear in your document is called the Stage.
2. The area which displays your document's frame and layer information is called the Timeline.
3. The Hand tool is used for moving the view of the Stage and Work Area.
4. Dragging the playhead back and forth in the Timeline to test a document is called scrubbing.
5. A new Flash document starts with one frame and one layer.
6. The Property inspector changes to display different options depending on which tool or object is selected.
7. Layers are used to organize the images, animations, and other objects that are part of a document.
8. The default dimensions for a Flash document are 550 pixels in width and 400 pixels in height.
9. To access the magnification levels to change the view of the Stage you can click View on the menu bar, point to Magnification, and select one of the levels. Or you can access the levels from the Zoom control list arrow in the right side of the Edit bar.

10. False. The grid lines do not become part of your document.

11. To display the rulers, click View on the menu bar, and then click Rulers.

12. To create a horizontal guide, drag your pointer from the top ruler down to the Stage window.

Session 1.3

1. Strokes refer to lines and outlines, while fills refer to the areas enclosed by lines and outlines.

2. False. The blue oval cuts away at the ungrouped red rectangle.

3. False. Grouped objects can be edited in group-edit mode.

4. By default, 216 Web-safe colors are shown in the color pop-up window.

5. The Color Mixer panel is used to create custom colors.

6. You can select both the stroke and the fill of an oval at the same time by double-clicking on either the stroke or fill. Or, you can draw a rectangular marquee around the oval with the Selection tool.

7. To select several objects at the same time using the Lasso tool, drag a marquee around the objects.

8. The How Do I tab displays a Quick Start book with lessons that can be followed to learn more about Flash.

OBJECTIVES

In this tutorial you will:

- Draw lines, curves, ovals, and rectangles

- Apply stroke and fill colors

- Modify strokes and fills

- Transform graphic objects using the Free Transform tool

- Create text blocks

- Export a graphic for use on a Web site

- Learn how to use the History panel

- Create symbols and instances of symbols

- Organize symbols in the Library panel

DRAWING, ADDING TEXT, AND CREATING SYMBOLS

Creating a Banner for the Flounders Pet Shop Web Site

CASE

Admiral Web Design

Admiral Web Design has developed a number of different Web sites for its clients. The focus of the company has been to design easy-to-use, informative, and effective Web sites. Each Web site has been designed with the needs of the client in mind and the clients have been very pleased with the results. Now several of the clients have requested some enhancements to their Web sites. One of these clients is Flounders Pet Shop, a small business specializing in selling pets and related pet supplies. The owner of the pet shop, Joe Flounders, has requested that a new banner be developed for his Web site to promote a special sale on fish and aquariums. As a result, Gloria Adamson has asked Aly to work on this request along with Chris Johnson, one of Admiral's Web designers.

Aly and Chris hold a planning meeting with Joe Flounders to discuss his request. You are invited to the planning meeting because you will be working under Aly's supervision to create the banner. At the meeting, Joe expresses his wish for a colorful banner with graphic images of fish. Aly suggests the banner resemble an aquarium with several fish and plants inside the aquarium. Joe is very excited about this idea and Chris thinks that such a banner will blend well with the current design of the pet shop's home page. Aly sketches a draft of the banner so everyone can see what it will look like. After further discussion and revisions to the sketch, everyone is in agreement and you are assigned the task of creating the banner using Flash according to the sketch shown in Figure 2-1.

Figure 2-1   **SKETCH OF THE BANNER FOR THE FLOUNDERS PET SHOP WEB SITE**

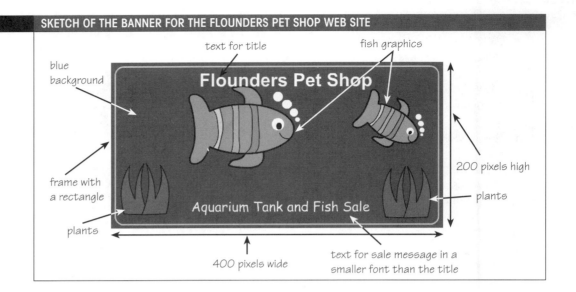

As you use Flash to create the banner for the Flounders Pet Shop in this tutorial, you will learn how to use the drawing tools, text tools, and tools for modifying graphic objects. You will also learn how to select and apply colors. You will modify existing graphics, create new graphics for the banner, and then export the banner for use on the Flounders Pet Shop's Web site.

SESSION 2.1

In this session you will learn how to use the main drawing tools in Macromedia Flash. You will use some of these tools to create graphic elements for the Flounders Pet Shop banner. You will learn how to draw lines, curves, ovals, rectangles, and paint brush strokes. In addition to the drawing tools, you will learn how to apply and change the colors of strokes and fills, and how to apply properties of one object to another object.

Drawing Lines and Shapes

When working with Flash, you will often have to create graphic images from scratch by using the drawing tools. To draw lines and curves you use the Line, Pen, and Pencil tools. If you create an enclosed shape as you draw with these tools, the enclosed areas will be filled with the currently selected fill color (as shown in the Fill Color control on the toolbar). To draw shapes you use the Oval, Rectangle, PolyStar, and Brush tools. These tools allow you to create shapes of various sizes and colors. The ovals, rectangles, and polygons you draw can include strokes as well as fills, or you can draw them with only a stroke or only a fill.

Refer to Figure 2-1 which shows the sketch of the banner you are to create. In this session you will use the Oval, Pencil, Paint Bucket, Eyedropper, and Pen tools to create the fish and plant graphics. You will also use the Rectangle tool to create a frame around the banner. You will use the Selection tool to modify the shapes you draw, and you will display the grid which will be useful as you draw and align objects on the Stage.

Oval, Rectangle, and PolyStar Tools

Drawing simple shapes is easy with the Oval, Rectangle, and PolyStar tools. These tools all work in a similar manner. You simply select the tool on the toolbar, select colors for the stroke and fill using the Stroke and Fill Color controls, and then click and drag the pointer on the Stage. The size of the shape is determined by where you release the pointer. The

PolyStar tool has an additional option where you can specify whether you want to draw a polygon or a star shape. You can also indicate the number of sides the shape will have. The number of sides can range from three to 32. For star shapes, you can also specify the star point size in values ranging from zero to one. This number specifies the depth of the star points. A number closer to zero creates deeper star points, as shown in Figure 2-2.

Figure 2-2	STAR SHAPES WITH DIFFERENT POINT SIZES

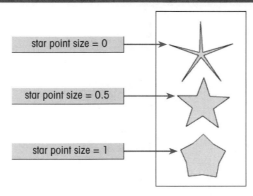

Each shape you draw may contain both a stroke and a fill, or you can draw shapes that contain only a fill or only a stroke. If, for example, you select the no color option for the stroke, then the drawn shape contains a fill but no stroke. Once you draw a shape you can still change its stroke or fill color. Recall from Tutorial 1 that you can also apply colors to existing strokes and fills using the Color Mixer panel, the Property inspector, or the Fill Color and Stroke Color controls on the toolbar.

You can also use the Oval and Rectangle tools to draw a perfect circle or a perfect square. You do this by first selecting the Snap to Objects command on the View menu. For example, as you draw with the Oval tool, a small solid ring appears next to the pointer to let you know when you have drawn a perfect circle. The same thing happens when you draw with the Rectangle tool to let you know you have drawn a perfect square.

When you select the Rectangle tool, the Round Rectangle Radius modifier becomes available in the options area of the toolbar. If you click this modifier, a dialog box opens in which you can enter a value for the number of points by which you want to round the corners of the rectangle. The higher the value, the more rounded the corners will be. See the rectangle examples in Figure 2-3.

| Figure 2-3 | RECTANGLES WITH ROUNDED CORNERS |

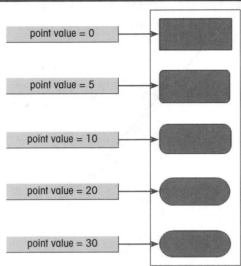

You are now ready to begin creating the banner for Flounders Pet Shop. You will first set the document properties and display the rulers. You will then save the banner file to the location where your Data Files are stored.

To set the document properties, show the rulers, and save the document:

1. Start Flash, click **File** on the menu bar, and then click **New**. On the General tab of the New Document dialog box, click **Flash Document**, if necessary, and click **OK** to create a new document.

2. Click **Window** on the menu bar, point to **Panel Sets**, and click **Default Layout**. Click the **Timeline's** title bar to collapse it. Now you will set the document dimensions according to the banner sketch. These dimensions are 400 by 200 pixels.

3. Click **Modify** on the menu bar, and then click **Document**.

4. When the Document Properties dialog box opens, the value in the width text box should be selected. If it is not, click the value in the width text box, type **400** for the width value, and then double-click the value in the height text box and type **200** for its value. Do not press Enter or click OK yet.

   You will now set the background color to blue as shown in the sketch.

5. Click the **Background color** control list arrow to open the color pop-up window. Using the eyedropper [eyedropper icon], click the **blue** color swatch in the first column, ninth row.

6. Leave the Frame rate at 12 frames per second and the Ruler units at Pixels, and then click the **OK** button to close the dialog box. The Stage changes to match your document settings.

7. Click **View** on the menu bar, and then click **Rulers**. The rulers display on the Stage window. Your Stage window should look like the one shown in Figure 2-4.

Figure 2-4

DOCUMENT WINDOW SHOWING RULERS AND NEW STAGE PROPERTIES

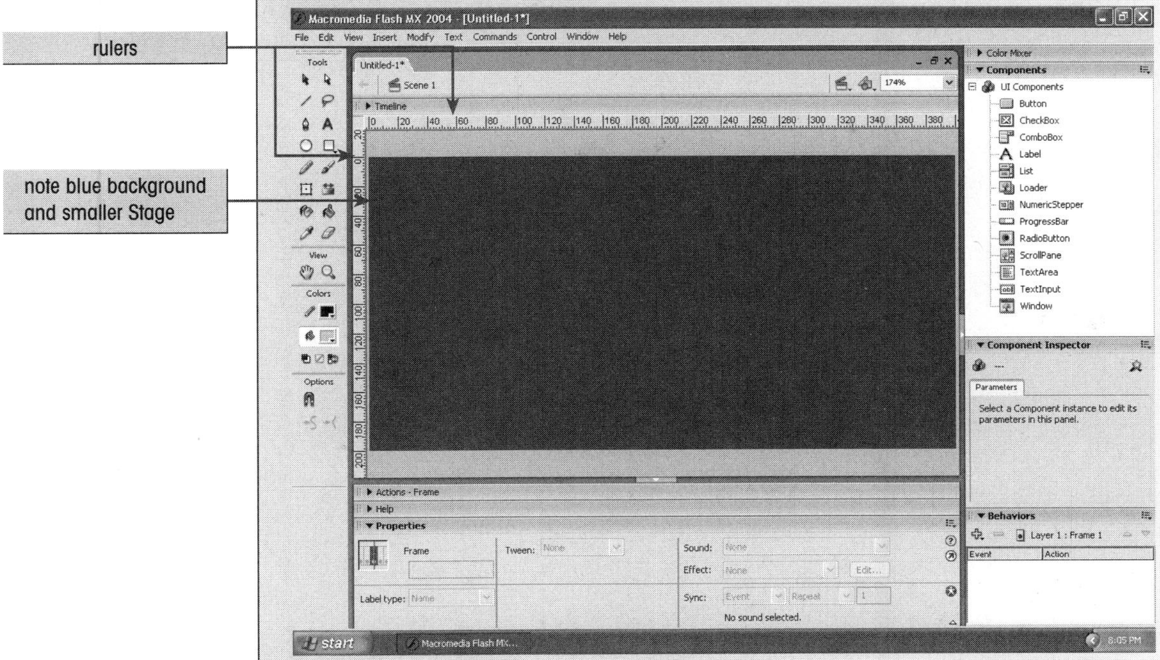

rulers

note blue background and smaller Stage

8. Save your document as **Banner.fla** in the **Tutorial.02\Tutorial** folder included with your Data Files.

Now that you have the document ready, you will create the large fish in the center of the banner Aly sketched. Aly suggests that you use the Oval tool to draw a large oval for the body of the fish and a smaller oval that will become the fish's tail. You can create guide lines to guide you as you draw. You can then use the Selection tool to modify the smaller oval to resemble the tail.

To draw the fish using the Oval tool and guide lines:

1. Click the **top horizontal ruler** and drag a horizontal guide onto the Stage. Use the vertical ruler on the left to place the guide approximately 50 pixels from the top of the Stage. Drag another horizontal guide and place it approximately 110 pixels from the top of the Stage.

2. Click the **vertical ruler** and drag a vertical guide onto the Stage. Use the horizontal ruler to place the guide approximately 100 pixels from the left of the Stage. Drag another vertical guide and place it approximately 220 pixels from the left of the Stage. See Figure 2-5.

Figure 2-5   GUIDES

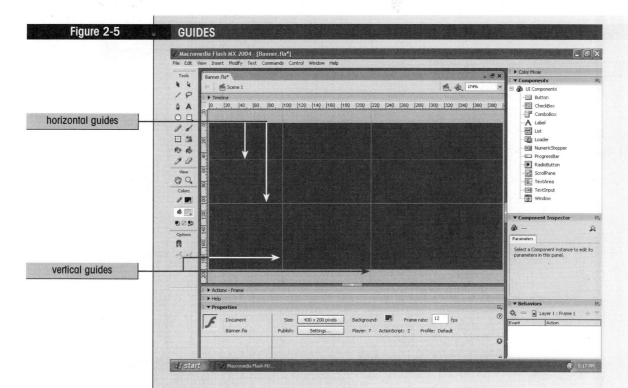

horizontal guides

vertical guides

Next, using the guides to help you draw, you will use the Oval tool to create the fish body.

3. Click the **Oval** tool ⬭ on the toolbar. If necessary, click the **Stage** once to display the Oval tool properties in the Property inspector. Before drawing the oval that will be the body of the fish, select the stroke and fill colors.

4. In the Property inspector, click the **Stroke color** control list arrow to open its color pop-up window, and then click the **black** swatch in the first column, first row. Enter **2** in the Stroke height list box, and make sure the Stroke style is set to **Solid**.

5. In the Property inspector, click the **Fill color** control list arrow, and then click the **orange** swatch in the seventh row from the top, third column from the right. You will now draw the fish body.

6. Use the ╂ to draw an oval on the Stage starting at the upper-left corner of the rectangular area formed by the guides. Drag the pointer to the lower-right corner of the rectangular area formed by the guides. Release the mouse button at this lower-right corner to create the oval, as shown in Figure 2-6.

Figure 2-6   OVAL

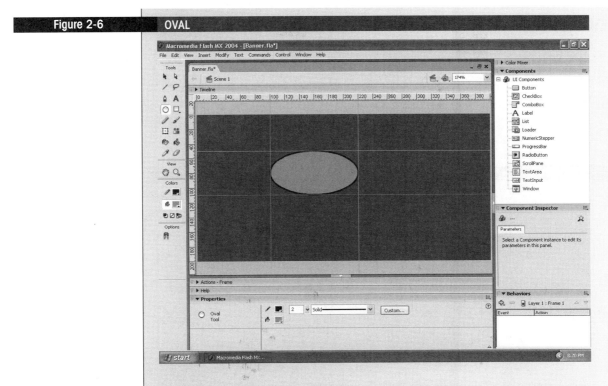

7. Draw another smaller oval that overlaps the left end of the first oval. Draw it so that it is centered on the left vertical guide, as shown in Figure 2-7.

Figure 2-7   OVERLAPPING OVALS

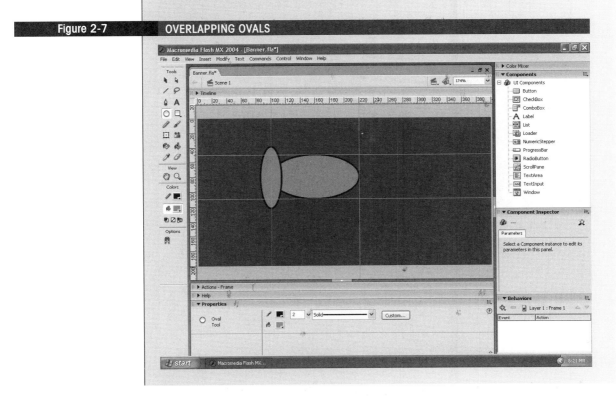

Now that you have drawn these two ovals, you will use the Selection tool to modify them to more closely resemble the fish Aly sketched for you. For example, the stroke segment of the smaller oval that overlaps the larger oval can be removed. Then, the stroke segment on the left edge of the smaller oval needs to be modified to curve inward, toward the larger oval.

To modify the ovals using the Selection tool:

1. Click the **Selection** tool 🅡 on the toolbar, and then click the part of the small oval's stroke that is inside the larger oval, as shown in Figure 2-8. The stroke segment that is inside the larger oval is selected.

Figure 2-8   STROKE SEGMENT SELECTED

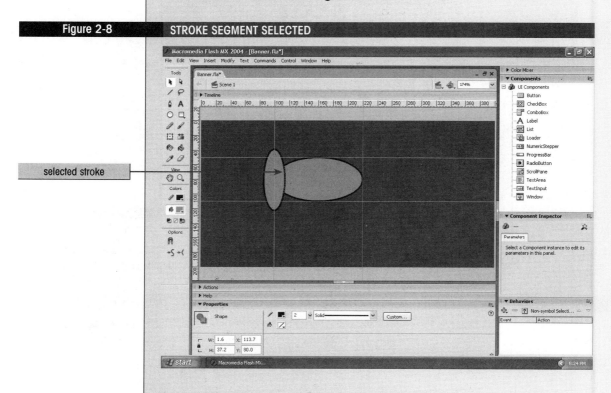

selected stroke

2. Press the **Delete** key to delete this stroke segment.

3. Move the pointer to the stroke on the left edge of the smaller oval until you see a curve pointer 🅡. Drag the line to the right to about the center point of the small oval. The center point should be at the left vertical guide, as shown in Figure 2-9.

| Figure 2-9 | MODIFYING THE OVAL'S STROKE |

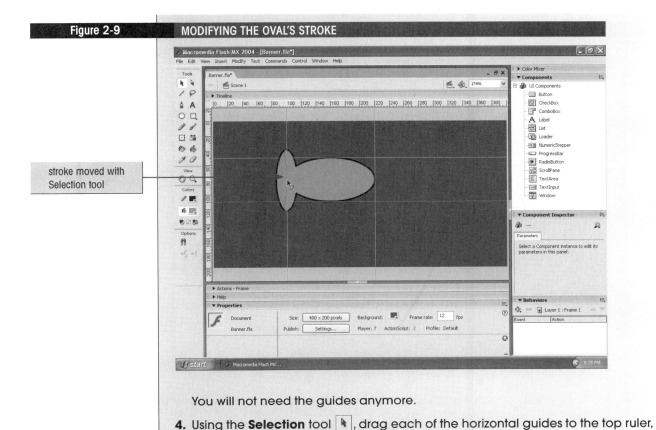

stroke moved with
Selection tool

You will not need the guides anymore.

4. Using the **Selection** tool, drag each of the horizontal guides to the top ruler, and then drag each of the vertical guides to the left ruler.

Now you are ready to draw the eye for the fish. You can use the Oval tool for this.

To use the Oval tool to draw the eye for the fish:

1. Click the **Zoom** tool on the toolbar, make sure the **Enlarge** modifier is selected, and then click the right side of the fish shape once to zoom in.

2. Click the **Oval** tool on the toolbar, and then in the Property inspector, set the Stroke color to **No Color** and the Fill color to **white**. Now you can draw the eye. Flash helps you draw a perfect circle if the Snap to Objects command is turned on.

3. If necessary, click **View** on the menu bar, point to **Snapping**, and then click **Snap to Objects** to select this option.

4. Use the ┼ to draw a small circle on the right end of the fish shape, as shown in Figure 2-10.

| Figure 2-10 | FISH EYE |

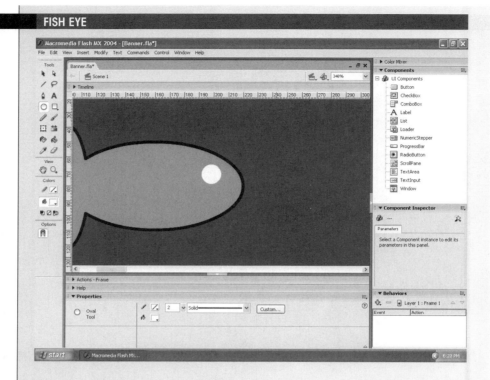

To make it easier to draw a small oval for the pupil, you will turn off the Snap to Objects command.

5. Click **View** on the menu bar, point to **Snapping**, and then click **Snap to Objects** to remove the check mark and deselect this option.

6. With the Oval tool ⭕ still selected on the toolbar, use the Fill Color control on the toolbar to change the fill color to **black**.

7. Draw a smaller oval inside the eye to represent the eye's pupil.

TROUBLE? If you make a mistake and draw over the orange fill of the fish, click Edit on the menu bar, click Undo, and then draw the oval again.

Now you have completed the fish. As shown in the sketch of the banner, several bubbles need to be drawn coming from the fish's mouth. Again, you can use the Oval tool. Because you want these bubbles to appear as perfect circles, you need to select the Snap to Objects command to turn this feature on.

To draw bubbles using the Oval tool and the Snap to Objects command:

1. Make sure the Oval tool ⭕ is still selected on the toolbar, and then use the Fill Color control on the toolbar to change the fill color to **white**. Now ensure the ovals you draw will appear as perfect circles.

2. Click **View** on the menu bar, point to **Snapping**, and then click the **Snap to Objects** command.

3. Draw four circles of varying sizes on the right side of the fish. These circles represent bubbles, as shown in Figure 2-11.

| Figure 2-11 | FISH WITH BUBBLES |

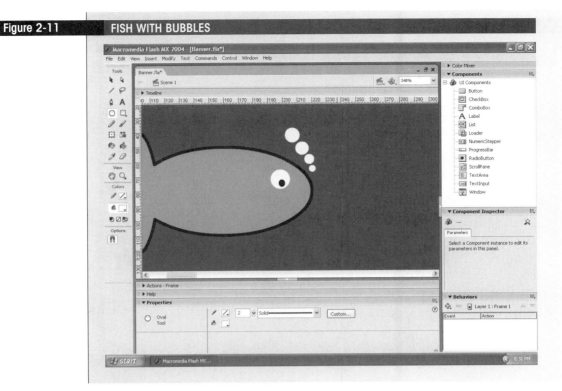

Next you will create a rectangle shape around the banner to provide a frame around all of the graphic elements. As indicated in Aly's sketch, the rectangle will have a stroke and no fill and will have rounded corners.

To draw a rectangle to frame the banner:

1. Double-click the **Hand** tool on the toolbar to make all of the Stage visible.

2. Click the **Rectangle** tool on the toolbar.

3. Click the **Stroke color** control in the Property inspector. In the color pop-up window select the **light gray** color swatch located in the first column, fifth row. Set the stroke height to **2** and the stroke style to **Solid**, if necessary.

4. Click the **Fill Color** control on the toolbar, and then click the **No Color** button.

5. Click the **Round Rectangle Radius** modifier in the options area of the toolbar. In the Rectangle Settings dialog box, enter **10** in the Corner radius text box. Recall that the point values entered for the Corner radius determine how much to round the corners of the rectangle. Click the **OK** button to close the dialog box.

6. On the Stage draw a **rectangle** that forms a border just inside the Stage area, as shown in Figure 2-12.

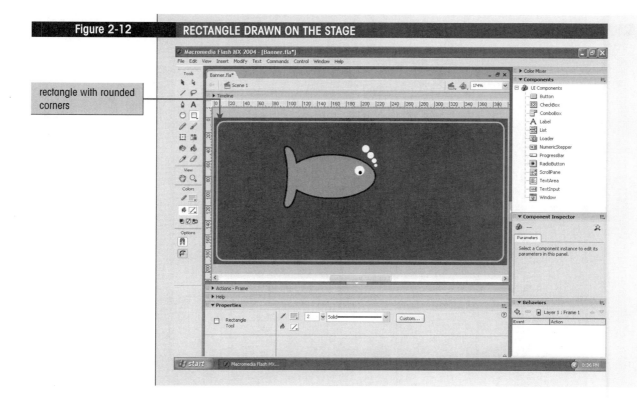

| Figure 2-12 | RECTANGLE DRAWN ON THE STAGE |

rectangle with rounded corners

You show Aly the work you have completed thus far on the banner. She thinks everything looks great, but notices you forgot to draw the fish's mouth and fins. She suggests you use the Pencil tool to add these elements to the drawing.

Pencil Tool

The **Pencil** tool works in a similar way to the Line tool, however, you are not limited to drawing straight lines. The Pencil tool allows you to draw lines and shapes in a free-form manner as if you were using an actual pencil to draw on paper. As is the case with the Line tool, you can select a color, height, and style for the lines drawn with the Pencil tool. You make these selections using the Property inspector. When you select the Pencil tool, the pointer changes to a pencil 🖉 as you move it over the Stage. You click and drag the pointer to draw lines. The Pencil tool has the **Pencil Mode** modifier in the options area of the tool-bar that you can use to control the way your lines appear as you draw them. Figure 2-13 summarizes the options for this modifier.

Figure 2-13	PENCIL MODE MODIFIER OPTIONS	
MODIFIER BUTTON	**OPTION**	**DESCRIPTION**
↳	Straighten	The program helps straighten the lines you draw
S	Smooth	The program smoothes out the lines and curves you draw
⤵	Ink	The program provides minimal assistance as you draw

Now use the Pencil tool to add a mouth and fins to the fish. You will zoom in on the fish to make it easier to work with it.

To add the fins, mouth, and lines to the fish using the Pencil tool:

1. Click the **Zoom** tool on the toolbar, select the **Enlarge** modifier, if necessary, and click the center of the fish once.

2. Click the **Pencil** tool on the toolbar to select it. You will select the Smooth option for the Pencil Mode modifier so that the lines you draw will be smooth.

3. Click the **Pencil Mode** modifier in the options area of the toolbar, and then click the **Smooth** option from the list of pencil modes. Now use the Property inspector to set the stroke color, height, and style before drawing lines.

4. In the Property inspector, make sure the stroke color is **black**, the height is **2**, and the style is **Solid**. You will draw the fins first.

5. Draw a fin on the top side of the fish and another one on the bottom side, as shown in Figure 2-14.

Figure 2-14	FINS ON THE FISH

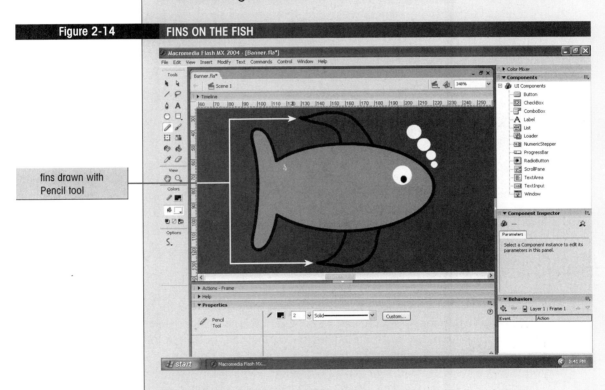

fins drawn with Pencil tool

Now set the stroke height for the fish's mouth.

6. In the Property inspector, change the stroke height to **1**, and draw a small curved line for the fish's mouth starting right below the eye and ending on the stroke in the lower-right side of the fish.

7. Using the , draw three pairs of lines in the middle of the fish starting on the top part of the stroke and ending on the bottom stroke. The fish should look similar to that in Figure 2-15.

Figure 2-15   **FISH WITH FINS, MOUTH, AND LINES**

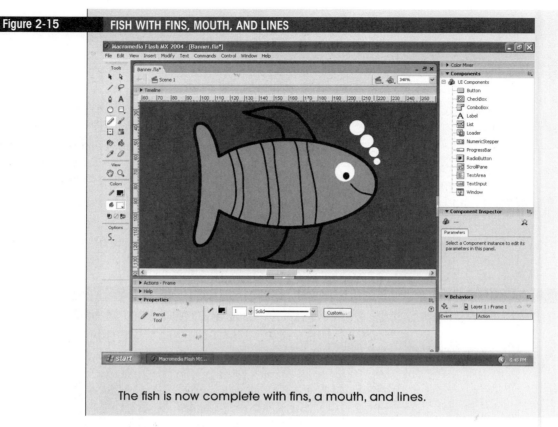

The fish is now complete with fins, a mouth, and lines.

In reviewing the sketch of the banner, you realize the lines on the fish should actually be bands of color. You can add the color to these parts of the fish using the tools on the toolbar that apply color to strokes and fills—the Paint Bucket tool, the Ink Bottle tool, and the Eyedropper tool. You will use the Paint Bucket and the Eyedropper tools on the banner.

Changing Strokes and Fills

Once you draw an object, you can still change its stroke and fill. You can change the stroke's color, height, or style, and you can change a fill's color. You can even add a fill or a stroke to an object that does not have one or the other. The tools used for changing existing strokes and fills include the Paint Bucket, Ink Bottle, and Eyedropper tools. The **Paint Bucket tool** is used to modify an existing fill's color or to apply a fill to an enclosed area that does not have a fill. The **Ink Bottle tool** changes the attributes or properties of a stroke, or it applies a stroke to an object that has no stroke. The **Eyedropper tool** copies the attributes of a stroke on one object to the stroke of another object. It also copies a fill's color from one object to another. In this tutorial we will discuss the Paint Bucket and Eyedropper tool in more detail as these tools will be used to complete the banner for the Flounders Pet Shop.

Paint Bucket Tool

The **Paint Bucket** tool can be used to change the color of a fill or to create a fill for an enclosed area. To use the Paint Bucket tool, you simply select it from the toolbar, select a fill color using the Fill Color control on the toolbar, in the Property inspector, or in the Color Mixer panel, and then click an object's enclosed area using the Paint Bucket pointer. The Paint Bucket tool also has a Gap Size modifier and a Lock Fill modifier in the options area of the toolbar. The **Gap Size modifier** determines how the tool will paint areas that are not completely enclosed. The **Lock Fill modifier** affects gradient and bitmap fills. Gradients and bitmaps will be covered in Tutorial 6. The Paint Bucket modifiers and their options are described in Figure 2-16.

Figure 2-16	PAINT BUCKET TOOL MODIFIERS AND OPTIONS			
MODIFIER BUTTON	**MODIFIER**	**OPTION**		**DESCRIPTION**
⊙	Gap Size	Don't Close Gaps option		Areas not completely enclosed are not painted
⊙	Gap Size	Close Small Gaps option		Areas not enclosed, but with small gaps, are painted
⊙	Gap Size	Close Medium Gaps option		Areas not enclosed, but with medium gaps, are painted
⊙	Gap Size	Close Large Gaps option		Areas not enclosed, but with large gaps, are painted
⊿	Lock Fill			Causes gradient or bitmap fills to extend across multiple objects

You will use the Paint Bucket tool to fill the bands on the fish with some bright colors.

To apply fills to the fish with the Paint Bucket tool:

1. Click the **Paint Bucket** tool 🪣 on the toolbar. Now select a fill color to apply to the fish.

2. Click the **Fill Color** control list arrow on the toolbar to open the Fill Color pop-up window. Select the **yellow** swatch (first column, tenth row) for the fill.

3. Using 🪣, click the area enclosed by the two lines on the far left, as shown in Figure 2-17. The fish now has a yellow stripe.

   TROUBLE? A padlock icon next to the paint bucket pointer means the Lock Fill modifier is selected. This will not affect the way the tool works in these steps.

   TROUBLE? If the yellow color fills other areas of the fish, the lines may not be connected to the fish body outline. If so, make sure that Snap to Objects is turned on and redraw the lines so that they snap to the fish body outline.

Figure 2-17   **APPLYING A FILL COLOR**

paint bucket pointer

yellow stripe

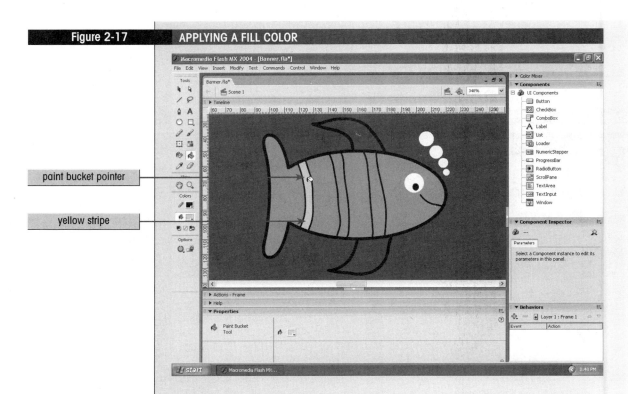

4. Click the **Fill Color** control list arrow on the toolbar to open its color pop-up window, click the **green** swatch (first column, eighth row), and then click the area enclosed by the middle two lines on the fish to make a green stripe.

5. Repeat Step 4 to apply the **pink** color (first column, twelfth row in the color pop-up window) to the area enclosed by the two lines on the far right to give the fish a bright pink stripe. See Figure 2-18.

Figure 2-18   **FISH WITH COLORED STRIPES**

yellow stripe

green stripe

pink stripe

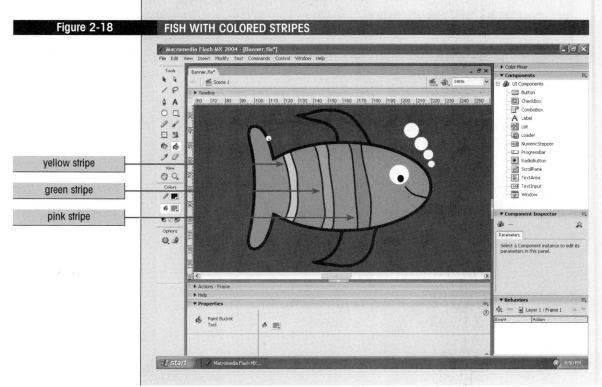

Next, you will learn about the Eyedropper tool.

Eyedropper Tool

The **Eyedropper** tool is used to copy the fill or stroke properties of one object and then apply them to another object. You can also use the Eyedropper tool to copy the properties of a text block and apply them to another text block. You will learn more about creating and working with text in the next session. When you select the Eyedropper tool, the pointer changes to an eyedropper . If you move the eyedropper over a stroke, the pointer changes to include a small pencil next to it indicating that you are about to copy the stroke's attributes. Once you click the stroke, the pointer changes to an ink bottle . You then use the ink bottle to click another object to apply the copied stroke attributes.

You follow a similar process to copy the fill attributes of one object to another. First you select the Eyedropper tool, and then move the eyedropper over a fill. The pointer changes to include a small paintbrush next to it; this indicates that you are about to copy the fill's attributes. When you click the fill whose attributes you want to copy, the pointer changes to a paint bucket . The pointer may include a padlock if the Lock Fill modifier is selected. You then use the paint bucket to click another object to apply the copied fill attributes.

REFERENCE WINDOW	RW
Using the Eyedropper Tool: ■ Click the Eyedropper tool on the toolbar. ■ Click the stroke or fill whose attributes you want to copy. ■ Click the stroke or fill to apply the copied attributes.	

You compare the work you have completed thus far on the banner to Aly's sketch. The fins of the fish need to have the same color as the fish's tail. You can use the Eyedropper tool to copy the fill color of the tail to the fins.

To apply a color using the Eyedropper tool:

1. Click the **Eyedropper** tool on the toolbar.

2. Click the **orange** fill color on the tail of the fish. The pointer changes to to indicate that you can now apply the orange color to another part of the fish.

   TROUBLE? If the paint bucket pointer does not have a padlock icon next to it, that means the Lock Fill modifier is not selected. This will not affect the way the tool works in these steps.

3. Click the blank area enclosed by the top fin, as shown in Figure 2-19. The top fin now has the same color as the rest of the fish.

Figure 2-19   **APPLYING A COPIED COLOR**

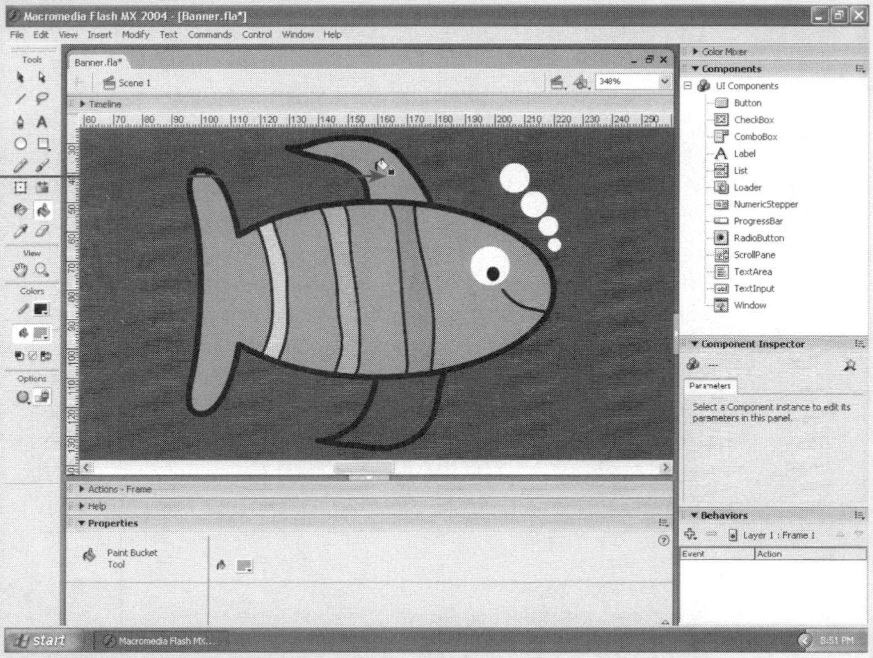

pointer changes to paint bucket to apply fill color

4. Click the bottom fin with the 🪣 to apply the orange fill color to the fin.

You have completed drawing the fish by applying colors to the fins to match its body. To keep the various parts of the fish and the bubbles together, you will group them so that they are treated as one object. This will allow you to modify the fish graphic as a whole or to create copies of the fish graphic without having to work with each of its individual elements.

To group the fish graphic and bubbles:

1. Using the Selection tool, draw a selection marquee around all of the fish and bubbles.

2. Click **Modify** on the menu bar, and then click **Group**. The graphic elements are now grouped and a thin rectangular blue line surrounds the grouped object to show it is selected. See Figure 2-20.

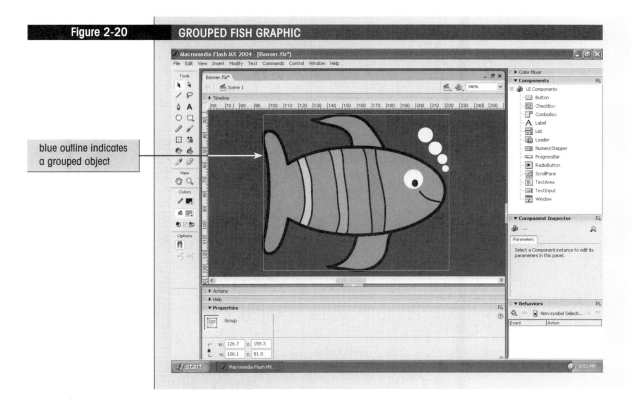

Figure 2-20   **GROUPED FISH GRAPHIC**

blue outline indicates a grouped object

You have completed the fish graphic and grouped it to make it easier to work with. In reviewing the sketch you see that plant leaves are still needed for the banner. Aly suggests that you use the Pen tool to draw the plant leaves because the Pen tool can be used to draw line segments that can then be modified to resemble leaves.

Pen Tool

The **Pen** tool can be used to draw shapes consisting of straight and curved lines connected by anchor points. Areas that are enclosed when you draw these lines are filled with the fill color currently selected in the Fill Color control on the toolbar. When you select the Pen tool, the pointer changes to a pen icon 🖊ₓ with a small x next to it indicating that you are about to start a new line or curve. Clicking the Stage with the Pen tool pointer creates points that are then connected with straight lines. To draw curved lines you click and drag instead of just clicking points. As you drag the pointer, a curved line is drawn. Drawing curved lines can be tricky especially because you cannot always see the curve as you are drawing it. To make it easier to see what you are drawing, you can select the Show pen preview command, which is located on the Editing tab of the Preferences dialog box. To open the Preferences dialog box, you click Edit on the menu bar, and then click Preferences.

You will use the Pen tool to draw the plant leaves Aly sketched as part of the banner.

To draw with the Pen tool:

1. Double-click the **Hand** tool 🖐 to change the Stage view to make all of the Stage visible.

2. Click the **Selection** tool 🔖 on the toolbar and then click a blank area of the Stage to deselect the fish.

3. Click the **Pen** tool 🖊 on the toolbar. Before using the Pen tool to draw the leaves, set the stroke and fill colors.

4. In the Property inspector, set **black** as the stroke color, and **dark green** (located in the fourth column, first row of the color pop-up window) for the fill color. Set the stroke height to **1** and the stroke style to **Solid**. Now you are ready to draw the object that will become the plant leaves.

5. On the left side of the Stage above the gray rectangle's bottom side, click to create the anchor points shown in Figure 2-21. Click the points in the shape of the letter M. Do not worry about the exact shape as you can modify the shape later. Your last click should be back on the beginning anchor point to complete the shape.

| Figure 2-21 | ANCHOR POINTS DRAWN WITH PEN TOOL |

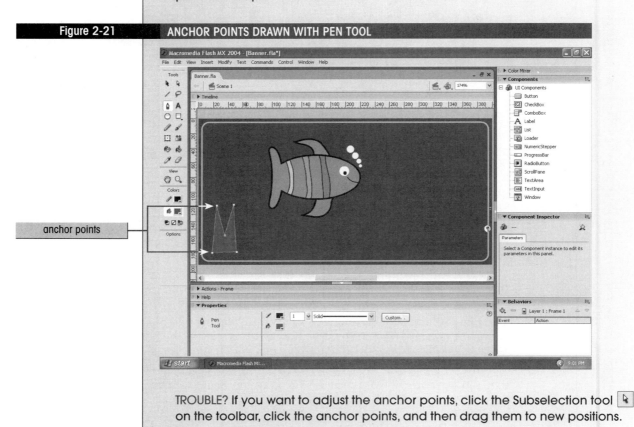

anchor points

TROUBLE? If you want to adjust the anchor points, click the Subselection tool ▷ on the toolbar, click the anchor points, and then drag them to new positions.

Now you will use the Selection tool to modify the lines you have drawn so they appear curved like plant leaves.

To modify the lines using the Selection tool:

1. Click the **Selection** tool ▶ on the toolbar.

2. Point to the left edge of the plant leaves shape. When the pointer changes to ⤵, drag the line slightly to the left to curve it, as shown in Figure 2-22.

Figure 2-22   LINE MODIFIED WITH SELECTION TOOL

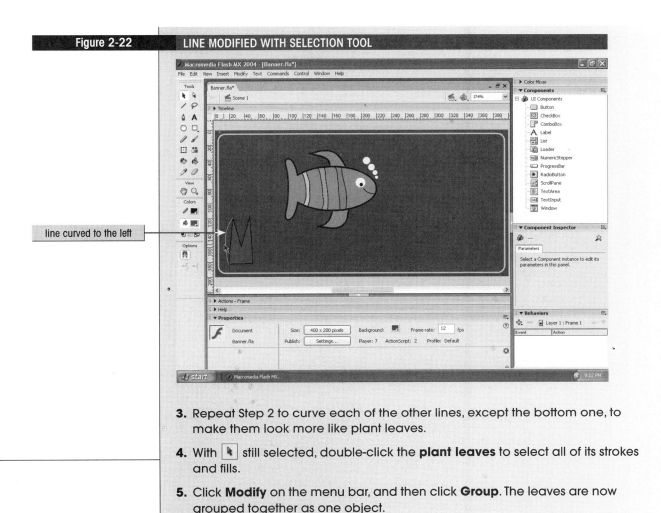

line curved to the left

3. Repeat Step 2 to curve each of the other lines, except the bottom one, to make them look more like plant leaves.

4. With ⟨�⟩ still selected, double-click the **plant leaves** to select all of its strokes and fills.

5. Click **Modify** on the menu bar, and then click **Group**. The leaves are now grouped together as one object.

Now you will make a copy of the plant leaves you created and you will transform the copy by using the Flip Horizontal command on the Transform menu which is found on the Modify menu. You will then create a copy of the two sets of plant leaves and move the copy to the right side of the banner.

To create more plant leaves:

1. Click the **plant leaves** group with the Selection tool ⟨�⟩ to select it, if necessary. Click **Edit** on the menu bar, and click **Copy**. Click **Edit** again, and then click **Paste in Center** to create the copy.

2. Drag the **copy** of the plant leaves to the right side of the original plant leaves. Now you will use the Transform command to flip the selected leaves horizontally.

3. Click **Modify** on the menu bar, point to **Transform**, and then click **Flip Horizontal**. See Figure 2-23.

Figure 2-23   **PLANT LEAVES**

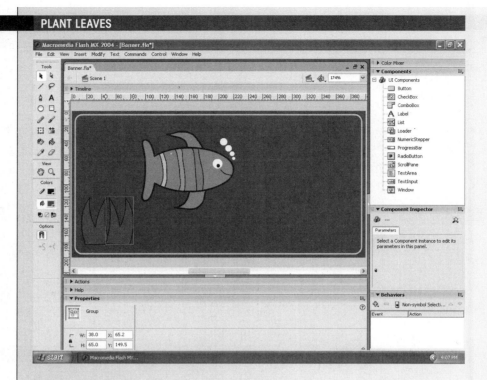

4. Draw a rectangular marquee around the two groups of plant leaves to select both of them at the same time. Make sure you do not select any other objects.

5. Click **Edit** on the menu bar, click **Copy**, click **Edit** on the menu bar again, and then click **Paste in Center**. A copy of the set of plant leaves is placed on the center of the Stage.

6. Move the new set of plant leaves to the lower-right corner of the Stage, as shown in Figure 2-24.

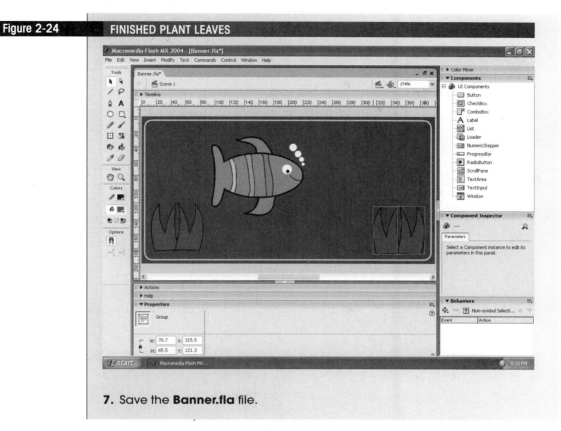

Figure 2-24 **FINISHED PLANT LEAVES**

7. Save the **Banner.fla** file.

Free Transform Tool

Once you draw objects, you may want to modify them in various ways other than just changing their color. Flash provides several tools to modify an object's strokes and fills. One of these is the **Free Transform tool**. This tool allows you to move, rotate, scale, skew, or even distort objects. You can transform a particular stroke or fill of an object, or you can transform the entire object at one time. When you select an object with the Free Transform tool, a bounding box with selection handles surrounds the object, as shown in Figure 2-25.

Figure 2-25   **BOUNDING BOX ON AN OBJECT**

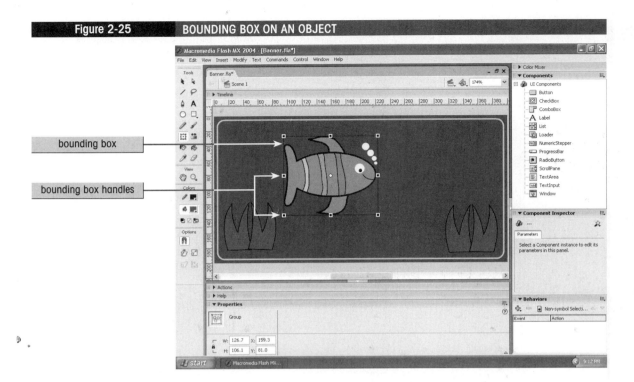

bounding box

bounding box handles

You drag the handles of the bounding box to transform the object. These selection handles are different from the anchor points you used with the Pen tool and Subselection tool. The anchor points are used to modify the curves, lines, or specific shapes. The selection handles on the bounding box affect the whole object at one time.

As you move the pointer near a handle, the pointer changes to indicate how the object will be modified when you drag the handle. For example, when you point just outside a corner handle, the pointer changes to a Rotate pointer ↻, meaning you can rotate the object by dragging the corner. The Free Transform tool also has several modifiers in the options area of the toolbar. These include the **Rotate and Skew**, **Scale**, **Distort**, and **Envelope** modifiers, and they are described in Figure 2-26.

Figure 2-26   **FREE TRANSFORM TOOL MODIFIERS**

MODIFIER BUTTON	OPTION	DESCRIPTION
	Rotate and Skew	Allows you to freely rotate an object by dragging a corner handle or to skew it at a different angle by dragging an edge handle
	Scale	Allows you to change the size of an object by dragging a corner or edge handle
	Distort	Allows you to reposition the corner or edge of an object by dragging its handle
	Envelope	Displays a bounding box with points and tangent handles; you can then adjust these points or tangent handles to warp or distort the object

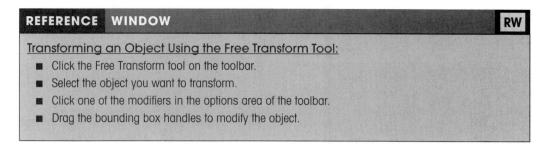

REFERENCE WINDOW **RW**

Transforming an Object Using the Free Transform Tool:
- Click the Free Transform tool on the toolbar.
- Select the object you want to transform.
- Click one of the modifiers in the options area of the toolbar.
- Drag the bounding box handles to modify the object.

The sketch for the banner shows another smaller fish swimming next to the larger fish you already drew. Instead of drawing the smaller fish from scratch, you can simply copy the existing fish, and then use the Free Transform tool to resize the copied fish.

To make a copy of the fish:

1. To create a copy of the fish, click the **fish** once to select it.

2. Click **Edit** on the menu bar, and then click **Copy**. Click **Edit** on the menu bar again, and then click **Paste in Center**. A copy of the fish is placed in the center of the Stage.

3. Use the **Selection** tool to drag the copy and position it to the right of the original fish, as shown in Figure 2-27.

| Figure 2-27 | COPY OF FISH |

fish copy

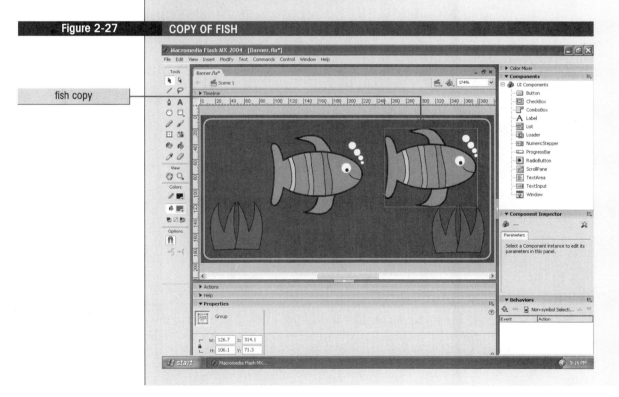

Now that you have a copy of the fish, you can use the Free Transform tool to modify it.

To modify the copied fish with the Free Transform tool:

1. Click the **Free Transform** tool ⊞ on the toolbar, and then click the **Scale** modifier ⬚ in the options area of the toolbar.

   A bounding box with selection handles appears around the fish. You can use this to reduce the size of the copied fish.

2. Drag a corner handle to reduce the size of the fish to about half the size of the original.

3. Click the **Rotate and Skew** modifier ⬚ in the options area of the toolbar, click the copied fish, and drag the lower-right corner handle down to rotate the fish so that it appears to be swimming in a downward direction, as shown in Figure 2-28.

| Figure 2-28 | ROTATING THE FISH |

bounding box handles used to rotate object

4. Save the **Banner.fla** file.

You decide to show Aly the work you have completed thus far on the banner. She is very pleased with the fish and the plants and suggests you now turn your attention to the text that is to appear at the top of the banner. You will add the text to the banner in the next session.

In this session you learned how to use the drawing tools and to add colors to strokes and fills. You saw how you can change a fill's color and a stroke's color, height, and style. You also learned how to modify an object by scaling and rotating it. In the next session you will learn how to work with text, how to export a graphic, and you will see how to undo, replay, and save steps as commands.

Session 3.1 QUICK CHECK

1. When drawing a shape with the Oval tool, Flash helps you draw a perfect circle when the Snap to Grid option is selected. True or False?

2. How can you draw a rectangle with rounded corners?

3. The _____ tool is used to draw line and curve segments by creating anchor points that connect them.

4. The _____ modifier helps straighten lines you draw with the Pencil tool.

5. Describe how to use the Eyedropper tool to copy a stroke's attributes to another object.

6. Which tool can you use to add a fill to an enclosed area that has no fill?

7. Which modifier can be used with the Free Transform tool to resize a selected object?

8. The Free Transform tool is used to modify an object's gradient fill. True or False?

SESSION 2.2

In this session you will learn how to use the Text tool to create different types of text boxes, and you will learn how to export a graphic for use on a Web page. You will also learn how to undo, replay, and save the steps you perform while working with a document.

Adding Text

As you have seen, Flash gives you the tools to easily create graphic images. However, graphic images alone may not communicate the message you are trying to convey with your Flash document. Many of the images and animations you create will also need to include text. Fortunately, in Flash you can easily create text blocks in a variety of colors, sizes, and fonts. You use the Text tool to add static text blocks to a document. A **static text block** is simply an object that contains text which is entered when you create the document but does not change once you publish the document. You can also create dynamic text fields or input text fields. A **dynamic text field** is an advanced feature where the text can be updated automatically with information from a Web server when the document is published and displayed in a Web browser. An example of this would be a text field that displays up-to-the-minute sports scores retrieved from a Web server. An **input text field** allows the user to enter text in forms or surveys. You will only work with static text blocks in this tutorial.

You create a text block using the Text tool located on the toolbar. To set or change the properties of text such as the font size, color, alignment, and spacing between characters, you need to use the Property inspector. These properties will be displayed in the Property inspector when the Text tool or a text block is selected.

Text Tool

The **Text** tool is used to create text blocks for your documents. Text can be created in a **fixed-width** text block or in a **single-line** text block that extends as you type. If the width of the text block is fixed, the text wraps around to create new lines as needed. To create a fixed-width text block, you click the Text tool on the toolbar, and then you click and drag the text pointer on the Stage. The text block has a square handle in its upper-right corner indicating that the width of the text block will remain fixed. As you type, the words wrap around to the next line when you reach the right margin of the block. To create a single-line text block, click once on the Stage with the text pointer where you want the text to appear and begin typing. The text block has a round handle on the upper-right corner which indicates that the width of the text block extends as you type.

You can change a fixed-width text block to a single-line text block by double-clicking its square handle. The text block changes to one line and its handle becomes round. Similarly, if you drag the round handle of a single-line text block to adjust the width of the block, the handle becomes square indicating that the width of the block is now fixed.

Once you create a text block, you can move it on the Stage using the Selection tool, and you can also resize, rotate, and skew it using the Free Transform tool. The font, size, color, and other properties of the text are determined by the settings you specify in the Property inspector. You can set these properties before you type the text or you can select existing text and then change its properties. The Property inspector has many options for text. The main options you will work with are Font, Font Size, Text (fill) color, and text style. You choose the color for the text using the various Fill Color controls on the toolbar, the Color Mixer panel, or the Property inspector. The text options in the Property inspector are indentified in Figure 2-29.

Figure 2-29   **TEXT OPTIONS IN THE PROPERTY INSPECTOR**

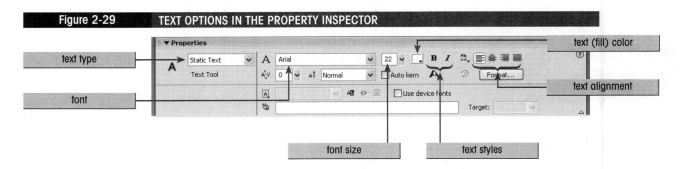

Use the Text tool to add two text blocks to the banner. You will set the Property inspector options before you create the text.

To add text to the banner:

1. If you took a break after the last session, open the **Banner.fla** file located in the **Tutorial.02\Tutorial** folder included with your Data Files. If necessary, collapse the Timeline by clicking its titlebar.

2. Click the **Text** tool A on the toolbar. Now set the text properties.

3. Using the Property inspector, set the font to **Arial**, the font size to **22**, and the text fill color to **white**. Also, click the **Bold** button **B** to apply bold, if necessary.

4. Click once in the top area of the Stage to create a single-line text box. Type **Flounders Pet Shop**, as shown in Figure 2-30.

| Figure 2-30 | TEXT BLOCK FOR BANNER |

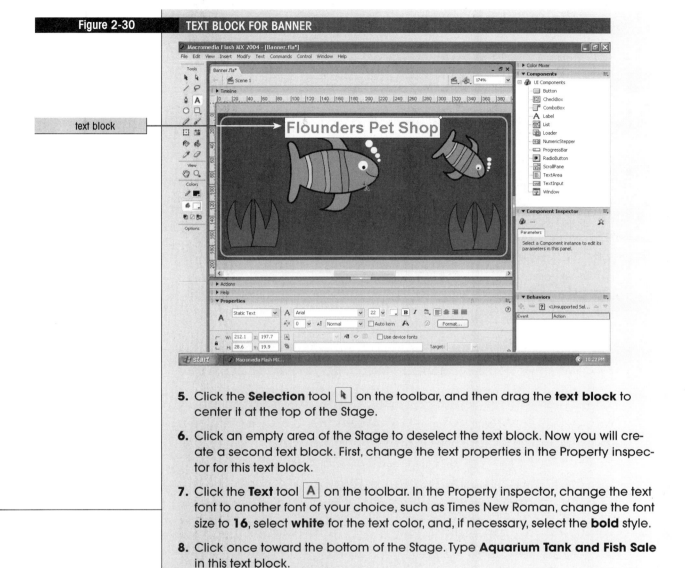

text block

5. Click the **Selection** tool 🔓 on the toolbar, and then drag the **text block** to center it at the top of the Stage.

6. Click an empty area of the Stage to deselect the text block. Now you will create a second text block. First, change the text properties in the Property inspector for this text block.

7. Click the **Text** tool A on the toolbar. In the Property inspector, change the text font to another font of your choice, such as Times New Roman, change the font size to **16**, select **white** for the text color, and, if necessary, select the **bold** style.

8. Click once toward the bottom of the Stage. Type **Aquarium Tank and Fish Sale** in this text block.

9. If necessary, use the Selection tool to center the text block. The banner is now complete, and matches the sketch Aly provided.

10. Save the **Banner.fla** file.

Once you have added text to your document, you can have Flash check your spelling.

Spellchecking Text

To check spelling, you use the Check Spelling command on the Text menu. This command will check the spelling in each of your document's text blocks. It can also check the spelling of text in other parts of your document such as symbol names and layer names. Symbols are covered in the next session and layers are covered in the next tutorial. Before you use the Check Spelling command for the first time, you need to specify some options in the Spelling Setup dialog box, as shown in Figure 2-31. To open the Spelling Setup dialog box, click the Spelling Setup command on the Text menu.

Figure 2-31 **SPELLING SETUP DIALOG BOX**

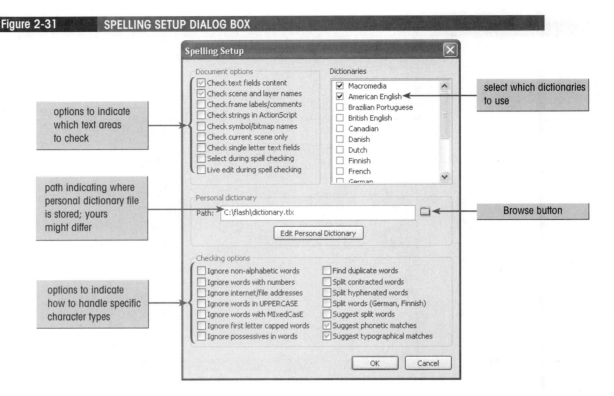

Under Document options in the Spelling Setup dialog box you specify which text areas to check such as the content of text fields and the names of layers. You also select which built-in dictionaries to use such as the Macromedia terms dictionary and a language dictionary such as American English. The Path for the Personal dictionary specifies where you want Flash to create a file that will contain words and phrases you add yourself. You click the Browse button to navigate to a location on your hard drive where the file will be created. The personal dictionary can contain words that are not in the Macromedia or language dictionaries but are spelled correctly. For example, a company name may be spelled correctly but may be considered misspelled by Flash. You can add the name to your personal dictionary so it will not be considered misspelled. You can also edit your personal dictionary once it is created. Finally, in the Spelling Setup dialog box, you can also specify Checking options that tell Flash how to handle specific character types such as words with numbers or words with all uppercase letters. You can have Flash ignore such words when spellchecking your document. You can also select options, such as Suggest phonetic matches, to have Flash provide a list of suggestions when it encounters a misspelled word. You can then choose one of the suggested words to replace the misspelled word.

Once you have specified the options in the Spelling Setup dialog box you are ready to check the spelling in your document. To begin checking, click Text on the menu bar and then click Check Spelling. If Flash finds a word that is mispelled or not contained in its dictionaries, the Check Spelling dialog box opens, as shown in Figure 2-32.

Figure 2-32   **CHECK SPELLING DIALOG BOX**

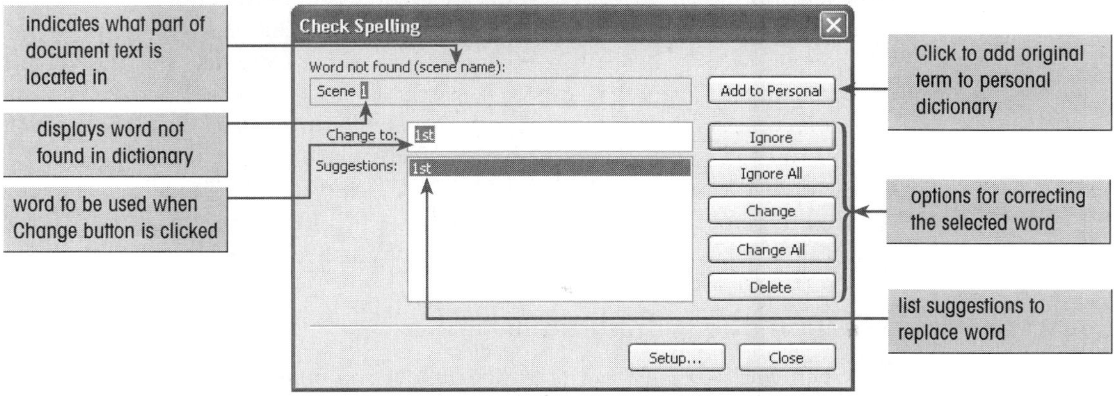

The options in the Check Spelling dialog box are described in Figure 2-33.

Figure 2-33

OPTION	DESCRIPTION
Word not found text box	Displays the word not found in the selected dictionaries; will also indicate in parentheses if the word is in a text field, scene name, or layer name depending on the options selected in the Spelling Setup dialog box
Change to text box	Contains the word that will replace the misspelled word when the Change button is clicked
Suggestions list box	Lists suggested words to replace the misspelled word
Add to Personal button	Adds the selected word to your personal dictionary
Ignore button	Ignores the selected word
Ignore All button	Ignores all occurrences of the selected word
Change button	Changes the selected word with the word in the Change to text box
Change All button	Changes all occurrences of the selected word with the word in the Change to text box
Delete button	Deletes the selected word from your document

Depending on the options you select in the Spelling Setup dialog box, the Check Spelling dialog box will display a word not found in its dictionaries and may offer suggestions for replacing the word. You can choose to add the word to your personal dictionary, ignore the word, change it, or delete it. The Check Spelling dialog box also shows in what element of the document the word not found is located. For example, it may show that the word not found is in a text field, a scene name, or a layer name.

You have completed the banner by adding text and you learned about spell checking text. Aly is very pleased with your work. She asks you to export the banner for use on the pet shop's Web site. Chris has recommended that the banner be exported in the GIF file format. Recall from Tutorial 1 that most Web pages use graphics that are in the GIF or JPG file format because these formats do not require a plug-in to display on a Web page.

Exporting a Graphic for Use on the Web

A document you create in Flash is saved in the FLA format. This format contains all of the different elements you create in Flash. When you need to revise the document, you open the FLA file. When you are ready to place the image on a Web page, however, it needs to be published or exported. Publishing a document will be covered in more detail in Tutorial 3 when you add animations to your documents. A published document is in the SWF file format and is called a Flash movie. It requires the Flash Player plug-in to play in a Web browser. When you create a document such as the Flounders Pet Shop banner that does not have animation, you can export it instead of publishing it. **Exporting** means that the program converts the document into another file format such as GIF or JPG. Exporting also combines all of the individual elements of your document into one graphic. You cannot edit the individual elements of the image in an exported file. To edit the image's elements, you need to go back to the corresponding FLA file. Once you export the document into a GIF or JPG file format, it can be placed on a Web page using HTML code.

Export Image Command

When you are ready to export a document you point to Export on the File menu and select Export Image. When you select this command an Export Image dialog box opens in which you specify the location where the file will be saved, and the name of the exported file. You specify the type of file you want to export in the Save as type list box. The list box contains formats such as GIF and JPG, as well as formats specific to other drawing programs such as Adobe Illustrator. When you click the Save button, another dialog box may open, depending on the export format you selected. This dialog box, which is different for each export format, has additional options and settings from which to select depending on the particular file format.

Because you need to export the Banner.fla file to a GIF file format, you will use the Export Image command.

To export the banner to a GIF file format:

1. Click **File** on the menu bar, point to **Export**, and then click **Export Image** to open the Export Image dialog box.

2. In the Export Image dialog box, navigate to the **Tutorial.02\Tutorial** folder included with your Data Files. Enter **Banner** as the name of the file, and select **GIF Image** from the **Save as type** list box, as shown in Figure 2-34. Click the **Save** button. An Export GIF dialog box opens.

Figure 2-34	EXPORT IMAGE DIALOG BOX

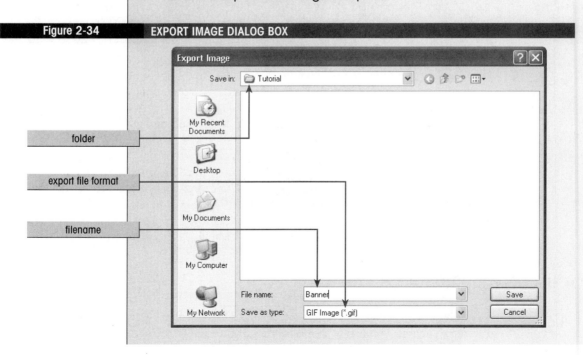

folder

export file format

filename

3. Click the **Include** list arrow, click **Full Document Size**, and then click the **OK** button. The banner is exported as a GIF file.

4. Click **File** on the menu bar, and then click **Close** to close the file. If you are prompted to save your changes, click the **Yes** button.

You have exported the banner as a GIF file. Aly gave this GIF file to Chris, and had him place it in a Web page with the HTML needed to display the Banner.gif image. You can preview this Web page in your Web browser.

To preview the Banner.gif file in a Web browser:

1. Start your Web browser.

2. Click **File** on the menu bar, and then click **Open**. In the Open dialog box, click the **Browse** button, and navigate to **Tutorial.02\Tutorial** folder included with your Data Files.

3. Select the **Flounder.htm** file, click **Open**, and then click **OK** in the Open dialog box. The Web page opens in the browser and the Banner.gif file displays as part of the page, as shown in Figure 2-35.

Figure 2-35   WEB PAGE WITH EXPORTED BANNER

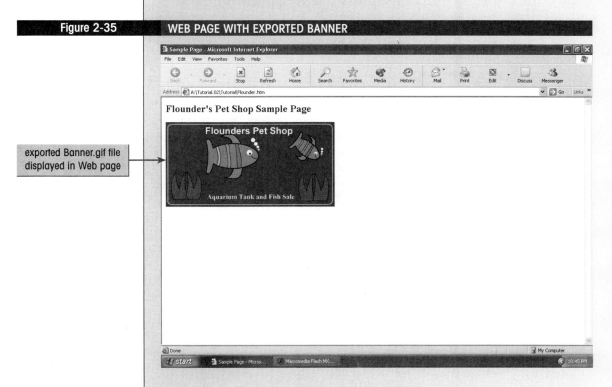

exported Banner.gif file displayed in Web page

4. Close the browser when you are done viewing the Web page with the banner.

Once you view your document in a Web browser, you might want to go back to the document, review it, and make some changes. The History panel in Flash is a useful tool for reviewing and editing your work.

Using the History Panel

The History panel allows you to undo, replay, and save steps you have performed in the current document. Once you open or create a document, each step is recorded and displayed in the History panel with an icon that reflects the particular step, as shown in Figure 2-36.

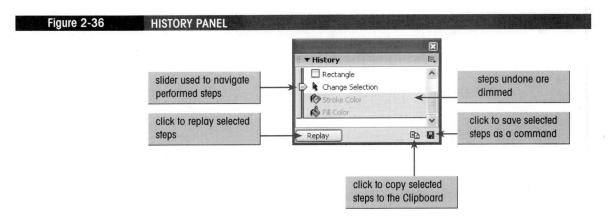

Figure 2-36   HISTORY PANEL

slider used to navigate performed steps

click to replay selected steps

steps undone are dimmed

click to save selected steps as a command

click to copy selected steps to the Clipboard

These steps can then be undone, replayed, or even saved as commands. The History panel only displays the steps for the current document. If you switch to another document, the History panel changes to display the steps taken in creating or editing that document.

Undoing Steps

As you work with the various tools in Flash to create and modify graphic images, you will often want to undo one or more steps within a document. This may occur if you make a mistake and you want to go back to the previous step. Flash gives you the ability to undo one or more steps by simply clicking the Undo command on the Edit menu or by using the keyboard shortcut Ctrl + Z. By default, Flash allows you to undo up to 100 steps. As a result, you can backtrack though a series of steps which you performed until you get back to a particular state of the document at which you want to start over. You can change the default number of steps that can be undone using the Preferences dialog box which you open by clicking the Preferences command on the Edit menu.

If after you have performed a series of steps you decide you want to change the document back to how it was before you performed the steps, you can use the History panel. The slider in the History panel shown in Figure 2-36 initially points to the last step you performed. You can drag the slider to go back to a previous step. As you move the slider to point to a step, it will be undone and the document on the Stage will change based on the steps being undone. That step will also appear dimmed in the History panel.

Replaying Steps

You can also apply one or more steps in the History panel to an object on the Stage. You do this by selecting an object on the Stage, selecting one or more steps in the History panel, and then clicking the Replay button in the panel. The steps are then applied to the selected object in the order shown in the panel. Steps displayed with an icon that includes a small red x cannot be replayed.

Selected steps can also be applied to objects in other documents. You first select one or more steps in the History panel and then click the Copy selected steps to the clipboard button. This copies the selected steps to the Windows Clipboard. You can then open another

Flash document, select an object on the Stage, and use the Paste in Center command on the Edit menu to apply the copied steps to the selected object in the document.

Saving Steps

The History panel also allows you to save selected steps as commands. If you have a series of steps you expect to use frequently, you can create a command based on those steps. You select the steps in the History panel, click the Save selected steps as a Command button, and assign a name for the command. To use the command in the same document or in another document, you click the Commands menu on the menu bar. You can then click the name of the command which is displayed on the menu. This and other commands you save are available each time you use Flash.

Aly wants you to become familiar with the History panel by working with a document she has created for another Admiral Web Design client, Jackson's Sports.

To use the History panel with a sample document:

1. Navigate to the **Tutorial.02\Tutorial** folder included with your Data Files and open the **sports1.fla** document. The Jackson's Sports banner opens.

2. Click **Window** on the menu bar, point to **Other Panels**, and then click **History**. The History panel opens. If necessary, move the panel to the right side of the screen. Before you can work with the document, you need to unlock the layers in the document. You do this using the Timeline.

3. If necessary, click the **Selection** tool on the toolbar, display the **Timeline**, then click the **Lock/Unlock All Layers** icon in the Timeline to unlock the layers. Notice that a step labeled Lock Layers is added to the History panel. Next you will modify the top text block.

4. Click the **Jackson's Sports** text block to select the block and use the Text (fill) color control in the Property inspector to change the text color to yellow (first column, tenth row). The letters in the text block change color. Now increase the size of the text block.

5. Click the **Free Transform** tool on the toolbar, and then click the **Scale modifier** button . Drag the bottom right corner handle on the text block to make the text block slightly larger. Now you can replay these steps from the History panel.

6. In the History panel, click and drag to select the Fill Color and Scale. Do not drag the slider on the left side of the History panel as this will undo steps you have performed. See Figure 2-37.

Figure 2-37   STEPS SELECTED IN HISTORY PANEL

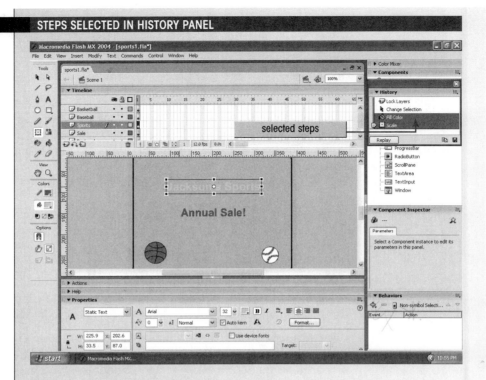

7. Click the **Annual Sale** text block in the center of the Stage to select it. Click the **Replay** button in the History panel. The text block increases slightly in size and the text color changes to yellow.

8. Click ▶ on the toolbar, click the **basketball** to select it, and then drag the basketball to the upper-left corner of the Stage.

9. Press and hold the **Ctrl** key on the keyboard, and then click the **Move** step in the History panel to select this step. With the Ctrl key still pressed, click **Fill Color** in the History panel to deselect it, and make sure that **Scale** is still selected.

10. Click the **baseball** on the Stage to select it, and then click the **Replay** button in the History pane to replay the selected steps. The baseball becomes slightly larger and moves to the top of the Stage. Finally, you will use the History panel to undo steps.

11. Drag the slider in the History panel up so that it points to the Scale step. The steps below the Scale step are dimmed indicating that they have been undone. The objects on the Stage also change to reflect that the steps were undone.

12. Close the **sports1.fla** document. Do not save the changes you have made.

In this session you learned how to create text blocks, how to set the properties for the text, and how to check for spelling errors. You added text blocks to the banner for the Flounders Pet Shop and exported the finished banner as a GIF file which was previewed in a Web page. Finally, you learned how to undo, replay, and save steps using the History panel.

Session 3.1 QUICK CHECK

1. What is the difference between a static text block and a dynamic text field?

2. How do you create a fixed-width text block?

3. Which panel is used to set text attributes such as the font and size?

4. How can you change a single-line text block into a fixed-width text block?

5. If a text block displays a square handle in its upper-right corner, what type of text block is it?

6. Which option do you select in the Spelling Setup dialog box so that Flash will check the spelling of the text in your text blocks?

7. What is the purpose of the personal dictionary path in the Spelling Setup dialog box?

8. How can you undo a series of steps using the History panel?

SESSION 2.3

In this session you will learn how to create and edit symbols and instances of symbols. You will also learn how to use the Library panel to organize the symbols by creating library folders.

Symbols

Symbols are elements such as graphics and buttons that can be used more than once in your document. You can create a symbol from an existing object by selecting the object on the Stage and then using the Convert to Symbol command on the Insert menu. You can also create a new symbol by using the New Symbol command on the Insert menu. You can also use symbols from other Flash documents in your current document.

Symbol Behavior Types

The symbols in your document are characterized as having one of three types of behavior. These include movie clip, graphic, and button. **Movie clips**, the default behavior, contain their own Timeline and operate independently of the Timeline of the movie in which they appear. For example, a movie clip may contain an animation sequence that spans 10 frames within its own Timeline. When the movie clip is used in the document, its 10 frames do not occupy 10 frames in the document's Timeline. Instead, the movie clip occupies only one frame within the document's Timeline and yet it still plays its own 10-frame animation. Most of the symbols you create can be movie clips. **Graphic** symbols can be static images or animated images. They operate in sync with the Timeline of the movie in which they appear. A graphic symbol with a 10-frame animation sequence occupies 10 frames in the document's Timeline. **Button** symbols have their own four-frame Timeline. You will learn more about buttons in Tutorial 5. Most of the time, you can select the default behavior of Movie Clip for the symbols you create. When you need to have a symbol's animation synchronized with the rest of the document's Timeline, then you choose Graphic. And when you want to make a symbol into an interactive button, you choose Button. You can easily change a symbol's behavior at any time.

Symbols are stored in the document's library and are accessible from the Library panel.

The Library

The **library** stores symbols you create for a document. You view, organize, and edit symbols stored in the library from the Library panel. When you create a symbol for a document, you assign a name to it, and you specify certain properties based on the behavior of the symbol. These properties of the symbol are stored with the symbol in the library. Symbols created within a document are saved with that document. However, you can share symbols with other documents by making them part of a shared library. Shared libraries are an advanced topic and are not covered in this tutorial. You can modify a symbol's properties using the Library panel. The Library panel, as shown in Figure 2-38, displays a list with the names of all the symbols in the library for the sports document.

Figure 2-38	LIBRARY PANEL

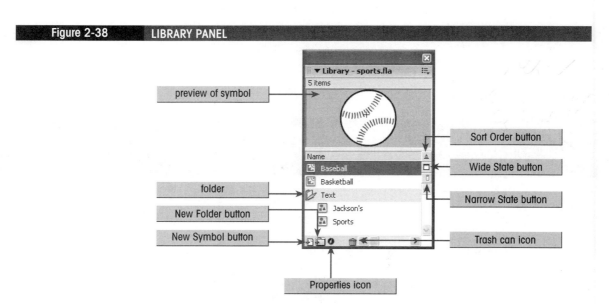

To view the Library panel, click the Library command on the Window menu. Each symbol in the Library panel has an icon to the left of its name to show what type of symbol it is. A symbol's type is the same as its behavior. You can click the name of a symbol to see a thumbnail preview of the symbol at the top of the Library panel.

The options available from the Library panel are described in Figure 2-39.

Figure 2-39	LIBRARY PANEL OPTIONS

BUTTON	OPTION	DESCRIPTION
⊡	New Symbol	Click to create a new symbol; opens the Create New Symbol dialog box in which you enter the symbol's name and behavior type; it then takes you into symbol-editing mode to create the symbol
⊡	New Folder	Click to create a new folder; a folder can be used to organize related symbols
🗑	Trash can	Click to delete a symbol; be careful when deleting symbols because you cannot undo this action
ⓘ	Properties	Click to view and edit a symbol's properties in the Symbol Properties dialog box; the Symbol Properties dialog box allows you to change the symbol's name and behavior type (movie clip, graphic, or button)
⬆	Sort Order	Click to change the order in which the symbols are listed; toggle between A–Z and Z–A order based on the symbol names
☐	Wide State	Click to expand the view of the Library panel to show more details about each symbol, such as the date it was last modified
▯	Narrow State	Click to contract the view of the Library panel to show only the Name column; this is the default view

As you work with a document, you will often create many symbols. Some of these symbols may be related to a particular graphic in the document. For example, you may have multiple symbols that make up a button on the Stage. As your document gets more complex, the number of symbols in the library can increase significantly and become unmanageable. To make it easier to manage and organize the symbols in the Library panel, you can create folders that can group and hold related symbols. You create a folder by clicking the New Folder button in the Library panel or by clicking New Folder from the Library panel's options menu. Folders display in the Library panel with a folder icon. Any symbols inside a folder will appear indented under the folder name. You can double-click a folder's icon to collapse it so that its contents are not displayed and you double-click it again to expand the folder so that its contents display.

The Library panel can also be expanded to show several columns of information about each symbol. Figure 3-14 shows the Library panel in wide view. To switch to wide view, you click the Wide State button identified in Figure 2-40.

Figure 2-40	WIDE VIEW OF THE LIBRARY PANEL

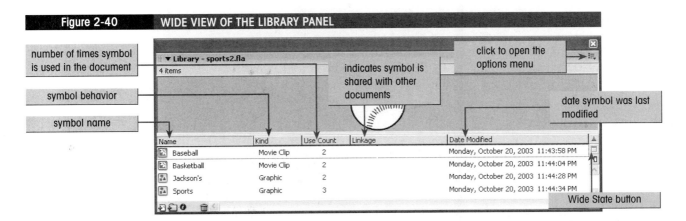

This view displays additional columns listing the symbol's behavior (Kind column), the number of times the symbol is used in the document (Use Count column), whether the symbol is shared with other documents (Linkage column), and the date it was last modified (Date Modified column). You can also sort the symbols according to a column by clicking the column's header. For example, if you wanted to sort the symbols by date, you would click the Date Modified header to sort the symbols. The order of the dates would be from most recent to oldest. This order can be reversed by clicking the Sort Order button. To get back to the default view of the Library panel, click the Narrow State button.

Additional Library panel options can be accessed using the Library panel's options menu. This menu includes options to create new symbols, rename, edit, or delete symbols, as well as to create duplicates of a symbol.

To become familiar with the Library panel, you will explore a sample document's library to see how symbols are stored, and you will change the behavior of one of the symbols using the Library panel.

To open a sample document and explore its library:

1. Open the **sports2.fla** document located in the **Tutorial.02\Tutorial folder** included with your Data Files. Another version of the Jackson's Sports banner opens.

2. Click **Window** on the menu bar and then click **Library** to open the document's library. The Library panel opens and displays the symbols for this document. If necessary, separate the Library panel into its own window by dragging it from the left corner of its title bar and placing it in the center of the Stage.

3. Click the **Basketball** symbol in the Name column of the Library panel. A preview of the basketball is displayed in the preview window. Next change the view of the Library panel.

4. Click the **Wide State** button ☐ to expand the view of the Library panel. You may need to reposition the Library panel to see all of it. See Figure 2-41. Now sort the symbols by behavior.

| Figure 2-41 | SPORTS BANNER LIBRARY PANEL |

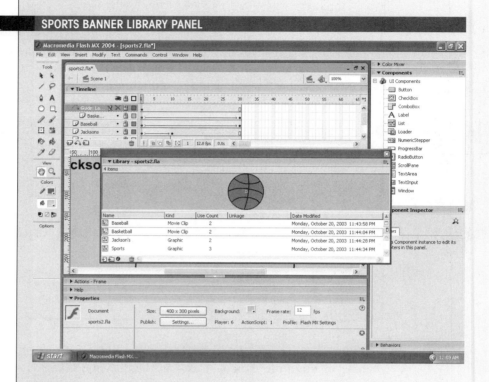

5. Click the **Kind** column header. The symbols are listed according to their behavior: buttons, graphics, and movie clips. To view the properties of a symbol, you use the Properties icon.

6. Click the **Properties** icon 🛈. The Symbol Properties dialog box opens for the Basketball symbol. Try changing this symbol's behavior.

7. Click the **Graphic** option button under Behavior, and then click the **OK** button to close the Properties dialog box. The basketball symbol's icon and Kind reflect the new behavior, as shown in Figure 2-42. Return the Library to its default view.

Figure 2-42   SYMBOLS IN LIBRARY PANEL

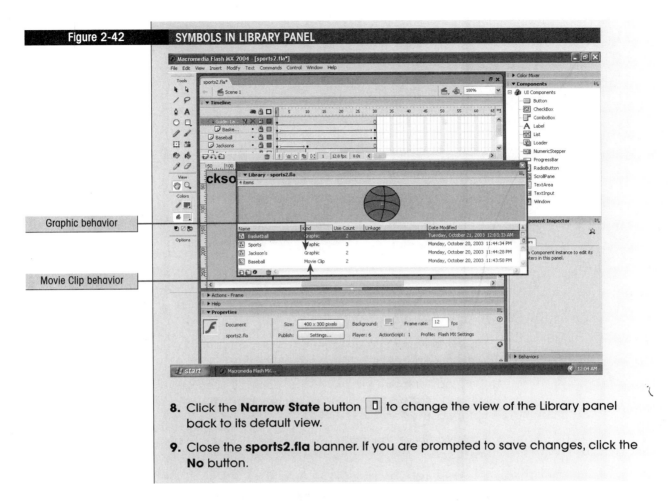

Graphic behavior

Movie Clip behavior

8. Click the **Narrow State** button ▯ to change the view of the Library panel back to its default view.

9. Close the **sports2.fla** banner. If you are prompted to save changes, click the **No** button.

Now that you understand what symbols are and how to use the Library panel to view and work with symbols, you are ready to create symbols for the Flounders Pet Shop banner.

Creating Symbols for the Flounders Pet Shop Banner

Aly wants you to modify the banner you have created for the Flounders Pet Shop Web site. You will convert the fish graphic you created into a symbol to see how instances of the fish symbol can used. You will also create a copy of the fish symbol and change its color.

REFERENCE   WINDOW

Creating a Symbol
- Select an existing graphic, click Modify on the menu bar, and then click Convert to Symbol.
- In the Convert to Symbol dialog box, enter a symbol name in the Name text box, select a behavior by clicking the appropriate behavior option button, and click the OK button.

or

- Click Insert on the menu bar, and then click New Symbol.
- In the New Symbol dialog box, enter a symbol name in the Name text box, select a behavior by clicking the appropriate behavior option button, and then click the OK button to enter into symbol-editing mode.
- Create the graphic(s) for the symbol.
- Click Insert on the menu bar, and then click Edit Document.

To create symbols for the banner and view them in the Library panel:

1. Open the **Banner.fla** document from the **Tutorial.02\Tutorial** folder included with your Data Files.

2. Click the **Selection** tool 🡒 on the toolbar, if necessary, and click the fish graphic on the center of the Stage to select it. You will ungroup this graphic before converting it to a symbol.

3. Click **Modify** on the menu bar and then click **Ungroup**. The fish is still selected, but it is no longer grouped. Now you can convert the fish graphic to a symbol.

4. Click **Modify** on the menu bar, and then click **Convert to Symbol**. The Convert to Symbol dialog box opens. In this dialog box, you can specify a name for the symbol and select a behavior.

5. In the Convert to Symbol dialog box, type **Fish1** in the Name text box, and click the **Movie clip** option button, if it is not already selected. You will use this behavior for most of the symbols you create in Flash unless you specifically need to create a graphic or button symbol. See Figure 2-43.

Figure 2-43   **CONVERT TO SYMBOL DIALOG BOX**

symbol's name

behavior options

Convert to Symbol
Name: Fish1
Behavior: ○ Movie clip   Registration: ▪□□ / □□□ / □□□
○ Button
○ Graphic
OK / Cancel / Advanced

indicates symbol's Registration point; when the symbol is transformed, such as rotated, it will do so around this point

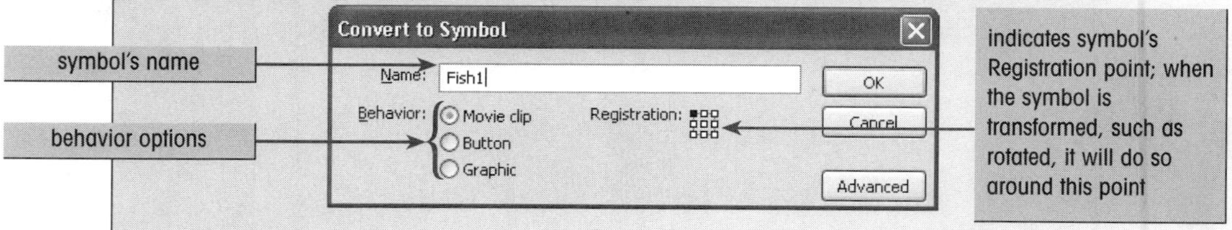

6. Click the **OK** button to close the dialog box. Now the symbol has been created and added to the library of symbols for this document. View the symbol in the Library panel.

7. Click **Window** on the menu bar, and then click **Library**. The Library panel opens. Click the **Fish1** symbol to see its preview.

TROUBLE? The Library panel may open in Wide State. If this is the case, click the Narrow State button to change to the default view.

Once a symbol is added to a document's library, you can create a duplicate of it. The duplicate symbol must have a different name. You can create a duplicate of a symbol by clicking the Duplicate command on the Library panel's option menu or by right-clicking the symbol in the Library panel to display its context menu, and then clicking the Duplicate command.

Aly suggests you create a duplicate symbol of the Fish1 symbol that you can then edit, thereby creating a second, different fish symbol.

To create a duplicate of a symbol:

1. Click the **Fish1** symbol in the Library panel to select it, if necessary.

2. Click the Library panel's **options menu** button ≔ to open the options menu, and then click **Duplicate**. The Duplicate Symbol dialog box opens.

3. In the Duplicate Symbol dialog box, enter **Fish2** in the Name text box, and then click the **OK** button.

Instances of Symbols

Once you create a symbol it is automatically stored in the document's library. To use the symbols in your document, you create instances. An **instance** is a copy of a symbol. To create an instance of a symbol, you drag it from the Library panel to the Stage. You can either drag the thumbnail from the preview window or drag the symbol's name from the list of symbols. Each time you drag the symbol onto the Stage you are creating an instance of the symbol in your document. The symbol, however, is stored only once in your document regardless of how many instances you have created. So if you have a graphic that will be used in a document multiple times, convert it into a symbol. Then insert instances of the symbol wherever that graphic is needed in your document. This helps keep the size of the file to a minimum.

Each of the instances created in your document can be edited without changing the original symbol stored in the document's library. For example, if you have several instances of a symbol in the same document, you can make one instance smaller than the others. Or you can rotate each instance to appear at a different angle. You can also change the color tint or brightness of one instance without affecting the other instances or the original symbol. If you modify the original symbol, however, then all the instances of that symbol are also changed.

Aly suggests you edit the Fish2 symbol in the document's library so that it has a unique appearance from the Fish1 symbol.

Editing a Symbol

Once you create a symbol you may still need to modify it. You can do this in one of several ways. If an instance of the symbol is on the Stage, you can select it and use the Edit in Place command on the Edit menu. You can also double-click the instance of the symbol on the Stage to edit it in place. Even though you double-click the instance, you are actually editing the symbol. When you do this, the other objects on the Stage will be dimmed and the Edit bar at the top of the Stage window will show the symbol's name after a link called Scene 1, as shown in Figure 2-44.

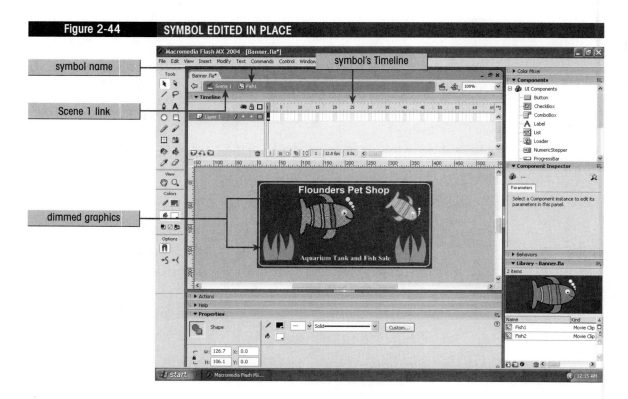

Figure 2-44   SYMBOL EDITED IN PLACE

symbol name

Scene 1 link

symbol's Timeline

dimmed graphics

You can also edit a symbol by right-clicking an instance of it on the Stage and selecting Edit, Edit in Place, or Edit in New Window from the context menu. **Edit** places the symbol in symbol-editing mode. **Edit in Place** dims all other objects on the Stage while you edit the symbol, and **Edit in New Window** places the symbol in a separate window for editing. You have to close this window when you finish editing the symbol. After you edit the symbol, you can return to the document by clicking the Edit Document command on the Edit menu or by clicking the Scene 1 link on the Address bar. The Scene 1 link identifies the current scene. Flash documents may be divided into multiple scenes and every document has at least one scene. The Scene 1 link takes you back to the document. You can also double-click an empty area of the Stage to get back to editing the document.

Another way to edit a symbol is to select the symbol in the Library panel and then double-click the symbol's icon. This will place the symbol in symbol-editing mode so that it can be edited, as shown in Figure 2-45.

Figure 2-45	SYMBOL-EDITING MODE

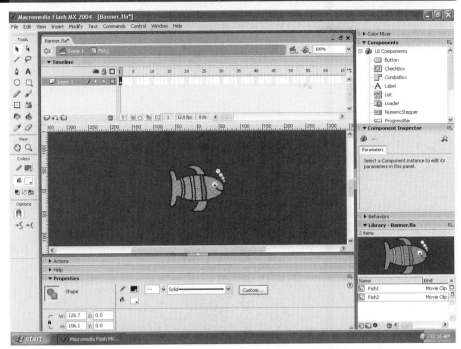

Once you are done editing the symbol, you can click the Scene 1 link to return to the document or you can click the Edit Document command on the Edit menu.

Now that you have two fish symbols in the library, you will change one of the symbols so that it has a different color and is smaller in size. This will distinguish the two fish symbols when they are used in the banner.

To edit a symbol in the document's library:

1. Make sure the **Fish2** symbol is selected in the Library panel. Click the Library panel's **options menu** button, and then click **Edit** to open the symbol in symbol-editing mode. Click an empty area of the Stage to deselect it. Next, you will apply a different color to the fish2 symbol.

2. Click the **Paint Bucket** tool on the toolbar. Using the Fill color control in the Property inspector, change the fill color to a **light blue** color (seventh column, sixth row, in the color pop-up window).

3. Click each of the orange areas of the fish to change them to light blue. Now select the fish graphic so you can make it smaller.

4. Click **Edit** on the menu bar, and then click **Select All**. All of the fish is selected.

5. Click **Window** on the menu bar, point to **Design Panels**, and then click **Transform** to open the Transform panel.

6. In the Transform panel, click the **Constrain** check box, if necessary, to select it. Constrain keeps the width and height proportional when either one is changed. Double-click the **Width** value in the upper-left text box to select it and change it to **50%.** Press the **Enter** key to accept the new value, and then close the Transform panel. The fish has become smaller, as shown in Figure 2-46. Now that you are done editing the Fish2 symbol, exit symbol-editing mode.

Figure 2-46   **REVISED FISH2 SYMBOL**

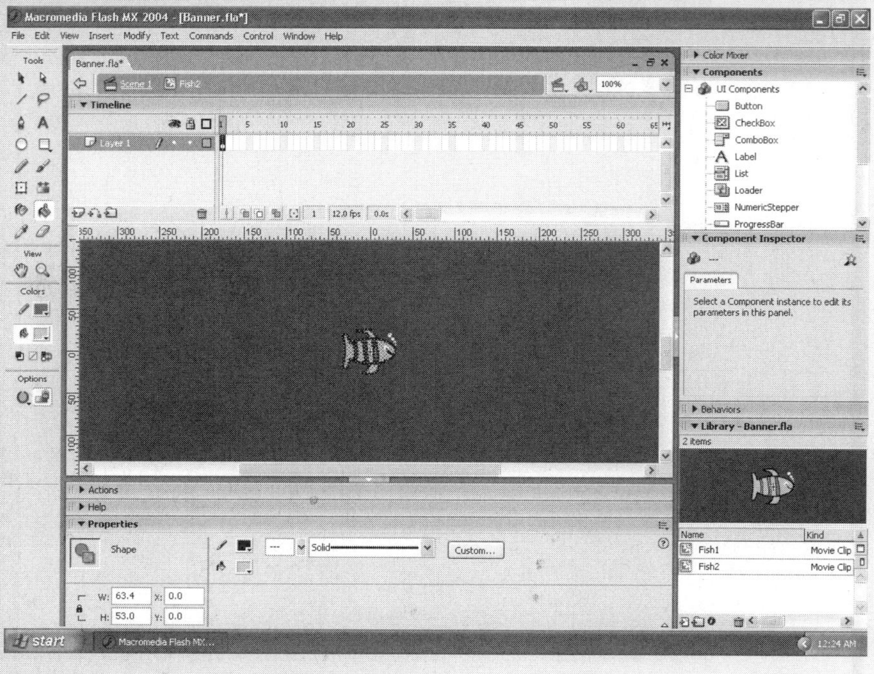

7. Click **Edit** on the menu bar, and then click **Edit Document** to exit the symbol-editing window.

8. Save the **Banner.fla** file.

In this session you have learned about symbols and how to use the Library panel to work with the symbols in your document's library. In the next tutorial, you will learn how to create animations with the symbols in the Flounders Pet Shop banner.

Session 2.3 QUICK CHECK

1. What are the three behavior types for symbols?

2. What is the purpose of the Library panel?

3. How do you delete a symbol from the Library panel?

4. What two buttons can change the view of the Library panel?

5. What is the difference between a symbol and an instance of a symbol?

6. When you modify a symbol, the instances created from that symbol are not affected. True or False?

REVIEW ASSIGNMENTS

Aly is very pleased with the progress you have made in learning the basic tools of Macromedia Flash. She is especially pleased with the banner you created for the Flounders Pet Shop's Web site. She asks you to modify the banner by changing the color of one fish, adding a third fish, modifying one of the plant leaves, and changing one of the text blocks. She also wants you to change the color and style of the rectangle and to draw several lines.

If necessary, start Macromedia Flash and then do the following:

1. If necessary, open the **Banner.fla** file which you created in the tutorial from the Tutorial.02\Tutorial folder, set the panels to their default layout, and collapse the Timeline.

2. Open the Library panel, and drag the Fish2 symbol from the Library panel into the Stage to create an instance of it. Place the instance on the left side of the banner and rotate it so that it appears to be swimming in an upward direction.

3. Use the Paint Bucket tool to change the orange color of the small fish on the right side of the banner to pink. Change the color of its stripes so that the left one is blue, the middle one is dark green, and the right one is yellow. (*Hint:* You need to double-click the fish first to get into group-edit mode to make the changes. Double-click an empty area of the Stage to exit group-edit mode.)

4. Select the first group of plant leaves on the left side of the banner and convert the group into a symbol. Name the symbol **plant1**. Select the second group of plant leaves on the left side of the banner and also convert the group into a symbol. Name this symbol **plant2**.

5. Select and delete the two groups of plant leaves on the right side of the banner. Drag an instance of the plant1 symbol from the Library panel to the right side of the banner. Also, drag an instance of the plant2 symbol to the right side of the banner.

6. Edit the plant2 symbol in the library to change its size to about one-third its original size. The two plant2 instances on the Stage will also change in size.

Explore   7. Select and then delete the bottom text block. Add three new text blocks with the same-text properties as the text block you deleted. One text block should read **Fish**, the other should read **Aquarium Tanks**, and the third should read **On Sale Now!**. Place the first text block on the left side below the blue fish. Place the second text block on the right side below the pink fish, and place the third text block in the center below the larger fish.

8. Use the Pencil tool to draw horizontal lines under each of the three new text blocks. The lines should be yellow, have a height of 2, and appear as underlines for the text.

Explore   9. Use the Property inspector and the Text tool to change the text in the top text block so that Flounders Pet Shop is in italics and has a font size of 26. (*Hint:* Select the text first before you apply the Italics style). Center the text block, if necessary.

Explore   10. Use the Ink Bottle tool to change the color, height, and style of the rectangle's stroke. First, choose a bright-green color, set the stroke height to 3, and choose a stroke style other than Solid in the Property inspector.

11. Save your revised banner to the Tutorial.02\Review folder included with your Data Files. Name it **Banner2.fla**.

12. Close the Banner2.fla file.

CASE PROBLEMS

Case 1. Creating a Banner for Sandy's Party Center Sandy's Party Center has just opened and is preparing for its grand opening celebration and sale. Sandy Rodriguez, owner of the store, meets with John Rossini to discuss the development of the store's Web site. John suggests that a banner be developed first that will set the tone for the rest of the Web site. Sandy agrees and also asks John to develop the banner so that it helps promote the grand opening celebration she is planning. She asks John to include graphics on the banner that depict a party and to add text about the grand opening. John asks you to help him develop the banner. An example of the completed banner is shown in Figure 2-47, which you can refer to as you complete this case problem.

Figure 2-47   **SANDY'S PARTY CENTER BANNER**

If necessary, start Flash and then complete the following:

1. Start with a new document. Change the document properties so that the width is 500 pixels and the height is 150 pixels. Change the background color to a light yellow (use #FFFF99).

2. Add a text block at the top of the Stage. Use a font such as Comic Sans MS, a font size of 40, and blue text. Bold and italicize the text. Type **Sandy's Party Center** in the text block.

3. Add a second text block with a smaller font size of 18 and black text. Type **Grand Opening this Saturday!**, and on a separate line in the same text block type **Come celebrate with us!**. Make sure this text is centered within the text block.

4. Draw three balloons on the left side of the Stage using the Oval tool with different colors for each balloon. Do not include a stroke for the balloons. Draw a string for each balloon using the Pencil tool with a light-gray color for the stroke. Draw three more balloons on the right side of the Stage with different colors.

5. Draw a party hat by first drawing a triangle shape with the Pen tool. Use a black stroke and a red fill. Once you have drawn the triangle shape, use the Selection tool to curve the triangle's bottom line. Curve it slightly in a downward direction to make it look like a party hat, referring to Figure 2-47, if necessary.

6. Make several copies of the hat and change the fill color of each copy. When you copy the hat, make sure you select both its stroke and fill. Position the hats in different locations of the Stage.

Explore   7. Use the Brush tool to draw confetti on the Stage. Select a small brush size from the Brush Size modifier in the options area of the toolbar. Select a brush color using the Fill Color control on the toolbar. Then click dots with the tool on the banner to create the confetti. Create different colored dots throughout the Stage.

8. Create a rectangle as a border around all of the objects on the Stage. The rectangle should have slightly rounded corners, a pink stroke, no fill, a stroke height of 3, and a solid style. Draw the rectangle so that it is just inside the edges of the Stage.

9. Save the banner in the Tutorial.02\Cases folder included with your Data Files. Name the file **spcbanner.fla**.

10. Use the Export Image command to export the image to the Tutorial.02\Cases folder in GIF file format. Use the same name as the FLA file, and accept the default settings in the Export GIF dialog box. When you are done, close the FLA file.

Case 2. Creating a Banner for River City Music   Janet Meyers, manager of River City Music, asks Alex Smith to develop a new banner for the River City Music Web site. The new banner will be used to advertise an upcoming piano sale that will be held in conjunction with their anniversary sale. After meeting with Janet, Alex decides that the banner and its graphic elements can be developed using Flash. The banner will contain text with the store's name and sale information as well as graphic elements depicting piano keys and musical notes. Alex asks you to help him develop the banner. An example of the completed banner is shown in Figure 2-48, which you can refer to as you complete this case problem.

Figure 2-48   RIVER CITY MUSIC BANNER

If necessary, start Flash and then complete the following:

1. Open the **music.fla** document, located in the Tutorial.02\Cases folder included with your Data Files. This document is a partially completed banner. Save the document as **rcmbanner.fla** in the Cases folder.

2. Change the document properties so that the width is 300 pixels and the height is 200 pixels. Change the background color to a light blue by entering #0099FF in the color pop-up window's hexadecimal text box.

3. Use the rectangles contained in the document to create the piano keys graphic. The rectangles are grouped so that their strokes and fills can be copied and moved together as one object. Start by creating two copies of the larger white rectangle.

4. Display the rulers and drag a horizontal guide line and place it about 50 pixels from the top of the Stage. Drag a vertical guide line about 80 pixels from the left of the Stage. Make sure Snap to Guides is turned on. Move the three white rectangles to the middle of the Stage below and to the right of the guide lines. As you move the rectangles drag them from their top edges so they will snap to the horizontal guide. The rectangles should be placed right next to each other without overlapping.

5. Create one copy of the smaller black rectangle. Place the copy of the black rectangle on top of the two white rectangles on the far left so that it equally overlaps both of them. As you move the black rectangle, drag it from its top edge so that it snaps to the horizontal guide.

6. Move the original black rectangle on top of the two white rectangles on the far right so that it equally overlaps them. Adjust its position so that it is lined up with the first black rectangle. If the black rectangle is behind the white rectangles, use the Arrange options on the Modify menu to bring it forward.

7. Select all of the objects on the Stage and convert them to a symbol. Name the symbol piano keys and use Movie Clip as the behavior type. Create two instances of the symbol on the Stage and line up all of the instances so that they form the piano keys graphic.

Explore

8. To draw the musical notes, use the Oval tool. In the lower-left side of the Stage, draw a small oval with a black stroke and white fill. Make the oval about 10 pixels high and 15 pixels wide. You may need to turn off Snap to Objects to keep the program from drawing a perfect circle. Use the Line tool to draw a vertical line about 30 pixels high for the note's stem. Draw the line on the right side of the oval so that the note resembles the letter "d". Select the entire note and convert it into a symbol. Name the symbol note1 and use Movie Clip as the behavior type.

9. Create a duplicate of the note1 symbol and name it note2. Edit the note2 symbol to change the fill color of the oval to black.

10. Drag one instance of the note1 symbol and two instances of the note2 symbol into the Stage next to the existing note1 instance. Rotate one of the note1 instances and one of the note2 instances so that they resemble the letter "p".

11. In the lower-right corner of the Stage, draw a horizontal line about 100 pixels in length. The line should be black, have a stroke height of 1, and a solid style. Create four copies of the line. Arrange the lines so that they are approximately 15 pixels apart. Then use the Align options under the Modify menu so that the lines are aligned on their left sides and that they are distributed equally.

12. Move the musical notes between the horizontal lines. Use Figure 2-48 as a guide.

13. Create a single-line text block for the name of the store. Place the text block on the top part of the Stage. Use a font such as Monotype Corsiva, a font height of 36, and make the text bold and italic. Type **River City Music** in the text block. Create a fixed-width text block on the lower-left side of the Stage. Use the same font as before, but with a font height of 22. Type **Piano Sale! Now through the end of the month!**.

14. Create a rectangle as a border around all of the objects on the Stage. The rectangle should have a dark-blue stroke, no fill, a stroke height of 3, and a dotted style. Draw the rectangle so that it is just inside the edges of the Stage.

15. Save the banner.

16. Use the Export Image command to export the image to the Tutorial.02\Cases folder in GIF file format. Use the same name as the FLA file and accept the default settings in the Export GIF dialog box. When you are done, close the FLA file.

Case 3. Creating a Logo for Sonny's Auto Center Sonny's Auto Center is a used car dealership offering competitive prices and a friendly no-pressure atmosphere. Sonny Jackson, owner of the auto center, has been in business for 10 years and has gradually built his business from a small corner lot with a few dozen cars to a large commercial lot with hundreds of cars. Sonny attributes his success to his focus on customer service. Customers are able to look through the auto center's inventory in a relaxed environment. When they are ready to buy, they find friendly, competent sales personnel willing to help them through the whole purchasing process.

Amanda Lester was recently contracted by Sonny to update the company's Web site. As other car dealers have developed new Web sites, Sonny wants to make sure his company's Web site stays up to date and remains an effective marketing tool for his business. Amanda meets with Sonny and he requests that she first develop a new logo for his business. The logo should contain the business name, phone number, and an appropriate slogan, along with some graphics. Amanda decides that Macromedia Flash is an ideal program to use to develop the logo. An example of the completed banner is shown in Figure 2-49, which you can refer to as you complete this case problem.

Figure 2-49   SONNY'S AUTO CENTER LOGO

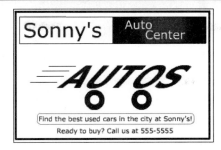

If necessary, start Flash and then complete the following:

1. Start with a new document. Change the document properties so that the width is 300 pixels and the height is 200 pixels.

2. Create a rectangle across the top of the Stage. Use a black stroke with a height of 1 and a solid style. Do not include a fill color. Make the rectangle about 280 pixels wide and about 50 pixels high. Place the rectangle about 10 pixels from the left of the Stage and 10 pixels from the top.

3. Create a text block inside the rectangle. Use Verdana or a similar font. Make the font size 30 and use black text. Type **Sonny's** in the text block. Position the text block on the left side of the rectangle.

4. Draw a straight vertical line inside the rectangle to the right of the text block. One end of the line should snap to the top of the rectangle and the other end should snap to the bottom of the rectangle. This line effectively splits the rectangle into two sections.

5. Apply a new fill to the right section of the rectangle. The fill should be a blue radial gradient. Use the fifth gradient from the left on the color palette.

6. Create a new text block on the inside of the rectangle over the gradient. The text should be white with a font size of 18. Type **Auto** in the text block. Position the text in the upper-left area of the rectangle.

7. Create another text block the same as in the previous step. Type **Center** in this text block. Position the text so that the "C" is right below the "o" in the "Auto" text block.

Explore ▷ 8. Create a text block in the center of the Stage with a font size of 46 and black text. Type **AUTOS** in this text block. Using the Free Transform tool, skew the text block so that the letters are slanted to the right.

9. Add four straight horizontal lines of about 40 pixels in length each. Draw the lines to the left of the letter "A" in the center text block. Space the lines equally apart and place each one approximately the same distance from the letter "A".

10. On the bottom part of the Stage, draw a circle of about 30 pixels in diameter. The circle should have a black fill and no stroke.

11. Draw another circle of about 15 pixels in diameter. This circle should have a white fill and a black stroke. Group the stroke and fill for this second circle. Then move the smaller grouped circle into the middle of the larger circle to form the image of a car tire.

12. Select both of the circles that make up the tire and then make them into a group. Make a copy of this grouped object. Then move the two tire graphics right below the text block on the center of the Stage. Place one tire right below the "U" on the "AUTOS" text. Place the other one right below the "O".

13. Add a single-line text block below the tire graphics. Use a font size of 10 and black text. Type **Find the best used cars in the city at Sonny's!** into the text block. Center the text block on the Stage. Draw a rectangle around this text block. The rectangle should have a light-gray stroke with a height of 1 and no color for the fill. It should have rounded corners.

14. Below the previous text block create another text block with the same attributes as in the previous step. Type **Ready to buy? Call us at 555-5555** into the text block.

15. Add a rectangle to frame all of the graphic elements for the logo. Use a black stroke with a height of 3 and no color for the fill. Do not round the corners. Draw the rectangle so that is just inside the edges of the Stage.

16. Save the logo in the Tutorial.02\Cases folder included with your Data Files. Name the file **saclogo.fla**.

17. Use the Export Image command to export the image to the Tutorial.02\Cases folder in GIF file format. Use the same name as the FLA file and accept the default settings in the Export GIF dialog box. When you are done, close the FLA file.

Case 4. Creating a banner for LAL Financial Services LAL Financial Services, headquartered in San Antonio, Texas, is one of the state's largest commercial banking organizations and has been in business for more than 20 years. The company operates through an extensive distribution network in many of the major cities in Texas. LAL's primary businesses include deposit, credit, trust, and investment services. Through various subsidiaries the company also provides credit cards, mortgage banking, and insurance.

Christopher Perez, head of Marketing, is leading a new effort to improve the company's Web site. After meeting with Webmaster Elizabeth Danehill, they decide to start by developing a new banner to be used on the company's home page. Elizabeth assigns the task to the graphics designer, Mia Jones. The new banner is to portray the financial strength of the company and will include the company's name, as well as keywords highlighting their services. Mia decides to use Macromedia Flash to develop the banner. An example of the completed banner is shown in Figure 2-50, to which you can refer as you complete this case problem.

| Figure 2-50 | LAL FINANCIAL SERVICES BANNER |

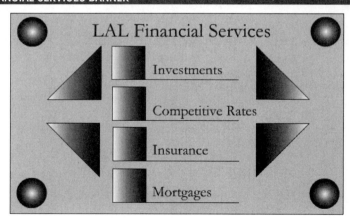

If necessary, start Flash and then complete the following:

1. Start with a new document. Change the document properties so that the width is 500 pixels and the height is 300 pixels. Change the background color to a light gray.

2. Create a circle in the upper-left corner of the Stage. Use the gray radial gradient fill found in the color pop-up window. Do not use a color for the stroke. Make the circle about 45 pixels in diameter.

3. Convert the circle to a Movie Clip symbol and name it circle. Create three instances of the circle symbol and place each of the four circles in a separate corner of the Stage.

Explore
4. Create a square of about 90 pixels on each side. Use the gray linear gradient fill found in the color pop-up window and use a thin black stroke. Convert this square into a triangle by moving one of its corner anchor points to the center of the square until the two lines adjacent to the corner point merge.

Explore
5. Convert the triangle into a Movie Clip symbol and name it triangle. Create three instances of the triangle symbol and place each instance in a separate quadrant of the Stage. Use the Transform submenu located on the Modify menu to rotate and arrange the four triangles as shown in Figure 2-50.

6. Create a square in the middle of the Stage. Use the same gray linear gradient as before and a stroke of 1. Make the square approximately 50 pixels on each side. Convert the square into a Movie Clip symbol and name it square. Create three instances of the square symbol and line all four squares vertically.

7. Draw a straight horizontal line from the lower-right corner of the first square to extend to the right about 140 pixels. Copy this line three times and snap each copy to the lower-right corners of each of the copied squares.

8. Create a text block at the top of the Stage. Use a font such as Garamond, with a font size of 30, and black text. Type **LAL Financial Services** in the text block. Center the text block within the Stage.

9. Create another text block right above the top horizontal line, to the right of the square. Use the same font as in the previous step but reduce the font size to 22. Type **Investments** in this text block. Create three more text blocks in the same way. Type **Competitive Rates** in one, **Insurance** in the next, and **Mortgages** in the third. Position each block so that it is about 10 pixels from its respective square.

10. Save the banner in the Tutorial.02\Cases folder included with your Data Files. Name the file **lfsbanner.fla**.

11. Use the Export Image command to export the image to the Tutorial.02\Cases folder in GIF file format. Use the same name as the FLA file, and accept the default settings in the Export GIF dialog box. When you are done, close the FLA file and exit Flash.

QUICK | **C**HECK ANSWERS

Session 2.1

1. False. When drawing a shape with the Oval tool, Flash helps you draw a perfect circle when the Snap to Objects options is selected.

2. To draw a rectangle with rounded corners, click the Round Rectangle Radius button, and enter a point value in the Rectangle Settings dialog box.

3. The Pen tool is used to draw line and curve segments by creating anchor points that connect them.

4. The Pencil Mode modifier helps straighten lines you draw with the Pencil tool.

5. Click an object's stroke with the Eyedropper tool. The pointer turns into an ink bottle. Then click the other object to apply the stroke's attributes.

6. You can use the Paint Bucket tool to add a fill to an enclosed area that has no fill.

7. The Scale modifier can be used with the Free Transform tool to resize a selected object.

8. False. You use the Fill Transform tool to modify an object's gradient fill.

Session 2.2

1. A static text block has text that does not change once the document is published, whereas a dynamic text field's content may be changed as it is updated from a Web server.

2. To create a fixed-width text block, click and drag the Stage to set the desired width.

3. You use the Property inspector to set the text attributes such as the font and size.

4. You can change a single-line text block into a fixed-width text block by dragging its round corner handle.

5. A text block that displays a square handle in its upper-right corner is a fixed-width text block.

6. You check the Check text fields content checkbox in the Spelling Setup dialog box.

7. The personal dictionary path specifies where on your disk the personal dictionary file will be saved.

8. In the History panel, you can drag the slider up to a previous step. The steps that are dimmed in the History panel are undone.

Session 2.3

1. The three behavior types for symbols are Movie Clip, Graphic, and Button.

2. The Library panel stores and organizes the symbols contained in a document.

3. You delete a symbol by selecting it and then clicking the trash can icon at the bottom of the Library panel.

4. The Wide State button and the Narrow State button change the view of the Library panel.

5. Symbols are reusable elements such as graphics, buttons, and sound files that can be used more than once in your document. An instance is a copy of a symbol.

6. False. Modifying a symbol will also change the instances created from that symbol.

CREATING ANIMATIONS

Developing Animations for Admiral Web Design Clients

course.com * to down load files → window

CASE

Admiral Web Design

At the weekly staff planning meeting for Admiral Web Design, Aly Garcia, graphics designer, reports that she is pleased with the Flounders Pet Shop banner you created using the program's drawing and painting tools, which she shows to the rest of the staff. Gloria Adamson, co-owner of Admiral Web Design, asks Aly to meet with Joe Flounders, owner of Flounders Pet Shop, to show him the banner. She also mentions that in a previous conversation with Joe he expressed an interest in having animation added to the banner. He has recently seen some Web sites that use animated graphics and thinks that animation could attract more attention to the sale the banner will be promoting. Aly meets with Joe to show him the banner and to discuss what type of animation he had in mind. After this meeting, Aly revises the banner you previously created for Flounders Pet Shop and uses it to put together a partially completed banner which will be the basis for the new animated banner. In a meeting with Aly, it is decided that the banner will be revised so that there will be an initial animation of a fish pulling a sale sign while the words "Fish" and "Aquarium" display one after the other. Then there will be an animated fish swimming in the tank. The plant will also be animated by making the leaves move slightly back and forth. Figure 3-1 shows a printout of the preliminary banner with instructions on what needs to be done to complete it.

Figure 3-1   FLOUNDERS PET SHOP PARTIALLY COMPLETED BANNER

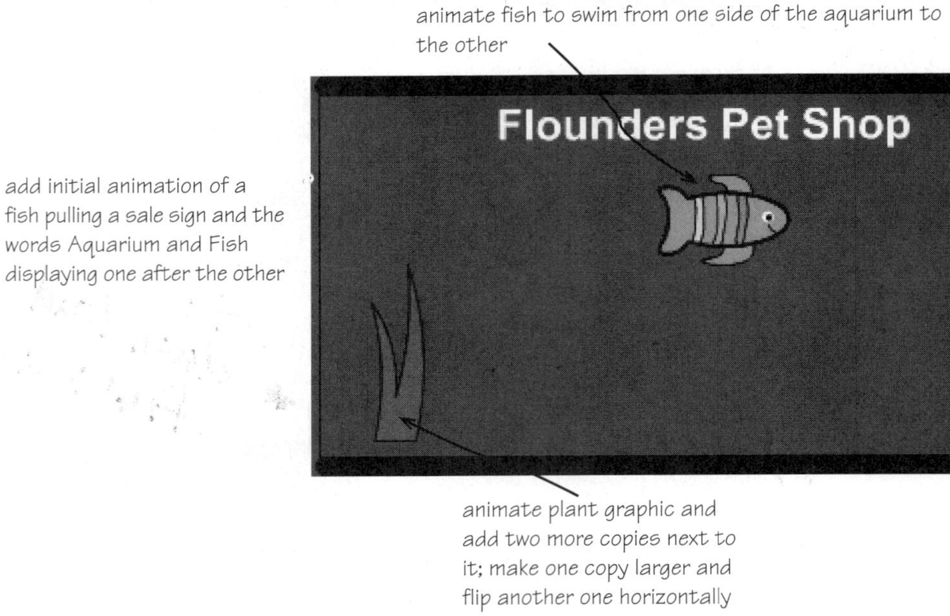

animate fish to swim from one side of the aquarium to the other

add initial animation of a fish pulling a sale sign and the words Aquarium and Fish displaying one after the other

Flounders Pet Shop

animate plant graphic and add two more copies next to it; make one copy larger and flip another one horizontally

You will continue your training in Flash by learning how to create animations and by adding the fish and plant animations to the Flounders Pet Shop banner. You will also add a duplicate scene for the sale sign animation. Before completing the animation for the Flounders Pet Shop banner, Aly suggests you study the animation she has recently created for another Admiral client, Jackson's Sports.

In this tutorial, you will learn the basics of creating Flash animations and how to coordinate these animations in the Timeline using frames and layers. You will also learn how to extend a document using scenes. You will learn how to create animations using Timeline effects, and how to create frame-by-frame, motion tweened, and shape tweened animations. Finally, you will learn how to create animations using graphic symbols.

SESSION 3.1

In this session, you will learn about the different elements that make up a Flash animation. You will explore the Timeline and work with layers and frames. Finally, you will learn how to work with multiple scenes.

Elements of Animation

Recall one of the most powerful features of Flash is its ability to create animation. Animation is achieved by changing the content of an object from one moment in time to the next. In order to create an animation you need to review some basic elements of a Flash document. A document is made up of layers, frames, and the graphic objects, such as symbols, that display on the Stage. The document's Timeline is used to coordinate these elements, as shown in Figure 3-2.

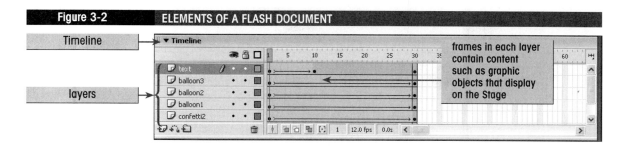

Figure 3-2   **ELEMENTS OF A FLASH DOCUMENT**

Layers

Layers are used to organize the content of your document. A Flash document starts with one layer. You can add more layers as you add more graphic objects to a document and then place these objects on the different layers to keep them from interacting with each other. Recall from Tutorial 1 that objects you draw or move on top of other objects will split or merge with those objects. Placing objects on separate layers prevents this and allows you to overlap the objects on the Stage. Objects on different layers can also be moved in front or in back of each other by changing the order in which the layers are organized. Layers are especially useful when animating more than one object at the same time. An object on one layer can be animated to move in one direction while an object on another layer can be animated to move in a different direction. Both animations can occur at the same time, but do not impact one another in any way. In certain types of animations, which will be covered later in this tutorial, an object that is animated must reside on its own layer.

Guide Layers

A **guide layer** is a special type of layer that may be used to align objects on other layers to the objects on the guide layer. The contents of the guide layer do not appear in the published SWF file. For example, if you draw a rectangle on a guide layer, you can use the rectangle to guide you as you draw all the objects of the document. The rectangle appears on the Stage in your document but does not show in the published SWF file. Any layer can be converted to a guide layer by selecting Guide in the Layer Properties dialog box.

A guide layer may also be used to provide a path for an animated object to follow. This is called a **motion guide layer**. You can add a motion guide layer by clicking the Motion Guide command located on the Timeline submenu, which is accessible from the Insert menu, or by clicking the Add Motion Guide button at the bottom of the Timeline. The layer below a motion guide layer is called a **guided layer**. You will be creating a guide layer in Tutorial 4.

Mask Layers

Another special type of layer is a mask layer. A **mask layer** contains a graphic object through which the content of the **masked layer** shows. The masked layer is below the mask layer. The contents of the masked layer are hidden except for the area covered by the object on the mask layer. The object can be a filled shape such as an oval, or it can be text. The content of the masked layer only shows through when the object is over it. You can convert a layer into a mask layer by selecting Mask from the Layer Properties dialog box for that layer. You will work with mask layers in Tutorial 4.

Frames

Frames contain the content for an animation and represent a particular instant in time. For example, at the default frame rate of 12 frames per second (fps), one frame is displayed for 1/12 of a second during the animation. Placing different content on each frame or slightly modifying the content from one frame to the next creates the perception of movement. This movement is what makes up an animation. To create an animation you start by adding more frames to a layer. The frames you add are used to create new content or to change the content from previous frames. As you add more frames, you are extending the life of the animation. Initially, a document contains just one frame and that one frame is called a keyframe. A **keyframe** is a frame that represents a change in the content from the previous frame. If you add regular frames, the content remains the same in the new frames. If you want the content to change, then you add a keyframe. You add frames using the Timeline.

The **Timeline**

The **Timeline**, which appears above the Stage in the Flash program window, is used to control and coordinate the timing of the animation by determining how and when the frames for each layer are displayed. The Timeline is also a means of creating, modifying, and organizing layers and frames. Figure 3-3 shows the Timeline for an animation Aly has created for Jackson's Sports. Figure 3-4 identifies and describes the components of the Timeline.

Figure 3-3	TIMELINE OF A SAMPLE DOCUMENT

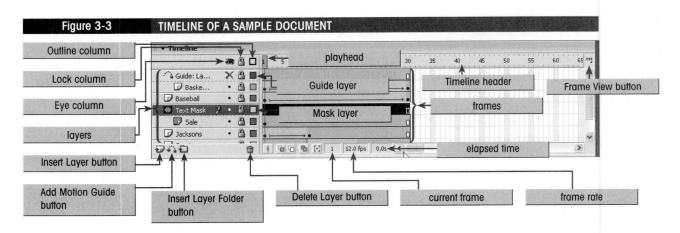

Figure 3-4	ELEMENTS OF THE TIMELINE

TIMELINE ELEMENT	PURPOSE
Layers	Used to organize the various graphic objects that are part of a document
Eye column	Hides or displays the content for all layers
Lock column	Locks or unlocks the content for all layers; you must unlock a layer before it can be edited
Outline column	Displays the content for all layers in Outline view or Normal view
Playhead	Indicates which frame is currently being displayed
Header	Displays the frame numbers; you can click a frame number in the header to select the frame
Frames	Contain content to be displayed for each instant in time
Frame View button	Displays the Frame View pop-up menu with options for controlling the way frames are displayed
Insert Layer button	Adds a new layer above the current layer
Add Motion Guide button	Inserts a motion guide layer above the current layer; the current layer becomes the guided layer
Insert Layer folder button	Inserts a layer folder above the current layer
Delete Layer button	Deletes the current layer
Current frame	Indicates the current frame being displayed on the Stage
Frame rate	Number of frames displayed in each second of time
Elapsed time	Shows how much time has elapsed since the start of the animation

The layer controls are displayed in the area on the left side of the Timeline. Each row within this column represents one layer. Above the list of layers there are three icons. The icon in the first column is the eye icon and is used to show or hide all the layers. When you click the dot in this column for a particular layer, a red x is displayed in place of the dot and the layer's content is temporarily hidden. You click the red x to display the content again. The padlock icon in the next column represents the Lock column. When you click a dot in this column a padlock icon replaces it to indicate the layer is locked and cannot be edited. It is a good idea to lock a layer once you finish editing its content. You click the layer's padlock icon again to unlock the layer. The icon in the third column represents the Outline column. When you click the colored square in this column for a particular layer, the layer's content is displayed in Outline view. When you select Outline view, the layer's contents on the Stage change so that only outlines of its objects display. Each layer has its own outline color to distinguish its contents on the Stage when it is in Outline view. The color of the outline is the same as the Outline view control square's color. This is useful when working with a complex animation and you want to see how the objects from the various layers overlap each other. You click a layer's square in the Outline column to return to Normal view where the contents are not in outline form. Each of these properties may be set at one time for all of the layers by clicking the icons at the top of the columns.

The frames for a layer are shown in a row to the right of the layer. Regular frames that are empty are white. Those that have some content are gray. Keyframes contain a white dot when they are blank and a black dot when they have content. The layer icon to the left of a layer's name indicates the type of layer it is. For example, regular layers have a page icon, while a mask layer has a mask icon. A guide layer has a guide icon and a motion guide layer appears with a motion guide icon.

Another important element of the Timeline is the playhead. The **playhead** indicates which frame is currently being displayed. The playhead is represented in the Timeline header by a red rectangle with a red vertical line below it. When you play an animation the playhead moves along the Timeline header to display the different frames that make up the animation.

Aly wants you to explore the Timeline of the Jackson's Sports banner she has been developing.

To explore the Timeline of the sports banner:

1. Open the **sports2.fla** file located in the **Tutorial.03\Tutorial** folder included with your Data Files.

2. Position the panels to their default positions by clicking **Window** on the menu bar, pointing to **Panel Sets**, and then clicking **Default Layout**. See Figure 3-5.

Figure 3-5	SPORTS BANNER

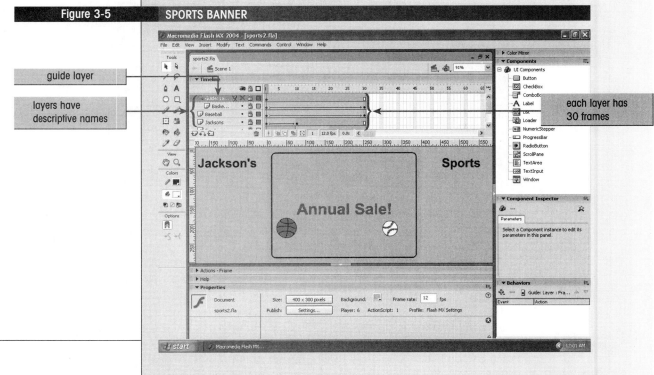

The document's Timeline contains several layers and each layer has 30 frames. The layers include animations of a baseball, basketball, and text. Notice that each layer has a name descriptive of its contents. You will see later in this session how to change the name of a layer. The Timeline also shows an example of a guide layer. Now play the animation and watch the Timeline as it displays the elements of the document.

3. Click **Control** on the menu bar, and then click **Play**. As the playhead moves from Frame 1 to Frame 30 in the Timeline, the baseball and basketball move in different directions on the Stage, the baseball decreases in size, and the text moves in from the sides of the Stage.

The Timeline displays useful information that you need to monitor as you view an animation. The Elapsed Time control displays the time that has elapsed from Frame 1 to the frame the playhead is currently on. The elapse time depends on the frame rate, which is also shown at the bottom of the Timeline. By default, the frame rate is 12 frames per second, which means that an animation that spans 12 frames takes one second to play. The length of the Sports banner animation you just viewed can be determined by looking at the elapsed time when the playhead is in the last frame. In this case the length of the animation is 2.4 seconds.

As you can see from the sports banner animation, a document can have a large number of frames, and the contents of the frames may look very similar from one frame to the next. As you work with content on the Stage it is important to always be aware of which frame is being displayed, because that is the frame whose content you are working with. Because the Stage and its contents may look very similar from one frame to the next, it is easy to get confused. If you are not careful you can change or create the content for the wrong frame. The Timeline makes it easy for you to determine which frame you are working with. Recall you can check the location of the playhead in the Timeline header. In Figure 3-6 the playhead in the Timeline header is on Frame 30, which means the contents of Frame 30 are currently displayed on the Stage. You can also see which frame is currently being displayed by looking at the Current frame indicator at the bottom of the Timeline window. This changes as the playhead moves to a different frame.

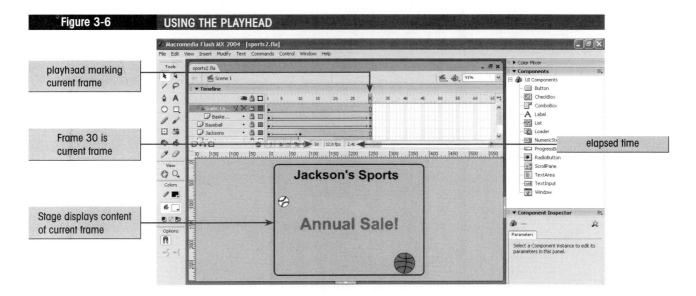

Figure 3-6 USING THE PLAYHEAD

As you develop your animation, the number of frames can grow very rapidly, as well as the number of layers. So there may come a time when you need to change the view of the Timeline in order to work more efficiently with the elements of your animation.

Changing the View of the Timeline

The Timeline can be modified in several ways. For example, you can extend the Timeline to show more frames by closing the panels on the right side of the Flash program window. Recall that to close a panel you click its options menu control to display the options menu, and you then click Close Panel. You can also temporarily hide the panels by pressing the F4 key on your keyboard. You press the F4 key again to redisplay the panels.

Another way to modify the view of the Timeline is by selecting one of the options on the Timeline's Frame View pop-up menu, as shown in Figure 3-7.

Figure 3-7   TIMELINE'S FRAME VIEW POP-UP MENU

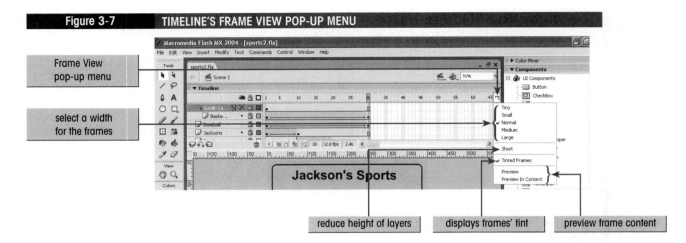

Frame View pop-up menu

select a width for the frames

reduce height of layers   displays frames' tint   preview frame content

The first set of options, **Tiny**, **Small**, **Normal**, **Medium**, and **Large** change the width of the frames. Tiny and Small allow you to see more frames within the Timeline window. Medium and Large can be used when you need to see more of the frame's contents. An example of this is when you are working with sounds. (Sounds will be covered in Tutorial 5.) A sound's waveform, which is a representation of the sound, is displayed in a frame when you add it to a document. Making the frames wider makes it easier to see more of the waveform. The **Short** option reduces the height of the layers. This can be useful when you have many layers and you need to fit more of them into the Timeline window. If you deselect the **Tinted Frames** option, the color tints on the frames are removed. By default, the frames are tinted different colors depending on the type of content they contain. For example, the frames of a motion tweened animation are tinted blue. You will learn about motion tweened animations later in this tutorial. Finally, if you use the **Preview** or **Preview in Context** options, the frames in the Timeline will show thumbnail previews of their content. The Preview command shows a thumbnail of the frame's content that is scaled to fit the Timeline's frame. The Preview in Context command shows a preview of the entire frame's contents including white or empty space. The thumbnails for this command are generally smaller than for the Preview command.

Because you will be working extensively with the Timeline, you will practice changing the view of its frames and layers. You will continue to practice with the sports banner created by Aly.

To change the view of the Timeline:

1. To make more room for the Timeline, press the **F4** key on your keyboard. The panels close and the Timeline and Stage windows expand across the width of the program window. Now resize the Timeline window so that all the layers for the sports banner are visible.

2. Position the pointer on the bottom border of the Timeline until the pointer changes to ‡, then drag the bottom border until the Rectangle layer is visible, as shown in Figure 3-8. Next you want to increase the size of the frames.

Figure 3-8   **RESIZING THE TIMELINE WINDOW**

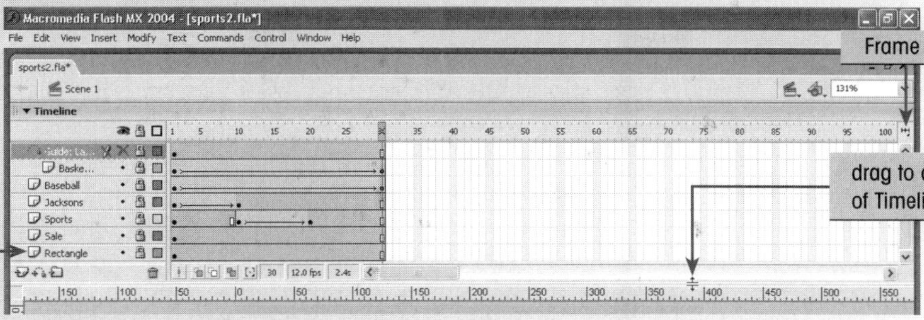

rectangle layer visible

Frame View button

drag to adjust height of Timeline window

3. Click the Timeline's **Frame View** button ⊞ to display the Frame View pop-up menu, and then click **Medium** to increase the size of the frames.

4. Click ⊞ again and then click **Preview**. The frames increase in size to show the content of each keyframe. You may need to use the Timeline window's scroll bars to see all of the frames. See Figure 3-9.

Figure 3-9   **FRAMES IN PREVIEW VIEW**

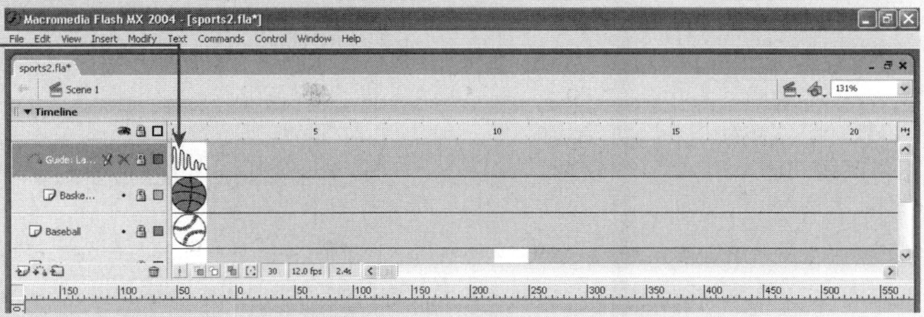

preview of frame's content

5. Click ⊞ again, click **Normal** to display the frames in their default or Normal view, and then press the **F4** key to redisplay the panels.

When working with a complex document, the number of layers can become difficult to manage. The Timeline is a useful tool in managing and organizing multiple layers in an animation.

Organizing Layers Using the Timeline

Recall that when you open a new document in Flash, it contains one layer and one frame within that layer. As you create your animation, you add more layers to the document. In a particularly lengthy or complex animation, you could have a large number of layers. Therefore, you need to know how to use the Timeline to work with the different layers in your document most efficiently.

To select a layer you click it in the Timeline. The layer is then highlighted and a pencil icon is displayed to the right of the layer's name. To delete a layer, you select it and then click the Delete Layer button at the bottom of the Timeline. You can also drag the layer to the Delete Layer button or right-click the layer to display a context menu. You can then click Delete Layer from the context menu.

To add more layers to a document you can use the Layer command on the Timeline submenu, which is accessible from the Insert menu or you can click the Insert Layer button in the lower-left corner of the Timeline. As you add more layers to the Timeline it is a good idea to name each one according to the content it contains. This helps you keep the content organized as the complexity of the animation increases. To change the name of a layer, you double-click its name in the Timeline and type a new name. You can also select the layer by clicking it, and then open the Layer Properties dialog box by clicking Layer Properties on the Timeline submenu, which is accessible from the Modify menu. You can also open this dialog box by double-clicking the Layer icon to the left of a layer's name. In the Layer Properties dialog box, as shown in Figure 3-10, you can type a new name for the layer as well as change some of its other properties such as whether the layer is hidden or locked.

| Figure 3-10 | LAYER PROPERTIES DIALOG BOX |

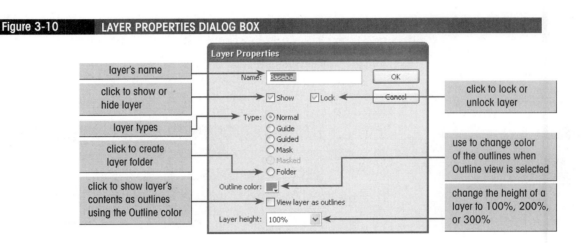

As your document gets more complex and the number of layers increases, you may want to temporarily hide some layers as you work with the content of other layers. Also, once you finish working with the content of one layer, you can lock it so that you do not accidentally change it. You can also change the layer type, the outline color, and the height of the layer. There are different types of layers, as mentioned earlier. There are guide layers and mask layers, as well as guided and masked layers. You can select each of these layer types within the Layer Properties dialog box. Another option is the Outline Color. This determines the color of the layer's contents on the Stage when the View layer as outlines option is selected. Viewing the contents on the Stage in outline form can be helpful when you want to see how the different objects on the Stage relate to each other throughout the animation. Also in this dialog box, you can increase an individual layer's height as represented in the Timeline from the default of 100% to 200% or 300%. This only affects the individual layer and is useful when you need to see more of the layer's contents in Preview or Preview in Context mode.

The number of layers you have in a document can quickly increase as you add more content or animation to your document. In fact, it is best to insert new layers as you add new content to your document. This helps you work with and organize your document's contents more easily. The additional layers do not add to the overall size of your finished file. Keep in mind that you want to keep the size of the final published SWF file as small as possible so it will download quickly from the Web server to the viewer's computer. When you have multiple layers in the document's Timeline, you can create layer folders to help you work more efficiently.

Adding Layer Folders

A **layer folder** is a container in the Timeline in which you can place layers. The names of layers placed in a layer folder are displayed indented under the layer folder in the Timeline, as shown in Figure 3-11.

| Figure 3-11 | LAYER FOLDER |

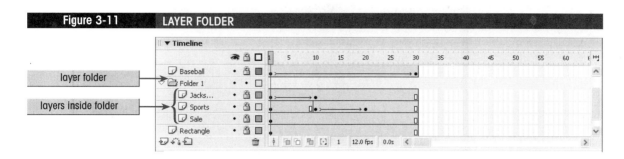

Using layer folders is similar to how you use a folder on your computer's hard drive—you place related files into the folder to make the files easier to find and manage. You can use a layer folder to keep related layers together. For example, you can create a folder to place all of the layers that contain text. Then you can quickly find the text layers when you need to edit them. You can also name a layer folder the same way you name a layer, thereby making it easier to know what each folder contains. Once you have placed layers in a layer folder, you can collapse the layer folder so that the layers in the folder are not visible. This makes the Timeline less cluttered and makes it easier to work with the other layers in the document. Collapsing the folder's layers does not affect the view of the layers' content on the Stage. To collapse a folder, you click the folder's Collapse arrow in the Timeline. To expand the folder's contents and display the layers you click the folder's Expand arrow.

Aly wants you to practice working with layer folders using the sports2 document.

To insert a layer folder:

1. Click the **Jacksons** layer in the Timeline, click **Insert** on the menu bar, point to **Timeline**, and then click **Layer Folder**. A layer folder name Folder 1 is inserted above the Jacksons layer.

2. To rename the folder, double-click the folder name and then type **Text layers**. Press the **Enter** key. The name of the folder changes. Once a folder is created, you can move the related layers into it.

3. Click and drag the **Jacksons** layer to the Text layers folder, releasing the mouse when the Text layers folder's icon changes to a dark color. The Jacksons layer is indented underneath the folder, as shown in Figure 3-12.

Figure 3-12   **JACKSONS LAYER INSIDE FOLDER**

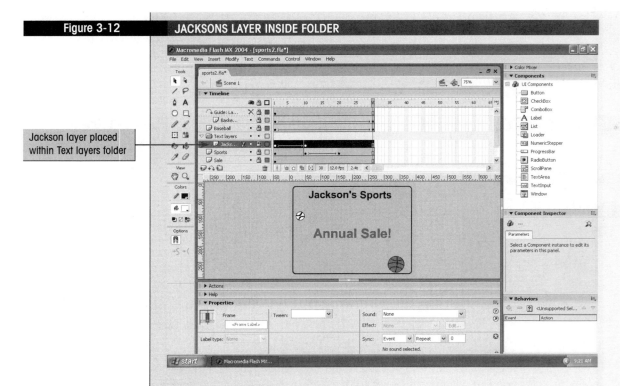

Jackson layer placed within Text layers folder

4. Move the **Sports** layer and the **Sale** layer into the Text layers folder. Each of the text layers now appear indented underneath the Text layers folder.

5. Click the Text layers folder's **Collapse arrow** ▽. The folder's icon changes to a closed folder and the text layers are no longer visible.

Now that you know how to manipulate layers using the Timeline, Aly wants you to learn how to use the Timeline to work with frames.

Selecting, Copying, and Moving Frames

A document's frames may be copied or moved within the same layer or from one layer to another. To copy or move frames, you must first select them. You can select individual frames by clicking the frame in the Timeline. To select multiple frames, click and drag the mouse pointer across the frames you want to select. You can select frames within one layer or across multiple layers. To copy the selected frames, right-click the frames and select Copy Frames from the context menu. To move the frames, select Cut Frames from the context menu, and then right-click the frame where you want to move or copy the selected frames and click Paste Frames.

Aly suggests you practice with the sports2 document to select and copy frames.

To select, copy, and paste frames:

1. Select the **Baseball** layer and click the **Insert Layer** button ⊞ in the Timeline. A new layer is inserted above the Baseball layer. Rename this new layer **Baseball 2**.

2. Click the name of the **Baseball** layer. All of the frames for the layer are selected and you can now copy them to the new layer.

3. Right-click the selected frames to display the context menu, as shown in Figure 3-13.

Figure 3-13   **FRAMES CONTEXT MENU**

selected frames

context menu

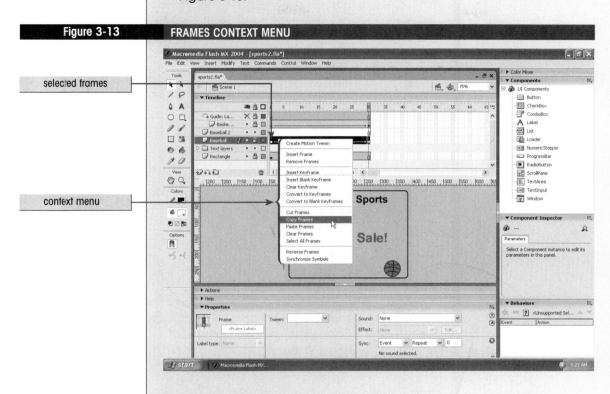

4. Click **Copy Frames** on the context menu.

5. Click the name of the **Baseball 2** layer to select all of its frames. Right-click the selected frames and click **Paste Frames** on the context menu. The layer's frames are replaced with the copied frames from the Baseball layer.

6. Click the **dot** in the Eye column for the Baseball layer to hide it temporarily. Notice that the baseball instance is still shown on the Stage. This baseball is the content of the copied frames that are now in the Baseball 2 layer.

7. Close the file without saving the changes you have made.

You have seen how to work with the document's Timeline and its layers and frames. A Flash document may contain more than one Timeline when the document is divided into separate scenes.

Scenes **and Multiple Timelines**

Scenes provide a way to break up a long or complex document into smaller sections that are more manageable. Every Flash document starts with one scene that contains a Timeline. For more complex animations, a document can have more than one scene, and each scene has its own Timeline, as shown in Figure 3-14. A document may be divided into scenes similar to a motion picture. Just like the scenes in a motion picture are played in order, the scenes in a document are also played one after the other. The frames in a scene's Timeline are then played one after the other. By adding new scenes to a document you are essentially adding new Timelines which contain their own frames.

| Figure 3-14 | **MULTIPLE SCENES IN ONE DOCUMENT** |

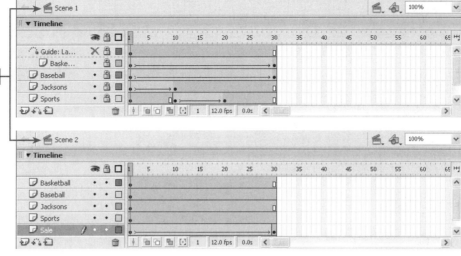

scene name

Once a document with multiple scenes is published, the SWF file plays in a Web page using the Flash Player. The player treats all of the scenes in a SWF file as one long Timeline. So, for example, if a Flash document has two scenes and each scene has 30 frames, the Flash Player will treat this as one long Timeline with 60 consecutive frames and play them according to the order of the scenes in the Scene panel.

Using the Scene Panel

Scenes can be added, deleted, and moved using the Scene Panel. The Scene panel and its options are shown in Figure 3-15.

| Figure 3-15 | **SCENE PANEL** |

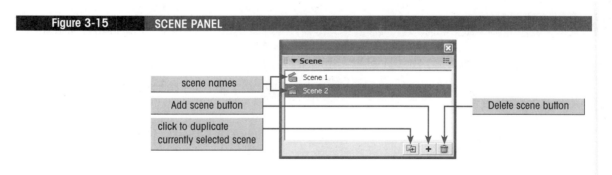

scene names

Add scene button

Delete scene button

click to duplicate
currently selected scene

The Scene panel options are described in Figure 3-16.

| Figure 3-16 | **SCENE PANEL OPTIONS** |

OPTION	DESCRIPTION
Duplicate scene	Creates a copy of the currently selected scene
Add scene	Adds a new blank scene to the document
Delete scene	Deletes the currently selected scene

The Scene panel, which can be displayed by pointing to Design Panels on the Window menu and then clicking the Scene command, lists the scenes in the current document in the order in which they will play. You can change the order the scenes will play by dragging a scene within the panel and placing it before or after other scenes. The Scene panel also allows you to duplicate, add, and delete scenes. A duplicate scene will have the same name as the original with the word "copy" added to its name and it will have the same contents as the original. When you add a new scene it will have the name Scene followed by a number that is one higher than the previous scene. Using the default scene names such as Scene 1, Scene 2, and Scene 3 may be okay if you have a small number of scenes, but if a document has many scenes it is better to assign more meaningful names to each scene to make it easier to manage your document. If you have 10 scenes, for example, you may not remember the content of each of the 10 scenes. You would then have to search through several scenes to find the one containing the content you want to work with. By giving each scene a meaningful name, you can more easily remember what each scene contains. You can change the name of a scene by double-clicking the scene's name in the Scene panel and typing a new name.

When you add a new scene or create a duplicate of a scene, the Stage automatically displays the new scene. You can tell which scene is currently displayed by the scene number in the upper-left corner of the Stage window or by looking at the Scene panel to see which scene is currently selected. To switch to a scene different from the currently displayed scene, you click the name of the scene you want to switch to in the Scene panel. Another way to navigate from one scene to another is to use the Edit Scene button located in the upper-right corner of the Stage window. Clicking this button displays a list of the scenes in the document, as shown in Figure 3-17. You can then switch to a different scene by clicking its name.

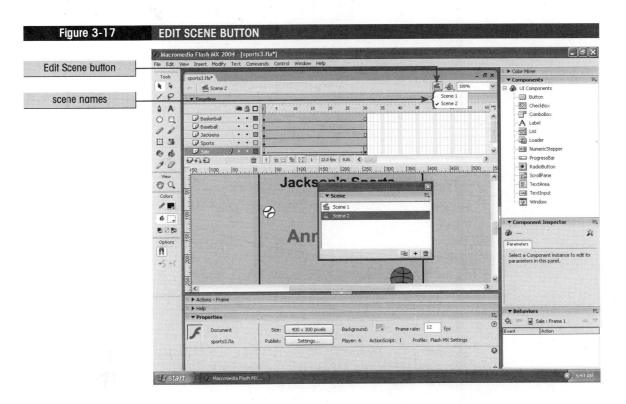

Figure 3-17   EDIT SCENE BUTTON

Edit Scene button

scene names

To practice with scenes Aly asks you to open another version of the Jackson's Sports document that contains two scenes.

To work with scenes:

1. Open the **sports3.fla** document in the **Tutorial.03\Tutorial** folder included with your Data Files.

2. Click **Window** on the menu bar, point to **Design Panels**, and then click **Scene** to open the Scene panel. The Scene panel shows two scenes named Scene 1 and Scene 2. You will start by renaming the scenes with more meaningful names.

3. Double-click **Scene 1** in the Scene panel, type **Start** to rename the scene, and then press the **Enter** key.

4. Double-click **Scene 2**, type **End** to rename that scene, and then press the **Enter** key. The scene names change in the Scene panel. Changing the name of the second scene also switched the Stage view to that scene. Notice the scene name changed in the upper-left corner of the Edit bar and the contents of the Timeline also changed, as shown in Figure 3-18.

Figure 3-18	CURRENT SCENE

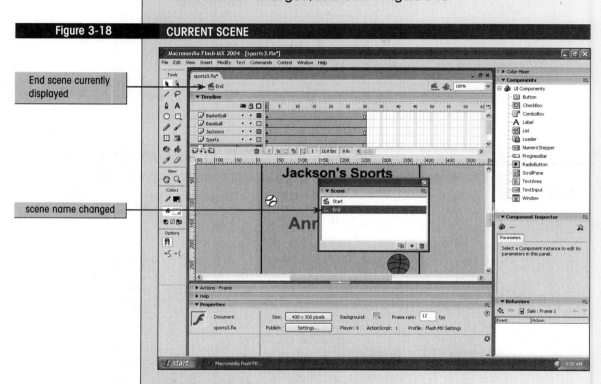

End scene currently displayed

scene name changed

5. Move the Scene panel to the right of the Stage, click **Control** on the menu bar, and then click **Play**. The animation for the End scene plays showing the Annual Sale text rotating. Now test the animation to see how both scenes play one after the other.

6. Click **Control** on the menu bar and then click **Test Movie**. A new window opens showing the SWF file as it plays the animation of the Start scene followed by the animation of the End scene. Close the new window to return to the document. You can also use the Scene panel to reorder the scenes in your document.

7. In the Scene panel, click and drag the **Start** scene so that it follows the End scene. Click **Control** on the menu bar and then click **Test Movie** to see how the sequence of the animations has changed based on the order of the scenes in the Scene panel. The Annual Sale rotating text animation plays first followed by the animation in the Start scene. Close the new window to return to the document.

8. Click the **Edit Scene** button 📇 in the Timeline and then click **End** scene, as shown in Figure 3-19. The Timeline and Stage for the End scene display.

Figure 3-19	SELECTING A SCENE USING THE EDIT SCENE BUTTON

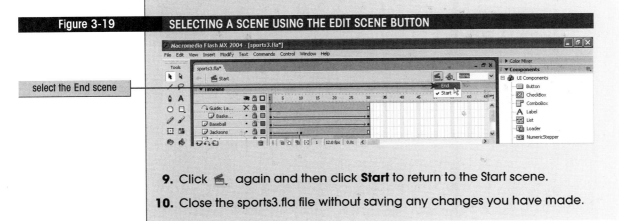

select the End scene

9. Click 📇 again and then click **Start** to return to the Start scene.

10. Close the sports3.fla file without saving any changes you have made.

Now that you have practiced working with the Timeline and with multiple Timelines for scenes, you are ready to begin your work to create the animations for the Flounders banner. You will begin by adding a duplicate scene to the banner.

Adding a Duplicate Scene to the Flounders Banner

Based on the planning instructions Aly provided, the banner will have two different animation sequences. The first sequence will show a fish swimming across the Stage with a sale sign. The second animation sequence will show several fish swimming in the aquarium and plant leaves moving. To make it easy to manage the two animation sequences, Aly suggests you create each in a separate scene. She asks you to add a new scene to the banner she has started by duplicating the initial scene.

To create a duplicate scene:

1. Open the **Banner.fla** document located in the **Tutorial.03\Tutorial** folder included with your Data Files.

2. If necessary, open the Scene panel. The Scene panel shows one scene named Scene 1. You need to create a duplicate of Scene 1.

3. Click the **Duplicate scene** button in the Scene panel. The Scene panel shows the duplicate scene with the name Scene 1 copy. Rename the scenes with more meaningful names.

4. Double-click **Scene 1** in the Scene panel, type **Intro** to rename the scene, and then press the **Enter** key. Double-click **Scene 1 copy** in the Scene panel, type **Fish Swimming**, and then press the **Enter** key. The Scene panel displays the new scene names.

5. Save the file.

Now that you have added a new scene to the Flounders banner document, you are ready to create the animations. You will do that in the next session.

In this session, you learned about the basic elements of Flash that are used in creating animations—layers and frames. You have learned how to work with these elements using the Timeline. You also learned how scenes can help you manage a longer or more complex document. In the next session, you will learn how to create animations that are based on a series of frames that contain graphics.

Session 3.1 QUICK CHECK

1. What is the purpose of the Timeline?

2. How can you tell which is the current frame in the Timeline?

3. What is the default frame rate for a Flash document?

4. What is the difference between frames and layers?

5. List two ways to insert a new layer.

6. What is the purpose of a layer folder?

7. What is a scene?

8. List two methods you can use to change from one scene to another.

9. How can you change the name of a scene?

SESSION 3.2

In this session, you will learn how to create animations in Flash. You will learn how to use Timeline effects to create a simple animation, and then you will learn how to create a frame-by-frame animation. Finally, you will learn the different ways to test an animation.

Creating Animation

As you learned in the previous session, animation is accomplished by displaying the content of different frames one after another. Each frame contains some graphic element that is displayed for a short instant in time. As the content of each frame is displayed in succession, the graphic elements appear to be moving. There are several ways to create animations in Flash. The easiest way is to use one of the pre-built Timeline effects. **Timeline effects** allow you to quickly and easily create animations by selecting from various options in a dialog box. Based on the options selected, Flash creates the animation for you.

To create the animation yourself, there are basically two methods. You can create a **frame-by-frame animation** in which you create the content for each individual frame. Or, you can create a **tweened animation** in which you create the content for the beginning and ending frames, and Flash creates the content for the in-between frames. A tweened animation is quicker and easier to create than a frame-by-frame animation because you only need to create the content for two frames, the one at the beginning of the animation and the one at the end. Each of these two frames is a keyframe. Frame-by-frame animations take more time to create because you need to create all of the content for all the frames in the animation. Frame-by-frame animations are usually used to build more detailed animations where you need to control the content of each step in the animation. Frame-by-frame animations also tend to produce larger-sized files than tweened animations.

Recall from Aly's sketch, shown in Figure 3-1, there is an initial animation sequence for the Flounders Pet Shop banner in which a fish pulls a sale sign across the Stage. This animation will be created with a Timeline effect. In the second animation sequence the plant leaves will be animated so that the leaves' tips appear to be moving. This will be done with a frame-by-frame animation because you need to specify the positions of the leaves at different moments in time. The fish in the banner will be animated using tweened animations in the next session. You will start by exploring Timeline effects.

Timeline Effects

Timeline effects allow you to create an animation or a special effect by selecting from options in a dialog box. You can apply Timeline effects to objects on the Stage and Flash will create the necessary elements for the animation. This saves you time and does not require that you understand how the animation works. Each Timeline effect is created on its own layer and the layer name indicates the type of effect created. To create a Timeline effect, you first select an object on the Stage to which you want to apply the effect. You then access the various Timeline effects from the Timeline Effects submenu, located on the Insert menu. The Timeline Effects submenu provides a list of Timeline effects organized by category. These categories include Assistants, Effects, and Transform/Transition. When you point to one of these categories, a submenu of Timeline effects for that category appears. Figure 3-20 lists and describes the Timeline effects categories and their Timeline effects.

Figure 3-20

TIMELINE EFFECT	DESCRIPTION
ASSISTANTS	
Copy to Grid	Duplicates the selected object across a grid; you specify the number of rows and columns in the grid plus the spacing between rows and columns
Distributed Duplicate	Creates duplicates of an object and distributes them according to settings such as offset distance, rotation, and color
EFFECTS	
Blur	Animates an object by duplicating it and increasingly blurring each duplicate; you set the number of duplicates to create and the direction in which to display them throughout the animation
Drop Shadow	Creates a drop shadow of an object; you select the color of the shadow, how much transparency to apply to it, and what distance to offset it from the object
Expand	Creates an animation where an object, such as a text block, expands and/or contracts; includes settings to specify the number of frames to use for the animation as well as whether to expand or contract the object and in what direction to move the object
Explode	Breaks an object into pieces simulating an explosion of the object; you can specify the direction, arc, and rotation the exploded pieces will move in, the size of the pieces, and the amount of transparency to apply to the pieces
TRANSFORM/ TRANSITION	
Transform	Creates an animation where an object is transformed; you can also specify that the object change position, rotate, scale in size, change color, or change amount of transparency; you can control how slow it starts or ends the animation
Transition	Creates a fade or wipe transition for an object; you specify what direction to fade or wipe and you can control how slow it starts or ends the animation

Once you select one of these Timeline effects, a dialog box opens displaying a preview of the effect along with default settings specific to the effect. Figure 3-21 shows an example of the transform Timeline effect.

Figure 3-21	EXAMPLE OF A TIMELINE EFFECT DIALOG BOX

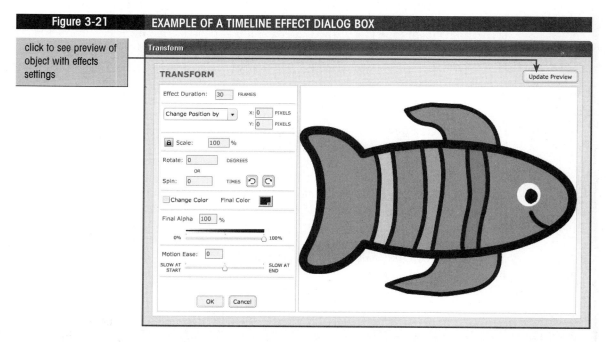

click to see preview of object with effects settings

In the dialog box you change the settings you want to apply. You can then update the preview to see the effect within the dialog box. If you make additional changes to the settings, click the Update Preview button again to see how the changes affect the Timeline effect. When you are satisfied with the settings in the dialog box, click the OK button. Flash then creates a new layer in the Timeline and creates the frames with the appropriate content for the animation, as shown in Figure 3-22.

Figure 3-22	TIMELINE EFFECT LAYER

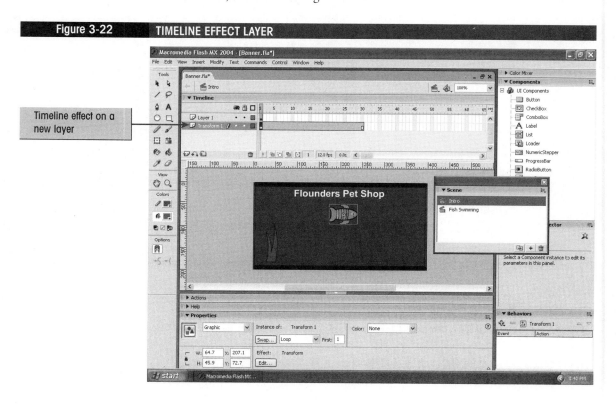

Timeline effect on a new layer

In addition to the new layer created in the Timeline, Flash creates a new symbol for the Timeline effect and adds this symbol to the document's library. Flash also creates a new folder called Effects Folder in the Library panel, which holds the graphic symbols used to create the animation. You can see the symbol and folder by opening the Library panel, as shown in Figure 3-23.

| **Figure 3-23** | **LIBRARY WITH NEW SYMBOL AND EFFECTS FOLDER** |

new folder

new symbol

Once the Timeline effect is created you may need to modify or remove it. This can be done by clicking Modify on the menu bar, pointing to Timeline Effects, and then selecting Edit Effect or Remove Effect. Selecting the Edit Effect command opens the same dialog box that was used to create the effect allowing you to change the settings. If you select Remove Effect, Flash removes the effect from the Timeline and also removes the effect's symbols and the Effects Folder from the document's library.

Adding a Timeline Effect to the Flounders Pet Shop Banner

Recall that the first animation sequence for the Flounders Pet Shop banner will have an animation where a fish moves across the Stage pulling a sale sign. Aly suggests you create this animation using the Transform Timeline effect. The animation will be created in the first scene.

To draw the graphics for the animation:

1. If you took a break after the last session, open the **Banner.fla** file located in the **Tutorial03\Tutorial** folder included with your Data Files.

2. If necessary, switch to the **Intro** scene to make it the current scene. Use the **Selection** tool to select the entire plant leaves graphic on the Stage and then delete it. The leaves will not be used in this scene.

3. Click the **Rectangle** tool on the toolbar. If necessary, click the **Black and White** modifier on the toolbar to change the stroke color to black and the fill color to white. Use a stroke height of **2** and a **solid** stroke style. Draw a rectangle to the left of the fish. Make the rectangle approximately 75 pixels wide and 40 pixels high. This will be the sign the fish pulls across the banner. Add the words to the sign next.

4. Click the **Text** tool A on the toolbar, and if necessary, change the text color to **black**. Use **Arial** for the text font and **22** for the text size. Create a text block inside the rectangle you drew in Step 2. Type **SALE!** in the text block, and center it in the rectangle, if necessary. Now modify the lines of the rectangle.

5. Using ▶, drag the top line of the rectangle downward slightly to curve it. Then drag the bottom line of the rectangle upwards slightly to curve it also. Do not curve the lines past the text in the text box. You now need to draw a line to connect the sign to the fish.

6. Select the **Line** tool ∕ on the toolbar and draw a line from the left side of the fish to the right side of the rectangle. Set **black** as the line color, **2** for the line height, and **solid** for the line style. See Figure 3-24.

Figure 3-24	FISH WITH SALE SIGN

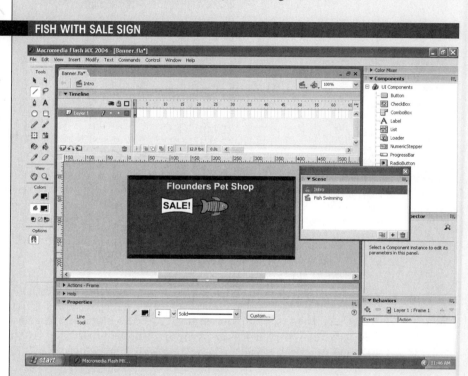

The graphic of the fish pulling the sign is now complete. You are ready to apply the animation to it using the transform Timeline effect. You must first select the sign, the line, and the fish all at once.

To add a Timeline effect to the Flounders banner:

1. Use ▶ to draw a marquee around the sign, line, and fish graphic to select all of the objects at one time.

2. Click **Insert** on the menu bar, point to **Timeline Effects**, point to **Transform/ Transition**, and then click **Transform**. The Transform dialog box opens. You will change the settings so that the animation will occupy 30 frames in the Timeline, move horizontally 300 pixels, and slow down at the end of the movement.

3. In the Transform dialog box, make sure that the number of frames in the Effect Duration text box is **30**. If necessary, select the **Change Position by** option in the Position list box, and change the X position value to **300**.

4. Enter **80** in the **Motion Ease** text box. The Motion Ease value determines whether the animation starts slowly and goes faster at the end or it starts fast and then goes slower at the end. This gives the movement a more natural look, more so than if you had the object move at the same rate throughout the entire animation sequence. The settings in the Transform dialog box should match those shown in Figure 3-25.

Figure 3-25   **SETTINGS FOR TRANSFORM TIMELINE EFFECT**

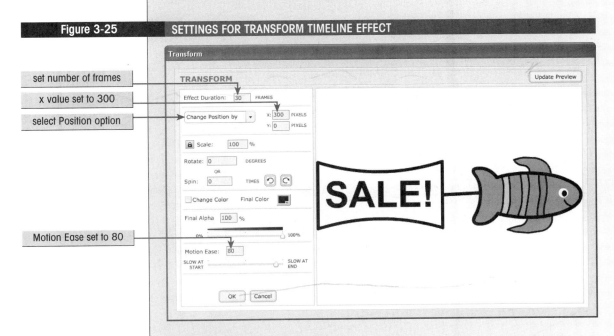

set number of frames

x value set to 300

select Position option

Motion Ease set to 80

5. Click the **Update Preview** button to see how the animation will work. Click the **OK** button to close the dialog box and create the effect in the Timeline. A new layer named Transform 1 is created in the Timeline and the selected objects on the Stage are converted into a symbol. Next, position the symbol instance.

6. Click **Frame 1** of the Transform 1 layer and use the **Selection** tool to move the symbol instance to the left so that the sale sign is off the Stage, as shown in Figure 3-26.

Figure 3-26 | **POSITION FISH AND SALE SIGN**

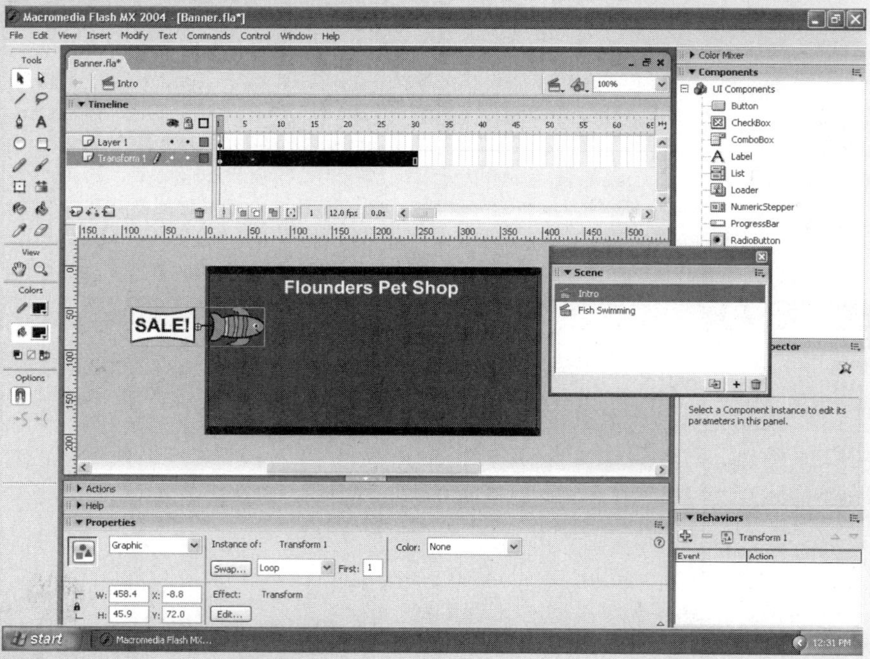

(handwritten margin note: how could not click play, word not highlighted)

7. Click **Control** on the menu bar and click **Play** to test the animation. The fish and sale sign move across the Stage from the left to the right slowing down slightly when they reach the end of the animation. To complete the animation, extend Layer 1 so that it exists for 30 frames.

8. Click **Frame 30** of Layer 1, click **Insert** on the menu bar, point to **Timeline**, and click **Frame** to insert a regular frame. The graphics in Layer 1 are displayed through Frame 30.

You have completed the Timeline effect for the first scene of the banner. Next, you will continue your work with the banner by adding the animation to the second scene. You will animate the plant leaves using frame-by-frame animation.

Frame-by-Frame **Animation**

To create a frame-by-frame animation, you need to create the graphic elements for the animation in each of its individual frames. If, for example, your animation is to have 15 frames, then you need to create the content for each of the 15 frames. Some of the content can be the same from one frame to the next, but other content can be slightly modified. As the frames are displayed one after the other, the perception of movement is achieved. To create a frame-by-frame animation you start with a graphic object in the initial frame. Then for each place in the animation where you need the object to change, you add a keyframe. Recall that a frame that has different content from the previous frame is called a keyframe. Depending on the animation, every frame may be a keyframe or you may have intervening frames where the graphic object does not change. As you add keyframes, you change the position of the graphic object. Once you have all of the keyframes created you test the animation. Figure 3-27 shows the Timeline for a sample frame-by-frame animation. Notice the keyframes where the content changes throughout the animation.

Figure 3-27	SAMPLE FRAME-BY-FRAME ANIMATION

keyframes indicate content changes in each frame

Adding Frame-by-Frame Animation to the Flounders Pet Shop Banner

The Fish Swimming scene of the banner contains a graphic element that looks like a plant. You will convert this plant graphic into a symbol with a movie clip behavior, and you will animate the plant's leaves so that they appear to be moving inside the aquarium tank. You will do this by creating a frame-by-frame animation. The plant's leaves will be animated within the Timeline of the plant symbol and not in the main Timeline of the document. Recall from the previous tutorial that a movie clip symbol has its own Timeline which is independent of the document's Timeline. By adding the animation in the symbol's Timeline, every instance of the symbol automatically includes the animation. This means that each plant instance you create on the document's Stage will have the same animation built-in as part of the instance.

To create the animation of the plant leaves, Aly suggests you add keyframes to every other frame of the plant leaves layer from Frame 1 through Frame 9. This will be sufficient to create the movement of the leaves. She further suggests that in each keyframe you move the tips of the leaves slightly, first in one direction and then in the opposite direction.

Before you can create the frame-by-frame animation of the plant leaves, you need to convert these objects to symbols.

To convert the objects in the Fish Swimming scene to symbols:

1. If necessary, click the **Fish Swimming** scene in the Scene panel to make it the current scene, then close the Scene panel. You will create symbols of the plant and fish graphics.

2. Use the **Selection** tool to select all of the plant graphic. Make sure you select both its stroke and its fill. Click **Modify** on the menu bar and then click **Convert to Symbol**. In the Convert to Symbol dialog box, type **Plant** in the Name text box, and make sure the **Movie clip** option button is selected. Click the **OK** button to close the dialog box.

   The fish graphic also needs to be converted to a symbol. Recall from Aly's planning sketch that this fish will be animated to swim from one side of the tank to the other. (You will complete this animation in Session 3.3.)

3. Select the entire fish graphic, making sure to select all of its strokes and fills. Click **Modify** on the menu bar and then click **Convert to Symbol**. In the Convert to Symbol dialog box, type **Fish1** for the name of the symbol and make sure the **Movie clip** option button is selected. Click the **OK** button to close the dialog box.

Now you are ready to animate the plant symbol. You need to first open the Library panel to work with the Plant symbol.

To create a frame-by-frame animation of the plant symbol:

1. If necessary, click **Window** on the menu bar and then click **Library** to open the Library panel. You need to first select the Plant symbol from the Library panel, so you can edit it to create an animation within its Timeline.

2. Double-click the **Plant** symbol's icon in the Library panel to open the symbol in symbol-editing mode.

3. In the symbol's Timeline, click **Frame 3**, as shown in Figure 3-28. You will add a keyframe at Frame 3.

Figure 3-28	SELECTING A FRAME

click Frame 3

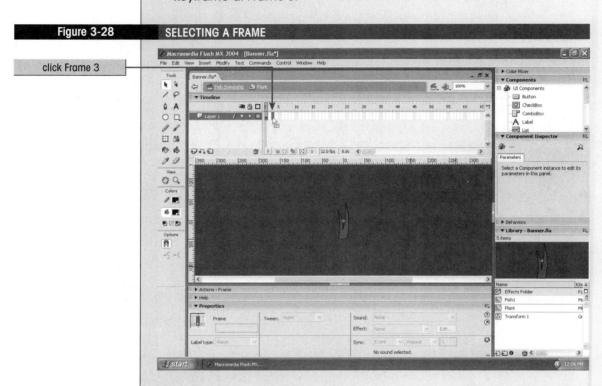

4. Click **Insert** on the menu bar, point to **Timeline**, and then click **Keyframe**. A keyframe is inserted in Frame 3 and a regular frame is added in Frame 2. When you add any kind of frame to a layer, Flash will add intervening frames. So when you added a keyframe in Frame 3, Flash automatically added a regular frame, not a keyframe, in Frame 2. The plant graphic is also automatically copied to all of the new frames. See Figure 3-29.

Figure 3-29   **KEYFRAME ADDED TO PLANT SYMBOL TIMELINE**

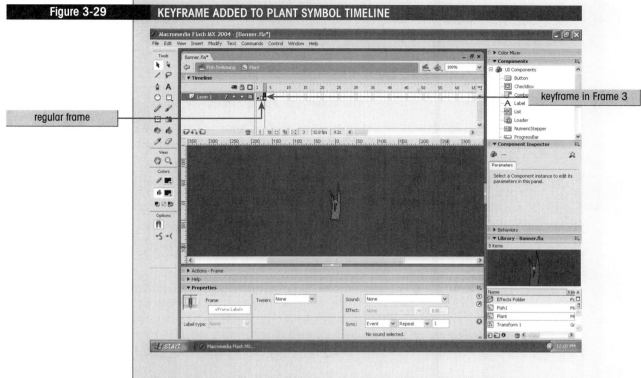

regular frame

keyframe in Frame 3

In this frame, move the tips of the leaves slightly to the right.

5. Using the **Selection** tool , deselect the plant by clicking an empty area of the Stage. Position the mouse pointer over the tip of one of the leaves until you see the corner pointer . Once you see the , click and drag the tip of the leaf slightly to the right. Repeat this for the other leaf's tip to reposition it slightly to the right. See Figure 3-30.

Figure 3-30   **MODIFYING THE PLANT LEAVES**

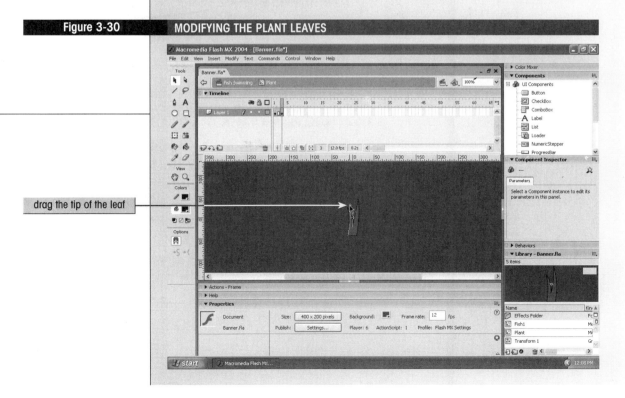

drag the tip of the leaf

You will now add keyframes in every other frame.

6. Click **Frame 5** and insert a keyframe. Repeat Step 5 to reposition both of the leaves' tips slightly more to the right.

7. Click **Frame 7** and insert a keyframe. Repeat Step 5, but this time, reposition the leaves' tips back slightly to the left. Now you will finish the animation with another keyframe moving the leaves' tips to their starting position.

8. Click **Frame 9** and insert another keyframe. This time move the leaves' tips slightly more to the left to almost the same position where they started in Frame 1.

9. Drag the playhead back and forth through these frames to get a sense of what the animation looks like. You are done creating this frame-by-frame animation. You can exit symbol-editing mode.

10. To exit the symbol-editing mode, click **Edit** on the menu bar, and then click **Edit Document**.

You have created a frame-by-frame animation within the Plant symbol. Because the animation was created within the symbol's Timeline, each instance of the symbol has the same animation. You can, therefore, place several instances of the plant symbol in the document and all of the instances will be animated.

Recall from Aly's instructions that the banner should have three animated plants in the lower-left corner of the tank. You will therefore add three instances of the animated plant symbol. The second instance will need to be modified to make it larger than the first, and the third instance will need to be modified such that its leaves point to the right of the tank.

To create instances of the animated plant symbol and then modify them:

1. Click **View** on the menu bar, point to **Magnification**, and click **Show All** to fit all of the contents to the Stage. First you will delete the instances of the plant and fish from the first layer. These were the original graphic objects. When you created symbols using these objects, they became instances of the symbols. You will be placing instances of these symbols onto separate layers.

2. Click the **plant** instance on the Stage, and press the **Delete** key to remove it. You are only deleting one instance of the symbol. The symbol itself is still in the document's library. Next delete the fish instance.

3. Click the **fish** instance on the Stage, and press the **Delete** key. Before you insert the plant instances into the document, create a new layer for the plant instances.

4. Click **Insert** on the menu bar, point to **Timeline**, and then click **Layer**. To change the name of the new layer, double-click **Layer 2** in the Timeline, type **Plant** as the new name for this layer, and press the **Enter** key.

5. Make sure the Plant layer is the current layer, and drag an instance of the Plant symbol from the Library panel to the lower-left corner of the Stage.

6. Drag another instance of the Plant symbol from the Library panel and place it to the right of the first, as shown in Figure 3-31.

Figure 3-31   **PLANT ARRANGEMENT**

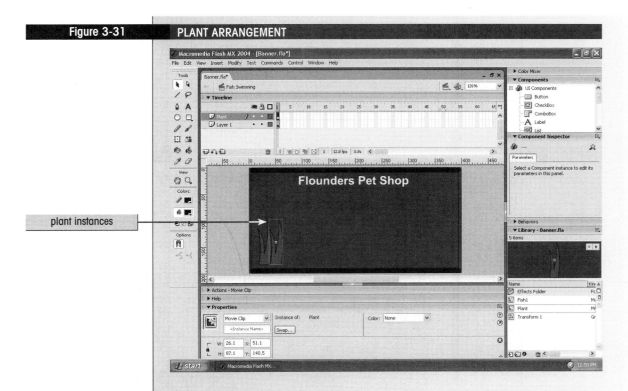

plant instances

7. With this instance still selected, click the **Free Transform** tool 🔲 on the toolbar, and then click the **Scale** modifier button 🔲 in the options area of the toolbar. Drag one of the corners of the bounding box around the plant to make this plant instance slightly larger than the first. See Figure 3-32. If necessary, reposition the instance to align it with the bottom edge of the other plant instance.

Figure 3-32   **ENLARGING THE PLANT INSTANCE**

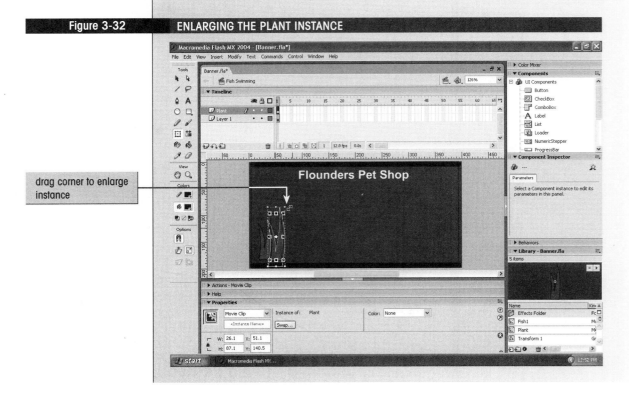

drag corner to enlarge instance

8. Click the **Selection** tool ▶ on the toolbar, then drag one more instance of the Plant symbol from the Library panel, and place it to the right of the other two. Next you will flip the horizontal position of the third instance.

9. With this instance still selected, click **Modify** on the menu bar, point to **Transform**, and click **Flip Horizontal**. Be sure to line up the bottoms of the plants with the bottom part of the tank outline. See Figure 3-33.

Figure 3-33   **INSTANCES OF PLANT SYMBOL**

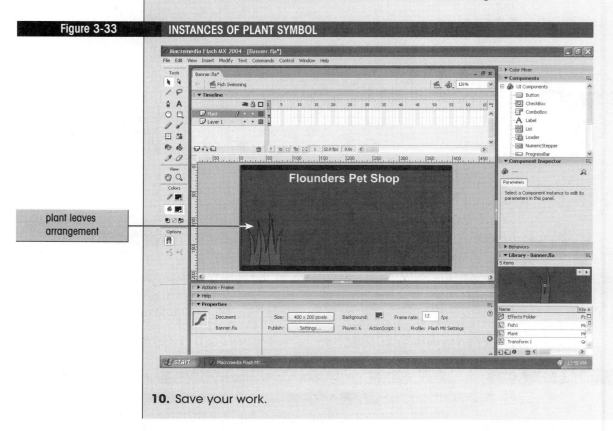

plant leaves arrangement

10. Save your work.

Once you create an animation, it is important to test it to make sure it works correctly when the movie plays.

Testing a Document's Animation

Once you create a document with animation, you need to test it to make sure it works correctly. To test your document's animation, you click the Play command on the Control menu or press the Enter key on the keyboard. This plays the animation on the Stage. You can also test the animation by dragging the playhead with the mouse pointer back and forth through the frames. This is known as **scrubbing** and is useful when you need to test a short animation sequence. Another way to test your document's animation is to click the Test Movie command on the Control menu. When you use this command, Flash actually creates an SWF file and then plays the file using the Flash Player plug-in. Finally, you can test your animation on a Web page by clicking the Default (HTML) command on the Publish Preview submenu, which you open from the File menu. Flash publishes the document as an SWF file and also creates a Web page. The Web page with the SWF file is then displayed in your computer's default browser. After viewing the animation in the Web page, you can close the browser window to return to the document.

REFERENCE   WINDOW   **RW**

<u>Testing a Document's Animation</u>

- ■ To test the document's animation within the program window, click Control on the menu bar, and then click Play.
- ■ To test a few frames of animation, scrub by dragging the playhead along the Timeline header.
- ■ To test the animation in a Flash Player plug-in window, click Control on the menu bar, and then click Test Movie.
- ■ To test the animation in a Web page, click File on the menu bar, point to Publish Preview, and click Default - (HTML).

Because the plant symbol's animation is within its own Timeline, you need to test the animation as a SWF file. If you test the animation within the Flash program window, the plant symbol's animation will not play. You will use the Test Movie command on the Control menu to test the document's animation.

To test the document's animation:

1. Click **Control** on the menu bar, and then click **Test Movie**. The movie plays in a Flash Player window starting with the Intro scene. The plant leaves animation, however, is only visible for a fraction of a second. This is because the second scene only has one frame. You will stop the animation loop and advance to the plant leaves.

2. Click **Control** on the menu bar and click **Loop** to stop the animation. Press the **Period** key on your keyboard repeatedly to advance the animation one frame at a time. Stop when you see the plant leaves animation, as shown in Figure 3-34. The plant leaves display their animation.

Figure 3-34   **FLASH PLAYER WINDOW**

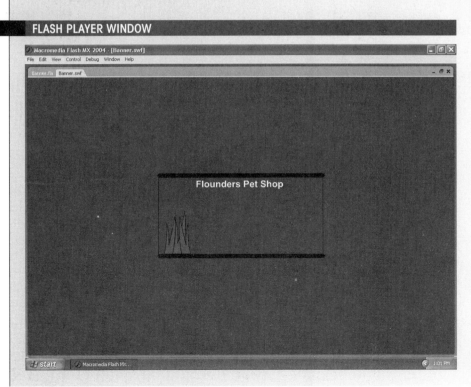

3. Click **File** on the menu bar, and then click **Close** to close the Flash Player window. Now test the animation in a Web page.

4. Click **File** on the menu bar, point to **Publish Preview**, and then click **Default – (HTML)**. Your computer's default browser opens and the animation plays in a Web page.

5. Close the browser window when you are finished viewing the animation.

You have completed two of the three animations for the Flounders Pet Shop banner using Timeline effects and frame-by-frame animation. In the next session, you will create the third animation Aly asked for in her planning sketch.

Session 3.2 QUICK CHECK

1. What is a Timeline effect?

2. Each Timeline effect is created in its own layer. True or False?

3. Once you create a Timeline effect in your document, how can you change its settings?

4. In a frame-by-frame animation, what kind of frame do you need to have in the Timeline when the content changes on the Stage?

5. To create a frame-by-frame animation, the object being animated must first be converted to a symbol. True or False?

6. Can you include regular frames in a frame-by-frame animation? Why or why not?

SESSION 3.3

In this session, you will learn about tweened animations in Flash. You will learn how to create both a motion tween and a shape tween. You will also learn how to create animations using graphic symbols.

Tweened Animation

In the previous session, you learned how to create a frame-by-frame animation by creating the content for each frame yourself. However, this process can be tedious and time consuming if you have many objects that need to be animated. For most animations where you want an object to move, resize, rotate, or change certain properties over a period of time, it is best to create a tweened animation. Recall that tweened animation is where you create the content of the beginning frame and then change that content in the ending frame. The program then creates the in-between frames, varying the content evenly in each frame to achieve the animation. The beginning frame and the ending frame for a tweened animation must be keyframes. Many of the Timeline effects covered in the previous session are also created with tweened animations; however, you do not have as much control over the animation as you do when you create the tweened animation yourself.

There are two types of tweened animations. These are motion tweening and shape tweening. **Motion tweening** can be used to create an animation where an object changes its position, rotates, scales in size, or even changes in color. You can also make an object fade in or out. **Shape tweening** is used to change a shape into another shape over time. For example, you can create an animation where a circle shape is changed into a square shape.

Motion Tweening

The process for creating a motion tweened animation is relatively simple. You create an object in the beginning frame of the animation and convert the object to a symbol. In order for an object to be animated using motion tweening, the object must be a symbol. Also, you can only have one object in the layer in which you create the motion tween. If you have more than one object, Flash groups them and tries to animate them together. If an object is not to be part of a motion tween, then it should be placed on a separate layer. Once the object to be animated is a symbol, you create a keyframe in the frame where the animation will end. In this keyframe you move the object to a different position or you change its properties such as its color tint or color brightness. You create the animation in the first frame by selecting the Create Motion Tween command located on the Timeline submenu, which you access from the Insert menu. Flash then creates the tweened frames varying the content in each frame to change the object's position or properties slightly from one frame to the next. You can also create the motion tween by using the Property inspector. Once you click the first frame where the animation is to begin, the Property inspector displays the Tween list box. You then select Motion from the Tween list box, and additional options are displayed, as shown in Figure 3-35.

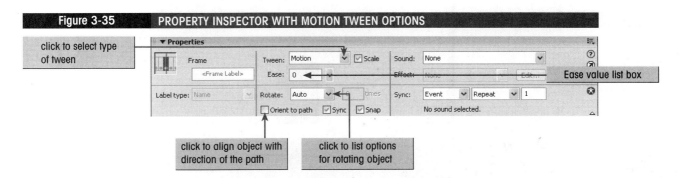

Figure 3-35   PROPERTY INSPECTOR WITH MOTION TWEEN OPTIONS

click to select type of tween

Ease value list box

click to align object with direction of the path

click to list options for rotating object

Two of these options are the Ease value list box and the Rotate list box. The **Ease** value makes an object accelerate or decelerate to create a more natural appearance of movement. With the default value of 0, the rate of change between the tweened frames remains constant. A negative value between –1 and –100 causes the object to begin slowly and accelerate toward the end of the animation. A positive value between 1 and 100 causes the object to begin rapidly and decelerate toward the end of the animation. The **Rotate** list box allows you to specify whether the object should also rotate during the motion tween. Selecting CW causes the object to rotate in a clockwise direction. Selecting CCW rotates the object in a counterclockwise direction. You then specify how many times to rotate the object throughout the motion tween in the times text box.

Once you create a motion tween, the frames in the Timeline will have a light-blue background and there will be a solid line across the frames. If there is a dashed line that means that the tween is broken or incomplete such as when there is no ending keyframe. Remember a motion tween starts at a keyframe and ends at a keyframe. If the ending keyframe is missing, the animation does not work and a dashed line appears in the Timeline. Also, if the object to be animated is not a symbol, a dashed line displays.

Creating a Motion Tweened Animation

You will now continue your work with the Flounders Pet Shop banner by adding a motion tweened animation of the fish graphic in the second scene. The fish will swim from one side of the tank, turn around, and swim back. In a discussion with Aly, she suggests making the animation approximately four seconds in length. At the frame rate of 12 frames per second this will take 48 frames. You will have the fish swim to the side of the tank and back in 48 frames. So you decide that the fish should arrive at the side of the tank at Frame 24 so that it can turn around and return to the other side during the second half of the animation.

To create a motion tween with the fish graphic:

1. If you took a break after the last session, open the **Banner.fla** file located in the **Tutorial.03\Tutorial** folder included with your Data Files. Select the **Plant** layer in the Timeline. You need to add a new layer for the motion tweened fish.

2. Click **Insert** on the menu bar, point to **Timeline**, and then click **Layer**. A new layer is added to the Timeline above the Plant layer. Double-click the layer's name to select it, and change the name to **Fish1**. You will add an instance of the fish to this layer.

3. Make sure that the Fish1 layer is selected. Drag the **Fish1** symbol from the Library panel to the left side of the Stage, just inside the tank outline. This will create an instance of the Fish1 symbol. See Figure 3-36.

Figure 3-36   **FISH1 INSTANCE CREATED ON THE STAGE**

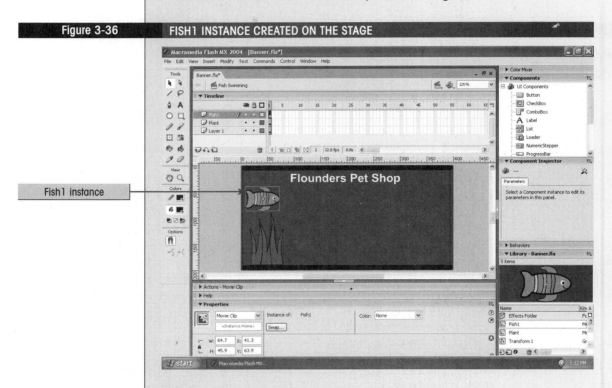

Fish1 instance

4. Click **Layer 1**, and then if necessary, use the Timeline horizontal scroll bar to make Frame 48 visible. Click **Frame 48** of Layer 1. Click **Insert** on the menu bar, point to **Timeline**, and then click **Frame**. A regular frame is added at Frame 48. Regular frames are also automatically added between Frames 1 and 48. The Layer 1 graphics from Frame 1 are copied to Frame 48.

Notice the fish and the plant disappeared when you added the frame in Frame 48. This is because these graphics do not exist in Frame 48 yet. They only exist in Frame 1. In order for the plant and fish to exist through Frame 48 you need to add frames to their respective layers.

5. Click **Frame 48** of the Plant layer. Click **Insert** on the menu bar, point to **Timeline**, and then click **Frame** to extend the layer through Frame 48. You will add a keyframe where the fish will arrive at the right side of the tank.

6. Click **Frame 24** of the Fish1 layer. Click **Insert** on the menu bar, point to **Timeline**, and then click **Keyframe**. A keyframe is added at Frame 24 and regular frames are automatically added between Frames 1 and 24. The Fish1 graphic is copied to Frame 24.

7. While still in Frame 24, drag the **Fish1** instance from the left side of the Stage to the right side. Be sure to stay within the tank outline, as shown in Figure 3-37.

Figure 3-37   **FISH1 INSTANCE REPOSITIONED FOR FRAME 24**

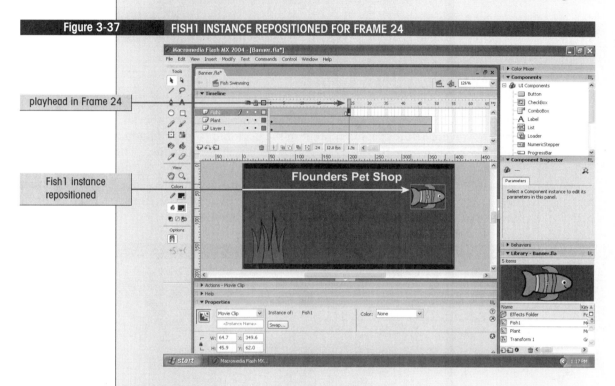

playhead in Frame 24

Fish1 instance repositioned

Now add a keyframe where the fish will turn around.

8. Click **Frame 25** and insert a keyframe. In this frame you will move the fish so that it faces in the opposite direction.

9. Click **Modify** on the menu bar, point to **Transform**, and then click **Flip Horizontal**. Next you need to add a keyframe at the end of the animation for the Fish1 layer.

10. Click **Frame 48** of the Fish1 layer, and insert another keyframe. In this keyframe, drag the **Fish1** instance so that it is back to its original starting position on the left side of the Stage. Now you can create a motion tween.

11. Click **Frame 1** of the Fish1 layer, click **Insert** on the menu bar, point to **Timeline**, and then click **Create Motion Tween**. A motion tween is created as evidenced by the line and light-blue background on Frames 1 through 24 in the Timeline. Now you need to create another motion tween.

12. Click **Frame 25** of the Fish1 layer, click the **Tween** list arrow in the Property inspector, and then click **Motion**. This has the same result as selecting Create Motion Tween from the Timeline submenu.

Now that you have created the motion tweens, you should test them.

To test the motion tweened animations:

1. Click **Control** on the menu bar, and then click **Rewind**. The playhead moves to Frame 1.

2. Click **Control** again and click **Play**. The fish moves from the left of the Stage to the right and then back again to the left.

3. Save your work.

You can create a shape tween in a way similar to the method used to create a motion tweened animation.

Shape Tweening

Recall a shape tween takes one shape and transforms it into another shape. To create a shape tween, you create the graphic content in the beginning and ending frames of the animation and Flash creates the tweened frames to complete the animation. The object you use in a shape tween must not be a symbol, or a grouped object. This is different from a motion tween where you first have to convert an object into a symbol. A shape tween is indicated in the Timeline by a line and a light-green color for the frames, as shown in Figure 3-38. The Flounders Pet Shop banner does not require a shape tween.

Figure 3-38	A SHAPE TWEEN IN THE TIMELINE

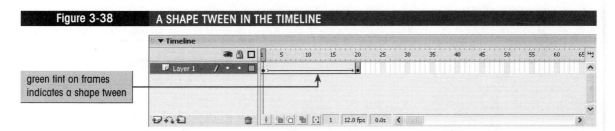

green tint on frames indicates a shape tween

Graphic **Symbol Animations**

Recall that when you create symbols, you have three options for their behavior. These are movie clip, button, and graphic. Most of the symbols you need to create will have a behavior of movie clip or graphic. Symbols with button behaviors are symbols that can be used to control an animation. You will learn how to create button symbols in Tutorial 5. You have already worked with movie clip symbols in Tutorial 2. In this session, you will learn about graphic symbols and their special characteristics.

Both movie clip and graphic symbols have their own Timeline. Recall in a movie clip symbol the frames in its Timeline play independently of the document's main Timeline. However, in a graphic symbol the frames of its Timeline are synchronized with the document's main Timeline. So, for example, suppose you insert a movie clip instance that contains an animation with ten frames into a document whose main Timeline consists of only one frame. Even though the main Timeline contains only one frame, the movie clip's ten frames will still play in their entirety. However, if you insert a graphic instance that contains an animation with ten frames into a document whose main Timeline has only one frame, then only one frame of the graphic instance will play. If you want all ten frames of the graphic instance to play you have to extend the length of the document's main Timeline to at least ten frames. Graphic symbols are useful when you want to synchronize the animations in the symbol to that of the main Timeline.

Another difference between graphic symbols and movie clips is that movie clip instances always start playing from their first frame. With a graphic instance, however, you can specify which of its frames to play first. As a result, if you create a graphic symbol animation and then create several instances of the symbol, each of the instances can have a different starting frame. For example, one instance can start playing at Frame 1 of its Timeline while another instance can start playing at Frame 20. Using this technique you can create multiple instances of one graphic symbol in the same scene and have each instance exhibit a different behavior.

Also, graphic symbol instances display their animation when you scrub the playhead in the document's main Timeline or play the animation within the Stage window of the main Timeline's animation. That is, you do not need to test the document in the Flash Player to see the animations contained in instances of graphic symbols. On the other hand, instances of movie clips appear as static objects and do not display their animations within the Stage window. You have to play the document in the Flash Player in order to see the movie clip animations. Again, this has to do with the fact that the frames of graphic symbols are synchronized with the document's main Timeline, while the frames of a movie clip symbol are independent of the document's main Timeline.

Creating Graphic Symbol Animations

You create a graphic symbol animation the same way you create a movie clip animation. You just specify Graphic as the symbol's behavior in the Create Symbol dialog box. The symbol will also display a different icon in the document's Library panel to indicate its behavior type. Once a graphic symbol animation is created, instances of the symbol can be created on the Stage in the same way you create instances of movie clip symbols. However, when you select an instance of a graphic symbol on the Stage, you can use the Property inspector to indicate what frame you want the instance's animation to begin. You do this by entering a value in the First Frame text box, as shown in Figure 3-39.

| Figure 3-39 | GRAPHIC INSTANCE PROPERTIES IN THE PROPERTY INSPECTOR |

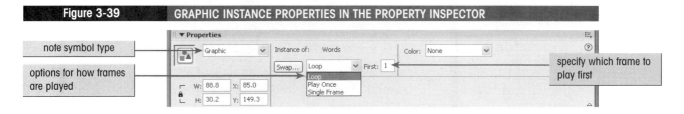

You can also specify whether you want the instance's animation to play continuously, play only once, or play only one frame. These graphic instance options are described in Figure 3-40.

| Figure 3-40 | GRAPHIC INSTANCE PLAY OPTIONS |

OPTIONS	DESCRIPTION
Loop	Plays all of the animation's frames in the current instance; the frames are played for as many frames as the instance occupies in the document's main Timeline
Play Once	Plays the animation's frames only one time starting with the frame specified in the First Frame text box
Single Frame	Displays only one frame of the animation; this frame is specified in the First Frame text box

Aly's instructions specified that the Flounders Web Site banner contain an animation with the words Fish and Aquarium displayed on the Stage. These words will display one at a time and continuously change from one word to another. The animation will be placed in several places in the document. To accomplish this and to create the animation only once, you will create a graphic symbol animation. You will then create several instances of this symbol in the Intro scene, and specify that each instance begin its animation in a different frame.

To create a graphic symbol animation:

1. If necessary, switch to the Intro scene, then click **Insert** on the menu bar, and then click **New Symbol** to open the Create New Symbol dialog box. Name this symbol **Words** and set its Behavior type to **Graphic**, and then click the **OK** button. The Stage changes to symbol-editing mode.

2. Use the **Text** tool [A] to create a text block with the word **Fish** on the center of the Stage. Set the following type settings in the Property inspector: Font: **Monotype Corsiva**, Font size: **24**, text color: **light gray (#CCCCCC)**. Click the **Selection** tool [↖] on the toolbar, and keep the text block selected.

3. Click **Window** on the menu bar, point to **Design Panels**, and click **Info** to open the Info panel. If necessary, click the **center registration** point for this object in the Info panel. Enter **0** for the X and Y values to center the text block, as shown in Figure 3-41.

Figure 3-41   SETTINGS IN THE INFO PANEL

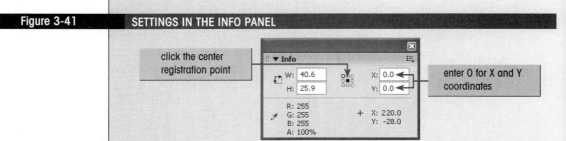

4. Close the Info panel. The text is now centered on the Stage. Next you will convert the text block to a movie clip and duplicate it.

5. With the text block still selected, click **Modify** on the menu bar, and then click **Convert to Symbol**. Name the symbol **Fish text** and change the behavior type to **Movie clip**. Click the **OK** button to create the symbol.

   You have created a movie clip symbol inside the graphic symbol. The text block has to be a symbol so that you can create a motion tweened animation. Create a duplicate of the symbol next.

6. If necessary, open the Library panel. Right-click the name of the **Fish text** symbol in the Library panel and click **Duplicate** to open the Duplicate Symbol dialog box. Name the duplicate **Aquarium text** and leave its behavior as Movie clip. Click the **OK** button to close the dialog box. You will now change the text in the duplicate symbol.

7. Click the **Edit Symbols** button [✍] in the Stage window and select the **Aquarium text** symbol to open it in symbol-editing mode. Double-click the text block and change the word to **Aquarium**. Open the Info panel and set the X and Y values to **0**, then close the Info panel. See Figure 3-42.

Figure 3-42 EDITING THE AQUARIUM TEXT SYMBOL

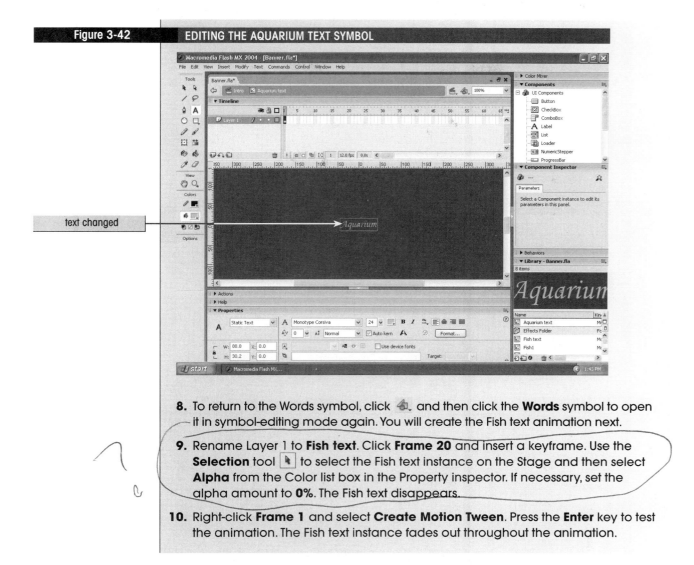

text changed

8. To return to the Words symbol, click 🔄 and then click the **Words** symbol to open it in symbol-editing mode again. You will create the Fish text animation next.

9. Rename Layer 1 to **Fish text**. Click **Frame 20** and insert a keyframe. Use the **Selection** tool ▶ to select the Fish text instance on the Stage and then select **Alpha** from the Color list box in the Property inspector. If necessary, set the alpha amount to **0%**. The Fish text disappears.

10. Right-click **Frame 1** and select **Create Motion Tween**. Press the **Enter** key to test the animation. The Fish text instance fades out throughout the animation.

Now that you have created the animation for the first word, you need to create a similar animation for the next word. But rather than repeating all of the steps in a new layer, you can copy the frames in the Fish text layer and paste them into a new layer. Then in the new layer, you can swap the instances of the Fish text symbol with instances of the Aquarium text symbol. You will need to swap the instance in the keyframe at the beginning of the motion tween and also in the keyframe at the end of the motion tween. Finally, you can reposition the frames that contain the motion tween so that the animation starts later than the animation for the first word. To reposition the frames, you first select them and then drag them to a new position with the mouse pointer.

You will duplicate the Fish text layer to create an animation for the Aquarium text symbol.

To copy the animation:

1. Click the name of the **Fish text** layer in the Timeline to select all of its frames.

2. Click **Edit** on the menu bar, point to **Timeline**, and then click **Copy Frames**. The frames are copied to the Windows Clipboard.

3. Insert a new layer and name it **Aquarium text**. Click the **Aquarium text** layer's name to select all of its frames. Click **Edit** on the menu bar, point to **Timeline**, and then click **Paste Frames**. The frames containing the Fish text animation are pasted into the Aquarium text layer. You now need to swap the Fish text, symbol with the Aquarium text symbol.

4. Click **Frame 1** of the Aquarium text layer and click the instance of the Fish text symbol at the center of the Stage. In the Property inspector click the **Swap** button to open the Swap Symbol dialog box, and then select **Aquarium text**, as shown in Figure 3-43.

| Figure 3-43 | SWAP SYMBOL DIALOG BOX |

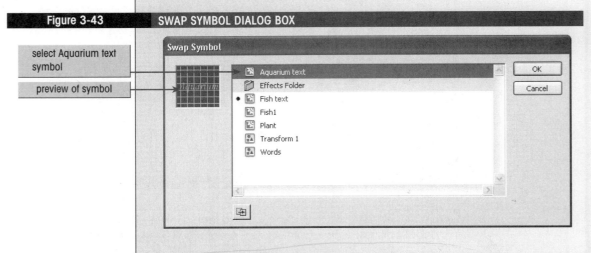

5. Click the **OK** button. The Fish text instance is replaced with the Aquarium text instance. The text blocks for the two layers are currently overlapped so you will see one word displayed on top of the other. You will fix this in the next set of steps. Next, swap the instance in the second keyframe.

6. Click **Frame 20** of the Aquarium text layer. Click the **Fish text** instance at the center of the Stage which is indicated by a blue outline. The word is not visible because you set the alpha amount to 0% at this keyframe. In the Property inspector, click the **Swap** button and then select **Aquarium text** in the Swap Symbol dialog box. Click the **OK** button. The Fish text instance is replaced with the Aquarium text instance.

The animation in the Aquarium text layer works the same as the one in the Fish text layer except that now the symbol being animated is the Aquarium text symbol and not the Fish text symbol. So instead of having to repeat the steps to create an animation in the Aquarium text layer, you copied an existing animation and swapped the instances in the keyframes.

Now that you have both of the animations, you need to reposition the Aquarium text animation so that the two animations do not occur at the same time. You want the Fish text animation to start first, and then the Aquarium text animation should begin before the Fish animation ends. Aly suggests that you keep the total number of frames at 30 to match the number of frames in the Intro scene's Timeline. This means that the Aquarium text animation will begin at Frame 11, so that its 20 frames end at Frame 30. You can easily change the location of frames within a layer by selecting the frames to be moved and than dragging the selected frames to a new location in the layer. You will do that next.

To reposition frames within a layer:

1. Click and drag the mouse pointer from **Frame 1** to **Frame 20** in the Aquarium text layer to select the frames that make up the Aquarium text animation in the Aquarium text layer.

   TROUBLE? If the keyframe in Frame 1 moves when you drag the mouse pointer, you released the mouse button after clicking the first keyframe and then started dragging from that same keyframe. This moved the keyframe instead of selecting the series of frames. Click Edit on the menu bar, click Undo, and then repeat Step 1.

2. Once you have selected the frames, release the mouse button to complete the selection. Then drag the selected frames so that the first keyframe starts on **Frame 11**, as shown in Figure 3-44.

Figure 3-44	MOVING SELECTED FRAMES

use mouse pointer to drag selected frames to start at Frame 11

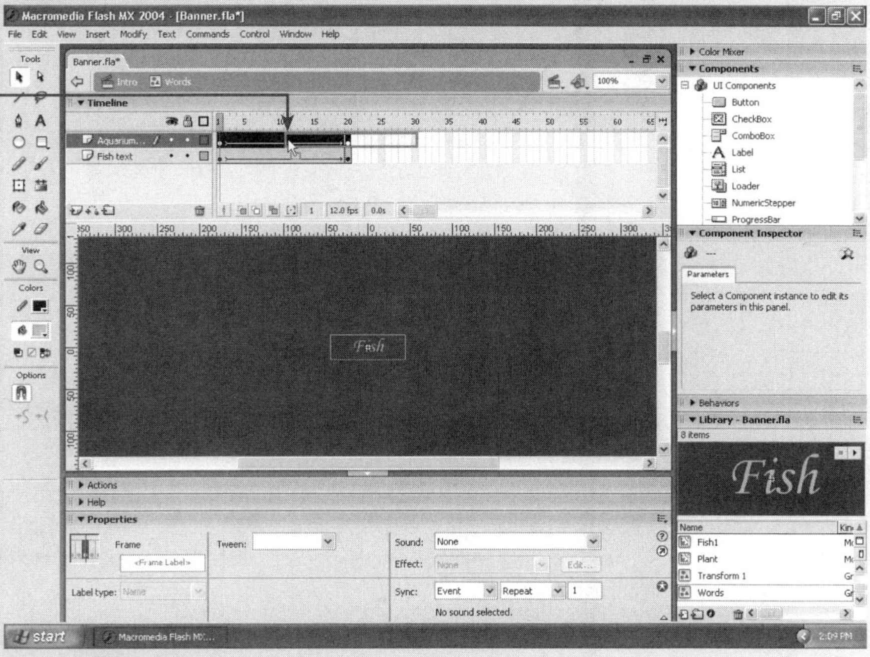

3. Drag the playhead to **Frame 1** and press the **Enter** key. The words appear and fade out in turn. The Words graphic animation is now complete.

4. Exit symbol-editing mode and return to the Intro scene.

Now you are ready to insert two instances of the Words symbol onto the Stage for the Intro scene. You will then change the starting frame for one of the instances. The instances will each start off displaying a different word and display the subsequent word in turn.

To insert graphic symbol instances and change their starting frame:

1. In the Intro scene, insert a new layer above Layer 1 and name it **Words**. Select **Frame 1** of the Words layer.

2. While still in the Words layer, drag two instances of the Words symbol from the Library panel to the bottom part of the Stage, as shown in Figure 3-45.

| Figure 3-45 | GRAPHIC SYMBOL INSTANCES |

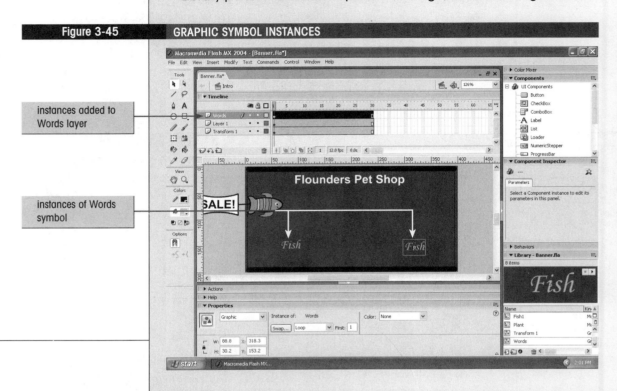

instances added to Words layer

instances of Words symbol

3. Select the instance of the **Words** symbol located on the right side of the Stage. In the Property inspector, change the value in the **First** text box to **11**. Also, make sure the instance's option is set to **Loop**. The text for the instance fades slightly.

4. Click an empty area of the Stage and then press the **Enter** key to test the animation. The Words instances each start at a different frame as they fade in and out.

Now that you have completed the animation for the Intro scene, you will test the banner to see how its various animations work. When you test the document's animation by using the Play command on the Control menu or by pressing the Enter key, Flash only plays the current scene. To see how all of the scenes work together, you need to use the Test Movie command on the Control menu. With this command, Flash generates a SWF file and then plays the animation in a new Flash Player window. Each scene plays in sequence with the animation repeating until you close the Flash Player window. You will test the completed document next.

To test the entire Banner.fla document's scenes:

1. Click **Control** on the menu bar and then click **Test Movie**. A Flash Player window opens within the Flash program window and each scene plays in sequence.

2. When you are finished viewing the animation, click **File** on the menu bar, and click **Close**. The Flash Player window closes and the Flash document displays.

3. Save your work.

In this session, you created animations using motion tweens and you learned how to create shape tweens. You also learned how to create animations using graphic symbols.

Session 3.3 QUICK CHECK

1. Briefly describe the difference between a frame-by-frame animation and a tweened animation.

2. How many objects can you have on a layer with a motion tween?

3. How can you animate a movie clip symbol so that each of its instances automatically contains the animation?

4. What type of tweened animation would you create to have an object move from one side of the Stage to the other?

5. To create a shape tween, the object being animated must first be converted to a symbol. True or False?

6. List two differences between a movie clip symbol and a graphic symbol.

REVIEW ASSIGNMENTS

After reviewing the revised animated banner, Aly asks you to modify the banner so that the words animation in the first scene includes the word "Sale". She also wants you to animate the title text block in the first scene to fade in as the fish pulls the sale sign. Finally, she asks you to add another animated fish in the second scene that swims in a direction opposite the current fish.

1. Open the **Banner.fla** file which you created in the tutorial from the Tutorial.03\Tutorial folder included with your Data Files, and set the panels to their default layout. Save the file as **Banner2.fla** in the Tutorial.03\Review folder included with your Data Files.

2. Select the Flounders Pet Shop text block in the Intro scene and insert a Transition Timeline effect. Set the Effect Duration to 30 frames and select the Fade In effect only so the text will fade in throughout the Intro scene.

3. Open the Library panel and make a duplicate of the Fish text symbol. Name this duplicate **Sale text**. Edit the Sale text symbol by changing the text to read **Sale** instead of **Fish**.

4. Edit the Words symbol by inserting a new layer in its Timeline. Name the layer **Sale text**. Select all of the Aquarium text layer's frames and copy them to the Clipboard. Select all of the Sale text layer's frames and paste the copied layers. Select Frames 11 through 30 of the Sale text layer, and then move them so they start on Frame 21 of the same layer.

5. Select Frame 21 of the Sale text layer and swap the Aquarium text instance on the Stage with an instance of the Sale text symbol. Select Frame 40 and also swap this Aquarium text instance with an instance of the Sale text symbol. Exit symbol-editing mode.

6. In the Intro scene, add one more instance of the Words symbol to the Stage between the existing Words instances. Have this instance start its animation in Frame 21.

7. In the Library panel, make a duplicate of the Fish1 symbol. Name this duplicate **Fish2** and edit this symbol by changing each of its orange colored fills to light green (#00FF99). Exit symbol-editing mode.

8. In the Fish Swimming scene, insert a new layer and name it **Fish2**. In this layer, drag an instance of the Fish2 symbol to the lower-right corner of the banner. Create two motion tweens for this Fish2 instance similar to the motion tweens in the Fish1 layer. You want the Fish2 instance to swim to the left, stop just before the plant leaves, then turn around and swim back to its starting point.

9. Save the revised Banner2.fla file.

CASE PROBLEMS

Case 1. Creating an Animated Banner for Sandy's Party Center   Planning is well underway at Sandy's Party Center for their grand opening celebration. Sandy Rodriguez, store owner, is expecting a good turnout for their celebration. Sandy meets with John Rossini to discuss the development of the banner for their new Web site. Sandy asks John to make the banner more festive by adding animation to it.

John has started developing the revised banner shown in Figure 3-46 and wants you to help him complete the task by adding animations for a text block, balloon graphics, and confetti graphics. The balloons will float up as the confetti comes down. The text block will move in from above the banner to the bottom of the banner.

Figure 3-46	INITIAL VERSION OF THE REVISED SANDY'S PARTY BANNER

If necessary, start Flash, and then do the following:

1. Open the **partybanner.fla** file located in the Tutorial.03\Cases folder included with your Data Files. The document contains some of the graphic elements that will be used to create the animated banner. Save the banner in the same folder with the name **partybanner2.fla**.

2. Select the confetti on the Stage, and convert it to a symbol. Make sure you select all of the confetti graphic at one time. Name the symbol **confetti**, and keep the default behavior type of Movie clip.

3. Select and convert the party hat to a symbol. Make sure you select both the fill and the stroke that make up the graphic. Name the symbol **party hat**. The behavior type should also be Movie clip.

4. Convert the balloon into a symbol, with the name of **balloon1** and behavior of Movie Clip.

5. Select the bottom text block and convert it to a symbol named **text**.

6. Delete the confetti, party hat, and balloon graphics, as well as the bottom text block from the Stage. Do not delete the top text block nor the rectangle around the banner.

7. Change the name of Layer1 to **background** and add regular frames to extend this layer through Frame 30.

8. Insert a new layer. Name this layer **confetti1**. Open the Library panel. Drag an instance of the confetti symbol to the upper-left corner of the banner. Create a motion tween so that the confetti instance moves from the upper-left to the lower left of the banner. The motion tween should span Frames 1 through 30.

9. Insert another layer and name it **confetti2**. Drag another instance of the confetti symbol, but this time place it in the upper-right corner of the banner. Create a motion tween so that the confetti instance moves from the upper-right to the lower-right corner of the banner.

10. Create a duplicate of the balloon1 symbol. Name this symbol **balloon2**. Edit the balloon2 symbol to change the color of the balloon to red. Create another copy of the balloon1 symbol and name it **balloon3**. Edit the balloon3 symbol to change its color to pink.

11. Insert a new layer and name it **balloon1**. On this layer, drag an instance of the balloon1 symbol to the lower-left corner of the Stage. Create a motion tween so that the balloon moves up to the top of the banner.

12. Insert a new layer and name it **balloon2**. On this layer, drag an instance of the balloon2 symbol to the middle of the Stage. Create a motion tween so that the balloon moves up to the top of the banner.

13. Insert a new layer and name it **balloon3**. On this layer, drag an instance of the balloon3 symbol to the lower-right corner of the Stage. Create a motion tween so that the balloon moves up to the top of the banner.

14. Insert a new layer and name it **text**. On this layer, drag an instance of the text symbol and place it above the center of the banner, outside the Stage. Create a motion tween so that the text block moves from above the banner to the bottom center of the banner. This tween should span Frames 1 through 10 and the text should remain visible through Frame 30.

15. Add several instances of the hat symbol to the background layer. Make sure you add them to the first frame.

16. Test your animation.

17. Save the file.

Case 2. Creating an Animated Banner for River City Music River City Music is getting ready for their upcoming anniversary sale and store manager, Janet Meyers, has met with Alex Smith to review the banner that Alex has developed. They agree to make the banner more interesting by adding animation to it.

Alex has started developing the revised banner, as shown in Figure 3-47, and he wants you to help him complete the task by adding two text blocks that will be animated and by animating the musical notes.

Figure 3-47   **INITIAL VERSION OF THE REVISED RIVER CITY MUSIC BANNER**

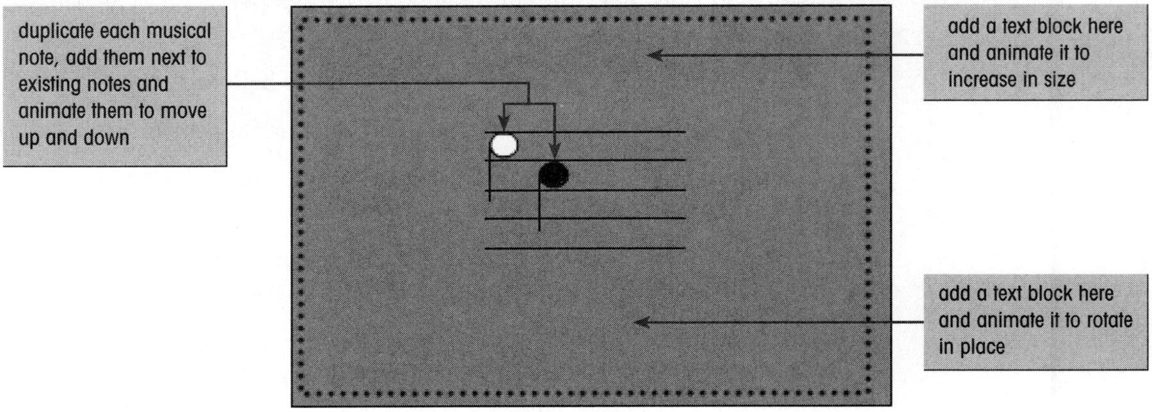

duplicate each musical note, add them next to existing notes and animate them to move up and down

add a text block here and animate it to increase in size

add a text block here and animate it to rotate in place

If necessary, start Flash, and then do the following:

1. Open the **musicbanner.fla** file located in the Tutorial.03\Cases folder included with your Data Files. The document contains some of the graphic elements that will be used to create the animated banner.

2. Save the banner with the name **musicbanner2.fla** in the same folder.

3. Select the left musical note on the Stage and convert it to a symbol. Name this symbol **note1**. Select the second musical note and convert it to a symbol also. Name this symbol **note2**.

4. Take note of the positions of the notes within the lines, and then delete them from the Stage. Rename the layer **background**, and add regular frames so that it extends to Frame 20.

5. Insert a new layer and name it **notes1**. Open the Library panel. Drag an instance of the note1 symbol to the left side of the lines so that it is in its original position between the top two lines.

6. In the notes1 layer, add keyframes in each of Frames 5, 10, 15, and 20. In Frames 5 and 15 move the note so that it is between the third and fourth lines from the top. Keep the horizontal position the same. Then create motion tweens between each keyframe. The motion tweens will be in Frames 1, 5, 10, and 15. Test the animation. The note should move up and down.

7. Insert a new layer and name it **notes2**. Drag an instance of the note2 symbol to the left side of the lines so that it is in its original position between the third and fourth lines from the top.

8. In the notes2 layer, add keyframes in every fifth frame just like you did for the notes1 layer. In frames 5 and 15 move the note so that it is between the first and second lines from the top. Keep the horizontal position the same. Now create motion tweens between each keyframe. Test the animation. This note should move up and down.

Explore

9. Insert another layer and name it **notes3**. Drag an instance of the note1 symbol to the right side of the last note so that it is between the second and third lines from the top. You will create motion tweens as before, but before you do, rotate the note 180 degrees so that its stem is pointing up. Then create the keyframes and motion tweens so that it moves up and down like the other notes. When the note moves down it should be between the bottom two lines.

10. Insert another layer and name it **notes4**. Drag an instance of the note2 symbol to the right side of the last note so that it is between the bottom two lines. Rotate the note

180 degrees so that its stem is pointing up. Then create the keyframes and motion tweens so that it moves up and down like the other notes. When the note moves up it should be between the second and third lines from the top.

11. Insert a new layer and name it **title**. In Frame 1 of this layer create a text block with the text **River City Music**. Use a fancy font such as Monotype Corsiva and use a text font size such as 20. Select a font color of your choice. The text block should be centered on the banner above the notes.

12. Select the text block and insert a Transform Timeline effect. Enter 20 for the effect duration and change the scale percent value to 200. Preview the effect to see the text increase in size. Once you create the effect, test the animation in your document. The text block should start out small and grow in size.

13. Insert one more layer and name it **sale**. Create a text block in this layer in Frame 1 with the text **Piano Sale!** using the same font and font size as the title text. Center the text below the notes. Select this text block and insert a Transform Timeline effect. Enter 20 for the effect duration and enter a spin value of 2 so that the text will rotate clockwise two times. Preview the effect to see the text rotate. Once you create the effect, test the animation in your document. The text block should rotate twice throughout the animation.

14. Test your animation and save the file.

Case 3. Creating an Animated Logo for Sonny's Auto Center Sonny Jackson, owner of Sonny's Auto Center, meets with Amanda Lester, who was contracted to update the company's Web site. Amanda shows Sonny the logo she developed and they both agree that the logo could be enhanced by adding some animation.

Amanda decides to revise the logo by adding a shape tween to the company name and a masking effect on the word Autos. She asks you to help her complete the task. The revised logo will use the same graphics as the current logo, but you will animate the Sonny's text and the AUTOS text. Each should be on a separate layer. The banner will look similar to that shown in Figure 3-48.

Figure 3-48 | **SONNY'S AUTO CENTER LOGO**

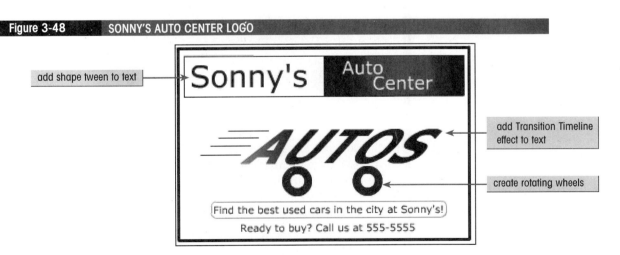

If necessary, start Flash and then do the following:

1. Open the logo file you created in Case 3 of Tutorial 2 for Sonny's Auto Center. The file is **saclogo.fla** and should be in the Tutorial.02\Cases folder included with your Data Files. Save this file as **saclogo2.fla** in the Tutorial.03\Cases folder. If you did not complete this case problem in Tutorial 2, see your instructor for assistance.

2. Rename Layer 1 to **Background**, and add regular frames so that the layer extends to Frame 30.

3. Insert a layer and name it **Sonny**. Insert another layer and name it **Autos**.

Explore ▶ 4. Select the Sonny's text block. Use the Cut command on the Edit menu to cut the text block. Then on Frame 1 of the Sonny layer, use the Paste in Place command on the Edit menu to place the text in the same relative position as it was in the Background layer.

5. Select the AUTOS text block in the center of the Stage. Make sure you do not select any other graphics besides the text. Use the Cut command to cut the text block. Then on Frame 1 of the Autos layer, use the Paste in Place command to place the text in the same relative position as it was on the Background layer.

6. Use the Scene panel to create a duplicate of Scene 1. Rename Scene 1 copy to **Wheel animation** and rename Scene 1 to **Sonnys animation**.

Explore ▶ 7. In the Sonnys animation scene select the Sonny's text and use the Break Apart command to break the text apart into individual letters. Use the command a second time to break the letters into filled shapes.

Explore ▶ 8. Insert a keyframe in Frame 20 of the Sonny layer. In the first frame draw a black filled rectangle over the Sonny's text block. The size of the rectangle should be just slightly larger than the text block itself. Insert a shape tween in Frame 1. Test the animation. The rectangle should transform into the text Sonny's.

Explore ▶ 9. In the same scene, select the AUTOS text in Frame 1 of the Autos layer and insert a Transition Timeline effect. Enter 30 for the effect duration and use the Wipe in effect only. Do not use the Fade effect. Change the direction of the wipe to be to the right and use -70 for the Motion Ease value. Preview the effect to see the text block appear from the left to the right. Once you create the effect, test the animation in your document. The text block should initially be transparent and then appear from left to right.

10. Switch to the Wheel animation scene. Select the left wheel graphic below the AUTOS text and convert it to a symbol. Name the symbol **Wheel** and use Graphic for its behavior type. Open the Wheel symbol in symbol-editing mode. Zoom in on the wheel graphic and then apply the Break Apart command twice to ungroup the two circles that make up this graphic.

11. Draw a short horizontal line across the middle of the white area of the wheel graphic to represent a wheel spoke. Use black as the color and 2 for the stroke height. Draw a short vertical line across the white area of the wheel graphic to represent another wheel spoke.

Explore ▶ 12. To create frame-be-frame animation to rotate the wheel, first open the Transform panel. Insert a keyframe in Frame 2. In the Transform panel enter a value of 30 for the number of degrees to rotate the wheel. (Be sure to press the Enter key to apply the Rotate value.) Insert another keyframe at Frame 3 and enter 30 for the rotate value in the Transform panel to rotate the wheel again. Continue this process of inserting a keyframe and entering 30 for the rotate value in the Transform panel until you reach Frame 13 and the wheel has been rotated 360 degrees. Exit symbol-editing mode and return to the Wheel animation scene.

13. Delete the original wheel under the O of AUTOS on the Stage and add an instance of the Wheel graphic symbol in the same position. Test the animation to see the wheels rotate.

14. Save the changes you have made to the logo.

Case 4. Creating an Animated Banner for LAL Financial Christopher Perez, head of Marketing at LAL Financial Services, meets with webmaster Elizabeth Danehill to discuss progress in the development of the new banner for the company's Web site. They decide that adding some animation to the banner will enhance its appearance. Elizabeth meets with the graphics designer, Mia Jones, and they ask you to help revise the banner. The banner will look similar to that shown in Figure 3-49, but the square, triangle, and circle shapes will be animated.

Figure 3-49	LAL FINANCIAL BANNER

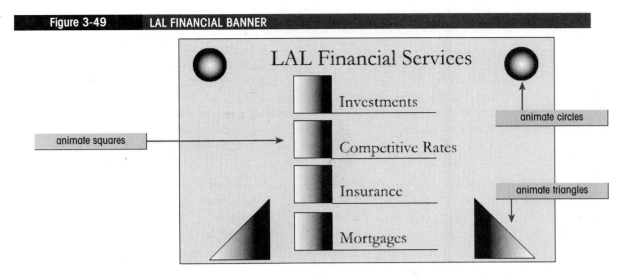

If necessary, start Flash and then do the following:

1. Open the banner file you created in Case 4 of Tutorial 2 for LAL Financial Services. The file is **lfsbanner.fla** and should be in the Tutorial.02\Cases folder included with your Data Files. Save this file as **lfsbanner2.fla** in the Tutorial.03\Cases folder. If you did not complete Case 4 of Tutorial 2, then see your instructor for assistance.

2. Start by adding a rectangle to frame all of the contents on the Stage. Draw the rectangle with no fill, a black solid stroke with a stroke height of 1. The sides of the rectangle should be close to the edges of the Stage and all of the contents on the Stage should be inside the rectangle. Create two duplicates of Scene 1. Name one duplicate **Intro**, the other **Main animation**, and the third **Triangles**.

3. Switch to the Intro scene. Delete all of the circles and squares from the Stage. Also delete the Investments, Insurance, and Mortgages text blocks. Leave the Competitive Rates text block. Delete the three lines whose words you deleted. Leave the line under Competitive Rates. Delete the two bottom triangles and the upper-right triangle. Move the upper-left triangle closer to the Competitive Rates text block and line up its bottom with the line.

4. Select the Competitive Rates text block and convert it to a symbol. Name the symbol **Words** and use Graphic as the behavior type. Edit the Words symbol to create a frame-by-frame animation that changes the text block to a different word or phrase every half second. Start by inserting a keyframe at Frame 7. Change the text block to read **Investments**. Insert a keyframe at Frame 13 and change the text to **Insurance**. Add another keyframe at Frame 19 and change the text to **Mortgages**. Add one more keyframe at Frame 25 and change the text to **This is LAL Financial**. Exit symbol-editing mode.

5. In the Intro scene extend Layer 1 so that it has 40 frames. Select the Words instance on the Stage and in the Property inspector change the Options for graphics to Play Once. Test the animation for the Intro scene.

6. Switch to the Main animation scene. Delete all of the circles, triangles, and squares from the Stage. Rename Layer 1 to **background** and extend it so it has 30 frames.

7. Use the circle symbol to create a motion tween where the circle moves from the lower-left corner of the banner to the upper-left corner. Create another motion tween using the circle symbol to have a circle move from the lower-right corner of the banner to the upper-right corner. Both of these tweens should occur at the same time and cover the first 20 frames.

8. Create four motion tweens using the square symbol. Each instance of the square should move individually from the left side of the banner, starting outside the Stage. Each square should move to the right and end up just to the left of the horizontal line for each text block. The bottom of the square should line up with the horizontal line. The squares should move in a straight horizontal line. (Hint: For the top square, the motion tween should span Frames 1 through 5. For the next square, the motion tween should span Frames 1 through 10. The third square should have a motion tween that spans Frames 1 through 15. The motion tween for the bottom square should span Frames 1 through 20.)

9. Create two motion tweens for the triangle symbol. Have each instance of the triangle move from the top of the banner to the bottom. One starts to the left of the banner's title and the other starts to the right of the banner's title. The triangle on the right should be flipped horizontally before creating its motion tween. Test the animation.

10. Switch to the Triangles scene. Select the top square and apply the Break Apart command so that it is no longer an instance of the square symbol. With the square still selected, convert it to a new symbol. Name this symbol **shape** and use Graphic as its behavior type. Delete the bottom three squares from the Stage.

11. Edit the shape symbol by inserting a keyframe at Frame 15 of its Timeline and then creating a shape tween in Frame 1. Drag a horizontal guide line to the center of the Stage so that it goes across the center of the square. You will use this guide line to help create the triangle shape.

Explore 12. To complete the shape tween, select Frame 15, make sure that Snap to Guides is turned on, and then use the Subselection tool to move the upper-right corner of the square straight down to the guide line. Then drag the lower-right corner straight up to the guide line to form a triangle. Test the animation to see the square change to a triangle.

13. Return to the Triangles scene, extend Layer 1 so that it has 30 frames. Add three more instances of the shape symbol where the original squares were located. Set each of the shape instances so that it plays only once. Test the animation in your Web browser.

14. Save your revised banner.

QUICK | CHECK ANSWERS

Session 3.1

1. The purpose of the Timeline is to coordinate and control the frames that make up an animation. It is also used to organize the layers that contain the different elements of a document.

2. You can tell what the current frame is by looking at the location of the playhead on the Timeline header. You can also see the current frame number displayed at the bottom of the Timeline.

3. The default frame rate is 12 fps.

4. Frames contain content that is displayed for an instant in time. Frames are displayed one after another to create the perception of movement. Layers are made up of one or more frames and are used to organize the graphic elements of a document.

5. You can insert a new layer by using the Layer command on the Insert menu. You can also insert a new layer by clicking the Insert Layer button on the Timeline.

6. A layer folder is a container in the Timeline in which you can place layers. This allows you to work more efficiently when you have a lot of layers.

7. A scene provides a way to break up a Flash document into separate mini-movies each with its own Timeline. The scenes are played according to the order they are listed in the Scene panel.

8. Two methods you can use to change from one scene to another include selecting a scene from the Scene panel and clicking the Edit Scene button to select a scene from the drop-down list.

9. To change the name of a scene you double-click the name of the scene in the Scene panel to select it and then type a new name.

Session 3.2

1. Timeline effects allow you to create an animation or a special effect by selecting from options in a dialog box without having to know how to create the animation yourself.

2. True. Each Timeline effect is created on its own layer.

3. Once the Timeline effect is created in your document you can still change it by clicking Modify on the menu bar, pointing to Timeline Effects, and then selecting Edit Effect. This opens the same dialog box that was used to create the effect allowing you to change the settings.

4. In a frame-by-frame animation, you need to have a keyframe when the content changes on the Stage.

5. False. The object being animated in a frame-by-frame animation does not need to be a symbol.

6. Yes, you can include regular frames in a frame-by-frame animation. Regular frames indicate that the content has not changed from the previous keyframe.

Session 3.3

1. A frame-by-frame animation requires that you create the content for each of the frames. With a tweened animation, Flash creates the frames between the beginning and ending keyframes.

2. A layer with a motion tween can only have one object.

3. Create the animation in the symbol's Timeline instead of in the document's Timeline. Each instance of the movie clip symbol then automatically contains the animation.

4. To have an object move from one side of the Stage to the other, you would create a motion tweened animation.

5. False. An object used in a shape tween must not be converted to a symbol.

6. A movie clip symbol's Timeline is independent from the document's main Timeline whereas a graphic symbol's Timeline is synchronized with the main document's Timeline. Also, when you test the document's animation within Flash, movie clip animations do not play, while graphic symbol animations do play. And you can also specify which frame a graphic instance's animation should start. A movie clip animation always starts from the first frame of its Timeline.

OBJECTIVES

In this tutorial you will:

- Create an animation using a motion guide layer

- Create an animation using a mask layer

- Animate text blocks

- Animate individual letters within a text block

- Test animations using onion skinning

- Create nested movie clip symbols

- Learn how to use the Movie Explorer

SPECIAL ANIMATIONS

Creating Special Animations for the Flounders Pet Shop Banner

CASE

Admiral Web Design

Aly Garcia, graphics designer, meets with you to review the work you have done for the Flounders Pet Shop banner. She is very pleased with your progress and asks you to develop a second banner for the Flounders Pet Shop Web site because she wants to give Mr. Flounders more than one banner from which to choose. She has started developing the second banner and wants you to complete it. The banner will consist of three scenes. The first scene will include an animation of the company name. This will be a complex animation where the individual letters of the name rotate one after another onto the screen and into place to form the word Flounders. As each letter moves into place, it will fade in and decrease in size. Aly has started work on the second scene and instructs you to complete this scene by changing the way the fish swims across the aquarium. Specifically, she tells you to have the fish swim along a curved path and not just in a straight line. You will also create a second animated fish that exhibits more natural movements of its fins and tail. The third scene requires you to create a new animation sequence which will consist of several text blocks with the store's name and a message promoting the aquarium tank and fish sale. You will also create an animation showing a spotlight effect on the Flounders Pet Shop name.

Aly has started working on the second scene in the banner, and she gives you the file containing this document. You will complete the work on the document using Aly's notes shown in Figure 4-1. You will create the text animations for Scene 1 and Scene 3 in Session 4.2. You will complete the complex animations of the fish for Scene 2 in Sessions 4.1 and 4.3.

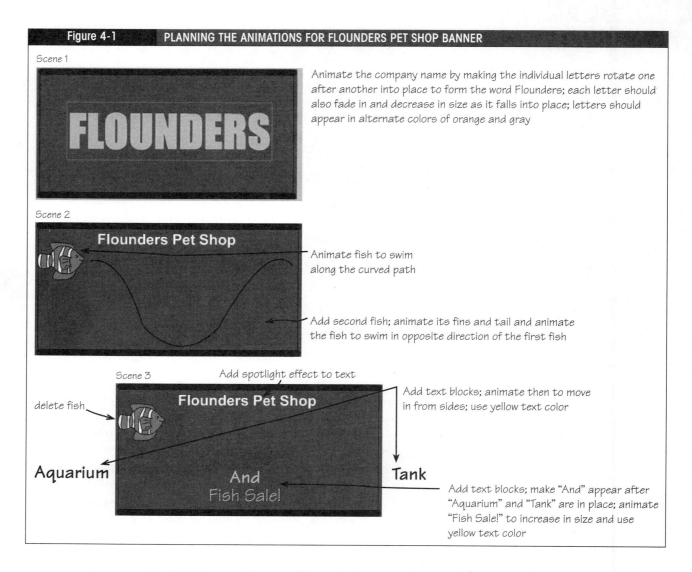

Figure 4-1   PLANNING THE ANIMATIONS FOR FLOUNDERS PET SHOP BANNER

Scene 1

Animate the company name by making the individual letters rotate one after another into place to form the word Flounders; each letter should also fade in and decrease in size as it falls into place; letters should appear in alternate colors of orange and gray

Scene 2

Flounders Pet Shop

Animate fish to swim along the curved path

Add second fish; animate its fins and tail and animate the fish to swim in opposite direction of the first fish

Scene 3   Add spotlight effect to text

delete fish

Flounders Pet Shop

Add text blocks; animate then to move in from sides; use yellow text color

Aquarium   And   Tank
Fish Sale!

Add text blocks; make "And" appear after "Aquarium" and "Tank" are in place; animate "Fish Sale!" to increase in size and use yellow text color

In this tutorial, you will learn how to create animations using a motion guide layer and a mask layer. You will learn how to work with text to create animations of text blocks and individual letters. You will also learn how to test an animation using onion skinning and how to work with nested movie clip symbols to create complex animations. Finally, you will learn how to use the Movie Explorer to review all of the document's elements.

SESSION 4.1

In this session, you will learn how to create animations using motion guide layers and mask layers. You will use these techniques to modify the fish animation Aly has created in Scene 2 of the Flounders banner, and you will create a spotlight effect animation with text.

Special Layers for Animation

As you learned in the previous tutorial, there are two special types of layers you can create in Macromedia Flash. These are guide layers and mask layers. A **guide layer** contains graphic elements that serve as a guide when creating content on other layers. A **mask layer** masks the contents of the layer below it which is called the **masked layer**. Both of these types of layers can also be used with animations. For example, you can create a guide layer which contains a path for an object on another layer to follow. You also can create an animation in a mask layer to show different areas of a masked layer throughout the animation. Both types of layers can be used with frame-by-frame and tweened animations.

Animation Using a Motion Guide Layer

When a guide layer is used together with a motion tween it is called a **motion guide layer**. A motion guide layer provides a path for an object in the guided layer to follow throughout the motion tween. This technique allows you to animate objects to move in a more natural way. Instead of having objects move only in straight lines, you can use a motion guide layer to have an object move along a curved path. For example, you can make a ball appear to be bouncing up and down while gradually coming to a stop. Or you can have a car move along a curved road, or a bird fly in a circular pattern. Whatever path you draw on the guide layer, you can attach an object to follow that path.

To create a motion guide layer for a motion tweened animation, you create the motion tween on one layer. You then select the layer and insert a motion guide layer above it by selecting the Motion Guide command, which you access by clicking Insert on the menu bar, pointing to Timeline, and then clicking Motion Guide. You can also click the Add Motion Guide button in the Timeline to add the motion guide layer. The layer with the motion tween will be indented and the motion guide layer will have a motion guide icon to the left of its name, as shown in Figure 4-2.

Figure 4-2   MOTION GUIDE LAYER

To draw a path for the animated object to follow you can use a tool such as the Pencil, Pen, Line, or Brush tool. You draw the path on the motion guide layer. To make the object on the guided layer follow the path, you need to attach it to the path. To do this, select the first frame of the guided layer which contains the motion tween and move the object to the beginning of the path. In the last frame of the animation, you move the object to the end of the path. In each case you need to make sure the center of the object snaps to the path. You can do this by first making sure that the Snap to Objects option on the Snapping submenu, located on the View menu, is selected. You can then drag the object from its center and have it snap to the path. Once you have the animated object following the path on the guide layer, you can also select the Orient to path option in the Property inspector, as shown in Figure 4-3.

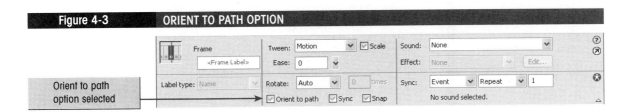

Figure 4-3   ORIENT TO PATH OPTION

The Orient to path option will cause the animated object to align itself to the slope of the curve of the path in the guide layer. This will make the movement in the animation appear more natural.

Adding a Motion Guide Layer to the Flounders Pet Shop Banner

Aly has started work on the alternate banner for Founders Pet shop. The file she gives you contains only the second scene in the banner that Aly has planned. In this document, there is a fish swimming across the banner in a straight line. Aly's notes shown in Figure 4-1 indicate this fish needs to swim along a curved path. Aly suggests you create this animation using a motion guide layer so that you can create a path for the animated fish to follow. You will add a motion guide layer that will guide the fish along a curved path from the upper-left corner of the banner, down towards the bottom and then back up to the upper-right corner.

To create a motion guide layer:

1. Open the **Banner3.fla** file located in the **Tutorial.04\Tutorial** folder included with your Data Files. Position the panels to their default layout.

2. If necessary, click **Frame 1** of the Fish1 layer.

3. Click **Insert** on the menu bar, point to **Timeline**, and then click **Motion Guide** to insert a motion guide layer above the Fish1 layer. Click **View** on the menu bar, point to **Snapping**, and make sure the **Snap to Objects** command is selected. You will use the Pencil tool to draw the path the fish will follow.

4. Click **Frame 1** of the Guide: Fish1 layer, and then click the **Pencil** tool 🖉 on the toolbar. Click the **Pencil Mode modifier** 🖫 in the options area of the toolbar, and then click **Smooth**. Click once on the Stage to display the Pencil tool properties in the Property inspector. If necessary, select **black** for the stroke color, **1** for the stroke height, and **Solid** for the style.

5. Draw a line starting at the center of the fish on the upper-left corner of the Stage curving down and then back up to the upper-right side of the Stage. See Figure 4-4. Now attach the fish to the end of the line.

Figure 4-4   **LINE DRAWN WITH PENCIL TOOL**

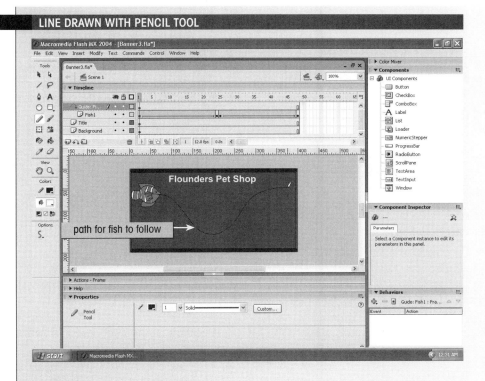

6. Click **Frame 1** of the Fish1 layer and make sure the center of the fish is snapped to the beginning of the line. If necessary, place it using the **Selection** tool on the toolbar.

7. Click **Frame 24** of the Fish1 layer. Use to drag the fish so that it snaps to the far-right endpoint of the line, as shown in Figure 4-5.

Figure 4-5   **CENTER POINT OF FISH SNAPS TO ENDPOINT OF LINE**

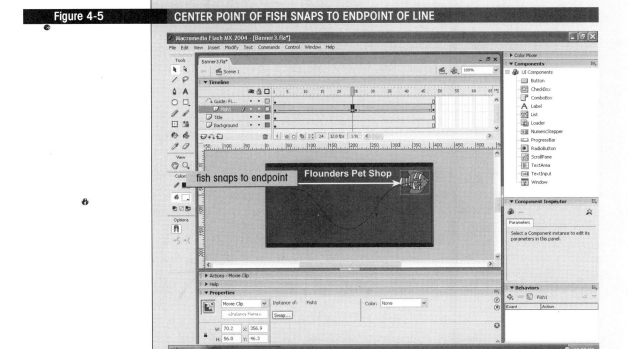

TROUBLE? If you move the endpoint of the line by mistake, just click Edit on the menu bar and click Undo, and then try moving the fish again.

8. Click **Frame 25** of the Fish1 layer and drag the fish again so that it snaps to the far-right endpoint of the line. This is where the fish starts a new motion tween to swim to the left side of the banner. Next position the fish at the end of the motion tween.

9. Click **Frame 48** of the Fish1 layer. This time drag the fish so that it snaps to the far-left endpoint of the line. This is where the fish ends its motion tween.

Now you can test the animation with the motion guide layer and make any necessary modifications.

To test the motion guide layer and make changes to it:

1. Press the **Enter** key to test the motion guide tween. The fish follows the path you drew in the guide layer.

   TROUBLE? If the fish does not follow the path, then its center point may not be snapped to the endpoints of the line. Check Frames 1, 24, 25, and 48 of the Fish1 layer to make sure the center point of the fish is snapped to the endpoints of the line. If necessary, move the fish again to snap it to the endpoints.

   You may notice that as the fish moves along the line, it stays in a horizontal position. You should change it so it moves in a more natural way. You can do this by selecting the Orient to path option in the Property inspector. This causes the object to align itself with the direction of the path and makes the movement appear more natural.

2. Click **Frame 1** of the Fish1 layer, and then click the **Orient to path** check box in the Property inspector to check it, if necessary.

   TROUBLE? If the Property inspector is not open, click Window on the menu bar, and then click Properties.

3. Click **Frame 25** of the Fish1 layer, and then click the **Orient to path** check box in the Property inspector to check it, if necessary.

   Before testing the animation again, hide the Guide layer so that the path is hidden.

4. Click the dot in the **Guide: Fish1** layer in the Eye column to hide its contents.

5. Move the playhead to Frame 1 and press the **Enter** key to test the animation again. This time the fish orients itself to the direction of the motion guide

Recall that another special type of layer is a mask layer. You can also create animations that incorporate a mask layer to create special effects.

Animation Using a Mask Layer

To create an animation using a mask layer, create the object that will be masked on one layer, and add a new layer above it that will contain the mask. You then right-click the top layer and select Mask from the context menu. The top layer will become the mask layer and the bottom layer will become the masked layer. The masked layer is displayed in the Timeline indented below the mask layer, as shown in Figure 4-6.

| Figure 4-6 | TIMELINE WITH MASK AND MASKED LAYERS |

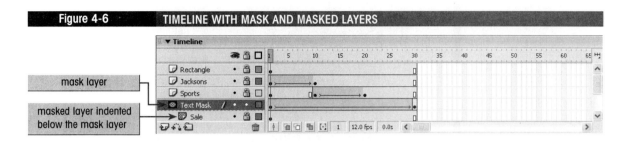

Another way to change a layer to a mask layer is to open the Layer Properties dialog box. You do this by right-clicking the layer's name and selecting Properties on the context menu. You can also click Modify on the menu bar, point to Timeline, and then click Layer Properties. In the Layer Properties dialog box you can select Mask or Masked to change the layer's type.

The object on the mask layer can be a filled shape such as an oval or rectangle. It can also be text or an instance of an object. The fill of the shape on the mask layer will reveal the content in the underlying masked layer. You can then animate either the object on the mask layer or the object on the masked layer. For example, you can animate an oval shape on the mask layer so that it moves over some stationary text on the masked layer. This technique creates a spotlight effect, as shown in Figure 4-7.

| Figure 4-7 | MASKED LAYER EXAMPLE |

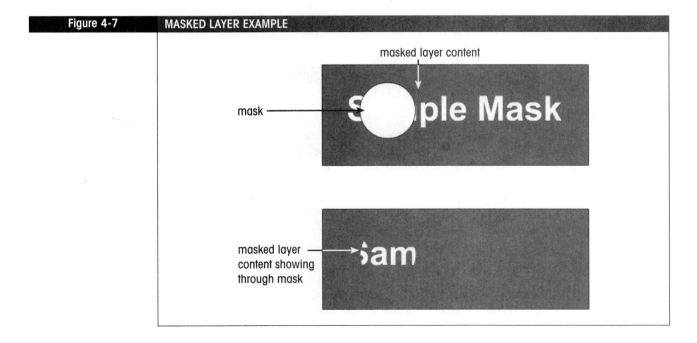

If you animate the object on the masked layer while the object on the mask layer remains stationary, you can create a different type of effect. For example, you can create a scrolling text effect by drawing a rectangle on the mask layer and then animating a block of text on the masked layer. As the text block moves across the mask, only the portion of the text behind the rectangle is visible, as shown in Figure 4-8.

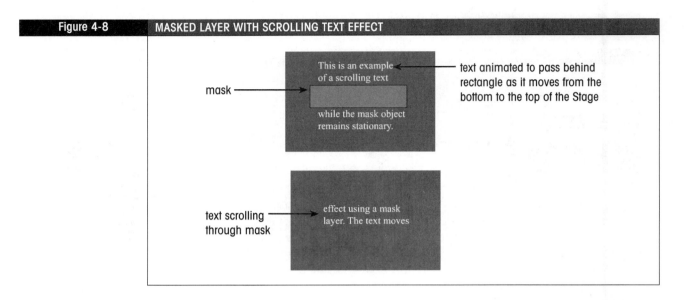

Figure 4-8   MASKED LAYER WITH SCROLLING TEXT EFFECT

You can also use text for the mask object and have another object show through the text itself. Using this technique, you can create an effect where the text acts like a window for the content behind it. For example, you can have an animated object on the masked layer such as a picture. As the picture moves, only the parts of the picture that are behind the text will be visible, as shown in Figure 4-9. You will learn how to use pictures in your Flash documents in a later tutorial.

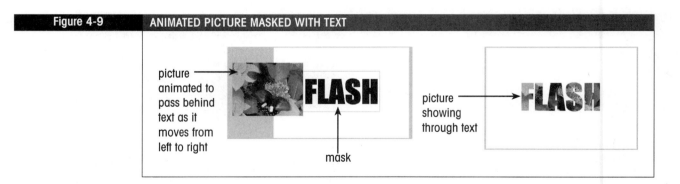

Figure 4-9   ANIMATED PICTURE MASKED WITH TEXT

When you first create a mask layer, Flash automatically locks both the mask and the masked layers. The layers must be locked in order to preview the effects of the mask within the Flash program window. When the layers are locked, the mask layer object is not visible, and only the content in the masked layer that is behind the mask layer object becomes visible. You unlock the layers to work with the objects on both layers and then lock the layers again to test the animation.

Aly suggests you explore a mask layer animation she has created for another Admiral client, Jackson's Sports to see how a mask layer animation works.

To explore the mask layer animation in the Jackson's Sports banner:

1. Open the **sports4.fla** file located in the Tutorial.04\Tutorial folder included with your Data Files.

2. If necessary, expand the height of the Timeline window so that the Text Mask and Sale layers are visible. Before you can view the mask layer's contents, you first need to unlock it.

3. If the Text Mask layer has a padlock icon in the Lock column, click it to unlock the layer. Unlocking the layer displays the contents of the Text Mask layer, as shown in Figure 4-10. When a mask layer is locked, the masking effect is visible in the Flash program window.

Figure 4-10	MASK LAYER ANIMATION

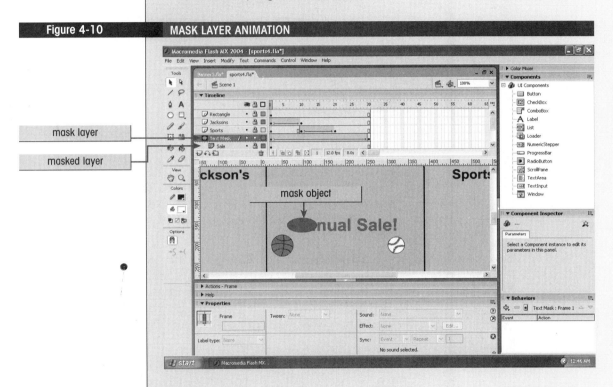

Notice that the content of the Text Mask layer is just a motion tween of an oval shape. The color of the shape is not significant because its color is not displayed. What is significant is its shape. This shape determines what part of the underlying Sale layer content is visible. As the oval moves from left to right, different parts of the underlying Annual Sale text become visible. Now test the animation. To do so, you must first lock the mask layer to test the mask effect.

4. Click the **dot** in the Lock column of the Text Mask layer to lock it.

5. Press the **Enter** key to test the animation. Notice how the part of the text that is under the oval is displayed as the oval moves across the Stage.

6. Close the sports4.fla file without saving any changes.

Now that you have previewed an existing mask animation, you will create a mask animation for the Flounders Pet Shop banner. As shown in Figure 4-1, Aly's notes for the banner indicate that in Scene 3, the Flounders Pet Shop text block should have a spotlight effect. To create this, you will first add a duplicate of the current scene in the file to create Scene 3, and then modify it by creating a spotlight effect where the spotlight moves across the Flounders Pet Shop text block.

To create a mask layer animation:

1. In the Banner3.fla file, click **Window** on the menu bar, point to **Design Panels**, and click **Scene** to open the Scene panel. Click the **Duplicate scene** icon to create a duplicate of Scene 1. Rename the scenes next.

2. Change the name of Scene 1 to **Fish Swimming**, and change the name of Scene 1 copy to **Animated Text**. If necessary, make the Animated Text scene the current scene. Close the Scene panel. You do not need some of the extra layers in the Animated Text scene.

3. If necessary, select the **Fish1** layer, click the **Delete Layer** button in the Timeline, select the **Guide: Fish1** layer and then click . Next you need to create a duplicate of the title text block.

4. Use the **Selection** tool to select the text block on the Stage. Click **Edit** on the menu bar and then click **Copy** to copy the text block to the Clipboard.

5. Select the **Background** layer, click **Insert** on the menu bar, point to **Timeline**, and then click **Layer** to insert a new layer above the Background layer. Change the name of the new layer to **Gray text**. Click **Edit** on the menu bar and then click **Paste in Place** to paste the text block in the new Gray text layer in the same relative position as it is in the Title layer.

6. Hide the content of the Title layer. Click **Frame 1** of the Gray text layer, click the **text block** to select it, change the color of the text block to **dark gray** (#666666) **and click** an empty area of the Stage to deselect the text. Lock the layer and unhide the content of the Title layer. The gray text will provide a background for the title as part of the spotlight effect. Next add a mask layer above the Title layer next.

7. Click **Frame 1** of the Title layer. Insert a new layer above the Title layer. Change the name of the new layer to **Mask**. The Mask layer's type needs to be changed to Mask.

8. Right-click the name of the Mask layer and then select **Mask** from the context menu. The layer changes to a mask layer and the Title layer changes to a masked layer and is indented below the Mask layer. Both layers are locked, as shown in Figure 4-11. Next you will draw a circle on the Mask layer to represent the spotlight.

Figure 4-11   **LOCKED LAYERS**

mask and masked layers are locked

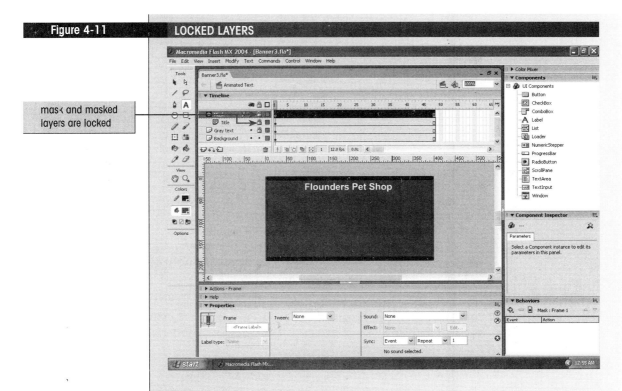

9. Unlock the Mask layer, click **Frame 1** of the Mask layer, and then click the **Oval** tool on the toolbar to select it. Select **white** as the fill color and select **No Color** for the stroke. Draw a small circle to cover the letters "Fl" on the Flounders Pet Shop text block, as shown in Figure 4-12.

Figure 4-12   **OVAL DRAWN TO MASK TEXT**

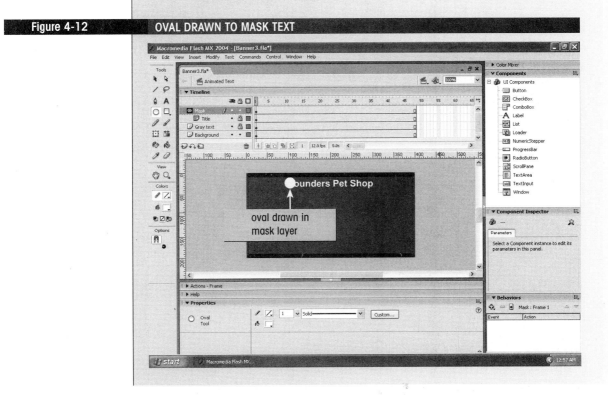

oval drawn in mask layer

10. Select the **circle**, click **Modify** on the menu bar, and then click **Convert to Symbol**. In the Convert to Symbol dialog box, name the symbol **Circle**, select **Movie clip** as its behavior type, and then click the **OK** button. Create two motion tweens for the circle so that it moves to the end of the title text block and then back to its starting point.

11. Insert a keyframe at **Frame 48** of the Mask layer. This is the end of the animation sequence and the circle will be back to this starting point at this frame. Additional keyframes are needed to complete the motion tweens.

12. Insert another keyframe at **Frame 24** of the Mask layer. Move the circle so that it covers the last two letters of the text block. Insert one more keyframe at Frame 25. Frame 24 represents the end of the first motion tween and Frame 25 represents the beginning of the second motion tween where the circle moves back to its starting point.

13. Right-click between Frames 1 and 24 and select **Create Motion Tween** from the context menu, and then right-click between Frames 25 and 48 and select **Create Motion Tween** again. Two motion tweens are created. Test the animation next.

14. Lock the Mask layer, move the playhead to **Frame 1**, and press the **Enter** key to test the animation. The circle creates a spotlight effect as it moves across and back over the title text.

15. Save your work.

In this session, you created a motion guide layer to have the fish instance swim along a curved path. You have also added a duplicate scene where you created a mask layer animation to create a spotlight effect. In the next session, you will continue your work on the banner by creating text animations.

Session 4.1 QUICK CHECK

1. List two ways to insert a motion guide layer.

2. Name two tools you can use to create a path on a motion guide layer.

3. How can you see the effect that a mask layer has on a masked layer when testing an animation within the Flash program window?

4. Text cannot be used as a mask in a mask layer. True or False?

5. When a guide layer is used together with a motion tween it is called a _____ layer.

6. What is the purpose of the Orient to path option in the Property inspector?

7. In a mask layer animation, the contents of the _____ layer are revealed when the object in the _____ layer moves over it.

SESSION 4.2

In this session, you will learn how to create various types of text animations, including how to animate the individual letters of a word. You will modify the Flounders banner by adding several animated text blocks.

Animating Text Blocks

Text can be animated in many interesting ways to create special effects. For example, a simple animation can be created where the text moves onto the Stage in a fly-in effect. Or in a more complex animation, the individual letters of a text block can rotate, fade in, and change in size as they appear one at a time on the Stage to form a word or phrase. Text can even be animated to increase and decrease in size creating a pulsating effect.

Text blocks can be animated using frame-by-frame or tweened animations. For example, you can have a text block move from one side of the Stage to the other. Using a motion tween you can animate a text block so that it rotates as the animation is played, or you can even have the text block change in size or color. To create a motion tween with a text block, you need to first convert the text block to a symbol. You then create the keyframes for the beginning and the ending of the animation and move the text block to its starting position in the first frame and to its ending position in the last frame. You then create the motion tween. This process is the same as you follow to create motion tweens for other symbols.

You can also apply a shape tween to text. To do so, however, you first need to convert the text to fills by using the Break Apart command located on the Modify menu. When you apply this command to a text block, each of the letters in the text block becomes an individual text block. You can then apply the command again to the individual letters to convert them to fills. Once converted to fills, you can apply a shape tween to them. For example, you can make the letters change into an oval shape, as shown in Figure 4-13. Note that once you convert the text to fills you can no longer edit the fills as text.

Figure 4-13	SAMPLE SHAPE TWEEN

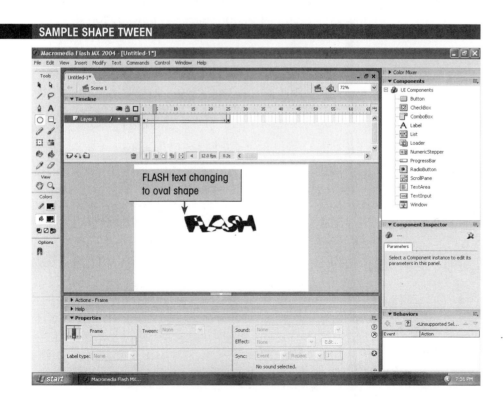

Adding Animated Text to the Flounders Pet Shop Banner

After reviewing Aly's notes for completing the banner, as shown in Figure 4-1, you see that you still need to add several text blocks to the banner. In the third scene there are to be four text blocks. The Aquarium text block and the Tank text block will move off the sides of the Stage to the center of the Stage. One text block, the And text block, will not be animated but will only appear halfway through the animation. The fourth text block, Fish Sale, will also appear halfway through the animation but will increase in size throughout the second half of the animation. Each text block will be on its own layer so you can animate them individually. You will start by adding four new layers, one for each text block, to the Animated Text scene.

To add a text block to the banner and use motion tweening to animate it:

1. If you took a break after the last session, start Flash and open the **Banner3.fla** file and set the panels to their default layout.

2. Select the **Mask** layer of the Animated Text Scene in the Timeline, and insert a new layer named **Aquarium**. Insert three more layers above the Aquarium layer, and name them **Tank**, **And**, and **Fish Sale**, respectively.

3. Click the **Zoom** control list arrow and click **100%** to change the view of the Stage. If necessary, display the rulers. You will want to have the work area visible to create the text blocks, and you will use the rulers for aligning the text blocks. Set the text properties next.

4. Select **Frame 1** of the **Aquarium** layer. Click the **Text** tool A on the toolbar and click an area to the left of the Stage to place a new text block. In the Property inspector, select **Arial** as the font, **26** for the font size, and **yellow** for the font color. If necessary, click the **Bold** button B, and then click the **Italic** button I to apply bold and italic formatting. Now you are ready to create the first block.

5. Type **Aquarium** for the text. If necessary, position the text block as shown in Figure 4-14. Before you can create a motion tween of this text block, it needs to be converted to a symbol.

Figure 4-14 AQUARIUM TEXT BLOCK

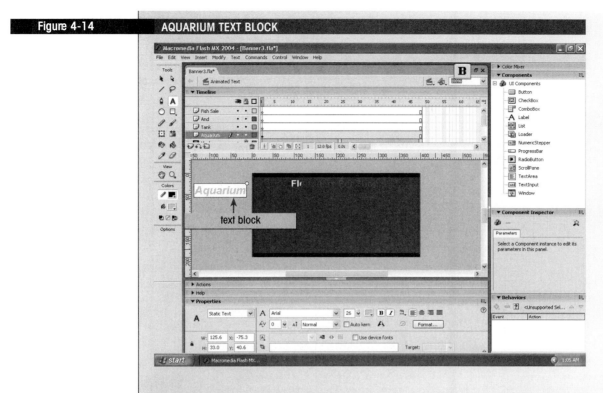

6. Convert the Aquarium text block to a symbol. Name the symbol **Aquarium text**, and assign **Movie clip** as the behavior. Recall movie clip is the behavior you will use for most of your symbols.

7. Click **Frame 10** of the Aquarium layer, and insert a keyframe. Move the Aquarium text block to the center of the Stage. Place it about 100 pixels from the left of the Stage and 75 pixels from the top, as shown in Figure 4-15.

Figure 4-15 END POSITION FOR TEXT

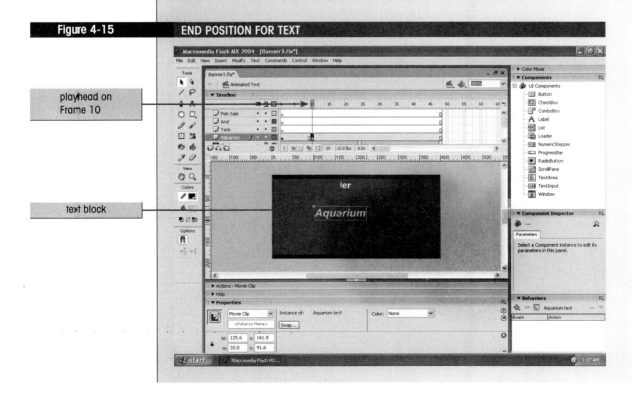

Now, create the motion tween for the text block.

8. Click **Frame 1** of the Aquarium layer. Click the **Tween** list arrow in the Property inspector, and then click **Motion**. A motion tween is created so that the text moves from the left of the Stage to the center of the Stage.

You have added a text block and then used a motion tween to animate it. Now you will repeat similar steps to add additional text blocks. You will use the other layers you created for these text blocks. You will start by creating a keyframe for the start of the Tank text.

To create more text animations:

1. Click **Frame 10** of the Tank layer. Insert a keyframe, and then click an empty area of the Stage.

2. Click the **Text** tool A on the toolbar. If necessary, select **Arial** as the font, **26** for the font size, and **yellow** for the font color in the Property inspector. Also, if necessary, select **bold** and **italic** styles.

3. Create a new text block to the right of the Stage with the word **Tank**, as shown in Figure 4-16.

Figure 4-16   **TANK TEXT BLOCK**

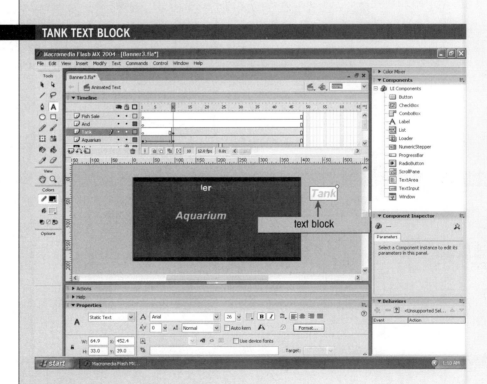

4. Select the text block and convert it to a symbol. Name the symbol **Tank text**, and assign **Movie clip** as the behavior.

5. Click **Frame 20** of the Tank layer. Insert a keyframe. Move the Tank text block to the right of the Aquarium text block. Line up the text horizontally with the Aquarium text. See Figure 4-17. Now create a motion tween.

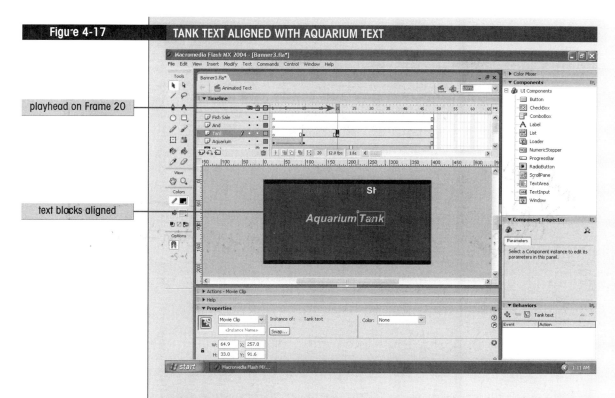

Figure 4-17   TANK TEXT ALIGNED WITH AQUARIUM TEXT

playhead on Frame 20

text blocks aligned

6. Click **Frame 10** of the Tank layer. Click the **Tween** list arrow in the Property inspector, and then click **Motion**. A motion tween is created so that the text moves from the right of the Stage to the right of the Aquarium text.

You will now repeat similar steps to add another text block. However, this text block will not have a motion tween because it will not be animated. Instead, it will only appear starting with Frame 25. This means that from Frame 1 to Frame 24 the text is not displayed. It is only displayed from Frame 25 through Frame 48.

To add a new text block:

1. Click **Frame 25** of the And layer and insert a keyframe.

2. Create another text block below the Aquarium and Tank text blocks.

3. Type the word **And** in this text block, and then click an empty area of the Stage to deselect the text.

Now you need to create one more text block. This text block will be animated with a motion tween. However, it will not move; instead, it will change in size throughout the animation. The text block will not be visible until Frame 25 at which point the motion tween will start.

To create a text block that increases in size:

1. Click **Frame 25** of the Fish Sale layer. Insert a keyframe. Click an area below the And text. If necessary, click the **Text** tool A on the toolbar, and in the Property inspector change the font size to **12**.

2. Create a text block below the And text block. Type **Fish Sale!** in this text block.

3. Click the **Selection** tool on the toolbar. With the text block still selected, convert this to a symbol named **Fish Sale text** with the behavior of Movie clip. Now you will add a keyframe for the end of the animation.

4. Click **Frame 35** of the Fish Sale layer. Insert a keyframe. In this frame you want to increase the size of the text.

5. Click **Window** on the menu bar, point to **Design Panels**, and then click **Transform** to open the Transform panel. Make sure that the Fish Sale text block is still selected. In the Transform panel, make sure that the **Constrain** checkbox is selected, and enter **300%** in the width box. Be sure to press the **Enter** key after you type 300. See Figure 4-18. Close the Transform panel. Now create a motion tween.

make sure right type end frame · *push enter, don't close*

Figure 4-18   **TRANSFORM PANEL**

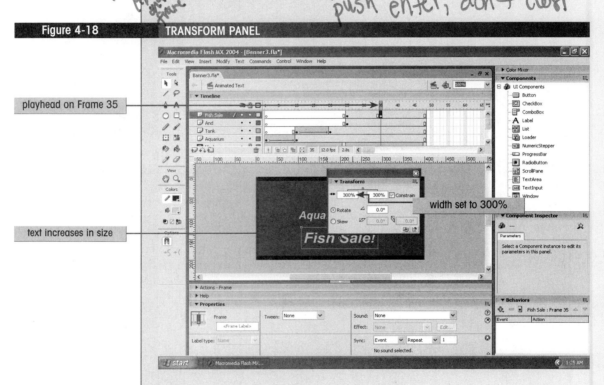

playhead on Frame 35

text increases in size

width set to 300%

6. Click **Frame 25** of the Fish Sale layer. Click the **Tween** list arrow in the Property inspector, and then click **Motion**. A motion tween is created so that the text increases in size throughout the animation.

7. Move the **playhead** to Frame 1, and then press the **Enter** key to test the animation.

8. Save the changes you have made to the document.

You have completed the text animations for the Animated Text scene. The next animation that needs to be created is one in which the individual letters of the name Flounders change one at a time. As shown in Aly's notes in Figure 4-1, this animation will appear in the first scene, which you need to create. Learning how to work with individual text letters will help you create a variety of interesting effects.

Animating **Individual Letters**

Animating individual letters in a word or phrase makes it possible to create interesting text effects. For example, you can animate the letters of a word to fall into place on the Stage one at a time. Or you can have a word explode with the individual letters flying off the Stage in different directions. Another example is to have the individual letters of a word increase and decrease in size to create a pulsating effect. To create most of these text effects you first need to break a word into its individual letters and then animate each letter separately. The easiest way to animate each letter is to create motion tweens. This means that each letter must be converted to a symbol and must reside on its own layer. Recall that you cannot have motion tweens on a layer with more than one symbol. To get more familiar with the process used to create an individual letter text animation, Aly suggests you look at a banner she has been working on for Jackson's Sports. This banner shows how each letter has the same motion tweens applied to it to create a pulsating effect.

To explore an individual letter text effect:

1. Open the **sports5.fla** file located in the Tutorial.04\Tutorial folder included with your Data Files.

2. Click **Control** on the menu bar and click **Play**. The text animation plays showing each letter increase and decrease in size one after the other. Notice that each letter resides on its own layer.

3. Click **Frame 1** of the J layer. Notice the size of the letter J on the Stage. Click **Frame 5** of the same layer. The letter J increases in size.

4. Click **Frame 10**. In this frame, the letter goes back to its original size. At the same time the next letter, A, has increased in size, as shown in Figure 4-19.

Figure 4-19   **SAMPLE LETTERS ANIMATION**

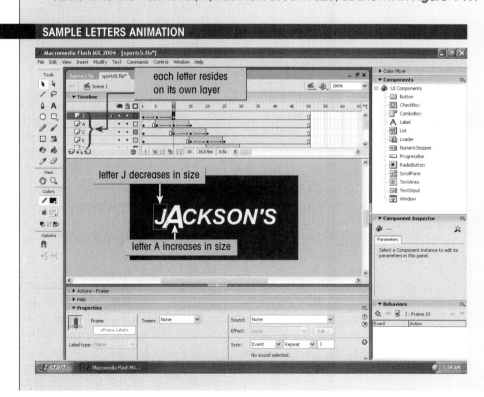

Aly suggests you look at the document's library to see the symbols created for this animation.

5. Click **Window** on the menu bar, and click **Library** to open the library. Notice that the library contains a series of symbols named Tween 1, Tween 2, etc.

These symbols are created automatically by Flash when you apply a motion tween to a grouped object such as a text block that was not first converted to a symbol. Aly explains that instead of first creating a symbol for each letter, she created the motion tweens and let Flash generate the graphic symbols to represent each tween. Because these symbols are not used in any other part of the animation, the names of the symbols are not important. Letting Flash generate the symbols automatically can save you time especially when creating animations of words or phrases with many letters.

6. Close this file without saving any changes.

As you observed in the Jackson's Sports banner example, the motion tweens applied to the letters overlap such that one letter's animation begins before the previous letter's animation ends. This gives the animation a smoother effect.

Animating a word's individual letters similar to the Jackson's Sports banner requires that each letter be placed on its own layer. A quick way to get each of the letters into its own layer is to use the Distribute to Layers command.

Distribute to Layers

The Distribute to Layers command will take a group of selected objects and place each individual object onto its own layer. Each new layer is named based on its new content. For example, if the objects distributed are text blocks, then the names of the new layers will be the same as the text in the text blocks. If the objects are symbols, the new layers will have the same name as the name of the symbols. Other layers will be named Layer followed by a number. This helps you to identify which layers the selected objects have been distributed to. The layer that originally contained the grouped objects will be empty after you apply the Distribute to Layers command. You select the Distribute to Layers command by clicking Modify on the menu bar, pointing to Timeline, and then clicking Distribute to Layers. Before you apply this command be sure to select all of the objects you want to distribute to individual layers. If you have many new layers as a result of applying this command, it is a good idea to place all of the new layers in a layer folder. This will make it easier to work with the document's Timeline and any other layers in your document.

Creating a Complex Text Animation for the Flounders Banner

One of the animations you have been instructed to create for the Flounders Pet Shop banner consists of individual letters in the Flounders name rotating into place one after the other to form the word Flounders. This animation will appear in the first scene, as described in Aly's planning notes shown in Figure 4-1. Each letter will fade in and decrease in size as it falls into place. This effect involves animating the individual letters of the word in a similar way to the animated text in the banner Aly created for Jackson's Sports. To create the animations for the individual letters, you will first create the Flounders text block, convert each letter in that text block into its own individual text block, and then distribute these individual letter text blocks onto their own layers. To convert the text block into individual letters you need to use the Break Apart command. This command breaks a text block into separate text blocks, one for each letter. The Break Apart command is located on the Modify menu. Once each letter is in its own text block, you then apply the Distribute to Layers command to the selected text blocks so that each letter is placed on its own layer. You then can create the necessary motion tween animations for each of the letters. For the motion tweens, Aly instructs you to start each letter rotated at a -45 degree angle, slightly faded, and twice as large as the ending size. Then each letter will rotate into its upright position, while fading in, and reducing in size. This will create the effect of the letters falling into place to spell the word Flounders.

Also, before animating the letters, Aly suggests you change the colors of the letters alternating between a light gray and an orange color for every other letter in the Flounders text block. She thinks this will enhance the special effect. Aly also suggests you initially create the text block in a new layer folder. Then when you distribute the letters to individual layers, all of the new layers will be inside the folder. This new animation will reside in its own scene, which will play before the other two scenes in the document.

To create the individual letters animation for the word Flounders:

1. Click **Window** on the menu bar, point to **Design Panels**, and click **Scene** to open the Scene panel.

2. In the scene panel, select the **Fish Swimming** scene and then click the **Duplicate scene** icon 🔲 to create a duplicate of the scene. A duplicate scene named Fish Swimming copy is created. Rename and move the duplicate scene so it is the first scene in the document.

3. Double-click the **Fish Swimming copy** scene in the Scene panel and change its name to **Title**. Drag the Title scene and position it above the Fish Swimming scene. Close the Scene panel.

4. In the Title scene, delete the **Fish1** and **Guide: Fish1** layers. Also, delete the text block in the Title layer. Next, create a new layer folder for the new text block.

5. If necessary, select the **Title** layer and then click **Insert** on the menu bar, point to **Timeline**, and click **Layer Folder**. A new layer folder is created above the Title layer.

6. Rename the layer folder **Letters** and then drag the Title layer so that it is inside the Letters folder.

7. Click **Frame 1** of the Title layer and then click the **Text** tool 🅰 on the toolbar. Click the center of the Stage. In the Properties inspector, select **Impact** for the font, **70** for the font size, and **light gray** (#CCCCCC) for the text color. Also, select the bold style.

8. Create a text block with the word **FLOUNDERS** on the Stage. Use the **Selection** tool 🔺 to center the text block and position it about 50 pixels from the top of the Stage, as shown in Figure 4-20. Change the color of the letters next.

Figure 4-20   **FLOUNDERS TEXT BLOCK**

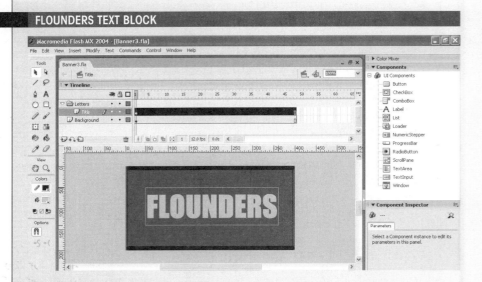

9. Double-click the **text block** and then click and drag to select just the letter **L** in the text block. Change its color to **orange** (#FF6600), and then change the color of the letters U, D, and R to the same color orange.

10. Click the **Selection** tool and keep the text block selected. Now you will separate the letters into individual text blocks.

11. Click **Modify** on the menu bar and then click **Break Apart**. Each letter is placed in its own text block, as shown in Figure 4-21.

Figure 4-21   **INDIVIDUAL LETTER TEXT BLOCKS**

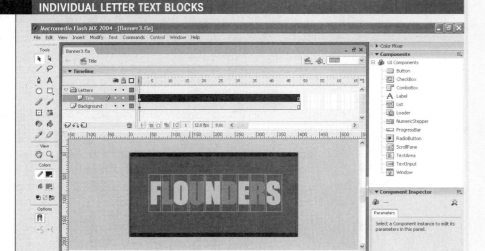

12. With all of the letters still selected, click **Modify** on the menu bar, point to **Timeline**, and then click **Distribute to Layers**. Each of the letters is placed on its own layer and each layer is named with the letter it contains.

13. Delete the **Title** layer because it is empty and it is no longer needed.

Now that the letters have been split into individual text blocks and onto separate layers, you can animate each one of them to create the Flounders letters animation. You will convert each letter into a symbol and create a motion tween to cover 15 frames. In discussing this special effect with Aly, she points out that each letter should start its animation a few frames after the previous letter. This means that the starting keyframe for each subsequent letter needs to be moved to a later frame in the Timeline. Aly suggests having each motion tween start every three frames. The first letter, F, starts in Frame 1 of the F layer. Then the second letter, L, will start in Frame 3 of its layer. The letter, O, will start in Frame 6 of its layer. The letter, U, will start in Frame 9 of its layer, and so on. This way, the animation effect is that of the letters dropping in one after the other. You will create the motion tween animations for the letters. First you will extend all of the layers so that they exist for five seconds by adding regular frames to Frame 60.

To animate the letters: —— control and highlight

1. In the Timeline, drag from Frame 60 of the F layer down to Frame 60 of the Background layer to select each frame. Click **Insert** on the menu bar, point to **Timeline**, and then click **Frame**. Each layer is extended to Frame 60.

   Instead of letting Flash create each tween symbol automatically as was done with the Jackson's Sports banner, you will create the symbols yourself so that they are easily identifiable in the document's library. This is helpful when you already have other symbols in the library.

2. Select the letter **F** in Frame 1 of the F layer and convert it to a symbol. Name the symbol **F** and specify **Movie clip** as its behavior. The symbol is added to the document's library. Next, convert the rest of the letters to symbols.

3. Repeat Step 2 for each of the other letters. Name each symbol the same as the letter it represents. Next you will move the starting keyframes for each of the letters except F.

4. Click **Frame 1** of the L layer. Drag the keyframe to **Frame 3** of the same layer, as shown in Figure 4-22.

Figure 4-22	REPOSITION KEYFRAME

move keyframe to Frame 3

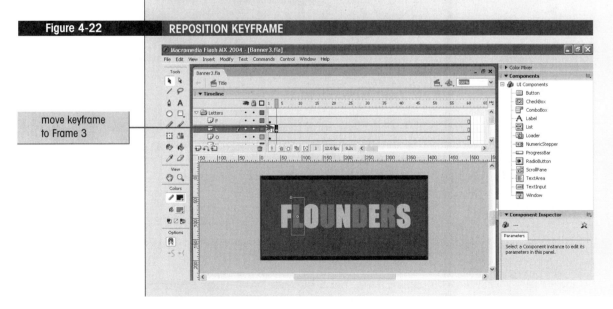

5. Repeat Step 4 to move the first keyframes for each of the subsequent letters in their respective layers. The keyframes are to be arranged as follows: O - Frame 6, U - Frame 9, N - Frame 12, D - Frame 15, E - Frame 18, R - Frame 21, S - Frame 24.

The motion tween for each letter will occupy 15 frames in their respective layers. That means that each layer should have another keyframe added 15 frames after the first one. You will add the ending keyframes.

6. Insert a keyframe at **Frame 15** of the F layer. This where the motion tween for the F will end. Add ending keyframes for the rest of the layers.

7. Insert keyframes for each of the other layers according to the following: L- Frame 18, O - Frame 21, U - Frame 24, N - Frame 27, D - Frame 30, E - Frame 33, R - Frame 36, S - Frame 39. Next you will add the motion tweens.

8. Right-click between **Frame 1** and **Frame 15** of the F layer and select **Create Motion Tween** from the context menu. The motion tween is created for the letter F.

9. Repeat Step 8 for each of the other layers by right-clicking between their respective starting and ending keyframes and selecting Create Motion Tween from the context menu. You will have a motion tween for each layer, as shown in Figure 4-23.

Figure 4-23	MOTION TWEENS FOR EACH LAYER

motion tweens

Now that each layer has a motion tween, you need to change the starting instance of the letter in each layer so that it is different from the ending instance. The instance at the end of each layer does not need to change. You will change the starting instance by increasing its size, rotating it to the left, and making it slightly transparent.

To change the starting instance in each layer:

1. Select **Frame 1** of the F layer and click the **F** symbol instance on the Stage to select it.

2. Click **Window** on the menu bar, point to **Design Panels**, and click **Transform** to open the Transform panel. Move the panel to the right side of the Stage. If necessary, click the **Constrain** check box to select it.

3. Enter **200** for the width value. The height value also changes to 200. Enter **-45** for the Rotate value and press the **Enter** key. The letter F changes in size and orientation.

4. Click the **F** instance to select it, click the **Color** list arrow in the Property inspector, and then select **Alpha**. Change the Alpha amount to **20%**, and then press the **Enter** key. The letter becomes slightly transparent. See Figure 4-24.

Figure 4-24   **CHANGES TO F INSTANCE IN FRAME 1**

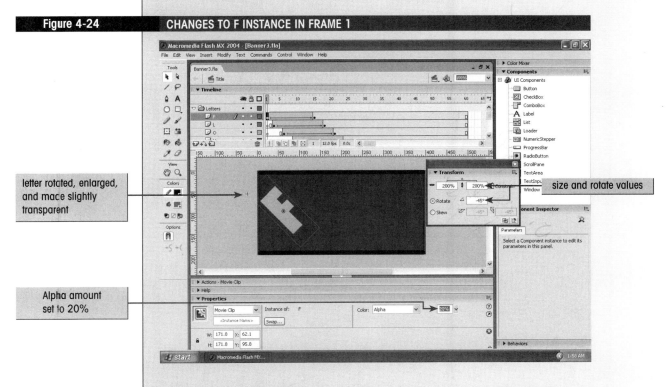

letter rotated, enlarged, and made slightly transparent

size and rotate values

Alpha amount set to 20%

---

5. Test the animation for the letter F by scrubbing the playhead between Frames 1 and 15. The F starts out large, slightly transparent, and tilted to the left then moves into place as it fades in and decreases in size. Change the rest of the starting instances for each letter.

6. For each letter, select it in its starting keyframe and then repeat Steps 3 and 4 to create the same animation effect as you did for the letter F. Close the Transform panel. Test the animation next.

7. Move the playhead to **Frame 1** and press the **Enter** key to view the animation, as shown in Figure 4-25.

Figure 4-25   INDIVIDUAL LETTERS ANIMATION

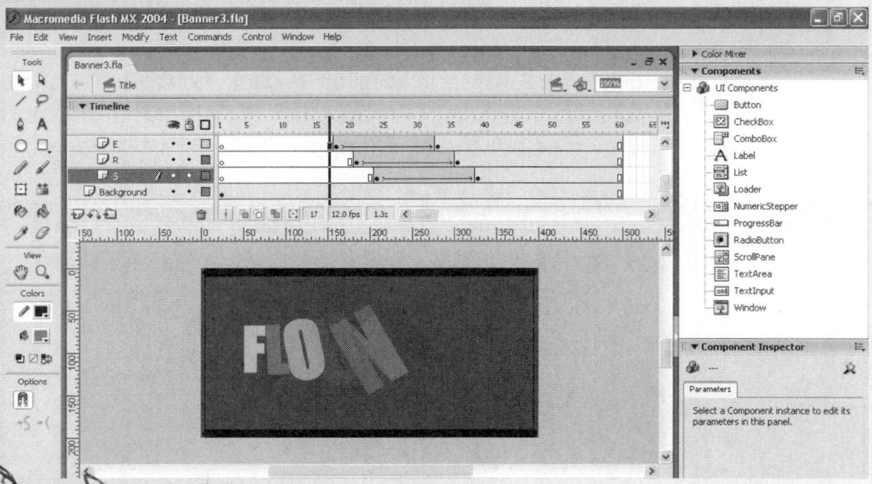

[handwritten annotations: "? my O is missing?", "what does dotted line mean", and a drawn face]

8. Save your work.

The special effect for the Flounders text has now been created. As a result of your work, nine new layers have been created inside the Letters folder.

In this session, you animated several text blocks in the last scene of the banner. You have also created a new scene with an animation of the individual letters of the Flounders name. In the next session, you will complete the banner by adding a complex animation to the second scene.

Session 4.2 QUICK CHECK

1. List two examples of how text may be animated.

2. To apply a shape tween to a text block what must you do first to the text?

3. If you apply the Distribute to Layers command to a group of selected text blocks how will the new layers be named in the Timeline?

4. Why must you have each letter that is to be animated on its own layer?

5. Why is it a good idea to have all of the individual letter layers contained in a layer folder?

SESSION 4.3

In this session, you will learn how to create a complex movie clip animation where one or more symbols are nested inside another movie clip symbol. You will also learn how to use onion skinning as you create and test complex animations. Finally, you will learn how to use the Movie Explorer to examine all the elements of a Flash document.

Creating and Testing Animations Using Onion Skinning

When working with complex animations it is often helpful to turn on onion skinning. **Onion skinning** displays more than one frame at one time on the Stage. This can be especially helpful when creating a frame-by-frame animation where you need to compare the current frame's contents to the previous frame's contents. Normally, you only see the current frame's contents on the Stage. With onion skinning, Flash will display the current frame plus two or more frames on the Stage at once. The content of the current frame, indicated by the position of the playhead, appears in full color as it normally does. The contents of the frames before and after the current frame appear dimmed. Figure 4-26 shows the onion skin options available on the Timeline and the effect that onion skinning has on how the document appears on the Stage.

Figure 4-26	ONION SKIN OPTIONS

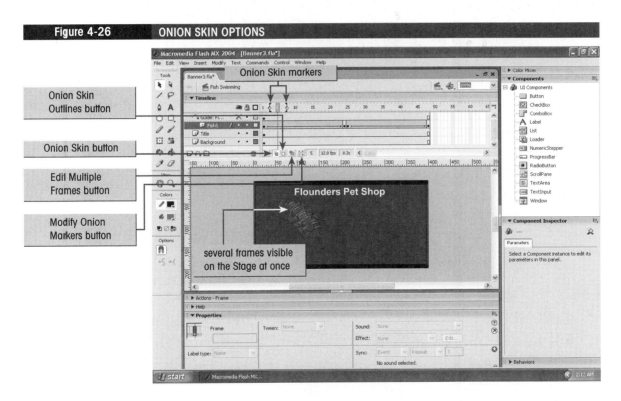

Figure 4-27 describes the onion skin options.

Figure 4-27

BUTTON	OPTION	DESCRIPTION
	Onion Skin	Turns onion skin effect on and off
	Onion Skin Outlines	Displays the frames' content as outlines
	Edit Multiple Frames	Allows you to edit all selected objects of the frames within the onion skin markers at one time
	Modify Onion Markers	Opens a context menu with the following options: ■ Always Show Markers – displays onion skin markers on the Timeline header even if onion skinning is turned off ■ Anchor Onion – locks onion skin markers in their current position and prevents them from moving with the playhead ■ Onion 2 – sets the onion skin markers to display two frames before and after the current frame ■ Onion 5 – sets the onion skin markers to display five frames before and after the current frame ■ Onion All – sets the onion skin markers to display all frames before and after the current frame
	Start Onion Skin marker	Marker that indicates the frame at which onion skinning begins
	End Onion Skin marker	Marker that indicates the frame at which onion skinning ends

To activate onion skinning, click the Onion Skin button on the Timeline. The Start Onion Skin marker and End Onion Skin marker appear on the Timeline header on either side of the playhead. The content displayed on the Stage is determined by the frames that are within the onion skin markers. The number of frames to display before and after the current frame can be changed by dragging the onion skin markers left or right on the Timeline header. You can also select Onion 2, Onion 5, or Onion All from the Modify Onion Markers menu to specify that two, five, or all frames, respectively, be displayed. If you select Onion Skin Outlines, the content on the Stage will display in outline form which can be helpful when working with complex animations. Another option is Edit Multiple Frames which can be used to change the content of more that one frame at a time. For example, suppose you need to move all of the graphics of an existing animation to a different part of the Stage. If you move the contents of all of the frames and layers, you would have to realign all of the graphics for the animation to be the same. Rather than doing this you can move all of the graphics for the animation at one time. You do this by clicking the Edit Multiple Frames button and then changing the onion skin markers to select all of the frames whose content you want to modify. You then select all of the graphics of the animation within these frames and move them all at once to the desired location. You will use onion skinning as you develop the animations in the next section.

Complex Animation with Nested Symbols

As you have seen, complex animations can be created by animating objects on separate layers. For example, you can animate one object to move across the Stage on one layer while at the same time another object on another layer rotates and increases in size. As a result, you can create complex animation effects just by adding more layers to the document's main Timeline. Sometimes, however, you cannot get the desired special effect by just adding more layers with more animations. For example, in the Flounders banner you have a fish swimming across the Stage. Its fins and tail, however, remain stationary in relation to the fish. It would be better if the fins and the tail would have their own animation to make the fish move in a more realistic way. You could separate the fins and the tail from the body of the fish, convert them to movie clip symbols, and then create animations for each one on separate layers.

Then you could animate the fish body, fins, and tail to move across the Stage at the same time as one object to achieve a more natural look. This is difficult to do, however, because it requires that you synchronize all of the animations to work together. A simpler way to do this is to create a nested symbol. A **nested symbol** is one which contains instances of other symbols within its Timeline. Recall that each symbol has its own Timeline. In the case of movie clip symbols, their Timelines are independent of the document's main Timeline. Within the Timeline of a movie clip symbol you can insert instances of other symbols which in turn can contain their own animations within their own Timelines. The nested movie clip instances are referred to as the **child movie clips** and the movie clip they are nested within is referred to as the **parent movie clip**. Instances of the parent movie clip can then be inserted into the document's main Timeline, and can be modified and animated just like any other symbol instance. Any modifications or animations applied to the parent movie clip also affect the child movie clips. In the case of the fish, the parent movie clip can consist of the fish body plus nested instances of the fins and the tail, as shown in Figure 4-28.

| Figure 4-28 | EXAMPLE OF NESTED MOVIE CLIP |

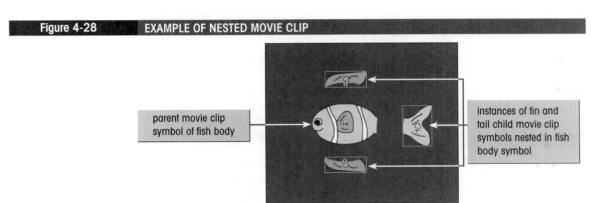

The fins and tail movie clip instances can contain their own animations to have them change slightly to simulate the movement of a real fish. These animations are independent of the fish body. The whole fish, which is the parent movie clip, can then be inserted in the document's main Timeline and animated to move across the Stage. When you apply a motion tween to the whole fish to make it move across the Stage, the motion tween is also applied to its nested instances. As a result, the fish body, fins, and tail all move across the Stage as one object while at the same time the fins and tail exhibit their own animations.

Creating a Nested Movie Clip for the Flounders Banner

One of the required elements you are to add to the second scene of the banner is another fish which has its fins and tail animated to appear more natural. To create this fish Aly suggests you create a nested movie clip symbol using several symbols she has already created. The symbols include a fish body, fin, and tail. You are to create frame-by-frame animations for the fin and the tail. Then you will add two instances of the fin movie clip and one instance of the tail movie clip to the fish body. The resulting nested movie clip symbol will then be inserted into the Fish Swimming scene of the Flounders banner.

You will start by creating a frame-by-frame animation for the fin. You will turn onion skinning on to help you as you create the animation. To create the animation for the fin, Aly suggests you add keyframes at every other frame of the fin Timeline starting at Frame 3. You will then change the shape of the fin slightly at each keyframe for a total of nine frames.

To create the fin frame-by-frame animation:

1. If you took a break after the previous session, open the **Banner3.fla** file from the **Tutorial.04\Tutorial** folder included with your Data Files. Set the panels to their default layout.

2. Click the **Edit Symbol** button ![icon] on the Timeline and then select the **Fin** symbol on the Edit Symbol menu. The Fin symbol opens in symbol-editing mode. Change the magnification level of the Stage.

3. Click the **Zoom** control and select **200%** to make it easier to see the Fin symbol on the Stage.

4. Insert keyframes at Frames 3, 5, 7, and 9 of Layer 1. The fin is copied to each of the new frames.

5. Click the **Onion Skin** button ![icon] on the Timeline. The onion skin markers display in the Timeline header. If necessary, click the **Modify Onion Markers** button ![icon] and select **Onion 2** to show the two frames before and after the current frame.

6. Click **Frame 3** and, if necessary, click the **Selection** tool ![icon] on the toolbar. Click an empty area of the Stage to deselect the fin and then use ![icon] to move the right side of the fin slightly to the left, as shown in Figure 4-29. Use the onion skinned frames as a reference when changing the fin.

Figure 4-29	MODIFYING THE FIN MOVIE CLIP

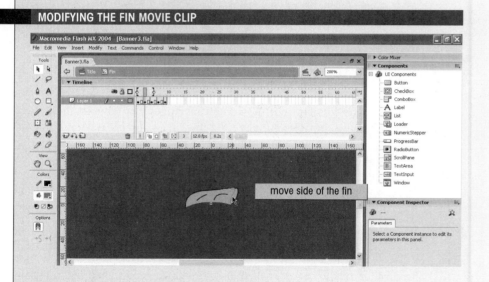

move side of the fin

7. Click **Frame 5**, deselect the fin, and move the top edge of the fin slightly up, as shown in Figure 4-30.

Figure 4-30	MODIFYING THE TOP OF THE FIN

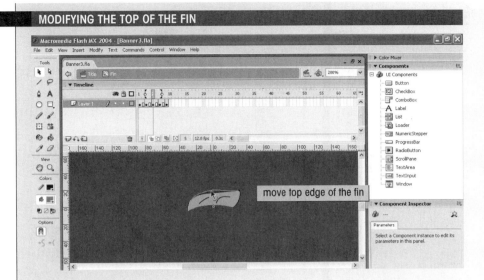

8. Click **Frame 7**, deselect the fin, and move the upper-right tip of the fin slightly to the right. Test the animation next.

9. Press the **Enter** key to test the frame-by-frame animation. The fin changes slightly at each keyframe throughout the animation.

You have created the frame-by-frame animation for the fin. Instances of the Fin symbol will be added to the fish body, but before doing that you will create a similar frame-by-frame animation for the Tail symbol. Aly suggests you use the same number of keyframes for the Tail symbol as you did for the Fin symbol and to change the shape of the tail slightly at each keyframe.

To create the tail frame-by-frame animation:

1. Click the **Edit Symbol** button and then select the **Tail** symbol. The Tail symbol opens in symbol-editing mode.

2. Insert keyframes at Frames 3, 5, 7, and 9 of Layer 1. The tail is copied to each of the new frames.

3. Click **Frame 3** and then click an empty area of the Stage to deselect the tail. Use to move the two tips on the right side of the tail slightly inward, as shown in Figure 4-31. Use the dimmed tail from the previous frame as a reference in changing the shape of the tail.

Figure 4-31   MODIFYING THE TAIL MOVIE CLIP

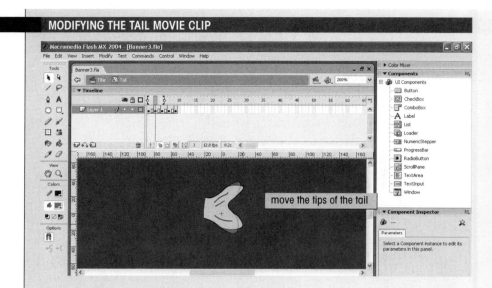

4. Click **Frame 5**, deselect the fin, and move the tail's top edge near the left side of the tail slightly down, as shown in Figure 4-32.

Figure 4-32   MODIFY THE TOP OF THE TAIL

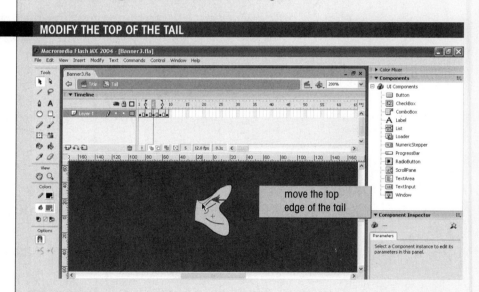

5. At the same frame move the tail's bottom edge near the left side of the tail slightly up. The mid section of the tail is narrower.

6. Click **Frame 7**, deselect the fin, and move the two tips on the right side of the tail slightly inward as you did in Step 3. Click the **Onion Skin** icon to turn onion skinning off. Test the animation next.

7. Click **Frame 1** and then press the **Enter** key to test the frame-by-frame animation. The tail changes slightly at each keyframe throughout the animation.

Now that you have created the animations for the Fin movie clip symbol and the Tail movie clip symbol, you are ready to insert instances of these symbols in the Fish2 symbol which contains the fish body. The instances will be the nested inside the Fish2 symbol.

To create the nested movie clip symbol:

1. Click the **Edit Symbol** button and then select the **Fish2** symbol. The Fish2 symbol opens in symbol-editing mode.

2. If necessary, open the Library panel. Drag an instance of the **Fin symbol** from the Library panel and place it directly above the fish body, as shown in Figure 4-33. If necessary, use the arrow keys on the keyboard to nudge the fin into place.

Figure 4-33   **PLACING THE FIN INSTANCE**

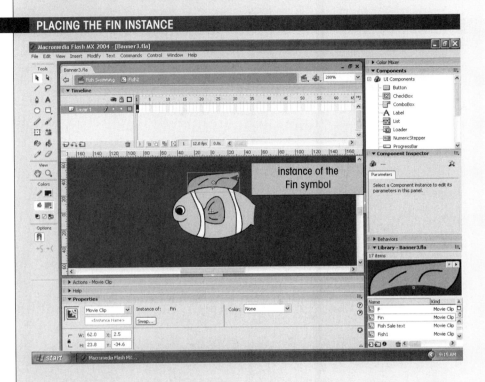

3. Drag another instance of the **Fin symbol** from the Library panel and place it below the fish body. With the Fin instance still selected, click **Modify** on the menu bar, point to **Transform**, and click **Flip Vertical**. Position the Fin instance right below the fish body. Add the tail next.

4. Drag an instance of the **Tail symbol** from the Library panel and place it just to the right side of the fish. If necessary, use the Selection tool to position the tail precisely against the fish body. The fish is now complete.

Now that the Fish2 symbol is complete with its nested movie clip symbols, you will place the complete fish in the Fish Swimming scene and apply motion tweens to make it swim across the Stage. The fins and tail will move together with the fish.

To insert and animate the Fish2 symbol in the Fish Swimming scene:

1. Change to the Fish Swimming scene, which is the second scene in the document.

2. Select the **Guide: Fish1** layer and insert a new layer above it. Name this new layer **Fish2**.

3. With the Fish2 layer selected, drag an instance of the Fish2 symbol from the Library panel and place it in the lower-right corner of the Stage.

4. Click the **Free Transform** tool on the toolbar and then click the **Scale** modifier in the options area of the toolbar. Drag a corner handle of the Fish2 symbol to reduce the size of the instance so that it is about the same size as the Fish1 instance on the Stage, as shown in Figure 4-34. Next you will create motion tweens to animate the fish.

Figure 4-34   NESTED MOVIE CLIP INSTANCE ADDED TO STAGE

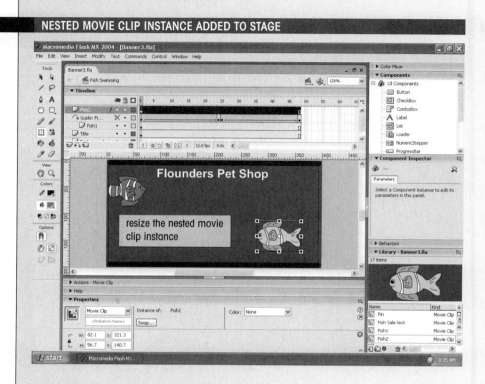

5. Click **Frame 24** of the Fish2 layer and insert a keyframe. Use the **Selection** tool to move the Fish2 instance to the lower-left corner of the Stage.

6. Click **Frame 25** of the Fish2 layer and insert a keyframe. Click **Modify** on the menu bar, point to **Transform**, and click **Flip Horizontal**. The fish flips to face the right side.

7. Click **Frame 48** of the Fish2 layer and insert a keyframe. Move the Fish2 instance back to the lower-right corner of the Stage. Next create the motion tweens.

8. Right-click between **Frames 1** and **Frame 24** of the Fish2 layer and select **Create Motion Tween** from the context menu. Right-click between Frames 25 and 48 and select **Create Motion Tween** again. The motion tween animation is complete for the Fish2 instance. Test the animation next.

9. Click **Frame 1** and press the **Enter** key to test the motion tween animation.

The Fish2 instance moves across the Stage and back; however, the nested fin and tail animations do not play. This is because the Fin and Tail symbols are movie clip symbols and their Timelines are independent of the main document's Timeline. In order to view the animations of the fin and tail you need to use the Test Movie or Test Scene commands on the Control menu. The Test Scene command plays the current scene as a SWF file in a Flash player window. Use this command to test the nested movie clip animations.

10. Click **Control** on the menu bar and then click **Test Scene**. The Fish Swimming scene plays in a Flash player window.

    The Fish2 instance moves across the Stage and back as before, but this time its fins and tail also exhibit their animations. To better see these animations you can stop the main document's Timeline from playing. Since the Fin and Tail instances have their own independent Timelines, their animations will continue to play.

11. Press the **Enter** key. The fish stop swimming; however, the fins and tail of the Fish2 instance continue their animations. Press the **Enter** key again to have the fish swim again.

12. Click **File** on the menu bar and click **Close** to close the Flash player window and return to the banner.

13. Save the file.

You have completed the nested movie clip symbol and added it to the Flounders banner. The alternate banner for Flounders Pet Shop is complete. Before Aly presents this second banner to Mr. Flounders, she wants you to to use the Movie Explorer to review all of the elements of the document with her.

Using the Movie Explorer

As your Flash document gets more complex with an increasing number of symbols, text blocks, layers, and scenes, it may become increasingly difficult to manage all of its elements or to easily find specific elements. When working with complex documents you may find it helpful to use the Movie Explorer panel. The Movie Explorer is a panel that displays all of a document's elements in a hierarchical view allowing you to manage and easily locate any of the individual elements. You can use the Movie Explorer to view each of the document's elements, to search for a specific element, to find all instances of a particular symbol, or even to print a list of the document's elements as listed in the Movie Explorer. To open the Movie Explorer you click the Movie Explorer command from the Other Panels submenu, which is located on the Window menu. The panel displays, as shown in Figure 4-35.

| Figure 4-35 | MOVIE EXPLORER |

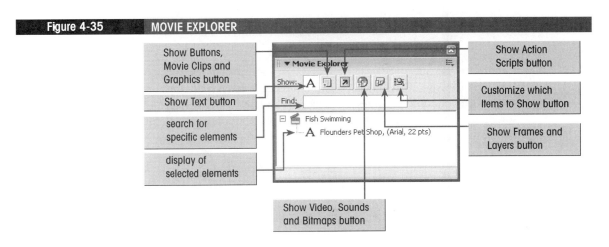

The display options of the Movie Explorer are described in Figure 4-36.

Figure 4-36 | **MOVIE EXPLORER ELEMENTS**

ELEMENT	OPTION	DESCRIPTION
A	Show Text	Displays all occurrences of text blocks in the document
▢	Show Buttons, Movie Clips and Graphics	Displays the symbols used in the document; symbols in the document's library that are not used in the document are not displayed
↗	Show Action Scripts	Displays Action scripts used in the document; Actions scripts will be discussed in a later tutorial
🔊	Show Video, Sounds and Bitmaps	Displays occurrences of video, sounds, and bitmaps used in the document
🎬	Show Frames and Layers	Displays the documents layers and the keyframes within each layer
🔍	Customize which Items to Show	Opens a dialog box where you can select specific items to display
Find text box	Find	Searches for specific elements in the Movie Explorer; displays results in the Movie Explorer

The display options in the Movie Explorer allow you to select which elements to display in the Movie Explorer panel. For example, if you only want to see the text blocks used in your document you can click the Show Text button, but not the other buttons in the Movie Explorer panel. The panel will display each text block with information about the font and font size used in the text block. If you want to see each instance of the symbols used in the document select the Show Buttons, Movie Clips and Graphics button. Each instance used in the current scene is displayed. If you select an instance in the Movie Explorer, information about where the instance is located in your document will be displayed, as shown in Figure 4-37.

Figure 4-37 | **SELECTING A FISH2 INSTANCE IN THE MOVIE EXPLORER**

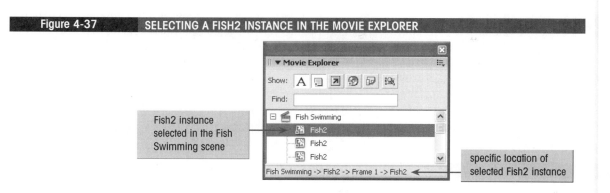

Fish2 instance selected in the Fish Swimming scene

specific location of selected Fish2 instance

Additional options can be selected from the Movie Explorer's options menu. For example, you can specify whether to show the document's elements or the symbol definitions or both. The document's elements include the layers, frames, and instances used in the document. The symbol definitions display below the document's elements with each symbol and its elements listed, as shown in Figure 4-38.

Figure 4-38 ▪ SYMBOL DEFINITIONS IN THE MOVIE EXPLORER

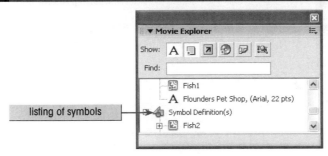

listing of symbols

The following are some of the other options available on the Movie Explorer's options menu.

- Go to Location – moves the playhead to the keyframe the selected instance resides in
- Find in Library – displays the selected symbol in the Library panel
- Show Movie Elements – displays the document's elements such as its layers, frames, and symbol instances
- Show Symbol Definitions – displays the symbols used in the document; also displays the elements of the symbols
- Show All Scenes – displays the elements and symbols for all scenes in the document not just the current scene
- Print – prints a list of the contents of the Movie Explorer; only those elements displayed in the Movie Explorer are printed

Because the banner you have created for the Flounders Pet Shop has increased in the number of scenes, layers, and symbols, Aly wants you to use the Movie Explorer to show her all of the its elements and view how all the various symbol instances used throughout the document are organized.

To use the Movie Explorer to examine the banner's elements:

1. Click **Window** on the menu bar, point to **Other Panels**, and click then **Movie Explorer**. The Movie Explorer panel opens.

2. If necessary, click the **Show Text** button [A] to select it. If necessary, click the other Show buttons to deselect them.

3. Click the **Movie Explorer** options menu control ▥ and, if necessary, click **Show Movie Elements** from the options menu to select it. If necessary, click ▥ again to select **Show Symbol Definitions** and **Show All Scenes**.

4. To see more of the elements in the Movie Explorer window, increase its size by dragging the bottom edge of the panel window down. If necessary, click the plus sign next to a scene name to expand its contents. The Movie Explorer displays all of the text blocks for all of the document's scenes as well as the document's symbols, as shown in Figure 4-39.

Figure 4-39   MOVIE EXPLORER PANEL DISPLAYING TEXT BLOCKS

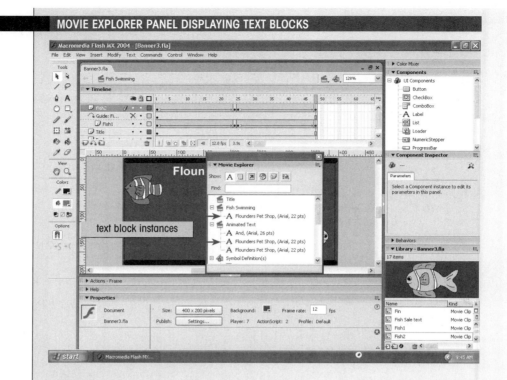

5. Click the **Show Frames and Layers** button 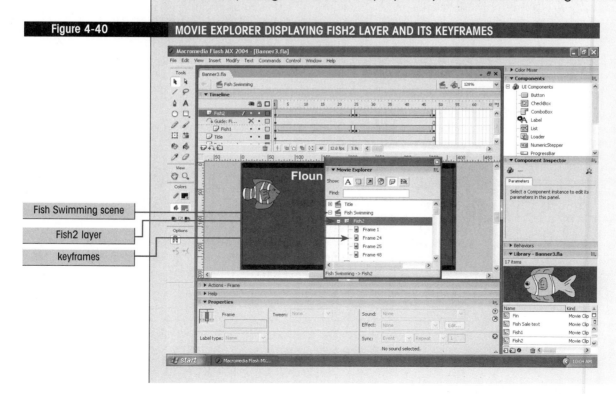 to select it. If necessary, click the minus sign next to the Title scene to collapse its display. Also, if necessary, click the plus sign next to the Fish Swimming scene to expand its display.

6. Click the **Fish2** layer name under the Fish Swimming scene and, if necessary, click the plus sign next to it to display its keyframes, as shown in Figure 4-40.

Figure 4-40   MOVIE EXPLORER DISPLAYING FISH2 LAYER AND ITS KEYFRAMES

7. Click the **Show Buttons, Movie Clips and Graphics** button ▣ to select it. Select the **Fish2** instance in Frame 1 of the Fish2 layer, as shown in Figure 4-41.

Figure 4-41   FISH2 INSTANCE IN FRAME 1 OF FISH2 LAYER

8. Scroll the Movie Explorer panel and select the **Fish1** instance under Frame 1 of the Fish1 layer.

9. Click the **Movie Explorer** options menu control ☰ and click **Go to Symbol Definition**. The Movie Explorer shows the Fish1 symbol under the Symbol Definitions area.

10. Click ☰ again and click **Find in Library**. The Fish1 symbol is displayed in the Library panel.

11. Close the Movie Explorer.

Aly thinks the document elements look great and that they are well organized. Before she shows it to Mr. Flounders, view it in a Flash player window.

To view the finished banner in a Flash player window:

1. Click **Control** on the menu bar and click **Test Movie**. The banner display in a Flash player window, playing each of its scenes.

2. Click **File** on the menu bar and click **Close** to close the window and return to the Flash document.

3. Save and close the Banner3.fla file.

In this session, you learned how to use onion skinning to display the contents of more than one frame at one time on the Stage. This is useful when working with complex animations. You also learned how to create nested movie clips which contain instances of other movie clips within their Timelines. Finally, you learned how to use the Movie Explorer to manage the elements of your documents as they increase in complexity.

Session 4.3 QUICK CHECK

1. How can you change the position of the onion skin markers in the Timeline header?

2. How can onion skinning help you when working with a complex animation?

3. What is a nested movie clip?

4. Why will the animations of movie clips embedded in a nested movie clip not play when you test them within the Flash program window?

5. How can you use the Movie Explorer to find the definition of a particular symbol?

REVIEW ASSIGNMENTS

Aly has showed Mr. Flounders the two banners you created for the Pet Shop's Web site. After reviewing the two banners, he has decided to use the second banner which was created in this tutorial. He does want a few changes made, and Aly describes these to you. Aly asks you to change the second fish in the Fish Swimming scene to swim along a curved path similar to the first fish. In this same scene, you are to add a new mask effect to the Flounders Pet Shop title. The effect will make the text block appear gradually from left to right. She also asks you to create a new animation of a small sign in the shape of a bubble that contains rotating text inside. Two instances of the bubble sign will be animated to move in the Animated Text scene.

If necessary, start Flash, and then do the following:

1. Open the **Banner3.fla** document which you created in the tutorial from the Tutorial.04\Tutorial folder included with your Data Files. Save the file with the new name **Banner4.fla** in the Tutorial.04\Review folder included with your Data Files.

2. If necessary, switch to the Fish Swimming scene. Add a new motion guide layer above the Fish2 layer and draw a path that curves from the lower-left corner of the Stage up to the center of the Stage and then back down to the lower-right corner. Attach the Fish2 instance at Frame 1 to the lower-right endpoint of the path. Then attach the Fish2 instance at Frames 24, 25, and 48 so that it swims along the path as it goes from the right to the left and back. Make sure the fish orients itself to the path. Hide the contents of the guide layer.

3. Add a new layer above the Title layer. Change the name of the new layer to **Mask** and change its type to Mask. Make sure the Title layer's type is changed to Masked and that it is indented below the Mask layer.

4. Unlock the Mask layer and draw a rectangle that covers the entire Flounders Pet Shop text block. The rectangle's width should be the same width as the text block and its height should only be as high as the text block. Do not include a stroke with the rectangle. The fill can be any color. Convert this rectangle to a movie clip symbol and name it Rectangle.

5. Insert a keyframe at Frame 24 of the Mask layer. Select Frame 1 and move the rectangle to the left of the text block to reveal the text block. Create a motion tween between Frames 1 and 24. The rectangle should move from left to right to gradually cover the text block. Lock the Mask layer and test the mask animation effect. The text block should appear gradually from left to right.

6. Create a new movie clip symbol and name it Rotating Text. In symbol-editing mode, add a text block to the center of the symbol's Stage. Use Arial for the font, 12 for the font size, and white for the text color. Also apply the bold and italic styles to the text. Type **Fish** in the text block. Set the text block's X and Y coordinates to 0 to center it.

7. Insert a keyframe at Frame 10 and create a motion tween between Frames 1 and 10. Set the text to rotate clockwise 360 degrees one time. Insert a keyframe at Frame 11 and change the text to **Tank**. Add another keyframe at Frame 20 and create a motion tween between Frames 11 and 20. Set this text block to rotate counter-clockwise 360 degrees one time.

8. Insert a keyframe at Frame 21 and change the text to **Sale**. Add another keyframe at Frame 30 and create a motion tween between Frames 21 and 30. Set this text block to rotate clockwise 360 degrees one time. Exit symbol-editing mode.

9. Create a new movie clip symbol and name it **Bubble Sign**. In symbol-editing mode, add a small circle to the center of the symbol's Stage. Use blue (#0099FF) for the fill of the circle and do not add a stroke. Use the Property inspector to make the circle 40 pixels wide and 40 pixels high. Also, set its X and Y coordinates to 0 to center it. Drag an instance of the Rotating Text symbol to the center of the circle. Exit symbol-editing mode.

10. Switch to the Animated Text scene. Insert a new layer and name it **Bubble Sign1**. On this layer drag an instance of the Bubble Sign symbol to the lower-left side of the work area just to the left of the Stage. Insert a keyframe at Frame 20 and create a motion tween between Frames 1 and 20. Use the Property inspector to set the X and Y coordinates for the Bubble Sign instances. At Frame 1 set the X coordinate to -50 and the Y coordinate to 150. At Frame 20 set the X coordinate to 50 and the Y coordinate to 150.

11. Insert a new layer and name it **Bubble Sign2**. On this layer drag an instance of the Bubble Sign symbol to the lower-right side of the work area just to the right of the Stage. Insert a keyframe at Frame 20 and create a motion tween between Frames 1 and 20. At Frame 1 set the X coordinate to 450 and the Y coordinate to 150. At Frame 20 set the X coordinate to 350 and the Y coordinate to 150. Test the new animations for the document using the Test Movie command.

12. Test, save, and then close the revised banner.

CASE PROBLEMS

Case 1. Developing a New Animated Banner for Sandy's Party Center Sandy Rodriquez, owner of Sandy's Party Center is very pleased about the banner developed for the store's Web site. She asks John Rossini about creating a new Flash document that will serve as an advertisement on the store's Web site. In particular she would like text information promoting the store's services.

John asks you to create the advertisement by starting with a document he has developed. He instructs you to add new text messages promoting the grand opening sale and the services provided by the store. The store's name will be animated so that it displays one letter at a time. After the store's name appears, the next text message will fade-in. Another text message will appear and will increase in size and change in color. There will also be several instances of the balloon and confetti symbols added.

If necessary, start Macromedia Flash and then do the following:

1. Open the **partyad.fla** file located in the Tutorial.04\Cases folder included with your Data Files. Save the document as **partyad2.fla** in the Tutorial.04\Cases folder.

2. Extend the layers in the Timeline so that they each have 60 frames.

3. Select the text block in Frame 1 of the Title layer. Convert the text block to individual text blocks, one for each letter. Distribute the letters to individual layers. Move the keyframes for each of the letters so that each letter starts one frame after the previous letter. The first letter, S, starts in Frame 1. The second letter, a, starts in Frame 2. The third letter, n, starts in Frame 3, and so on. The letters will appear one at a time to form the complete store name.

4. Rename the Title layer to **Sale**. Insert a keyframe at Frame 15 of this layer and in this frame drag an instance of the Sale symbol from the Library panel to the center of the Stage. Animate the text block instance to fade in over the next 10 frames. To do this, insert a keyframe at Frame 25 on the same layer. Create a motion tween between Frames 15 and 25 and then at Frame 15, change the Alpha amount of the Sale instance to 0%. This will cause the text block to fade in throughout the animation.

5. To further animate the Sale text block, add a keyframe at Frame 35 and also at Frame 45. Create motion tweens between Frames 25 and 35 and also between Frames 35 and 45. At Frame 35 change the tint of the Sale text instance to red. The text will change from black to red between Frames 25 and 35 and then change back to black between Frames 35 and 45.

6. Insert a new layer and name it **Supplies**. On this layer, insert a keyframe at Frame 25 and drag an instance of the Supplies symbol to the lower part of the Stage. Insert keyframes at Frames 35 and 45. Create a motion tween between Frames 25 and 35. Select Frame 25 and then use the Transform panel to reduce the size of the Supplies instance to 50% of its original size. Also in Frame 25, change the Alpha amount of the instance to 0%. The text block will fade in as it increases in size from Frame 25 and 35.

7. Insert another keyframe at Frame 40 of the Supplies layer and reduce the size of the Supplies instance in this frame to 80% of its original size. Create motion tweens between Frames 35 and 40 and also between Frames 40 and 45. The text block will decrease in size slightly in the first motion tween and increase back to its original size in the second motion tween.

8. Insert a new layer above the Background layer and name it **Balloon1**. Drag an instance of the Balloon symbol to the lower-left side of the Stage. Insert a keyframe at Frame 30 and create a motion tween between Frames 1 and 30. Add a motion guide layer above the Balloon1 layer and make sure the Balloon1 layer becomes the guided layer. In the Guide: Balloon1 layer draw a smooth wavy line from the lower-left side of the Stage to the upper-right side for the balloon to follow. Attach the balloon to the line so that it follows the path.

9. Insert another layer above the Background layer and name it **Balloon2**. Drag an instance of the Balloon symbol to the lower-right corner of the Stage. Insert a keyframe at Frame 30 and create a motion tween between Frames 1 and 30. Add a motion guide layer above the Balloon2 layer and make sure the Balloon2 layer becomes the guided layer. In the Guide: Balloon2 layer draw a smooth wavy line from the lower-right corner to the upper-left corner of the Stage. Attach the balloon to the line so that it follows the path.

10. To complete the elements of this document, add several instances of the confetti symbol to the Background layer.

11. Test the animation and then save and close the file.

Case 2. Creating an Advertising Banner for River City Music Janet Meyers, store manager for River City Music, has been very pleased with the recently developed graphics for her company's Web site. She meets with Alex Smith and asks that a new advertising banner be developed. In particular, she would like to see some new animations that highlight the River City Music company name. She also would like several text messages displayed on the banner promoting the company's services.

Alex asks you to help him create the new advertisement based on a banner that he started to develop. He instructs you to use his draft and to add a spotlight effect where the spotlight starts small at the center of the banner and increases to reveal the banner. He also asks you to develop a special text effect for the store name where the letters increase in size one after the other to give it a pulsating effect. Finally, he instructs you to add the text messages promoting the company.

If necessary, start Flash, and then do the following:

1. Open the **musicad.fla** file located in the Tutorial.04\Cases folder included with your Data Files. Save the document as **musicad2.fla** in the Tutorial.04\Cases folder.

2. Create a new movie clip symbol and name it **Circle**. In symbol-editing mode, draw a circle at the center of the Stage. The circle should have a white fill and no stroke. Make its dimensions 40 pixels wide and 40 pixels high and set its X and Y coordinates to 0. Exit symbol-editing mode.

3. Extend the Company Name layer to 20 frames. Insert a new layer named **Mask** above the Company Name layer. Select Frame 1 of the Mask layer and drag an instance of the Circle symbol from the Library panel to the center of the Stage. Set the instance's X and Y coordinates to 150 each to center it on the Stage.

4. Insert a keyframe at Frame 20 of the Mask layer. Select the Circle instance at Frame 20 and change its size to 300 pixels wide by 300 pixels high. Create a motion tween between Frames 1 and 20.

5. Select all of the frames on the Mask layer, then copy the frames to the Clipboard. Insert a new layer above the Mask layer and select all of its frames. Paste the copied frames to the new layer. Rename the new layer **Circle**.

6. Temporarily hide the contents of the Mask layer to work with the contents of the Circle layer. Click Frame 1 of the Circle layer, select the Circle instance on the Stage and change its Alpha amount to 40%. Click Frame 20 of the Circle layer, select the Circle instance and change its Alpha amount to 40%. Move the Circle layer so that it is below the Company Name layer.

7. Right-click the Mask layer and change its type to Mask. Make sure the Company Name layer is masked. Test the animation. The mask gradually reveals the company name. The motion tween on the Circle layer displays the dimmed circle to coincide with the circle on the Mask layer to create the special effect.

8. Hide the Mask layer temporarily and select the company name text block in the Company Name layer. Copy the text block. Insert a new layer and name it **Name**. Insert a keyframe at Frame 20 of the Name layer and in this frame paste the company name text block.

9. Insert a layer folder above the Name layer and then move the Name layer to the new folder. Rename the layer folder **Letters**.

10. Select the text block at Frame 20 of the Name layer and convert the text to individual letters. Then distribute the letters to individual layers. Delete the empty Name layer. When the letters are distributed to individual layers, the keyframes for each letter are moved to Frame 1of their respective layers. Move them all to Frame 20 by selecting all Frame 1's of the individual letter layers and dragging them all to start in Frame 20. This is where the individual letters animation will begin.

11. Extend all of the layers, except the Mask and Company layers, by adding regular frames at Frame 100 of each layer.

Explore ▷ 12. To make each letter change in size for a brief moment you will add two keyframes to each layer where the size of the letter is increased slightly in the first of the two new keyframes. So for the R layer, add a keyframe at Frame 22 and another at Frame 24. Then use the Transform panel to change the size of the instance in Frame 22 to be 130% larger. For the next letter in layer i, add a keyframe at Frame 26 and another at Frame 28. Increase the size of the instance in Frame 26 to 130%. For the letter v in layer v, add a keyframe at Frame 30 and another at Frame 32. Then increase the size of the letter in Frame 30 to 130%.

Explore ▷ 13. Continue Step 12 for each letter, starting two frames after the previous letter. The last letter in layer c (for the c in Music) will have keyframes added at Frames 74 and 76. Unhide the Company Name layer that was hidden earlier and then test the animation. The individual letters should increase in size one at a time after the mask effect.

14. Insert three new layers above the Letters folder and name them **Text1**, **Text2**, and **Text3**. Insert a keyframe at Frame 20 of the Text1 layer. Create a new text block centered at about 50 pixels from the top of the Stage. Use the Monotype Corsiva font, with a font size of 20 and text color of black. Use bold and italic styles. Type **Piano Lessons!** in the text block.

15. Convert the text block to a symbol and name it **Text1**. Insert a keyframe at Frame 25 of the Text1 layer and create a motion tween between Frames 20 and 25. At Frame 20, reduce the size of the Text1 instance to 50% of its original size. The text will increase in size throughout the motion tween.

16. Insert a keyframe of Frame 25 of the Text2 layer. Create a new text block in the work area to the left of the Stage about 90 pixels from the top. Use the same text settings as in Step 13 and type **Musical Instruments!** in this text block.

17. Convert the text block to a symbol and name it **Text2**. Insert a keyframe at Frame 30 of the Text2 layer and create a motion tween between Frames 25 and 30. At Frame 30 move the text instance to the Stage about 90 pixels from the top and centered on the banner. The text will fly in from the left of the Stage throughout the motion tween.

18. Create one more text motion tween in the Text3 layer between Frames 30 and 35. Create a text block with the words **Sheet Music!** in the work area to the right of the Stage about 200 pixels from the top. This text block should fly in from the right of the Stage to the center of the banner about 200 pixels from the top.

19. Insert a new layer above the Text3 layer and name it **Note1**. Insert a keyframe at Frame 35. Drag an instance of the Note1 symbol to the upper-left corner of the banner, staying within the large circle. Add another keyframe at Frame 40 and move the Note1 instance towards the bottom so that it is below the Sheet Music text. Create a motion tween between Frames 35 and 40 and have the Note1 instance rotate clockwise twice as it moves from the top to the bottom.

20. Insert a new layer above the Note1 layer and name it **Keys**. Insert a keyframe at Frame 40. Drag an instance of the Piano Keys symbol to the top of the banner right above the Piano Lessons text. Add another keyframe at Frame 45 and move the Piano Keys instance towards the bottom so that it is below the Sheet Music text and to the right of the Note1 instance. Create a motion tween between Frames 40 and 45 so that the Piano Keys instance moves from the top to the bottom.

21. Insert a new layer above the Keys layer and name it **Note2**. Insert a keyframe at Frame 45. Drag an instance of the Note2 symbol to the upper-right side of the banner, staying within the large circle. Add another keyframe at Frame 50 and move the Note2 instance towards the bottom so that it is below the Sheet Music text and to the right of the Piano Keys instance. Create a motion tween between Frames 45 and 50 and have the Note2 instance rotate clockwise twice as it moves from the top to the bottom.

22. Test the banner's animation to make all animations play correctly.

23. Save and close the banner.

Explore   *Case 3. Developing a Web Ad for Sonny's Auto Center* Sonny's Auto Center is expanding and opening a new center at a new location. To advertise the new location and promote his business, Sonny has started a new marketing campaign. As part of this campaign he wants to place an ad on the local newspaper's Web site. He has been pleased with the work Amanda Lester has done in creating various graphics using Flash and he asks her to develop the new ad.

Amanda asks you to help her create the ad banner. You will create several animations including one where the letters in the word "Sonny's" fall into place followed by an animation of the words Auto Center to create the title for the ad. Then several animated text blocks will move into place on the ad, followed by a graphic of the word Autos that will move across the ad banner simulating a car. The graphic will have animated tires.

If necessary, start Macromedia Flash, and then do the following:

1. Create a new document of 400 by 400 pixels in size and a white background. Save this file as **sonnyad.fla** in the **Tutorial.04\Cases** folder included with your Data Files.

2. Draw a rectangle that covers the entire Stage. Do not include a stroke and use a dark blue color (#000099) for the fill. If necessary, use the Property inspector to set the width of the rectangle to 400 and the height to 400 and position the rectangle so that the Stage is completely covered. Then rename Layer 1 to **Background**, extend this layer to Frame 120 and lock the layer.

3. Create horizontal guidelines at 50 pixels and at 200 pixels from the top of the Stage.

4. Insert a new layer named **Title1** and create a text block with the word **Sonny's**. Use white for the text color, Impact for the font, 40 for the font size, and apply bold and italic styles. Center the word on the guideline 200 pixels from the top of the Stage.

5. Insert a layer folder above the Title1 layer. Name this folder **Sonny's text**. Move the Title1 layer to the new layer folder. Then select the Title1 text block, break it apart and distribute the individual letters to separate layers. The new layers for the letters should be inside the layer folder. Delete the Title1 layer.

6. Convert each of the letters into symbols with movie clip behavior. Use the following names for the symbols to match the letter it represents: S1, O, N1, N2, Y, Apostrophe, and S2.

7. Each of the letters will be animated to drop in from the top part of the Stage to its current location 200 pixels from the top. The letters will move one at a time, rotating, and fading in as they move to form the word Sonny's. The first letter will start in Frame 1 and every other letter will start every 10 frames. Move each of the letters' keyframes that are in Frame 1of their respective layers to start every 10 frames. The keyframes should be moved to the following frames: S – Frame 1; o – Frame 11; n – Frame 21; n – Frame 31; y – Frame 41; ' (apostrophe) – Frame 51; s – Frame 61. Be sure to keep each letter in its own layer.

8. Insert ending keyframes for each letter in its corresponding layer as follows: S – Frame 10; o – Frame 20; n – Frame 30; n – Frame 40; y – Frame 50; ' (apostrophe) – Frame 60; s – Frame 70. Then create motion tweens between the two keyframes on each layer.

9. For each letter, select its first keyframe and move the letter to the guideline 50 pixels from the top of the Stage. This is where the letters will start. Each letter will drop in one at a time to form the word Sonny's at the center of the Stage. At the beginning keyframe for each letter, also change the Alpha amount to 0% for the letter instance and use the Property inspector to add a clockwise rotation in each motion tween. Each letter should rotate twice. Test the animations. The letters for the word Sonny's will drop into place one at a time. They will fade in and rotate as they fall. Collapse the Sonny's text folder to make it easier to work with the other layers in the Timeline.

10. Insert another layer above the Sonny's text layer folder and name it **Title2**. Insert a keyframe at Frame 71. Create a text block using the same type settings as in Step 4. Type **Auto Center** in the text block. Center this text block on the guideline 50 pixels from the top of the Stage. The Auto Center text block should move from the top of the Stage to right below the Sonny's text at the center of the Stage.

11. Convert the Auto Center text block to a movie clip symbol and name it **Title2**. Insert a keyframe at Frame 80 of the Title2 layer. Create a motion tween on this layer between Frames 71 and 80. Select the Title2 instance at Frame 71 and change its Alpha amount to 0%. Select Frame 80 of the layer and move the Title2 instance so that it is centered below the Sonny's text. The Auto Center text should move from its initial position down to below the Sonny's text and should fade in as it moves into position.

12. Insert a new layer and name it **Text1**. Insert a keyframe at Frame 80 of this layer and then create a text block in this frame. The text should be white, use Impact for the font, and 30 for the font size. It should be bold, but not italic. Place the text block on the work area to the left of the Stage about 50 pixels from the top. Type **Great Deals!** in this text block. Convert the text block to a symbol and name it **Text1**.

13. Insert a keyframe at Frame 85 of the Text1 layer and move the text block to the center of the Stage, keeping it about 50 pixels from the top. Create a motion tween between Frames 80 and 85 so that the Text1 instance moves in from the left of the Stage.

14. Insert a new layer and name it **Text2**. Insert a keyframe at Frame 85 and create a text block using the same settings used in Step 12. Place the text block in the work area to the right of the Stage about 370 pixels from the top. Type **Great Service!** in this text block. Convert the text block to a symbol and name it **Text2**.

15. Insert a keyframe at Frame 90 of the Text2 layer and move the text block to the center of the Stage, keeping it about 370 pixels from the top. Create a motion tween between Frames 85 and 90 so that the Text2 instance moves in from the right of the Stage.

16. To create a graphic that will simulate a car moving across the Stage you will start by creating a rotating wheel symbol. This symbol will then be embedded in the car graphic. Create a new movie clip symbol and name it **Rotating Wheel**. In symbol-editing mode, use the Oval tool to draw circle at the center of the Stage. The circle should be about 22 pixels in diameter. Use a black stroke color with a stroke height of 2 and a white fill color. If necessary, set the circle's X and Y coordinates to 0 so that it is centered on the Stage.

17. Use the Line tool to draw a line horizontally across the center of the circle and another vertically across the center. Keep the lines inside the circle. These lines represent the spokes for the wheel. Select both the circle and the lines at the same time and convert them to a movie clip symbol. Name this symbol **Wheel**.

18. While still in symbol-editing mode for the Rotating Wheel symbol, insert a keyframe at Frame 12 and then create a motion tween between Frames 1 and 12. In Frame 1 set the Wheel instance to rotate clockwise one time. The Rotating Wheel symbol is complete. Exit symbol-editing mode.

19. Create a new movie clip symbol and name it **Auto**. In symbol-editing mode, create a text block using Impact for the font, 40 for the font size, and red for the font color. Make the text bold and italic. Type the word **AUTO** in all uppercase.

20. Use the Line tool to draw a short horizontal line about 30 pixels wide using a stroke color of red and a stroke height of 1. Draw the line about five pixels to the left of the letter A. Create three copies of this line and place the lines to the left of the letter A. Each line should be about the same distance from the letter A and they should be equally spaced from each other. The lines will add to the effect of the AUTO text moving.

21. Now drag an instance of the Rotating Wheel instance to the Stage and place it right below the letters A and U in AUTO. Drag another instance and place it below the letters T and O. These instances will be the wheels for the AUTO. The Auto symbol is complete. Exit symbol-editing mode.

22. Insert a new layer above the Text2 layer and name it **Auto**. Insert a keyframe at Frame 70 and drag an instance of the Auto symbol in the work area to the lower-left corner of the Stage. Insert another keyframe at Frame 100 and then create a motion tween between Frames 70 and 100.

23. Insert a motion guide layer above the Auto layer. Make sure the Auto layer becomes the guided layer. On the Guide: Auto layer insert a keyframe at Frame 70. Use the Pencil tool to draw a smooth line starting from where the Auto instance is located and ending at the center of the Stage above the Sonny's text. This is the path the Auto graphic will follow. Make sure the Auto instance is attached to the beginning of the line at Frame 70 and to the end of the line at Frame 100. Click the Orient to path option in the Property inspector at the beginning of the motion tween.

24. Test your document's animation.

25. Save and close the file.

Case 4. Creating an Animated Banner for LAL Financial Christopher Perez, head of Marketing at LAL Financial Services meets with webmaster Elizabeth Danehill to discuss the development of a new advertisement banner they can use to place in various Web sites promoting the company. The ad will contain the company's name, an animation of a dollar sign going around the name, and several graphics containing text messages.

Elizabeth asks you to create the new ad with instructions from the graphics designer, Mia Jones.

If necessary, start Macromedia Flash, and then do the following:

1. Create a new document of 250 by 250 pixels in size and a dark green (#006633) background. Save this file as **LALad.fla** in the **Tutorial.04\Cases** folder included with your Data Files.

2. Create a text block at the center of the Stage. Use Garamond for the font, 40 for the font size, black for the text color, and make the text bold. Type **LAL Financial Services** in the text block where each word is in a separate line and all three lines are centered within the text. Change the name of Layer 1 to **Text** and extend the layer to Frame 60.

3. Insert a new layer and name it **Mask**. On this layer create a rectangle with a black fill and no stroke. Make the rectangle the same size as the text block and draw it so that it completely covers the text block. Select the rectangle on the Stage and convert it to a movie clip symbol. Name the symbol **Mask rectangle**.

4. Insert a keyframe at Frame 30 of the Mask layer and create a motion tween between Frames 1 and 30. At Frame 1 move the rectangle above the text block. The rectangle will move from above the text block down to cover the text block. The rectangle mask will reveal the text block as it moves over it.

5. Change the Mask layer's type to Mask. Make sure the Text layer becomes a masked layer. Test the mask animation to see the text block revealed as the mask goes over it.

6. Unlock the Text layer and select the text block in Frame 1. Copy the text block to the Clipboard. Lock the Text layer again. Insert a new layer and name it **Gray text**. If necessary, move the Gray text layer to below the Text layer. The Gray text layer should not be masked. At Frame 1 of the Gray text layer use the Paste in Place command to place the text block in the same relative position as the original in the Text layer.

7. Select the text block in the Gray text layer and change its color to gray (#CCCCCC). The gray text will show first and will then be replaced by the black text as the rectangle mask moves over the black text.

8. Insert a new layer above the Mask layer and name it **Rectangle**. Draw a rectangle using gray (#CCCCCC) for the stroke color, no fill, and rounded corners. Use 20 for the corner radius points. The rectangle should be larger than the text block so that the text block is completely inside the rectangle.

9. Insert a new layer above the Rectangle layer and name it **Dollar sign**. In Frame 1 create a text block at the bottom of the Stage. Use Arial for the font, 40 for the font size, gray (#CCCCCC) for the text color, and apply the bold style. Type **$** in this text block. Select the text block and convert it to a movie clip symbol. Name the symbol **Dollar sign**. Insert a keyframe at Frame 60 of the Dollar sign layer and create a motion tween between Frames 1 and 60.

Explore   10. You will animate the Dollar sign instance to move around the text block following the rectangle as a path. To do so first copy the existing rectangle in Frame 1 of the Rectangle layer. Then insert a motion guide layer above the Dollar sign layer. Make sure the Dollar sign layer becomes the guided layer. In Frame 1 of the Guide: Dollar sign layer use the Paste in Place command to paste the copy of the rectangle in the same relative position as the original rectangle.

Explore   11. Hide the contents of the Rectangle layer to work with the copied rectangle in the guide layer. Use the Eraser tool with a small eraser size to erase a small section of the rectangle in the middle of its bottom side.

12. In Frame 1 of the Dollar sign layer, attach the Dollar sign instance to the bottom of the rectangle at the left endpoint that was created by the eraser. At Frame 60 of the Dollar sign layer, attach the Dollar sign instance to the bottom of the rectangle at the right endpoint.

13. Hide the contents of the Guide: Dollar sign layer and unhide the contents of the Rectangle layer. Test the animation to see the Dollar sign instance move around the banner following the rectangle path.

14. Create a new movie clip symbol and name it Text animation. In symbol-editing mode create a text block using Arial as the font, 12 for the font size, and white for the text color. Do not use bold or italic styles, but do center align the text within the text block. Type **Mortgages** in the text block and then center the text block on the Stage by setting its X and Y coordinates to 0.

15. Insert a keyframe at Frame 11 and change the text in the text block to **Bank Loans.** Insert another keyframe at Frame 21 and change the text again to **Investments**. The text block will change every 10 frames. Exit symbol-editing mode.

16. Create a new movie clip symbol and name it **Button**. In symbol-editing mode create a rectangle with rounded corners at the center of the Stage. Use black for the stroke color and dark gray (#666666) for the fill color. The stroke height should be set to 1 and the corner radius points should be 10. The size of the rectangle should be 100 pixels wide and 25 pixels high. Select all of the rectangle and set its X and Y coordinates to 0 to center it on the Stage. Then drag an instance of the Text animation symbol to the center of the rectangle. Exit symbol-editing mode.

17. Insert a new layer, name it **Button**, and move it so that it is below the Gray text layer. In Frame 1 of this layer drag an instance of the Button symbol to the top of the Stage. Place its left edge about 70 pixels from the left of the Stage. Insert a keyframe at Frame 30 of the Button layer and create a motion tween between Frames 1 and 30. At Frame 30 move the Button instance so that it is at the bottom of the Stage and so that its left edge is still about 70 pixels from the left of the Stage. The Button instance will move from the top to the bottom of the Stage. Test the document's animation in a separate Flash player window to see the Text animation which is nested inside the Button movie clip.

18. Save and close the file.

QUICK | CHECK ANSWERS

Session 4.1

1. You can insert a motion guide layer by using the Motion Guide command on the Insert menu or by clicking the Motion Guide button in the Timeline.

2. To create a path in a motion guide layer you can use the Pencil, Pen, Oval, Rectangle, or Brush tool.

3. To see the effect that a mask layer has on a masked layer when testing an animation within the program window lock both layers.

4. False. Text can be used as a mask in a mask layer.

5. When a guide layer is used together with a motion tween it is called a motion guide layer.

6. The Orient to path option is used to make a motion tweened object orient itself to the slope of the path it is following.

7. In a mask layer animation, the contents of the masked layer are revealed when the object in the mask layer moves over it.

Session 4.2

1. Text may be animated to move from one part of the Stage to another. It may also be animated to rotate, fade in or fade out, and increase or decrease in size. You can also animate the individual letters of a text block to create special effects.

2. To apply a shape tween to a text block you must first break it apart twice.

3. If you apply the Distribute to Layers command to a group of selected text blocks the new layers will be named according to the text in each text block.

4. To animate individual letters, each letter must be on its own layer because you cannot have more than one object or symbol on a layer with a motion tween.

5. It is a good idea to have all of the individual letter layers inside a new folder so that they will be easier to work with and organize in the Timeline. You can also collapse the folder to hide its layers and make it easier to work with the other layers.

Session 4.3

1. You can change the position of the onion skin markers on the Timeline header by dragging them left or right with the mouse pointer. You can also use the Modify Onion Markers menu to change how many frames will be onion skinned.

2. Onion skinning can help you when working with a complex animation because you can see the contents of the frames before and after the current frame. This helps you compare what the current frame contents should be in comparison to the other frames.

3. A nested movie clip contains other movie clips in its Timeline that may have their own animations in their respective Timelines. Any change you apply to a nested movie clip in the main Timeline will also affect the movie clips it contains.

4. The animations of movie clips embedded in a nested movie clip will not play within the Flash program window because each has its own Timeline that is independent of the document's main Timeline.

5. You can select an instance of a symbol in the Movie Explorer and then use the Go to Symbol Definition command on the options menu to find its definition.

OBJECTIVES

In this tutorial you will:

- Create buttons and add them to a document

- Learn about behaviors and how to use the Behaviors panel to add behaviors to buttons

- Use the Behaviors panel to add behaviors to frames

- Learn about different types of sound effects and how to acquire sounds for your documents

- Add sound effects to buttons

- Add a background sound to a document

ADDING
BUTTONS, BEHAVIORS, AND SOUNDS

Making the Flounders Pet Shop Banner Interactive

CASE

Admiral Web Design

The staff of Admiral Web Design holds a meeting every week to discuss the status of projects they are working on for their clients. During a recent meeting, Aly presented the results of the two animated banners developed for their client, Flounders Pet Shop. Everyone was impressed with the work done to develop the banners and with the capabilities of the Macromedia Flash program. They were able to see what can be created with the program, and they were excited about how their other client Web sites could be improved with the use of animation.

Joe has contacted Aly to request a new banner for a fish supplies page being developed for his shop's Web site. He wants the new banner to have a similar design to the animated banner created in Tutorial 4 and to include a background sound in addition to animation. Aly suggests that because the banner will be on a page where visitors may have to spend some time reviewing the available fish supplies, it may be a good idea to give the visitor the option to turn off the animation and the background sound. This can keep the visitor from getting distracted while they view the information on the page. She suggests adding several buttons to the banner to control the animation and to mute the sound. She also suggests that the buttons can include their own sound effects to help the visitor know when the button has been clicked. Joe agrees to Aly's suggestions and approves the development of the new banner.

Aly then holds a planning meeting with you to discuss the requested banner for the fish supplies Web page. In discussing the new banner requested by Joe, Aly explains how Flash enables you to add buttons to a movie to allow the user to control it. Buttons can be an easy way to make an animation interactive and they can take many forms, can include sound effects, and can even change in appearance or behavior when the user places the mouse pointer over them. Aly also mentions that she has recently seen some Web sites that use background sounds and thinks the same can be added to the banner. She has developed the initial design of the banner and gives you a printout with instructions on what needs to be done to complete it. See Figure 5-1.

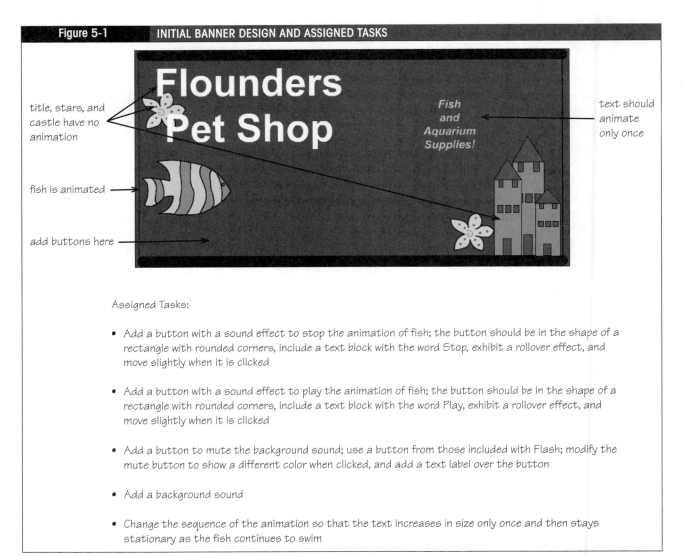

Figure 5-1   INITIAL BANNER DESIGN AND ASSIGNED TASKS

title, stars, and castle have no animation

fish is animated

add buttons here

text should animate only once

Assigned Tasks:

- Add a button with a sound effect to stop the animation of fish; the button should be in the shape of a rectangle with rounded corners, include a text block with the word Stop, exhibit a rollover effect, and move slightly when it is clicked

- Add a button with a sound effect to play the animation of fish; the button should be in the shape of a rectangle with rounded corners, include a text block with the word Play, exhibit a rollover effect, and move slightly when it is clicked

- Add a button to mute the background sound; use a button from those included with Flash; modify the mute button to show a different color when clicked, and add a text label over the button

- Add a background sound

- Change the sequence of the animation so that the text increases in size only once and then stays stationary as the fish continues to swim

In this tutorial, you will continue your training in Macromedia Flash by learning how to create buttons, including buttons that change in response to the mouse pointer. You will add buttons to a document and then add behaviors to the buttons so they can be used to control the animation. You will also learn how to change the way the animation plays by using frame behaviors, and finally you will add sound effects to the buttons and a background sound to the animation.

SESSION 5.1

In this session, you will create buttons that will be used to control the animation of the Flounders Pet Shop fish supplies banner. You will use a button from a library of existing buttons that are included with Flash, and you will also create your own buttons. You will align these buttons using the Align panel, and you will review the visual effects of the buttons.

Buttons

An exciting feature of Macromedia Flash is its ability to make a movie interactive. **Interactive** means that the user has some level of control over the movie, such as being able to stop or play its animation. Adding interaction to a movie draws the viewer in because the viewer is able to do more than passively watch the movie. One of the easiest ways to do this is to add buttons that perform an action. **Buttons** are symbols that contain a Timeline with only four frames. Each frame represents a different state of the button and may contain different content, as shown in Figure 5-2.

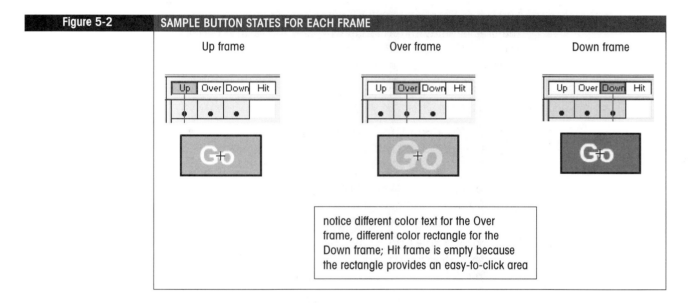

Figure 5-2 | SAMPLE BUTTON STATES FOR EACH FRAME

Up frame   Over frame   Down frame

notice different color text for the Over frame, different color rectangle for the Down frame; Hit frame is empty because the rectangle provides an easy-to-click area

The content in each frame is displayed in response to the mouse pointer's action. The **Up** frame contains the button's default state. This is what the button initially looks like to the user, before the user has used the button to take an action. When the pointer is over the button, the content in the **Over** frame is displayed. If you make the contents of the Over frame different from that in the Up frame, you create a **rollover effect**—that is, when the user rolls the pointer over the button, the button changes to show what is in the Over frame. The contents of the **Down** frame show what the button looks like when you click it. Making the contents of the Down frame different from the other frames gives the user a visual clue that the button has been clicked. Finally, the **Hit** frame does not change the appearance of the button. Instead, it represents the clickable or active area of the button. This is the area of the button that responds to a mouse click and displays the hand pointer 🖑 when the mouse pointer is over it. This is useful when the button is not a solid shape. For example, if the button consists of text, then the user has to click the letters in the text in order to activate the button. This may be difficult if the text is small. You can make it easier for the user to click the button by drawing a rectangle in the Hit frame. The rectangle represents the area that can be clicked to activate the button.

You will create buttons from scratch later in this session, but first you will use prebuilt buttons found in the Buttons library.

Adding a Button from the Common Libraries

A quick way to add buttons to your document is by using one of the buttons in the Buttons library. The Buttons library is one of the Flash Common Libraries. The Common Libraries have symbols that install with Flash and can be copied to your documents. These libraries include Buttons, Learning Interactions, and Classes. Learning Interactions and Classes are not covered in this book. The Common Libraries can be accessed from the Other Panels submenu on the Windows menu. To use the Buttons library you click Buttons from the Common Libraries menu. The library opens and its button symbols can then be copied to your document's library and used within your document. Recall from Tutorial 2 that symbols are stored in the document's library and then copies of the symbol, called instances, are added to the Stage.

Aly has asked you to make the Flounders Pet Shop banner interactive by adding buttons to control the animation. She also wants a button added that allows the user to mute the background sound that will be added later. She indicates this would be a good option to give the user because not everyone will want to listen to background sounds when visiting the Web site. She instructs you to add a button from the Buttons library and to add a text block indicating this button mutes the sound.

To add a button from the Buttons library:

1. Start Flash and open the **petshop2.fla** file located in the **Tutorial.05\Tutorial** folder included with your Data Files. Next you want to change the view so that the complete contents of the Stage are visible.

2. Change the magnification level of the Stage to **Show All**, position the panels to their default layout, and display the rulers. The view of the Stage changes to show all of the contents, and the panels are positioned in their default layout.

   You will now add a new layer to the Timeline where the buttons will be placed. It is best to keep different elements of a Flash document on separate layers. This helps you keep them organized.

3. Click the **Store** layer in the Timeline, click **Insert** on the menu bar, point to **Timeline**, and then click **Layer** to add a new layer. Change the name of this new layer to **Buttons**. The button you are going to add is part of the Common Libraries. Once you add it to your document, it is copied into your document's library of symbols.

4. Click **Window** on the menu bar, and then click **Library** to open the document's Library panel. The document's library contains five items, including the castle, fish, star, supplies text, and title symbols.

5. Click **Window** on the menu bar, point to **Other Panels**, point to **Common Libraries**, and then click **Buttons**. The Buttons library panel opens below the document's Library panel. The library contains 122 items organized into folders which represent categories of buttons such as Key Buttons or Circle Buttons. See Figure 5-3. You double-click a folder to list the buttons inside that folder.

Figure 5-3 BUTTONS LIBRARY

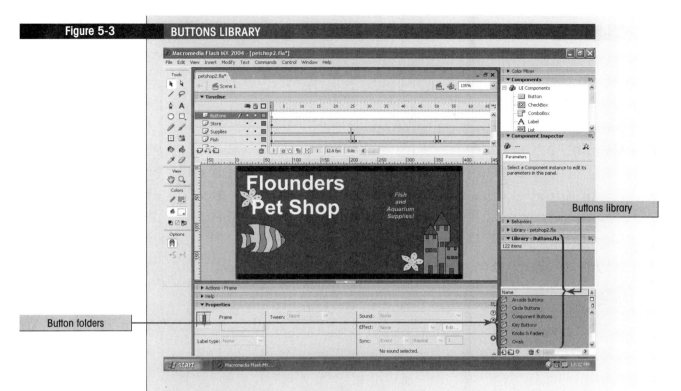

Button folders

Buttons library

6. Locate the Playback folder in the Buttons library panel. Double-click the **Playback** folder icon 📁 to display the list of buttons contained in that folder. Scroll down until you see the playback - stop button. Now you will copy the button to your document.

7. Make sure that the Buttons layer in the Timeline is still selected and then drag the **playback - stop** button from the Buttons library panel to the lower-left corner of the Stage to create an instance of the button. Place the button instance approximately 10 pixels from the left edge of the Stage and approximately 170 pixels from the top. Once you add the button instance to the Stage, the button symbol is also added to your document's library. You do not need the Buttons library any more, so you should close it.

8. Click the **Buttons Library panel options menu** control 📇 and then click **Close Panel.** If necessary, click the document's **Library panel** title bar to expand it and move the Library panel off and to the right of the Stage. Notice that the document's Library panel now contains six items. The playback - stop button has been added as a symbol with a Button behavior type, as shown in Figure 5-4.

Figure 5-4 **DOCUMENT'S LIBRARY WITH NEW SYMBOL**

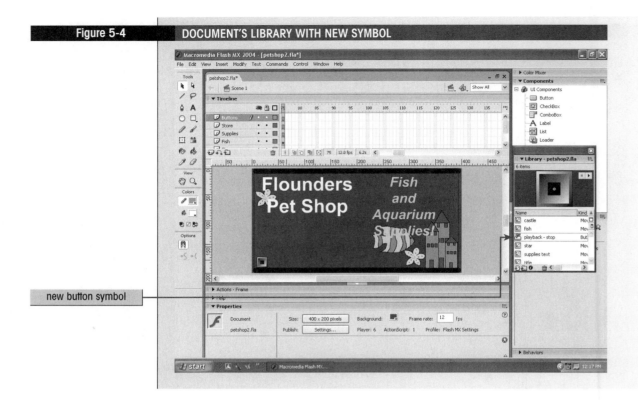

new button symbol

Once you have added a button instance to a document, it is a good idea to see how it works. You can do this within the Flash program window by turning on the Enable Simple Buttons command on the Control menu. When you turn this command on, the button exhibits its behavior on the Stage. When you move the mouse pointer over the button it changes to a hand pointer 🖑 and displays any rollover effects that are part of the button. You can use this feature to make sure that the button works properly. Once you have reviewed the button's behavior, you need to turn the Enable Simple Buttons command off if you want to select the button instance. You cannot select it with the hand pointer 🖑.

Use the Enable Simple Buttons command to see how the new button instance works.

To view the playback - stop button's behavior:

1. Click **Control** on the menu bar, and then click **Enable Simple Buttons**.

2. Click a blank area of the Stage away from the button to deselect the button. Now see what happens when the mouse pointer is over the button.

3. Position the pointer over the playback - stop button instance on the Stage. The pointer changes to a hand 🖑 indicating to the user that when the button is clicked, an action will occur.

4. Click the **playback - stop** button. When you click it, the button shifts in such a way that it appears as if the button was depressed and released.

Now you are going to edit the button. Recall Aly's instructions that you are to modify the playback - stop button so that it uses a different color for its Down frame. This is the frame that is displayed when the button is clicked, thus giving the user visual feedback that the button has been clicked. Because the button is a symbol, you need to be in symbol-editing mode to make changes to it.

To edit the playback - stop button to change its color:

1. Double-click the **playback - stop** button's icon 🖱 in the Library panel to open the button in symbol-editing mode. The button is displayed on the Stage along with its four-frame Timeline. Change the magnification level and examine the button's frames.

2. Increase the magnification level to **400%** to get a better view of the button, as shown in Figure 5-5. Drag the playhead back and forth between the Up frame and the Down frame in the Timeline to see how the button changes.

Figure 5-5	PLAYBACK - STOP BUTTON

Button frames

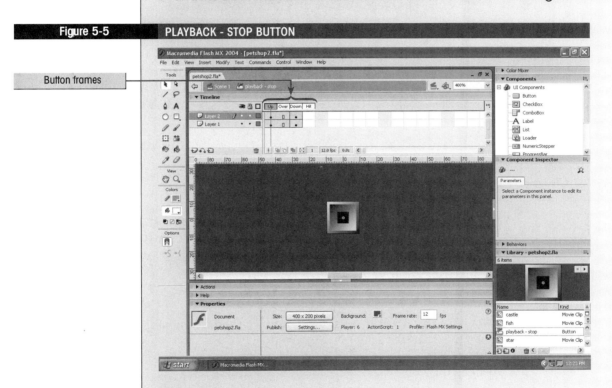

3. Click the **Down** frame of Layer 2 in the Timeline. The small black square in the center of the button appears selected, which is indicated by the fine dot pattern. Change the color of this square to **green** using the Fill Color pop-up window on the toolbar, as shown in Figure 5-6.

Figure 5-6   **CHANGING THE BUTTON**

Down frame

color will affect
small square in
button's Down frame

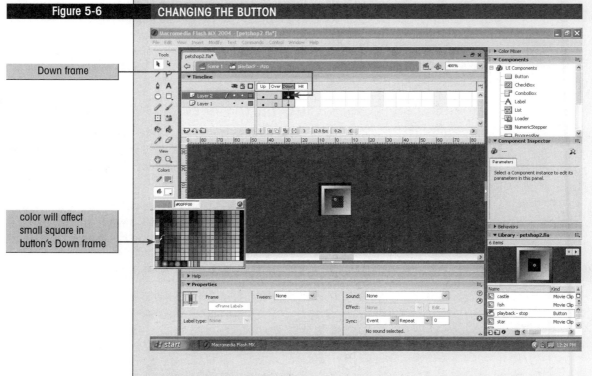

4. Click the **Scene 1** link in the Address bar to exit symbol-editing mode and return to the document.

Now you can see how the button works with the change you made.

5. Click the **button** instance on the Stage. When you click the button instance, the small black square in its center turns green. Now you will turn off the Enable Simple Buttons command.

6. Click **Control** on the menu bar, and then click **Enable Simple Buttons** to deselect this option.

Now that you have modified the button, you should add text above the button instance on the Stage that labels it as the Mute button. This tells the viewer what happens when the button is clicked. Otherwise, the viewer may not know what purpose the button serves. Providing this visual clue is an element of good design.

To add text to identify the button instance:

1. Set the magnification level to **200%**, and then use the **Hand** tool 🖐 to move the view of the Stage so that the button instance is centered in the Stage window. Now you will set the text properties and add a text block above the button.

2. Using the **Text** tool **A**, add a text block above the button with the text **Mute**. Use **Arial** for the font, **10** for the font size, **white** for the text color, and apply the **bold** text attribute. See Figure 5-7.

Figure 5-7	TEXT ADDED ABOVE BUTTON

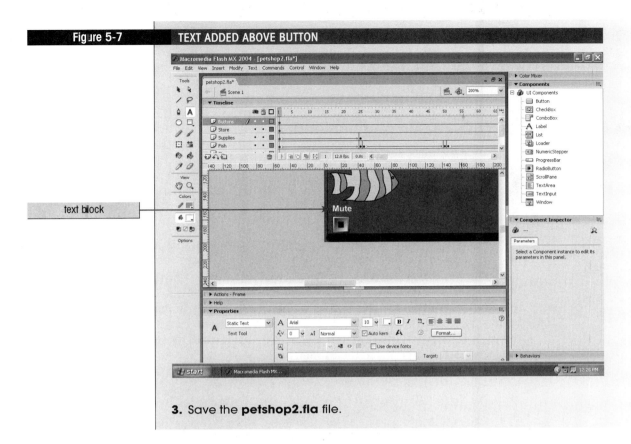

text block

3. Save the **petshop2.fla** file.

You have added a button from the Buttons library. Now you will create a button from scratch.

Creating a Button

The buttons in the Common Buttons Library provide you with many choices to use in your documents. However, you often need to create unique buttons that match your project's design. Macromedia Flash has the tools to create almost any kind of button you need. Buttons can be in the shape of rectangles, ovals, or even in the form of text. You are limited only by your imagination.

To create a button, you can use the Convert to Symbol command on the Modify menu or the New Symbol command on the Insert menu. If you first create an object on the Stage, such as a rectangle, you can convert it into a button symbol and then edit it in symbol-editing mode. If you use the New Symbol command to create the button, you do so in symbol-editing mode. In either case, you name the button just like you do any other symbol you create, and you assign Button as its behavior. Recall that symbols can have one of three behavior types, Movie Clip, Button, or Graphic. In symbol-editing mode you create or modify the content for each of the button's four frames. Once you create the button it is stored in the document's library. To use the button in your document, you must create instances of the button. If you convert an object on the Stage to a button symbol, then the object on the Stage becomes an instance once the button symbol is added to the library. If you create a new button symbol in symbol-editing mode, the button is stored in the document's library but no instances are created on the Stage.

REFERENCE WINDOW   **RW**

Creating a Button
- Create the button's shape on the Stage and select the shape.
- Click Modify on the menu bar, and then click Convert to Symbol.
- In the Convert to Symbol dialog box, name the symbol and assign the Button behavior to it.

or

- Click Insert on the menu bar, and then click New Symbol.
- In the New Symbol dialog box, name the symbol and assign the Button behavior to it.
- Create the button's shape on the Stage.

After reviewing the tasks assigned to you by Aly, you see that you now need to create two new buttons and then add these buttons to the banner. These buttons have the same general appearance in that they are both rectangles with rounded corners. However, one button is a Stop button, which the user clicks to stop the animation while it is playing. The second button is a Play button, which the user can click to start the animation playing at any time. Because these two buttons have a similar appearance, you can create the Stop button, and then make a copy of it that you can then modify to create the Play button. You will then add instances of these buttons to the banner.

To create a new button:

1. Click the **Buttons** layer in the Timeline. Before drawing the button on the Stage, select the appropriate settings using the Property inspector.

2. Click the **Rectangle** tool on the toolbar. In order to have rounded corners for the rectangle, you need to specify how much rounding to apply.

3. Click the **Rectangle Radius** modifier in the options area of the toolbar to open the Rectangle Settings dialog box, and then enter **10** for the Corner radius. Click the **OK** button to close the dialog box.

4. Create a rectangle in the lower left of the Stage to the right of the Mute button.

5. In the Property inspector, select **black** for the stroke color and **red** for the fill color. Also, make the stroke height **2** and make sure the stroke style is set to **Solid**. Compare your screen to Figure 5-8. Now that you have created the button shape, you need to convert it to a symbol.

Figure 5-8   RECTANGLE

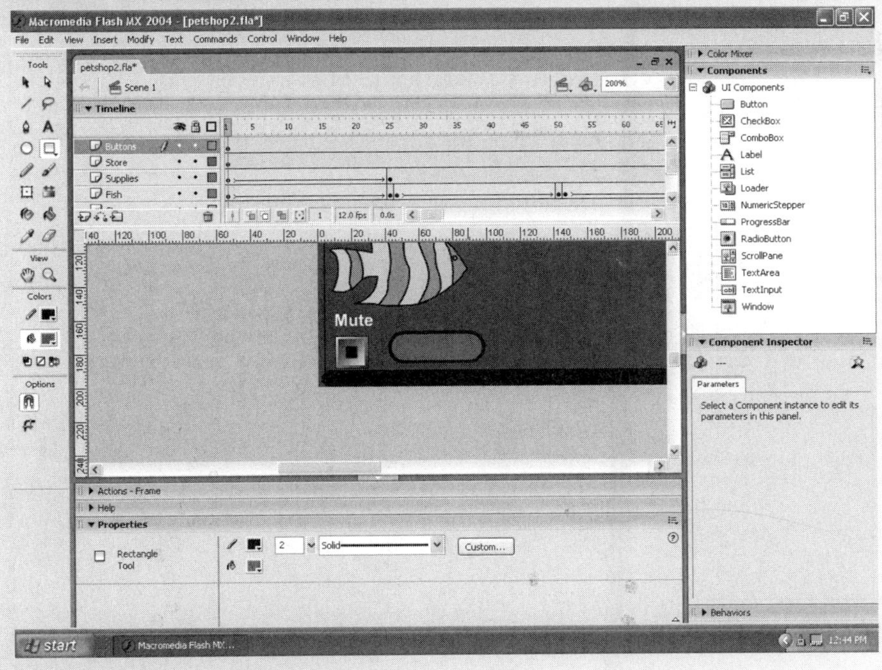

6. Click the **Selection** tool [⬚] on the toolbar. Double-click the **rectangle** to select both its fill and its stroke.

7. Click **Modify** on the menu bar, and then click **Convert to Symbol**. In the Convert to Symbol dialog box, enter **Stop** in the Name textbox to name the symbol, and then make sure that **Button** is selected as the behavior type. Click the **OK** button. The new button is added to the document's library.

Now you need to edit this button to add a text label and to create the different states of the button. The button should have a rollover effect. When you roll the pointer over the button, it should change from a red fill to a red radial gradient fill. This provides a visual clue to the user that something will happen if the button is clicked. The button should also move when it is clicked, providing visual feedback that reinforces the user's action. Remember that the button is a symbol, and to edit a symbol, you need to first enter symbol-editing mode.

To add text to the Stop button and create the different states of the button:

1. Double-click the **Stop button** icon [⬚] in the Library panel to open it in symbol-editing mode. Set the magnification level to **200%**. See Figure 5-9.

Figure 5-9 | **BUTTON SYMBOL IN EDITING MODE**

Button's four frames

button name

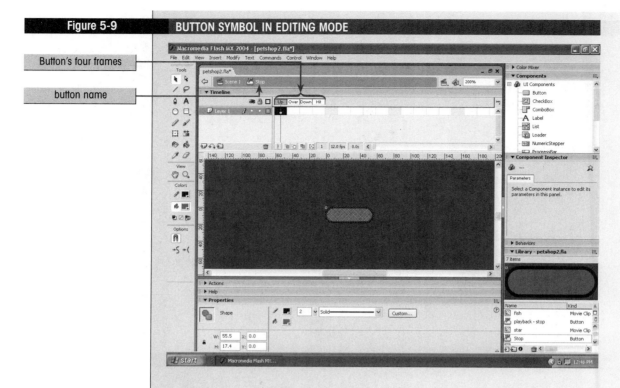

There are four frames in the Timeline for the button. The Up frame has a keyframe and contains the rectangle you created which represents the default state of the button. You will now add text to the button and then add keyframes to the Over and Down frames to create the different states of the button. First set the text properties.

2. Click the **Text** tool **A** on the toolbar. In the Property inspector, select **Arial** as the font, **10** as the font size, **white** as the text color, and apply the **bold** text attribute.

3. Create a text block inside the rectangle with the word **Stop**. Next you will position the text block such that it is centered inside the rectangle.

4. Click the **Selection** tool and if necessary, click the **Snap to Objects** modifier in the options area of the toolbar to deselect this option. Use the to move the text block so that it is centered inside the rectangle, as shown in Figure 5-10. Now you can create the contents for the Over frame.

Figure 5-10   **TEXT ADDED TO RECTANGLE**

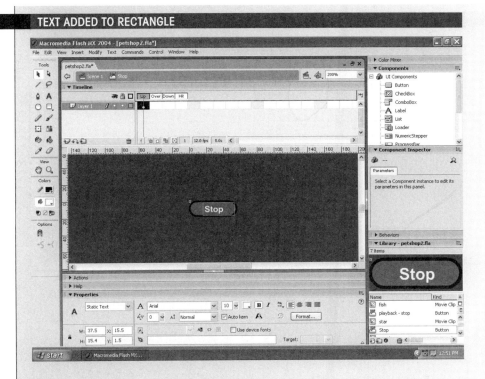

5. Click the **Over** frame in the Timeline to select it. Insert a **keyframe**. The contents of the Up frame are automatically copied to the Over frame. Recall from Tutorial 3 that each time you add a regular frame or a keyframe in a layer, the contents of the previous frame are copied into the new frame.

You want the button's appearance to change from the default state to the Over state, meaning when the user moves the pointer over the Stop button, you want the color of the button to change. So, now you will change the button's fill color in the Over frame.

6. With the rectangle still selected, click the **Fill Color control** list arrow on the toolbar to open the color pop-up window. Click the **red radial gradient** located at the bottom of the pop-up window. It is the third swatch from the left in the bottom row. The red radial gradient replaces the rectangle's red fill, as shown in Figure 5-11. Now add content to the Down frame.

Figure 5-11   RECTANGLE'S FILL CHANGED IN OVER FRAME

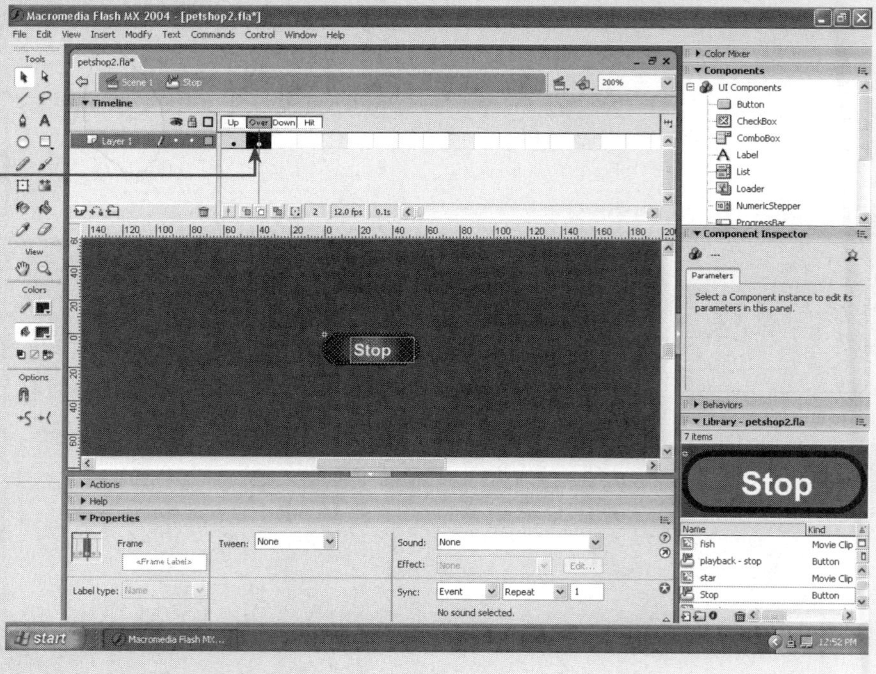

Over frame

7. Click the **Down** frame in the Timeline. Insert a **keyframe**. The contents of the Over frame are copied to the Down frame. When the user clicks the Stop button, you want the button to appear as if it has been depressed and released. To create this effect, you need to change the button's position in the Down frame.

8. With the rectangle and text block still selected, press the **Down Arrow** key on your keyboard three times, and then press the **Right Arrow** key three times. This changes the position of the rectangle three pixels down and three pixels to the right. Now you will exit symbol-editing mode. There is no need to add anything to the Hit frame because the rectangle shape provides the clickable or active area for the button.

9. Click the **Scene 1** link to exit symbol-editing mode and return to the document.

Now that you have finished creating the button and its different states, preview the button instance's behavior on the Stage to make sure the different effects you have created appear correctly. You use the Enable Simple Buttons command to preview the effects.

To test the button instance's rollover effects:

1. Click **Control** on the menu bar, click the **Enable Simple Buttons** command to select this option, and then click a blank area of the Stage to deselect the button.

2. Move the pointer over the **Stop** button to see the rollover effect, as shown in Figure 5-12, and then click the **Stop** button to see how it changes and moves. The rollover effects work well. Now that you are done creating and testing the visual effects of the button, you can turn off the Enable Simple buttons command.

Figure 5-12	BUTTON'S ROLLOVER EFFECT

rollover effect

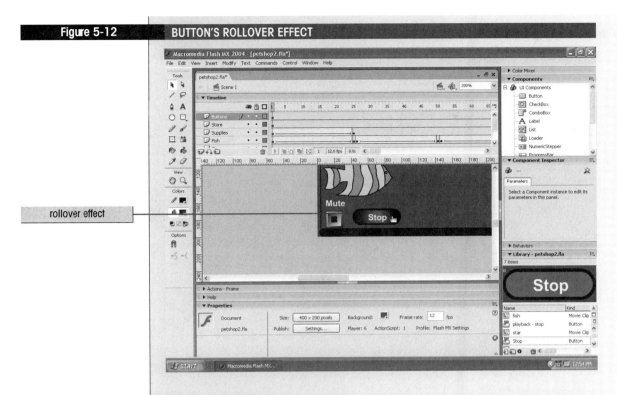

3. Click **Control** on the menu bar, and then click the **Enable Simple Buttons** command to deselect it.

You have created the Stop button and reviewed its rollover effects. Now you need to create one more button—the Play button. Recall from Aly's instructions, the Play button should look very similar to the Stop button. Therefore, instead of creating a new button, you can make a copy of the Stop button you just created, and modify it appropriately to create the Play button.

To create a copy of the Stop button:

1. In the Library panel, click the **Stop** button. Now use the options menu to create a copy of the button.

2. Click the **Library panel's options menu** control [icon] and then click **Duplicate**. The Duplicate Symbol dialog box opens showing the duplicate button's name, Stop copy. You want to change the name of the button.

3. In the Duplicate Symbol dialog box, select **Stop copy** in the Name text box if necessary, type **Play**, and then click the **OK** button to close the dialog box. A new symbol is added to the document's library, as shown in Figure 5-13.

Figure 5-13   **PLAY BUTTON SYMBOL**

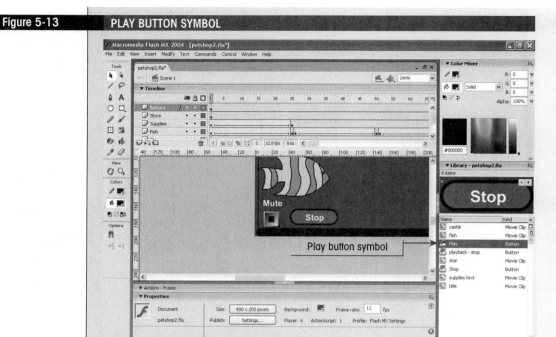

Now that you have created the Play button by making a copy of the Stop button, you need to modify the Play button so that it is green in its default state and so that it changes to a radiant green color when the user positions the mouse pointer over the button.

To edit the Play button:

1. Double-click the **Play button** icon 👆 in the Library panel. The button opens in symbol-editing mode.

2. Increase the magnification level to **200%** to make it easier to edit the button.

   To make changes to the button's colors you need to be sure you have selected the appropriate frame. You also want to make sure you do not change the text block. For the Up frame you only want to change the color of the rectangle's fill to green. So make sure the Up frame is selected and the button is deselected.

3. If necessary, select the **Up** frame and deselect the button by clicking a blank area of the Stage. Now select the color to be applied to the button.

4. Using the Fill Color control on the toolbar, change the fill color to a **dark green** (fourth column, first row), as shown in Figure 5-14.

Figure 5-14   **FILL COLOR POP-UP WINDOW**

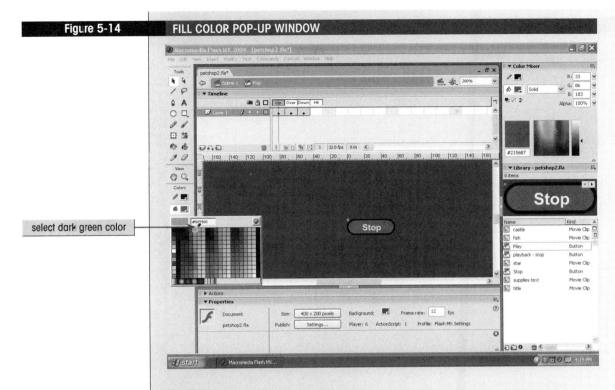

select dark green color

5. Click the **Paint Bucket** tool and then click the **Play** button on the Stage to apply the green color to the button's fill, replacing the button's red color. Now you need to change the text block on the button.

6. Click the **Text** tool A on the toolbar, click the **Stop** text block, and then change the text to **Play**. Make sure the text font is **Arial**, the text height is **10**, the text color is **white**, and the text style is **bold**.

   You have only changed the color and text of the Up frame. The Over and Down frames still contain the red fill and the Stop text. Now you need to also change the color and text of the button's Over and Down frames.

7. Drag the playhead to the **Over** frame in the Timeline. Click the **Selection** tool on the toolbar, and then if necessary, click a blank area of the Stage to deselect the button.

8. Using the Fill Color control on the toolbar, select the **green radial gradient** for the fill color. It is the fourth gradient swatch from the left in the bottom row of the color palette.

9. Click and then click the button on the Stage to apply the gradient to the button's fill. Finally, you need to change the button's text.

10. Change the Stop text to **Play** as you did for the Up frame. See Figure 5-15.

Figure 5-15   **OVER FRAME CHANGED**

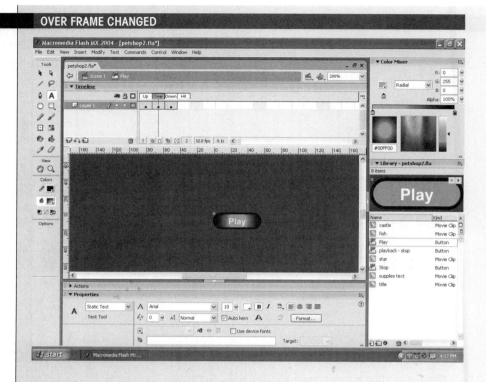

11. Drag the playhead to the **Down** frame in the Timeline. If necessary, deselect the button, and then repeat Steps 9 and 10 to apply the green radial gradient to the button's fill and change the text to Play.

12. Click the **Scene 1** link in the Address bar to exit symbol-editing mode.

You have modified the Play button by changing its color and its text label. Recall that a button symbol resides in the document's library. To use it in the document you need to create an instance of the button symbol. You can easily create an instance by dragging the button from the Library panel to the Stage. Now you can add an instance of the Play button to the document.

To add an instance of the Play button to the document:

1. Drag the **Play** button from the Library panel to the Stage. Place the instance to the right of the Stop button instance, as shown in Figure 5-16.

Figure 5-16	PLAY BUTTON INSTANCE ADDED TO DOCUMENT

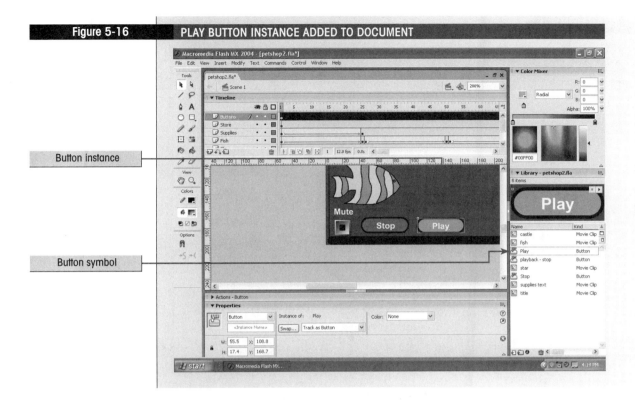

You have changed all of the Play button's frames by making them different from those in the Stop button, and you have added an instance of the Play button to the banner.

Aligning the Buttons

When adding several similar objects to a document you should align the objects. A set of objects like buttons that are close to each other on the Stage should be lined up vertically or horizontally and they should be evenly spaced to give your document a professional appearance. You can accomplish this alignment using the Align panel. The Align panel includes different options used to align a group of selected objects on the Stage. You can align objects by their edges or centers and you can also distribute them so that they are evenly spaced. In order to align objects you need to select them first. You then click one of the buttons in the Align panel. Figure 5-17 describes the different alignment options on this panel.

Figure 5-17	ALIGN PANEL OPTIONS

BUTTON	BUTTON NAME	DESCRIPTION
ALIGN		
	Align left edge	Align selected objects vertically along their left edges
	Align horizontal center	Align selected objects vertically along their horizontal centers
	Align right edge	Align selected objects vertically along their right edges
	Align top edge	Align selected objects horizontally along their top edges
	Align vertical center	Align selected objects horizontally along their vertical centers
	Align bottom edge	Align selected objects horizontally along their bottom edges

Figure 5-17	ALIGN PANEL OPTIONS (CONTINUED)	
BUTTON	**BUTTON NAME**	**DESCRIPTION**
DISTRIBUTE		
	Distribute top edge	Distribute selected objects so that their top edges are evenly spaced
	Distribute horizontal center	Distribute selected objects so that their horizontal centers are evenly spaced
	Distribute bottom edge	Distribute selected objects so that their bottom edges are evenly spaced
	Distribute left edge	Distribute selected objects so that their left edges are evenly spaced
	Distribute vertical center	Distribute selected objects so that their vertical centers are evenly spaced
	Distribute right edge	Distribute selected objects so that their right edges are evenly spaced
MATCH SIZE		
	Match width	Resize selected objects so that the widths of all objects match those of the largest selected object
	Match height	Resize selected objects so that the heights of all objects match those of the largest selected object
	Match width and height	Resize selected objects so that the widths and heights of all objects match those of the largest selected object
SPACE		
	Space evenly horizontally	Evenly spaces the selected objects horizontally
	Space evenly vertically	Evenly spaces the selected objects vertically
TO STAGE		
	To stage	Applies alignment relative to the Stage dimensions

Aly reviews the three button instances you have created and instructs you to align them by their bottom edges. She also tells you to make sure that they are positioned with an equal amount of space between them. You will use the Align panel to horizontally align and evenly space the Mute, Stop, and Play buttons.

To align the three buttons using the Align panel:

1. Click **Window** on the menu bar, point to **Design Panels**, and then click **Align** to open the Align panel. If necessary, move the panel so that you can see the three buttons on the Stage. Before you can align the three buttons, you must select them.

2. Using the **Selection** tool , click the **Mute** button instance on the Stage, press and hold the **Shift** key on the keyboard, click the **Stop** button instance, and then click the **Play** button instance to select all three buttons instances at one time, as shown in Figure 5-18.

Figure 5-18 | **THREE BUTTONS SELECTED**

3. Make sure the **To Stage** button ⊡ on the Align panel is not selected. To Stage aligns the selected objects relative to the Stage and not relative to each other. You want to align the button instances by their bottom edges.

4. With the three button instances selected, click the **Align bottom edge** button ⬚ in the Align panel. This icon is the far-right button in the Align section. Now apply an even amount of space between the button instances.

5. Click the **Space evenly horizontally** button ⬚. This is the far-right button in the Space section. The button instances should now have an equal amount of space between them.

6. Close the **Align** panel, and save the changes you have made to your document.

The buttons you have added to the banner do not control anything yet. When you click them the animation does not change. In order for the buttons to control the animation, they need programming instructions called Actions. **Actions** are instructions that are used to control how a movie plays. For example, if you create a button that stops an animation, you need to add a Stop action to the button instance. You can create Actions yourself using the Actions panel, or you can use pre-coded instructions, called behaviors, using the Behavior panel. You will use the Actions panel in Tutorial 7. You will add Actions to the buttons in the next session using the Behavior panel.

Session 5.1 QUICK CHECK

1. What is a button?

2. Why would you add buttons to a document?

3. How can you add a button from the Buttons library to your document's library?

4. How many frames are in a button's Timeline? List their names.

5. How do you create a rollover effect for a button?

6. How can you test a button in your document while in Macromedia Flash?

7. Which Macromedia Flash tool can help you to easily align several objects on the Stage?

SESSION 5.2

In this session, you will use the Behaviors panel to add behaviors to the buttons you created in the previous session. You will add a Play behavior to the Play button and a Stop behavior to the Stop button. You will also add a behavior to a frame. Finally, you will test these behaviors in your browser.

Understanding **Actions and Behaviors**

The buttons you added to the banner in the previous session look great and have some nice effects such as the rollover effect, but they do not yet allow the user to control the document's animation. When the button is clicked the animation does not change. The document still plays sequentially one frame after another until it reaches the end. According to Aly's instructions, the buttons should allow the user to stop and play the animation. In order for the buttons to be fully functional and interactive, you need to add instructions called Actions. **Actions** are instructions that are used to control a document while its animation is playing. Actions are part of Flash's programming language called **ActionScript**. The ActionScript language is very similar to the Web language **JavaScript**, which is used to add interactive elements to Web pages. Many of these actions are simple and can be used to create basic navigation controls to control a document's animation. For example, you can add actions that stop or play an animation. With ActionScript you create scripts that tell Flash what action to take when a certain event occurs. A **script** is a set of one or more actions that perform some function. An **event** is a situation where the user is interacting with a button such as clicking a button with the mouse and then releasing it. These events can be recognized by Flash and can be used to trigger or start the execution of the actions in a script.

Fortunately, you do not need any experience with computer programming or Web languages such as ActionScript to use actions in your Flash documents. With Flash, you can either write the ActionScript code for the actions in your documents, or you can use pre-coded actions provided in Flash. These pre-coded actions are called behaviors. **Behaviors** are actions with pre-written ActionScript scripts which assign controls and transitions to an object on the Stage. You can use behaviors to control an object in your document without writing any ActionScript coding yourself. There are a variety of behaviors available for Flash objects, including movie clips, video, and sound files.

To assign a behavior to an object, you must first select the object, and then display the Behaviors panel, which you access by clicking Window on the menu bar, pointing to Development Panels, and then clicking Behaviors. You can click the Add Behavior button in the Behaviors panel to open a menu of categories of behaviors. When you select a behavior from one of these submenus, a dialog box opens, in which you can select specific options for the action.

Figure 5-19 shows the Behaviors panel with a button that has a Goto and Play action and an On Release event handler assigned to it. An **event handler** tells Flash how to handle an event. The event handler in this case indicates that the button's action will execute when the user clicks the button, and then releases the mouse button.

Figure 5-19   BEHAVIORS PANEL

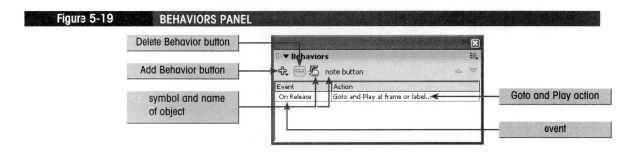

The script created by Flash when the GotoAndPlay behavior is assigned to a button instance, as shown in Figure 5-20.

Figure 5-20   SAMPLE SCRIPT

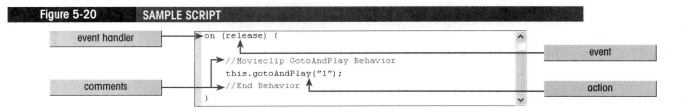

The script consists of several lines of code. The first line has the mouse event handler `on` followed by the event `release` in parentheses. The lines with the two forward slashes are comments and do not affect the behavior of the button. In this Play button example, the event handler is triggered when the user clicks and then releases the button causing the `gotoAndPlay` action to execute. The word `this` is just a reference to the instance the action is assigned to. When the action is executed the document's animation starts playing at Frame 1.

When you plan your document, you also plan what interactions will be part of the document and where these interactions will be placed. If you plan to use buttons to give the user control over the animation, then you need to also plan what actions will be needed to make the buttons functional. Once you create the buttons and add instances of them to the document, you can add the appropriate actions to the instances.

In Session 5.1 you added three buttons to the banner advertising fish supplies. According to Aly's planning notes, you need these buttons to be interactive. In this session, you will add the actions to the Stop and Play buttons that will make them interactive. Because you are a new Flash user and are inexperienced at writing computer programming code, Aly suggests you use the Behaviors panel to add the `gotoAndStop` action to the Stop button and the `gotoAndPlay` action to the Play button.

Adding Behaviors Using the Behaviors Panel

Before adding behaviors to your document, you need to specify where to add the behaviors. If you want the user to click a button you created and for that button to cause an action to execute, then the behavior containing the code for that action must be attached to the button instance. When adding behaviors to a button, you add them to the button instance on the Stage and not to the button symbol in the library. If you want an action to execute at a certain point in the animation, then attach it to the frame where you want it to start. Adding actions to frames is discussed later in this session.

Aly likes the buttons you have added to the banner. She tells you that the buttons now need actions so they can be used to control the animation as originally planned. She instructs you to add the `gotoAndStop` action to the Stop button and to add the `gotoAndPlay` action to the Play button using the Behaviors panel.

To add behaviors to the Stop and Play buttons:

1. If you took a break after the last session, start Flash and open the **petshop2.fla** banner stored in the **Tutorial.05\Tutorial** folder include with your Data Files.

2. Set the panels to their default layout and change the magnification level to show all of the Stage.

3. Click the **Stop** button instance on the Stage to select it. Make sure no other buttons or banner elements are selected.

4. Click the **Behaviors panel** title bar to expand this panel. The Behaviors panel is located to the right of the Stage. You need to assign a behavior.

5. Click the **Add Behavior** button ✥ in the Behaviors panel, point to **Movieclip**, and then click **Goto and Stop at frame or label**, as shown in Figure 5-21.

| Figure 5-21 | GOTO AND STOP BEHAVIOR |

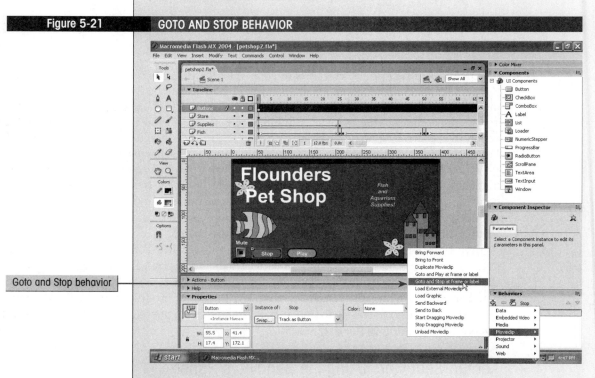

Goto and Stop behavior

6. In the Goto and Stop at frame or label dialog box, make sure **1** appears in the text box, and then click the **OK** button. The Stop button now has the Stop behavior assigned to it.

Now you can add the Goto and Play behavior to the Play button. To do so, you first need to select the button instance.

7. Using the **Selection** tool ▶, click the **Play** button instance on the Stage to select it.

8. Click the **Add Behavior** button ⊕ in the Behaviors panel, point to **Movieclip**, and then click **Goto and Play at frame or label**.

9. In the Goto and Play at frame or label dialog box, make sure **1** appears in the text box, and then click the **OK** button. This behavior is now assigned to the Play button.

Now that you have added the appropriate behaviors to the Play and Stop buttons, you should test them to make sure they work correctly.

To test the button behaviors:

1. Click **Control** on the menu bar, and then click **Test Movie**. The animation plays and the fish swims across the banner.

2. While the animation plays, click the **Stop** button to stop the animation. You can click the Play button again to play the animation. Click **File** on the menu bar and click **Close**. Now test the buttons by playing the SWF File on a Web page.

3. To test the movie in a Web page, click **File** on the menu bar, point to **Publish Preview**, and then click **HTML**. Your computer's default browser opens and the animation plays in a Web page.

4. Test the buttons by clicking them to stop and play the animation.

5. Close the browser window to return to Flash. Save the changes you have made to your document.

Behaviors that have been added to buttons are executed when certain events occur, such as when the user clicks the button. Another place where you can add behaviors is in individual frames.

Adding Behaviors to Frames

Behaviors in a frame execute when that particular frame is played. Scripts created for frame behaviors are different from those created for buttons in that no event handler is required. For example, if you add a Stop behavior to a frame, the script only contains one line with `stop();`. Frame behaviors do not depend on an event to occur. Instead they execute as soon as the frame they are in is played.

Frame behaviors can be used to change the sequence in which the frames are played in the Timeline. Ordinarily a movie plays sequentially starting with Frame 1, going through the last frame, and then repeating again at Frame 1. However, you may want to create a different animation effect by playing the frames in a different order. For example, you can create an animation in which a group of frames is played repeatedly by having the playhead go back to an earlier frame. This is called a **loop**. You can do this by placing a behavior in the last frame of the group that causes the animation to go back to the earlier frame, as shown in Figure 5-22. The frame behavior is indicated by a small **a** in the frame. Every time the last frame is played the playhead in the Timeline jumps back to Frame 25.

7. Using the **Selection** tool , click the **Play** button instance on the Stage to select it.

8. Click the **Add Behavior** button in the Behaviors panel, point to **Movieclip**, and then click **Goto and Play at frame or label**.

9. In the Goto and Play at frame or label dialog box, make sure **1** appears in the text box, and then click the **OK** button. This behavior is now assigned to the Play button.

Now that you have added the appropriate behaviors to the Play and Stop buttons, you should test them to make sure they work correctly.

To test the button behaviors:

1. Click **Control** on the menu bar, and then click **Test Movie**. The animation plays and the fish swims across the banner.

2. While the animation plays, click the **Stop** button to stop the animation. You can click the Play button again to play the animation. Click **File** on the menu bar and click **Close**. Now test the buttons by playing the SWF File on a Web page.

3. To test the movie in a Web page, click **File** on the menu bar, point to **Publish Preview**, and then click **HTML**. Your computer's default browser opens and the animation plays in a Web page.

4. Test the buttons by clicking them to stop and play the animation.

5. Close the browser window to return to Flash. Save the changes you have made to your document.

Behaviors that have been added to buttons are executed when certain events occur, such as when the user clicks the button. Another place where you can add behaviors is in individual frames.

Adding Behaviors to Frames

Behaviors in a frame execute when that particular frame is played. Scripts created for frame behaviors are different from those created for buttons in that no event handler is required. For example, if you add a Stop behavior to a frame, the script only contains one line with `stop();`. Frame behaviors do not depend on an event to occur. Instead they execute as soon as the frame they are in is played.

Frame behaviors can be used to change the sequence in which the frames are played in the Timeline. Ordinarily a movie plays sequentially starting with Frame 1, going through the last frame, and then repeating again at Frame 1. However, you may want to create a different animation effect by playing the frames in a different order. For example, you can create an animation in which a group of frames is played repeatedly by having the playhead go back to an earlier frame. This is called a **loop**. You can do this by placing a behavior in the last frame of the group that causes the animation to go back to the earlier frame, as shown in Figure 5-22. The frame behavior is indicated by a small **a** in the frame. Every time the last frame is played the playhead in the Timeline jumps back to Frame 25.

Figure 5-22 **LOOP CREATED WITH FRAME BEHAVIOR**

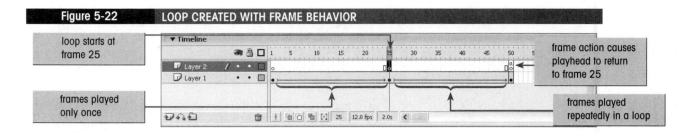

loop starts at frame 25

frames played only once

frame action causes playhead to return to frame 25

frames played repeatedly in a loop

In cases like these you need to refer to a specific frame when creating a behavior. Although you can refer to frames by their numbers, it is a good idea to assign labels to these frames and to then refer to the labels instead of the numbers. If you use frame numbers in your behavior and then later add or delete frames from the Timeline, the behavior may end up referring to the wrong frames. This is because adding or deleting frames causes other frames to be renumbered. You would then have to change each of the behaviors that refer to the wrong frame numbers. However, if you use frame labels, as shown in Figure 5-23, adding or deleting frames does not affect those frames. They will still have the same labels attached to them. Any behaviors that refer to the frames by their labels still work and, therefore, do not have to be changed. Frame labels are added to keyframes using the Frame Label text box in the Property inspector.

Figure 5-23 **FRAME LABEL**

Frame 25 with a label

It is also a good idea to create a separate layer in which to add your frame behaviors. Although this is not required, it makes it easier to keep track of the behaviors, especially when you have more than one in a document. If you then have to make changes to other parts of the document, the behaviors are not affected.

Recall from the planning meeting with Aly that the banner contains three motion tweens to make the fish swim back and forth, as shown in Figure 5-24. It also contains a motion tween that animates the Supplies text block.

Figure 5-24 **BANNER TIMELINE**

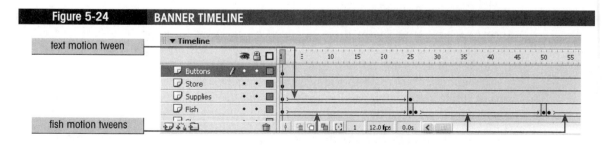

text motion tween

fish motion tweens

When the banner is published, the text and fish motion tweens repeat continuously because the movie plays from Frame 1 to Frame 75 and then back to Frame 1 to start again. Aly's instructions are for you to change the sequence of the animation so that the text animates only once and then remains stationary as the fish continues to swim. This means that the text motion tween should not be repeated. To accomplish this you need to change the sequence of the animation so that instead of going back to Frame 1 when it repeats, it should instead go to Frame 25, which is where the text animation ends. The animation should then continue from Frame 25 to Frame 75 and then back to Frame 25 to repeat. To do this you add a frame behavior to the last frame in the document. That frame behavior causes the playhead to move to Frame 25. The playhead then continues from Frame 25 to Frame 75 again. As a result, the playhead does not replay the text block's animation, but instead continues with the last two fish motion tweens. Since it is possible that frames may be added or deleted from the banner at a later date, the frame behavior in the last frame should refer to a frame label and not to a frame number. You can add a frame label at Frame 25 that can be referred to by the frame behavior in Frame 75. To keep things organized in your document, you will place the frame behavior and the frame label on their own separate layers.

To add behaviors to a frame:

1. Select the **Buttons** layer in the Timeline. Insert a new layer and name it **Behaviors**. Insert another new layer and name it **Labels**. If necessary, make the Labels layer the current layer.

   Before adding a label at Frame 25, you need to make Frame 25 a keyframe. Without a keyframe at Frame 25, the label is added to Frame 1. Remember, anytime there is to be a change in a frame, such as adding a label, a keyframe needs to be inserted at that frame.

2. In the Timeline, click **Frame 25** of the Labels layer, and then insert a keyframe. Now create the label for Frame 25.

3. In the Property inspector, type **Loop Start** in the Frame text box, as shown in Figure 5-25, and then press the **Enter** key. The frame label is added to Frame 25 of the Labels layer.

Figure 5-25	ADDING A FRAME LABEL

type the frame label in the Frame text box

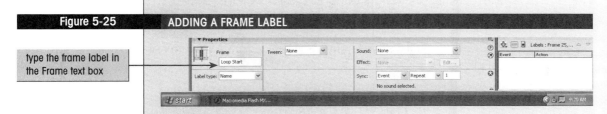

Now you will add a frame behavior to the last frame of the Behaviors layer. This frame behavior directs the animation to go back to the Loop Start frame. This last frame also needs to be a keyframe.

4. Click **Frame 75** of the Behavior layer and then insert a keyframe. You may need to use the Timeline's horizontal scroll bar to see Frame 75. Now add the frame behavior using the Behaviors panel.

5. Click the **Behaviors** panel title bar to expand this panel. Click the **Add Behavior** button ⊹ in the Behaviors panel, point to **Movieclip**, and then click **Goto and Play at frame or label**.

   You want to change the action so that the animation goes back to Frame 25 because this is where the text block motion tween ends. But rather than referring to a frame number in the script, you want to refer to the frame label you added to Frame 25.

6. In the Goto and Play at frame or label dialog box, make sure **Loop Start** appears in the text box, and then click the **OK** button.

The frame behavior you just added is indicated by a small a in Frame 75 of the Behavior layer in the Timeline, as shown in Figure 5-26.

| Figure 5-26 | FRAME BEHAVIOR |

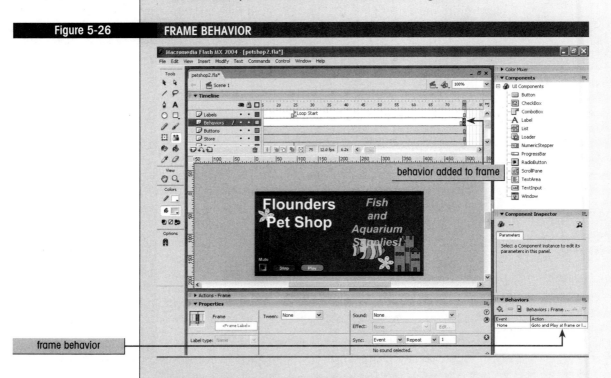

7. Click the **Behaviors** panel title bar to collapse it.

Now that you have added the frame behavior, you need to test it to make sure the animation plays properly.

To test the frame behavior:

1. Click **Control** on the menu bar, and then click **Test Movie**. The animation plays and when the playhead reaches Frame 75, it goes back and starts again at the frame labeled Loop Start, which is Frame 25.

2. Click **File** on the menu bar, and then click **Close** to return to the document.

3. Save the changes you made to the petshop2.fla document.

In this session, you learned how to add behaviors to button instances and to frames. You learned that actions are part of Macromedia Flash's ActionScript language and that you can add preprogrammed actions called behaviors using the Behaviors panel. You added behaviors to the banner to control the animation, and you tested the behaviors. In the next session, you will add sound to the banner.

Session 5.2 Quick Check

1. What is ActionScript?

2. In order to use ActionScript you need to know JavaScript. True or False?

3. What are behaviors?

4. Which panel is used to add behaviors?

5. Behaviors are added to a button symbol and not to an instance of the symbol. True or False?

6. What is an example of an event that triggers a behavior on a button to execute?

7. Why is it better to refer to a frame label in a behavior instead of a frame number?

8. What is the difference between a frame behavior and a button behavior?

SESSION 5.3

In this session, you will learn about the different sound file formats, how to adjust the various sounds you add to your document, and how to compress these sounds before publishing the document. You will add sound effects to the buttons you created in the previous sessions, and you will add a background sound to the Flounders Pet Shop fish supplies banner. You will also add an action to the Mute button to allow the user to stop the background sound.

Sound

Macromedia Flash offers several ways to use sounds. For example, you can add sounds to your document that play continuously and that are independent of the Timeline, such as a background sound. You can add sound effects to instances of buttons to make them more interactive. For example, a sound can be added that plays when a user clicks a button. You can also add sounds that are synchronized with the animation such as a sound simulating a clap of thunder that coincides with an animation of a lightning bolt. Sounds can even be added in the form of a voice narration to supplement the information being displayed on the Web page as text or graphics.

Types of Sounds

There are basically two types of sounds in Flash. These are event and stream sounds. **Event sounds**, which are the default type, will not play until the entire sound has downloaded completely. You add event sounds to keyframes so that the sound plays each time the keyframe is played. Event sounds are not synchronized with the Timeline which means that once an event sound is started it continues to play regardless of the Timeline until all of the sound is played or until the user takes an action to explicitly stop it. If you have a long event sound, it may continue to play even after all of the frames in the Timeline have finished playing.

Stream sounds are synchronized with the Timeline and begin playing as soon as enough data has downloaded. Stream sounds are useful when you need the animation in your movie to coincide with the sound. For example, if you have a voice narration with your animation, and you want the narration to match the text or graphics throughout the document, then you need to make the voice narration a stream sound.

Finding Sounds for Your Documents

Adding sound to an animation can have a very powerful effect, bringing another level of excitement to a well-designed document. The sound you use can be subtle or loud. You can create sounds with a separate sound-editing program and then import the sounds, or you can acquire prerecorded sounds from other sources. There are many different vendors of prerecorded sound files. Most vendors offer a wide variety of sound effects and music that may be purchased on CD-ROM. Sounds are also available for purchase on the Web. You can even download sounds for free from some Web sites such as Flash Kit's Web site at *www.flashkit.com*. Flash Kit provides a wealth of resources for Macromedia Flash developers. At their site, shown in Figure 5-27, you can find sounds under Sound FX and under Sound Loops.

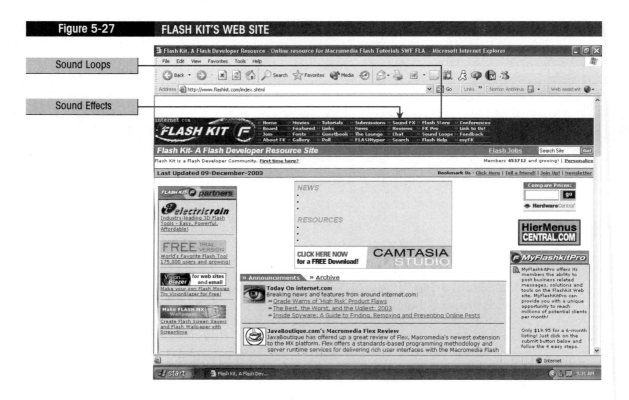

Figure 5-27   FLASH KIT'S WEB SITE

Sound Loops

Sound Effects

You can search for sounds using keywords or browse for sounds by category. Sounds listed at their site can also be previewed before being downloaded. If you download a sound file you may need to decompress the file, using a utility such as WinZip, before using the sounds in your document.

Other Web sites offer sounds for purchase. These Web sites have preproduced sounds from which you can select; they will even create customized sounds for a fee. Two examples of such sites are **Killersound** at *www.killersound.com* and **SoundShopper.com** at *www.soundshopper.com*. These sites also have a few sounds you can download for free to use in your personal projects.

However you acquire sounds, it is important to carefully examine the license agreement that determines how you can use the sounds. Even though a sound file may be downloaded for free there may be restrictions on how you may use it, especially if you plan to distribute the sound with your document. It is best to look for sounds that are royalty free. **Royalty free** means that there are no additional usage fees when you distribute them with your projects. An alternative to downloading free sounds or purchasing sounds is to record your own. This may not always be possible, but if you record a sound file yourself then you do not have to worry about licensing issues.

Sounds to be used with your documents must first be imported into Flash. The sounds that Flash accepts for import must be in a file format that is compatible with Flash. The file formats that it can import include Windows Waveform (WAV), Audio Interchange File Format (AIFF) used with Macintosh computers, and MP3 which plays on both Windows and Macintosh operating systems. The first two formats are not compressed and tend to be larger in size than MP3 files, which are compressed. Compressed files are smaller because the parts of the sound data that you are not likely to notice have been removed. Compressing a sound file basically means that its size has been reduced without sacrificing too much of the sound quality. The size of sound files is an issue you need to be aware of because adding sounds to your Flash documents can significantly increase the overall size of the published files and will, therefore, affect their download time. You can import a WAV file into your document and then compress it to MP3 format within the program. The MP3 is an ideal format for your Flash movies because it produces very small sound files, retains very good sound quality, and is compatible with both Windows and Macintosh computers.

Adding Sounds to Your Documents

Because you cannot create sounds in Flash, the sound files you use in your documents must first be imported. When you import a sound file it is placed in the document's library along with any symbols and buttons you may already have. You can identify the sound in the library by the sound's icon and also by the waveform that is displayed in the Library panel's preview window, as shown in Figure 5-28. A waveform is a graphical representation of a sound.

Figure 5-28 **SAMPLE SOUND IN LIBRARY PANEL**

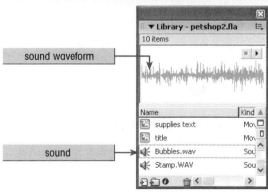

Once you have a sound file in your document's library you can use it as many times as you need in your document. Only one copy of the sound is stored. Before you add a sound to your document it is best to create a separate layer for each sound. This makes it easier to identify the sound in the Timeline. Also, sounds can only be added to keyframes. These can be keyframes in the main Timeline or keyframes in a button's Timeline. To add a sound, first select the keyframe in the Timeline where you want to place the sound, and then drag the sound from the Library panel to the Stage. You can also select the sound from the Sound list box in the Property inspector. The Sound list box in the Property inspector includes all the sounds currently in the document's library. Once you add a sound to a keyframe, it will play when the playhead reaches the keyframe.

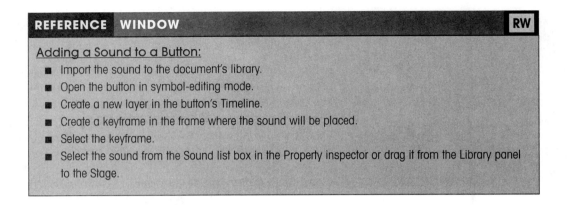

REFERENCE WINDOW RW

Adding a Sound to a Button:

- Import the sound to the document's library.
- Open the button in symbol-editing mode.
- Create a new layer in the button's Timeline.
- Create a keyframe in the frame where the sound will be placed.
- Select the keyframe.
- Select the sound from the Sound list box in the Property inspector or drag it from the Library panel to the Stage.

Based on the planning discussion for this banner, Aly wants you to add sound effects to the Stop and Play buttons for the banner.

To add a sound effect to the Stop button:

1. If you took a break after the last session, start Macromedia Flash and open the **petshop2.fla** document located in the **Tutorial.05\Tutorial** folder included with your Data Files.

2. Set the panels to their default layout and change the magnification level to show all of the Stage.

3. Click **Window** on the menu bar, and then click **Library** to open the document's Library panel.

4. Click **File** on the menu bar, point to **Import**, and then click **Import to Library** to open the Import to Library dialog box. In the Import to Library dialog box, navigate to the **Tutorial.05\Tutorial** folder included with your Data Files.

5. In the file list, click the **Stamp** sound file, and then click the **Open** button. The **Stamp.wav** file is added to the document's library, as shown in Figure 5-29.

Figure 5-29 STAMP SOUND FILE ADDED TO DOCUMENT'S LIBRARY

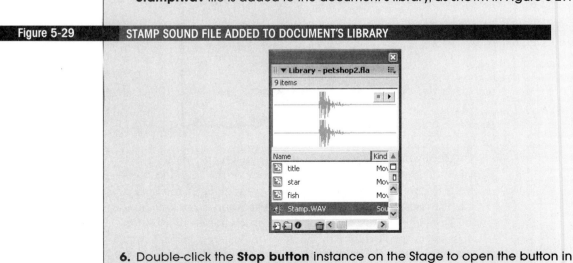

6. Double-click the **Stop button** instance on the Stage to open the button in symbol-editing mode.

7. Insert a new layer in the Stop button's Timeline and name this layer **Sound**. Now you need to insert a keyframe where the sound will be added.

8. Click the **Down** frame in the Sound layer to select it, and then insert a keyframe.

9. In the Property inspector, click the **Sound** list arrow to display the available sounds, and then click **Stamp.WAV**. This sound is added to the Down frame, as shown in Figure 5-30.

| Figure 5-30 | SOUND WAVEFORM IN FRAME |

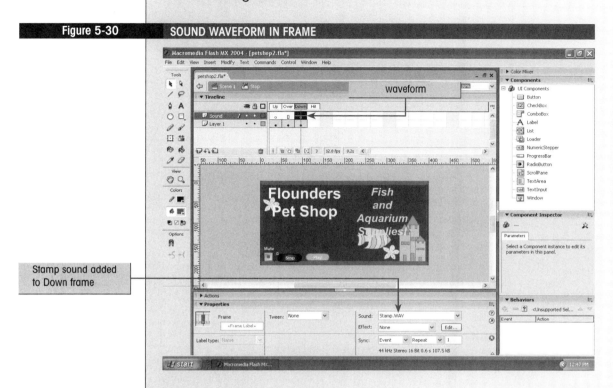

Stamp sound added to Down frame

10. Click the **Scene 1** link in the Address bar to return to the document and exit symbol-editing mode.

Now that you have added the sound to the Stop button, you should test it to make sure it works correctly. You can test the sound within the Flash program window by selecting the Enable Simple Buttons command on the Control menu and then clicking the button on the Stage. The button should exhibit its rollover effects and should also play the Stamp sound when clicked.

To test the sound effect you added to the Stop button:

1. If necessary, click **Control** on the menu bar, and then click **Enable Simple Buttons** to select this command. Now test the Stop button.

2. Click the **Stop** button on the Stage to hear the Stamp sound.

TROUBLE? If you do not hear a sound when you click the Stop button, make sure your computer's speakers are turned on, and the volume control is turned up.

Now you can add the same sound effect to the Play button. Because you are using the same sound effect, the Stamp sound, you do not need to import it to the library. This sound file is already part of your document's library. All you need to do is add the sound to the Play button the same way you added it to the Stop button. You start by opening the Play button in symbol-editing mode.

To add a sound effect to the Play button and then test it:

1. Double-click the **Play button** icon ⏏ in the Library panel. First add a new layer for the sound.

2. In the Play button's Timeline insert a new layer and name it **Sound**.

3. Click the **Down** frame of the Sound layer and insert a keyframe.

4. In the Property inspector, click the **Sound** list arrow, and then click **Stamp.WAV**.

5. Click the **Scene1** link in the Address bar to return to the document. You should now test the button.

6. Click the **Play** button on the Stage to hear the sound.

7. Click **Control** on the menu bar, and then click **Enable Simple Buttons** to deselect this command and turn this feature off.

You have added a sound effect to the Stop and Play buttons using a sound you imported to the library. In addition to adding sounds to your document you can also apply different settings to the sound files within Flash.

Sound Settings

Once you have added a sound to your document, you can control the way it plays by using the sound settings found in the Property inspector. The settings, shown in Figure 5-31, include **Effects**, **Sync**, and **Loop**.

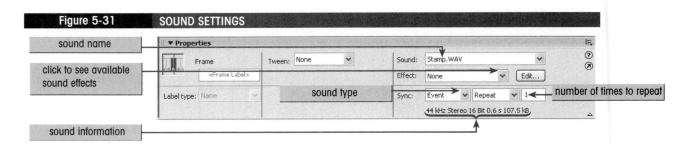

Figure 5-31   SOUND SETTINGS

The **Effect** list box offers the settings described in Figure 5-32.

Figure 5-32	SOUND EFFECTS
Left Channel/Right Channel	Specifies that the sound play in only one channel, either the left or the right; if set to left channel, the sound plays in the left speaker; if set to right channel, the sound plays in the right speaker
Fade Left to Right/Fade Right to Left	Specifies that the sound start on one channel (speaker) and then gradually shift to the other channel
Fade In	Specifies that the sound gradually increase in volume over its duration
Fade Out	Specifies that the sound gradually decrease in volume over its duration
Custom	Lets you customize the sound effects by changing the starting point and volume

The **Sync** list box lets you set a sound as an **Event** sound or as a **Stream** sound, the two main types of sounds used in Flash. In addition to this, you can also control event sounds by using the **Start** and **Stop** sync settings. By default, sounds are set to Event. Once an event sound starts it continues to play until it is stopped by the user or until it finishes. As a result, it is possible to have several instances of the same sound playing at the same time. Recall that event sounds play independently of the Timeline. An event sound will start playing when the playhead reaches the sound's keyframe. The sound will play completely until it is finished. If some button or frame action causes the playhead to play the sound's keyframe again before the sound has finished playing, another instance of the sound starts playing at the same time. This means one sound instance will overlap the other. To prevent this, you can change the sync setting of the sound to Start instead of Event. With the Start sync setting, the first instance of the sound will be stopped before a new instance starts, to prevent overlap. Finally, the Stop sync setting stops a sound that is playing. For example, you may have a sound that starts playing in Frame 1 but you want it to stop playing in Frame 10. You can add the same sound to Frame 10 but use a Sync setting of Stop. When the playhead reaches Frame 10, the sound stops playing.

Another sound setting available in the Property inspector is **Loop**. If you want a sound to play continuously for a period of time, then enter a number in the Repeat text box that specifies how many times you want the sound to play. For example, if a sound is 10 seconds long and you enter 12 for the number of times to loop, then the sound will play 12 times for a total of 120 seconds or two minutes. It is not a good idea to loop sounds with the Stream sync setting. Recall that a stream sound is synchronized with the Timeline. If you loop the sound and it extends beyond the length of the movie's Timeline, Flash adds frames to the Timeline, thus increasing the size of the movie.

In reviewing the tasks assigned for completing this banner, you see that a sound needs to be added that plays in the background. Aly has acquired a bubbling sound that she wants you to use for this task. This sound file is in the WAV format. You will import it into your document's library and add it as a background sound.

To add a background sound to the banner and then test it:

1. Import the **Bubbles.wav** sound from the **Tutorial.05\Tutorial** folder included with your Data Files.

   The Bubbles.wav sound file is added to the document's library.

2. Insert a new layer above the Labels layer, and name this new layer **Sound**. You will add the bubbles sound to the new layer.

3. Click **Frame 1** of the Sound layer. In the Property inspector, click the **Sound** list arrow to view the available sounds, and then click **Bubbles** (or Bubbles.wav). The Bubbles sound is added to the Sound layer, as shown in Figure 5-33.

Figure 5-33   **BUBBLES SOUND WAVEFORM IN LAYERS**

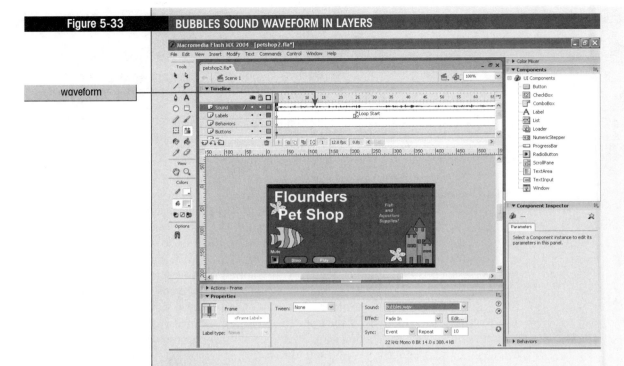

4. In the Property inspector make sure **Event** appears in the Sync text box. Event is the default setting and is used when you do not need the sound synchronized with the Timeline. Enter **10** in the Repeat text box to set how many times the sound should repeat.

As indicated by the information below the Sync list box, the Bubbles sound is 14 seconds long. If you leave the Repeat setting at 0, the sound ends if the user views the animation for more then 14 seconds. By changing the Repeat setting to 10, you are assured that the sound continues playing for a longer period of time. To test the sound you need to play the movie in a Flash Player window or in a Web page. The sound does not play within the Flash program window because it is not synchronized with the Timeline. Test the sound in a Flash Player window.

5. Click **Control** on the menu bar and then click **Test Movie**. The movie opens in a Flash Player window. If your computer's speakers are on, you will hear the bubbling background sound. Close the Flash Player window to return to your document.

You can modify the way a sound plays by changing the settings in the Effect list box. For example, you can change the sound so that it plays only in the left channel or only on the right channel. The Left Channel setting causes the sound to play only in the left speaker. The Right Channel setting causes the sound to play only in the right speaker. You can also use the Fade Left to Right or Fade Right to Left settings. With Fade Left to Right the sound starts in the left speaker and gradually moves to the right speaker. Fade Right to Left starts the sound in the right speaker and gradually moves to the left speaker. Other effects include Fade In and Fade Out. Fade In will gradually increase the sound while Fade Out gradually decreases the sound. Finally, the Custom setting allows you to create your own sound effects by adjusting the starting point of a sound and by controlling its volume.

Aly suggests you explore the various Effect settings to see how they impact the background sound for the banner.

To explore the Effect settings with the background sound:

1. Click **Frame 1** of the Sound layer to select it. Now change the sound Effect setting.

2. Click the **Effect** list arrow to display the list of effects. Click the **Fade Left to Right** effect. Now test the sound.

3. Click **Control** on the menu bar, and then click **Test Movie** to play the movie and hear the background sound. Close the Flash Player window to return to the document.

4. Select different Effect settings and use the Test Movie command each time to hear how the sound is played.

   Aly listens along with you as the background sound plays with different Effect settings applied. She decides that the Fade In effect fits well with the overall design and purpose of the banner and instructs you to apply that setting.

5. Click the **Effect** list arrow to display the list of effects, and then click **Fade In** to select this effect.

Even though the background sound may be nice to listen to, some viewers may not want to hear it. So you want to give the viewer the option to turn off the sound. You have already added a Mute button, but now you need to add an action to the Mute button instance to turn off the sound. To do this you will select the Mute button and then, using the Behaviors panel, you will add a behavior that will stop all sounds. This behavior will not affect the sound effects you added to the Stop and Play buttons.

To add a behavior to mute the background sound and then test it:

1. Click **Control** on the menu bar, and make sure that the **Enable Simple Buttons** command is not selected. This command must be off for you to be able to select the Mute button with the Selection tool.

2. Click the **Mute button** on the Stage to select it. Be sure to select the button and not the Mute text block.

3. Click the **Behaviors panel's** title bar to expand the panel. Now display the basic movie control behaviors.

4. Click the **Add Behavior** button ⊕ in the Behaviors panel, point to **Sound**, and then click **Stop All Sounds**.

5. Click the **OK** button in the Stop All Sounds dialog box. The behavior is added to the button instance, as shown in Figure 5-34.

| Figure 5-34 | STOP ALL SOUNDS BEHAVIOR |

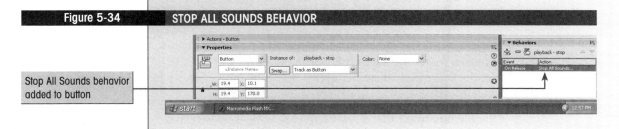

Stop All Sounds behavior added to button

> Now test the Mute button. Recall that the background sound will not play within the Flash program window. So to test the Mute button, you need to play the movie in a Flash Player window or in a Web page.
>
> 6. Click **Control** on the menu bar, and click **Test Movie**. As the animation and the background sound play, click the **Mute** button. The sound stops, but the animation continues to play.
>
> 7. Close the Flash Player window to return to the document, save the changes you have made to the banner, and close the file.

In this session, you learned how to acquire sounds and how to add them to your documents. You added sounds to buttons and you added a background sound to your document. You imported a sound to the document's library. You learned about the types of sounds that Macromedia Flash uses and about the different sound file formats that can be imported into a document. You also learned how to change the sound settings using the Property inspector and finally, you saw how to add a behavior to a button to stop all sounds from playing.

Session 5.3 QUICK CHECK

1. List two Web sites from which you can download sounds to use with your documents.

2. What are the two main types of sounds used in a Macromedia Flash document?

3. What are the three sound file formats that may be imported into Flash?

4. When you import a sound into your document, where is it stored?

5. Sounds can only be added to keyframes. True or False?

6. List three simple effects you can add to a sound in your document.

7. What is the purpose of assigning the Start Sync setting to a sound?

REVIEW ASSIGNMENTS

After reviewing the revised interactive banner, Aly asks you to make some changes to it. She wants you to remove the button below the Mute text block, to modify the text to read Mute Sound, and to make the text into a button. She also asks you to change the Play button so that when it is clicked the animation starts again from Frame 1. The background sound should not overlap each time that Frame 1 is played. Finally, she wants you to select a different sound effect for the Stop and Play buttons and to change the text on the Play button to Start.

If necessary, start Macromedia Flash and then do the following:

1. Open the **petshop2.fla** banner which you created in the tutorial from the Tutorial.05\ Tutorial folder included with your Data Files, set the panels to their default layout, and set the Stage magnification level to show the entire banner in the Stage window.

2. Save the banner in the Tutorial.05\Review folder included with your Data Files. Name the file **petshop3.fla**.

Explore
3. Select the Mute button instance on the Stage and delete it. Also, delete the playback - stop button from the library. You will not use these in this document.

4. Select the Mute text block and change the text to **Mute Sound,** where the word "Sound" is on a second line. Move the text block down to where the deleted button used to be.

5. Convert the text block to a symbol. Name the symbol **Mute**, and select **Button** as the behavior type.

6. Open the new Mute button in symbol-editing mode. Modify the button so that the text changes to a yellow color when the pointer is over the button.

Explore ▷ 7. Add a rectangle to the Hit frame so that it covers the text block. This way the user can click any part of the rectangle to activate the button. The rectangle can be any color because it will not be visible. Exit symbol-editing mode.

8. Use the Behaviors panel to add a Stop All Sounds Action to the Mute Sound button instance.

9. Create a frame label in Frame 1 of the Labels layer. Name this label **Start**.

Explore ▷ 10. Select the Play button. Select the Goto and Play behavior in the Behaviors panel, then click the Delete Behavior button. Add a Goto and Play behavior that refers to the Frame label "Start."

11. To prevent the background sound from playing more than once at the same time, click the Sound layer in the Timeline, then change its Sync setting to Start.

12. Import the **Door.wav** file from the Tutorial.05\Review folder. Edit the Stop and Play buttons to change the sound in each button from Stamp to Door.

13. Edit the Play button to change its text block to read **Start** instead of **Play**. Be sure to change the text in each of its frames.

14. Test the banner to make sure each of the buttons works properly.

15. Save the changes you have made to the petshop3 banner, and close the file.

CASE PROBLEMS

Case 1. Making the Banner for Sandy's Party Center Interactive Sandy Rodriquez, owner of Sandy's Party Center, is excited about the graphics developed for the store's Web site. She asks John Rossini to make changes to the banner he developed earlier. She would like it to be interactive to generate more interest from visitors to the Web site. Sandy also asks John if sounds can be added to the banner. John agrees to make the banner interactive and to add sounds to it.

John asks you to make the revisions to the animated banner you previously completed. He instructs you to add two buttons from the Buttons library: a Stop button and a Play button. The buttons should be similar in design. You are also to add a short sound effect that plays when the buttons are clicked. Also, add the appropriate behaviors to the buttons so that they will control the animation. John has provided a sound file that you are to add to the banner as a background sound. Finally, you will add a frame behavior so that the Grand Opening text block only animates one time.

If necessary, start Macromedia Flash and then do the following:

1. Open the **partybanner2.fla** file that you completed in Case 1 of Tutorial 3. You should have saved it in the Tutorial.03\Cases folder included with your Data Files. If

you did not complete Case 1 of Tutorial 4, then see your instructor for assistance. Save the document as **partybanner3.fla** in the Tutorial.05\Cases folder included with your Data Files.

2. Add a new layer and name it **Buttons**.

3. Open the Buttons library, open the Playback folder and scroll down to the gel Stop button. Make sure the Buttons layer is selected and drag the gel Stop button to the lower-left corner of the banner. Also drag the gel Right button so that it is next to the first button.

4. Add a text block below each button instance on the banner. The text for the gel Stop button should read **Stop** and the text for the gel Right button should read **Play**. Use a small font size for the text and make the text black.

5. Edit the gel Stop button. Insert a new layer and name it **Sound**. Import the **Door** sound from the Tutorial.05\Cases folder included with your Data Files into the Down frame of the Sound layer. Repeat these steps to add the same sound to the Down frame of the gel Right button.

6. Use the Behaviors panel to add the Goto and Stop behavior to the gel Stop button instance. Add the Goto and Play behavior to the gel Right button.

7. Insert a new layer and name it **Background Sound**. Import the **Party** sound file from the Tutorial.05\Cases folder. Add this sound to start at Frame 1 of the Background Sound layer. Make its Sync setting Start, and enter **10** for the number of times to Repeat.

8. Insert a new layer and name it **Labels**. Create a label in Frame 10. Enter **Loop** as the label. Frame 10 should be the same frame where the animated text in the Text layer finishes its motion tween.

9. Insert a new layer and name it **Behaviors**. Use the Behaviors panel to add a Goto and Play behavior in the last frame of the Behaviors layer. Use the frame label Loop as the destination of the behavior.

10. Test the changes to the banner. Make sure the buttons work properly and that the sounds play. Also make sure that the balloons and confetti continue to move after the Grand Opening text stops.

11. Save and close the revised banner.

Case 2. Adding Interaction and Sound to the River City Music Banner Janet Meyers, store manager for River City Music, is very pleased with the animated banner developed for their Web site. She meets with Alex Smith who developed the banner and asks if some additional enhancements can be added to the banner. In particular, she thinks musical sounds will make the banner more interesting. Alex agrees to add sound to the banner and suggests adding some interactivity as well.

Alex asks you to help him revise the banner by adding a behavior that repeats the movement of the musical notes without repeating the text animations. He instructs you to add a button that can be clicked to start the animation from the beginning. The button should resemble a musical note. You also will add a background sound to the banner and a sound effect to the button.

If necessary, start Macromedia Flash and then do the following:

1. Open the **musicbanner2.fla** file that you completed in Case 2 of Tutorial 3. You should have saved it in the Tutorial.03\Cases folder included with your Data Files. If you did not complete Case 2 of Tutorial 4, then see your instructor for assistance. Save the document as **musicbanner3.fla** in the Tutorial.05\Cases folder included with your Data Files.

2. Add a new layer to the Timeline and name it **Labels**. Insert a label in Frame 1 of the Labels layer. Enter **Start** for the label name. Also insert a label in Frame 15. This is where the motion tweens for the text finish. Enter **Loop** for the label name. These labels will be used when you add actions.

3. Insert another layer and name it **Behaviors**. Add a Goto and Play behavior to the last frame, Frame 20, of the Behaviors layer. The behavior should make the playhead go to the Loop frame to repeat the last group of frames that keep the animated musical notes moving.

4. Now add another layer and name it **Music**. Import the **Piano loop** sound from the Tutorial.05\Cases folder. Add the Piano loop sound to the first frame of the music layer. Change its Sync setting to Start and have it repeat two times.

5. To create a new button, copy the note1 symbol in the library. Name the copy **note button** and make sure its behavior is set to Button. Open the note button in symbol-editing mode.

6. Add a keyframe in the Over frame and change the size of the note graphic so that it is slightly larger. Use the Transform panel and enter a value of **110%** for both the height and the width.

7. Add a keyframe in the Down frame and use the arrow keys on the keyboard to move the note graphic three pixels down and three pixels to the right.

Explore ▸ 8. Add one more keyframe in the Hit frame. Draw a rectangle that covers the note graphic. This will be the clickable area of the button.

9. Insert a new layer into the button's Timeline. Name this layer **Sound**. Import the **Piano1** sound from the Cases folder just like you did the Piano loop sound. Add the Piano1 sound to the Down frame of the Sound layer. Exit symbol-editing mode.

10. Add an instance of the note button symbol to the banner. Place the instance in the lower-left corner of the banner. Select the button instance and open the Behaviors panel. Add the Goto and Play behavior. Change the behavior so that it refers to the Start frame. Now when the button is clicked, the playhead goes to the Start frame and repeats all of the animation.

11. Add a text block over the note button with the text **Start Over**. Use a small font and black text.

12. Test your animation to make sure the background music plays and that the button works.

13. Save and close the revised banner.

Case 3. Enhancing the Logo for Sonny's Auto Center Amanda Lester meets with Sonny Jackson and several of his employees to show them the animated logo for their Web site. The feedback is excellent. Sonny and his employees have several suggestions including adding sound and some interactive components. Amanda takes their suggestions and starts revising the logo.

Amanda asks you to help her complete the revisions by adding a background sound to the logo, adding a Stop button and a Go button, each with a sound effect. You also will add a frame behavior to control how the animation plays. The wheels should continue to rotate after the Sonny text shape animation has finished. The Stop button will stop the wheel animations, and the Go button will start the wheel animations.

If necessary, start Macromedia Flash, and then do the following:

1. Open the **sonnylogo.fla** file located in the Tutorial.05\Cases folder included with your Data Files. Save this file as **sonnylogo2.fla** in the same folder.

2. Insert three layers. Name one layer **Behaviors**, another **StopLabel**, and the third **LoopLabel**.

3. Add a label in Frame 19 of the StopLabel layer. Enter **Stop** for the label. Add a label in Frame 20 of the LoopLabel layer. Enter **Loop** for the label.

4. Add a behavior in the last frame of the Behavior layer that makes the playhead go to the frame with the Loop label.

5. Import the **auto loop** sound from the Tutorial.05\Cases folder included with your Data Files. Add this sound to a new layer, and set it to play several times without over-lapping itself.

6. Create a new button and name it **Stop**. This button should be in the shape of a circle, about 20 pixels in diameter with a red fill and black stroke. This button represents a red stop light. Add the **carhorn** sound located in the Tutorial.05\Cases folder included with your Data Files to the button's Down frame.

7. Duplicate the Stop button. Name the duplicate **Go**, and change its fill to green.

8. Insert a new layer in Scene 1 and name it **Buttons**.

9. With the Buttons layer selected, add an instance of the Stop button to the logo. Place it to the right of the "S" in AUTOS on the right side of the logo. Also, add an instance of the Go button and place it right below the instance of the Stop button.

10. Add a behavior to the Stop button instance. The behavior should cause the playhead to go to the frame with the Stop label and the animation should stop at that point.

11. Add a behavior to the Go button instance. The behavior should cause the playhead to go to the frame with the Loop label and continue to play the animation.

12. Test the logo animation making sure the sounds play and that the buttons work properly.

13. Save and close the changes you have made to the logo.

Explore ▷ **Case 4. Adding Sounds and Buttons to the Banner for LAL Financial** Christopher Perez is very pleased with the animations added to the banner for LAL Financial Services. He asks webmaster Elizabeth Danehill to add some interaction with appropriate sounds to enhance the impact that the banner can have when viewers visit their Web site.

Elizabeth asks you to modify the banner so that the animation stops when it reaches the last frame. She also instructs you to add a button that will repeat the animation. The button should resemble the circles that are part of the banner's design. She asks you to search the Web to find a background sound for the banner and a sound effect to be added to the button.

If necessary, start Macromedia Flash and then do the following:

1. Open the **lfsbanner** file from the Tutorial.05\Cases folder included with your Data Files. Save the document as **lfsbanner2** in the same folder.

Explore ▷ 2. Go to the Flash Kit Web site at *www.flashkit.com* or another site of your choice that has sound files you can download. Find two sound files appropriate for your banner. One sound should be short and will be used as a sound effect on a button. The other should be a sound loop that will be used as a background sound. Download the sounds to your Cases folder.

3. Extend the length of the banner by adding regular frames at Frame 45 of each layer in the Timeline.

4. Add a new layer and name it **Sound**. Add another layer and name it **Behaviors**.

5. Add a Goto and Stop behavior to Frame 45 of the Behaviors layer. This behavior should stop the animation and keep it from repeating.

6. Add the sound loop you downloaded to Frame 1 of the Sound layer.

7. Create a new button symbol and name it **Repeat**. Use the circle symbol's shape as the normal state for this button. (*Hint*: Double-click one of the circle symbol instances on the Stage so that you can make a copy of its shape. Then paste the shape into the Up frame of the button.)

8. Change the circle shape in the Over frame so that it has a green gradient fill. Change the shape in the Down frame so that it is offset by a few pixels. Also add the sound effect you downloaded to the Down frame.

9. Add a new layer to Scene 1 and name it **Buttons**. Add a Repeat button instance to Frame 45 of this layer. Place the button instance so that it covers the circle symbol in the upper-right corner of the banner. When the animation stops at Frame 45 the button instance should completely cover the circle symbol. It will look the same as the circle symbol until the mouse pointer is moved over it. Then the rollover effect changes the way it looks.

10. Add a behavior to the button instance. The behavior should cause the playhead to go to Frame 1 and play the animation again.

11. Test the banner animation making sure the sounds play and that the buttons work properly.

12. Save the changes you have made to the banner.

QUICK CHECK ANSWERS

Session 5.1

1. A button is a special symbol that contains its own four-frame Timeline.

2. Buttons provide an interactive element to a Macromedia Flash document. They allow the user to control how he or she watches the published movie.

3. Open the Buttons library from the Common Libraries menu in the Windows menu. Then drag a button from the Buttons library to the Stage. The button is automatically added to the document's library. Or drag a button from the Buttons library to the document's library.

4. A button contains four frames in its Timeline. They are the Up, Over, Down, and Hit frames.

5. You can create a rollover effect by making the Over frame's content different from the Up frame's content. When the pointer is over the button, the content in the Over frame is displayed in place of the content in the Up frame.

6. You can turn on the Enable Simple Buttons option found on the Control menu. This allows you to test a button while still in Flash without publishing the movie.

7. You can use the Align panel to easily align several objects on the Stage.

Session 5.2

1. ActionScript is Flash's scripting language and is used to create scripts to control how a movie plays.

2. False. You do not need to know JavaScript or any other scripting language in order to use ActionScript.

3. Behaviors are precoded instructions that are used to control how a movie plays.

4. Use the Behaviors panel to add behaviors.

5. False. Behaviors are added to a button instance and not to the symbol.

6. An example of an event that triggers a behavior on a button to execute is when the user clicks and releases a button.

7. It is better to refer to a frame label in a script instead of a frame number because if you later add or delete frames, the scripts will not have to be changed.

8. You add a frame behavior to a keyframe, whereas you add a button behavior to a button's instance.

Session 5.3

1. Many Web sites have sounds you can download. These include *www.flashkit.com*, *www.killersound.com*, and *www.soundshopper.com*.

2. The two main types of sounds used in a Flash document are event and stream.

3. The three sound file formats that may be imported into Flash are WAV, AIFF, and MP3.

4. When you import a sound into your document it is stored in the document's library.

5. True. Sounds can only be added to keyframes.

6. Simple effects you can add to a sound in your document can be found under Effect in the Property inspector and include Left Channel, Right Channel, Fade Left to Right, Fade Right to Left, Fade In, and Fade Out.

7. The Start Sync setting can be applied to a sound to prevent several instances of the sound from playing at the same time.

USING
BITMAPS, GRADIENTS, AND PUBLISHING

Creating and Publishing a New Banner and Logo for Flounders Pet Shop

CASE

Admiral Web Design

Joe Flounders has been very satisfied with the results of the banners created for his fish and aquarium sale and for his Web site's pet supplies page. He and Aly previously discussed the possibility of creating a more permanent banner for his Web site to use after the sale. He also had mentioned developing a new logo that can be used in a variety of areas on the company's Web site. Aly and Joe discuss what he wants in a new banner and logo. Up until now, the Flounders Pet Shop banners have only included graphic objects created within Macromedia Flash. Now Joe would like to see photos of some live animals used as part of the banner and logo designs. Aly tells him that it is possible to use photos and even suggests that the photos can be part of an animation.

Aly presents Joe's requests at the regular Admiral's Web Design staff meeting and suggests that Flash be used to create the banner and logo with photos of pets. Aly also suggests a sample Web page be developed that you can use to place the new banner and logo. Up until now, Chris has taken the banners and added them to the existing Flounder's Web site. As part of your training, Aly would like for you to get some experience incorporating Flash graphics into a Web page. She asks Chris to develop a sample Web page you can use.

Aly holds a planning meeting with you and invites Chris to attend. As a result of the meeting, some specific needs are outlined. These include the use of pictures or bitmaps that are representative of Flounders Pet Shop. Chris also suggests using a gradient for the background of the banner. He says he has seen some examples of how gradients have been used to create professional-looking designs. Aly started developing the new Flounders banner. She will have you complete the banner and create the logo. In particular, you will be working on adding bitmaps, creating gradients, and preparing the final movies for use in the pet shop Web site.

Aly has given you a sketch of the banner and logo requested by Joe Flounders for his Web site, as shown in Figure 6-1.

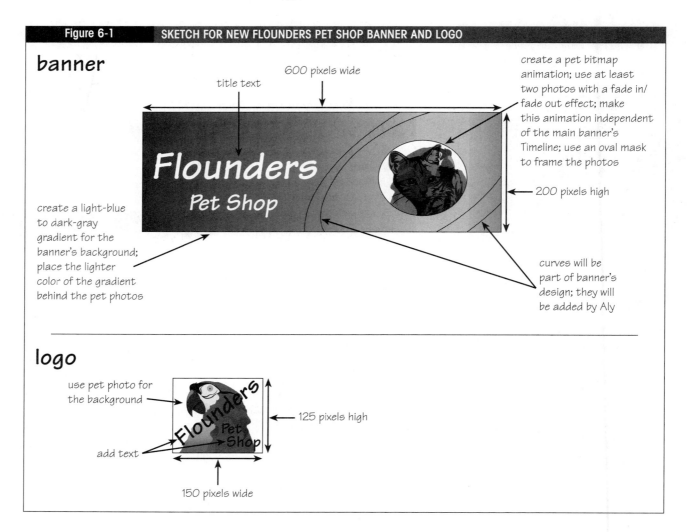

Figure 6-1   **SKETCH FOR NEW FLOUNDERS PET SHOP BANNER AND LOGO**

banner

title text

600 pixels wide

create a pet bitmap animation; use at least two photos with a fade in/fade out effect; make this animation independent of the main banner's Timeline; use an oval mask to frame the photos

Flounders
Pet Shop

200 pixels high

create a light-blue to dark-gray gradient for the banner's background; place the lighter color of the gradient behind the pet photos

curves will be part of banner's design; they will be added by Aly

logo

use pet photo for the background

Flounders Pet Shop

125 pixels high

add text

150 pixels wide

For the banner, she has instructed you to add two photos of pets—one of a cat and one of a parrot. Aly has edited the pictures in a separate image-editing program so that they are both the same size. These pictures will be combined into one animation where each picture is displayed in turn within an oval mask, using a fade in and fade out effect. The pet animation should be independent of any other animation that may be added later to the banner. You are also to create a radial gradient for the banner's background. The gradient will be a blend of a light-blue color that transitions into a dark-gray color. The gradient's light-blue center will be positioned behind the photos of the pets, giving the photos a highlighted effect.

In addition to the banner you are to complete, Aly asks you to create the logo Joe has requested. The logo will have the store name over a picture of a pet in the background. You will create a special effect with the picture to make it different from the pictures used on the banner.

In this tutorial, you will continue your training in Macromedia Flash by learning how to import bitmap graphics into a Flash document, change the bitmaps' properties, convert a bitmap into a vector graphic, and create animations using bitmaps. You will also learn how to create, modify, and use gradients to add a special effect to the banner. Finally, you will explore the various export and publish options available with Flash, and you will incorporate the banner and logo into an existing Web page.

SESSION 6.1	In this session, you will import bitmap graphics into a Flash document. You will change the bitmap properties and then use the bitmaps in an animation. You will also convert a bitmap graphic to a vector graphic and use the resulting graphic to create a logo.

Using Bitmaps

Recall from Tutorial 1 that Flash creates vector graphics that are stored as mathematical instructions. These instructions describe the color, outline, and position of all the shapes in the graphic. Vector graphic files tend to be small and consequently download quickly. They also tend to be mostly geometric in nature, consisting of ovals, rectangles, lines, and curves. In many situations, however, you may want to add more natural looking images such as photographs to your Flash documents. Using a photograph can sometimes greatly enhance the graphics you are creating with Flash. Recall also from Tutorial 1 that a photograph is an example of a bitmap graphic and that a bitmap graphic is stored as a row-by-row list of every pixel in the graphic, along with each pixel's color. Bitmap graphics do not resize well and their file sizes tend to be larger than vector graphics, so using bitmaps in a Flash movie increases the movie's download time. However, this should not keep you from using bitmap graphics in your Flash documents; it just means you should make sure that the graphic is really needed in your document's design. You also cannot create or easily edit bitmap graphics within Flash, so you should use another program such as Adobe Photoshop or Macromedia Fireworks to edit and size the bitmaps before bringing them into a Flash document.

Because you cannot create bitmap graphics in Flash, you need to import them into your documents. Once a bitmap has been imported into Flash, you can change its properties, such as its compression settings, use it in animations, and even change it into a vector graphic.

Importing Bitmaps

Importing a bitmap into your Flash document is a fairly straightforward process. You can use the Import to Stage command or the Import to Library command, both located under Import on the File menu. Both commands place the bitmap in the document's library. The only difference between these two commands is that the Import to Stage command also places an instance of the bitmap on the Stage in addition to placing the bitmap in the document's library. Once the bitmap is in the document's library you can create multiple instances of it on the Stage, yet only one copy of the bitmap is stored with the file. A bitmap in the document's library is not considered a symbol, although the copies you drag onto the Stage are called instances of the bitmap. An instance of a bitmap on the Stage can be converted into a symbol so that it can be used in a motion tween animation. This symbol is then stored in the document's library separately from the original bitmap.

REFERENCE WINDOW

<u>Importing a Bitmap</u>

- Click File on the menu bar, point to Import, and then click Import to Stage or Import to Library.
- In the Import or Import to Library dialog box, navigate to the location of the bitmap file, and then select the bitmap file in the file list.
- Click the Open button to import the bitmap into the document's library.

Based on the planning sketch shown in Figure 6-1 and Aly's instructions, you are to use two photos of pets in the new Flounders Pet Shop banner. To use these photos you need to import them into the document's library. You will open the partially completed banner that Aly has created and import the parrot and cat photos she has provided.

To import bitmap images into a document:

1. Start Flash and open the **flounders.fla** file located in the **Tutorial.06\Tutorial** folder included with your Data Files. Next you want to change the view so that the complete contents of the Stage are visible.

2. If necessary, change the magnification level of the Stage to **100%** and position the panels to their default layout. When you import a bitmap, it is stored in the document's library.

3. Click **Window** on the menu bar and then click **Library** to open the Library panel.

4. Click **File** on the menu bar, point to **Import**, and then click **Import to Library**. In the Import to Library dialog box, click the **Files of type** list arrow, click **All Formats** if necessary, and then navigate to the **Tutorial.06\Tutorial** folder included with your Data Files.

5. Click the **cat.bmp** file, press and hold the **CTRL** key on the keyboard, and then click the **parrot.jpg** file.

6. With the two files selected, as shown in Figure 6-2, click the **Open** button. The two bitmap files are imported into the document's library and now appear in the Library panel.

| Figure 6-2 | IMPORT TO LIBRARY DIALOG BOX |

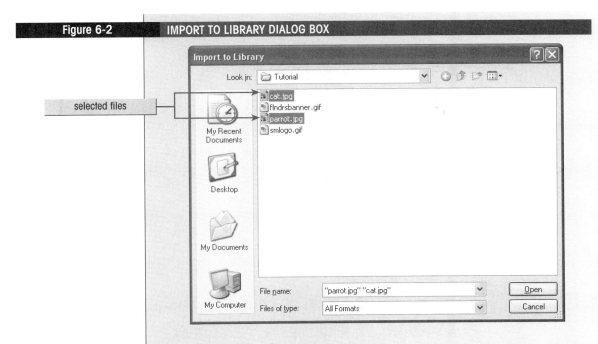

selected files

7. Click the **cat** bitmap in the Library panel to display its picture in the preview area. See Figure 6-3.

| Figure 6-3 | BITMAPS IN THE LIBRARY PANEL |

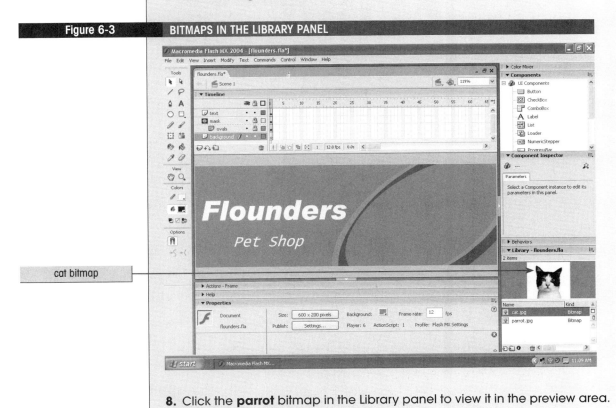

cat bitmap

8. Click the **parrot** bitmap in the Library panel to view it in the preview area.

Now that the bitmaps are in the document's library, you will change their properties using the Bitmap Properties dialog box. Aly suggests you reduce the JPEG quality to reduce the overall size of the final movie. You can check what effect the new JPEG quality value will have on the pictures within the dialog box.

Setting a Bitmap's Properties

You can modify a bitmap's properties using the Bitmap Properties dialog box. You can change the name of the bitmap, update the bitmap if the original file has been changed, and even change its compression settings. Recall from Tutorial 1 that compression means taking away some of the file's data to reduce its size. You can compress a bitmap while still maintaining its quality. To open the Bitmap Properties dialog box you select the bitmap in the Library panel and then click the Properties icon, or you can double-click the bitmap's icon in the Library panel. The options in the dialog box change depending on the file type of the selected bitmap. Figure 6-4 shows two versions of the Bitmap Properties dialog box, one for a JPEG bitmap and one for a PNG bitmap.

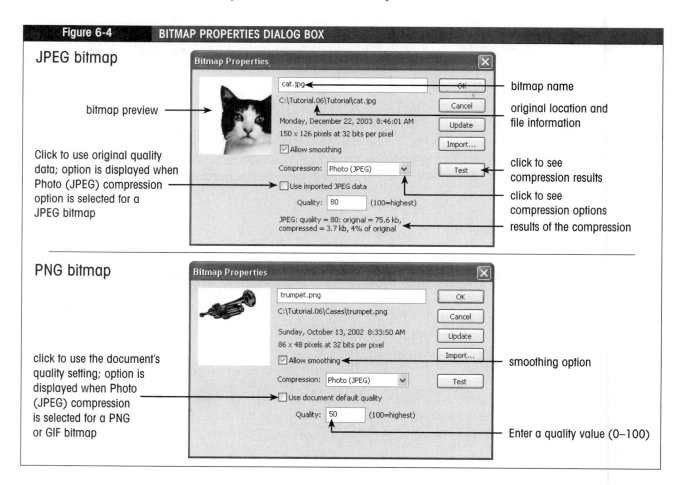

Figure 6-4   BITMAP PROPERTIES DIALOG BOX

The Bitmap Properties dialog box options are described in Figure 6-5.

Figure 6-5	BITMAP PROPERTIES OPTIONS

OPTION	DESCRIPTION
Allow smoothing check box	Smooth the edges of the bitmap so they do not appear jagged
Compression list box	Photo (JPEG): compress the image in JPEG format Lossless (PNG/GIF): compress the image with no data loss
Use imported JPEG data check box	Use the compression quality value specified with the original imported bitmap; check box is displayed for JPEG bitmaps when the Photo (JPEG) compression option is selected
Use document default quality check box	Use the compression quality value specified in the Publish Settings dialog box for the document; check box is displayed for PNG or GIF bitmaps when the Photo (JPEG) compression option is selected
Quality text box	Specify a quality value for compression; higher values (0-100) preserve more of the image and result in larger files; text box is displayed when the Use imported JPEG data check box or the Use document default quality check box is not checked
Location information	Indicates where the original bitmap is stored
Update button	If a bitmap has been modified with an external editor such as Macromedia Fireworks, update the bitmap in Flash without importing it again
Import button	Import a different bitmap to replace the current one; the newly imported bitmap keeps the same name as the one being replaced
Test button	Apply the compression settings; use the preview window to see the resulting image
Compression results	Displays the compressed file size compared to the original file size

In the Bitmap Properties dialog box the name of the bitmap is given, as well as information such as when the file was created or last modified, and its size and current compression rate. You can change the compression settings by choosing either Lossless (PNG/GIF) or Photo (JPEG) from the Compression list box. You can use Lossless (PNG/GIF) compression for bitmaps that are in the PNG or GIF file format or for bitmaps with large blocks of single colors. Use Photo (JPEG) compression for bitmaps with many colors or many color transitions such as photographs.

Imported bitmaps that have a JPEG file format, indicated by a .jpg extension, have the Photo (JPEG) compression option selected in the Bitmap Properties dialog box. The **Use imported JPEG data** check box will also be checked which means the quality JPEG settings of the original bitmap will be used within Flash. When you import bitmaps of other file formats, such as PNG (.png) or GIF (.gif), they will have the Lossless (PNG/GIF) compression option selected in the Bitmap Properties dialog box and the Use imported JPEG data check box will not appear. However, you can change the compression option for a PNG or GIF to Photo (JPEG). Doing so displays the **Use document default quality** check box. When this check box is selected, the bitmaps are displayed using the quality value specified for the whole document. This value is set in the Publish Settings dialog box, which is discussed later in this tutorial.

If the Use imported JPEG data check box or the Use document default quality check box is deselected, then the Quality text box is automatically displayed with a default value of 50. You can change this setting using a range of values from 0 to 100, where 0 yields the lowest result and 100 yields the highest. The Quality setting determines how much compression to apply to the bitmap. The more compression that is applied, the more data that is lost. Smaller values apply more compression while larger values apply less compression. You can experiment with this setting by changing the value and then clicking the Test button. When you click the Test button the bitmap's preview changes to reflect the new compression settings. Keep in mind that a bitmap in the JPEG file format has already been compressed and compressing it further degrades the picture. So you need to balance compression with the quality of the picture. You can use the preview of the bitmap in the Bitmap Properties dialog box to see the impact of the selected quality setting on the bitmap. If you move the pointer over the preview area, it turns into a hand pointer 🖑 which you can drag to adjust the view of the bitmap. You can also right-click the preview to zoom in to see more detail of the bitmap as you apply compression.

Before placing the bitmaps in the banner, Aly recommends you try to minimize the size of the final movie by changing the compression settings for each bitmap using the Bitmap Properties dialog box. The pictures you are using do not have to be of the highest quality because they are small and will be used as part of a larger graphic, the banner. So you can apply some additional compression to the bitmaps to reduce the overall size of the final movie. You start by selecting a bitmap in the document's Library panel and then clicking the Properties icon to open the Bitmap Properties dialog box.

To change a bitmap's properties:

1. Click the **cat** bitmap in the Library panel, and then click the **Properties** icon 🛈 to open the Bitmap Properties dialog box. Now adjust the view of the bitmap in the preview window so you can more readily see the effects of your changes to the picture's properties.

2. Right-click the **bitmap preview** in the upper-left corner and click **Zoom In** on the context menu. Because you want to adjust the compression of the bitmap to suit your needs, you do not want to use the bitmap's imported compression data.

3. Click the **Use imported JPEG data** check box to remove the check and deselect this option. The Quality text box shows the default value of 50. Next, see how the bitmap appears with a lower-quality value.

4. Double-click **50** in the Quality text box, type **20**, and then click the **Test** button to apply the new quality value. See Figure 6-6. Notice in the preview window how the quality of the picture is adversely affected. The picture is of poor quality because some of its colors have changed significantly and it has less detail as evidenced by the small blocks that appear throughout the picture. By contrast, a good quality picture would have most of its original colors and detail.

| Figure 6-6 | TESTING A COMPRESSION VALUE |

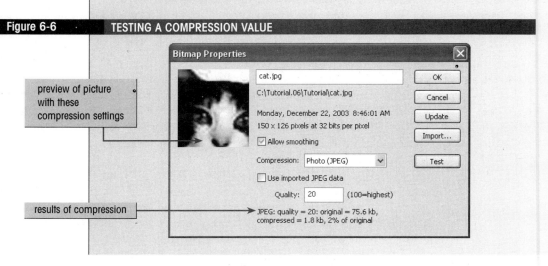

preview of picture with these compression settings

results of compression

Deciding on the best quality value is a subjective effort. There is no specific value that you have to use over another. Instead, you should try several values to compare how the quality of the picture is affected. Select the value that maintains the quality of the picture needed for the particular graphic design while at the same time compressing the bitmap as much as possible. For the cat bitmap, Aly suggests using a quality value of 80.

5. Enter **80** in the Quality text box and then click the **Test** button again. Notice that the compressed size shows the size of the bitmap smaller than the original and that the quality of the picture as seen in the preview window is not adversely affected.

6. Click the **OK** button to accept the compression value. Now you need to adjust the quality for the other bitmap.

7. Click the **parrot** bitmap in the Library panel and open its Bitmap Properties dialog box. Deselect the **Use imported JPEG data** check box and enter a value of **80** in the Quality text box.

8. Click the **Test** button to see how the parrot picture is affected. The parrot picture looks fine with this setting.

9. Click the **OK** button to accept the compression value.

You have changed the compression settings for the two bitmap files. These bitmaps can now be used to create an animation for the new Flounders banner.

Animating Bitmaps

Once you have imported a bitmap into your document you can animate it the same way you animate any other object. For instance, you can create a motion tween that causes the bitmap to move, rotate, change in size (scale), or fade in or out. To animate a bitmap in a motion tween you first need to convert the bitmap instance on the Stage to a symbol. You then create the motion tween the same as you would with any other symbol.

In reviewing Aly's instructions for creating the new banner, you see that you need to use the cat and parrot bitmaps in an animation where one bitmap appears and then fades away while the second bitmap fades in over the first. To accomplish the fade effect you change the alpha amount for each instance. The **alpha amount** controls the transparency of an image. You set the alpha amount by selecting Alpha from the Color list box in the Property inspector and then using the Alpha text box to specify an amount. The alpha amount is a percentage from 0 to 100. An amount of 0% makes the object completely transparent. An amount of 100% makes the object completely opaque, which means it has no transparency. You can create a motion tween that starts the object at an alpha amount of 100% and changes it at the end of the tween to 0%. This makes the object appear to fade out of view. You reverse the amounts to make the object appear to fade into view. Also according to Aly's instructions, this animation of the pet pictures is to be independent of any other animation that may be added to the banner. This means that you should create a movie clip symbol that contains the pet pictures animation within its own Timeline, independent of the main document's Timeline. (Recall that symbols with the movie clip behavior have their own independent Timeline.)

To create a new movie clip symbol and convert the cat bitmap into a symbol:

1. Click **Insert** on the menu bar, and then click **New Symbol**. In the Create New Symbol dialog box, enter **pet animation** as the symbol name, and select **Movie clip** as the behavior type. Click the **OK** button to create the symbol and to enter into symbol-editing mode. Now you will create an instance of the bitmap on the Stage.

2. If necessary, move the Library panel to the right of the Stage, then drag an instance of the **cat** bitmap from the Library panel to the center of the Stage. You need to specify an exact location for the bitmap in the Info panel to center the bitmap.

3. Click **Window** on the menu bar, point to **Design Panels**, and then click **Info**. In the Info panel enter **0** in both the X and Y text boxes and make sure the center registration point is selected in the Registration icon, as shown in Figure 6-7. This centers the bitmap within the editing window.

Figure 6-7	X AND Y COORDINATES SET TO 0

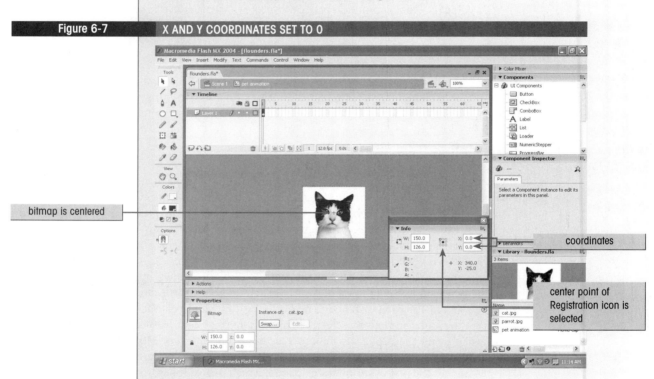

bitmap is centered

coordinates

center point of Registration icon is selected

Now you will convert the cat bitmap instance on the Stage into a symbol so that it may be used in a motion tween animation.

4. If necessary, select the **cat bitmap** instance on the Stage. Click **Modify** on the menu bar, and then click **Convert to Symbol**. In the Convert to Symbol dialog box, enter **cat symbol** for the name, select **Movie clip** for the behavior, and make sure the center registration point in the Registration icon is selected, as shown in Figure 6-8. Click the **OK** button to create the symbol.

Figure 6-8	REGISTRATION POINT SELECTED

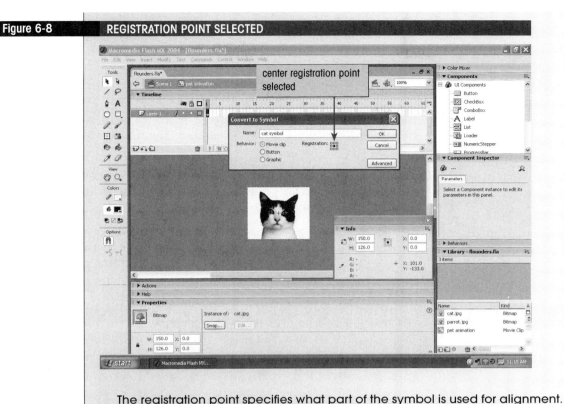

The registration point specifies what part of the symbol is used for alignment. Because the two images, the cat and the parrot, are to be aligned with each other such that they have the same position on the Stage, you want to specify a point in the cat image that can be used for alignment when you position the parrot.

Next you will create an animation in which the cat bitmap fades out of view after a period of time. Aly has given you a sketch that shows how the animation occurs, as shown in Figure 6-9.

Figure 6-9	FADE ANIMATION

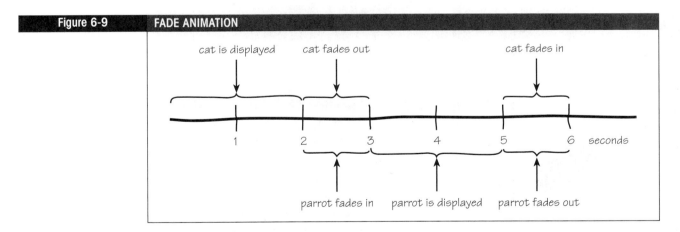

Based on the sketch, the animation of the pictures is to take place over a period of six seconds. During the first two seconds, the cat picture is displayed. Then during the third second, the cat picture fades out, while at the same time the parrot picture fades in. Then during the next two seconds, the parrot picture is displayed. Finally, during the last second, the parrot picture

fades out and the cat picture fades back in. Because the frame rate is 12 frames per second, each second requires 12 frames. Converting these time specifications to frame numbers means that you should have keyframes at Frames 1, 24, 36, 60, and 72. These are the frames where a change occurs from the previous frames.

To create the cat animation:

1. Change the name of Layer 1 to **cat layer**. Next you add key frames for the animation.

2. In the cat layer, insert keyframes at **Frame 24** and **Frame 36**. Next, set the alpha values for the cat instance, which control the transparency of the cat, allowing you to create the fade in and fade out effect.

3. Click **Frame 36** in the Timeline and click the **cat** instance on the Stage to select it. In the Property inspector, select **Alpha** from the Color list box, enter **0%** in the Alpha amount list box, and then press the **Enter** key. The cat instance becomes transparent and thereby no longer appears on the Stage, as shown in Figure 6-10.

| Figure 6-10 | ALPHA AMOUNT SET TO 0% |

transparent cat

alpha option

alpha amount

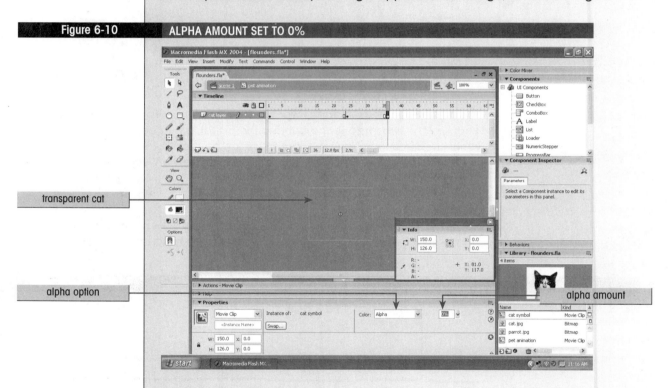

4. Click **Frame 24**, click **Insert** on the menu bar, point to **Timeline**, and then click **Create Motion Tween**.

5. Move the playhead to Frame 1 and then press the **Enter** key to preview the motion tween. The cat instance is displayed and then fades out throughout the motion tween. See Figure 6-11. Recall that the cat is supposed to fade out, and then fade back into view at the end of the animation. You will create another motion tween to fade in the cat.

Figure 6-11   **CAT ANIMATION**

motion tween

cat fading out during
motion tween

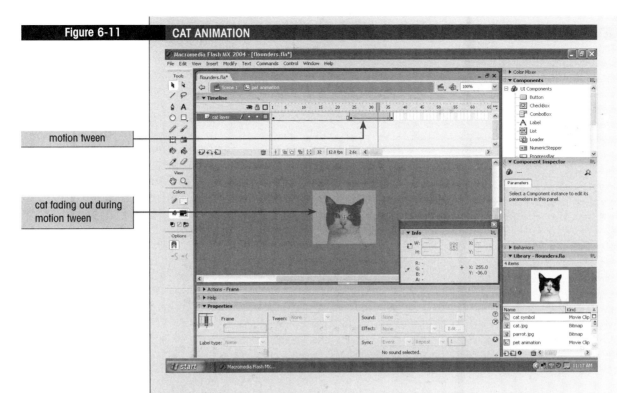

6. Insert keyframes at **Frame 60** and **Frame 72**. Click **Frame 72** in the Timeline, and then click the **cat** instance to select it. In the Property inspector, set its alpha amount to **100%**.

7. Click **Frame 60**, click **Insert** on the menu bar, point to **Timeline**, and then click **Create Motion Tween**. Now preview the two motion tweens.

8. Move the playhead to Frame 1 and then press the **Enter** key. The cat instance is displayed, fades out, and then fades back in at the end of the animation.

You have created an animation where the cat bitmap fades out and then fades in. Now you will repeat similar steps to make the parrot bitmap fade in while the cat bitmap fades out. The parrot bitmap will then fade out while the cat bitmap fades back in. First you need to create a separate layer to hold the parrot animation.

To add the parrot bitmap to the animation:

1. Add a new layer to the Timeline, name it **parrot layer**, and then insert a keyframe at **Frame 24**.

2. Drag a copy of the **parrot bitmap** from the Library panel to the center of the Stage. Next, you use the Info panel to center the parrot bitmap instance and place it in the exact same location as the cat bitmap instance.

3. In the Info panel enter **0** in both the X and Y text boxes and make sure the center registration point is selected in the Registration icon to center the bitmap instance within the editing window, as shown in Figure 6-12.

Figure 6-12   **PARROT ADDED TO FRAME 24**

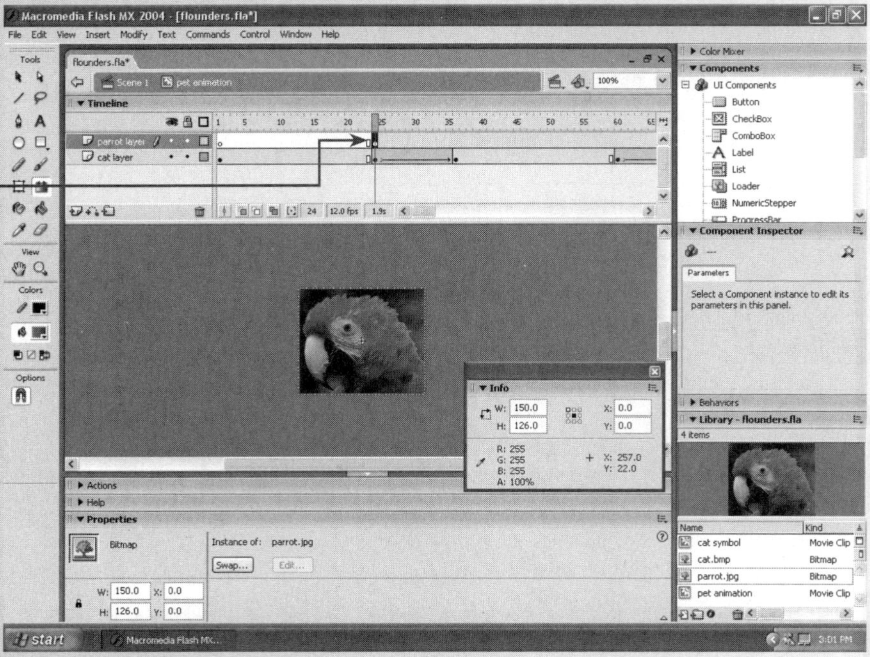

keyframe in Frame 24

4. Close the Info panel; you will no longer need it. Next you convert the parrot bitmap to a symbol.

5. If necessary, select the **parrot** bitmap on the Stage. Click **Modify** on the menu bar, and then click **Convert to Symbol**. Enter **parrot symbol** for the name, select **Movie clip** for the behavior, and make sure the center registration point is selected in the Registration icon. Click the **OK** button. Now add the necessary keyframes.

6. In the parrot layer, insert a keyframe at **Frame 36**. Next, you will set the alpha amount to make the parrot transparent.

7. Click **Frame 24** and, if necessary, select the **parrot** instance on the Stage, and then in the Property inspector select **Alpha** from the Color list box. Enter **0%** in the Alpha amount list box.

8. Make sure Frame 24 of the parrot layer is selected, click **Insert** on the menu bar, point to **Timeline**, and then click **Create Motion Tween**. Now drag the playhead between Frame 24 and Frame 36 and notice how the parrot is fading in while the cat is fading out. See Figure 6-13. Now create the motion tween for the cat to fade back in to view.

Figure 6-13 **MOTION TWEEN FOR THE PARROT**

motion tween

notice parrot fades
in as cat fades out

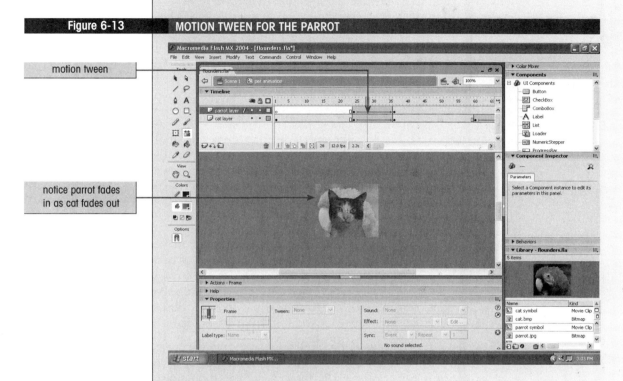

9. In the parrot layer, insert keyframes at **Frame 60** and **Frame 72**. Click **Frame 72** and then click the parrot instance to select it. Use the Property inspector to set its alpha amount to **0%**.

10. Click **Frame 60**, click **Insert** on the menu bar, point to **Timeline**, and then click **Create Motion Tween**.

11. Move the playhead to Frame 1 and then press the **Enter** key. The cat is displayed and then fades out when the parrot fades in. Then the cat fades back in while the parrot fades out.

The pet animation is now complete. Based on Aly's instructions, however, a mask still needs to be added. Recall from previous tutorials that a mask is created on a separate mask layer. The layer below the mask layer becomes the masked layer. The contents of the masked layer that are covered by the shape in the mask layer are displayed when the movie is played. In this case you need to create a mask layer, draw a filled oval that covers the pet animation, and make both the cat layer and the parrot layer masked layers. The filled oval determines how much of the pet animation shows through. This essentially creates a frame for the animation.

To create a mask layer:

1. In the Timeline, select the **parrot layer** and then insert a new layer named **mask**. Now make this new layer a mask layer.

2. Right-click the **mask layer**, and then click **Mask** from the context menu. The mask layer's icon changes to a checkerboard pattern overlaid with an oval shaped frame representing the layer's property. Also, the parrot layer is indented, and its icon changes to a checkerboard pattern indicating it is now a masked layer. Next you need to change the cat layer's properties so that it too is masked.

3. Right-click the **cat layer**, and then click **Properties** on the context menu. In the Layer Properties dialog box, click the **Masked** option button to select this type. Click the **OK** button to close the dialog box. The cat layer is now indented in the Timeline, and its icon also changes to a checkerboard pattern indicating it is now a masked layer. Next, to draw the oval, you need to unlock the mask layer because it is initially locked to display its effect.

4. Click the **mask layer** in the Timeline, and then click the padlock icon to unlock the layer. Next you draw the shape for the mask. Recall that a mask can be any shape that contains a fill. The area covered by the shape's fill determines what part of the masked layers' content is displayed. The shape's fill can be any color because it is not displayed. You choose a light-blue color.

5. Click the **Oval** tool ⭕ on the toolbar. If necessary, use the Fill Color control on the toolbar to select a light-blue color. You need to draw an oval shape so that the pet animation appears as though it is framed by the oval.

6. Position the crosshair pointer on the upper-left corner of the selection box that appears around the cat, and then drag the pointer to draw an oval to cover the cat, as shown in Figure 6-14. Cover as much of the picture as you can but keep the oval inside the picture area.

| Figure 6-14 | MASK COVERING PICTURE |

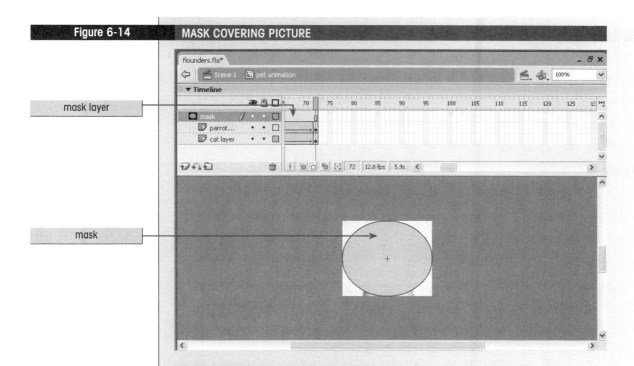

mask layer

mask

7. Lock all of the layers in the Timeline. Locking the layers displays the result of the mask. The cat shows through the mask.

   The mask for the pet animation is now complete. Return to the document and its main Timeline.

8. Click the **Scene 1** link in the Address bar to exit symbol-editing mode and return to the document.

9. Save the document.

Now that you have created the pet animation movie clip, you need to add it to the banner. Recall from the specifications for this banner that the pet animation is to be placed on the right side of the banner inside the large curves.

To add the pet animation to the banner and preview it:

1. Click the **background layer** in the Timeline and drag the pet animation symbol from the Library panel to the right side of the Stage and place it inside the ovals, as shown in Figure 6-15.

Figure 6-15   PET ANIMATION IN BANNER

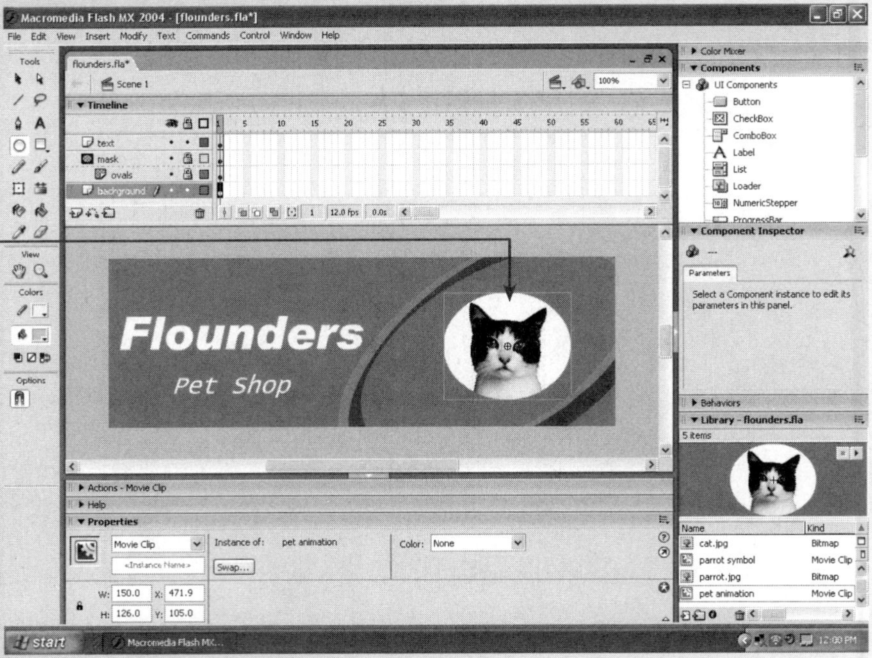

pet animation instance

Because the animation was created inside the movie clip's Timeline, you cannot preview it within the main document's Timeline. To preview the pet animation with the banner, you need to create a SWF file and play it in a separate window or in a Web page. Use the Test Movie command to preview the banner.

2. Click **Control** on the menu bar, and then click **Test Movie**. A separate window opens with the banner and the pet animation.

3. After viewing the banner, close the window to return to Flash.

4. Save the banner.

Another option when working with bitmaps is to convert them to vector graphics. The Flash vector drawing and painting tools can then be used to modify the graphics.

Converting a Bitmap to a Vector Graphic

A bitmap instance on the Stage can also be converted to a vector graphic. Once converted, the graphic can be modified just like any other vector graphics created in Flash. Converting a bitmap to a vector graphic may be useful if the imported bitmap is geometric in nature and you can use the Flash editing tools to edit the graphic. It may also be useful if you want to create a different visual effect with the image. Once you convert a bitmap instance on the Stage to a vector graphic, it is no longer linked to the imported bitmap in the document's library. The original bitmap in the library is not affected and can still be used to create instances of the bitmap on the Stage. Converting a bitmap instance to a vector graphic may also help reduce the file size of the final movie.

You convert a bitmap instance on the Stage into a vector graphic using the Trace Bitmap command. When you select the Trace Bitmap command from the Bitmap submenu on the Modify menu, the Trace Bitmap dialog box opens, as shown in Figure 6-16. You then specify values and select options to indicate how the bitmap is to be converted. The Trace Bitmap command then compares each pixel in the graphic to assign it a color.

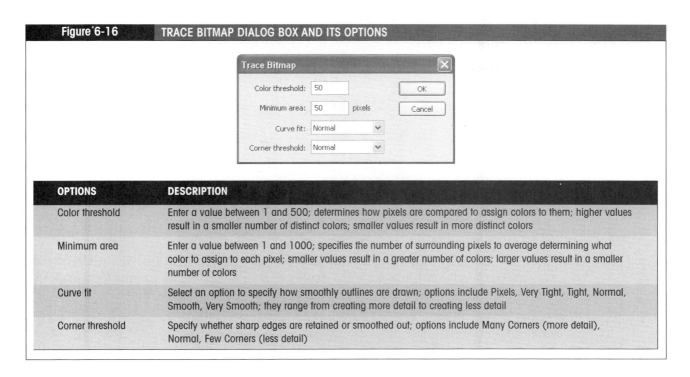

Figure 6-16   TRACE BITMAP DIALOG BOX AND ITS OPTIONS

OPTIONS	DESCRIPTION
Color threshold	Enter a value between 1 and 500; determines how pixels are compared to assign colors to them; higher values result in a smaller number of distinct colors; smaller values result in more distinct colors
Minimum area	Enter a value between 1 and 1000; specifies the number of surrounding pixels to average determining what color to assign to each pixel; smaller values result in a greater number of colors; larger values result in a smaller number of colors
Curve fit	Select an option to specify how smoothly outlines are drawn; options include Pixels, Very Tight, Tight, Normal, Smooth, Very Smooth; they range from creating more detail to creating less detail
Corner threshold	Specify whether sharp edges are retained or smoothed out; options include Many Corners (more detail), Normal, Few Corners (less detail)

When you convert a bitmap to a vector, pixels with similar colors are converted into areas of one color, essentially reducing the number of colors in the picture. Also, areas of contrasting color are converted to lines and curves. You specify how you want Flash to do this conversion through the settings in the Trace Bitmap dialog box. The **Color threshold** value determines how pixels are compared to assign colors to them. A higher value means that the colors of adjacent pixels have to vary more before they are considered to be a different color. Higher Color threshold values result in a smaller number of distinct colors. Smaller values result in more distinct colors. The **Minimum area** value specifies the number of surrounding pixels to average determining what color to assign to each pixel. Using a smaller value for the Minimum area means less surrounding pixels are compared and results in a greater number of colors. A larger value means a greater number of surrounding pixels are compared and results in a smaller number of colors. The **Curve fit** list box provides options for specifying how curves are drawn. The options range from Pixels, which results in more detail, to Very Smooth, which results in less detail. Finally, the **Corner threshold** list box provides options for specifying how many corners or sharp edges are retained in the converted image. The Many Corners option results in more detail and the Few Corners option results in less detail. Applying different values creates different effects on the end result. For example, applying the Trace Bitmap command on the cat bitmap using a Color threshold of 50, a Minimum area of 50, Curve fit at Normal, and Corner threshold at Normal creates a special effect, as shown in Figure 6-17.

Figure 6-17	THE CAT BITMAP CONVERTED TO A VECTOR

original bitmap   vector bitmap

In Aly's discussions with Joe Flounders, Joe indicated that he would like to have a photo of a bird used with the new company logo. Aly instructs you to use the parrot photo as a background for the new logo and to convert the bitmap to a vector graphic to create a special effect. First you will create a new document and set its dimensions as specified in the planning sketch that Aly provided. You will then apply the Trace Bitmap command with values and options suggested by Aly.

To convert the parrot bitmap to a vector:

1. Click **File** on the menu bar, and then click **New**. Click **Flash Document**, then click the **OK** button in the New Document dialog box if necessary. Now change the new document's dimensions to match those given by Aly in her sketch shown in Figure 6-1.

2. Click **Modify** on the menu bar, and then click **Document**. In the Document Properties dialog box enter **150** in the width text box and **125** in the height text box. Click the **OK** button to close the dialog box.

3. Save the file as **petlogo.fla** in the **Tutorial.06\Tutorial** folder included with your Data Files.

4. Change the magnification level of the Stage to **200%**, and then scroll the Stage window so that all of the Stage is visible. If necessary, expand the flounders document's Library panel. The logo will use the parrot bitmap stored in the flounders document's library.

5. Drag a copy of the **parrot bitmap** from the flounders Library panel to the Stage. It should fill all of the Stage. The bitmap is also added to the petlogo document's library. Now you will convert the parrot bitmap to a vector graphic.

   TROUBLE? If the parrot instance on the Stage has a thin blue outline instead of a gray dotted outline, you dragged the parrot symbol instead of the parrot bitmap. Delete the parrot symbol instance from the Stage and repeat Step 5.

6. With the parrot instance selected on the Stage, click **Modify** on the menu bar, point to **Bitmap**, and then click **Trace Bitmap**. The Trace Bitmap dialog box opens.

7. Enter a value of **50** in the Color threshold text box, and then enter a value of **50** in the Minimum area text box.

8. Click the **Curve fit** list arrow, click **Very Tight**, click the **Corner threshold** list arrow, and then click **Many corners**.

9. Click the **OK** button to convert the bitmap to a vector. Deselect the graphic by clicking the Work Area. The parrot picture is now a vector graphic, as shown in Figure 6-18.

Figure 6-18   **PARROT AS A VECTOR GRAPHIC**

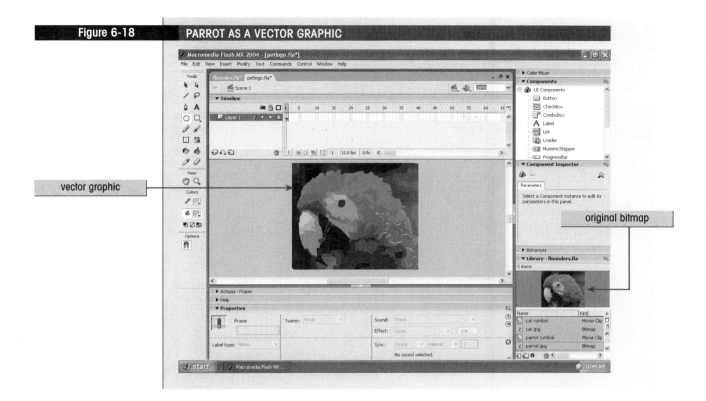

vector graphic

original bitmap

Now that you have converted the parrot bitmap on the Stage to a vector graphic you can complete the logo by adding text on top of the graphic as shown in Aly's planning sketch. The graphic is the background for the logo. You will add the text on separate layers.

To complete the logo by adding text:

1. Insert a new layer and name it **flounders**.

2. Click the **Text** tool A on the toolbar. Click the left-center area of the parrot and type **Flounders**. Now set the text properties.

3. Select the **Flounders** text, and then in the Property inspector, change the font to **Arial Black**, the font size to **26**, and then use the color pop-up window to change the text color to a shade of **yellow** (last column on the right, third row from the bottom). Click the **Left alignment** button, and make sure the Bold and Italic buttons are not selected. Next you make the first letter in the text block larger.

4. Select the letter **F** and then change the font size in the Property inspector to **42**.

5. Click the **Free Transform** tool ⊞ on the toolbar, and then click the **Rotate and Skew** modifier ⟳ in the options area of the toolbar. Drag one of the corner handles on the bounding box around the text to rotate the text block. If necessary, reposition the text block so that it is on the center of the picture. See Figure 6-19.

Figure 6-19	ROTATED AND CENTERED TEXT BOX

bounding box

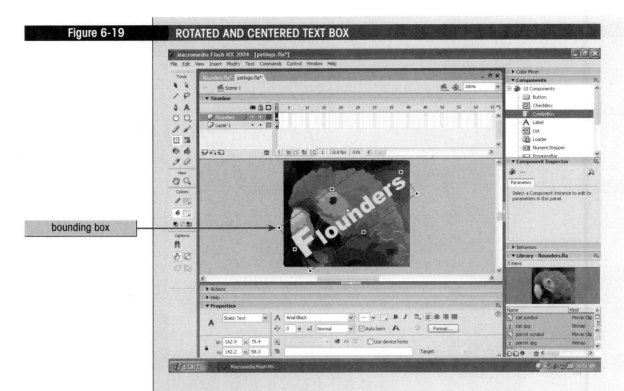

Now you need to create two more text blocks, one for the word "Pet" and one for the word "Shop." Each will have a slightly different color.

6. Deselect the Flounders text block. Click **A** on the toolbar, and then create a text box at the bottom center of the Stage. Type **Pet** for the text.

7. Select the **Pet** text, change the font size to **16**, and the text color to **gray** (fourth row, first column in the color pop-up window). Click the **Work area** to deselect the Pet text block.

8. Use the color pop-up window in the Property inspector to change the text color to a **lighter gray** (fifth row, first column, in the color pop-up window), and then create another text block below the Pet text. Type **Shop** in this text block, and then reposition the two text blocks, as shown in Figure 6-20.

Figure 6-20	LOGO WITH TEXT

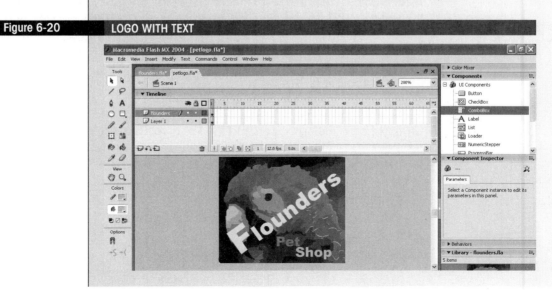

9. Save and close the logo file. You will export this logo and add it to a Web page later in this tutorial.

In this session, you learned that in order to use bitmaps in a Flash document, they have to be imported. Once imported, the bitmaps are stored in the document's library and instances can then be created on the Stage. You also learned how to change a bitmap's properties, how to convert a bitmap to a vector graphic, and how to create an animation using bitmaps. Finally, you learned how to use the alpha amount to create a fade effect animation with the bitmaps.

Session 6.1 QUICK CHECK

1. What is a bitmap?

2. What is the difference between the Import to Stage and the Import to Library commands?

3. How do you access a bitmap's properties within Flash?

4. For what type of bitmaps should you use the Photo (JPEG) compression setting?

5. What alpha amount makes an object transparent?

6. What command do you use to convert a bitmap to a vector graphic?

7. When converting a bitmap to a vector graphic how does the Color threshold value affect the resulting graphic?

SESSION 6.2

In this session, you will learn how to create and use gradients. You will create a custom gradient using the Color Mixer panel, save the gradient, and then apply the gradient to an object on the Stage. You will also learn how to modify a gradient once it has been applied to an object.

Using Gradients

A **gradient** is a gradual blend or transition from one color to another. Using gradients can help you create special effects and add a professional touch to your documents. For example, you can use a gradient for a banner's background, create a gradient to simulate a sunset or a rainbow, or use a gradient as part of an animation. Gradients can be added as fills to any object the same way you add solid color fills. You can select the gradient first for the fill color and then draw an object such as a rectangle that contains the gradient as a fill. You can also use the Paint Bucket tool to apply a gradient to an existing object.

There are two types of gradients you can create in Flash, linear and radial. A **linear** gradient blends the colors from one point to another in a straight line. A **radial** gradient blends the colors from one point outwards in a circular pattern. Figure 6-21 shows examples of linear and radial gradients.

Figure 6-21 **GRADIENT EXAMPLES**

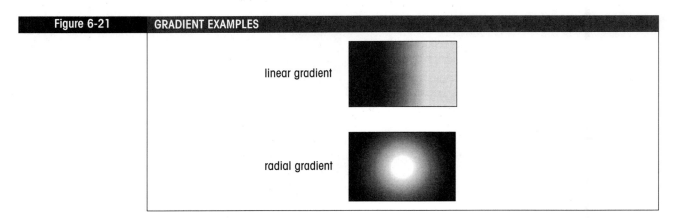

linear gradient

radial gradient

Flash includes several preset gradients located below the color swatches in the color pop-up window. You can use these gradients as fills for any closed shape. You can also create your own custom gradients using the Color Mixer panel.

Creating and Editing Gradients

The Color Mixer panel can be used to create new gradients. With the Color Mixer you specify linear or radial gradient as the fill style and then select the colors for the gradient. Once you select a gradient as the fill style, the gradient definition bar is displayed in the middle of the panel. Gradient pointers are displayed below the gradient definition bar and specify which colors are used in the gradient. If you need to create a gradient with more than two colors, you just add more gradient pointers. You add gradient pointers by clicking the area below the gradient definition bar, as shown in Figure 6-22.

Figure 6-22 **GRADIENT POINTERS IN COLOR MIXER**

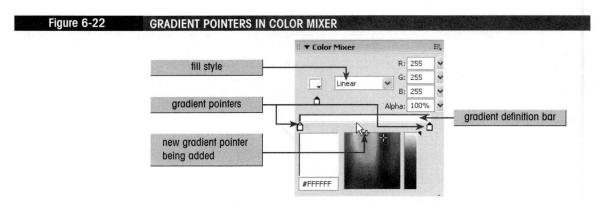

To remove a gradient pointer you drag it down, away from the gradient definition bar. Also, you can reposition a gradient pointer by dragging it to the left or the right. Doing so changes the gradient's **fall off point**, which is the point where the gradient shifts from one color to another.

There are several ways in which you can specify the colors for the gradient. Before specifying a color, however, you should first click the gradient pointer for the color you want to change. You then select a color using the color pop-up window, by entering the color's Red, Green, Blue (RGB) values, or by clicking the Color Space in the Color Mixer. You can also adjust the brightness of a color using the brightness control in the lower-right corner of the Color Mixer.

Once you have created a gradient you can save it with the Add Swatch command located on the Color Mixer's options menu. This command adds the new gradient to the document's color swatches that appear in the color pop-up window. The gradient is only stored with the current document.

Aly's instructions for creating the new banner for the Flounders Pet Shop state that the background should be a radial gradient using a blend of a light-blue color that transitions into a dark-gray color. You need to create the radial gradient and then create a rectangle with the gradient as its fill for the banner's background. You will create the rectangle on a separate layer.

To create a gradient for the banner:

1. If you took a break after the last session, start Flash, and open the **flounders.fla** document. Change the magnification level of the Stage to **100%** and position the panels to their default layout. Expand the Color Mixer panel if necessary.

2. Click the **Fill style** list arrow in the Color Mixer panel, and then click **Radial**. Now you can use the Color Swatches panel to view the preset gradients.

3. If necessary, click the **Color Swatches** panel title bar to expand it or open it using the Window menu. You will select a preset gradient as a starting point.

4. Click the **gray radial** gradient in the Color Swatches panel with the eyedropper pointer ⌖. This gradient appears as the second gradient from the left below the color swatches. See Figure 6-23.

Figure 6-23	SELECTING A PRESET GRADIENT

The Color Mixer changes to display the preset gray radial gradient and its gradient pointers. Next you change these gradient pointers to create a new gradient based on the colors specified in the planning sketch.

5. Click the **left gradient pointer** below the gradient definition bar to select it. When a gradient is selected, its small triangle appears black.

6. Click the panel's **color control** list arrow to open the color pop-up window.

7. Click the color swatch in the bottom row, seventh column from the left, as shown in Figure 6-24.

Figure 6-24   **CHOOSE THE LEFT GRADIENT COLOR**

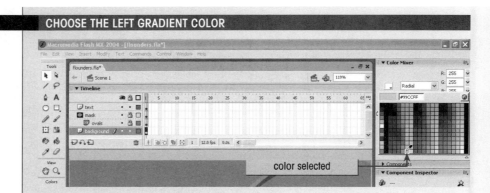

8. Click the **right gradient** pointer under the gradient definition bar, open the color pop-up window, and then click the color swatch in the second row, first column from the left.

   The Color Space in the Color Mixer shows the new gradient based on the colors you selected. You should save this gradient with the document.

9. Click the Color Mixer panel's **options menu** control 📇, and then click **Add Swatch** from the menu. The gradient is now added to the gradients in the Color Swatches panel, as shown in Figure 6-25.

Figure 6-25   **NEW GRADIENT IN COLOR SWATCHES PANEL**

You have created a gradient and added it to the document's color swatches. Now you are ready to use this gradient to create a background rectangle for the banner.

Applying a Gradient Fill

To apply a gradient fill to an object you follow the same process as when applying a solid fill. You can select the gradient for the fill color and then when you draw a shape such as a rectangle, the rectangle has the gradient as its fill. If the shape already exists on the Stage, you can use the Paint Bucket tool to apply the gradient. When using the Paint Bucket tool to apply a radial gradient, you can specify where the gradient's center point should go. The center point of a radial gradient is where the first color begins. The point where you click determines the gradient's center point, as shown in Figure 6-26.

| Figure 6-26 | RADIAL GRADIENT'S CENTER POINT |

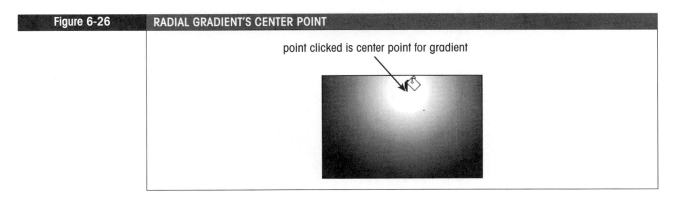

point clicked is center point for gradient

You can also apply a linear gradient by drawing a straight line with the Paint Bucket pointer 🪣. The line you draw determines the direction of the gradient.

Another option you can use when applying gradients is the Lock Fill modifier which is displayed in the options area of the toolbar when the Paint Bucket tool is selected. Using the Lock Fill modifier paints one gradient across several objects on the Stage rather than one gradient for each object. See Figure 6-27.

| Figure 6-27 | EFFECT OF LOCK FILL MODIFIER ON GRADIENTS |

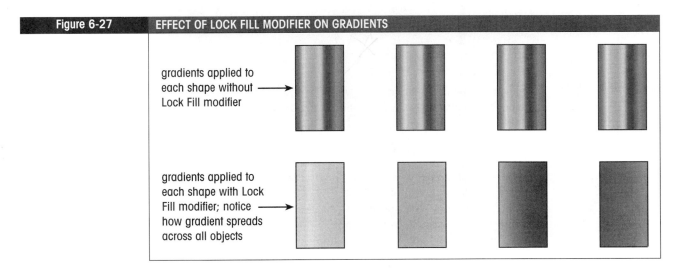

gradients applied to each shape without Lock Fill modifier

gradients applied to each shape with Lock Fill modifier; notice how gradient spreads across all objects

Now you will create a rectangle that uses the gradient you created earlier. The rectangle will serve as the banner's background. The rectangle will be added to the background layer.

To add a rectangle with the custom gradient:

1. If necessary, select the **background** layer, and then click the **Rectangle** tool 🔲 on the toolbar. Click the **Stage** once to display the Rectangle tool properties in the Property inspector.

2. If necessary, use the Property inspector to select the new gradient you created for the fill. The gradient is located in the bottom row, eighth column of the color pop-up window on the toolbar. Set the stroke to **no color**.

3. Draw a large rectangle that is the same size as the Stage. The rectangle should cover the entire Stage. See Figure 6-28

Figure 6-28	GRADIENT AS BACKGROUND

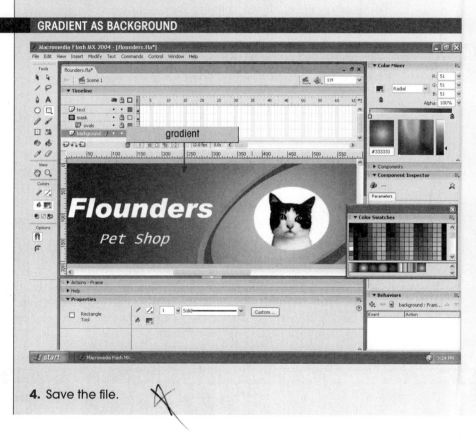

4. Save the file.

You now have a rectangle with the new gradient that serves as a background for the banner. This gradient can be modified to create a different effect using the Fill Transform tool.

Transforming Gradient Fills

A gradient fill in an object can be modified by using the Fill Transform tool on the toolbar. You can move a gradient's center, change its size, or change its direction. When you select a linear gradient with the Fill Transform tool, a bounding box is displayed around it. For a radial gradient a bounding circle is displayed around it. The gradient's center point is also displayed along with editing handles, as shown in Figure 6-29. You drag these handles to transform the gradient.

6. Click the Work Area to hide the bounding circle, and then return the magnification level to **100%**.

7. Save the flounders.fla banner.

The gradient has now been transformed. You show the banner to Aly and she is very pleased with your work and thinks it will look great on the Flounders Pet Shop Web site.

In this session, you learned about gradients. You learned how to create a gradient and how to use a gradient by drawing an object or by applying it to an existing object. You also learned how to modify a gradient's position, size, and width using the Fill Transform tool. In the next session, you will publish the banner.

Session 6.2 QUICK CHECK

1. What is a gradient?

2. Which panel is used to create a gradient?

3. How do you save a gradient?

4. When you save a gradient it is only saved with the current document. True or False?

5. If you have a gradient with two colors, how do you add another color?

6. Which tool is used to apply a gradient to an existing object?

7. Which tool is used to modify a gradient fill?

8. Which handle do you change on a linear gradient to rotate the gradient?

SESSION 6.3

In this session, you will learn about the publishing options in Macromedia Flash. You will explore the various settings available and then you will publish the new Flounders banner as a SWF file and export the new logo as a JPEG file. You will also learn how to incorporate the banner and logo into an existing Web page.

Publishing Options

As you have learned, the native file format for your Macromedia Flash documents is the FLA format. When you are done creating a FLA document you want to make it available for use on the Web. To do so, the document has to be published or exported into a format readable by a Web browser. You have already done this when you published your FLA documents as SWF movie files in previous tutorials. You have done this using the Test Movie command on the Control menu and also when you used the Default – (HTML) command on the Publish Preview menu. Recall the Test Movie command creates a SWF file and plays it in a separate window. The Default – (HTML) command creates both a SWF file and an HTML file to play the movie. The browser uses the Flash Player plug-in to play the movie. In most cases, if you are creating movies for the Web, you want to publish a SWF file. However, there are times when you need to publish or export your document in a different file format. Flash has other publishing and exporting options that allow you to publish your Flash documents in such file formats as JPEG, GIF, and PNG. A Flash file can even be published as a projector file, which is a stand-alone file with an .exe extension. A projector file has the Flash Player incorporated into it and plays the movie in its own window, not in a Web browser.

You specify how you want your FLA documents published using the Publish Settings dialog box. You can also save the publishing settings as a profile that you can use with other documents.

Publish Settings

The Publish Settings dialog box shown in Figure 6-32 lists the many file formats you can use to publish a Flash document.

Figure 6-32   **PUBLISH SETTINGS DIALOG BOX**

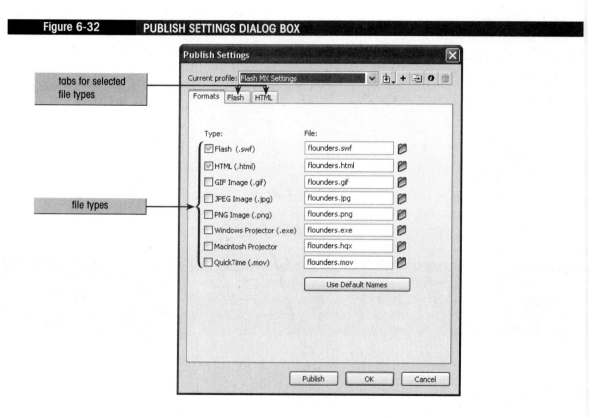

By default, only the first two Type options are selected. These are Flash (.swf) and HTML (.html). Most of the time, the documents you create are meant to be played on a Web page so these two options are the only two you will select. However, if you need to publish a document in a different format, you should select the check box for that format. For example, if you need to publish the document as a JPEG file, then you select the JPEG Image (.jpg) check box. Upon selecting a new Type option, its corresponding tab is displayed at the top of the dialog box. Each of the tabs has additional options for the associated file type. For example, when you click the Flash tab, its options are displayed. The Flash options and the default settings are shown in Figure 6-33.

Figure 6-33   FLASH FORMAT OPTIONS

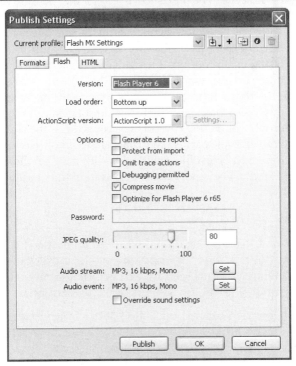

The Flash options are described in Figure 6-34.

Figure 6-34   FLASH FILE OPTIONS

OPTION	DESCRIPTION
Version list box	Select the Flash Player version to publish to
Load order list box	Select either Bottom up or Top down; determines the order the movie's layers are displayed
ActionScript version list box	Specifies version of ActionScript
Options:	
Generate size report check box	Create text file with information about the size of the published file and its components
Protect from import check box	Prevent the SWF file from being imported and converted back to a FLA file
Omit trace actions check box	Advanced option used when troubleshooting a movie
Debugging permitted check box	Advanced option used to troubleshoot a movie
Compress movie check box	Compress a Flash movie; the resulting movie only plays in Flash Player 6 or later
Optimize for Flash Player 6 r65	Optimize the movie for the specific release of Flash Player 6
Password text box	Add password for protection; use when Debugging Permitted is selected
JPEG quality	Specify the JPEG quality value for all JPEG images in the document; settings applied to individual images with the Bitmap Properties dialog box override this setting
Audio stream	Specify the compression settings for stream sounds
Audio event	Specify the compression settings for event sounds
Override sound settings check box	Override the sound settings set for individual sounds with the Sound Properties dialog box

The new banner you created will be added to the home page of the Flounders Pet Shop Web site so it needs to be published as a SWF file. Because the Web page already exists, you are to publish a SWF file only. Aly also instructs you to use the Publish Settings dialog box to specify what to publish and how to publish the movie. She wants you to make the SWF file compatible with all Flash Player plug-ins starting with version 5. You are to accept the Load Order default setting of Bottom up. This movie contains a small number of layers so the order they are loaded is insignificant. Also, the JPEG quality and sound settings do not have to be changed. Recall the bitmap properties were individually set and they override the JPEG settings in this dialog box. Also, there are no sounds in this movie so the Audio settings are not used. The only option that Aly instructs you to set is the Generate size report option. She wants you to see an example of this report that shows the size of the different parts of the movie. The report is created as a text file and is saved with the FLA file's name plus the word Report and an extension of .txt. The report is also displayed in the Output panel when the file is published.

To publish a SWF file:

1. If you took a break after the last session, start Flash and open the **flounders.fla** file. Change the magnification level of the Stage to **100%** and position the panels to their default layout. Click **File** on the menu bar, and then click **Publish Settings**. The Publish Settings dialog box opens.

2. On the **Formats** tab, click the **HTML (.html)** check box to deselect this option, and then make sure that the **Flash (.swf)** check box is checked. Now you will specify the name for the SWF file.

3. Enter **banner.swf** in the File text box to the right of Flash (.swf), as shown in Figure 6-35. Next you set the publishing options Aly has requested.

| Figure 6-35 | ENTERING A NEW NAME FOR THE SWF FILE |

new file name

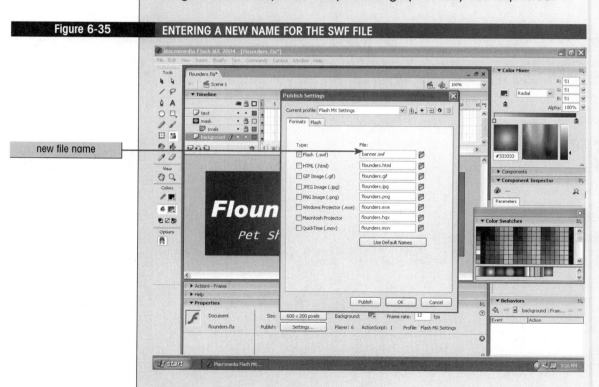

4. Click the **Flash** tab to display the settings for this format. Click the **Version** list arrow, click **Flash Player 6**, click the **Compress movie** check box to deselect it, and then click the **Generate size report** check box to select it. See Figure 6-36.

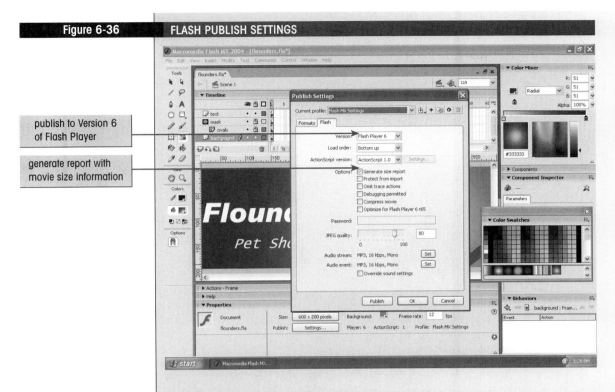

Figure 6-36   FLASH PUBLISH SETTINGS

publish to Version 6
of Flash Player

generate report with
movie size information

5. Click the **Publish** button to create the SWF file and the size report. The files are
   created in the same folder as the FLA file. The Output panel also opens. You will
   view its contents later in this session.

Aly tells you that Flash allows you to save your preferred publish settings for the document
as a publishing profile. When you save publish settings as a publishing profile, the settings are
available to any document you create in Flash. Aly decides to show you how to create a
publishing profile.

To save the publishing profile:

1. Click the **Create New Profile** button ⊞ in the Publish Settings dialog box to
   open the Create New Profile dialog box.

2. Enter **Pet Shop** in the Profile name text box, and then click the **OK** button.

   Pet Shop appears in the Publish Settings dialog box as the current profile, as
   shown in Figure 6-37.

Figure 6-37 PUBLISH PROFILE SAVED

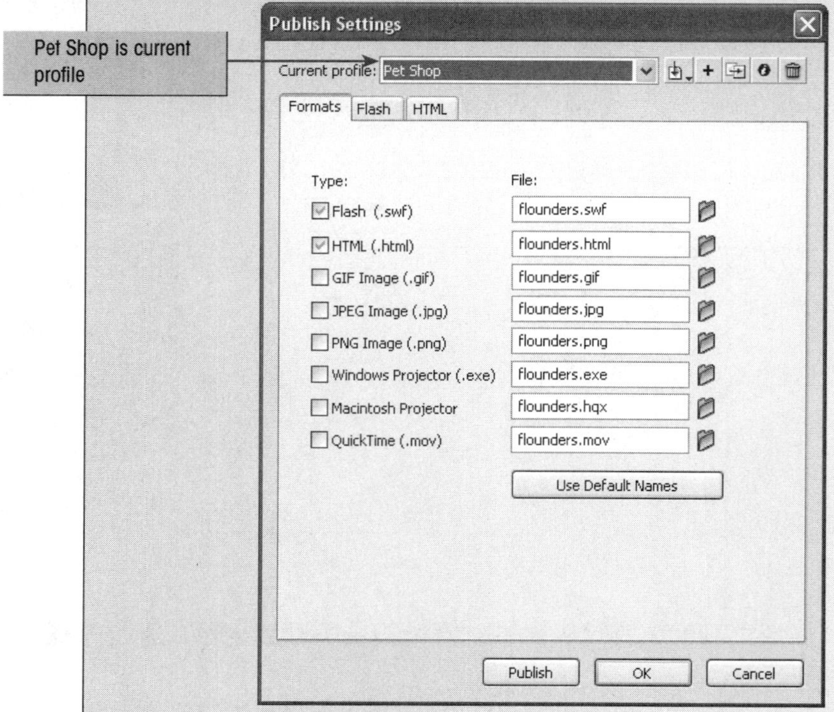

Pet Shop is current profile

If you are working in a computer lab on a shared computer, you should delete this publishing profile.

3. Click the **Delete Profile** button 🗑 in the Publish Settings dialog box, then click the **OK** button in the Flash MX dialog box asking you to confirm the deletion.

The profile is not saved for future use, but you can go back and save a new profile any time you need to.

4. Click the **OK** button to close the Publish Settings dialog box.

5. Save and close the flounders.fla file.

You have changed the publish settings for this file. The next time you need to publish, you can click the Publish command on the File menu instead of using the Publish Settings command. The Publish command publishes the files according to the settings in the Publish Settings dialog box. Also, because you deselected HTML (.html) from the Formats list, the Publish Preview command on the File menu no longer reads Default (HTML). Instead it reads Default (Flash) indicating that the default now creates a SWF file only and not an HTML file.

Aly instructs you to view the size report text file generated by Flash. The file displays automatically in the Output panel, but you can also open it in the Notepad program which is part of Windows.

To view the size report file in the Output panel:

1. Place the pointer over the edges of the Output panel and drag to enlarge it to view the text, as shown in Figure 6-38.

| Figure 6-38 | OUTPUT PANEL WITH MOVIE SIZE REPORT |

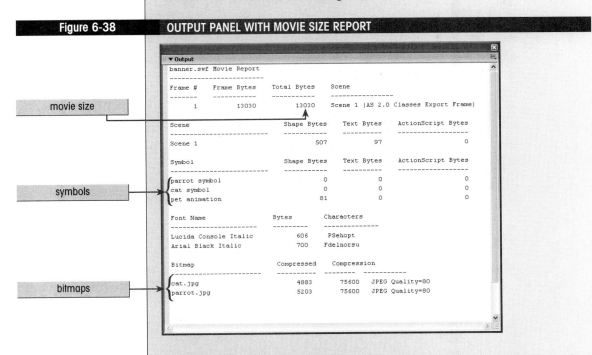

The report file shows information about the movie including its number of frames. Recall the main Timeline for the banner only has one frame. It also shows the total size of the movie in number of bytes, a list of the symbols in the movie, and a list of the bitmaps. This information can be useful when optimizing a larger, more complex movie to find ways of reducing its size.

2. Click the Output panel's **option menu** control ▤, and then click **Close Panel** to close the report.

Now that you have published the banner and viewed its size report, you turn your attention to the logo you created earlier in this tutorial. The logo can be published as a SWF file, but because it does not have any animation Aly wants you to export it as a JPEG file.

Exporting an Image

The JPEG and GIF file formats are the most common file formats used for images on Web pages. JPEG format is best for images that include many colors such as the photograph of the parrot. GIF format is best for images with fewer colors. You can use the Publish Settings dialog box to select JPEG or GIF as the format to publish. You can also use the Export Image command on the File menu. The Export Image command allows you to specify the type of format you want to export to and then displays settings you can change based on the file format you select. Some of the formats you can export to are listed in Figure 6-39.

Figure 6-39 **EXPORT FORMATS**

FILE TYPE	EXTENSION
Flash movie	.swf
Enhanced metafile	.emf
Windows metafile	.wmf
Adobe Illustrator	.ai
Bitmap (BMP)	.bmp
JPEG image	.jpg
GIF image	.gif
PNG image	.png

Because the logo you created earlier is static and includes only a picture and some text, you can export it as a JPEG image using the Export Image command.

To export the logo as a JPEG image:

1. If necessary, display the Flash program window. Open the **petlogo.fla** document stored in the **Tutorial.06\Tutorial** folder included with your Data Files. The Export Image command is located on the File menu.

2. Click **File** on the menu bar, point to **Export**, and then click **Export Image**. The Export Image dialog box opens.

3. If necessary, navigate to the **Tutorial.06\Tutorial** folder included with your Data Files. Enter **petlogo** in the File name text box, click the **Save as type** list arrow, and then click **JPEG Image (*.jpg)**.

4. Click the **Save** button. The Export JPEG dialog box opens. See Figure 6-40.

Figure 6-40 **EXPORT SETTINGS**

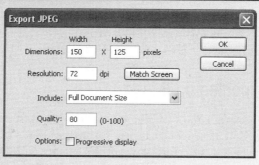

> Notice the Include list box has options of **Minimum Image Area** or **Full Document Size**. If the document has empty space, the Minimum Image Area setting will not export the empty space. The Quality value specifies how much compression is applied to the whole image.
>
> 5. If necessary, click the **Match Screen** button to change the dimensions to **150** by **125** pixels and the resolution to **72**. Also, if necessary, set the Include option to **Full Document Size** and enter **80** for the Quality value, as shown in Figure 6-40.
>
> 6. Click the **OK** button to save the image and close the dialog box.
>
> 7. Close the petlogo.fla file.

The published banner and exported logo are now ready to be placed in a Web page.

Adding Flash Graphics to a Web Page

The final outcome of creating movies with Macromedia Flash is a Web page that displays the movies along with text, hyperlinks, and other graphics. Once you complete a Flash graphic such as a banner or a logo you need to incorporate its file information into the Web page's HTML. When you publish a movie with the HTML format option, Flash automatically creates a simple Web page to display the movie. However, to add the SWF file to an existing Web page you need to edit the actual Web page. You can do this with a Web page editing program such as Macromedia Dreamweaver or Microsoft FrontPage. You also can edit the HTML itself in a text editor such as Notepad.

Chris has created a sample Web page for you to use to add the banner and the logo you have created. The Web page has a simple banner and logo that you will replace. You will edit the Web page using Notepad.

To add the banner and logo to a sample Web page:

1. Click the **Start** button on the taskbar, point to **All Programs**, point to **Accessories**, and then click **Notepad** to start the program.

2. Click **File** on the Notepad menu bar, and then click **Open**. The Open File dialog box opens.

3. Click the **Files of type** list arrow, click **All Files**, navigate to the **Tutorial.06\Tutorial** folder included with your Data Files, click **sample.htm** in the file list, and then click the **Open** button. The HTML for the sample Web page is displayed in the Notepad window.

4. Click the **Maximize** button ▣ to maximize the program window. See Figure 6-41.

Figure 6-41 **SAMPLE WEB PAGE HTML**

replace image tag

change logo name and dimensions

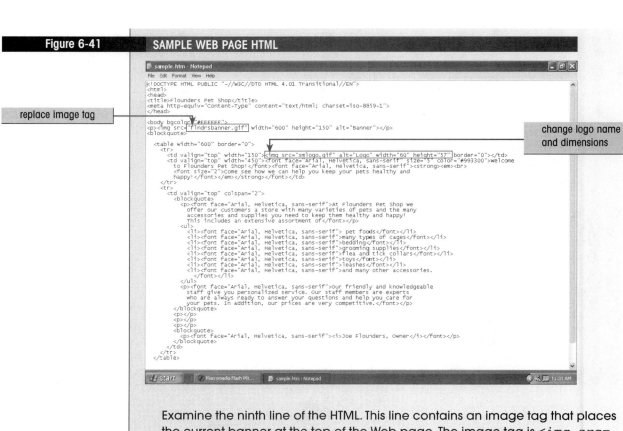

Examine the ninth line of the HTML. This line contains an image tag that places the current banner at the top of the Web page. The image tag is `<img src= "flndrsbanner.gif" width="600" height="150" alt="Banner">`. You need to replace this tag with a special EMBED tag for the SWF file. EMBED is not a standard HTML tag, but instead is used to load external media such as a SWF movie that requires the use of a plug-in.

5. Replace everything between the two angle brackets in the image tag with

   `<embed src="banner.swf" width="600" height="200">`

   Next you need to replace the reference for the current logo with a reference for the new logo file, petlogo.jpg.

6. On the 14th line, replace `smlogo.gif` with `petlogo.jpg`. Next you change the width and height values.

7. On the same line, replace `width="60" height="57"` with `width="150" height="125"`.

8. Save the changes, close the file, and exit Notepad.

Now that you have made the changes to the HTML of the sample Web page, you can test it by opening the page in your browser.

To preview the sample.htm Web page:

1. Start your browser.

2. Click **File** on the menu bar, and then click **Open**.

3. In the Open dialog box, click the **Browse** button, and then navigate to the **Tutorial.06\Tutorial** folder included with your Data Files.

4. Click **sample.htm** in the file list, and then click the **Open** button. Click the **OK** button in the Open dialog box. The page is displayed in the browser window, as shown in Figure 6-42.

| Figure 6-42 | SAMPLE WEB PAGE WITH FLASH GRAPHICS |

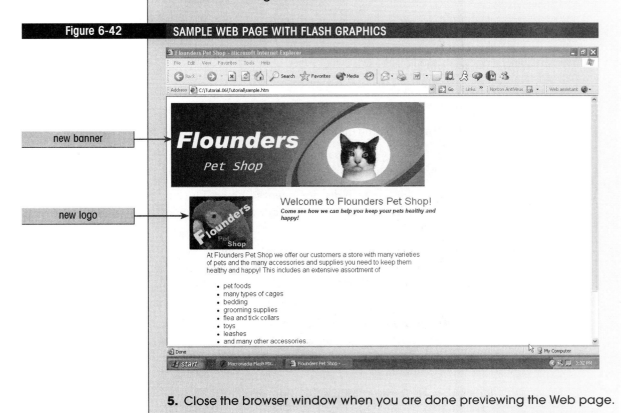

5. Close the browser window when you are done previewing the Web page.

In this session, you learned about the different options available in Flash to publish and export movies and graphics. You changed the publish settings for the banner and then you published the banner movie. You also changed the export settings to export the logo as a JPEG file. Finally, you edited the HMTL for a sample Web page to incorporate references for the new Flounders Pet Shop banner and logo.

Session 6.3 QUICK CHECK

1. What is the native file format for Flash documents?

2. What is the file format for published Flash movies?

3. How do you get the GIF tab to be displayed in the Publish Settings dialog box?

4. What information is contained in the size report generated when the Generate size report option is selected in the Flash publish settings?

5. What types of files are published by the Publish command?

6. List five file formats you can export with the Export Image command.

7. To add a SWF file to an existing Web page you must use Notepad. True or False?

REVIEW ASSIGNMENTS

Aly is very pleased with the new Flounders banner and asks you to make some changes before she shows it to Joe Flounders. She instructs you to replace the parrot bitmap with a dog bitmap in the pet animation. The dog bitmap will have the same properties as the other bitmaps and will have the same fade effect in the animation. She also asks you to change the Flounder text block so that it has a gradient instead of a solid color for the fill of the letters.

If necessary, start Macromedia Flash and then do the following:

1. Open the **flounders.fla** banner file which you created in the tutorial. It is located in the Tutorial.06\Tutorial folder.

2. Save the banner in the Tutorial.06\Review folder. Name the file **flounders2.fla**.

3. Import the **dog** bitmap into the document's library. The bitmap is in the Tutorial.06\Review folder included with your Data Files. Modify the dog bitmap's properties using a Quality value of 80.

4. Open the pet animation movie clip in symbol-editing mode. Delete the parrot layer and add a new layer above the cat layer. Name this layer **dog layer** and make sure it is indented under the mask layer just like the cat layer. Temporarily hide the contents of the mask layer while you work with the other layers.

5. Add a keyframe at Frame 24 of the dog layer. At Frame 24 drag a copy of the dog bitmap to the Stage. Use the Info panel to make sure that the position of the dog bitmap is the same as that of the cat bitmap. Convert the dog bitmap into a symbol and name it dog symbol.

6. Add another keyframe at Frame 36 of the dog layer. Change the alpha amount of the dog symbol at Frame 24 to 0%. If necessary, change the alpha amount of the dog symbol at Frame 36 to 100%. Create a motion tween at Frame 24.

7. Add two more keyframes to the dog layer, one at Frame 60 and another at Frame 72. At Frame 72 change the alpha amount of the dog symbol to 0%. Create another motion tween at Frame 60. Exit symbol-editing mode and return to the main document.

8. To add a gradient fill to the Flounders text, you need to convert the text to fills. Select the Flounders text block and apply the Break Apart command twice to convert the text to fills.

9. With the text still selected, create a gradient using the Color Mixer panel. Select linear gradient for the fill style. If necessary, click the gray linear gradient in the Swatches panel. Then in the Color Mixer panel change the color of the right gradient pointer to blue (ninth row, first column).

10. Save the changes you have made to the banner. Set the Flash publish settings to select Flash Player 6 and do not generate a size report. Publish the banner as a SWF file with the name **newbanner.swf**. Do not create an HTML file.

11. Open the **sample2.htm** Web page in Notepad. The file is in the Tutorial.06\Review folder included with your Data Files. Replace the image tag that has the flndrsbanner.gif reference to an EMBED tag with the newbanner.swf reference so that the Web page will display the new banner. Save the sample2.htm file and close Notepad.

12. Preview sample2.htm in your browser.

CASE PROBLEMS

Case 1. Creating a Logo for Sandy's Party Center Sandy Rodriquez, owner of Sandy's Party Center, asks John Rossini to develop a new logo for her store's Web site. She would like a logo with festive colors using some of the elements previously created for the banner such as the balloons and confetti. John suggests also incorporating the use of a picture for the letters on the logo and adding a gradient to the background. Sandy likes John's suggestions and tells John to develop the logo as soon as possible.

John develops an initial draft of the logo and instructs you to complete the logo by adding a bitmap that can be used as a fill for the letters. You also will create a gradient and use it as the background for the logo.

If necessary, start Macromedia Flash and then do the following:

1. Open the **partylogo** file from the Tutorial.06\Cases folder included with your Data Files.

2. Save the document as **partylogo2** in the Tutorial.06\Cases folder.

3. Import the jellybeans.jpg bitmap from the Tutorial.06\Cases folder directly into the document's library. Do not place a copy of the bitmap on the Stage.

4. Modify the bitmap's properties by changing its compression Quality value to 80%.

5. Select and change the text to fills by applying the Break Apart command twice to the text. Keep the text selected.

Explore
6. Use the Color Mixer panel to select bitmap as the fill style, and then if necessary, click the bitmap thumbnail in the Color Mixer panel. The text now has the jellybeans bitmap as its fill. Deselect the text.

7. Insert a new layer and name it **background**. If necessary, move the background layer to the bottom of the Timeline. In the Color Mixer panel create a new linear gradient. Use white as the color for the left gradient pointer and use yellow as the color for the right gradient pointer.

8. Draw a rectangle starting from the upper-left corner of the Stage to the lower-right corner to cover the entire Stage. The rectangle should have no stroke color and have the gradient as its fill.

9. Rotate the gradient using the Fill Transform tool so that the lighter or white area of the gradient is towards the bottom of the Stage.

10. Save the revised banner.

11. Publish the logo as both a SWF file and a JPEG file. Also, let Flash create a temporary HTML file.

12. Preview the logo in your browser using the HTML file created by Flash.

13. Close any open files.

Case 2. Revising the River City Music Banner with Bitmaps and a Gradient Janet Meyers, store manager for River City Music, is very happy with the interactive banner developed for the store's Web site. She meets with Alex Smith who developed the banner and asks him to add pictures of musical instruments and to change the Piano Sale text to read "Instruments". Alex suggests that the pictures of the instruments can also be animated and further suggests that a gradient can be added to the background to enhance the look of the banner.

Alex asks you to help him revise the banner that was previously developed. He instructs you to import two bitmaps of musical instruments, to add one to the left side of the banner and the other to the right side. Each bitmap will be animated to fade in and then to rock back and forth as the musical notes move up and down. He also instructs you to add a rectangle with a radial gradient to cover the banner within the current rectangle in the background. The gradient should start with white and end with the blue color used for the background.

If necessary, start Macromedia Flash and then do the following:

1. Open the **musicbanner3** file that you completed in Case 2 of Tutorial 5. You should have saved it in the Tutorial.05\Cases folder included with your Data Files. If you did not complete Case 2 of Tutorial 5, then see your instructor for assistance.

2. Save the document as **musicbanner4** in the Tutorial.06\Cases folder included with your Data Files.

3. Import the **trumpet.png** and **violin.png** bitmaps from the Tutorial.06\Cases folder on your Data Disk to the documents library.

4. Select the background layer and insert a new layer above it. Name the new layer **trumpet**.

5. Drag a copy of the trumpet bitmap from the Library panel to the left side of the animated musical notes. Convert the trumpet to a symbol and name it **trumpet symbol**. Add a keyframe at Frame 15 and at Frame 20 of the trumpet layer.

6. Select Frame 1 of the trumpet layer and change the alpha amount of the trumpet symbol instance to 0%. Create a motion tween at Frame 1. The trumpet will fade in throughout the motion tween.

7. Select Frame 20 of the trumpet layer and rotate the trumpet symbol instance slightly to the right. Create a motion tween at Frame 15.

8. Insert a new layer and name it **violin**.

9. Repeat Steps 5 through 7 using the violin bitmap on the violin layer. The violin should be placed on the right side of the animated musical notes. At Frame 20, the violin should be rotated slightly to the left. This way the trumpet and the violin will rock back and forth in opposite directions.

10. Insert a new layer and name it **gradient**. Move this layer below the background layer.

11. Create a new radial gradient. The gradient should start with the color white. The second color should be the same as the blue color currently used for the background.

12. Draw a rectangle in the gradient layer. The rectangle should have no stroke and it should use the gradient as its fill. Draw it so that it is the same size as the current rectangle that has a dotted stroke and is framing the banner.

13. Save the revised banner.

14. Publish the banner as a SWF file. Also, let Flash create a temporary HTML file.

15. Preview the banner in your browser using the HTML file created by Flash. Make sure the trumpet and violin fade in and then rock back and forth as the musical notes move up and down.

16. Close any open files.

Case 3. Revising the Sonny's Auto Center Logo with Bitmaps and a Gradient Sonny Jackson and his staff are excited about the interactive logo developed for their Web site. He talks to Amanda Lester and asks her about the possibility of using pictures of cars as part of the animation. Amanda suggests adding some sample pictures of cars so that he can see how the logo will look. Amanda also suggests changing the title of the logo to make it more dynamic. Sonny agrees to Amanda's suggestions. Amanda asks you to help her complete the revisions by creating an animation with the car bitmaps and adding a new, more dynamic title.

If necessary, start Macromedia Flash and then do the following:

1. Open the **sonnylogo2** file that you completed in Case 3 of Tutorial 5. You should have saved it in the Tutorial.05\Cases folder included with your Data Files. Save this file as **sonnylogo3** in the Tutorial.06\Cases folder. If you did not complete Case 3 of Tutorial 5, see your instructor for assistance.

2. Delete all layers except the Sound layer and Layer 1. Clear the contents of the keyframe at Frame 40 of Layer 1. (*Hint:* Right-click the frame and select Clear Keyframe.) Also in Layer 1, delete the Auto and Center text blocks, as well as the blue gradient rectangle. Delete the small vertical line inside the top rectangle.

3. Edit the Masked Autos symbol. Change the text in the text block of the autotext1 layer and the autotext2 layer. The text should read **Sonny's Autos**. Use the same font, keep it italic, and make sure the Align Center button is selected in the Property inspector before you type the new text. Both text blocks should be exactly the same and in the same position.

Explore ▷ 4. Create a new gradient as follows. Make it linear and select the gray linear gradient from the Swatches panel as a starting point. Add two more gradient pointers in the center of the gradient definition bar. Make these two new gradient colors white. Make the far left gradient color black. You should have a narrow white band in the middle of the gradient. Apply this new gradient to the rectangle on the Stage. (*Hint:* Double-click the gradient rectangle movie clip to change its fill.)

5. In the main document, in Layer 1, Frame 1, add an instance of the Masked Autos symbol to the Stage so that it is inside the top rectangle. Use the Transform panel to change the width and height of the instance to 60% of its original size. If necessary, reposition the instance so that it is centered within the rectangle. This is the title for the logo.

Explore ▷ 6. Import the **view1.png**, **view2.png**, and **view3.png** files from the Tutorial.06\Cases folder. Import to the library only and not to the Stage.

Explore ▷ 7. Create a new symbol, name it **car animation**, and use Movie clip as its behavior. In the car animation edit window drag a copy of the view1 bitmap onto the Stage, center it, and then reduce its size to 30%. (*Hint:* Use the Property inspector and the Transform panel.)

Explore ▷ 8. At Frame 15 delete the view1 instance and add a view2 instance. At Frame 30 delete the view2 instance and add a view3 instance. The view3 instance should exist through Frame 45. Make sure each instance is centered and reduced to 30%. The resulting animation has each view of the car appear for 15 frames and then be replaced by a different view.

9. In the document's main Timeline, insert a new layer and name it **car**. Drag an instance of the car animation symbol to Frame 1 of the car layer. Center the car animation instance on the Stage.

10. Save the revised logo.

11. Publish the logo as a SWF file. Also, let Flash create a temporary HTML file.

12. Preview the logo in your browser using the HTML file created by Flash. Make sure the views of the car change and the Sonny's Auto text has the gradient moving through its letters.

13. Close any open files.

Case 4. Modifying the LAL Financial Banner with Gradients Christopher is very pleased with the interactive banner created for LAL Financial Services. He asks webmaster Elizabeth to modify the banner so that it has more of a green color instead of the gray color. He also asks Elizabeth if she can find a way to highlight the company name more than it is in the current banner. Elizabeth tells him that a motion tween with a gradient can be used to provide a highlight effect and agrees to modify the banner.

Elizabeth asks you to help her modify the various gradients on the different banner elements and to create a motion tween with a gradient that will highlight the company name.

If necessary, start Macromedia Flash and then do the following:

1. Open the **lfsbanner2** file that you completed in Case 4 of Tutorial 5. You should have saved it in the Tutorial.05\Cases folder included with your Data Files. If you did not complete Case 4 of Tutorial 5, then see your instructor for assistance.

2. Save the document as **lfsbanner3** in the Tutorial.06\Cases folder included with your Data Files.

3. Rename the background layer as **text**. Insert a new layer and name it **background**. Move the background layer below the text layer.

4. On the background layer create a rectangle that covers all of the Stage. Use no color for the stroke and a dark green for the fill (use the swatch on the sixth column, first row, or hexadecimal #009900).

5. Insert a new layer above the background layer. Name this layer **highlight**. Draw a rectangle in the highlight layer. Draw it below the Stage in the Work Area, with no stroke and the same fill color as before. This fill color will be replaced. Make the rectangle 500 pixels wide and 30 pixels high.

6. Create a new linear gradient. Use the gray linear gradient from the Swatches panel as a starting point. Add one more gradient pointer to the middle of the gradient definition bar. Use the dark-green color (#009900) for the left gradient pointer. Use the same color for the right gradient pointer. Use white as the color for the middle gradient pointer. Add this gradient to the Swatches panel.

Explore

7. Apply the new gradient to the rectangle you created in Step 5. You want the top and bottom areas of the rectangle to have the dark-green color and the middle to have the white color. The result should be a narrow horizontal white band across the width of the rectangle. (*Hint:* Draw a vertical line with the Paint Bucket tool.)

8. Convert the rectangle with the gradient to a symbol. Name the symbol **highlight** and use Movie clip as its behavior type.

9. Create a motion tween in the highlight layer that moves the highlight symbol from below the Stage to the top of the Stage. It should stop right over the LAL Financial Services text block. The motion tween should span Frames 1 to 45.

10. Change the text color to white in each of the text blocks in the text layer. Then in the last frame of the text layer, change the LAL Financial Services text color to black. (*Hint:* Add a keyframe where you make the change.)

11. Edit the circle symbol. Replace its gradient fill with the green radial gradient found in the fill color pop-up window. It is the fourth gradient from the left. Then move the gradient's center point to the upper-left part of the circle.

12. Edit the repeat button. Replace the circle in the Up Frame with the circle symbol from the library. Center the circle symbol instance.

13. Edit the square symbol. Replace its gray gradient fill with a new linear gradient. Use green (eighth row, first column, or #00FF00) for the left gradient pointer and use black for the right gradient pointer. Rotate the gradient fill on the square so that the green area is in the lower-right corner of the square.

14. Edit the triangle symbol. Change the linear gradient you used for the square so that its left gradient pointer is moved to the middle of the gradient definition bar effectively increasing the green area of the gradient. Replace the triangle's gray gradient fill with the new gradient.

15. Save the revised banner.

16. Publish the logo as a SWF file. Also, let Flash create a temporary HTML file.

17. Preview the logo in your browser using the HTML file created by Flash. Make sure the highlight gradient moves throughout from the bottom to the top and stops on the title text.

18. Close any open files.

QUICK CHECK ANSWERS

Session 6.1

1. A bitmap is a graphic that is stored as a row-by-row list of pixels, along with each pixel's color information.

2. Both commands place the imported bitmap into the library. The Import to Stage command also places an instance of the bitmap on the Stage.

3. Select the bitmap in the library and then double-click the bitmap icon in the Library panel, or single-click the properties icon.

4. Use Photo (JPEG) compression for bitmaps with many colors or many color transitions such as photographs.

5. The alpha amount that will make an object transparent is 0%.

6. Use the Trace Bitmap command to convert a bitmap to a vector graphic.

7. The Color threshold value determines how many colors are used. A smaller value results in more colors.

Session 6.2

1. A gradient is a gradual blend or transition from one color to another.

2. Use the Color Mixer panel to create a gradient.

3. Click Add Swatch from the options menu in the Color Mixer panel.

4. True. A gradient is only saved with the current document.

5. To add another color you add another gradient pointer by clicking below the gradient definition bar.

6. Use the Paint Bucket tool to apply a gradient to an existing object.

7. Use the Fill Transform tool to modify a gradient fill.

8. You drag the circular handle on a linear gradient to rotate the gradient.

Session 6.3

1. The native file format for Flash documents is FLA.

2. The file format for published Flash movies is SWF.

3. To get the GIF tab to display in the Publish Settings dialog box you click the GIF Image (.gif) check box.

4. The size report contains information about the published movie such as the number of frames, the total size of the movie, and the size of individual elements in the movie such as each symbol and bitmap.

5. The Publish command publishes files according to the selections in the Publish Settings dialog box.

6. File formats you can export with the Export Image command include JPEG, GIF, PNG, SWF, AI, WMF, and BMP.

7. False. You can also add a SWF file to an existing Web page using Macromedia Dreamweaver or Microsoft Frontpage.

New Perspectives on

MACROMEDIA
FLASH MX 2004

Read This Before You Begin

To the Student

Data Files

To complete Tutorials 7-9 of this text you will need the starting student Data Files. Your instructor will either provide you with these Data Files or ask you to obtain them yourself. Tutorials 7-9 require the folders shown to complete the Tutorials, Review Assignments, and Case Problems. You will need to copy these folders from a file server, a standalone computer, or the Web to the drive and folder where you will be storing your Data Files. Your instructor will tell you which computer, drive letter, and folder(s) contain the files you need. You can also download the files by going to www.course.com; see the inside back or front cover for more information on downloading the files, or ask your instructor or technical support person for assistance.

Flash MX 2004
Tutorial.07
Tutorial.08
Tutorial.09

System Requirements

If you are going to work through this book using your own computer, you need:

■ **System Requirements** This text assumes a default installation of Macromedia Flash MX 2004 and Macromedia Flash Player 7. The screenshots in this book were taken using a computer running Windows XP Professional, and when showing a browser, Internet Explorer 6. If you are using a different operating system or a different browser, your screen might differ from the figures shown in the book.

Macromedia recommends the following Windows system configuration for Flash MX 2004: 600 MHz Intel Pentium III processor or equivalent; Windows 98 SE (4.10.2222 A), Windows 2000, or Windows XP; 128 MB RAM (256 MB recommended); and 275 MB available disk space.

■ **Data Files** You will not be able to complete the tutorials or exercises in this book using your own computer until you have the necessary starting Data Files.

To the Instructor

The Data Files are available on the Instructor Resources CD for this title. Follow the instructions in the Help file on the CD to install the programs to your network or standalone computer. See the "To the Student" section above for information on how to set up the Data Files that accompany this text.

You are granted a license to copy the Data Files to any computer or computer network used by students who have purchased this book.

OBJECTIVES

In this tutorial you will:

- Plan and create a Flash Web site

- Create a Flash template and use the template to create Flash documents

- Work with external libraries

- Create a navigation bar with complex buttons

- Load external SWF files into the Flash Player using levels

- Learn basic ActionScript commands

- Use the Actions panel

- Load external image files into the Flash Player using a movie clip

CREATING A FLASH WEB SITE

Creating a Web Site for Jackson's Sports

CASE

Admiral Web Design

Jackson's Sports is a local sports equipment and supplies company with a special interest in local youth sports teams. Over the years they have developed a relationship with many local teams formed by youth organizations and they provide discounted equipment, team uniforms, and player trophies to basketball, baseball, softball, volleyball, and soccer teams. Dan Jackson, owner of the company, has been discussing the development of a new Web site with Gloria Adamson, co-owner of Admiral Web Design. He wants the Web site to be accessible through links provided on their existing site and to focus on the services they provide to local youth sports. He wants to highlight his company's services to local teams and include information about some of the teams, such as team names and photos. Gloria asks graphics designer Aly Garcia and site developer Chris Johnson to work together to develop the new Web site. Aly and Chris meet with Dan to discuss his request. Based on their meeting, Aly and Chris determine the Web site will have a home page with appropriate graphic elements and a navigation scheme that will lead to the other key areas of the site. Chris suggests that Flash is the ideal tool to use to develop the entire site—not just the graphic elements of the site. With Flash, they can make the site more visually interesting and also include some multimedia elements requested by Dan, such as the team photos that will be changed regularly to showcase different teams and players. The use of Flash will also make it easier to incorporate Dan's request to eventually have short video clips added to the site.

Aly and Chris develop a sketch showing the general design of the Jackson's Sports Web site, as shown in Figure 7-1.

Figure 7-1	PRELIMINARY SKETCH OF WEB SITE FOR JACKSON'S SPORTS

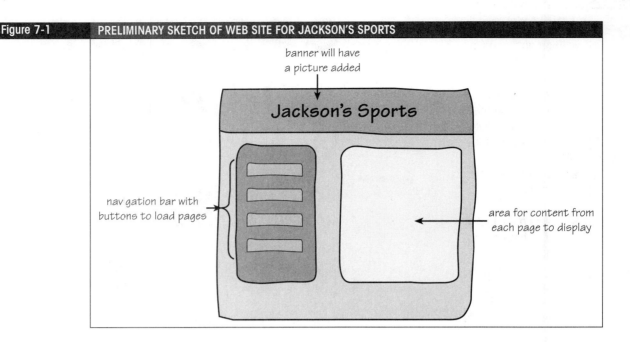

banner will have
a picture added

Jackson's Sports

navigation bar with
buttons to load pages

area for content from
each page to display

Aly recommends that you be assigned to work on this project because of the skills you have developed using Flash. This is a great opportunity for you to learn more advanced features of the program. As part of the planning process, Aly will help you through the initial planning phase used to develop a Web site.

In this tutorial, you will continue your training in Flash by learning how to plan and design a Flash Web site based on the requirements of the client. You will create a Flash Web site with a navigation bar. You will learn how to use levels to load one SWF file on top of another in the Flash Player and how to use ActionScript commands to control how a SWF file is loaded. You will learn how to create a Flash template to create additional documents. You will also learn how to load external image files into a movie clip.

SESSION 7.1

In this session, you will review the process for developing a new Flash Web site. You will learn how a Flash Web site differs from a non-Flash Web site. You will identify the purpose and objectives of a site for Jackson's Sports and then develop a storyboard showing the major parts of the Jackson's Sports Web site and its navigation system.

Structure of a Flash Site

Many of the Web sites you see on the Internet consist mainly of HTML documents. These HTML documents or Web pages contain text, graphics, and hyperlinks and may also contain multimedia elements such as those created with Flash. The animations and graphic elements you have created so far with Flash are all meant to be part of an HTML document. However, as stated in Tutorial 1, Flash can also be used to create a complete Web site in which all of the Web site pages are actually Flash SWF files and not HTML documents. The SWF files work together based on a navigation system using buttons or other graphic elements that can be clicked to navigate to the various SWF files. In some cases, a Web site is built in two versions, one using mostly HTML and one using mostly Flash. The user is given the option of which site to view, as shown in the example in Figure 7-2.

Figure 7-2   **NASA MARS WEB SITE**

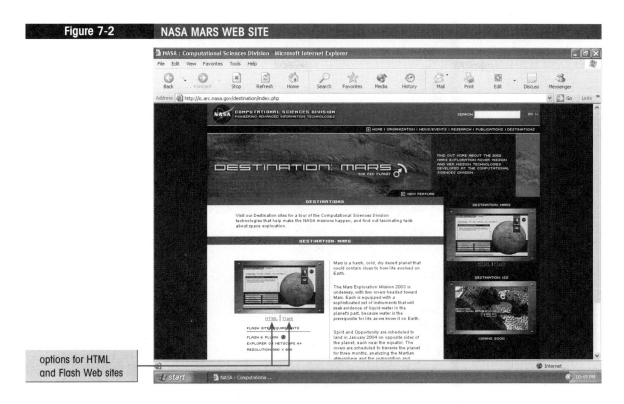

options for HTML
and Flash Web sites

The two versions of the NASA Mars Web site are shown in Figure 7-3a and b.

Figure 7-3a   **TWO VERSIONS OF THE NASA MARS WEB SITE**

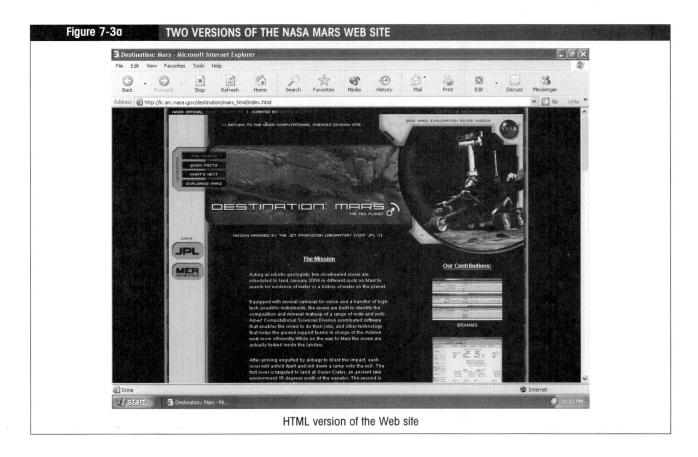

HTML version of the Web site

Figure 7-3b   TWO VERSIONS OF THE NASA MARS WEB SITE CONTINUED

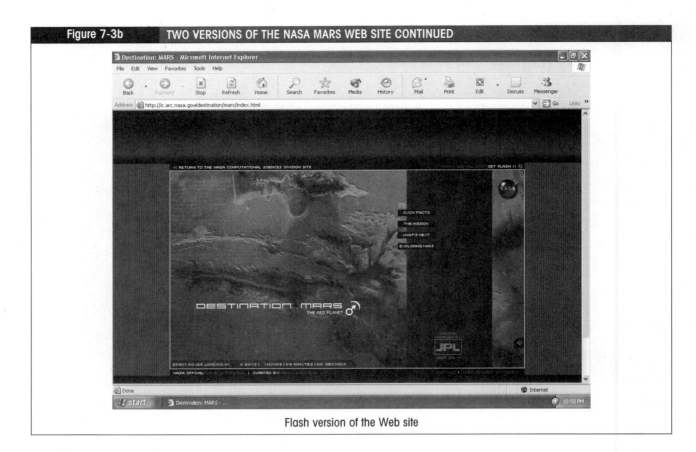

Flash version of the Web site

The SWF files that make up the Web site are referenced from an HTML document. The HTML document is usually created by the site developer using a program such as Macromedia Dreamweaver. It can also be created using Flash by selecting the HTML format in the publish settings for the document. Notice that the URL of the Flash site shown in Figure 7-3 does not reference a SWF file. Instead, the URL shows Index.html as the name of the document. The HTML document displays in the Web browser and then calls or references the SWF file that causes the Flash Player to activate. Recall that the Flash Player is a plug-in that is used to enable the Web browser to play the SWF files. Within the HTML document, the Flash Player plays the SWF file that is the home or main page of the Web site. When the user clicks the Quick Facts button on the NASA Mars page, another SWF file containing the Quick Facts page is loaded into the Flash Player using the same HTML document. Figure 7-4 shows the Quick Facts file loaded in the Flash Player in the same HTML document.

Figure 7-4 QUICK FACTS PAGE ON FLASH VERSION OF MARS SITE

note URL stays the
same as main page

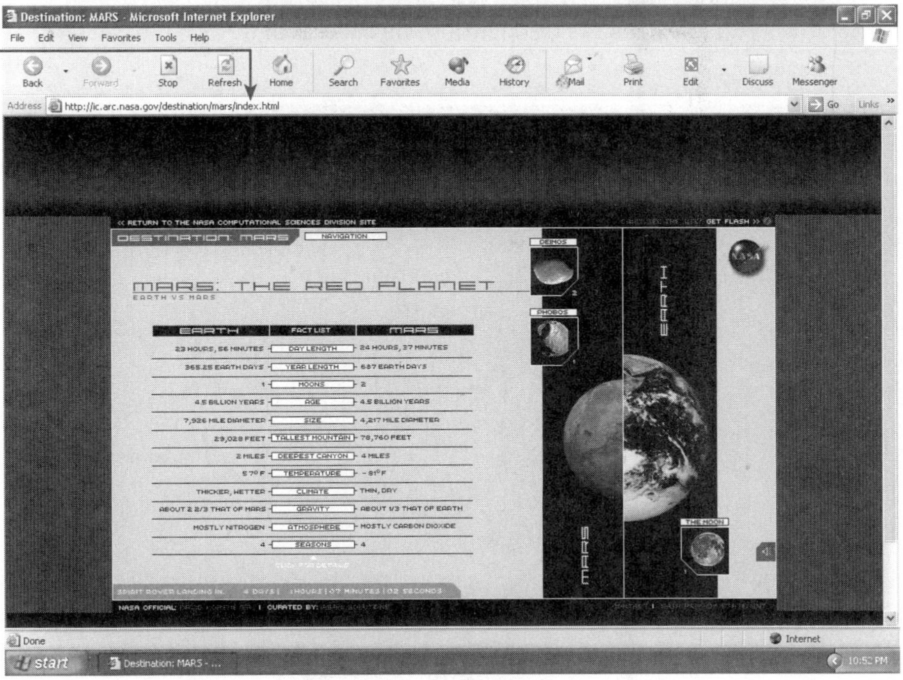

Because a Flash Web site does not consist of a series of HTML documents but instead uses only one HTML document, the Back and Forward buttons on the Web browser toolbar do not provide the same functionality as they do when you are visiting an HTML Web site. When viewing a traditional HTML Web site, each time you navigate to a different Web page within the Web site, the browser keeps track of which Web pages you visited in its history and the Address bar displays a slightly different URL based on the filename of the Web page. For example, when you click the Back button, the browser displays the page most recently visited. When you are visiting a Flash Web site, however, only one HTML document might be displayed and the URL does not change. What does change is the SWF files being displayed in the Flash Player within the HTML document. The HTML document displayed in the Web browser only acts as a container for the SWF files. So, even after the user has navigated to several parts of the Flash Web site, using the Back button does not display the most recently visited SWF file but instead the most recently visited URL, which may not be part of the Flash Web site. As a result, it is vitally important to provide a clear navigational system within the Flash Web site so that the user can easily understand how to navigate within the site without using the browser navigation buttons.

Using Levels

The navigation system for a Flash Web site is simply a set of buttons that, when clicked, cause the Flash Player to play a different part of the current SWF file, such as a different scene, or cause a different SWF file to be loaded into the Flash Player. You can create a button that causes a SWF file to be loaded into the Flash Player to replace the currently playing SWF file or to load a SWF file on top of the currently playing SWF file. A SWF file can play on top of another SWF file through the use of levels. The Flash Player uses levels to play more than one SWF file at the same time. The first SWF file loaded into the Flash Player is loaded at level 0 and is usually considered the home or main page of the Flash Web site. Other SWF files can then be loaded at higher levels. For example, if you specify that a SWF file be loaded at level 1, it plays on top of the SWF file that is already playing at level 0 and the content of the SWF file at level 0 shows through any empty areas of the SWF file at level 1, as shown in Figure 7-5.

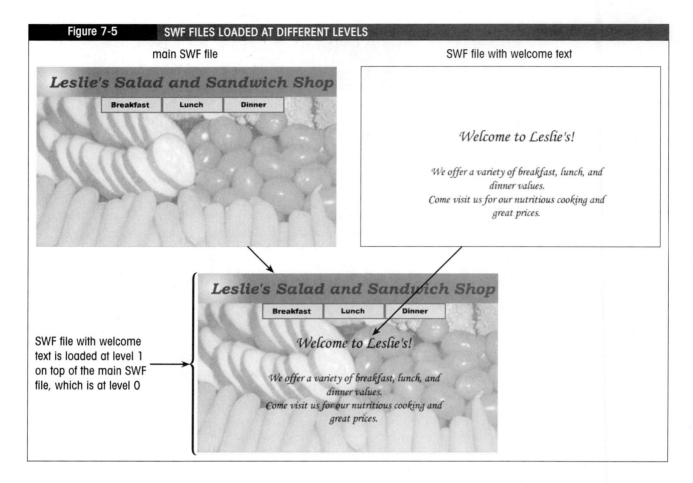

Figure 7-5   SWF FILES LOADED AT DIFFERENT LEVELS

main SWF file

SWF file with welcome text

Leslie's Salad and Sandwich Shop

Breakfast   Lunch   Dinner

Welcome to Leslie's!

We offer a variety of breakfast, lunch, and dinner values.
Come visit us for our nutritious cooking and great prices.

SWF file with welcome text is loaded at level 1 on top of the main SWF file, which is at level 0

Leslie's Salad and Sandwich Shop

Breakfast   Lunch   Dinner

Welcome to Leslie's!

We offer a variety of breakfast, lunch, and dinner values.
Come visit us for our nutritious cooking and great prices.

If you load a SWF file at a level that already has a SWF file playing, the new SWF file replaces the file currently playing. When a SWF file is loaded on top of another SWF file at a different level, the properties of the SWF file at level 0 take precedence over those of the SWF files loaded at higher levels. For example, if the SWF file at level 0 has a green background and a SWF file with a blue background is loaded at level 1, then the loaded SWF file also has a green background. The same applies to the dimensions of the Stage. The dimensions of the SWF file at level 0 take precedence over the dimensions of the loaded SWF files. It is important, therefore, that you make certain the contents of the loaded SWF files do not interfere with those of the SWF file loaded at level 0.

Exploring a Sample Flash Web Site

To get a better idea of how a Flash Web site works and how the site for Jackson's Sports will be created, Aly suggests you explore a sample site she has been working on with Chris. The site is for another of Admiral Web Design's clients, Leslie's Salad and Sandwich Shop, and is under development, but Aly thinks this will help you as you work on the new Jackson's Sports site.

To explore a sample Flash Web site:

1. Start Flash and open the **leslie.fla** file located in the **Tutorial.07\Tutorial** folder included with your Data Files, and set the panels to their default layout.

2. Click **File** on the menu bar, point to **Publish Preview**, and then click **Default - (HTML)**. Your browser opens and displays the leslie.html file with the leslie.swf file playing in the Flash Player plug-in.

3. Click the **Breakfast** button. The breakfast menu displays in the Flash Player. Notice that the URL in the browser's Address bar does not change. It still shows leslie.html as part of the URL. See Figure 7-6.

| Figure 7-6 | LESLIE'S SALAD AND SANDWICH SHOP WEB SITE |

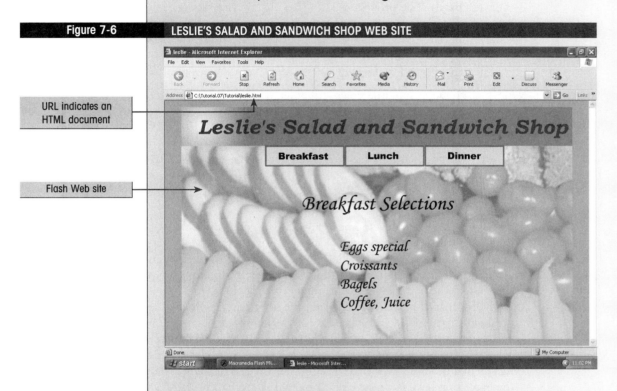

URL indicates an HTML document

Flash Web site

4. Click the **Dinner** button. The menu changes to display dinner items. Again, the URL does not change.

5. Click the **Lunch** button to view this page. When you are finished viewing the Web site, close the browser window to return to Flash.

6. To view one of the other documents used in this Web site, open the **breakfast.fla** file from the **Tutorial.07\Tutorial** folder included with your Data Files.

   Notice that the breakfast.fla document only contains the breakfast menu items and not the navigation buttons. It also does not contain any of the graphic elements of the Web site. The buttons, background, and title banner of the Web site are only contained in the leslie.fla file. When the buttons are clicked, other SWF files are loaded into the Flash Player and play on top of the leslie.swf file.

7. Close the leslie.fla and breakfast.fla files. Do not save any changes you may have made to the files.

Now that you understand the structure of a Flash Web site, you are ready to begin work on the Jackson's Sports Web site. The first and most crucial step is to plan the structure and content for the site.

Planning a Flash Web Site for Jackson's Sports

As discussed, a Flash Web site consists of a series of Flash SWF files that work together to present the desired information. Each SWF file is a published Flash document and represents a page of the Web site just like a non-Flash Web site consists of pages that are HTML documents. A Flash Web site also includes a navigation system with options to view each of the site's pages. The process used to plan the development of a new Flash Web site is similar to that of planning the development of a non-Flash Web site. The goal in either case is to develop a site that meets the needs of the client. It is these needs that must first be determined before any design or development begins.

The process used to develop a Flash Web site includes the following steps:

- Determine the goals and objectives of the Web site.
- Determine the site's contents.
- Design the site pages and develop a storyboard.

After the site planning has been completed, you build the site and test it.

Determining the Goals and Objectives of the Site

The first step in the development process is to determine the goals of the site. It is essential that the goals be clearly defined. Otherwise, a site may be developed that does not meet the needs of the client. You start defining the goals of the site by meeting with the client and discussing what he or she wants the site to accomplish. For example, the client may want the site to help the company sell a product or to provide information about the services offered by the company. The client may want the site to increase brand awareness for the company's products or to provide information for the company's employees, such as company policies and procedures. Another possible goal may be to disseminate information to customers about how to use certain products. Each of these examples requires a different approach and results in a different type of Web site. The success of the site depends on how well it meets the goals that have been developed and agreed to by the client.

Aly and Chris meet with Dan Jackson to determine his needs, and based on their meeting, Aly identifies the goals shown in Figure 7-7 for the Jackson's Sports Web site.

Figure 7-7	JACKSON'S SPORTS WEB SITE GOALS

Goals for Jackson's Sports Web Site

- Promote the Jackson's Sports name.
- Increase sales to local youth sports teams.
- Provide a site dedicated to serving local youth sports.

These goals impact the overall design of the Web site and determine how the site is developed. After the goals have been determined, a list of objectives can be developed based on the goals. These objectives more clearly define the information the Web site will contain, the types of media that are required, and the number of Web pages needed to provide the information and fulfill the needs of the client. The objectives also help determine how the Web site pages will be organized and what types of pages need to be developed. For example, one type of site may require pages with many pictures, whereas another type of site may require pages with more text and only a few pictures. Other sites may require pages that display animations or even videos.

The objectives must be clear and measurable so that after the site is complete, you can determine whether each objective has been met. For example, if one of the goals of the site is to enhance a company's brand awareness, then one of the objectives might be to include a list of the benefits of using the company's products. Another objective might be to highlight the company's logo that appears on all of its products. These objectives are clear and measurable. You can easily develop a page that has a list of the benefits of using the company's products. You can also include the company's logo on all of the pages of the Web site, thereby increasing the company's brand awareness.

As part of the planning process, you must consider the intended audience. That is, what are the characteristics of the audience that will be using the site? These characteristics impact how the information is presented on the Web site. The characteristics could be based on demographic information, such as the age group, education level, or economic level of the audience. A young audience may mean that more engaging animations need to be included, whereas a more mature audience may mean less animation and perhaps a more conservative color scheme. You can also try to determine what the expectations are of the intended audience. Do they expect to be entertained or do they expect to obtain detailed information about a product? This determines whether to include interactive games and graphics or detailed information in the form of text.

Based on both the goals developed by Aly for the Jackson's Sports Web site and the information gathered by Aly and Chris in their meeting with Dan Jackson, objectives for the Web site are identified, as shown in Figure 7-8.

Figure 7-8	JACKSON'S SPORTS WEB SITE OBJECTIVES

Objectives for Jackson's Sports Web Site

- Include the message that Jackson's Sports supports local youth sports.
- Provide a list of products and services offered by Jackson's Sports.
- Provide the names of local teams doing business with Jackson's Sports.
- Include pictures of the teams; these pictures will change every few weeks.

The goals and objectives developed early in the Web site development process guide the rest of the process. They determine which Flash documents need to developed, what information each should contain, and how the documents should be organized. The next step is to determine the site's contents.

Developing the Web Site Content

Based on the goals and objectives identified earlier and partly on who the intended audience is, your next step is to determine what content the site's pages will contain. The content to be included is determined in large part by what the client wants the site to accomplish. This is why identifying the site's goals and objectives is very important in the planning process. These goals and objectives help determine the required pages and required media to be included on the Web site. For example, each of the objectives listed for the Jackson's Sport site will result in one or more separate Web pages designed to meet the specific objective. One of the pages will display pictures that need to change regularly, so that capability has to be designed as part of the page. One way to determine the site's contents is to develop an outline with categories and subcategories. Each category may correspond to an objective or you may have more than one category for a stated objective. The categories in the outline can correspond to the pages that will be developed for the site and also help determine the navigation system for the site. Aly and Chris have developed an outline based on the goals and objectives for the Jackson's Sports Web site, as shown in Figure 7-9.

Figure 7-9	JACKSON'S SPORTS WEB SITE OUTLINE

Outline for Jackson's Sports Web Site

1. Home page
    a) Banner
    b) Message about Jackson's Sports' support to local youth sports
    c) Navigation bar with buttons exhibiting rollover effects and animation
2. Services
    a) List of products and services
3. Teams
    a) Names of local teams
4. Photos
    a) Pictures of local teams

After you have developed an outline, you can start to gather and organize the required information, bitmaps, videos, or other graphics to be included on the site. Much of the information to be included on the site, such as the products and services available, will be provided by the client. Graphic elements, such as bitmap files of pictures or video files, need to be prepared by the developer of the site or by someone else such as a graphic designer. The development of the outline leads to the next step in the process, which is to storyboard the Web site.

Developing a Storyboard and Navigation System

After you have outlined the main areas of content to be included on the Web site, you create a **storyboard**, which is simply a diagram showing the site's pages and the way they are organized. The storyboard shows a sketch of each page with lines indicating how each page links to the other pages. The way the pages link to each other determines the navigation system for the site. As you develop the navigation system, you should keep in mind the characteristics of the intended audience. For example, if a large segment of your intended audience has limited Internet skills, you should keep the navigation simple and easy to understand.

Based on the outline of the content developed for the Jackson's Sports Web site, Aly and Chris have developed a storyboard for the site, as shown in Figure 7-10.

Figure 7-10   **JACKSON'S SPORTS WEB SITE STORYBOARD**

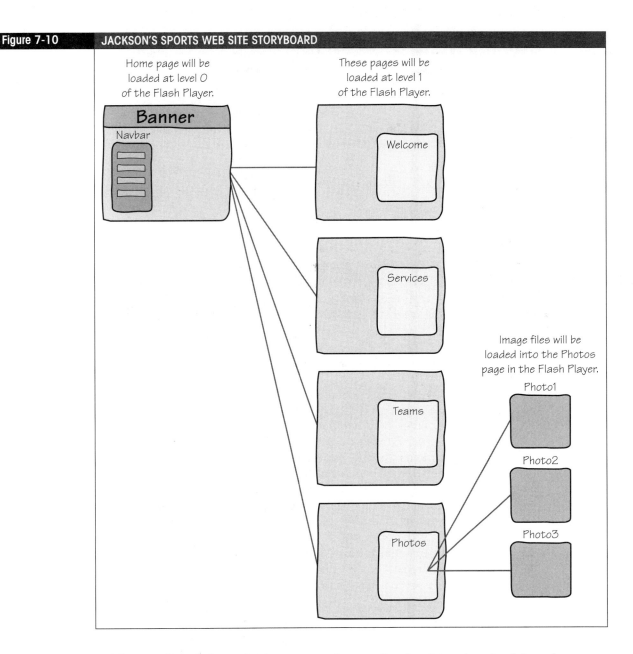

The storyboard shows the home or main page for the site and each of the other pages that will be developed. The home page will be loaded at level 0 in the Flash Player. The other pages, which will be loaded at level 1, include the Teams' Names page, the Services page, and the Photos page. In addition, a Welcome page will display initially when the home page is first displayed. The Welcome page will be replaced when one of the other pages is loaded at level 1. Then, when the site visitor clicks the Home button, the Welcome page will load again replacing the page currently at level 1.

Now that the planning for Jackson's Sports Web site is complete, you are ready to create the Flash documents that will make up the Jackson's Sports Web site. You will begin this task in the next session.

In this session, you have reviewed the process for the development of a Flash Web site. You have learned about the importance of developing the goals and objectives for a site. You have also learned the purpose of developing an outline of the site's contents and creating a storyboard to show the sites pages and navigation system. In the next session, you will create the pages for the Jackson's Sports Web site and the navigation bar.

Session 7.1 QUICK CHECK

1. A Flash Web site consists mostly of SWF files. True or False?

2. The Flash Player uses _____ to load more than one SWF file at one time.

3. When you load a SWF file at the same level that already has a SWF file playing, the new SWF file plays on top of the currently playing file. True or False?

4. What is the first step in the planning process for developing a Web site?

5. How can you start to define the goals of the site?

6. What is a storyboard?

SESSION 7.2

In this session, you will learn how to create a Flash Web site. You will create the Jackson's Sports home page, a template to be used for the additional pages, and a navigation bar for the site.

Creating the Web Site's Contents

To create the site's contents, you start by creating a Flash document that will be the main or home page that is displayed when the user first enters the Web site. You create the document in the same way you have created other Flash documents. The only difference is that you are creating a document that will have a navigation system to work with other Flash documents. Because you want the site's documents to work together and to provide a consistent viewing experience for the user, you want each of the documents to be the same size and have the same background. As seen in the Leslie's Salad and Sandwich Shop example, the main document will contain the background, banner, and navigation buttons. The other documents on the Web site will contain only the elements specific to the particular component of the Web site. Each of the documents can have any number of graphic elements, including animations. Because the documents will play on top of the main document, you need to make certain that the elements on one document do not hide or overlap the elements of the main document.

Creating the Web Site's Main Document

Based on Aly's instructions, the main page of the Jackson's Sports Web site will have a banner with an animation of the store's name and a background picture that she has prepared. It will also contain a navigation bar consisting of a set of buttons. You start to create the Web site's main document by creating the banner.

To create the Web site's banner:

1. Create a new Flash document with a width of **700 pixels** and a height of **500 pixels**. Use **dark green** (#006600) for the background color. Save this document with the name **Main.fla** in the **Tutorial.07\Tutorial** folder included with your Data Files. Set the panels to their default layout. Next create the banner as a symbol.

2. Create a new symbol. Name the symbol **Banner** and use **Movie clip** as its behavior.

3. With the symbol in symbol-editing mode, draw a rectangle on the center of the Stage. Use the Property inspector to make the rectangle **700 pixels** wide and **80 pixels** high. Use a **maroon color** (#663300) for the rectangle's fill and do not include a stroke. Aly has provided a bitmap picture to be used as part of the banner.

4. Click **File** on the menu bar, point to **Import**, and then click **Import to Library**. In the Import to Library dialog box, locate and double-click the **Ball&Glove.jpg** bitmap stored in the **Tutorial.07\Tutorial** folder included with your Data Files.

5. If necessary, open the Library panel. Drag an instance of the **Ball&Glove.jpg** bitmap from the Library panel to the Stage and place it inside the left edge of the rectangle. You now need to align the objects on the Stage.

6. Click **Edit** on the menu bar and then click **Select All**. Both the bitmap and the rectangle are selected.

7. Click **Modify** on the menu bar, point to **Align**, and make sure To Stage is not selected. If it is, then click it to deselect it. Click **Modify** on the menu bar, point to **Align**, and then click **Left**. Click **Modify** again, point to **Align**, and then click **Top**. Click an empty area of the Stage to deselect the objects. The left and top sides of the two objects are aligned. Lock Layer 1 to prevent its objects from being moved accidentally. Now add text to the banner.

8. Insert a new layer and name it **Text1**. Create a text block on this layer by selecting the **Text** tool **A** on the toolbar and clicking the left side of the picture once. Use the Property inspector to select **Verdana** for the font, **26** for the font size, **white** for the text color, **Bold** and **Italic** attributes, and **Align Left**. Type **Jackson's** in the text box.

9. Create another text block below and slightly to the right of the Jackson's text with the same attributes as the text block created in Step 8 and type **Sports**. Place the two text blocks using Figure 7-11 as a guide. Finally, you will modify each of the two text blocks so that the first letter in each word (J and S) is slightly larger than the rest of the letters of the word.

Figure 7-11 TEXT BLOCKS ADDED TO BANNER

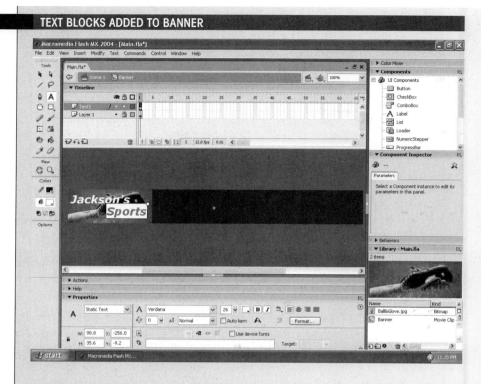

10. Change the font size for the letter **J** in Jackson to **35**, and then change the font size for the letter **S** in Sports to **35**.

Now that you have created the text over the picture, Aly instructs you to create an animation using the text. The text will be animated to increase in size over a short period of time and then decrease. Aly suggests making the animation two and one-half seconds long. You will create a motion tween in which the text starts out 50% smaller than its original size and then increases to its original size. Then, after a short pause, it will decrease back to 50% of its original size.

To animate the Jackson's Sports text:

1. Use the **Selection** tool to select the **Jackson's** text block. While pressing the **Shift** key, select the **Sports** text block. Both text blocks are selected.

2. Convert these text blocks to a symbol. Name the symbol **JS Title** and use **Movie clip** as the symbol's behavior.

3. Insert a keyframe at **Frame 10** of the Text1 layer. The text will start small at Frame 1; the text will be back to its original size at Frame 10. Insert another keyframe at **Frame 25**. This is where the text will start to decrease in size. Finally, insert another keyframe at **Frame 30**. This is where the text will be back to its original size.

4. Create motion tweens at **Frame 1** and at **Frame 25**.

5. Select **Frame 1** of the Text1 layer. Click **Window** on the menu bar, point to **Design Panels**, and then click **Transform** to open the Transform panel. In the Transform panel, make certain that the Constrain check box is checked, type **50** for the width percentage of the object, and press the **Enter** key. The JS Title text block decreases in size.

6. Select **Frame 30** of the Text1 layer, type **50** for the width percentage in the Transform panel, and press the **Enter** key. Close the Transform panel.

7. Move the playhead to **Frame 1** and press the **Enter** key to test the animation.

8. Insert a regular frame at **Frame 30** of Layer 1 to extend the layer. The text animation is now complete.

The final part of the banner is a text block over the rectangle with a message about Jackson's Sports' support of youth sports. This text block will use a smaller font than the title text.

To create another text block for the banner:

1. Insert a new layer above the Text1 layer and name it **Text2**. On this layer, create a text block on the rectangle to the right of the picture. Use the Property inspector to change the text color to **light yellow** (#FFFFCC), use **Verdana** for the font, and use **20** for the font size. Also, if necessary, select the **Bold**, **Italic**, and **Align Left** text attributes. Type **Supporting Youth Sports in our Community!** in this text block.

2. Use the **Selection** tool to center the text block over the maroon rectangle area, as shown in Figure 7-12.

| Figure 7-12 | NEW TEXT BLOCK ON BANNER |

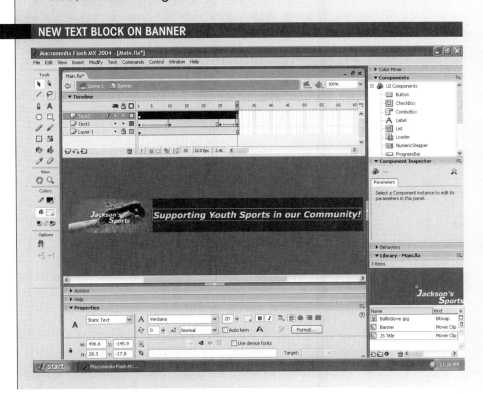

3. Click **Scene 1** on the Address bar to exit symbol-editing mode and return to the main document.

4. Drag an instance of the **Banner symbol** from the Library panel to the top of the Stage. Change the name of Layer 1 to **Banner**. Next, align the banner with the Stage.

   The banner needs to be aligned so that its left edge is even with the left edge of the Stage and its top edge is even with the top edge of the Stage. To do this, you can use the Align options under the Align command of the Modify menu. To align objects to the Stage, first select the To Stage option. The To Stage option applies the Align commands relative to the Stage. Otherwise, the Align commands apply relative to the selected objects. After you select the To Stage option, select the object to be aligned and apply one of the Align options, such as Top or Left. Use the Align options to position the banner precisely at the top of the Stage.

5. Click **Modify** on the menu bar, point to **Align**, and, if necessary, click the **To Stage** command. If the To Stage command already has a check mark next to it, it is already selected.

6. If necessary, select the **Banner** instance. Click **Modify** on the menu bar, point to **Align**, and then click **Left**. The banner aligns with the left edge of the Stage.

7. Click **Modify** on the menu bar, point to **Align**, and then click **Top**. The banner is now aligned with the top edge of the Stage.

The next step in creating the Web site's main page is to add a background to the Stage. This will enhance the appearance of the content that is to appear on the Stage for each of the documents on this Web site. Aly suggests you create a rectangle over the Stage to cover all of the area not covered by the banner. Because the Stage is 700 pixels wide, the rectangle should also be 700 pixels wide. Because the Stage is 500 pixels high and the banner is covering the top 80 pixels, the rectangle should be 420 pixels high. The rectangle should be aligned to the bottom-left edge of the Stage. Aly also suggests that you use a gradient fill for the rectangle. You will do this next.

To add a rectangle to the Stage:

1. Insert a new layer and name it **Rectangle**.

2. Use the **Rectangle** tool ▭ to draw a rectangle on the Rectangle layer. The rectangle should cover all of the Stage except for the area covered by the banner. Use the **green radial gradient** (last row, fourth column from the left) for the fill. Do not include a stroke for the rectangle.

3. Use the **Selection** tool ▸ to select the rectangle, and then use the Property inspector to more precisely set the dimensions of the rectangle to **700 pixels** wide by **420 pixels** high.

4. Click **Modify** on the menu bar, point to **Align**, and then click **Left**. The rectangle aligns to the left edge of the Stage.

5. Click **Modify** once more, point to **Align**, and then click **Bottom**. The rectangle aligns with the bottom edge of the Stage. See Figure 7-13.

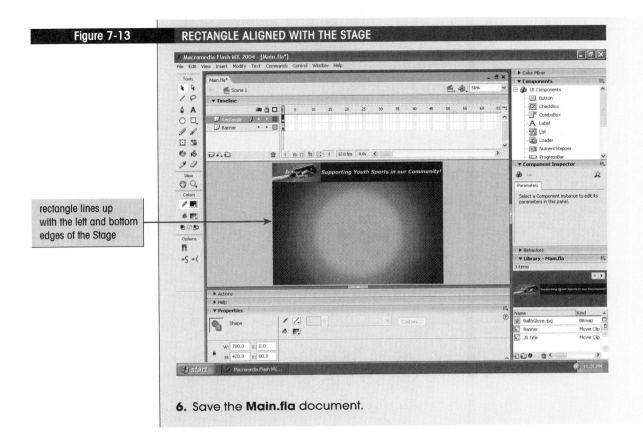

Figure 7-13 RECTANGLE ALIGNED WITH THE STAGE

rectangle lines up with the left and bottom edges of the Stage

6. Save the **Main.fla** document.

The graphics for the Main.fla document are now complete. The only item missing is the navigation bar with the buttons that will control how the Web site pages are loaded. Before creating the navigation bar, you will create the additional pages that are part of the Web site.

Creating Additional Pages Using a Flash Template

Recall that the additional documents for the Web site will be loaded on top of the main document. The main document will be at level 0 and its contents will still be visible on the Stage as other documents are loaded at higher levels. These additional documents, therefore, do not need to include the banner or other background graphics that are contained in the main document. They only need to have the content that is to be displayed. For the Jackson's Sports Web site, you will make each of the documents the same size. The background color of the loaded documents does not matter because they will automatically use the green background of the main document. To ensure that each of the additional documents have the same dimensions as the main document and to make it easier to create new documents that will be part of this Web site, you can create a Flash template. **Templates** are pre-built documents that can be used as a starting point for many Flash projects. Flash installs with several templates, and you can also create your own Flash templates. By starting with a template that installs with Flash, you can quickly develop a new document that looks professional and that can be customized based on your requirements. To create a document based on a template, you select a category from the Create from Template column on the Start page and then select the template from the New from Template dialog box. You can also click the New command on the File menu to open the New Document dialog box. You then click the Templates tab in the dialog box to display the available template categories. When you select a category, a list of the available templates in that category displays. Clicking a template name displays a preview and description of the template, as shown in Figure 7-14.

Figure 7-14   SELECTING A FLASH TEMPLATE

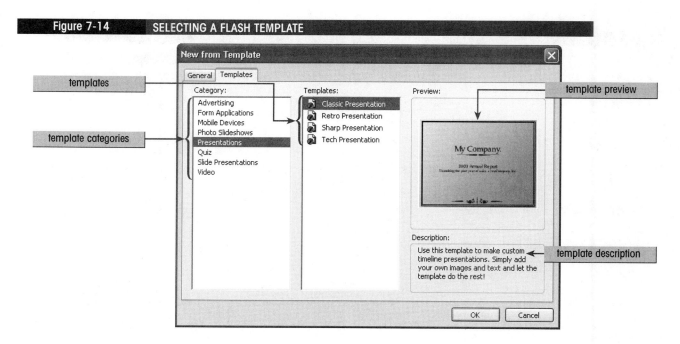

After you select a template and click the OK button, a Flash document based on the template opens in the Flash program window just like any other document. The document's elements can then be modified and saved with a new name.

In addition to using the templates that install with Flash, you can also create your own templates based on your own document. Creating your own templates allows you to create new documents based on the template and thus saves development time. For example, you can create a template that contains the basic graphic elements, background, or animations you want to include in other documents. Then, each time you create a new document based on the template, the graphic elements, background, and animations are automatically included with the new document. To create your own Flash template, create a document and then simply save it as a template. You assign the new template to an existing template category or create a new category. You also include a description of the template that displays when the template is selected in the New from Template dialog box. The new template is listed in the template category in which it is saved. The template can then be used as a starting point to create other documents.

Because you need to create several documents for the Jackson's Sports Web site and because each document will have the same dimensions as well as other similar elements, Aly suggests you create a template. You will first create the document with the basic graphic elements and then save it as a template, which will be used to create the other documents. The template will have the same dimensions as the Main.fla document, a rectangle to serve as a background for the document's content, and a simple animation. The documents created based on the template will be loaded on top of the main document and will assume the same background color as the main document. As a result, it does not matter what background color you use for the template.

The banner of the main document occupies the top 80 pixels of the main document and the navigation bar that will be added will be 200 pixels wide and will be placed on the left side of the Stage. Therefore, the content of the new documents must be placed below the banner and to the right of the navigation bar so it will not interfere with the content on the main document. To help you place the contents of the new documents correctly, you will place a horizontal guide line 100 pixels from the top edge of the Stage and a vertical guide line 250 pixels from the left edge of the Stage. The new content will be added below the horizontal guide line and to the right of the vertical guide line.

REFERENCE   WINDOW   **RW**

Creating a Flash Template
- Create a Flash document.
- Click File on the menu bar and then click Save as Template.
- In the Save as Template dialog box, enter a name for the template.
- Select an existing template category or create a new category.
- Type a description for the template and then click the OK button.

To create a Flash template:

1. Create a new document with a width of **700 pixels** and a height of **500 pixels**, which are the same dimensions as the Main.fla document. Click the **Zoom control** list arrow and click **Show Frame** to display all of the Stage.

2. Display the rulers. Drag a horizontal guide line from the top ruler and place it **100 pixels** from the top edge of the Stage. Drag a vertical guide line from the left ruler and place it **250 pixels** from the left edge of the Stage. Each of the documents based on this template will have a rectangular area within which the content will display.

3. Draw a rectangle using **light yellow** (#FFFFCC) for the rectangle's fill color. Do not include a stroke. Set a Corner radius of **10** points so that the rectangle has rounded corners. Draw the rectangle so that its left and top edges align with the vertical and horizontal guide lines respectively.

4. Select the **rectangle** and use the Property inspector to more precisely set its width and height by entering **400** for its width and **350** for its height. If necessary, reposition the rectangle to align it with the guide lines, as shown in Figure 7-15.

Figure 7-15	ALIGNING THE RECTANGLE WITH THE GUIDE LINES

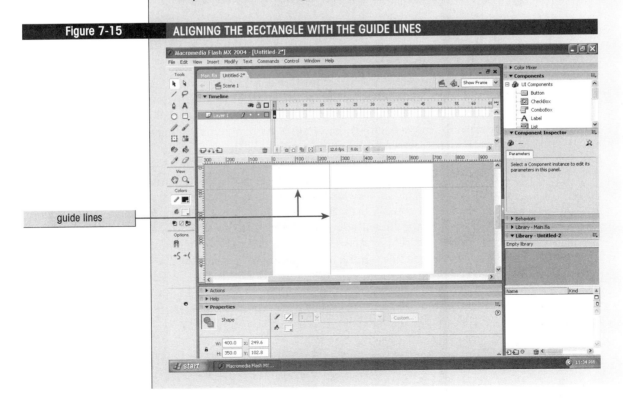

guide lines

5. Change the name of Layer 1 to **Rectangle** and lock the layer. Insert a new layer and name it **Contents**. This layer will be empty and will be used to create the contents of each new Web site document. The document is now ready to be saved as a template.

6. Click **File** on the menu bar and then click **Save as Template**. The Save as Template dialog box opens, as shown in Figure 7-16.

| Figure 7-16 | SAVE AS TEMPLATE DIALOG BOX |

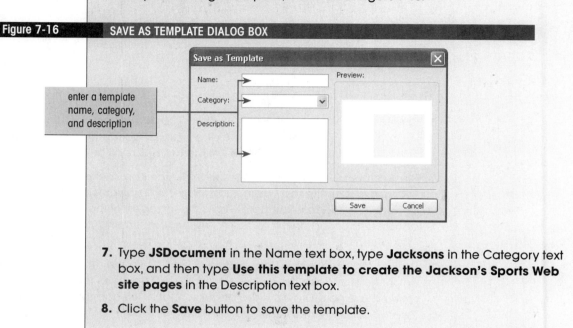

enter a template name, category, and description

7. Type **JSDocument** in the Name text box, type **Jacksons** in the Category text box, and then type **Use this template to create the Jackson's Sports Web site pages** in the Description text box.

8. Click the **Save** button to save the template.

The template will contain an animation of a baseball. Rather than creating a new graphic object of the ball, you can copy the ball from an existing symbol in another Flash document.

Using External Libraries

Aly has created a sample document for Jackson's Sports that contains a basketball symbol and a baseball symbol. You will copy these symbols to your template document. Both of these symbols will then be available to every document created using the template. To copy symbols from an existing document, you open the document's library as an external library. An **external library** contains the symbols for a stored document and makes these symbols available to the currently active document. To open a document's library as an external library, point to Import on the File menu, and then click the Open External Library command. The external library opens in a Library panel separate from the Library panel for the current document. After the external library is open, you can drag instances of the symbols from the external library's Library panel to the Library panel for the current document. You can also simply drag the symbols from the external library's Library panel to the Stage of the current document. The symbols are then copied to the library of the current document. You will copy the basketball and the baseball symbol so that both are available in the template.

To copy symbols from an external library:

1. Click **File** on the menu bar, point to **Import**, and then click **Open External Library**. The Open as Library dialog box opens.

2. Locate and select the **sports3.fla** document in the **Tutorial.07\Tutorial** folder included with your Data Files and then click the **Open** button. The sports3.fla Library panel opens as an external library directly below the Library panel for the current document, as shown in Figure 7-17.

| Figure 7-17 | OPENING AN EXTERNAL LIBRARY |

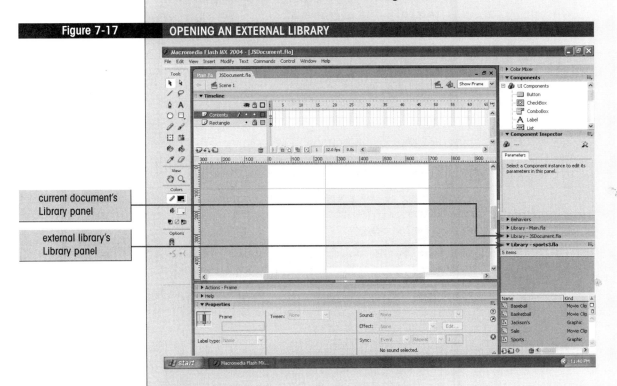

current document's Library panel

external library's Library panel

3. Point to the left side of the **sports3.fla** Library panel title bar until the pointer changes to a four-headed arrow pointer ✥ and then drag the panel to the middle of the screen to place it in its own window. Click the title bar of the JSDocument's Library panel to expand it. You will copy symbols from the external library to the JSDocument's library.

4. Drag the **Baseball** symbol from the sports3.fla Library panel to the JSDocument's Library panel. Also, drag the **Basketball** symbol from the sports3.fla Library panel to the JSDocument's Library panel. Both symbols are now copied and the external library can now be closed.

5. Click the **Close window** button ☒ on the sports3.fla Library panel's title bar to close the external library. Both the basketball and the baseball symbols are now stored in the current document's library. You will use the baseball in the animation for the template. You will use the basketball symbol in an animation created later in the tutorial.

Now, you are ready to create the baseball animation that will be part of the JSDocument template.

To create an animation with the baseball symbol:

1. Insert a new layer above the Rectangle layer and name it **Animation**. Drag an instance of the **baseball** symbol from the Library panel to the Stage and place it in the lower-left corner of the yellow rectangle.

2. Add a regular frame at **Frame 30** of the Rectangle layer to extend it. Also, add a regular frame at **Frame 30** of the Contents layer to extend it.

3. Insert a keyframe at **Frame 15** of the Animation layer and another at **Frame 30**. At **Frame 15**, move the baseball to the lower-right corner of the rectangle. Create a motion tween at **Frame 1** and another at **Frame 15**. The baseball will move from the left side of the rectangle to the right side and back. Next, you will add a rotation effect.

4. Select **Frame 1** of the Animation layer. In the Property inspector, click the **Rotate** list arrow and then click **CW**. The baseball will rotate clockwise one time as it moves to the right side of the rectangle.

5. Select **Frame 15** of the Animation layer, click the **Rotate** list arrow, and then click **CCW** so that the baseball will rotate counterclockwise one time as it goes back to the left side.

6. Move the playhead to **Frame 1**, and press the **Enter** key. The baseball moves back and forth as it rotates. The animation is complete.

7. Save and close the **JSDocument.fla** file. You return to the Main.fla document.

Now that you have created the template for the Web site's pages, you are ready to begin creating the pages according to Aly's instructions. You will start by creating the page that will load initially with the main document. This page's content will display the first time the Web site is visited and each time the Home button is clicked. The Home button will be created later in this session.

To create the initial page using a template:

1. Click **File** on the menu bar and then click **New**. In the New Document dialog box, click the **Templates** tab and then click **Jacksons** in the Category list box. The JSDocument template displays in the Templates list box, along with a preview of the template and a description, as shown in Figure 7-18.

Figure 7-18   SELECTING A TEMPLATE

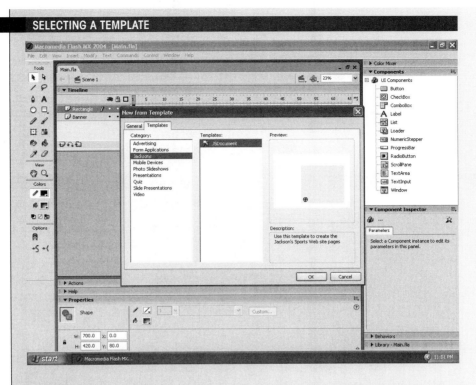

2. If necessary, click **JSDocument** in the Templates list box to select it, and then click the **OK** button. A new untitled document opens based on the JSDocument template. Click the **Zoom control** list arrow, and select **Show All** to display all of the contents on the Stage.

3. If necessary, select the **Contents** layer. Create a text block at the top of the yellow rectangle, placing it about **300 pixels** from the left edge of the Stage. Use the Property inspector to select **Times New Roman** for the font, **24** for the font size, and **black** for the text color. Also, if necessary, select the **Bold** and **Align Left** attributes and make certain the Italic attribute is not selected. Type **Welcome to Jackson's Sports!** in the text block.

You have been given some text by Aly based on information provided by the staff of Jackson's Sports. You will type the text into a text block in the document. The text block should have a fixed width so when you type the text, it wraps around onto separate lines within the text block as opposed to the text appearing on one long line. To create a fixed-width text block, you click and drag the Text tool pointer $+_A$ across the Stage to create a text block of specific dimensions. Then, you can type the text inside the text block.

4. Click the **Text** tool [A] on the toolbar and then click once in an empty area of the Stage. Use the Property inspector to select **Times New Roman** for the font, **14** for the font size, and **black** for the text color. Make certain the Bold attribute is not selected. Click and drag the **Text tool** pointer $+_A$ starting about **300 pixels** from the left edge of the Stage and below the text block created in Step 3. Drag it to the right to about **600 pixels** from the left edge of the Stage. A fixed-width text block with a width of about 300 pixels appears on the Stage.

5. Type the following paragraphs of text in the text block, making certain to press the **Enter** key twice after the first paragraph.

At Jackson's Sports we value your business and we'll do our best to provide you the best sports equipment and supplies at the best prices.

We are proud to support our local youth sports teams. We have been supplying equipment and sports supplies to many of the local teams for over 15 years.

Your screen should match the one shown in Figure 7-19.

Figure 7-19   TEXT BLOCKS ALIGNED

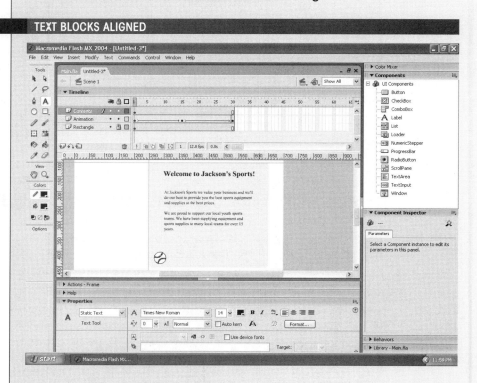

6. Click **Text** on the menu bar and then click **Check Spelling**. If spelling errors are detected, make the appropriate corrections. If an alert box displays asking if you want to continue checking from the beginning of the document, click the **Yes** button. When an alert box displays indicating that the spelling check is completed, click the **OK** button. If the Movie Explorer is opened as a result of the spelling check, close it.

TROUBLE? If a dialog box opens telling you that, based on your settings, there is nothing to check, click Text on the menu bar and then click Spelling Setup. In the Spelling Setup dialog box, select the Check text fields content check box under Document options, click the OK button, and then repeat Step 6.

7. Save this file as **Initial.fla** in the **Tutorial.07\Tutorial** folder included with your Data Files.

You have created the page that displays initially on top of the Main document when the Main document is first displayed. According to Aly's instructions, there are three other pages that you need to create. One contains the names of local sports teams that have done business with Jackson's Sports. The second is a list of services offered by the store. The third contains pictures of local teams and players. You will create each of the pages using the JSDocument template as a starting point.

To create the Teams' Names page:

1. Create a new document using the JSDocument template. A new untitled document opens based on the JSDocument template. Click the **Zoom control** list arrow and click **Show All** to display all of the contents on the Stage.

2. If necessary, select the **Contents** layer. Create a text block centered at the top of the yellow rectangle. Use the Property inspector to select **Times New Roman** for the font, **24** for the font size, and **black** for the text color. Also, if necessary, select the **Bold** and **Align Left** attributes. Type **Local Sports Teams** in the text block.

3. Create a fixed-width text block below the text block created in Step 2. Use the Property inspector to select **Times New Roman** for the font, **14** for the font size, and **black** for the text color. Make certain the Bold attribute is not selected. Place the text block about 300 pixels from the left edge of the Stage and make it about 300 pixels wide.

4. Type the following paragraphs of text in the text block, making certain to press the **Enter** key twice after the first paragraph and once between the other paragraphs.

Jackson's Sports is proud to support the following youth sports teams. For more information about these teams, contact our staff.

The Stars Basketball Team

The Sting Volleyball Team

The Tigers Softball Team

The Angels Baseball Team

Your screen should match the one shown in Figure 7-20.

Figure 7-20	TEAM NAMES ON SEPARATE LINES

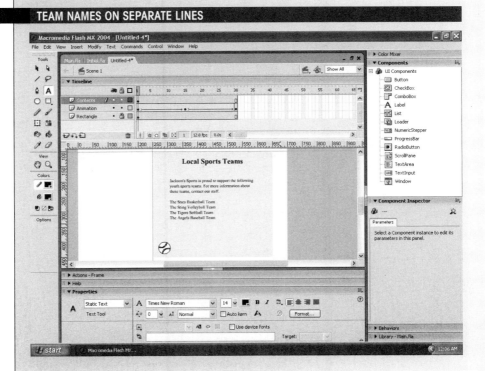

5. Check the spelling. Correct any misspelled words, and close the Movie Explorer if necessary. Next, you will change the color of the yellow rectangle to make it easier to see that a different page has loaded.

6. Unlock the **Rectangle** layer and select the **rectangle** on the Stage. Use the Property inspector to change the color of the rectangle's fill to a **peach color** (#FFCC99). Relock the Rectangle layer.

7. Save this file as **Teams.fla** in the **Tutorial.07\Tutorial** folder included with your Data Files.

The next document contains a list of the main services offered by Jackson's Sports. This document will be similar in format to the Initial.fla and Teams.fla documents, but you will change the animation to use the basketball graphic instead of the baseball.

To create the Services page:

1. Create a new document using the JSDocument template. A new untitled document opens based upon the JSDocument template. Click the **Zoom control** list arrow and select **Show All** to display all of the contents on the Stage.

2. If necessary, select the **Contents** layer. Create a text block centered at the top of the yellow rectangle. Use the Property inspector to select **Times New Roman** for the font, **24** for the font size, and **black** for the text color. Also, if necessary, select the **Bold** and **Align Left** attributes. Type **Jackson's Sports Services** in the text block.

3. Create a fixed-width text block below the text block created in Step 2. Use the Property inspector to select **Times New Roman** for the font, **14** for the font size, and **black** for the text color. Also, make certain the Bold attribute is not selected. Place the text block about 300 pixels from the left edge of the Stage and make it about 300 pixels wide.

4. Type the following paragraphs of text in the text block, making certain to press the **Enter** key between paragraphs.

- **Sale of equipment and supplies at a discount**

- **Team and individual trophies, including engraving of players' names**

- **Sponsorship of tournaments**

- **Team and player pictures**

Your screen should match the one shown in Figure 7-21.

Figure 7-21	EACH SERVICE LISTED ON SEPARATE LINES

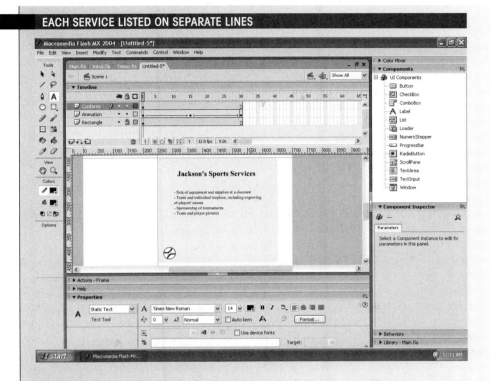

5. Check the spelling. Correct any misspelled words, and then close the Movie Explorer if necessary.

6. Unlock the **Rectangle layer** and select the **rectangle** on the Stage. Use the Property inspector to change the color of the rectangle's fill to a **light green color** (#99FFCC). Relock the Rectangle layer. Now, you will change the animated graphic to the basketball symbol you copied from the external library earlier in the session.

7. Select **Frame 1** of the Animation layer, click the **Baseball** instance on the Stage, and then click the **Swap** button in the Property inspector. Click the **Basketball** symbol in the Swap Symbol dialog box, and then click the **OK** button. The Baseball instance changes to a Basketball instance on the Stage. Swap the other Baseball instances.

8. Repeat Step 7 for **Frame 15** and **Frame 30** of the Animation layer. Test the animation to view the basketball moving from the left of the rectangle to the right and then back while rotating at the same time.

9. Save this file as **Services.fla** in the **Tutorial.07\Tutorial** folder included with your Data Files.

The next document will contain buttons that load pictures of local teams or players. This document will be similar in format to the previous documents, but it will not include the animation.

To create the Photos page:

1. Create a new document using the JSDocument template. A new untitled document opens based on the JSDocument template. Click the **Zoom control** list arrow and select **Show All** to display all of the contents on the Stage.

2. If necessary, select the **Contents** layer. Create a text block centered at the top of the yellow rectangle. Use the Property inspector to select **Times New Roman** for the font, **24** for the font size, and **black** for the text color. Also, if necessary, select the **Bold** and **Align Left** attributes. Type **Team and Player Photos** in the text block. The animation will not be used with this page.

3. Select the **Animation** layer and delete it.

4. Save this file as **Photos.fla** in the **Tutorial.07\Tutorial** folder included with your Data Files.

The Photos.fla page will be completed later in this tutorial. Now that you have created the main document and the Web site's pages, you need to create the navigation bar that will allow visitors to the Web site to navigate from one document to another within the site.

Creating the Site's Navigation Bar

A Web site is not complete without a means of navigating from one Web page to another. In a regular HTML-based Web site, hyperlinks load another HTML document into the Web browser when clicked. In a Flash Web site, the hyperlinks are replaced with buttons that load other SWF files into the Flash Player when clicked. These buttons are created the same way as the buttons you created to control animations in Tutorial 5. The buttons for a Flash Web site have ActionScript programming code that instructs the Flash Player as to which SWF file to load and how to load it. This programming code will be added in the next session. The buttons must include obvious visual clues that indicate how the buttons can be used to navigate the site. It is also helpful if the buttons have some sort of animated effect that occurs when you move the mouse pointer over the button, indicating that something will happen when you click the button.

For the Jackson's Sports Web site, Aly instructs you to create a navigation bar, which is simply a set of related buttons grouped together. Many Web sites have navigation bars with buttons, arranged horizontally or vertically, that look the same but have different text indicating what action will occur when clicked. For the Jackson's Sports Web site, the buttons will be arranged vertically on a rectangle placed on the left side of the Main document. The navigation bar will have four buttons; each button will load a different page when clicked. The buttons will be labeled Home, Services, Teams, and Photos. The navigation bar's rectangular background will be large enough to allow for additional buttons if new pages are created for the Web site. The navigation bar will be created as a symbol and an instance of it will be added to the Main document. The navigation bar will always be displayed as long as the Main document is being played in the Flash Player.

To create a navigation bar for the Jackson's Sports Web site:

1. Return to the **Main.fla** document. Create a new symbol for the navigation bar by clicking **Insert** on the menu bar and then clicking **New Symbol**. Name the symbol **Navbar**, select **Movie clip** for the symbol's behavior, and click the **OK** button to create the symbol and enter symbol-editing mode.

2. Draw a rectangle on the center of the Stage. Use the Property inspector to select a **light green color** (#00CC66) for the fill and a **light gray color** (#CCC-CCC) for the stroke. Select a **solid** stroke style with a stroke height of **1**. Also, if necessary, set the corner radius value to **10** so that the rectangle will have rounded corners.

3. Select the **rectangle** and use the Property inspector to set its dimensions to **200 pixels** wide by **250 pixels** high. If necessary, reposition the rectangle so it is centered on the Stage.

4. Rename Layer 1 **Background** and lock the layer. Insert a new layer and name it **Buttons**.

5. Draw a small rectangle centered at the top of the larger rectangle. Use the Property inspector to select a **light gray color** (#CCCCCC) for the stroke and a **dark gray color** (#666666) for the fill. Also, if necessary, set the corner radius value to **10** so that the rectangle will have rounded corners.

6. Select the **rectangle** and use the Property inspector to set its width at **150** pixels and its height at **20** pixels. See Figure 7-22.

Figure 7-22   BUTTON SHAPE ON NAVIGATION BAR

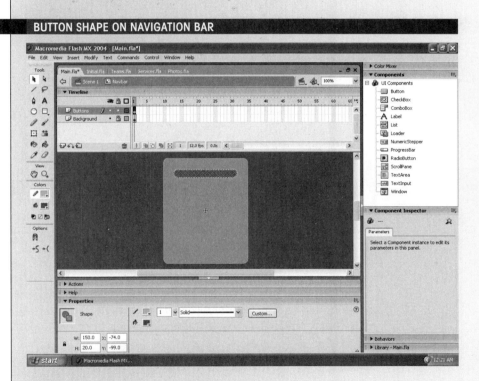

7. Convert the small rectangle to a symbol. In the Convert to Symbol dialog box, name the symbol **Home button**, select **Button** as the symbol's behavior, and, if necessary, select the upper-left corner square for the Registration point. Click the **OK** button.

8. Click the **Edit Symbols** button and click **Home button** to open it in symbol-editing mode. You need to add a rollover effect to the button.

9. Insert a keyframe in the **Over frame** of Layer 1. With the rectangle still selected, use the Property inspector to change the fill color to **yellow** and the stroke color to **black**.

10. Rename Layer 1 to **Background** and lock it. Insert a new layer and name it **Text**. Now, you will add text to the button on the new layer.

11. Create a text block in the Up frame of the Text layer. Use the Property inspector to select **Verdana** for the font, **16** for the font size, and **white** for the text color. Do not apply the Bold or Italic attributes. If necessary, set the alignment to **Align Left**. Type **Home** in the text block and position it about 10 pixels from the left side of the rectangle, as shown in Figure 7-23.

Figure 7-23   **TEXT ON BUTTON**

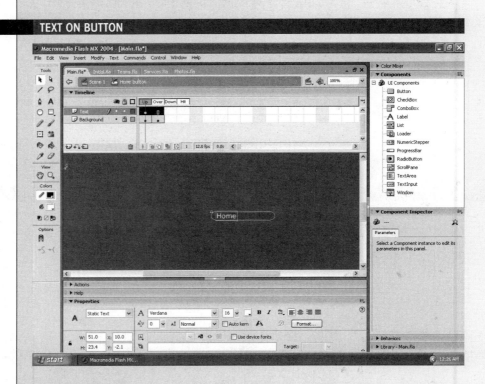

12. Insert a keyframe in the **Over frame** of the Text layer. Change the text color to **black**. The rollover effect is now complete.

You have created the Home button for the navigation bar; you will use this button to create additional buttons. But before you create the additional buttons, Aly asks you to add an animation to the button that displays only when the mouse pointer is over the button.

Adding an Animation to a Button Frame

Creating a button with a rollover effect is fairly straightforward, and the rollover effect reinforces the fact that clicking the button causes something to happen. In addition to a simple rollover effect, you can also add animations to any of the Up, Over, or Down frames of the button's Timeline. One effect that is commonly used is to have an animation in the Over frame of the button. When the mouse pointer is over the button, the animation displays. When the mouse pointer is not over the button, the animation does not display. To do this, you need to create a separate movie clip symbol with an animation in its Timeline and then place an instance of the symbol in the Over frame of the button symbol. The animation of the movie clip only displays when the Over frame is active, which is when the mouse pointer is over the button. This effect is similar to the nested movie clip animations that you created in Tutorial 4, in which you had an instance of a movie clip inside the Timeline of another symbol. In the case of buttons, you will also have an instance of another symbol inside the button's Timeline.

Aly suggests you create an animation in a movie clip symbol to add to the Home button. This animation will be a simple motion tween of a small circle.

To create a movie clip animation:

1. Create a new symbol. Name the new symbol **Button animation** and select **Movie clip** as its behavior type.

2. In symbol-editing mode, use the **Oval** tool ⊙ on the toolbar to create a small circle in the center of the Stage. Use the **green radial gradient** located in the bottom of the color pop-up window for the fill. Do not include a stroke. Position and set the size of the circle.

3. Select the **circle** and use the Property inspector to set its width and height to **18 pixels**. If necessary, reposition the circle so it is centered on the Stage. To animate the circle using a motion tween, it must first be converted to a symbol.

4. With the circle still selected, click **Modify** on the menu bar and then click **Convert to Symbol**. Name the symbol **Circle** and leave the behavior type as **Movie clip**. Click the **OK** button to create the symbol. Click the **Color** list arrow in the Property inspector and select **Alpha**. Set the Alpha Amount to **30%**. Now, you need to add the keyframes for the animation.

5. Insert keyframes at **Frames 5**, **10**, **15**, and **20**.

6. Select **Frame 5** and click the circle on the Stage once to display its properties in the Property inspector. Change the X coordinate of the circle to **50** and press the **Enter** key. The circle moves to the right, as shown in Figure 7-24.

Figure 7-24   **CHANGING THE SYMBOL'S POSITION**

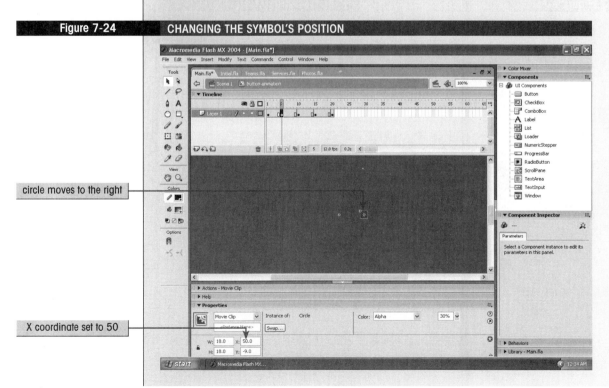

circle moves to the right

X coordinate set to 50

7. Select **Frame 15** and click the **circle** on the Stage once. Change the X coordinate of the circle to **-50** and press the **Enter** key. The circle moves to the left.

8. Create motion tweens at **Frames 1, 5, 10**, and **15**. Now, you can test the animation.

9. Move the playhead to **Frame 1** and press the **Enter** key to see the animation. The circle moves to the right, moves to the left of center, and then returns to the center.

The button animation is now complete. Now, the movie clip animation needs to be added to the button symbol. It will be added to the Over frame of the button so that the animation displays only when the mouse pointer is over the button.

To add the button animation to the button:

1. Click the **Edit Symbols** button and then click **Home button** to open the Home button in symbol-editing mode. Add a new layer for the movie clip animation.

2. Insert a new layer above the Background layer and name it **Animation**. You want the Animation layer to be below the Text layer so that the animation will not cover the text. Now insert the keyframe for the animation.

3. Insert a keyframe in the **Over frame** of the Animation layer. Add the movie clip animation next.

4. If necessary, expand the Library panel to display the Button animation symbol. Drag an instance of the **Button animation** symbol to the center of the button, as shown in Figure 7-25.

| Figure 7-25 | ADDING AN INSTANCE OF THE BUTTON ANIMATION |

circle symbol instance on button

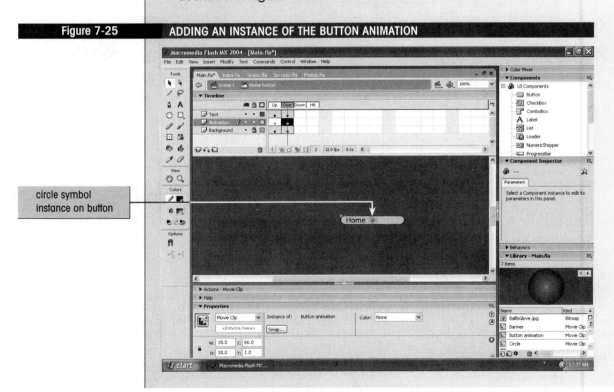

The Home button symbol is now complete. The other buttons needed for the navigation bar will be similar to this button. The only difference will be the text that displays on the buttons. Rather than creating the other buttons from scratch, you will make duplicates of the Home button symbol and then change the text for the duplicates. According to Aly's instructions, you are to have three more buttons. One button will be for the Teams' Names page, one for the Services page, and the third for the Photos page.

To create additional buttons for the navigation bar:

1. In the Library panel, locate and right-click the **Home button** and then click **Duplicate**. In the Duplicate Symbol dialog box, name the duplicate symbol **Teams button**, make certain the **Button** behavior is selected, and then click the **OK** button to close the Duplicate Symbol dialog box.

2. Repeat Step 1 to create a second duplicate named **Services button**. Then repeat Step 1 once more to create a third duplicate named **Photos button**.

3. Click the **Edit Symbols** button 🔲 and then click **Teams button** to open the Teams button symbol in symbol-editing mode. Change the button's text.

4. Select the **Up frame** of the Text layer. Click the **Text** tool 🅰 on the toolbar and then click the **Home** text block. Change the text to **Teams**. Do the same for the **Over frame** of the Text layer to change the Home text to **Teams**.

5. Click 🔲 and then click **Services button** to open the Services button symbol in symbol-editing mode.

6. Select the **Up frame** of the Text layer. Change the Home text to **Services**. Select the **Over frame** of the Text layer and change the Home text to **Services**.

7. Click 🔲 and then click **Photos button** to open the Photos button symbol in symbol-editing mode. Change the button's text.

8. Select the **Up frame** of the Text layer. Change the Home text to **Photos**. Select the **Over frame** of the Text layer and change the Home text to **Photos**.

The additional buttons are now complete. Next, you will add the button instances to the navigation bar. The navigation bar already contains the Home button, so you need to add the Teams, Services, and Photos buttons. You will add the buttons and then add the navigation bar to the Stage of the main document.

To complete the navigation bar and add it to the main document:

1. Click the **Edit Symbols** button 🔲 and then click **Navbar** to open the Navbar symbol in symbol-editing mode. Add instances of the buttons.

2. Drag an instance of the **Teams button** symbol from the Library panel to the rectangle and place it below the Home button. Drag an instance of the **Services button** symbol and place it below the Teams button. Then drag an instance of the **Photos button** symbol and place it below the Services button. Next, you need to align the button instances.

3. Select the **Home button** with the **Selection** tool 🔲, and in the Property inspector, change its X coordinate to **-75** and its Y coordinate to **-100**.

4. Repeat Step 3 for the **Teams button**, setting its X coordinate to **-75** and its Y coordinate to **-50**. Repeat Step 3 for the **Services button**, setting its X coordinate to **-75** and its Y coordinate to **0**. Repeat Step 3 one more time for the **Photos button**, setting its X coordinate to **-75** and its Y coordinate to **50**. The navigation bar contains button instances for each button, as shown in Figure 7-26. Now, you can add the navigation bar to the main document.

Figure 7-26   **BUTTONS ON NAVIGATION BAR**

5. Click the **Scene 1** link on the Address bar to return to the Main document's Timeline. Click the **Zoom control** list arrow and select **Show All** to display all of the contents on the Stage.

6. Insert a new layer above the Rectangle layer and name it **Navbar**.

7. Drag an instance of the Navbar symbol to the left side of the Stage and place it as shown in Figure 7-27.

| Figure 7-27 | NAVIGATION BAR ON STAGE OF MAIN DOCUMENT |

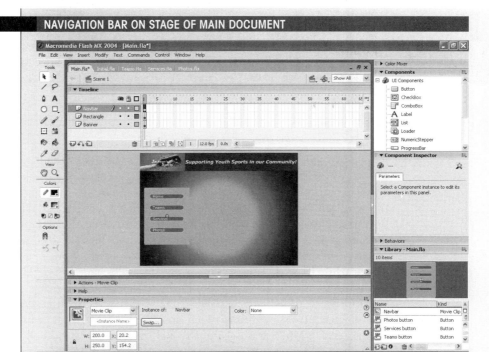

8. To test the navigation bar, click **Control** on the menu bar and then click **Test Movie**. The SWF file opens in a separate window. Move your mouse pointer over each of the four buttons. The buttons change colors and exhibit the circle animation while the mouse pointer is over them.

9. Click **File** on the menu bar and click **Close** to return to the Main.fla document, and then save the **Main.fla** file.

The navigation bar and its buttons are now complete. However, they do not yet control anything. You will add the ActionScript code to these buttons in the next session.

In this session, you created the documents that make up the Jackson's Sports Web site. You created the site's main document or home page, and then created a Flash template that was used to create the additional documents for the site. You also created the navigation bar with a set of buttons that will be used to navigate from one document to another in the Web site. The buttons include a movie clip animation that displays when the mouse pointer is over the buttons.

Session 7.2 QUICK CHECK

1. What is a Flash template?

2. What is the purpose of opening a document's library as an external library in another document?

3. A Flash Web site is displayed in the Flash Player within a(n) _____ document.

4. A Flash Web site's navigation bar contains _____ used to load different SWF files.

5. Briefly explain how you add an animation to a button that displays when the mouse pointer is over the button.

In this session, you will learn how to use the Actions panel to add ActionScript instructions to the buttons you created in the previous session. You will also complete the Photos page for the Web site that will be used to display pictures. You will add appropriate ActionScript instructions to control how the pictures are loaded into a movie clip in the Flash Player.

Using **ActionScript**

As you learned in the previous session, a Flash Web site's navigation system usually consists of a set of buttons. When you click a button, you want the Flash Player to load a different SWF file at the specified level. The navigation bar you created in the previous session has the required buttons, but the buttons do not yet control anything. To make the buttons operational, you need to add ActionScript instructions to them. Recall from Tutorial 5 that ActionScript is a programming language within Flash that allows you to add actions to objects or frames in your document. Actions are instructions that are used to control a document while its animation is playing. In Tutorial 5, you added behaviors to buttons to make the buttons control the animation. Recall that behaviors provide a limited set of actions that you can use without having to write ActionScript programs. However, adding actions to buttons to control how a movie loads into the Flash Player requires adding actions using the Actions panel. You use the Actions panel to add actions in the form of **scripts**, which can contain one or more actions as well as other programming code used to control how the actions are executed. You will learn more about ActionScript in Tutorial 8. For now, you will add simple scripts to the buttons to control how the Web site's pages are loaded. The actions will be added to the button instances on the Navbar symbol.

Using the loadMovieNum Action

Recall from Session 7.1 that the Flash Player uses levels to load a SWF file. The main document loads into the Flash Player at level 0 and other SWF files can then be loaded at different levels. A SWF file loaded at a higher level will be on top of the SWF file at level 0. Using this method, you can load the Web site's main document with the banner, background, and navigation bar at level 0 and then load the other pages of the Web site at level 1 or higher. For example, you will load the Services page at level 1 and it will display on top of the main document loaded at level 0.

To load a SWF file into the Flash Player at a specific level, you need to create an ActionScript script with the `loadMovieNum` action. The format of this action is `loadMovieNum("filename.swf", level)`. Within the parentheses, you specify the **parameters** of the action. The parameters give the action the information it needs to execute properly. In the case of the `loadMovieNum` action, the two parameters are the name of the SWF file to be loaded and the level number at which the file will be loaded. The name of the SWF file must be enclosed in quotes and a comma must separate the filename and the level number. For example, the action to load the Services page at level 1 is `loadMovieNum("Services.swf", 1)`. The `loadMovieNum` action is only executed when the button instance to which it is attached is clicked and released. For the action to work with the button, you must add an event handler that determines when to execute the action. Flash uses **event handlers** to check for events, such as when a button is clicked or when it is released. The event handler determines the action to take when a specific event occurs. To handle button events, you use the on event handler. The format of the on event handler is `on (mouseEvent)`, where the `mouseEvent` can include `press` or `release`. `Press` refers to a button being clicked. The event handler is followed by a pair of curly braces within which you place statements such as the `loadMovieNum` action. When you click a button with your mouse, you cause the `press` event to occur. When you release the mouse button, the `release` event occurs. So, to execute an action after the button is released, you code the on event handler as `on (release)`, followed by the statement to be executed within curly braces. The complete script to load the Services page is as follows:

```
on (release)  {
        loadMovieNum("Services.swf", 1);
}
```

The curly braces can be placed on the same lines as other statements or on separate lines. The preceding format is recommended to make the script easier to read. It is also recommended practice to end ActionScript statements with a semicolon. Flash helps you write the script when you use the options in the Actions panel.

Using the Actions Panel

To add an ActionScript script to a button, you first select the button instance on the Stage. Then, you select actions from the Actions panel shown in Figure 7-28.

| Figure 7-28 | ACTIONS PANEL ELEMENTS |

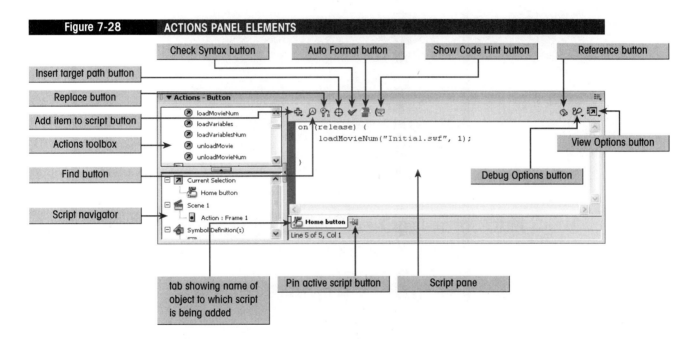

To open the Actions panel, you click the Actions panel title bar to expand the panel or you click Window on the menu bar, point to Development Panels, and then click Actions. The main elements of the Actions panel are described in Figure 7-29.

Figure 7-29   **ACTIONS PANEL ELEMENTS**

OPTION	BUTTON	DESCRIPTION
Actions toolbox		Lists actions and other ActionScript elements organized by categories; double-clicking an action adds its code to the Script pane
Script navigator		Lists elements in the FLA file that have ActionScript code
Script pane		Allows you to add and edit the ActionScript code
Add item to script button	⊹	Displays menu and submenus of actions and other ActionScript elements; selecting an action from a submenu adds its code to the Script pane
Find button	🔍	Provides a search function; finds instances of keywords in the currently displayed script in the Script pane
Replace button		Provides a search and replace function; finds instances of keywords in the currently displayed script in the Script pane and replaces them with the specified keyword
Insert target path button	⊕	Allows you to select an element in the FLA file such as a movie clip instance; it then creates the code to reference the element in the script
Check Syntax button	✓	Checks the ActionScript code in the Script pane for errors
Auto Format button	▤	Automatically formats the ActionScript code in the Script pane for improved readability; adds indentation to nested statements and removes unnecessary blank lines
Show Code Hint button		Displays code hints when typing ActionScript code in the Script pane
Reference button		Displays ActionScript information in the Help panel
Debug Options button		Provides options to troubleshoot advanced scripts
View Options button		Displays options to control the view of the Script pane such as adding line numbers to the ActionScript statements
Pin active script button		Keeps a script from closing when another script is opened; allows you to keep several scripts open at the same time

---

REFERENCE   WINDOW   **RW**

Adding ActionScript Code to a Button
- Select the button instance on the Stage.
- Open the Actions panel, select a category from the Actions toolbox, and then double-click an action to add its code to the Script pane.
- If necessary, type required code such as parameters that reference filenames.
- Click the Check Syntax icon to check the script for errors.

Because the navigation bar for the Jackson's Sports Web site has buttons that are designed to load a SWF file when clicked, you will add the `on` event handler with the `release` parameter. So when the button is clicked and then released, the event handler executes the `loadMovieNum` action to load the specified movie at a particular level. This script will be added to each button instance with the corresponding name of the SWF file.

To add ActionScript to the Home button:

1. If you took a break after the last session, open the **Main.fla**, **Initial.fla**, **Teams.fla**, **Services.fla**, and **Photos.fla** documents located in the **Tutorial.07\Tutorial** folder included with your Data Files. If necessary, switch to the **Main.fla** document and set the panels to their default layout.

2. Click the **Edit Symbols** button 🔄 and then click **Navbar** to open the symbol in symbol-editing mode. Select the **Home button** instance on the Stage. You will use the Actions panel to add the ActionScript to the button.

3. Click the **Actions panel** title bar to expand it. Click **Global Functions** in the Actions toolbox to expand this category, and then click **Movie Clip Control** to expand this category. A list of functions displays, including the on event handler.

4. If necessary, scroll down the list of actions in the Actions toolbox to locate the on event handler. Double-click the on event handler to add it to the Script pane, as shown in Figure 7-30.

Figure 7-30   ON EVENT HANDLER ADDED TO SCRIPT PANE

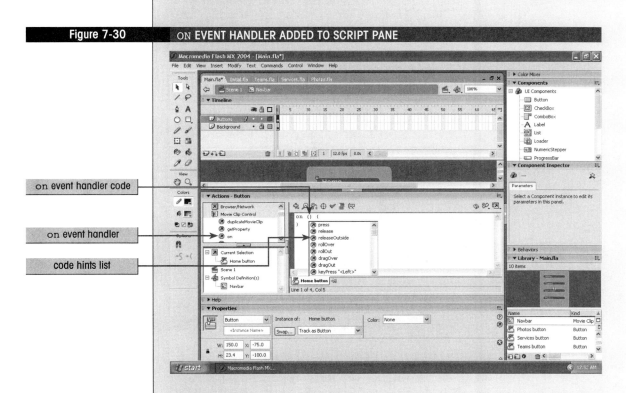

When the on event handler is added to the Script pane, the parentheses and curly braces are automatically added by Flash. In addition, a code hints list of events displays so that all you have to do is double-click the event you want to include in the script. In this case, you want to select the release event.

5. Double-click the release event from the list of events. The word release is added between the parentheses.

TROUBLE? If the list of events does not display, type the word release within the parentheses.

The loadMovieNum action must now be added between the two curly braces. You will insert a new line between the two curly braces and then add the action on the new line.

6. Use the **Right arrow** key on the keyboard to move the cursor in the Script pane to the end of the first line after the opening curly brace. Press the **Enter** key to add a new line.

7. Click **Browser/Network** in the Actions toolbox. A list of actions displays.

8. If necessary, scroll down the list of actions to locate the loadMovieNum action. Double-click the loadMovieNum action to add it to the script. Next, you must type the parameters for the filename and the level number.

9. Within the parentheses of the loadMovieNum action, type "Initial.swf" , 1 to complete the script, as shown in Figure 7-31.

| Figure 7-31 | COMPLETED SCRIPT FOR BUTTON |

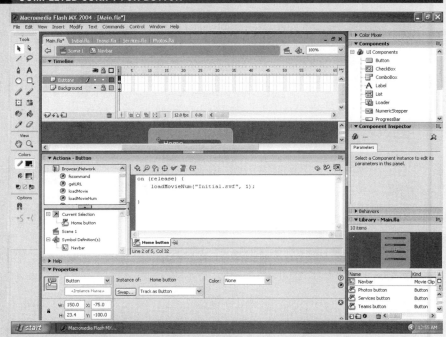

The Actions panel includes an option to check your script for errors. You will use this option to ensure your script does not contain any errors.

10. Click the **Check Syntax** button in the Actions panel.

If no errors are present, an alert box displays stating "This script contains no errors." If errors are present in your script, an alert box displays stating, "This script contains errors. The errors encountered are listed in the Output panel." The Output panel displays at the bottom of the screen with a list of the errors.

11. Click the **OK** button to close the alert box that displays. If the Output panel is open, close the panel and compare your script to that of Figure 7-31. Make the necessary corrections and repeat Step 10 until no more errors are encountered.

The Home button is now operational and when clicked, loads the Initial.swf file into the Flash Player at level 1. The same script must now be added to the rest of the buttons. The only difference will be the name of the SWF file within the parentheses of the `loadMovieNum` action. You will add the scripts to the buttons next.

To add ActionScript to the remaining buttons:

1. Collapse the Actions panel. Select the **Teams button** instance on the Stage and then expand the Actions panel again.

2. Double-click the **on** event handler from the Actions toolbox to add it to the Script pane and then double-click the `release` event from the list of events. The event handler and event are added to the Script pane.

3. Move the cursor in the Script pane to the end of the first line after the opening curly brace and press the **Enter** key to add a new line.

4. Double-click the `loadMovieNum` action from the Actions toolbox to add it to the script. The action is added to the script. Now type the parameters for the filename and the level number.

5. Within the parentheses of the `loadMovieNum` action, type `"Teams.swf", 1` to complete the script.

6. Click the **Check Syntax** button ☑ in the Actions panel to check the script for errors.

7. Click the **OK** button to close the alert box that displays. If the Output panel is open, close the panel and make the necessary corrections. Repeat Step 6 until no more errors are encountered.

8. Collapse the Actions panel to select the **Services button** instance on the Stage and then expand the Actions panel again. Repeat Steps 2 through 7 to create the script for this button. In Step 5, be certain to type `"Services.swf"` for the filename parameter in the `loadMovieNum` action. Create the script for the last button.

9. Collapse the Actions panel to select the **Photos button** instance on the Stage and then expand the Actions panel again. Repeat Steps 2 through 7 to create the script for this button. In Step 5, be certain to type `"Photos.swf"` for the filename parameter in the `loadMovieNum` action.

10. Click the **Scene 1** link in the Address bar to return to the Main.fla document, and collapse the Actions panel.

The ActionScript scripts for the buttons are now complete. To ensure that the buttons work as expected, you will test them next. To test them, you must first publish each of the site's documents as SWF files. Remember, the `loadMovieNum` action will load the SWF files named in the parameter portion of the action script code. You have created the Flash documents and saved them as FLA files. Now, you will publish them using the Publish Settings command on the File menu. After the documents have been published, you will use the Test Movie command for the Main.fla document to test the buttons in the navigation bar.

To test the buttons in the navigation bar:

1. Switch to the **Initial.fla** document.

2. Click **File** on the menu bar and then click **Publish Settings**. The Publish Settings dialog box opens. This file only needs to be published as a SWF file.

3. Select the **Flash (.swf)** option and make sure no other options are selected. Click the **Publish** button to publish the SWF file. The Initial.swf file is created and saved to the same folder as the Initial.fla file.

4. Click the **OK** button to close the Publish Settings dialog box.

5. Switch to the **Teams.fla** document and repeat Steps 2 through 4 to publish the **Teams.swf** file.

6. Switch to the **Services.fla** document and repeat Steps 2 through 4 to publish the **Services.swf** file.

7. Switch to the **Photos.fla** document and repeat Steps 2 through 4 to publish the **Photos.swf** file. The Main.fla document will be published using the Test Movie command.

8. Switch to the **Main.fla** document. Click **Control** on the menu bar and then click **Test Movie**. The Test Movie command creates the SWF file and displays the Main.swf file in a separate window.

9. Click the **Home** button on the navigation bar to display the Home.swf file, as shown in Figure 7-32.

 Figure 7-32   HOME PAGE IN JACKSON'S SPORTS WEB SITE

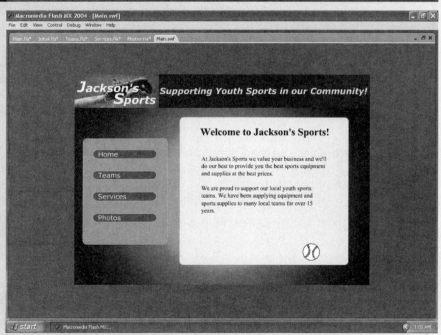

10. Click the **Teams, Services, and Photos** buttons to display their respective SWF files. The SWF files display when the buttons are clicked.

11. Click **File** on the menu bar and then click **Close** when you are finished testing the buttons.

When the Main.swf file first displayed in the preceding steps, the contents of the Initial.swf file did not display. It was not until you clicked the Home button that the Initial.swf file loaded into the Flash Player. When someone visits the Jackson's Sports Web site, you want the Initial.swf file to load right away without requiring the site visitor to click the Home button. What is missing is another `loadMovieNum` action to tell the Flash Player to load the Initial.swf file as soon as the Main.swf file is loaded. Because this action is not part of a button, it is not enclosed within an event handler. Instead, the action is added to Frame 1 of the Main.fla document's Timeline. Then, when the Main.swf file is loaded into the Flash Player and Frame 1 plays, the `loadMovieNum` action causes the Initial.swf file to load right away. You will add this action next.

To add an action to a frame:

1. Insert a new layer in the Main.fla document's Timeline. Name this layer **Action**.

2. Select **Frame 1** of the Action layer. Expand the Actions panel, and double-click the `loadMovieNum` action from the Actions toolbox to add it to the Script pane. Now type the parameters for the filename and the level number.

3. Within the parentheses of the `loadMovieNum` action, type **"Initial.swf", 1** to complete the action, as shown in Figure 7-33.

Figure 7-33	ACTION ADDED TO FRAME 1 OF MAIN DOCUMENT

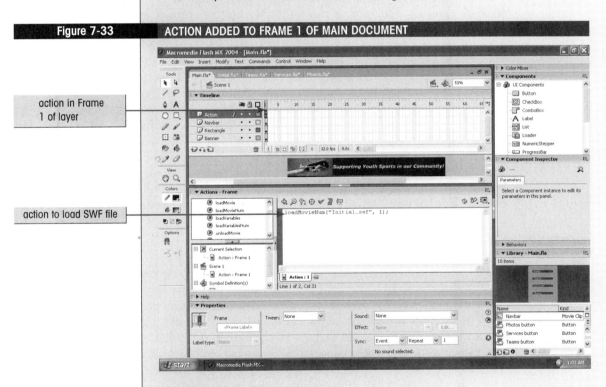

action in Frame 1 of layer

action to load SWF file

4. Click the **Check Syntax** button in the Actions panel to check the script for errors.

5. Click the **OK** button to close the alert box that displays. If the Output panel is open, close the panel and make the necessary corrections. Repeat Step 4 until no more errors are encountered. Collapse the Actions panel.

6. Click **Control** on the menu bar and then click **Test Movie**. The Main.swf file displays in a separate window and the contents of the Initial.swf also display.

7. Click **File** on the menu bar and then click **Close** to return to the Main.fla document.

8. Save the **Main.fla** document.

You have added the ActionScript scripts to make the navigation bar buttons operational and to load the Initial.swf file when the Main.swf file is first loaded into the Flash Player. The site is almost complete. Now, you only need to complete the Photos page so that it displays several pictures of local youth sports teams and events.

Loading **External Image Files**

The Photos page will display bitmap pictures of sports teams and individual players. The pictures will change on a regular basis as different teams submit pictures to Jackson's Sports. Ordinarily when you display a picture in a Flash document, you import the picture and it becomes part of the document. However, because this case requires the pictures to change regularly, you do not want to make the pictures part of the document. To do so would require the document to be modified each time a different set of pictures is to be displayed. A better option is to leave the pictures as separate files and to bring them into the Flash Player only when they are to be displayed. The external image files for the pictures that will be displayed on the Photos page should reside in the same folder as the Photos.swf file. This will make it easier to reference the files from within the Photos page. Also, because all of the pictures will be displayed in the same area of the Photos page, they should be no larger than the area in which they will be displayed. The images should be prepared in a separate image-editing program such as Macromedia Fireworks and then saved with a nonspecific filename such as Photo1.jpg. This way, when a picture is to be replaced, a new picture can be assigned the same name of Photo1.jpg and saved to the same folder. When the Photos.swf file loads the Photo1.jpg file, the new picture displays. The Flash document does not have to be modified each time the pictures are replaced.

Using the loadMovie Action

Loading external image files into a SWF file in the Flash Player can be accomplished by using the `loadMovie` action. The `loadMovie` action is similar to the `loadMovieNum` action but can be used to load image files into a movie clip instance instead of a level. You create an empty movie clip symbol in a document such as the Photos document, add an instance of the symbol to the Stage, and then use the `loadMovie` action to load a picture into the movie clip instance. The format of the `loadMovie` action is `movieclip.loadMovie("filename")`, where `movieclip` represents the name of the movie clip instance. To use this action, you must assign a name to the movie clip instance on the Stage in addition to the name of the symbol in the library. An instance can be assigned a name using the Property inspector. If you have a movie clip instance named Picture_mc, the action to load the picture file Photo1.jpg into the instance is `Picture_mc.loadMovie("Photo1.jpg")`. You can create this `loadMovie` action along with the event handler code using the Actions panel in a similar way to how you created the `loadMovieNum` action. However, this action can also be added to a button using the Behaviors panel, which is easier than using the Actions panel.

Note that when using the `loadMovie` action, the image files for the pictures need to be in the standard JPEG file format and not in the progressive JPEG format. The **progressive JPEG** format causes a picture that is downloading to a Web browser to appear to fade in by gradually downloading the data that makes up the picture. Aly has prepared two pictures to be used with the Jackson's Sports Web site. She suggests you use the Behaviors panel to add the `loadMovie` action to a new set of buttons you will create on the Photos page. You will add the movie clip, buttons, and behaviors to complete the Photos page. There will be two buttons, one for each picture. The buttons will be created as part of a navigation bar that will be placed at the bottom of the rectangle in the Photos page.

To create the navigation bar for the Photos page:

1. Display the **Photos.fla** document.

2. Create a new symbol. Name the symbol **Photos Navbar** and set its behavior type as **Movie clip**.

3. In symbol-editing mode, use the **Oval** tool ◯ on the toolbar to draw a small oval at the center of the Stage. Use the Property inspector to select **orange** (#FF9900) for the fill color and **black** for the stroke. Select a **solid** stroke with a stroke height of **1**.

4. Select the **oval** and use the Property inspector to make the oval **50** pixels wide and **40** pixels high. If necessary, reposition the oval to center it on the Stage.

5. Convert the oval to a symbol. Name the symbol **Button1** and use **Button** as its behavior type.

6. Click the **Edit Symbols** button 🐢, and click **Button1** to open the symbol in symbol-editing mode. Insert a keyframe in the **Over** frame of the button's Timeline. Use the Property inspector to change the fill color to **yellow**.

7. Insert a new layer and name it **Text**. In the Up frame of the Text layer, add a text block to the oval. Use the Property inspector to select **Verdana** for the font, **12** for the font size, and **black** for the text color. Set the alignment to **Align Left** and do not use the Bold or Italic attributes. Type **Photo 1**. If necessary, reposition the text to center it over the oval, as shown in Figure 7-34.

Figure 7-34

TEXT POSITIONED INSIDE THE OVAL

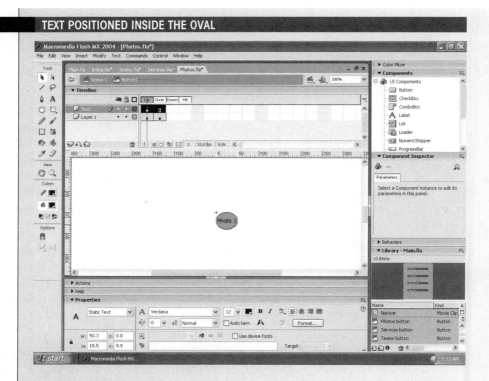

Figure 7-34   **TEXT POSITIONED INSIDE THE OVAL**

8. If necessary, open the Library panel. Right-click the **Button1** symbol in the Library panel and click **Duplicate**. In the Duplicate Symbol dialog box, name the duplicate symbol **Button2** and click the **OK** button to create the symbol.

9. Click 🔲, and then click **Button2** to open it in symbol-editing mode. Double-click the text block and change the text to **Photo 2**.

10. Click 🔲, and select **Photos Navbar** to open the navigation bar in symbol-editing mode. Drag an instance of the Button2 symbol to the Stage and place it to the right of the Button1 instance. Use the **Selection** tool 🔲 to position the Button2 instance so it is aligned with the Button1 instance.

11. Click the **Scene 1** link in the Address bar to return to the document's main Timeline.

12. Click the **Contents** layer to select it. Drag an instance of the **Photos Navbar** from the Library panel to the bottom of the rectangle on the Stage, as shown in Figure 7-35.

Figure 7-35 | **NAVIGATION BAR ADDED TO PHOTOS PAGE**

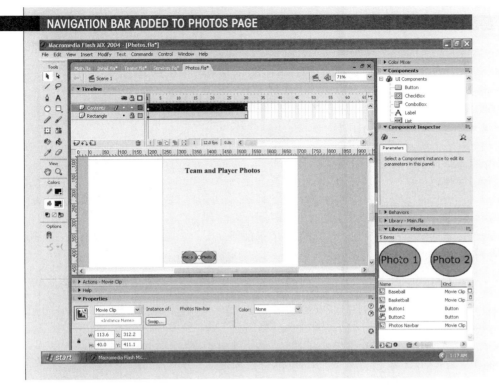

The buttons for the Photos page's navigation bar are now complete. To make them operational, however, you need to add the `loadMovie` action to each instance of the buttons. However, before you add the action, you need to create an empty movie clip symbol and place an instance of it on the Stage. The instance will be indicated by a small circle on the Stage, which is the symbol's registration point. When a picture is loaded into the movie clip instance, the upper-left corner of the picture will be aligned with the registration point of the instance. Also, the instance will have to be named so that the `loadMovie` action can refer to it when it loads the pictures to the instance on the Stage. You will create the movie clip next and add the actions to the buttons using the Behaviors panel.

To create a movie clip and add actions to the buttons:

1. Insert a new symbol. Name the new symbol **Picture movie clip** and use **Movie clip** as its behavior type. The symbol opens in symbol-editing mode. Because the movie clip will be empty, you can exit symbol-editing mode.

2. Click **Scene 1** in the Address bar to return to the document's main Timeline.

3. Drag an instance of the **Picture movie clip** symbol from the Library panel to the upper-left area of the yellow rectangle, under the title. The instance is indicated by a small circle.

4. In the Property inspector, type **Picture_mc** in the Instance Name text box and then press the **Enter** key. See Figure 7-36.

Figure 7-36 ASSIGNING A NAME TO THE MOVIE CLIP INSTANCE

empty movie
clip instance

name of instance

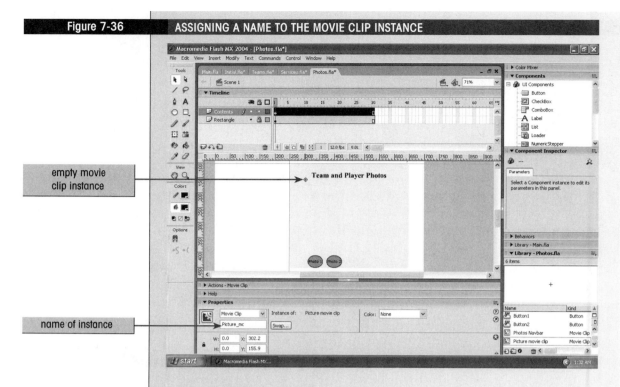

5. Click the **Edit Symbols** button, and select **Photos Navbar** to open it in symbol-editing mode. Select the **Photo 1 button** instance on the Stage.

6. If necessary, expand the Behaviors panel. Click the **Add Behavior** button. In the Behaviors panel, point to **Movieclip**, and then click **Load Graphic**. The Load Graphic dialog box opens.

7. Type **Photo1.jpg** in the Enter the URL to the .JPG to load text box, and then click the movie clip name, **Picture_mc**, from the list of movie clips. See Figure 7-37.

Figure 7-37 ADDING THE LOAD GRAPHIC BEHAVIOR

type filename of picture

select name of
movie clip instance

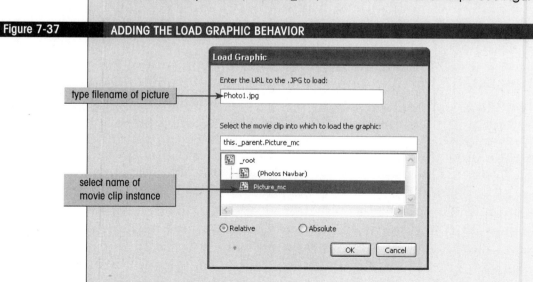

8. Click the **OK** button to create the behavior and close the Load Graphic dialog box. Add the behavior to the other button.

9. Select the **Photo 2 button** on the Stage and repeat Steps 6 through 8, typing **Photo2.jpg** in the Enter the URL to the .JPG to load text box in Step 7.

10. Click the **Scene 1** link in the Address bar to return to the Photo document's main Timeline.

   The Photos document needs to be saved and published as a SWF file so that it will work with the Main document.

11. Save the **Photos.fla** file, click **File** on the menu bar, and then click **Publish** to create the Photos.swf file.

The photo buttons and the Photos page are now complete. When the Photos page is loaded into the Flash Player, the buttons display. Then, the site visitor can click one of the photo buttons to load a picture into the Flash Player. Because the Web site is now complete, you will test it in your Web browser.

To save and publish the Main page:

1. Switch to the **Main.fla** document. Set the publish settings.

2. Click **File** on the menu bar and click **Publish Settings**. The Publish Settings dialog box opens. Make sure that the Flash (.swf) and the HTML (.html) check boxes are selected.

3. Click the **OK** button to close the dialog box.

4. Click **File** on the menu bar, point to **Publish Preview**, and then click **Default - (HTML)**. The Jackson's Sports Web site opens in your Web browser.

5. Click the **Photos** button to display the Photos page. Click the **Photo 1** button on the Photos page to display the first picture, as shown in Figure 7-38.

Figure 7-38   **PHOTOS PAGE DISPLAYED IN THE WEB BROWSER**

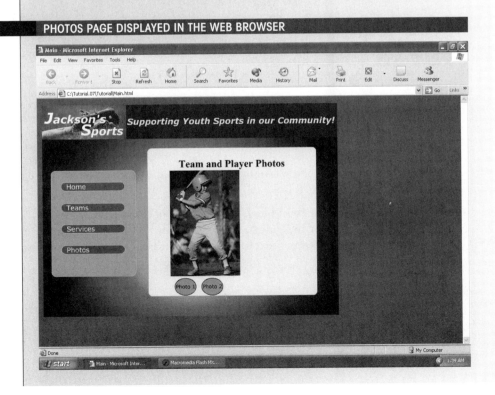

6. Close the browser window when you are finished testing the Web site.

7. Save and close all of the FLA documents.

In this session, you have you used the Actions panel to add ActionScript scripts to the buttons in the navigation bar to make them operational. You also used the Behaviors panel to add actions to buttons on the Photos page to load external image files into the Flash Player.

Session 7.3 QUICK CHECK

1. What is ActionScript?

2. Write the ActionScript statement to load the Staff.swf file to level 1 of the Flash Player.

3. What is the purpose of the on event handler?

4. What option in the Actions panel can be used to check for errors in your script?

5. What action can be used to load external image files into a movie clip instance?

6. When you use the Load Graphic behavior, you must assign a _____ to the movie clip instance where the picture will be loaded.

REVIEW ASSIGNMENTS

After reviewing the Web site, Aly asks you to make some changes to it. She wants you to add a new Specials page that includes information about the weekly sales promotion offered by Jackson's Sports. You also need to add a button to the Main document's navigation bar to load the Specials page. She also asks you to add the option to display a third photo in the Photos page. You will add a third button to the Photos page.

If necessary, start Flash and then do the following:

1. Create a new document using the JSDocument template located in the Jacksons template category. Save the document as **Specials.fla** in the Tutorial.07\Tutorial folder included with your Data Files.

2. Add a text block at the top of the yellow rectangle with the text **Specials of the Week!**. Use Times New Roman for the font, 24 for the font size, and black for the text color. Make the text bold and set its alignment to Align Left.

3. Add another text block in the center of the rectangle. Use Times New Roman for the font, 14 for the font size, and black for the text color. Do not make the text bold. Set the alignment of the text to Align Center. Enter the following text:

The following items are on sale this week.

Softball bats—as low as $89

Softballs—$3.99 each

Batting gloves—$12.99

4. Save and publish the document to create the **Specials.swf** file.

5. Open the **Main.fla** file, which you created in this tutorial, from the Tutorial.07\Tutorial folder included with your Data Files.

6. If necessary, open the Library panel and make a duplicate of the Home button symbol. Name the duplicate **Specials button**. Edit the Specials button symbol and change the text in the Up and Over frames of the Text layer to **Specials**.

7. Add an instance of the Specials button to the bottom of the navigation bar in the Navbar symbol. Place it below the Photos button and set the Specials button's X coordinate to -75 to align its left edge with the other buttons. Select all of the buttons on the Stage simultaneously and use the Distribute Heights option in the Align submenu of the Modify menu to distribute the buttons evenly.

8. Add the `loadMovieNum` action to the instance of the Specials button. Use the `on` event handler so that the action executes when the button is released after it has been clicked. The `loadMovieNum` action should load the **Specials.swf** file into level 1 of the Flash Player.

9. Save and publish the **Main.fla** file to update the **Main.swf** file.

10. Open the **Photos.fla** file from the Tutorial.07\Tutorial folder included with your Data Files.

11. Make a duplicate of the Button1 symbol and name the duplicate **Button3**. Edit the Button3 symbol and change the text to **Photo 3**.

12. Add an instance of the Button3 symbol to the Photos Navbar symbol so that it is to the right of the Button2 symbol.

13. Add the Load Graphic behavior to the Button3 instance so that it loads the **Photo3.jpg** file located in the Tutorial.07\Tutorial folder included with your Data Files. The picture should be loaded to the Picture_mc movie clip instance.

14. Save and publish the **Photos.fla** file to update the **Photos.swf** file.

15. Test the Web site to make sure the Specials button loads the Specials page and the Photos page displays a third photo using the third button.

CASE PROBLEMS

Case 1. Creating a Web Site for Sandy's Party Center Sandy Rodriquez, owner of Sandy's Party Center, is very pleased about the projects developed for the store's Web site. She asks John Rossini about creating a new Web site that will include information promoting some of their special services. She wants to make the site festive and easy to use for anyone wanting help in planning their next party. Based on John's meeting with Sandy and their discussion of her request, John develops the following list of goals for the Web site:

- Promote the Sandy's Party Center name.
- Increase awareness of their services.

Based on these goals, John puts together the following list of objectives:

- Provide a list of services.
- Highlight the party planning service available.
- Highlight the cake decorating services and classes.

Then John meets with you and shows you the outline he has prepared for the site, which includes a home page with a banner at the top with the name of the store and a navigation bar on the left side. The navigation bar will have buttons in the shape of balloons that link to a Party Supplies page, a Party Planning page, and a Cake Decorating page.

John asks you to create the Web site that will include the Main, Welcome, Supplies, Planning, and Cake pages. He instructs you to create the Supplies, Planning, and Cake pages based on the Welcome page that he has prepared. The banner and the navigation for the site will be on the site's Main page. John has also created a document with several symbols that you will use. These include a balloon symbol to be used for the buttons in the navigation bar, a picture and a confetti graphic to be used in the banner, and a party hat animation to be used on some of the pages.

If necessary, start Flash, and then do the following:

1. Create a new document 600 pixels wide by 400 pixels high. Use a light yellow (#FFFF99) for the background color. Save this document as **Spcmain.fla** in the Tutorial.07\Cases folder included with your Data Files.

2. Create a new symbol and name it **Banner**. In this symbol, create a rectangle 600 pixels wide by 100 pixels high. Use an orange color (#FFCC00) for the fill and do not include a stroke. Rename Layer 1 as **Background**.

3. Insert a new layer and name it **Graphics**. Open the **sandys.fla** file as an external library. The file is located in the Tutorial.07\Cases folder included with your Data Files. On the Graphics layer, add an instance of the **Jellybeans** bitmap picture from the external library to the left side of the banner. Align the picture with the left and top edges of the rectangle. Also, add three instances of the Confetti symbol spread over the orange area of the rectangle.

4. Insert a new layer above the Graphics layer and name it **Text**. On this layer, add a text block in the top-center area of the rectangle. Use Comic Sans MS for the font, 50 for the font size, and white for the text color. Type **Sandy's Party Center** in the text block. The banner is complete.

5. Insert an instance of the Banner symbol at the top of the Stage. Align the Banner instance with the top and left sides of the Stage. Rename Layer 1 to **Background**.

6. Insert a new symbol and name it **Navbar**. In the Navbar symbol, create a rectangle 100 pixels wide by 300 pixels high. Use an orange color (#FFCC00) for the fill and do not include a stroke. Center the rectangle on the Stage. Rename Layer 1 to **Background** and lock it.

7. Insert a new layer and name it **Buttons**. On the Buttons layer, drag an instance of the balloon symbol from the external library to the upper-left side of the rectangle. With the balloon instance selected, use the Break Apart command on the Modify menu to break it into a regular graphic. Convert the balloon graphic into a button symbol and name it Home button.

8. Edit the Home button symbol. In the button's Timeline, insert a keyframe in its Over frame and change the color of the balloon to red. Also, change the color of the string to green. Insert a keyframe in the Hit frame, and draw a rectangle to cover the balloon. Make the rectangle about 40 pixels wide by 100 pixels high. The rectangle's fill can be any color and will designate the clickable area of the button.

9. Insert a new layer and name it **Text**. On the Text layer, add a text block with the words **SPC Home** on two lines. Use Comic Sans MS for the font, 12 for the font size, and black for the text color. Do not use the Bold or Italic attributes. Use Align Center. Place the text block just below the circle that represents the balloon and on top of the balloon's string.

10. Make three duplicates of the Home button. Name one **Supplies button**, another **Planning button**, and the third **Cake button**. Change the text in the Supplies button to **Party Supplies**, keeping the words on separate lines. Change the text in the Planning button to **Party Planning**, also keeping each word on a separate line. Finally, change the text in the Cake button to **Cake Decorating**, also keeping each word on a separate line.

11. Add an instance of the Supplies button to the Navbar symbol. Place the instance below and to the right of the Home button instance. Place it close to the right edge of the rectangle. Add an instance of the Planning button and place it below and to the left of the Supplies button instance, near the left edge of the rectangle. Then add an instance of the Cake button and place it toward the lower-right side of the rectangle.

12. Select the Home button in the Navbar, open the Actions panel, and add a `loadMovieNum` action so that when the button is clicked and then released, the **Welcome.swf** file loads at level 1 of the Flash Player. Also, add `loadMovieNum` actions to the other button instances to load SWF files at level 1. The Supplies button should load the **Supplies.swf** file. The Planning button should load the **Planning.swf** file. The Cake button should load the **Cake.swf** file.

13. Return to Scene 1, insert a new layer, and name it **Navbar**. On this new layer, add an instance of the Navbar symbol to the left side of the Stage below the banner. Align the Navbar instance with the left and bottom edges of the Stage.

14. Insert a new layer and name it **Action**. Add a `loadMovieNum` action at Frame 1 of the Action layer that loads the **Welcome.swf** file at level 1 as soon as Frame 1 is played. This displays the **Welcome.swf** file as soon as the **Spcmain.swf** page plays in the Flash Player.

15. Open the **Welcome.fla** file located in the Tutorial.07\Cases folder included with your Data Files. Insert a new layer and name it **Hats**. Add an instance of the party hat symbol from the external library so that it is to the left of the top text block. Add another instance of the party hat symbol and place it to the right of the top text block. Save the **Welcome.fla** file as a template named **SPCTemplate**. Save it in a new template category called SPC with the following description for the template: **Template for the SPC Web site pages**. Close the **SPCTemplate.fla** file. The **Welcome.fla** document will remain unchanged.

16. Create a new document based on the SPCTemplate and save this document as **Supplies.fla** in the Tutorial.07\Cases folder included with your Data Files. Change the top text block to **Sandy's Party Supplies!**. Reposition the text block so that it is centered between the two party hat instances. Change the second text block to the following text:

    Sandy's has everything you could possibly need for your next party, including party favors, decorations, invitations, plates, napkins, balloons, costumes, and gift wrap. We also have theme party packs that include hats, paper goods, and decorations for themes such as baseball, western, Mardi Gras, casino, and more. Also, you'll find red, white, and blue decorations and party items for your Memorial Day and patriotic celebrations.

    Spell check the text and make the necessary corrections.

17. Create a new document based on the SPCTemplate and save this document as **Planning.fla** in the Tutorial.07\Cases folder included with your Data Files. Change the top text block to **Let Sandy's Plan Your Next Party!**. Make certain the text block is centered between the two party hat instances. Also, change the color of the text to blue. Then change the second text block to the following text:

Here at Sandy's, we can help you whether you're planning a small dinner party or a large wedding reception. We can suggest what party favors to use, how to arrange the seating for your guests, how to reserve rental equipment, how to plan games for the appropriate age group, how to arrange party decorations, and even how to get your party catered. Let our experts help you make your next party a success.

Also, change the color of the text to red. Be certain to spell check the text and make any necessary corrections.

18. Create a new document based on the SPCTemplate and save this document as **Cake.fla** in the Tutorial.07\Cases folder included with your Data Files. Change the top text block to **Sandy's Cake Decorating Tips!**. Make certain the text block is centered between the two party hat instances and change the color of the text to dark green (#006600). Then change the second text block to the following text:

Ask about our cake decorating tips. Our experts are always willing to help. We even offer recipes for all types of cakes, big and small, as well as step-by-step instructions to help you bake the perfect cake. We also have cake decorating classes. Be certain to ask one of our staff members for a schedule of upcoming classes.

19. Save and publish each of the documents to create the **Supplies.swf**, **Planning.swf**, and **Cake.swf** files. Open the **Welcome.fla** file and publish it to create the **Welcome.swf** file. Return to the **Spcmain.fla** document and test the Web site by using the Test Movie command. Test each of the buttons and make certain the individual pages are loaded. Make any necessary corrections.

20. Save and close all open files.

Case 2. Creating a Web Site for River City Music Janet Meyers, store manager for River City Music, has been very pleased with the recently developed graphics for her company's Web site. She meets with Alex Smith to discuss the development of a new Web site to showcase some special services available at her store. As a result of their discussion, they agree on the following goal for the Web site:

■ Promote some of the unique services available at River City Music.

Based on this goal, Alex puts together the following list of objectives:

■ Highlight the store's large selection of sheet music.
■ Highlight the recital hall available for rental.
■ Promote the monthly specials on musical instruments.

Alex asks you to help him create the new Web site based on the goals and objectives developed. Alex designs a background picture for the Web site as well as some of the graphics to be used. He provides these graphics in a Flash document. He suggests developing the main page and then a template for the remaining pages. He instructs you to develop a navigation system using a musical note graphic for the buttons with an animation effect that displays when the user moves the mouse pointer over the buttons.

If necessary, start Flash, and then do the following:

1. Create a new document 600 pixels wide by 400 pixels high. Use white for the background color. Save this document as **RCMmain.fla** in the Tutorial.07\Cases folder included with your Data Files.

2. Open the **Music.fla** document as an external library. The document is stored in the Tutorial.07\Cases folder included with your Data Files. Drag an instance of the **pianobk.jpg** bitmap onto the Stage. Align the picture to cover all of the Stage. Rename Layer 1 to **Rectangle**.

3. Create a new symbol and name it **Banner**. In this symbol, create a rectangle 600 pixels wide by 70 pixels high. Use the Color Mixer to create a radial gradient with a blue (#0066FF) inner color and a white outer color. Use this gradient for the fill of the rectangle. Use a stroke color of a dark blue (#006699) and a stroke height of 2. Center the rectangle on the Stage and rename Layer 1 as **Background**.

4. Insert a new layer and name it **Text**. Add a text block in the center of the rectangle. Use Monotype Corsiva for the font, 60 for the font size, and black for the text color. Apply the Bold and Italic attributes and use Align Left. Type **River City Music** in the text block. The banner is complete.

5. Return to Scene 1 and add an instance of the Banner symbol to the top of the Stage. Align the instance with the top and left edges of the Stage.

6. Insert a new button symbol and name it **Home button**. Drag an instance of the note1 symbol from the external library to the center of the Stage. Use the Property inspector to center the note1 symbol. Rename Layer 1 to **Note**. The note1 instance will only be present in the Up frame of the button's Timeline.

7. Insert a new layer and name it **Text**. Add a text block on the Text layer so that it is to the right of the note1 instance on the Stage. Use Monotype Corsiva for the font, 18 for the font size, and black for the text color. Type **Home** in the text block. Insert a keyframe in the Over frame of the Text layer. In this frame, change the text color to blue.

8. Insert a new layer and name it **Animation**. Insert a keyframe in the Over frame of the Animation layer. Drag an instance of the note1 symbol to the center of the Stage and center it using the Property inspector. Convert the note1 instance to a movie clip symbol and name it **Note animation**. Edit the Note animation symbol and add a keyframe in Frame 10 of its Timeline. Create a motion tween between Frames 1 and 10 and have the note rotate clockwise one time in the motion tween.

9. Edit the Home button by adding a blank keyframe in the Hit frame of the Text layer. Turn on onion skinning and extend the onion skin markers to cover all four frames of the Timeline. In the Hit frame of the text layer, draw a small rectangle to cover the area for both the note and the text. The Home button is complete.

10. Make three duplicates of the Home button. Name one **Sheet button**, another **Recital button**, and the third **Instruments button**. Change the text in both the Up and Over frames of the Sheet button to **Sheet Music**. Also, change the size of the rectangle in the Hit frame of the Text button to cover all of the text.

11. Change the text in the Recital button to **Recital Hall**, and also change the size of the rectangle in the Hit frame. Change the text in the Instruments button to **Musical Instruments**, and also change the size of the rectangle in the Hit frame. Be certain to change the text in the Up and Over frames for both buttons.

12. Insert a new movie clip symbol and name it **Navbar**. In the Navbar symbol, drag an instance of the Home button to the left side of the Stage. Drag instances of the Sheet button, Recital button, and Instruments button placing each one to the right of the previous button instance. Align them by using the Property inspector to set each instance's X and Y coordinates as follows: Home button (X=-175, Y=0), Sheet button (X=-110, Y=0), Recital button (X=0, Y=0), Instruments button (X=110, Y=0).

13. Select the Home button in the Navbar, open the Actions panel, and add a `loadMovieNum` action so that when the button is clicked and then released, the **Home.swf** file loads at level 1 of the Flash Player. Also, add `loadMovienum` actions to the other button instances to load SWF files at level 1. The Sheet button should load the **Sheet.swf** file. The Recital button should load the **Recital.swf** file. Finally, the Instruments button should load the **Instruments.swf** file. The Navbar is now complete.

14. Return to Scene 1 and drag an instance of the Navbar symbol to the Stage and place it centered right below the banner.

15. Insert a new layer and name it **Action**. Add a `loadMovieNum` action at Frame 1 of the Action layer that loads the **Home.swf** file at level 1 as soon as Frame 1 is played. This displays the **Home.swf** file as soon as the **RCMmain.swf** page plays in the Flash Player.

16. Create a new document that will be saved as the Home page and as a template. Make the document 600 pixels wide by 400 pixels high. Drag a horizontal guide line to about 110 pixels from the top edge of the Stage. Draw a rectangle below the guide line. This rectangle will be used to frame the contents of each page. Use a dark blue color (#006699) for the stroke, a stroke height of 2, and do not include a fill. Make the rectangle 500 pixels wide by 250 pixels high. Center the rectangle in the area below the guide line. Rename Layer 1 to **Rectangle**.

17. Insert a new layer and name it **Text**. Add a text block inside the rectangle. Place it close to the top of the rectangle. Use Monotype Corsiva for the font, 32 for the font size, and black for the text color. Also use the Bold and Align Left attributes. Type **RCM - Serving Musicians** in the text block. Add a fixed-width text block below the first text block. Use Arial for the font, 14 for the font size, and black for the text color. Use Align Left but do not use the Bold attribute. Type the following in this text block:

    River City Music provides musical instruments and supplies to musicians of all ages in the local region. Some of the special services offered by RCM include a large selection of sheet music, a recital hall, and musical instruments of all types.

18. Center the two text blocks within the rectangle. Save this page as **Home.fla** in the Tutorial.07\Cases folder included with your Data Files. Then save this same document as a template named **RCMTemplate**. Save it in a new template category called RCM with the following description for the template: **Template for the RCM Web site pages**. Close the **RCMTemplate.fla** file.

19. Create a new document based on the RCMTemplate and save this document as **Sheet.fla** in the Tutorial.07\Cases folder included with your Data Files. Change the top text block to **RCM's Sheet Music**. Keep the text block centered within the rectangle. Change the second text block to the following text:

    River City Music has one of the largest selections of sheet music in the local region. We have every type of sheet music from pop to classical, for everyone from beginners to professionals. Come visit our store and plan to spend some time browsing through our library.

20. Create a new document based on the RCMTemplate and save this document as **Recital.fla** in the Tutorial.07\Cases folder included with your Data Files. Change the top text block to **RCM's Recital Hall**. Keep the text block centered within the rectangle. Change the second text block to the following text:

River City Music has an intimate recital hall available for rental by small groups or music teachers. The hall seats 40 people and has a raised stage with a grand piano. Many local piano teachers use the hall to showcase their students' skills. Call 1-800-44-PIANO for more information about our recital hall and to check for available dates.

Change the text color in both text blocks to blue.

21. Create a new document based on the RCMTemplate and save this document as **Instruments.fla** in the Tutorial.07\Cases folder included with your Data Files. Change the top text block to **Musical Instruments**. Keep the text block centered within the rectangle. Change the second text block to the following text:

River City Music carries a wide variety of musical instruments. Here, you can find trumpets, clarinets, flutes, drums, trombones, guitars, violins, and much more. If we don't have it in stock, we will order it for you at no extra charge. We also service all musical instruments.

Change the text color in both text blocks to red.

22. Save and publish each of the documents to create the **Sheet.swf**, **Recital.swf**, and **Instruments.swf** files. Open the **Home.fla** file and publish it to create the **Home.swf** file. Return to the **RCMmain.fla** document and test the Web site by using the Test Movie command. Test each of the buttons and make certain the individual pages are loaded. Make any necessary corrections.

23. Save and close all of the files.

Case 3. Creating a Web Site for Sonny's Auto Center Sonny has been pleased with the work Amanda Lester has done in creating various graphics using Flash and he asks her about creating a new Web site to showcase his auto center's weekly specials. This Web site will be separate from their current Web site. Amanda discusses Sonny's request with him and she develops the following goals for the new Web site:

■ Promote the Sonny's Auto Center name.
■ Showcase weekly specials.

Based on these goals, Amanda develops the following list of objectives:

■ Provide a welcome message with contact information.
■ Showcase the vehicles currently on sale.
■ Display photos of the vehicles.

Amanda asks you to help her create the Web site. She meets with you and shows you the outline she has prepared for the site, which includes a home page with a banner at the top consisting of the Sonny's Auto Center name with an animation. The navigation bar will have buttons in the shape of a car wheel, which rotate when the mouse pointer is over them. She wants a link to the Photos page, with buttons to display each of three pictures. You will start with a document Amanda has created and use the graphics and photos she has provided.

If necessary, start Flash, and then do the following:

1. Open the **Sonnymain.fla** file located in the Tutorial.07\Cases folder included with your Data Files.

2. Create a new movie clip symbol and name it **Banner**. In this symbol, create a text block in the center of the Stage. Use Verdana for the font, 46 for the font size, and black for the text color. Apply the Bold and Italic attributes and use Align Left. Type **Sonny's Auto Center** in the text block. Use the Property inspector to center the text block. Change the name of Layer 1 to **Text1**.

3. Insert a new layer and name it **Text2**. Select the text block on the Text1 layer and copy it. Use the Paste in Place command to paste the copy on the Text2 layer in the same position as the original text block.

4. Insert a new layer and name it **Gradient**. Place this layer between the Text1 and Text2 layers. Drag an instance of the Gradient symbol to Frame 1 of the Gradient layer. Place the gradient rectangle on the right side of the text block so that the rectangle's left side covers the letter *r*. Insert a keyframe at Frame 20 of the Gradient layer. Also, add regular frames to Frame 20 of both the Text1 and Text2 layers to extend them.

5. At Frame 20 of the Gradient layer, move the gradient rectangle to the left side of the text block so that the rectangle's right side covers only the letter *S*. Create a motion tween at Frame 1 of the Gradient layer. The gradient rectangle will move across the text from the right to the left side.

6. Change the Text2 layer to a mask layer and make certain the Gradient layer becomes a masked layer. The banner is complete.

7. Return to Scene 1 and insert a new layer and name it **Banner**. On the Banner layer, add an instance of the Banner symbol to the top of the Stage. Center the instance and place it right below the top edge of the box created by the rectangle on the Stage.

8. Insert a new button symbol and name it **Home button**. Drag an instance of the Wheel symbol from the library to the center of the Stage. Use the Property inspector to center the Wheel symbol. Add a text block to the right of the Wheel instance on the Stage. Use Verdana for the font, 16 for the font size, and black for the text color. Type **Home** in the text block. Insert a keyframe in the Over frame; in this frame, delete the Wheel instance and change the text color to red.

9. Insert a new layer and name it **Animation**. Insert a keyframe in the Over frame of the Animation layer. Drag an instance of the Rotating Wheel symbol to the center of the Stage and center it using the Property inspector.

10. Add a blank keyframe in the Hit frame of Layer 1. Turn on onion skinning and extend the onion skin markers to cover all four frames of the Timeline. In the Hit frame of Layer 1, draw a small rectangle to cover the area for both the wheel and the text. The Home button is complete.

11. Make a duplicate of the Home button and name it **Photos button**. Change the text in both the Up and Over frames of the Photos button to **Photos**.

12. Insert a new movie clip symbol and name it **Navbar**. In the Navbar symbol, drag an instance of the Home button to the left side of the cross hair on the Stage. Drag an instance of the Photos button and place it to the right of the Home button. Select both symbol instances and align them so that there top edges are even.

13. Select the Home button in the Navbar, open the Actions panel, and add a `loadMovieNum` action so that when the button is clicked and then released, the **Autos.swf** file loads at level 1 of the Flash Player. Also, add a `loadMovieNum` action to the Photos button instance to load the **Photos.swf** file at level 1. The Navbar is now complete.

14. Return to Scene 1, insert a new layer, and name it **Navbar**. On this layer, drag an instance of the Navbar symbol to the Stage and place it centered right below the banner.

15. Insert a new layer and name it **Action**. Add a `loadMovieNum` action at Frame 1 of the Action layer that loads the **Autos.swf** file at level 1 as soon as Frame 1 is played. This displays the file as soon as the **Sonnymain.swf** page plays in the Flash Player.

16. Create a new document 600 pixels wide by 400 pixels high. Drag a horizontal guide line to about 100 pixels from the top edge of the Stage. The content for the page will be below this guide line.

17. Add a text block below the guide line. Place it about 150 pixels from the top edge of the Stage. Use Verdana for the font, 16 for the font size, and black for the text color. Also use the Bold and Align Left attributes. Type **Sonny's Specials of the Week!** in the text block. Add a fixed-width text block below the first text block. Use Verdana for the font, 14 for the font size, and black for the text color. Use Align Left but do not use the Bold attribute. Type the following in this text block:

    Welcome to Sonny's specials of the week. Here, we bring you information about some great deals on used cars. Each week, we highlight several great vehicles at discounted prices.

    Please call one of our friendly salespeople for more information.

18. Center the two text blocks on the Stage. Save this page as **Autos.fla** in the Tutorial.07\Cases folder included with your Data Files.

19. Create a new document 600 pixels wide by 400 pixels high. Drag a horizontal guide line to about 100 pixels from the top edge of the Stage. The content for the page will be below this guide line.

20. Insert a new movie clip symbol and name it **Photo MC**. Exit the movie clip's editing mode and return to Scene 1. Drag an instance of the Photo MC symbol to the Stage. Use the Property inspector to place the movie clip instance at the X coordinate of 150 and the Y coordinate of 100. Also, assign the name **Picture** to the movie clip instance.

21. Create a new movie clip symbol and name it **Photos Navbar**. In the Photos Navbar, draw a circle with a red fill and a black stroke. Make the circle 45 pixels in diameter. Convert the circle to a button symbol and name it **Photo button**. Edit the Photo button symbol and add a keyframe in the Over frame. In the Over frame, change the color of the circle's fill to green. Several instances of the same button will be used in the Photos NavBar.

22. Return to the Photos Navbar and add two more instances of the Photo button to the Stage. Arrange the instances vertically below the first instance. Add a text block above the buttons. Use Verdana as the font, 12 for the font size, and black for the text color. Do not use the Bold or Italic attributes. Type **Click below** in the text block.

23. Select the top button instance in the Navbar, open the Behaviors panel, and add a Load Graphic behavior to the button instance. The behavior should load the **Auto1.jpg** file into the Picture movie clip instance. The Behavior text box should display this._parent.Picture, indicating the graphic will load into the Picture instance on the Scene 1 Timeline. Also, add the Load Graphic behavior to the other two button instances on the Stage. One should load the **Auto2.jpg** file and the other should load the **Auto3.jpg** file. Both photos should load in the Picture movie clip instance.

24. Return to Scene 1 and drag an instance of the Navbar to the left side of the Stage. Place it right below the guide line and about 30 pixels from the left edge of the Stage. Save this page as **Autophotos.fla** in the Tutorial.07\Cases folder included with your Data Files.

25. Publish each of the documents to create the **Autos.swf** and **Autophotos.swf** files. Return to the **Sonnymain.fla** document and test the Web site by using the Test Movie command. Test each of the buttons and make certain the individual pages and photos are loaded. Make any necessary corrections.

26. Save and close all of the files.

Case 4. Creating a Web Site for LAL Financial Elizabeth Danehill, webmaster for LAL Financial Services, is tasked to develop a preliminary version of a new Web site that will highlight special services available at the company. She meets with Christopher Perez, head of Marketing, and Mia Jones, graphics designer, to discuss the development of the new Web site. Based on their discussions, the following goals are developed:

- Promote the company's main services.
- Promote the company name.

Based on these goals, they develop the following list of objectives for the Web site:

- Provide a welcome message with contact information.
- Provide information about investments opportunities.
- Provide information about loan rates.
- Provide information about insurance rates.
- Provide information about mortgages.
- Use a picture for the background of the content and allow for the picture to be changed periodically.

Elizabeth, with Mia's help, prepares some graphic elements to be used in the Web site. She assigns you the task of developing the Web site with her guidance. The Web site will be a preliminary version and the content for each page is under development.

If necessary, start Flash, and then do the following:

1. Create a new document 500 pixels wide by 300 pixels high. Use a dark green (#006600) for the background color. Save this document as **LALmain.fla** in the Tutorial.07\Cases folder included with your Data Files.

2. Draw a rectangle to cover all of the Stage. Use the green radial gradient (fourth gradient from the left on the bottom row of the color pop-up window) for the rectangle's fill and do not include a stroke. Make the rectangle 500 pixels wide by 300 pixels high. Use the Align options to align it with the Stage. Rename Layer 1 to **Rectangle** and lock the layer.

3. Insert a new layer and name it **Title**. On this layer, create a text block centered at the top of the Stage. Use Garamond for the font, 30 for the font size, and white for the text color. Apply the Bold attribute and use Align Left. Type **LAL Financial Services** in the text block.

4. Insert a new button symbol and name it **Investments button**. In the Up frame of the Investments button, draw a small square at the center of the Stage. Use the same green radial gradient as used in Step 2 and use a black solid stroke with a height of 1. Make the square 25 pixels wide by 25 pixels high. Convert the small square into a movie clip symbol and name it **Small square**.

5. Insert a new movie clip symbol and name it **Small animated square**. Add an instance of the Small square symbol to the center of the Stage for the Small animated square symbol. Insert a keyframe at Frame 10 and create a motion tween at Frame 1 so that the square rotates clockwise one time.

6. Edit the Investments button and insert a blank keyframe in its Over frame. Drag an instance of the Small animated square symbol in the Over frame and make certain it is centered on the Stage.

7. Insert a new layer in the Investments button Timeline and name it Text. Add a text block in the Up frame of the Text layer so that it is to the right of the square. Use Garamond for the font, 14 for the font size, and white for the text color. Do not apply the Bold attribute. Type **Investments** in the text block.

8. Insert a keyframe in the Over frame of the Text layer and change the Investments text by applying the Bold attribute to it. Insert a blank keyframe in the Hit frame of the Text layer. Use onion skinning to see the contents of all the frames and draw a rectangle in the Hit frame to cover both the small square and the text.

9. Make three duplicates of the Investments button. Name one **Rates button**, another **Insurance button**, and the third **Mortgages button**. Change the text in both the Up and Over frames of the Rates button to **Competitive Rates**. Also, change the size of the rectangle in the Hit frame of the Text button to cover all of the text.

10. Change the text in the Insurance button to **Insurance** and change the text in the Mortgages button to **Mortgages**. Be certain to change the text in the Up and Over frames for both buttons.

11. Insert a new movie clip symbol and name it **Navbar**. In the Navbar symbol, drag an instance of the Investments button to the left side of the Stage. Drag instances of the Rates button, Insurance button, and Mortgages button, placing each one to the right of the previous button instance. Align them by using the Property inspector to set each instance's X and Y coordinates as follows: Investments button (X=-200, Y=0), Rates button (X=-95, Y=-25), Insurance button (X=45, Y=-25), Mortgages button (X=140, Y=0).

12. Select the Investments button in the Navbar, open the Actions panel, and add a `loadMovieNum` action so that when the button is clicked and then released, the **Investments.swf** file loads at level 1 of the Flash Player. Also, add `loadMovieNum` actions to the other button instances to load SWF files at level 1. The Rates button should load the **Rates.swf** file. The Insurance button should load the **Insurance.swf** file. Finally, the Mortgages button should load the **Mortgages.swf** file.

13. Return to Scene 1 and drag an instance of the Navbar symbol to the Stage and place it centered right below the text title.

14. Insert a new layer and name it **Action**. Add a `loadMovieNum` action at Frame 1 of the Action layer that loads the **Investments.swf** file at level 1 as soon as Frame 1 is played.

15. Create a new document that will be saved as a template and be used to create the other pages. Make the document 500 pixels wide by 300 pixels high. Use a dark green (#006600) for the background color.

16. Create a new movie clip symbol and name it **Picture**. Leave the movie clip symbol empty, and drag an instance of it to the Stage. Set its X and Y coordinates to 100 and assign the name **Picture_mc** to the instance. Rename Layer 1 to **Background picture**.

17. Insert a new layer and name it **Picture mask**. On this layer, draw an oval. Use black for the fill and do not include a stroke. Make the oval 300 pixels wide by 200 pixels high. Set the X coordinate for the oval at 100 and its Y coordinate at 100. The oval should be centered in the lower part of the Stage. If necessary, use the Info panel to select the upper-left registration point for the oval.

18. Change the Picture mask layer to a mask layer. Make certain the Background picture layer is masked.

19. Insert a new layer and name it **Action**. Add a Load Graphic behavior to Frame 1 of the Action layer. The behavior should load the **Money.jpg** file into the Picture_mc movie clip. When the SWF file is played, the Money picture loads into the Picture_mc movie clip, and the area covered by the oval mask displays. Insert a new layer and name it **Content**. Also, add a horizontal guide line at about 100 pixels from the top edge of the Stage and add two vertical guide lines. Place one guide line at about 100 pixels from the left edge of the Stage and the other at about 400 pixels from the left edge of the Stage.

20. Save the document as a template. Use the name **LALTemplate** and save it in a new template category called **LAL**. Use the following description for the template: **Template to be used for LAL Financial Services Web site**. Close the **LALTemplate.fla** file.

21. Create a new document based on the LALTemplate and save this document as **Investments.fla** in the Tutorial.07\Cases folder included with your Data Files. Add a text block on the Content layer. Place the text block on the Stage below the horizontal guide lines and between the vertical guide lines. Use Garamond for the font, 26 for the font size, and black for the text color. Apply the Bold attribute and use Align Left. Type **Investment Opportunities** in the text block.

22. Create another document based on the LALTemplate and save this document as **Rates.fla** in the Tutorial.07\Cases folder included with your Data Files. Add a text block on the Content layer. Place the text block on the Stage below the horizontal guide lines and between the vertical guide lines. Use the same font text attributes as in the preceding step and type **Competitive Rates** in the text block.

23. Create two more new documents based on the LALTemplate. Save one as **Insurance.fla** and the other as **Mortgages.fla**. Save both in the Tutorial.07\Cases folder. For each document, add a text block on the Stage keeping it below the horizontal guide lines and between the vertical guide lines. Use the same text attributes as in the preceding step. For the **Insurance.fla** document, type **Insurance Plans** in the text block and for the **Mortgages.fla** document, type **Great Mortgage Rates** in the text block.

24. Save and publish each of the documents to create the **Investments.swf**, **Rates.swf**, **Insurance.swf**, and **Mortgages.swf** files. Return to the **LALmain.fla** document and test the Web site by using the Test Movie command. Test each of the buttons and make certain the individual pages are loaded. Make any necessary corrections.

25. Save and close all of the files.

QUICK | CHECK ANSWERS

Session 7.1

1. True. A Flash Web site consists mostly of SWF files.

2. The Flash Player uses levels to load more than one SWF file at one time.

3. False. When you load a SWF file at the same level that already has a SWF file playing, the new SWF file replaces the currently playing file.

4. The first step in the development process is to determine the goals of the site.

5. You start defining the goals of the site by meeting with the clients and discussing what they want the site to accomplish.

6. A storyboard is simply a diagram showing the site's pages and the way they are organized. The storyboard shows a sketch of each page with lines indicating how each page links to the other pages.

Session 7.2

1. A Flash template is a pre-built document that installs with Flash and provides a way to quickly develop a new Flash document.

2. The purpose of opening a document's library as an external library in another document is to add instances from the external library to the library of the current document.

3. A Flash Web site is displayed in the Flash Player within an HTML document.

4. A Flash Web site's navigation bar contains buttons used to load different SWF files.

5. To add an animation to a button that displays when the mouse pointer is over the button, you create a separate movie clip with an animation. You then place an instance of the movie clip in the Over frame of the button's Timeline.

Session 7.3

1. ActionScript is a programming language within Flash that allows you to add actions to objects or frames in your document. Actions are instructions that are used to control a document while its animation is playing.

2. The ActionScript statement to load the Staff.swf file to level 1 of the Flash Player is: `loadMovieNum("Staff.swf", 1);`

3. The on event handler determines what action to take when a specific button event occurs.

4. The Check Syntax option in the Actions panel can be used to check for errors in your script.

5. The `loadMovie` action can be used to load external image files into a movie clip instance.

6. When you use the Load Graphic behavior, you must assign a name to the movie clip instance where the picture will be loaded.

In this tutorial you will:

- Review the basics of ActionScript programming

- Use ActionScript to create links to access external Web sites

- Create input and dynamic text fields

- Use ActionScript to create an input form

- Create and test a Flash preloader

ADDING
INTERACTIVITY
WITH ACTIONSCRIPT

Adding Interactive Elements to Jackson's Sports Web Site

CASE

Admiral Web Design

Dan Jackson, owner of Jackson's Sports, is very pleased with the Flash Web site you created, and it has been well received by the company's clients. In a meeting with Aly and Chris, Dan requests additional pages for the site. One of the additional pages he has requested is a Resources page, which will contain hyperlinks to other Web sites that visitors to his site might find interesting. These include sites related to organizations promoting various youth sports. Jackson's Sports is also starting a new initiative to offer customized team jerseys to local teams. Therefore, he also wants to have a page that team coaches or managers can use to calculate the cost of team jerseys. This page will allow someone to enter the number of jerseys needed and to choose from various options. These selections will then be used to calculate and display the total cost.

Aly and Chris agree to make the design changes and ask you to help develop the new pages. They revise the design of the Web site and instruct you to start with the revised documents. Aly also asks you to add programming instructions to the main page to display a message along with a simple animation to tell the site visitors that the site is loading. This visual feedback is important for users with a slow connection as this message will display temporarily while the site contents are loading into the Flash Player.

Aly and Chris revise the sketch showing the storyboard with the new pages to be completed for the Jackson's Sports Web site, as shown in Figure 8-1.

Figure 8-1   **JACKSON'S SPORTS WEB SITE REVISED STORYBOARD**

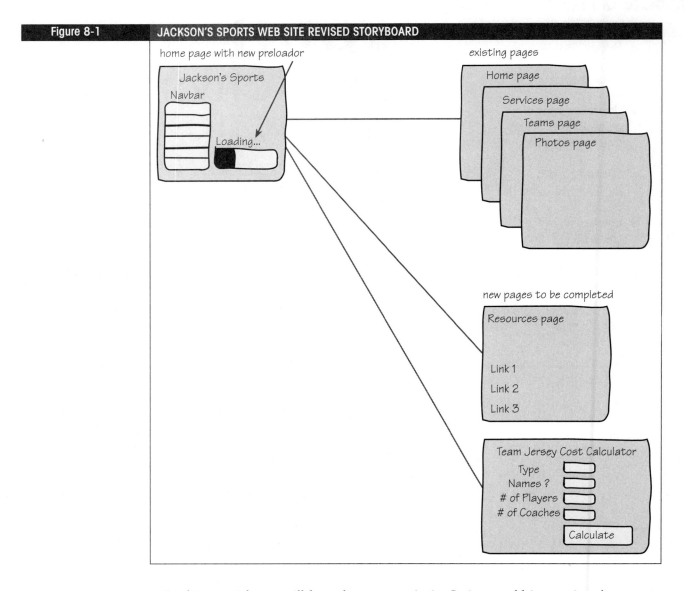

In this tutorial, you will learn how to use ActionScript to add interactive elements to Flash documents. You will learn about the structure and syntax of the ActionScript programming language, and you will write and create the ActionScript code for the Resources and Team Jersey Cost Calculator page for the Jackson's Sports Web site.

SESSION 8.1

In this session, you will learn the basic elements of ActionScript programming. You will learn how to create scripts to control objects in a Flash document. You will also learn about the structure of a script written in ActionScript and about the rules or syntax used. Finally, you will explore sample documents with ActionScript, and you will modify a script.

Programming **with ActionScript**

ActionScript is a robust programming language that gives the Flash developer an almost unlimited number of ways to make a Flash document interactive. ActionScript can be used to create actions to control multimedia elements, such as buttons, as you have done in previous tutorials.

This requires writing scripts that consist of actions, event handlers, and other programming statements to control how the actions are executed. For example, in Tutorial 5 you added behaviors, precoded ActionScript actions, to buttons. When you added a behavior to a button, actions were created by Flash to control how the animation played. Adding actions using the Behaviors panel is easy because you are not required to write any ActionScript code. However, the number of behaviors in the Behaviors panel is limited, and creating more complex interactions requires you to write the ActionScript code using the Actions panel, which you did in Tutorial 7 when you added ActionScript code to instances of buttons. The buttons were then used by the viewer to control when and how a SWF file was loaded into the Flash Player.

In addition to controlling the order frames play in a document's Timeline or making buttons operational, ActionScript can be used to allow the viewer to input data, and then have Flash process the data to return a result. It can also be used to change the properties of movie clips while they play in the Flash Player. For example, you can have a movie clip such as a graphic of a car that changes color when a button is clicked. With ActionScript, you can also test a condition and then execute different actions based on the result of the test. For example, you can create a script that checks the horizontal location of a movie clip instance by comparing its X coordinate against a set value. If the coordinate is greater than the set limit, actions in the script can be performed to change the X coordinate of the movie clip, thus changing its location on the Stage. This would be useful in a game in which objects on the Stage are moved by the user. The underlying ActionScript code could then determine and evaluate the location of the object, and then display a message providing feedback to the user as to whether he correctly placed the object.

ActionScript can also be used to write complete programming applications such as a shopping cart application in which the user can enter data, make selections, and then make a purchase, as shown in the example in Figure 8-2. Writing a complete programming application requires more advanced programming skills and is beyond the scope of this book.

Figure 8-2 **SAMPLE FLASH APPLICATION**

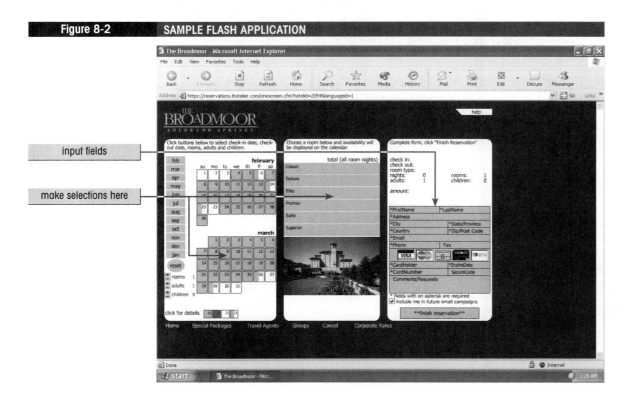

In this tutorial, you will write ActionScript code to control multimedia elements, to access external Web pages, and to provide the viewer a means of entering and processing information. Before creating the ActionScript code for these features of the Jackson's Sports Web site, Aly wants you to understand the basic components of the ActionScript programming language and some rules for writing ActionScript code.

Working with Objects and Properties

ActionScript is used to control and modify objects. An **object** is an element in Flash that has **properties** or characteristics that can be examined or changed with ActionScript. The multimedia elements you work with in Flash, such as buttons, movie clips, and text blocks, are considered objects. For example, a button has properties, such as its width, height, and location on the Stage. An instance of a movie clip symbol also has similar properties. ActionScript code can be written to read or change these properties in response to certain events, such as a mouse click, a key press, or when a certain frame in the Timeline is played. Properties in ActionScript are identified by an underscore character at the beginning of the property's name. For example, the property that controls the transparency of a movie clip is `_alpha`. Other properties include `_rotation`, which controls the orientation of a movie clip, and `_visible`, which controls the visibility of a movie clip. Many properties can be examined and modified using ActionScript. Some properties can be examined but not modified. For example, the `_ymouse` property identifies the vertical location of the mouse pointer. ActionScript can read or examine this property and then use it as part of an action, but the value of the property cannot be changed with ActionScript.

Working with objects in ActionScript often requires that you assign names to them. Recall that you can have multiple instances of one movie clip symbol, which means that you can have multiple objects based on one symbol. When using ActionScript to refer to a specific instance, you need to refer to its name. To assign a name to an instance, you select it on the Stage and then enter a name in the Instance Name text box in the Property inspector, as shown in Figure 8-3.

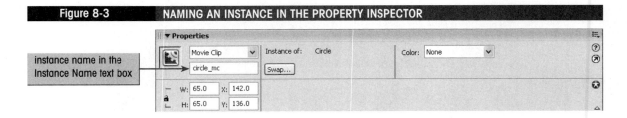

Figure 8-3   NAMING AN INSTANCE IN THE PROPERTY INSPECTOR

instance name in the Instance Name text box

When naming instances of objects, you should include a suffix that identifies what type of object it is. Flash recognizes the `_mc` suffix for movie clip instances, the `_btn` suffix for button instances, and the `_txt` suffix for text field instances. Although it is not required that you use these suffixes, doing so takes advantage of code hints in the Actions panel. When entering ActionScript code, Flash displays code hints based on what is typed. For example, if you assign the name `circle_mc` to a movie clip instance on the Stage, and then use the name in the Actions panel, Flash displays code hints, as shown in Figure 8-4.

Figure 8-4 CODE HINTS IN THE ACTIONS PANEL

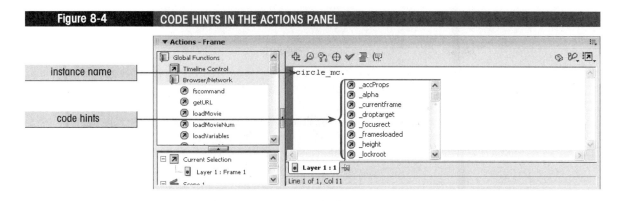

Double-clicking the desired code displayed in the code hints list causes the code to be added to the script. This makes it easier to enter the correct code and to avoid typing mistakes.

After an instance has a name, you can refer to it in the action using dot notation. **Dot notation** is used to link the object names to its properties and methods. (Methods are discussed later in this session.) For example, if a movie clip instance has the name circle_mc, the code to change the _alpha property of the instance to 30% is written as circle_mc._alpha = 30. The dot (.) links the property to the particular instance or object.

Using Actions, Methods, and Functions

As you know, an **action** is a statement, such as gotoAndStop(), that instructs a SWF file to do something. The terms actions and statements are often interchangeable.

Functions are blocks of statements that process information and return a value or perform some action. Flash includes a number of prebuilt functions, such as the getVersion() function, which returns the version number of the Flash Player, and the loadMovieNum() function, which you used in Tutorial 7. You can also create your own functions. For example, you can create a function that accepts the temperature value in Fahrenheit degrees and returns the value in Celsius degrees. Then, you can **call** or execute the function from different parts of the script in which it is defined. To use a function, you need to know what value or values to send to it and what value or values to expect in return. The values you send to a function are called **parameters** or **arguments** and are enclosed in parentheses. For example, the name of the SWF file and the level number in the action loadMovieNum("Welcome.swf", 1) are both considered arguments of the function.

Methods are functions specific to a particular object. They are built-in capabilities of the object that perform certain actions or respond to certain events. Methods are similar to other functions and actions, but methods are part of an object and can be used to control the object. For example, if you have a movie clip instance in the document's main Timeline and the movie clip has 20 frames in its own Timeline, you can control which of the 20 frames will play. You do this with the gotoAndPlay() method for the movie clip. If the movie clip instance has the name circle_mc, the code to tell the instance to start playing at Frame 10 of its Timeline is circle_mc.gotoAndPlay(10). Because gotoAndPlay() is a method of the movie clip object, the movie clip knows how to respond when the method is executed. The gotoAndPlay() method is also considered an action in the main Timeline. In actuality, it is a method of the main document, which is also considered an object. When using the gotoAndPlay() method for the document's main Timeline, it is not necessary to specify an object name.

Writing ActionScript Using Variables, Expressions, Operators, and Comments

To write ActionScript code, you need to first understand the main components that make up ActionScript statements. ActionScript statements are made up of variables, expressions, operators, and comments.

A **variable** is a container that holds information while the SWF file is playing. You can assign almost any name to a variable as long as it contains letters as part of the name and is not already a keyword in ActionScript. A **keyword** is a word or phrase that already has a specified use or meaning in ActionScript and cannot be reused in another context in a statement. An example of a keyword is `else`, `if`, `while`, `in`, and `this`, to name a few. Some examples of valid variable names include `UserName`, `Amount`, `x`, and `option1`.

An **expression** is a statement that is used to assign a value to a variable. For example, the expression `UserName = "Tom"` assigns the text "Tom" to the variable `UserName`. Note that when referring to text in an expression, it is enclosed in quotes. The characters within the quotation marks are considered string data, which is handled differently than numeric data. **String data** is a series of characters, such as letters, numbers, and punctuation, and is always enclosed in quotation marks. **Numeric data** is a number or numbers that are not enclosed in quotes. So, to assign a numeric value to a variable, you do not enclose the value in quotes. For example, the expression `Amount = 20` assigns the numeric value `20` to the variable named `Amount`.

The equal sign in the expression is an example of an operator. **Operators** are used in expressions to tell Flash how to manipulate the values in the expression. There are several types of operators. For example, the equal sign is an example of an **assignment operator** because it assigns a value to a variable. ActionScript also has **arithmetic operators**, such as +, -, *, and /. These are used to indicate addition, subtraction, multiplication, and division, respectively. In addition, ActionScript allows shortcuts that combine assignment and arithmetic operators. For example, if you want to increment the value in the variable `Amount` by 5, you can write the expression `Amount += 5`, instead of having to write `Amount = Amount + 5`. Both of these expressions provide the same result. Another type of operator is a comparison operator. A **comparison operator** is used in conditional statements. A **conditional statement** is one in which one value is compared to another. Based on the result of the comparison, certain actions are performed. An example of a comparison operator is ==, which is used to test for equality. This is different from the assignment operator, =, which is used to assign a value to a variable. Other examples of comparison operators include >, <, and !=, which are used to test for greater than, less than, and not equal to, respectively. An example of a conditional statement is the `if` action. The `if` action tests a condition; if the condition is true, it performs actions within the curly braces that follow it. For example, the following script checks if the value of the variable `x` is greater than 50. If it is, the `gotoAndPlay()` action is performed, which moves the playhead to Frame 1.

```
if (x > 50) {
    gotoAndPlay(1);
    }
```

Notice that the condition `x > 50` is enclosed in parentheses, and the statement or statements that are to be performed if the condition is true must be written inside the curly braces.

As scripts get longer and more complex, it is important to add comments. **Comments** are notes within the ActionScript code that explain what is happening. Comments do not cause any actions to be performed and are not necessary for the actions to work. However, they are very useful to the programmer writing the code and to other programmers who might have to modify the code at a later date. Comments are indicated by two forward slashes (//). Any text after the slashes is not interpreted by the Flash Player and appears dimmed in the Script pane, as shown in Figure 8-5.

Figure 8-5 COMMENT IN SCRIPT PANE

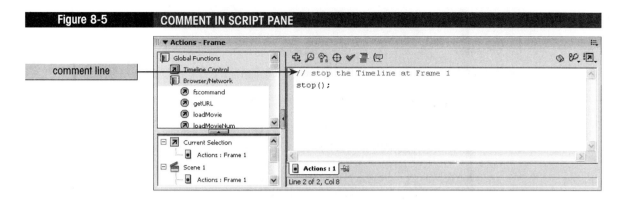

Writing ActionScript Code

When writing ActionScript code, you need to follow certain rules. These rules are also known as the **syntax** of the language. As you saw in previous examples, actions and functions are often written in mixed case. For example, the `gotoAndPlay()` function uses the uppercase letters A and P, whereas the remainder of the letters are lowercase. If you write this function as `gotoandplay()` with all lowercase letters, Flash does not understand it. This is because ActionScript is case sensitive. To avoid writing actions incorrectly, use the Actions toolbox on the left side of the Actions panel to select the actions. Also, as you have seen in previous examples, statements should end with a semicolon. Even though the statements work without the semicolon, it is good programming practice to include it. Other required syntactical elements are parentheses, which are used to group arguments in methods and functions, and curly braces, which group a block of related statements together. See Figure 8-6.

Figure 8-6 ACTIONSCRIPT SYNTAX

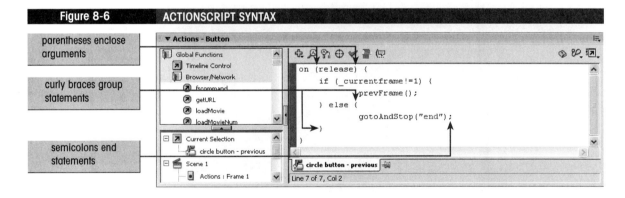

Recall from Tutorial 7 that the Actions panel is used to create the scripts to control the objects in your document. Before you create a script, however, you must determine where it will be placed. The placement of scripts depends on when you want the actions in the script to be performed. For example, if you want a script to be performed whenever the playhead reaches a particular frame, the script should be placed in that frame. If you want the script to be performed when a button is clicked, the script should be placed on the instance of the button. If you want a script to be performed as part of a movie clip, it should be placed on the movie clip. When you are writing scripts in the Actions panel, the title bar of the Actions panel indicates where the script is being applied, as shown in Figure 8-7.

Figure 8-7   **ACTIONS PANEL TITLE BARS**

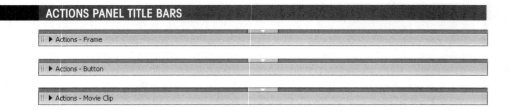

▶ Actions - Frame

▶ Actions - Button

▶ Actions - Movie Clip

Exploring ActionScript Examples

To get a better idea of interactivity created with ActionScript, Aly suggests you review a version of the Leslie's Salad and Sandwich Shop Web site. This site has been modified from the one you viewed in Tutorial 7. Specifically, the Web site contains a new Specials page with buttons that allow the site visitor to display daily specials for each day of the week. The buttons contain ActionScript code that controls how the playhead moves in the Timeline. Each of the buttons advances the playhead to the next or previous frame, and each frame contains the daily special for a different day of the week.

To explore the Leslie's Salad and Sandwich Shop Specials page:

1. Start Flash and open the **leslie.fla** file located in the **Tutorial.08\Tutorial** folder included with your Data Files. Set the panels to their default layout.

2. Click **Control** on the menu bar, and then click **Test Movie**. The Leslie's Salad and Sandwich Shop home page displays.

3. Click the **Specials** button on the navigation bar. The Daily Specials page displays with a Previous and a Next button located in the lower-right corner, as shown in Figure 8-8.

Figure 8-8   **SPECIALS PAGE WITH BUTTON CONTROLS**

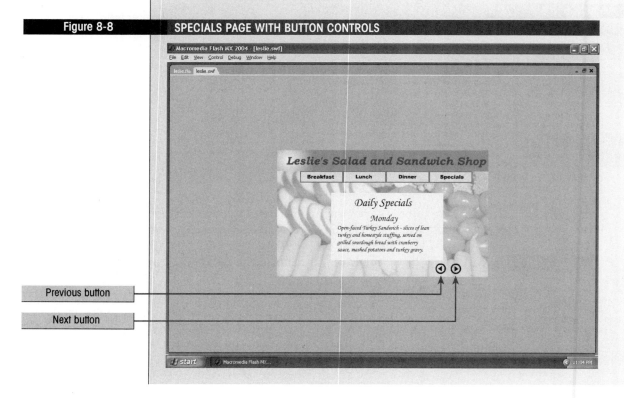

Previous button

Next button

4. Click the **Next** button to display the specials for Tuesday. Continue to click the **Next** button until you have viewed the specials for each day of the week.

5. When you are finished viewing the Specials page, click **File** on the menu bar and click **Close** to return to the leslie.fla file. Next open the Specials document so you can view the ActionScript code for the Next and Previous buttons.

6. Open the **specials.fla** file located in the **Tutorial.08\Tutorial** folder included with your Data Files.

7. Click the **Next** button located in the lower-right corner of the Stage to select it.

8. Click the **Actions panel** title bar to expand the panel. The ActionScript for the Next button displays, as shown in Figure 8-9.

| Figure 8-9 | ACTIONS PANEL FOR THE NEXT BUTTON |

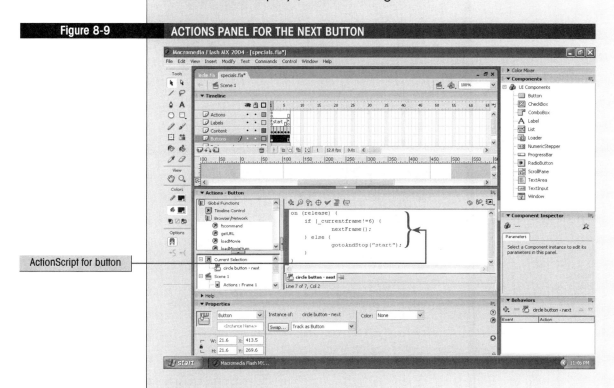

ActionScript for button

The first line contains an event handler like the ones you used in Tutorial 7. The on event handler checks for the `release` event. When the button is clicked and then released, the code that follows is executed. This code checks if the frame the playhead is on is not equal to 6. If true, the function `nextFrame()` is executed. This function causes the playhead to move to the next frame. If the current frame is equal to 6, the `gotoAndStop()` function moves the playhead to the frame that has the label `Start`. Recall that labels can be assigned to individual frames using the Property inspector.

9. Close the **leslie.fla** and **specials.fla** files. Do not save any changes you may have made to the files.

Another example that Aly suggests you review is one that Chris has created to test some ActionScript code. In this example, the `_x` property of a movie clip instance is modified using ActionScript. The `_x` property has the value of the movie clip's X coordinate or horizontal position on the Stage.

To explore the Basketball movie clip:

1. Open the **ballsample.fla** file located in the **Tutorial.08\Tutorial** folder included with your Data Files.

2. If necessary, select the **Basketball** instance on the Stage and expand the Actions panel to see the ActionScript code. Before exploring the code, test the SWF file.

3. Click **Control** on the menu bar, and then click **Test Movie**. The Basketball moves from left to right and repeats when it reaches the right side of the Stage.

4. When you are finished viewing the SWF file, click **File** on the menu bar, and click **Close** to return to the ballsample.fla file. Next open the Movie Explorer.

5. Click **Window** on the menu bar, point to **Other Panels**, and click **Movie Explorer**. The Movie Explorer panel opens.

6. Select the **Show Action Scripts** button 🔼 and deselect all of the other buttons in the Movie Explorer. If necessary, click the **+** symbol next to Actions for Basketball under Scene 1 in the Movie Explorer to display the ActionScript code. Also, if necessary, expand the size of the Movie Explorer panel to see all of the code, as shown in Figure 8-10.

Figure 8-10	ACTIONSCRIPT FOR MOVIE CLIP

ActionScript

```
// set initial values when the movie clip is loaded
onClipEvent (load) {
    x = 20;
}
// perform the following actions each time the frame is played
onClipEvent (enterFrame) {
    this._x = x;
    x += 5;
    if (x >= 400) {
        x = 20;
    }
}
```

Notice that the code contains comments that explain its various sections. The first part of the ActionScript code contains the `onClipEvent` event handler. This event handler checks for movie clip events and is similar to the `on` event handler you have used for buttons. In this case, the event handler checks to see if the movie clip has loaded into the Flash Player. This happens when the SWF file first starts to play in the Flash Player. When the movie clip loads, the expression `x = 20` is performed causing the variable x to be assigned a value of 20. The second event checked by `onClipEvent` is `enterFrame`. This event occurs each time the frame containing the movie clip is played. In this case, only one frame is in the Timeline, and it is played repeatedly in the Flash Player. As a result, the `enterFrame` event occurs every time the frame is played, and the code enclosed in curly braces under the `onClipEvent(enterFrame)` line is performed every time the frame is played. The first line of this code is `this._x = x`. Recall that `_x` is the horizontal position property of the movie clip. The word `this` is used to target the specific movie clip instance. In this case, `this` refers to the movie clip instance itself because the ActionScript code is attached to the instance. If the ActionScript code was not attached to the movie clip, you would have to use the name of the movie clip instance in the statement by writing `ball_mc._x = x` because the name of the instance is `ball_mc`. It is important to be clear as to which instance you are targeting because there could be more than one Basketball instance in the document. The first line, `this._x = x`, assigns the value of the variable `x`, which was initially set to `20`, to the `_x` property of the movie clip. This causes the Basketball instance to move horizontally to a point 20 pixels from the left side of the Stage. The next statement, `x += 5`, increments the value of the variable `x` by 5. The next statement, `if (x >= 400)`, is a conditional statement that compares the value in the variable `x` to 400. If the value of `x` is greater than or equal to 400, the statement in the next set of curly braces is performed. So, if the condition is true, the statement, `x = 20` is performed, which resets the value of `x` to 20. The code within the set of curly braces after `onClipEvent(eventFrame)` is repeated each time the frame is played. As a result, the horizontal position property of the Basketball instance is incrementally changed by 5, causing the instance to move across the Stage. When the x value reaches or passes 400, the x value is reset to `20` causing the instance to move back to the left side of the Stage and repeat its movement across the Stage.

Aly suggests you modify the ActionScript code to include the `_y` property of the instance. You will do that next.

To modify the Basketball's ActionScript code:

1. Close the Movie Explorer and click in the **Script pane** of the Actions panel. Place the cursor at the end of the `x = 20;` statement, and then press the **Enter** key. Type `y = 20;` to set an initial value for a variable that will be used to modify the vertical position of the instance.

2. Scroll down and place the cursor at the end of the statement `this._x = x;`, and press the **Enter** key. Type `this._y = y;` to assign the value of `y` to the `_y` property of the instance.

3. Place the cursor after the statement `x += 5;`, and then press the **Enter** key. Type `y += 5;` to increment the value of the variable `y` by 5.

4. Move the cursor down, place it after the statement `x = 20;`, and then press the **Enter** key. Type `y = 20;` to reset the value of y when the `if` condition is true. Check the code next.

5. Click the **Check Syntax** button ✔ to ensure the code has no syntax errors. If the code has errors, review the statements you typed and make the necessary corrections. If no errors are found, click the **OK** button to continue.

6. Click **Control** on the menu bar, and click **Test Movie** to play the SWF file. The Basketball instance moves diagonally from the upper-left side of the Stage to the lower-right side. When it reaches the lower-right side, it starts back at the upper-left side. Close the SWF file and collapse the Actions panel.

7. Save and close the **ballsample.fla** file.

In this session, you have learned the basic components and rules for the ActionScript programming language. You learned about actions, methods, functions, variables, expressions, and operators. You also explored two examples of ActionScript code used in sample documents. In the next session, you will write ActionScript code for the two new pages to be added to the Jackson's Sports Web site.

Session 8.1 Quick Check

1. What is ActionScript?

2. ActionScript code can be added to a button using the Behaviors panel. True or False?

3. Actions can be added to a button instance, a frame, or a _____.

4. A(n) _____ is an element in Flash that has properties or characteristics that can be examined or changed with ActionScript.

5. In naming button instances, it is best to add the suffix _____ to the names so that Flash will display _____ hints in the Actions panel when the names are used.

6. Write the expression to change the `_alpha` property of the `Car_mc` instance to 30.

7. Briefly explain the purpose of the ActionScript statement `Amount += 5;`.

SESSION 8.2

In this session, you will create the ActionScript code for the Jackson's Sports Resources page and Team Jersey Cost Calculator page. Specifically, you will learn how to create links to Web sites in a Flash document using ActionScript. You will also learn how to create and code input text fields that allow the viewer to enter data into a form. Finally, you will learn how to create and code a dynamic text field that calculates and displays the results of a calculation using ActionScript.

Linking to Web Sites Using the getURL( ) Function

Dan Jackson requested a Resources page for the Jackson's Sports Web site that will contain a list of links to Web sites on the Internet that might be of interest to their clients. A Flash document can include links in the form of buttons or movie clips with ActionScript code directing Flash to open the specified Web site. Aly has begun creating the Resources page, and she wants you to finish it by creating buttons that represent links to the external Web sites and the corresponding ActionScript code. When the viewer clicks a button, a new browser window will open displaying an external Web site. To create a link to an external Web site, you will use the `getURL()` function.

The `getURL()` function loads a document such as a Web page into a browser window. The format of the function is `getURL(url, window)` where `url` is the address of the Web site you want to open in the browser window. The argument `window` can be one of several options. These options are listed next.

- `_self`—Specifies that the Web site document be opened in the current browser window; this replaces the currently displayed document

- `_blank`—Specifies that the Web site document be opened in a new browser window; the currently displayed document remains opened in its own browser window

- `_parent`—Specifies that the Web site document be opened in the parent of the current frame; this applies when you are using frames to display your Web site; **frames** split the browser window into more than one window and allow you to display several Web documents at one time

- `_top`—Specifies that the Web site document be opened in the top-level frame in the current window; this applies when you are using frames to display your Web site

Because the Jackson's Sports Web site is not designed to use frames, the options _parent and _top will not be used. If you use the _self option with the getURL() function, the Web site document that is loaded replaces the Jackson's Sports Resources page in the browser window. The Web site visitor then uses the browser's Back button to return to the Jackson's Sports Web site. This might present a problem because instead of returning to the Resources page, the visitor returns to the Jackson's Sports Web site Initial.swf page. Recall from Tutorial 7 that the Jackson's Sports Web site pages consist of SWF files that play in the Flash Player and the Flash Player sits inside one HTML document. This document was named Main.html and was generated by Flash when you published the Main.fla document. As a result, if you use the _self option, when the site visitor clicks the browser's Back button to return to the Jackson's Sports Web site Resources page, the browser reloads the Main.html document. This document loads the Main.swf file into the Flash Player and the Main.swf file includes a loadMovieNum() function in its first frame to load the Initial.swf file into level 1 of the Flash Player. As a result, the Initial.swf page displays and not the Resources page. To avoid confusing the Web site visitors, you will not use the _self option and instead will use the _blank option. The _blank option will cause the Web site document specified by the URL to load into a new browser window. The advantage of this is that the Resources page of the Jackson's Sports Web site will remain opened in its own window. The Web site visitor can then return to the Resources page when the new window is closed. To make it easier for the site visitor, Aly suggests you add a message on the Resources page explaining that a new browser window will open when a Web site is visited. You will complete the Resources page next.

To add the URL links to the Resources page:

1. If you took a break after the last session, start Flash if necessary, and open the **Resources.fla** file located in the **Tutorial.08\Tutorial** folder included with your Data Files. Set the panels to their default layout.

2. Create a text block below the title so that it is about **220** pixels from the top edge of the Stage and about **220** pixels from the left edge of the Stage. Use **Arial** for the font, **16** for the font size, and **black** for the text color. Make certain the **Align Left** text attribute is selected. Make certain the Bold attribute is not selected. Type **US Youth Soccer Online**, and then click the **Selection** tool on the toolbar.

3. Click **Modify** on the menu bar, and click **Convert to Symbol**. In the Convert to Symbol dialog box, name the symbol **USSoccer** and select **Button** as its behavior type. Click the **OK** button to create the button.

4. Click the **Edit Symbols** button, and click **USSoccer** to open it in symbol-editing mode.

5. Insert a keyframe in the Over frame of the button's Timeline. Select the **US Youth Soccer Online** text, and click the **Bold** button **B** in the Property inspector to apply the Bold attribute to the text. This provides visual feedback when the user moves the mouse pointer over the button. Now, you will draw a rectangle over the text block to make it easier for the viewer to click the button. Otherwise, the viewer would have to move the mouse pointer directly over a letter to activate the button.

6. Insert a keyframe in the **Hit** frame. Draw a rectangle to cover the text block. See Figure 8-11.

Figure 8-11   **RECTANGLE IN HIT FRAME**

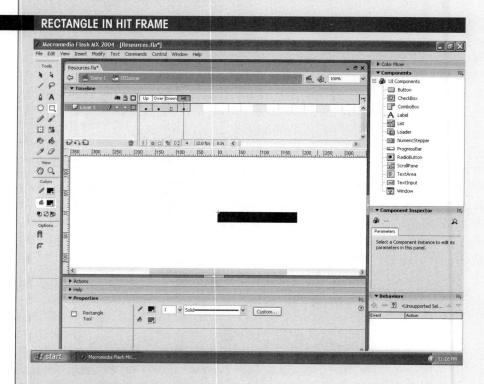

7. Click the **Scene 1** link in the Address bar to return to the document's main Timeline. Add the ActionScript to the button next.

8. Select the **button instance** on the Stage. Make certain the Actions panel title bar displays Actions - Button. Click the **Actions panel** title bar to expand the panel. If necessary, click **Movie Clip Control** in the Actions toolbox to display the list of actions. To add actions to a button instance, you need to first add an event handler.

9. Double-click the on event handler to add it to the Script pane, as shown in Figure 8-12.

Figure 8-12   ON EVENT HANDLER IN SCRIPT PANE

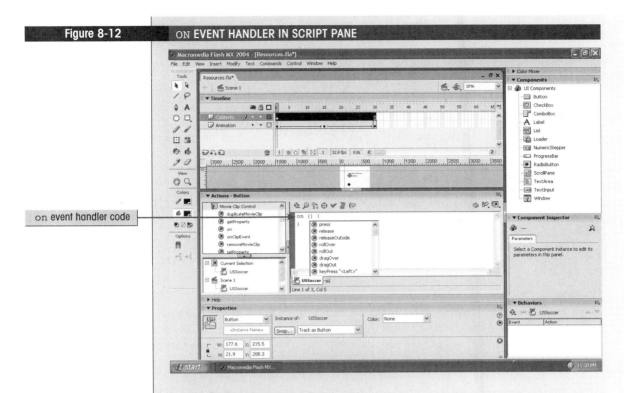

on event handler code

10. Double-click **release** from the code hints list. The button will perform an action when the user releases the mouse button after clicking the button.

11. Move the cursor to the end of the first line, and press the **Enter** key to add a new line. If necessary, click **Browser/Network** in the Actions toolbox to display the corresponding list of actions. Double-click the getURL function to add its code to the Script pane. Then type "http://www.usysa.org", "_blank" inside the function's parentheses, as shown in Figure 8-13.

Figure 8-13   getURL() FUNCTION

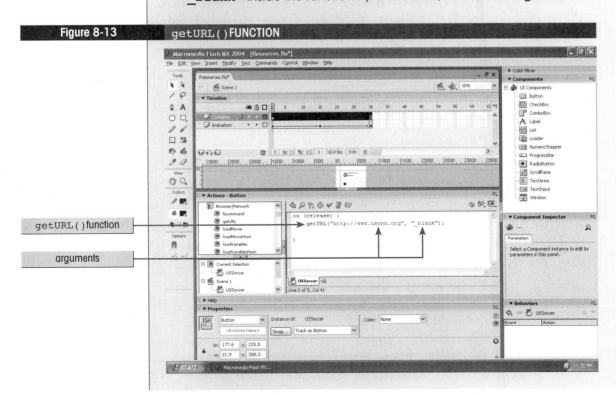

getURL() function

arguments

12. Click the **Check Syntax** button ✓ to check the ActionScript code syntax. If errors occur, compare your code with that of Figure 8-13, and make the necessary corrections. Otherwise, click the **OK** button to close the alert box.

13. Click **Control** on the menu bar, and click **Test Movie**. Click the **US Youth Soccer Online** button. The US Youth Soccer Web site opens in a new browser window.

> TROUBLE? If an error message appears stating the page cannot be displayed, your computer might not be connected to the Internet. If it is connected to the Internet, check the URL in the getURL() function to make certain it is correct.

> TROUBLE? If an error message appears stating the URL cannot be found, the URL address for the US Youth Soccer Online Web site might have changed since the printing of this book. See your instructor for assistance.

14. Close the Web browser window and close the Flash Player window in Flash to return to the Resources.fla document.

You have created a button with text and added an on event handler so that when the button is clicked and released, a Web site opens in a new browser window. You will add two more buttons to two other external sites. You will also add a message advising the site visitor that clicking a button will open a Web site in a new window.

To create additional buttons for the Resources page:

1. Click the **Actions panel** title bar to collapse the panel. Create a new text block below the US Youth Soccer Online button. Use **Arial** for the font, **16** for the font size, and **black** for the text color. Make certain the **Align Left** text attribute is selected. Make certain the Bold attribute is not selected.

2. Type **Amateur Softball Association** in the text block. Select the text and convert it to a button symbol. Name the symbol **ASA**. Place the button in symbol-editing mode, and insert a keyframe in its **Over** frame. Make the text bold in the Over frame. Insert a keyframe in the button's **Hit** frame, and draw a rectangle to cover the text block. Exit symbol-editing mode. Add the ActionScript code next.

3. Select the **ASA button instance** on the Stage, and expand the Actions panel. Double-click the on event handler in the Actions toolbox, and then double-click release in the code hints list for the event. Add a blank line after the first line, and double-click the getURL() function in the Actions toolbox. Type "http://www.softball.org", "_blank" between the parentheses for the function's arguments. You need to now create one more button.

4. Collapse the Actions panel and create another text block. Use **Arial** for the font, **16** for the font size, and **black** for the text color. Make certain the **Align Left** text attribute is selected. Make certain the Bold attribute is not selected. Type **National Alliance for Youth Sports** in the text block. Select the text and convert it to a button symbol. Name the symbol **NAYS**.

5. Place the NAYS symbol in symbol-editing mode, and insert a keyframe in its **Over** frame. Make the text bold in the Over frame. Insert a keyframe in the button's **Hit** frame, and draw a rectangle to cover the text block. Exit symbol-editing mode. Add the ActionScript code next.

6. Select the **NAYS button instance** on the Stage, and expand the Actions panel. Double-click the on event handler in the Actions toolbox, and then double-click `release` in the code hints list. Add a blank line after the first line, and double-click the `getURL()` function in the Actions toolbox. Type `"http://www.nays.org"`, `"_blank"` between the parentheses for the function's arguments. Now that the three buttons are in place, you need to align them.

7. Collapse the Actions panel, click the **Selection** tool ![cursor] on the toolbar, press and hold the **Shift** key, and then click each of the three buttons to select them all at the same time.

8. Click **Modify** on the menu bar and point to **Align**. If the To Stage command is checked, click it to deselect it. Click **Modify** again, point to **Align**, and then click **Left** to align the buttons along their left edges. Click **Modify** again, point to **Align**, and then click **Distribute Heights** to space the buttons equally.

9. Set the Zoom control to **100%**. Add a text block above the USSoccer button. Use **Arial** for the font, **10** for the font size, and **black** for the text color. Make certain the **Align Left** text attribute is selected, and apply the **Italic** attribute. Make certain the Bold attribute is not selected. Type **Clicking a button below will open the Web site in a new window.**, as shown in Figure 8-14.

| Figure 8-14 | TEXT BLOCK ABOVE BUTTONS |

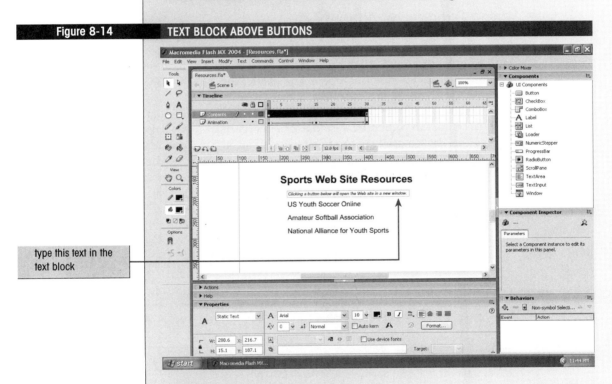

type this text in the text block

10. To test the links, click **Control** on the menu bar, and then click **Test Movie**. The SWF file plays in the Flash Player. Click each of the buttons. Each time you click a button, a new browser window opens to display the selected Web site. Close the browser windows.

   TROUBLE? If an error message appears stating the URL cannot be found, the URL address for the Web site might have changed since the printing of this book. See your instructor for assistance.

11. Close the Flash Player window to return to the Resources.fla file. Save and close the **Resources.fla** file.

The Resources.fla document is now complete. You have added the buttons and ActionScript code to open Web sites in new browser windows. Aly likes the work you have done with the document and asks you to complete the input form next.

Creating an Input Form

An input form is a common element found on many Web sites on the Internet. An input form allows the user to enter data into text boxes. The data can then be submitted for storage and processing on a Web server. The server software sends results of the processing back to the user's computer to be displayed on the same form or on another Web page. A page developed with Flash can also allow the user to enter data, have the data processed, and return a result directly from the Flash Player on the user's computer. The page developer uses ActionScript to write the underlying functions required to create a form with several input fields coded to accept data from the site visitor, such as the number and type of items to be purchased. Other fields on the form can display a total price based on the site visitor's input. Creating an input form requires the use of dynamic and input text.

Using Dynamic and Input Text

Text is an important element of a Flash document as you have seen in the projects you have worked on in this book. All of the text you have created so far has been static text. Static text cannot be changed after the document plays in the Flash Player. Recall, however, from Tutorial 2 that there are two other types of text in Flash: dynamic text and input text. Although static text cannot change, dynamic text can. **Dynamic text** can receive text in the form of characters or numbers from a Web server or from an expression in ActionScript and display the text on a Web page in the Flash Player. Dynamic text is defined to display the contents of a variable. The variable can be used in ActionScript to change the value displayed. For example, if a dynamic text block is assigned the variable `Amount`, you can code an expression in ActionScript to assign a value to the variable, such as `Amount = Price1 + Price2`. When the statement is performed in the script, the value stored in the variable `Amount` displays in the text block on the Web page. To create a dynamic text block, you use the Text tool just as you do for static text; however, you select Dynamic Text from the Text type list box in the Property inspector, as shown in Figure 8-15.

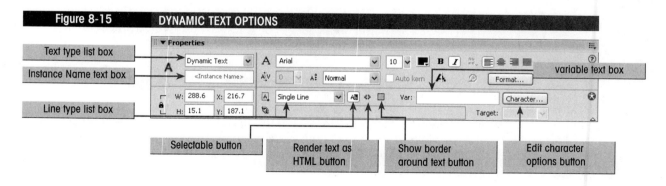

Figure 8-15   DYNAMIC TEXT OPTIONS

Text type list box

Instance Name text box

Line type list box

variable text box

Selectable button

Render text as HTML button

Show border around text button

Edit character options button

When you select Dynamic Text from the Text type list box, the Property inspector displays options specific to dynamic text, as described in Figure 8-16.

Figure 8-16	SUMMARY OF DYNAMIC TEXT OPTIONS	

OPTION	BUTTON	DESCRIPTION
Instance Name text box		Assigns a name to the instance of the text block on the Stage; the name can be used to change the properties of the instance using ActionScript
Line type list box		Specifies how many lines of text can be entered in the text block
Selectable button	![AB]	Allows the user to select the text when the SWF file is playing in the Flash Player
Render text as HTML button	![<>]	Interprets the text in the text block as HTML, allowing you to include HTML tags to format the text
Show border around text button	![border]	Displays a border around the text in the text block
Variable text box		Contains the name of the variable whose contents are displayed in the text block; use this variable name in ActionScript code to change the text being displayed
Edit characters options button	Character...	Opens a dialog box used to embed font outlines with the published SWF file; font outlines refer to information about the font used to create the text block; by default, font outlines are not embedded with the SWF file

Input text is used to allow the user to enter text into the text block. This text can then be stored in a variable and used in an ActionScript script. To create an input text block, use the Text tool and select Input Text from the Text type list box in the Property inspector, as shown in Figure 8-17.

Figure 8-17	ADDITIONAL OPTIONS FOR INPUT TEXT

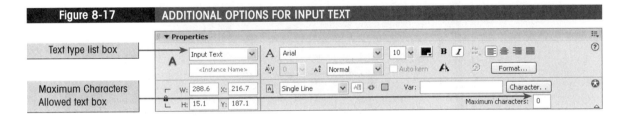

The options in the Property inspector for input text are the same as those for dynamic text, but input text also includes the Maximum Characters Allowed text box. You can specify the maximum number of characters the user can enter into the input text block. The initial setting of 0 does not limit the user to a specific number of characters.

Creating the Team Jersey Cost Calculator Page

Based on Dan Jackson's request, Aly has created a new document that will serve as the Team Jersey Cost Calculator page for the Jackson's Sports Web site. This document will allow the user, such as a team manager, to enter several values for the type and number of team jerseys the team will need to buy. The page will contain a button with ActionScript code that will use the entered values to calculate a total cost and display the result. One of the values that the user will enter is for the type of jersey desired, which is based on two options. One option is a team jersey for $10.00 with the team name only. The other option is a team jersey for $12.00 with both the team name and a player number. Then, the user will enter whether the jersey will contain the name of the player. Adding the player's name will cost an additional $1.50 per jersey. Finally, the user will enter the number of players and number of coaches to determine the number of jerseys needed.

Aly has started creating the Team Jersey Cost Calculator document. You will complete it by creating the input and dynamic text blocks. You will also create a Calculate button and write the ActionScript code for the button to calculate the total cost.

To create the input text boxes for the Team Jersey Cost Calculator document:

1. Open the **Calc.fla** file located in the **Tutorial.08\Tutorial** folder included with your Data Files. Set the panels to their default layout.

2. Insert a new layer above the Contents layer, and name it **Text fields**. Select the **Text** tool A on the toolbar, and create a text block to the right of the Type of jersey line.

3. Select **Input Text** from the Text type list box in the Property inspector. Use **Arial** for the font, **14** for the font size, and **black** for the text color. Make certain that the Bold and Italic attributes are not selected. Select the **Align Right** option.

4. Click the **Selection** tool ▶ on the toolbar. If necessary, use the Property inspector to change the width to **50** and the height to **20**. Also, if necessary, select **Single Line** from the Line type list box, and click the **Show border around text** button 🗐 to select it. In the Variable text box, type **JerseyType** making certain to use the specified letter case. Enter **1** in the Maximum characters text box. Only one character is allowed in the input text box. Now check the text block's registration point before setting its coordinates.

5. Click **Window** on the menu bar, point to **Design Panels**, and click **Info**. In the Info panel, make certain the upper-left registration point is selected. If it is not, click the **upper-left registration** point to select it. Close the Info panel. In the Property inspector, change the X coordinate to **450** and the Y coordinate to **224**. See Figure 8-18.

Figure 8-18   **INPUT TEXT BLOCK FOR COST CALCULATOR PAGE**

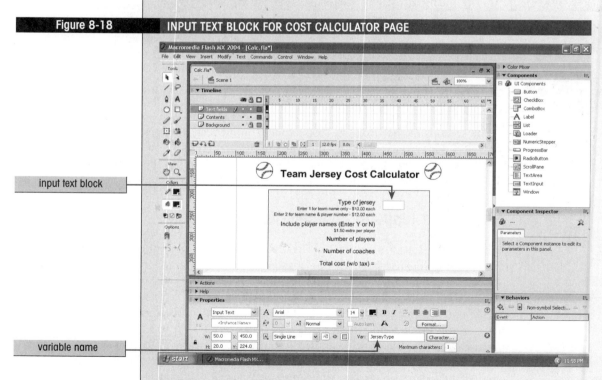

input text block

variable name

6. Create another text block and place it to the right of the Include player names (Enter Y or N) line. Select **Input Text** from the Text type list box in the Property inspector. Use **Arial** for the font, **14** for the font size, and **black** for the text color. Make certain that the Bold and Italic attributes are not selected. Select the **Align Right** option. Set the width to **50**, the height to **20**, the X coordinate to **450**, the Y coordinate to **270**, and type **PlayerNames** in the Variable text box. Also, enter **1** in the Maximum characters text box.

TROUBLE? If you have trouble changing the X and Y coordinates, click the Selection tool ⬚ first and then change the coordinate values.

7. Create a text block to the right of the Number of players line. Select **Input Text** from the Text type list box in the Property inspector. Use **Arial** for the font, **14** for the font size, and **black** for the text color. Make certain that the Bold and Italic attributes are not selected. Select the **Align Right** option. Use the Property inspector to set the width to **50**, the height to **20**, the X coordinate to **450**, and the Y coordinate to **305**. Type **NumberOfPlayers** in the Variable text box, and, if necessary, set the Maximum Characters Allowed text box to **0**.

8. Create a text block to the right of the Number of coaches line. Select **Input Text** from the Text type list box in the Property inspector. Use **Arial** for the font, **14** for the font size, and **black** for the text color. Make certain that the Bold and Italic attributes are not selected. Select the **Align Right** option. Use the Property inspector to set the width to **50**, the height to **20**, the X coordinate to **450**, and the Y coordinate to **335**. Type **NumberOfCoaches** in the Variable text box, and set the Maximum characters text box to **0**.

The text boxes the visitor will use to enter data are completed. You will add a dynamic text block next.

To create the dynamic text boxes for the Team Jersey Cost Calculator document:

1. Create a text block to the right of the Total cost (w/o tax) = line. Select **Dynamic Text** from the Text type list box in the Property inspector. Use **Arial** for the font, **14** for the font size, and **black** for the text color. Make certain that the Bold and Italic attributes are not selected. Select the **Align Right** option.

2. Use the Property inspector to set the width to **50**, the height to **20**, the X coordinate to **450**, and the Y coordinate to **365**. Type **TotalCost** in the Variable text box. If necessary, click the **Selectable** button 🔠 to deselect it. See Figure 8-19.

| Figure 8-19 | DYNAMIC TEXT BLOCK FOR COST CALCULATOR PAGE |

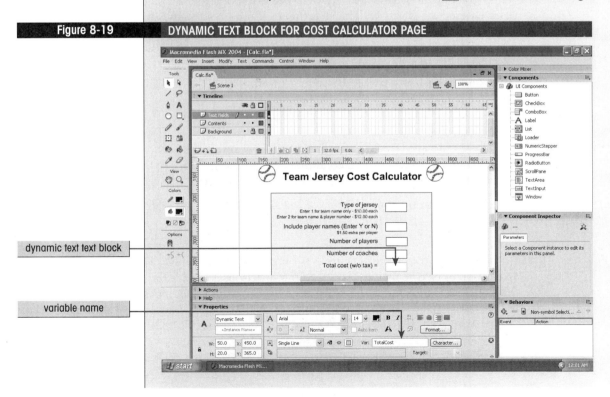

dynamic text text block

variable name

Now that you have created the input and dynamic text blocks, you need to add the button the user will click to calculate the total cost for the jerseys. Aly instructs you to add an instance of a button she created in the Calc.fla file and to add the ActionScript code to calculate the total cost based on the values entered in the input text blocks. The button will have an **on** event handler. When the button is clicked and then released, the total cost will be calculated based on the values in the input text blocks. The first input text block will contain either a 1 or a 2 for the type of jersey. To determine which price to use for the jersey, you must use an **if** conditional statement. The condition to check is whether the user entered a 1 or a 2. Aly suggests you only check for the value of 1. If 1 is not entered, you assume the user entered 2. This way, you will only have to check one condition (if the value entered is 1) and will not have to check a second condition (if the value entered is 2). The logic for this **if** statement is expressed in the following pseudocode. **Pseudocode** is an expression of programming logic using English sentences.

> If JerseyType is equal to 1
>> assign 10 to price
>
> else
>> assign 12 to price

The ActionScript statement for the **if** statement is as follows.

```
if (JerseyType == "1") {
        Price = 10;
} else {
        Price = 12;
}
```

Recall that `JerseyType` is the variable assigned to the first input text block and it contains the value entered by the user. The conditional operator == checks for equality. `Price` is a variable used within the ActionScript code to hold the price of the jersey. After this **if** statement is performed, `Price` will contain a value of `10` or `12` depending on the value entered by the user. The next action to perform is another **if** statement to determine if the user entered a Y or an N. This determines if the player names will be included on the jerseys. If the user entered a Y, you will add 1.50 to the price of the jerseys. Because ActionScript is case sensitive, you will need to check for both a lowercase y and an uppercase Y. This will allow for both possibilities depending on what is entered by the user. The pseudocode for this step is as follows.

> If PlayerNames equals y or Y
>> add 1.50 to the price

There is no need to check for the letter N because if the user entered an N, the price will not change. To check for two conditions within the same **if** statement, you use the logical operator ||, which represents **Or**. The ActionScript code is as follows.

```
if (PlayerNames == "Y" || PlayerNames == "y") {
        Price += 1.50;
}
```

Notice that the condition checks for both the value y and Y. The || operator causes the condition to be true if either one of the comparisons is true. If the condition is true, the variable `Price` is incremented by 1.50. The next two input text blocks contain values that represent how many players and coaches are on the team. These two values will be added together to get the total number of jerseys to be purchased. Before the values can be added, however, they need to be converted to numbers. Values entered into an input text block are considered string data and not numeric data. That is, the values are not treated as numbers, but instead are treated as text characters. Using the + operator to add the two values will not yield the correct result if the values are not first converted to numeric values. Flash includes the `parseFloat()` and the `parseInt()` functions that can be applied to the values to convert them to numbers. The `parseFloat()` function converts a number to a floating point number, which includes decimals. The `parseInt()` function converts a number to an integer, which is a whole number that does not include decimals. Because the number of players and number of coaches are whole numbers, you will use the `parseInt()` function. The statement to add the two values is as follows.

```
NumberOfJerseys = parseInt(NumberOfPlayers) +
parseInt(NumberOfCoaches);
```

The `NumberOfPlayers` and `NumberOfCoaches` variables were defined in the input text blocks and will contain the values entered by the user. These values are converted to integers and then added together. The result is then assigned to the variable `NumberOfJerseys`.

The final step to perform is to calculate the total cost by multiplying the `NumberOfJerseys` by the `Price`. The ActionScript code to do this is as follows.

```
TotalCost = NumberOfJerseys*Price;
```

After this step is performed, the value in the dynamic text block will change to reflect the value in the `TotalCost` variable because this is the variable name assigned to the text block. All of the ActionScript code used to perform this calculation needs to be inside the curly braces for the `on` event handler for the steps to be performed when the button is clicked and then released. You will add the button and the ActionScript next.

To add the button and ActionScript code to the Calc.fla file:

1. Open the document's Library panel, if necessary, and drag an instance of the **Calc_btn** symbol from the Library panel to the Stage. Place the instance below the dynamic text block for the total cost.

2. With the Calc_btn still selected, expand the Actions panel. The Actions panel title bar displays Actions – Button. You will add the event handler to the button instance next.

3. Double-click the `on` event handler in the Actions toolbox to add its code to the Script pane. Double-click `release` in the code hints list. Now, you will add the first part of the script.

4. Move the cursor to the end of the first line in the Script pane, and press the **Enter** key to add a new line. Click **Statements** in the Actions toolbox, and then click **Conditions/Loops**. Double-click the `if` action to add its code to the Script pane. Type `JerseyType == "1"` inside the parentheses for the condition. Move the cursor to the end of the line, and press the **Enter** key to add another blank line. Type `Price = 10;` on this line, and press the **Enter** key.

5. Double-click the `else` action in the Actions toolbox, and, if necessary, move the cursor to the end of the line. Press the **Enter** key again, and type `Price = 12;`. Compare your ActionScript code to the code shown in Figure 8-20.

Figure 8-20   **IF ACTIONSCRIPT CODE**

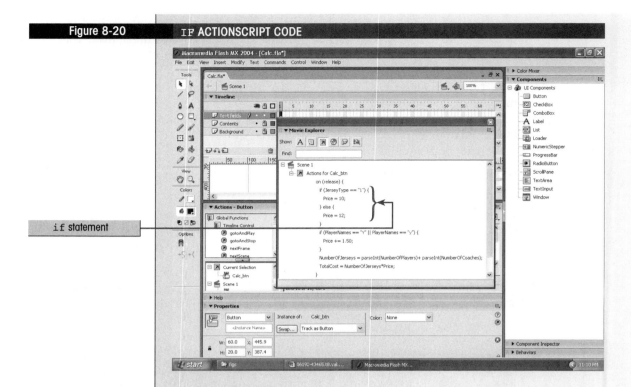

if statement

Extra blank lines and extra spaces will not affect the results. Continue entering the script.

6. Move the cursor to the right of the next curly brace, and press the **Enter** key. Double-click the `if` action in the Actions toolbox to add its code to the Script pane. Type `PlayerNames == "Y" || PlayerNames == "y"` inside the parentheses. (*Note:* To type the | character, press and hold the Shift key, and then press the \ key on the keyboard.) Move the cursor to the end of the current line, and press the **Enter** key. On the new line, type `Price += 1.50;`.

7. Move the cursor to the blank line below the next curly brace. Make certain you place the cursor before the final closing curly brace. Type `NumberOfJerseys = parseInt(NumberOfPlayers) + parseInt(NumberOfCoaches);`. Press the **Enter** key and type `TotalCost = NumberOfJerseys*Price;`. The complete code is shown in Figure 8-21.

Figure 8-21   **COMPLETE ACTIONSCRIPT CODE**

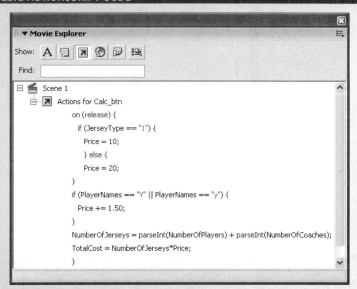

▼ Movie Explorer

Show:

Find:

```
Scene 1
  Actions for Calc_btn
    on (release) {
      if (JerseyType == "1") {
        Price = 10;
      } else {
        Price = 20;
      }
      if (PlayerNames == "Y" || PlayerNames == "y") {
        Price += 1.50;
      }
      NumberOfJerseys = parseInt(NumberOfPlayers) + parseInt(NumberOfCoaches);
      TotalCost = NumberOfJerseys*Price;
    }
```

8. To check for errors, click the **Check Syntax** button ☑ in the Actions panel. If errors occur, compare your code to that of Figure 8-21, and make the necessary corrections. Make certain that the variable names and ActionScript keywords have the same capitalization as shown in Figure 8-21. Also, make certain the parentheses and curly braces are organized as shown in the figure. You will test the form next.

9. Click **Control** on the menu bar, and click **Test Movie**. Enter **1** for the Type of jersey, **Y** for Include player names, **10** for the Number of players, and **2** for the Number of coaches. Click the **Calculate** button. The Total cost field displays 138. Try several other combinations of input values, clicking the **Calculate** button for each set of values.

TROUBLE? If you do not get the correct results, make sure you enter the correct input values and also check the variable names of your input and dynamic text boxes. Remember that ActionScript is case-sensitive. If the case of the variable names assigned to the text boxes is different from that used in the code, the result will not be correct.

10. Click **File** on the menu bar, and click **Close** when you are finished testing the form. Save and close the **Calc.fla** file.

You have completed and tested the input form document that allows the user to enter values in input text blocks, calculates the total cost of the jerseys based on the values entered, and displays the result in a dynamic text block.

In this session you used the `getURL()` function to create buttons for the Resources page with URL links to other Web sites on the Internet. You also learned about input and dynamic text blocks and used them to complete the Team Jersey Cost Calculator page that allows the user to enter values in input text blocks. You created and coded a Calculate button that the user can click to calculate the total cost of the jerseys based on the values entered in the input text blocks.

Session 8.2 QUICK CHECK

1. Write the ActionScript function to add to a button's event handler that will open the Web site *http://www.course.com* in the same window as the document containing the button.

2. What is the purpose of input text?

3. How can you limit the number of characters that can be entered in an input text block?

4. When you define dynamic text, what is the purpose of the Variable text box in the Property inspector?

5. Explain the purpose of the || operator in the following statement: if (Code == "1" || Code == "2").

6. What is the purpose of the parseInt() function?

SESSION 8.3

In this session, you will learn how to use ActionScript to create a preloader animation that will display while the content of a SWF file loads into the Flash Player. You will also add actions to buttons on the main page to complete the Jackson's Sports Web site.

Using a Flash Preloader

A SWF file, just like an HTML file, is downloaded over the Internet from a Web server to the user's computer, known as the **client computer**, where the files will reside. A major factor that affects the amount of time it takes a file to download is the size of the file, measured in kilobytes. A **kilobyte** is approximately 1000 bytes, and a **byte** is equivalent to one character of information. Flash Web sites typically contain various multimedia elements, such as graphics, animations, pictures, audio, and video. Each of these elements adds to the overall size of the published file. Even though the SWF files are compressed and contain vector graphics that tend to be small, they might still take some time to download. Another factor that affects download time is the type of Internet connection used by the client computer. The type of Internet connection can be a broadband connection using a cable or DSL modem, which provides high-speed download capability. Or, it could be a much slower dial-up connection using a telephone modem, as is still the case with many personal computers. When a SWF file starts to download from a Web server to a client computer, it is loaded into the Flash Player one frame at a time. The first frames start playing in the Flash Player as soon as they load even though other frames of the file are still downloading. This is because of the streaming capability of Flash files. **Streaming** means that as the file is downloading, the initial content can start playing while the rest of the content continues to be downloaded, which means the wait time for the user is reduced. A problem occurs, however, when the client computer plays all of the loaded frames and then has to wait for additional frames to load. This can happen if a particular frame has a large amount of content such as bitmap images. The wait causes the Flash Player to pause the playing of the SWF file while additional frames load. This delay affects the way the SWF file plays and might confuse or frustrate the user. Also, if the wait is more than a few seconds and there is no visual indication that something is still loading, the user may think the Web site is not working and decide to go to another site. To avoid losing site visitors, Flash developers usually add a **preloader**, which is a short animation or message located in the first few frames of the Flash file. The preloader typically contains a short animation and the word "Loading" to indicate to the site visitor that the Web site is still loading. This visual feedback helps assure the site visitor that the Web site is loading while the frames of the SWF file continue to download. After all of the content has downloaded, the preloader stops and the rest of the SWF file plays. Several examples of preloaders are shown in Figure 8-22.

Figure 8-22 | **SAMPLE PRELOADERS**

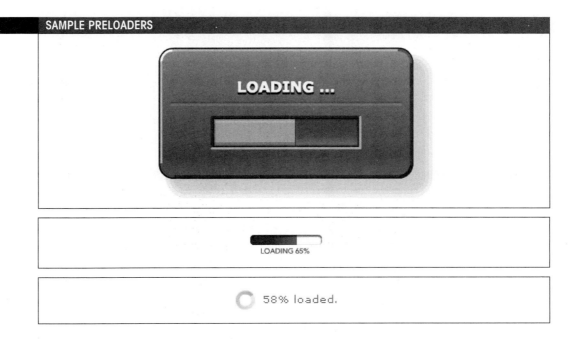

Creating the Preloader ActionScript

Adding a preloader to a Flash file requires writing ActionScript code. The loading message and animation should be placed in the first few frames of the Timeline. Then, an ActionScript script can be added to a later frame to control the preloader and to check if all of the content has downloaded. The basic logic involves knowing how much of the SWF file has loaded and comparing that with the total size of the file. The amount of content that has loaded and the total size of the file can be measured in either number of frames or number of bytes, both of which can be examined using ActionScript. By checking how much content has been loaded and comparing it to the total size of the file, different actions can be performed. For example, if the number of bytes that have loaded into the Flash Player is equal to the total number of bytes for the file, the entire SWF file has loaded. At that point, the SWF file can play as designed. Otherwise, the preloader continues to play.

If the SWF file contains a large number of frames, you can create a preloader that checks the number of frames loaded. In the case of the Jackson's Sports Web site, the number of frames is small, so it is best to check the number of bytes loaded. To examine the total number of bytes, you use the `getBytesTotal()` function. This function returns the total number of bytes contained in the SWF file. You can then assign the result to a variable such as `totalBytes = getBytesTotal()`. To check the number of bytes loaded, you use the `getBytesLoaded()` function. You can also assign this value to a variable such as `loadedBytes = getBytesLoaded()`. After you have these numbers, the rest of the ActionScript involves comparing the numbers and performing actions based on the result of the comparison. The pseudocode for this preloader logic is as follows.

> Get the total number of bytes
>
> Get the number of bytes loaded
>
> If the number of bytes loaded equals the total number of bytes
>
> > play the rest of the SWF file
>
> else
>
> > continue playing the preloader animation

The ActionScript code for the comparison requires using the `if` statement. The actions to be performed based on the result of the comparison will then direct the playhead to the first frame after the preloader animation or back to the start of the preloader animation, which is usually Frame 1. You use the `gotoAndPlay()` function to direct the playhead to a specific frame. Rather than using frame numbers as arguments in the `gotoAndPlay()` function, it is best to use frame labels. Recall that you can assign labels to frames using the Property inspector. The frame labels are indicated on the Timeline with a small red flag icon, as shown in Figure 8-23.

Figure 8-23	FRAME LABELS

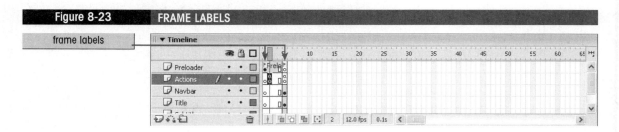

frame labels

For example, you can assign the frame label Preload to the first frame where the preloader animation begins. You can then assign the frame label Start for the frame where the rest of the content begins. Using these labels, the ActionScript for the `if` statement is as follows.

```
if (loadedBytes == totalBytes) {
    gotoAndPlay("Start");
} else {
    gotoAndPlay("Preload");
}
```

In addition to comparing the `loadedBytes` with the `totalBytes`, you can also use these values to control the animation used in the preloader. Recall from Session 8.1 that the properties of a movie clip instance can be modified using ActionScript. By creating a movie clip such as a small vertical bar, you can increase the bar's width by changing its `_width` property to reflect how much of the file has been loaded. To increase its width, you place the vertical bar inside a rectangle, as shown in Figure 8-24.

Figure 8-24	CHANGING THE WIDTH OF A MOVIE CLIP

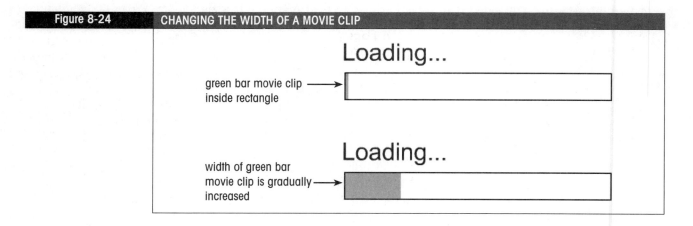

Both the vertical bar and the rectangle need to be converted to movie clips, and names must be assigned to each instance on the Stage. The width of the vertical bar will be increased gradually until it equals the width of the rectangle. To determine what value to assign to the width of the vertical bar, you first divide the `loadedBytes` by the `totalBytes`. The result of this division represents a percentage of how much of the file has loaded. It increases gradually until the two values are equal, which means all of the file's content has loaded. The result of the division, which is always less than one, can then be multiplied by the width of the rectangle. This results in a value that represents a percentage of the rectangle's width and can be used to set the width of the vertical bar. The resulting expression is shown in the following code, in which `loadBar` is the name of the vertical bar instance and `loadBarRect` is the name of the rectangle instance. Recall that to reference the property of a movie clip instance, you use the name of the instance followed by a dot and then the name of the property.

```
loadBar._width = loadBarRect._width*(loadedBytes/totalBytes);
```

Using this expression increases the width of the vertical bar each time the `loadedBytes` value changes. This expression is placed after values are assigned to the `loadedBytes` and `totalBytes` variables and before the `if` statement that checks the progress of the downloading.

Creating a Preloader for the Jackson's Sports Web Site

Now that you have seen how to create the preloader ActionScript code, Aly instructs you to create a preloader for the Jackson's Sports Web site on its main page. You will add the preloader to a revised version of the Main.fla file. The preloader will be placed on a new layer and will start in Frame 1 of the layer. The ActionScript script will be added to the second frame of the existing Actions layer.

To create a preloader for the Jackson's Sports Web site:

1. If you took a break after the last session, start Flash if necessary, and open the **Main.fla** file located in the **Tutorial.08\Tutorial** folder included with your Data Files. Set the panels to their default layout.

2. Insert a new layer above the Actions layer and name it **Preloader**. Insert a keyframe at **Frame 5** of the Preloader layer. Use the Property inspector to assign the name **Start** to this frame. Select **Frame 1** of the Preloader layer, and assign the name **Preload** to this frame.

3. Create a static text block at the center of the Stage. Use the Property inspector to select **Arial** for the font, **18** for the font size, **black** for the text color, and **Align Left** for alignment. Type **Loading...** in this text block, and then click the **Selection** tool. See Figure 8-25.

Figure 8-25   **LOADING MESSAGE FOR PRELOADER**

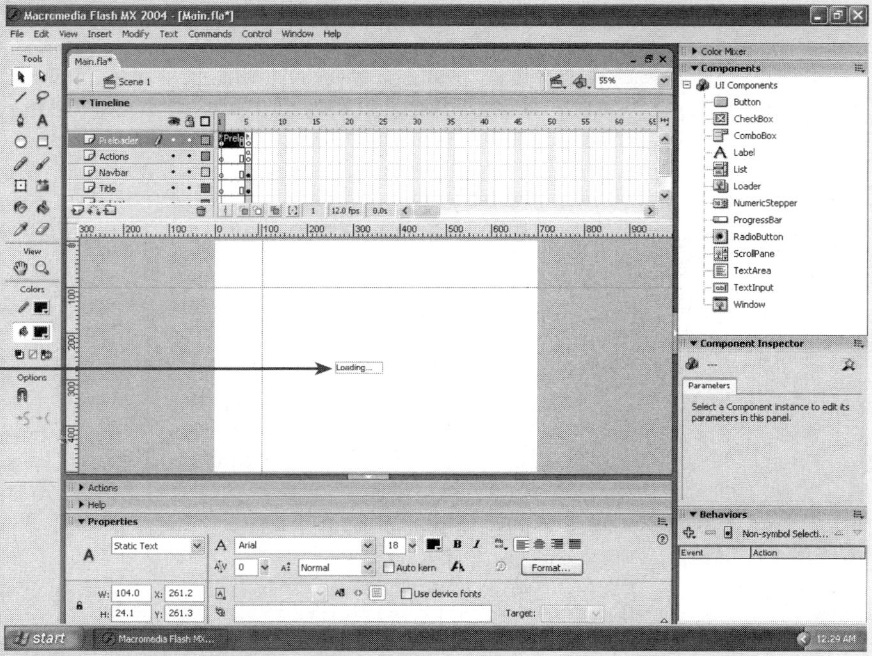

static text block

4. Create a new symbol. Name the symbol **Rectangle** and assign **Movie clip** as its behavior. In symbol-editing mode, create a rectangle at the center of the Stage. Use the Property inspector to select a **solid** stroke with **black** for the stroke color and **1** for the stroke height. Do not include a fill color. Make the rectangle **200** pixels wide by **20** pixels high, and center it on the Stage. Exit symbol-editing mode.

5. Create another new symbol named **Bar**, and assign **Movie clip** as its behavior. In symbol-editing mode, draw a small rectangle to resemble a vertical bar. Use no stroke color and use a **green (#009900)** fill color. Open the Info panel and if necessary, select the upper-left registration point. Then set the width to **2** the height to **20**, and the X and Y coordinates to **0**. Close the Info panel. Exit symbol-editing mode.

6. To make it easier to see the content on the Stage, click the **Zoom control** list arrow and click **200%**. If necessary, open the Library panel. Drag an instance of the **Bar symbol**, and place it below the letter L of the Loading text block. Type **loadBar** in the Instance Name text box in the Property inspector, and press the **Enter** key.

7. Drag an instance of the **Rectangle** symbol onto the Stage, and place it so that the Bar instance is inside the left edge of the Rectangle instance, as shown in Figure 8-26.

Figure 8-26   **PLACEMENT OF INSTANCES**

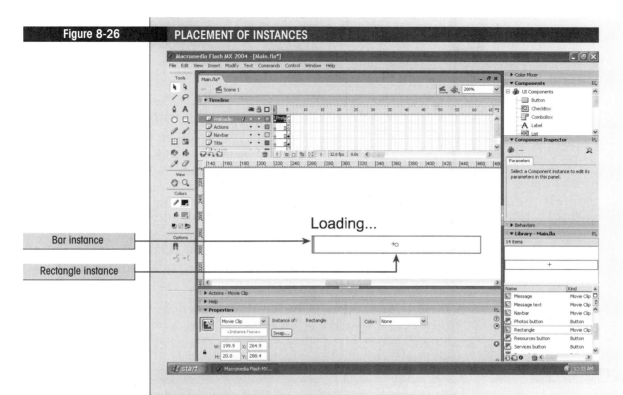

Bar instance

Rectangle instance

8. Type **loadBarRect** in the Instance Name text box in the Property inspector to name this instance, and press the **Enter** key. The preloader contents are now complete. You will add the ActionScript code next.

9. Click **Frame 2** of the Actions layer to select it and insert a keyframe. The ActionScript code will be placed in this frame. Click the **Actions panel** title bar to expand the panel. Type the script shown in Figure 8-27. Make certain to use the same letter case as shown in the figure.

Figure 8-27   **ACTIONSCRIPT FOR PRELOADER**

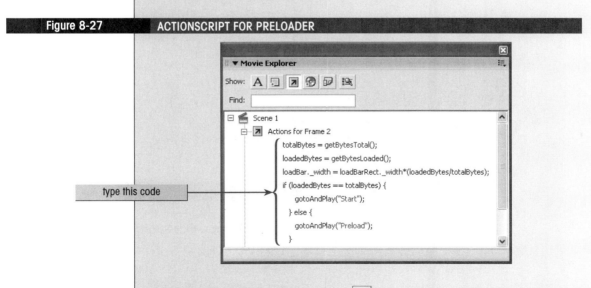

type this code

```
totalBytes = getBytesTotal();
loadedBytes = getBytesLoaded();
loadBar._width = loadBarRect._width*(loadedBytes/totalBytes);
if (loadedBytes == totalBytes) {
    gotoAndPlay("Start");
} else {
    gotoAndPlay("Preload");
}
```

10. Click the **Check Syntax** button ✅ in the Actions panel to check for errors. If errors occur, compare your code to that of Figure 8-27, make the necessary corrections, and click ✅ again.

11. Click **Frame 5** of the Actions layer. In the Actions panel, place the cursor below the `loadMovieNum("Initial.swf", 1);` line, and type `stop();` to prevent Frames 1 through 4 from repeating after Frame 5 is played. Collapse the Actions panel. Test the preloader.

12. Click **Control** on the menu bar, and click **Test Movie**. The SWF file plays in the Flash Player; however, the preloader displays for only a fraction of a second.

Because the SWF file is loading from your computer's drive, the file's content loads instantly. As a result, the preloader animation is only visible for a very short time. This will not be the case, however, when the SWF file is downloaded from the Internet. To test the preloader, you can use the Simulate Download command, which is located on the View menu in the Test Movie window. This command simulates the time it takes to download a SWF file based on the type of Internet connection you select. You select the type of Internet connection from the Download Settings submenu, which is on the View menu. These settings list several common types of connections, such as a 56K telephone connection and a DSL broadband connection.

13. Click **View** on the menu bar in the Test Movie window, point to **Download Settings**, and then click **56K (4.7 KB/s)**. Click **View** again and click **Simulate Download**. The preloader animation plays, as shown in Figure 8-28.

Figure 8-28	USING THE SIMULATE DOWNLOAD OPTION

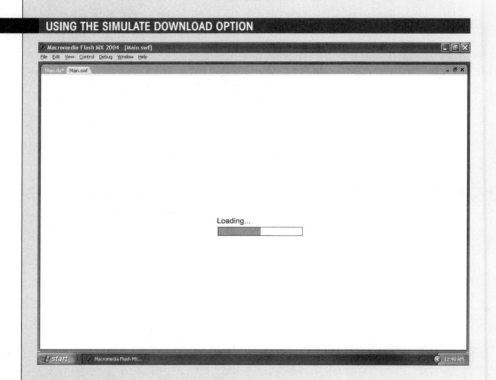

After the green bar fills the rectangle, the Jackson's Sports Web site displays.

14. Click **File** on the menu bar, and click **Close** to return to the Main.fla file.

Completing the Actions for the Jackson's Sports Web Site

Now that you have created the preloader, you can complete the Web site by adding the ActionScript code to the buttons for the new pages you worked with in Session 8.2. These were the Resources page and the input form. The SWF files for these pages need to be loaded into level 1 of the Flash Player in the same way the other pages of the site are loaded. This requires the use of the `loadMovieNum()` action. The buttons have already been added to the Main.fla file by Chris, and you now need to make the buttons operational.

To add ActionScript to the Resources and Calculate buttons:

1. Click the **Edit Symbols** button ⬦, and select **Navbar** to open it in symbol-editing mode.

2. Click the **Resources** button on the Navbar. If necessary, open the Actions panel. Double-click the on event handler located under Movie Clip Control in the Actions toolbox to add its code to the Script pane. Double-click the `release` event in the code hints list.

3. Move the cursor to the end of the first line, and press the **Enter** key to add a blank line. Double-click the `loadMovieNum` function located under **Browser/Network** in the Actions toolbox. Type `"Resources.swf", 1` inside the parentheses as the arguments for the function.

4. Collapse the Actions panel and click the **Calculate** button in the Navbar on the Stage. Expand the Actions panel, double-click the on event handler under Movie Clip Control in the Actions toolbox to add it to the Script pane, and double-click `release` in the code hints list.

5. Move the cursor to the end of the line, and press the **Enter** key. Double-click the `loadMovieNum` function in the Actions toolbox, and type `"Calc.swf", 1` inside the parentheses.

6. Click the **Scene 1** link on the Address bar to return to the Main document. Now test the file.

7. Click **Control** on the menu bar, and click **Test Movie**. The Jackson's Sports Web site displays in the Flash Player. Use the **Simulate Download** command to play the SWF file the way a user would see it using a 56K modem connection. After the main content loads, click the **Resources** and **Calculate** buttons to load the respective SWF files.

8. Close the browser window to return to the Main.fla document. Save and close the **Main.fla** document.

The additional pages for the Jackson's Sports Web site are completed, and you show them to Aly. She is very pleased with the pages, and looks forward to sharing them with Dan Jackson at their next meeting.

In this session, you created a preloader using ActionScript for the Jackson's Sports Web site. You tested the preloader by simulating the download speed of a 56K modem Internet connection. You also added the ActionScript needed to make the Resources and Calculate buttons operational in the navigation bar for the Web site.

Session 8.3 QUICK CHECK

1. What is the purpose of a preloader?

2. Which ActionScript function do you use to get the total number of bytes in a SWF file?

3. Which property do you use to modify the width of a movie clip instance?

4. The amount of content that has loaded from a SWF file can be measured in either number of _____ or number of _____.

5. Explain how you can simulate the downloading of a SWF file within Flash.

REVIEW ASSIGNMENTS

After showing the Resources and Team Jersey Cost Calculator pages to Dan Jackson, Aly asks you to modify some of the new content. She wants you to add a new link to the Resources page to display another youth sports Web site. You will also add a new input text block to the Team Jersey Cost Calculator page to include the option to enter a discount code. This code will be given to special customers for a 10% discount. She also asks you to add some more visual feedback to the preloader. You are to display a value that represents the percentage of the number of bytes that have loaded.

If necessary, start Flash, and then do the following:

1. Open the **Resources.fla** document from the Tutorial.08\Tutorial folder included with your Data Files. Save a copy of the file in the Tutorial.08\Review folder included with your Data Files.

2. Create a static text box below the National Alliance for Youth Sports button. Use Arial for the font, 16 for the font size, black for the text color, and Align Left for the alignment. Type **InfoSports.net** in the text block. Convert the text block into a button symbol named **ISN**. Edit the ISN button. Add a keyframe in its Over frame, and bold the text. Add a keyframe in the Hit frame, and draw a rectangle to cover the text block.

3. Return to Scene 1, select the ISN button instance on the Stage, and open the Actions panel. Add an on event handler with a `release` event. Add the `getURL()` function to open the Web site at *www.infosports.net* in a new browser window.

4. Test the SWF file and click the new button to make certain the Web site opens in a new browser window. *Note:* If an error message appears indicating an error opening the Web pages, the URLs for these Web sites might have changed since the printing of this text. See your instructor for assistance.

5. Close the **Resources.swf** file. Save and close the **Resources.fla** file.

6. Open the **Calc.fla** document from the Tutorial.08\Tutorial folder included with your Data Files. Save a copy of the file in the Tutorial.08\Review folder included with your Data Files.

7. Add a static text block to the lower-left corner of the yellow rectangle. Use Arial for the font, 14 for the font size, black for the text color, and Align Left for the alignment. Type **Discount Code** in the text block. Add an input text block to the right of the static text block. Use the same text properties as the first text block. Select the Show border around text button and assign the name **DiscCode** to the variable. Set the maximum number of characters to 4.

8. Select the Calculate button and open the Actions panel. The `TotalCost` will be reduced by 10% if the discount code is entered in the DiscCode variable. The discount code is 827. Add a blank line after the `TotalCost = NumberOfJerseys*Price;` statement. Type the following code.

```
if (DiscCode == "827") {
    TotalCost -= TotalCost * .1;
}
```

9. Test the SWF file. Enter **1** for the Type of jersey, **N** for the Include player names, **9** for the Number of players, and **1** for the Number of coaches text boxes. Also enter **827** for the discount code. Click the Calculate button. The total cost should be 90.

10. Close the **Calc.swf** file. Save and close the **Calc.fla** file.

11. Open the **Main.fla** document from the Tutorial.08\Tutorial folder included with your Data Files. Save a copy of the file in the Tutorial.08\Review folder included with your Data Files.

12. Select Frame 1 of the Preloader layer. Create a static text block below the rectangle on the Stage. Use Arial for the font, 16 for the font size, and black for the text color. Type **Percent done** in the text block. Create a dynamic text block to the right of the Percent done text. Use the same character properties as the first text block, and make it 50 pixels wide by 20 pixels high. Also assign the variable name **percentDone** to this text block. Add another static text block to the right of the dynamic text block. Type **%** in this text block.

Explore   13. Click Frame 2 of the Actions layer and open the Actions panel. Add a blank line after the `loadedBytes = getBytesLoaded();` line. On the blank line, type **`percentDone = Math.round((loadedBytes/totalBytes)*100);`**. *Note:* `Math.round` is a built-in function that rounds the number inside the parentheses to the nearest integer.

14. Test the file using the Test Movie command, and use the Simulate Download command to test the preloader animation. Close the SWF file.

15. Save and close the **Main.fla** file.

CASE PROBLEMS

Case 1. Adding Interactivity to Pages on the Sandy's Party Center Web Site Sandy is very happy with the new Web site you created to promote some of the store's special services. She meets with John to discuss adding two new elements to the Web site. She wants to have two hyperlinks added to the Cake Decorating page. These hyperlinks are for Web sites that provide more information about cake decorating. She also wants to have a way for the user to select from several party supplies packages on the Party Planning page. The user should be able to enter the number of people that will attend a party. The page will then display the cost of the party supplies based on the selections.

John meets with you to discuss the new requests and asks you to add the new elements to the Web site. He asks you to use a revised version of these pages that he has developed.

If necessary, start Flash, and then do the following:

1. Open the **Cake.fla** file located in the Tutorial.08\Cases folder included with your Data Files.

2. Add a new layer above the Hats layer and name it **Links**. Create a static text block within the pink rectangle on the Stage at about 210 pixels from the left edge of the Stage and 265 pixels from the top edge of the Stage. Use Comic Sans MS for the font, 14 for the font size, black for the text color, and Align Left for the alignment. Type **American Cake Decorating** in the text block.

3. Create another static text block below the first one with the same text properties. Place it about 210 pixels from the left edge of the Stage and 305 pixels from the top edge of the Stage. Type **Pastry Food Resource Center** in the text block. If necessary, select the two text blocks at the same time and align them by their left edges.

4. Convert each of the two text blocks into symbols. Assign button for the symbol behaviors. Name the first text block symbol **CakeMag** and the second text block symbol **PastryWiz**.

5. Edit the CakeMag symbol. Add a keyframe in its Over frame, and make the text bold in this frame. Add a rectangle in the button's Hit frame to make it easier to click the button. Edit the PastryWiz symbol, add a keyframe in its Over frame, and make the text bold in this frame. Add a rectangle in the button's Hit frame.

6. In Scene 1, select the CakeMag button instance on the Stage, and then expand the Actions panel. Double-click the `on` event handler in the Actions toolbox. Double-click `release` from the code hints list for the event. Add a new line after the opening curly brace, and insert a `getURL( )` function that will open the American Cake Decorating site in a new browser window. The URL for the site is *www.cakemag.com/*.

7. Select the PastryWiz button instance, and enter the same ActionScript code as you did for the CakeMag button instance, but use *www.pastrywiz.com/cakes/* for the URL.

8. Create a new static text block below the second button. Use the same text properties as used for the other text blocks, except that that font size should be 10. Also, apply the Italic attribute to the text. Type **Clicking the buttons above will open a new window.** in the text block.

9. Save the **Cake.fla** file in the Tutorial.08\Cases folder included with your Data Files. Test it to ensure the buttons open the linked Web sites in new browser windows. *Note:* If an error message appears indicating an error opening the Web pages, the URLs for these Web sites might have changed since the printing of this text. See your instructor for assistance.

10. Open the **Planning.fla** file located in the Tutorial.08\Cases folder included with your Data Files.

11. Insert a new layer above the Hats layer and name it **Text fields**. Create an input text block to the right of the second line in the light blue rectangle that states **Enter letter for type of party supplies package:**. Place the text block about 430 pixels from the left edge of the Stage and about 260 pixels from the top edge of the Stage. Make the text block 40 pixels wide by 20 pixels high. Use Comic Sans MS for the font, 12 for the font size, black for the text color, and Align Right for the alignment.

12. If necessary, select Single Line from the Line type list box. Select the Show border around text button, type **Package** in the Variable text box, and enter **1** in the Maximum characters text box.

13. Create a second input text block with the same dimensions and properties as the first one. Place this text block to the right of the How many party guests? line and about 300 pixels from the top edge of the Stage. Type **Guests** in the Variable text box, and, if necessary, enter **0** in the Maximum characters text box.

14. Create another input text block as in Step 13, and place it to the right of the Include a cake for $12.50 (Y- yes or N- no) line and about 325 pixels from the top edge of the Stage. Type **Cake** in the Variable text box, and enter **1** in the Maximum characters text box.

15. Create a dynamic text block to the right of the Total cost (w/o taxes): line and about 355 pixels from the top edge of the Stage. Use the same dimensions and text properties as the input text blocks. Type **Total** in the Variable text box.

16. In the Text fields layer, drag an instance of the Calc button from the document's Library panel to the lower-right corner of the light blue rectangle. With the button selected, add the on event handler code to the Script pane of the Actions panel, and then select `release` from the code hints list. Type the following ActionScript code inside the curly braces of the on event handler.

```
if (Package == "B" || Package == "b") {
        Price = 2.50;
    } else {
        Price = 2.89;
    }
Total = Price*Guests;
if (Cake == "Y" || Cake == "y") {
        Total += 12.50;
    }
```

17. Check the code for syntax errors, and make any necessary corrections.

18. Save the **Planning.fla** file and test it by entering **B** for the type of package, **7** for the number of guests, and **Y** for a cake. Clicking the Calculate button displays 30 for the total cost.

19. Close all open files.

Case 2. Adding Interactivity to the River City Music Web Site Janet is very happy with the Web site developed for her music store. She meets with Alex to request an additional element for the Web site. She wants to have the musical instruments page include several special sales where the site visitor can change the display from one special to another.

Alex asks you to help him modify the Instruments page of the Web site. He instructs you to add buttons to control the display of each special and to add each special on a separate frame. Each special will display a musical instrument picture and a short message about the special. River City Music currently has three instruments specials.

If necessary, start Flash, and then do the following:

1. Open the **Instruments.fla** file located in the Tutorial.08\Cases folder included with your Data Files.

2. Add three new layers above the Text layer. Name the first layer **Buttons**, the second layer **Labels**, and the third layer **Action**. Rename the Text layer to **Contents**. Select the Buttons layer.

3. Open the Buttons Common Library. (*Hint:* To access the Buttons Common Library, click Window on the menu bar, point to Other Panels, point to Common Libraries, and then click Buttons.) In the Buttons Library panel, open the Circle Buttons folder, and drag an instance of the circle button - next symbol to the Stage. Place the instance right above the bottom side of the rectangle centered within the rectangle. Drag an instance of the circle button - previous symbol and place it just to the left of the circle button - next instance.

4. Add a regular frame at Frame 4 of the Rectangle layer. Also, add a regular frame to Frame 4 of the Buttons layer.

5. Add a keyframe to Frame 2 of the Contents layer. Delete the bottom text block.

6. Import the **guitars.jpg** file to the document's library. The file is located in the Tutorial.08\Cases folder included with your Data Files. Drag an instance of the **guitars.jpg** bitmap from the document's Library panel to the center of the rectangle. Place it above the buttons.

7. Add a static text block to the left of the guitars picture. Make the text block's width about 100 pixels. Use Arial for the font, 14 for the font size, red for the text color, and Align Left for the alignment. Type **Guitars are now on sale. Save up to 30% on name brands.** in the text block.

8. Add a keyframe at Frame 3 of the Contents layer. Delete the picture of the guitars. Import the **piano.jpg** file to the document's library from the Tutorial.08\Cases folder included with your Data Files. Drag an instance of the **piano.jpg** bitmap to the same place where the guitars picture was located.

9. Change the text in the text block to the left of the picture to the following. **Used pianos on sale. Save 20% off their regular price. Tuned and refurbished.**

10. Add a keyframe at Frame 4 of the Contents layer. Delete the picture of the piano. Import the **trumpets.jpg** file to the document's library from the Tutorial.08\Cases folder included with your Data Files. Drag an instance of the **trumpets.jpg** bitmap to the Stage. Change the text in the text block to the following. **Take an extra 15% off all trumpets. Also, get a free lesson with the purchase of a trumpet.**

11. Select Frame 1 of the Labels layer. Assign the label **Begin** to this frame in the Property inspector. Insert a keyframe at Frame 4 of the Labels layer, and assign the label **End** to the frame.

Explore

12. Select the instance of the circle - button previous on the Stage. Expand the Actions panel, and double-click the `on` event handler from the Movie Clip Control book in the Actions toolbox. Select `release` for the event, and create a new line after the opening curly brace. Type the following code between the curly braces. This code will cause the playhead to move to the previous frame if the current frame is not Frame 1. Otherwise, the playhead will move to the last frame.

```
if (_currentframe!=1) {
        prevFrame();
    } else {
        gotoAndStop("End");
    }
```

13. Check the code for syntax errors, and make any necessary corrections.

Explore

14. Select the instance of the circle - button next on the Stage. In the Script pane of the Actions panel, add the on event handler with the `release` event. Type the following code between the curly braces. This code will cause the playhead to move to the next frame if the current frame is not Frame 4. Otherwise, the playhead will move to the first frame.

```
if (_currentframe!=4) {
        nextFrame();
  } else {
        gotoAndStop("Begin");
  }
```

15. Check the code for syntax errors, and make any necessary corrections.

16. Select Frame 1 of the Action layer. When the SWF file starts to play, you want the playhead to stop at Frame 1. In the Script pane of the Actions panel, type **stop();**.

17. Test the file. Click the buttons to display each of the specials in the frames. Close the SWF file. Save and close the **Instruments.fla** file.

Case 3. Adding a Photo Gallery and Preloader to the Sonny's Auto Center Web Site

Sonny is very happy with his new Web site and is very excited about the Photos page, which displays pictures of cars for sale. However, he tells Amanda that the number of pictures varies each week and the current page only has three buttons, one for each picture. He wonders whether adding more pictures will require adding more buttons. Rather than adding more buttons to the page, Amanda suggests having only one button. Each time the button is clicked, a different picture will display. Sonny likes the idea and asks Amanda to modify the Photos page.

Amanda asks you to help her modify the Photos page. To more easily control the display of the pictures, Amanda instructs you to first create a new document that will contain one picture per frame. This document will be published, and its SWF file will load into the movie clip instance on the Photos page. Amanda also instructs you to add a preloader to the new document. Because several pictures will be in the document, it will take longer to load. The preloader will show a message and an animation indicating the progress of the loading. You will complete a revised version of the Autophotos.fla document that Amanda has created. You will add ActionScript code to control which picture in the new document is displayed.

If necessary, start Flash, and then do the following:

1. Create a new document 350 pixels wide by 250 pixels high. Use white for the background color. Save the document as **Forsale.fla** in the Tutorial.08\Cases folder included with your Data Files.

2. Change the name of Layer 1 to **Pictures** and insert a keyframe at Frame 4. Use the Import to Stage command to import the **Auto1.jpg** file located in the Tutorial.08\Cases folder included with your Data Files. Click the Yes button when asked if you want to import all of the images in the sequence. This will place each of the three pictures in separate frames.

3. Insert a layer and name it **Price**. Insert a keyframe in Frame 4 of the Price layer and then create a static text block in the upper-left corner of the picture. Use Arial for the font, 14 for the font size, and select the Bold attribute. Type **$4,999** in the text block.

4. Insert a keyframe at Frame 5 of the Price layer, and change the price in the text block to **$14,995**. Add one more keyframe, this time in Frame 6 of the Price layer. Change the price to **$9,995**.

5. Insert a layer above the Price layer. Name the new layer **Actions**. Insert a keyframe in Frame 4 of the Actions layer. Expand the Actions panel and type `stop();` in the Script pane to keep the playhead from moving past the first picture when the document is loaded in the Flash Player.

6. Insert a new layer above the Actions layer, and name it **Preloader**. Select Frame 1 of the Preloader layer, and type **Preload** for its frame label. Insert a keyframe at Frame 4 of the layer, and type **Start** for its frame label.

7. Create a new movie clip symbol named **loadBar**. In symbol-editing mode, draw a small vertical bar in the center of the Stage using the Rectangle tool. Use red for the fill and no color for the stroke. Make the rectangle 1 pixel wide by 20 pixels high.

8. Create another new movie clip symbol, and name it **loadRectangle**. In symbol-editing mode, draw a rectangle in the center of the Stage. Use black for the stroke color and do not include a fill. Make the rectangle 100 pixels wide by 20 pixels high.

9. In Frame 1 of the Preloader layer, create a static text block. Use Arial for the font, 14 for the font size, red for the text color, and Align Left for the alignment. Place the text block about 130 pixels from the left edge of the Stage and 130 pixels from the top edge of the Stage. Type **Loading...** in the text block.

10. Drag an instance of the loadBar symbol from the Library panel to the center of the Stage right above the letter L of the Loading text. Drag an instance of the loadRectangle symbol and place it over the loadBar instance so that the small red vertical bar is just inside the left edge of the rectangle. If necessary, increase the Zoom level of the Stage to adjust the position of the rectangle.

11. Insert a keyframe at Frame 2 of the Actions layer. With Frame 2 selected, expand the Actions panel, if necessary, and type the following code. The code will check and compare the bytes loaded with the total bytes and increase the width of the small red vertical bar to fill the rectangle as the document is loaded.

```
totalBytes = getBytesTotal();
loadedBytes = getBytesLoaded();
loadBar_mc._width = loadRect_mc._width*(loadedBytes/totalBytes);
if (loadedBytes == totalBytes) {
        gotoAndPlay("Start");
    } else {
        gotoAndPlay("Preload");
    }
```

12. Test the file. Use the Simulate Download command to test the preloader. After the document loads, the first picture is displayed. The display of the other pictures will be controlled in the **Autophotos.fla** file.

13. Open the **Autophotos.fla** file located in the Tutorial.08\Cases folder included with your Data Files.

14. Insert a new layer and name it **Actions**. Select Frame 1 of the Actions layer, and, if necessary, expand the Actions panel. Type `pic_mc.loadMovie("Forsale.swf");` in the Script pane to load the **Forsale.swf** file into the empty pic_mc movie clip instance on the Stage.

15. Drag an instance of the Photo button symbol from the document's library and place it below the text block on the left side of the Stage.

Explore   16. With the button selected, expand the Actions panel, if necessary, and type the following code in the Script pane. The code controls which frame to display in the pic_mc movie clip instance, which contains the **Forsale.swf** file. Each time the button is clicked and released, the `picFrame` variable is incremented by 1 until it is equal to 6. The **Forsale.swf** file contains pictures in Frames 4, 5, and 6 of its Timeline.

```
on (release) {
    if (picFrame == 6) {
        picFrame = 4;
    } else {
        picFrame += 1;
        }
    pic_mc.gotoAndStop(picFrame);
}
```

Explore   17. Select Frame 1 of the Actions layer, and type `picFrame = 4;` below the `pic_mc.loadMovie("Forsale.swf");` line in the Script pane. This initializes the `picFrame` variable so that it starts with Frame 4 of the **Forsale.swf** Timeline.

18. Test the **Autophotos.fla** file and use the Simulate Download command to see the preloader display first. When the first vehicle picture displays, use the Next button to display the rest of the vehicle pictures.

19. Save and close the **Forsale.fla** and **Autophotos.fla** files.

Explore   **Case 4. *Adding Interactive Pages to the LAL Financial Web Site*** Elizabeth is pleased with the new Web site you developed for the company. While reviewing the Web site with Michael, the marketing director, he suggests adding interactive elements to enhance the site. As a result of their meeting, they decide that the site should have two simple calculators. The first calculator will allow the user to enter the loan amount, the number of months to pay the loan, and the yearly interest rate. The calculator will determine and display the amount of the monthly payment for the loan. The formula to determine the monthly payment is as follows.

$$\text{monthly payment} = \text{interest x amount} / (1 - (1 + \text{interest})^{-\text{months}})$$

The other calculator will determine how much someone can borrow based on the monthly payments he can afford to make, the number of months to make the payments, and the interest rate for the loan. The formula to determine the loan amount is as follows.

$$\text{amount} = \text{monthly payment}/\text{interest x} (1 - (1 + \text{interest})^{-\text{months}})$$

Elizabeth assigns you the task of developing the new pages for the Web site. You will start with a document she has developed.

If necessary, start Flash, and then do the following:

1. Open the **PaymentCalc.fla** file located in the Tutorial.08\Cases folder included with your Data Files.

2. Create an input text block to the right of the Loan Amount text. Use Garamond for the font, 14 for the font size, black for the text color, and Align Right for the alignment. Also, if necessary, select Single line from the Line type list box, and select the Show border around text button. Type **Principal** in the Variable text box, and, if necessary, type **0** in the Maximum characters text box. Place the text block about 200 pixels from the left edge of the Stage and about 160 pixels from the top edge of the Stage. Set the text block's dimensions at 80 pixels wide by 17 pixels high.

3. Create another input text block with the same properties as the one created in Step 2. Place this text block to the right of the No. of Months text at about 200 pixels from the left edge of the Stage and about 185 pixels from the top edge of the Stage. Type **Months** in the Variable text box.

4. Create one more input text block also using the same properties. Place this text block to the right of the Annual Rate text at about 200 pixels from the left edge of the Stage and about 208 pixels from the top edge of the Stage. Type **Rate** in the Variable text box.

5. Create a dynamic text block to the right of the dollar sign in the Monthly Payment text. Use the same properties as you did for the input text blocks except for the following. Use 16 for the font size and white for the text color. Deselect the Show border around text button. Make the text block about 60 pixels wide by 20 pixels high. Type **Payment** in the Variable text box.

6. Drag an instance of the Calc button from the document's Library panel to the lower-right side of the Stage. Set the button's X coordinate to 320 and its Y coordinate to 275.

7. With the button selected, expand the Actions panel, and add the on event handler with the `release` event. Insert a new line after the opening curly brace. Type the following comment. The comments will help you if you have to modify the ActionScript code at a later date.

```
// Remove any nonnumeric characters from the input values
```

8. Type the following lines after the comment. The values entered by a user might contain nonnumeric characters such as spaces. Using the `parseFloat()` and `parseInt()` functions will convert the input values to floating point numbers (decimal numbers) and integer numbers, respectively.

```
Rate = parseFloat(Rate);
Months = parseInt(Months);
Principal = parseInt(Principal);
```

9. Type the following comment and statement next. The user will enter an annual rate as a percentage. You convert it to a monthly rate by dividing it by 12 and converting it to a decimal value by dividing it by 100.

```
// Determine the monthly interest rate
MonthlyRate = (Rate/12)/100;
```

10. Type the following comment and statement next. The `Math.pow()` function uses two arguments. The first is `1 + MonthlyRate` and the second one is `-Months`. The function determines the value of raising the first argument to the power (or exponent) in the second argument. The result is placed in the variable `factor` to be used with the next part of the formula.

```
// Calculate part of the formula using the Math power function
factor = (1- Math.pow(1+MonthlyRate,-Months));
```

11. Type the following comment and statement next. The `Math.round()` function is used to round the final calculation to the nearest integer, which in this case results in a dollar amount. The result is placed in the `Payment` variable and displays in the dynamic text block.

```
// Calculate the payment; round to the nearest dollar
Payment = Math.round((MonthlyRate/factor)*Principal);
```

12. Check for syntax errors and make any necessary corrections.

13. Save the **PaymentCalc.fla** file and test it. Enter **19000** for the loan amount, **48** for the number of months, and **5** for the annual rate. Click the Calculate button. A monthly payment of 438 displays.

14. The second calculator page is similar to the first, so use the Save As command to save **PaymentCalc.fla** with the new name **AmountCalc.fla**.

15. Change the text, Loan Payment Calculator, in the title text block to **How Much Can I Afford?**. Change the Loan Amount text block to **Mo. Payment**. Select the input text to the right of Mo. Payment, and change its variable name to **Payment**.

16. Change the Monthly Payment = $ text to **You can afford $**. Select the dynamic text block to the right of this text, and change its variable name to **Amount**. Also, change the width of the text block to 80, and, if necessary, move it closer to the $.

17. Select the Calculate button and, if necessary, expand the Actions panel. Locate the statement `Principal = parseInt(Principal);`. Change the statement to `Payment = parseInt(Payment);`.

18. Locate the last statement `Payment = Math.round((MonthlyRate/factor) *Principal);`. Change the statement to **Amount = Math.round((Payment/ MonthlyRate)*factor);**. Also change the comment above this line to `// Calculate the amount; round to the nearest dollar`.

19. Check the syntax for errors, and make any necessary corrections.

20. Save the **AmountCalc.fla** file and test it. Enter **438** for the monthly payment, **48** for the number of months, and **5** for the annual rate. Click the Calculate button. An amount of 19019 displays.

21. Save and close all of the files.

QUICK | CHECK ANSWERS

Session 8.1

1. ActionScript is a programming language that allows you to make Flash documents interactive by manipulating objects.
2. True. ActionScript code can be added to a button using the Behaviors panel.
3. Actions can be added to a button instance, a frame, or a movie clip.
4. An object is an element in Flash that has properties or characteristics that can be examined or changed with ActionScript.
5. In naming button instances, it is best to add the suffix **_btn** to the names so that Flash will display code hints in the Actions panel when the names are used.
6. The expression to change the `_alpha` property of the Car_mc instance to 30 is `Car_mc._alpha = 30;`.
7. The purpose of the ActionScript statement `Amount += 5;` is to increment the value in `Amount` by 5.

Session 8.2

1. The ActionScript function to add to the button's event handler is: `getURL("http://www.course.com", _self)`.

2. Input text allows the user to enter values into the text block when the SWF file is playing in the Flash Player.

3. To limit the number of characters that can be entered in an input text block, enter a value other than 0 in the Maximum characters text box in the Property inspector.

4. With dynamic text, the Variable text box allows you to assign a variable name that can be used with ActionScript to change the value displayed in the text box.

5. The `||` operator allows the `if` statement to test for two conditions. If either condition is true, the statements in the curly braces that follow will be performed.

6. The `parseInt()` function converts a value entered into a text box to an integer.

Session 8.3

1. A preloader, located in the first few frames of a SWF file, displays a short animation or message while the rest of the file's contents load into the Flash Player. The preloader provides visual feedback to the site visitor.

2. The ActionScript function used to get the total number of bytes in a SWF file is `getBytesTotal()`.

3. You use the `_width` property to modify the width of a movie clip instance.

4. The amount of content that has loaded from a SWF file can be measured in either number of frames or number of bytes.

5. You can simulate the downloading of a SWF file within Flash by using the Download Settings command in the View menu of the Test Movie window. After you select a setting, you use the Simulate Download command found in the View menu.

OBJECTIVES

In this tutorial you will:

- Learn the basics of using digital video as it relates to Flash

- Import video into a Flash document

- Use Flash components

- Prepare Flash content for printing

USING
VIDEO, FLASH COMPONENTS, AND PRINTING

Adding Video, Revising the Photos Page, and Adding Coupons to the Jackson's Sports Web Site

CASE

Admiral Web Design

Aly and Chris meet with Dan Jackson to review the latest updates to the Jackson's Sports Web site. Now that many of the main elements of the Web site have been completed, Dan asks about adding video to his site to showcase brief video segments of local youth teams playing sports. He believes this will attract more attention to the site and will provide an incentive for his current customers to continue to visit the site and to do business with his store. He also wants to change the Photos page so that there can be more team and player photos available for viewing, and perhaps provide a list of photos for visitors to scroll through to find the photos they want to view. Finally, Dan also asks about adding a Coupons page to allow site visitors to print coupons that can be redeemed at the store.

Aly and Chris agree that these changes can be made to the site. Aly enlists your help in completing the work. You are to create a Videos page that will be used to display short video segments of a youth sports game. The page will contain buttons for starting and stopping the video. You will also modify the Photos page to add thumbnails, which are miniature views of photos, that when clicked, will expand to full size for easy viewing. Finally, you will create a page that displays coupons the visitor can print. In discussing these tasks with you, Aly and Chris suggest exploring the use of components to make these interactive elements in Flash.

Aly and Chris revise the sketch showing the storyboard with the new pages to be completed for the Jackson's Sports Web site, as shown in Figure 9-1.

Figure 9-1 | **JACKSON'S SPORTS WEB SITE REVISED STORYBOARD**

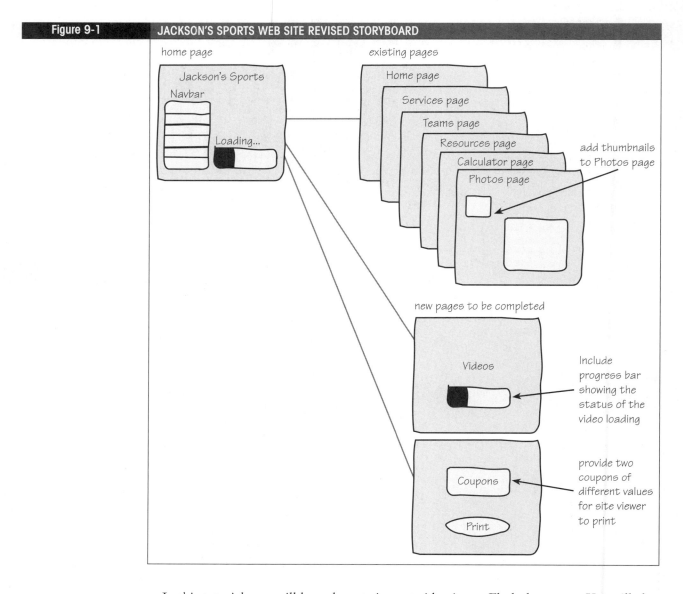

In this tutorial, you will learn how to import video into a Flash document. You will also learn how to use components to create interactive elements and how to control the printing of individual frames in a Flash document.

SESSION 9.1

In this session, you will learn the basics of digital video as it relates to Flash and you will learn how to add video to a Flash document.

Working with Video

As you have seen throughout this book, you can use a variety of multimedia elements, such as graphics, bitmaps, and sounds, in a Flash document. In addition to these elements, you can also use video in Flash. Adding video to your Web site can make your site more visually appealing and exciting. Adding video to a Flash document is a fairly straightforward process because Flash provides a wizard to guide you step-by-step as you import video.

Before you work with video in Flash, you should understand some basic terminology and concepts about how video is prepared and in what format it can be imported into Flash. You need to consider the frame size, frame rate, and file size of video files. You also need to understand that using video on your Flash Web site can significantly increase the file size of your files and, therefore, can increase a site's overall download time.

The most important part of using video in Flash has to do with the quality of the source file, which refers to the original video file with which you begin. The better the quality of the source file, the better the result when it is imported into Flash. If you use a digital camcorder to record video, the video needs to be transferred from the camcorder's media to the computer. You can also capture video directly by connecting a camcorder to a computer and recording video directly to the computer. In addition, you can also convert video from an analog format such as a VCR tape into a digital format for storing on your computer. However, whenever possible, it is best to use a digital source file. Converting from analog to digital can produce lower-quality video compared to video that is captured in digital format. Regardless of the video source, you should edit it using a video-editing program such as Adobe Premiere after it is transferred to the computer but before it is imported into Flash. Even though Flash provides some editing options when video is imported, the options are limited. A video-editing program allows you to trim unwanted parts of the video or just select part of the video depending on how you plan to use it. You can also change other attributes of the video, such as its frame rate and frame size. After you edit the video, you export it to a format that can be used in Flash.

Video Frame Rate and Frame Size

A video's **frame rate**, which is similar to the frame rate of a document in Flash, represents how many frames play each second. Video frame rates vary depending on where the video is played. For example, video played on television plays at 30 frames per second. However, video played on the Web plays at slower rates, typically varying between 10 and 15 frames per second. Frame rate also affects the size of the file. The higher the frame rate, the larger the size of the video file. For example, a 10-second video clip formatted at 30 frames per second contains 300 frames. The same 10-second video clip formatted at 12 frames per second contains 120 frames. Of course, the higher the frame rate, the better the quality of the video. Deciding on the frame rate to use is a balance between the quality of the video and the size of the file. Lowering the frame rate lowers the quality.

Some video can be played on the Web at rates of 10 or less frames per second if there is a minimal amount of movement. This could be a video of someone talking in front of the camera where there is very little motion. However, video with more movement such as children playing a sport is best played at frame rates between 12 and 15 frames per second. Another factor to consider with frame rate is the user's connection to the Internet. With a dial-up connection, high frame rates do not play well because the connection speed cannot download the frames fast enough to play smoothly on the client computer. If the user has a faster, broadband connection, higher frame rates can be supported. Another consideration is the capability of the client computer. If the user has a slow computer with minimal capabilities, the computer might not be able to support videos with high frame rates. So, it is important to consider who your intended audience is and to determine their typical connection speed and what their computer capabilities might be.

When editing video clips and preparing them for use in Flash, you should also determine what frame size to use. You can decide the frame size by considering the type of connection your users will have to the Internet and the length of your video. If you are targeting users with dial-up access to the Internet, you should limit the frame size of your videos. Typically, this is 160 pixels wide by 140 pixels high. If you know that the majority of your users have faster connections, you can set your video's frame size to 320 pixels wide by 240 pixels high.

Video Compression and Decompression

Another factor affecting the use of video over the Web is the size of the video file. The amount of data required to represent a few seconds of video can make downloading the video over the Internet a slow process. As a result, compression is used to reduce the size of the video file. Recall that compression refers to reducing the size of the file by removing redundant data. You can specify how much to compress a video when you edit it using a video-editing program. To compress video requires an encoder program, also known as a **compressor**. Before the video can be played, it has to be decompressed with a decoder program, also known as a **decompressor**. A video compressor/decompressor program is called a **codec**. Various codecs are available to work with video. Flash includes the Sorenson Spark compressor, which automatically starts when you bring video into a document. The Flash Player contains the Sorenson Spark decompressor to decompress video for playback.

Basically, two techniques are available for video compression: temporal and spatial. **Temporal compression** compares frames with adjacent frames. Keyframes are used in this compression technique. Keyframes in this context are not the same as keyframes in a Flash document's Timeline. In this instance, keyframes are specific frames in a video that are used to compare subsequent frames. A keyframe has minimal or no compression, and the surrounding frames in the video are compressed by comparing them to the keyframes. Any redundant data in the other frames is removed. Frames compressed with this technique are also known as **interframes**. When using this compression technique, you specify how many keyframes to include in a video. The more keyframes you include, the larger the resulting file size and the better the quality of the compressed video. The fewer the keyframes you include in a file, the smaller the file size and the lower the quality. Determining how many keyframes to use is often a trial-and-error process to find the right balance between file size and quality. **Spatial compression** compresses each frame independently without comparing it to other frames in the video. The result of spatial compression can mean better quality with smaller file size, but the compression process can take longer because each frame is individually compressed. Frames compressed with this technique are also known as **intraframes**. The Sorenson Spark codec in Flash uses a combination of temporal and spatial compression to reduce the size of a video file while retaining the best quality possible. Because Flash uses the Sorenson Spark codec to compress video, it is best to avoid compressing the video before bringing it into Flash. When editing the video with a video-editing program, you should export it using the least amount of compression as possible because after you bring the video into Flash it is compressed again, thus further reducing its quality.

After you edit a video clip, you export it in one of several formats. Flash accepts several different video file formats, including .mpg, .avi, and .dv. Other formats can also be used. For example, if your computer has the QuickTime plug-in installed, you can import video in the .mov format into Flash. Each video file format has different characteristics and might or might not include compression.

Embedded Versus Linked Video

After video is prepared using a video-editing program, the video can be imported into Flash. The process to import video is guided by a Video Import Wizard that is based on the Sorenson Spark codec. Two methods are available for importing video in Flash. Video is either embedded with the Flash document or linked as an external file. **Embedded video** is imported into a Flash document and becomes part of the document—similar to the way that bitmaps are imported and become part of the document. When you import a video clip, it is stored in the document's library just like bitmaps and sound files. **Linked video**, however, does not get embedded into the Flash document but instead is linked to external video files. Linked video files must be QuickTime files with the .mov extension. When you link video files with a Flash document, the document must be published as a QuickTime file and not as a SWF file. The resulting file plays using the QuickTime plug-in and not the Flash Player. The advantage to linking video files is that the published Flash document is much smaller than if the video files were embedded in it. The disadvantage is that because you cannot publish the file as a SWF file, you lose the ability to make the video file interactive.

To embed video files into a Flash document, you simply use the Import to Library or Import to Stage commands on the Import submenu. When you start the import process, the Video Import Wizard opens, as shown in Figure 9-2.

| Figure 9-2 | VIDEO IMPORT WIZARD |

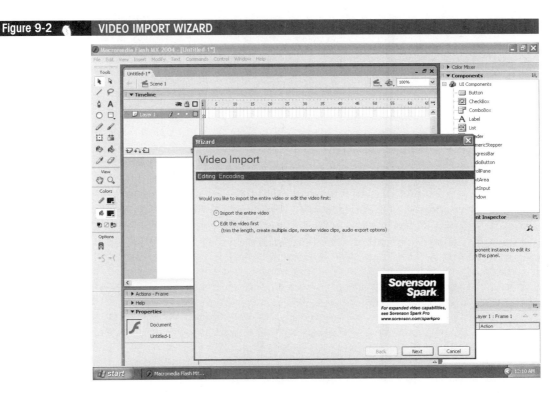

The Video Import Wizard presents a series of dialog boxes with options to import and edit the video. Depending on the type of file you are importing, the wizard presents different options. If you are importing a QuickTime movie, for example, you have the options to embed the video in the document or to link the video as an external QuickTime movie, as shown in Figure 9-3.

Figure 9-3   OPTION FOR LINKING EXTERNAL QUICKTIME VIDEO

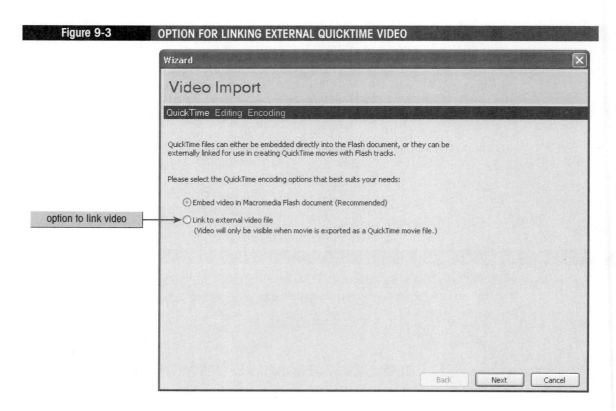

If you select to embed the file, the next dialog box allows you to specify whether to import the entire video or to edit the video first. If you choose to edit the video first, the next dialog box allows you to preview the video and either trim the beginning and ending points or to split the clip into smaller clips, as shown in Figure 9-4.

Figure 9-4   **VIDEO EDIT OPTIONS**

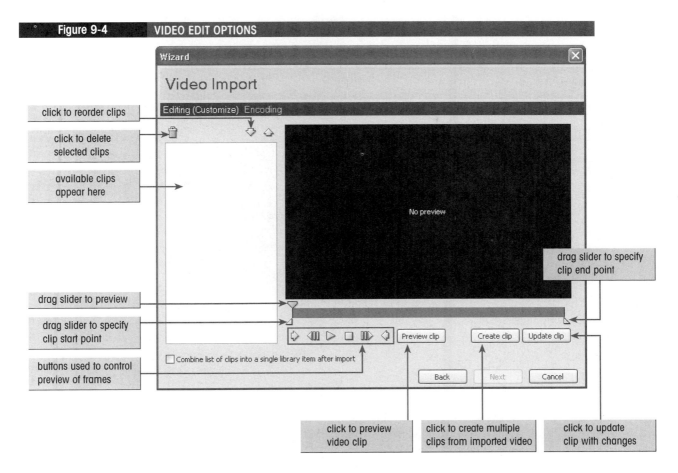

After you trim the video or create multiple clips, you are presented with options for compressing the video and for further editing the video. The Compression profile has a list of preset compression settings based on the type of connection you expect your typical site visitor will have. You can choose from a 56-kbps modem to a DSL/cable connection at 786 kbps. If you edit the Compression profile, you are presented with additional options, as shown in Figure 9-5.

Figure 9-5   **VIDEO COMPRESSION OPTIONS**

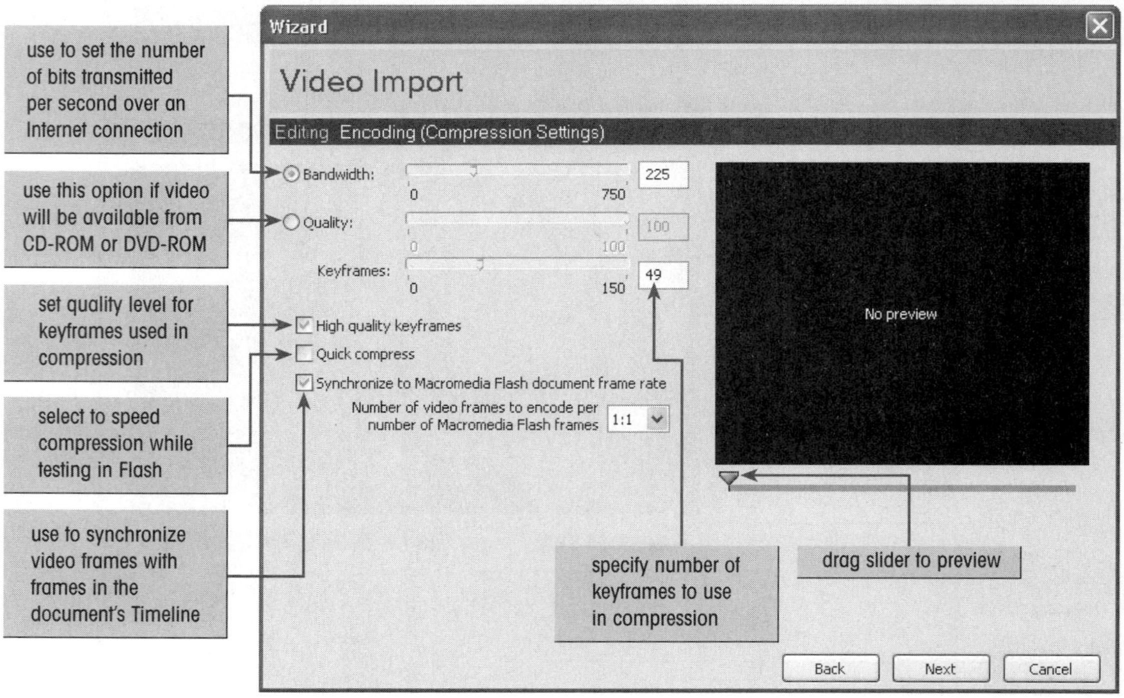

use to set the number of bits transmitted per second over an Internet connection

use this option if video will be available from CD-ROM or DVD-ROM

set quality level for keyframes used in compression

select to speed compression while testing in Flash

use to synchronize video frames with frames in the document's Timeline

Wizard

Video Import

Editing Encoding (Compression Settings)

○ Bandwidth: 0   750   225
○ Quality: 0   100   100
Keyframes: 0   150   49

☑ High quality keyframes
☐ Quick compress
☑ Synchronize to Macromedia Flash document frame rate
Number of video frames to encode per number of Macromedia Flash frames 1:1 ▾

No preview

specify number of keyframes to use in compression

drag slider to preview

Back   Next   Cancel

In this dialog box, you have the option to modify the bandwidth or quality settings. If your final file is to be downloaded over the Internet, choose the Bandwidth option button. This specifies the data rate of the file, which is the number of bits transmitted per second. If your file will be published for use from a CD and it does not have to be sent over the Internet, you can use the Quality settings. In this pane, you can also specify the number of keyframes to use in the compression process.

In addition, you can specify that the keyframes retain as much quality as possible by enabling the High quality keyframes check box. You enable the Quick compress check box to speed the compression process while you are testing the Flash document file. When you are ready to publish the final SWF file, you can deselect the Quick compress check box. Finally, in this dialog box, you can specify how the video file frames are synchronized with the frames in the Flash document. For example, a 1:1 setting means each video frame is encoded in one Flash frame. So if the video file has 100 frames, the video file occupies 100 Flash frames. If you change the compression settings in this dialog box, you can save the settings as a Compression profile so you can apply it to other videos you import.

You can also create an Advanced settings profile in which you specify color adjustments, dimensions (such as cropping), and tracking (which is where you specify the location to import the video and whether to keep the audio integrated in the video clip or to separate it). See Figure 9-6.

Figure 9-6	VIDEO ADVANCED OPTIONS

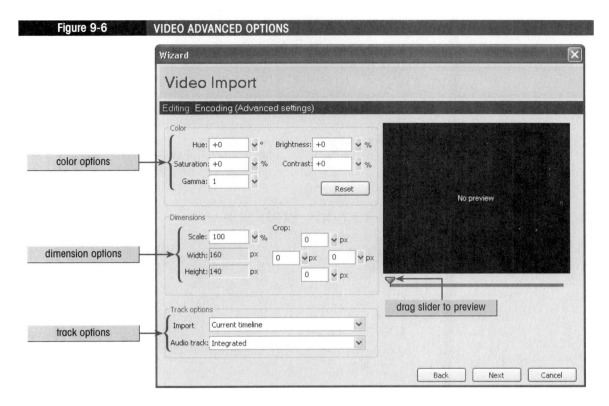

color options

dimension options

track options

After you finish making any edits to the video file, you click the Finish button, and the video is imported into the Flash document. Whether you embed or link the video to your Flash document, an entry for it appears in the Library panel. If the video is embedded, it becomes part of the document, and if it is linked, the document only contains a link to the external video file. The icon in the document's Library panel indicates if the video is embedded or linked, as shown in Figure 9-7.

Figure 9-7	VIDEO CLIPS DISPLAYED IN LIBRARY PANEL

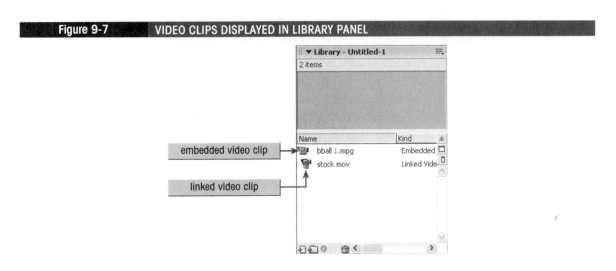

embedded video clip

linked video clip

After you embed a video file, you can create an instance of it the same way you create instances of movie clips and bitmaps. You simply drag the instance from the Library panel to the Stage. When you drag the video to the Stage, you might be prompted that the video requires more frames than are available in the Timeline. If you click the Yes button, Flash extends the Timeline the number of frames necessary to place the video frames. To have more control over the video clip in Flash, it is recommended that you place the video inside a movie clip symbol. As a movie clip symbol, you can modify the movie clip's attributes and control the video instances using ActionScript.

Now that you have learned the basic video concepts and terminology and about how to import a video into Flash, you are ready to add video to the Jackson's Sports Web site.

Adding **Video to the Jackson's Sports Web Site**

As requested by Dan, you are to add video to the Jackson's Sports Web site. Aly has prepared two short video clips of a local youth basketball game. You are to import each video clip into individual Flash documents. These documents will be published to create separate SWF files, one for each video clip. These SWF files will then be loaded into a document in the Jackson's Sports Web site. You will modify a Flash document started by Aly that will be used to display the SWF files. This document has buttons that will be used to control which video is loaded and to stop and play the videos. You will add the necessary ActionScript code to make the buttons operational.

To import video clips into Flash documents:

1. Start Flash and create a new document. Set the dimensions of the document to **160 pixels** wide by **140 pixels** high. Set the frame rate at **12** and the background color at **white**. Save the document as **Clip1.fla** in the **Tutorial.09\Tutorial** folder included with your Data Files. Set the panels to their default layout.

2. Click **File** on the menu bar, point to **Import**, and click **Import to Library**. In the Import to Library dialog box, select **All Video Formats** from the Files of type list box. Select **bball 1.mpg** from the **Tutorial.09\Tutorial** folder included with your Data Files, and then click the **Open** button. The Video Import Wizard opens.

3. Click the **Edit the video first** option button, and then click the **Next** button. The next dialog box in the wizard displays a preview window along with options to split the video into multiple clips.

4. Click the **Preview clip** button. The first time you preview, the clip loads and might not display. If necessary, click the **Preview clip** button a second time to preview the video clip. The video plays in the preview window. When the video stops playing, you notice extra areas above and below the video, as shown in Figure 9-8. You will remove the unwanted areas later in these steps. You will not be splitting this clip into multiple clips.

Figure 9-8   IMPORTING VIDEO CLIP

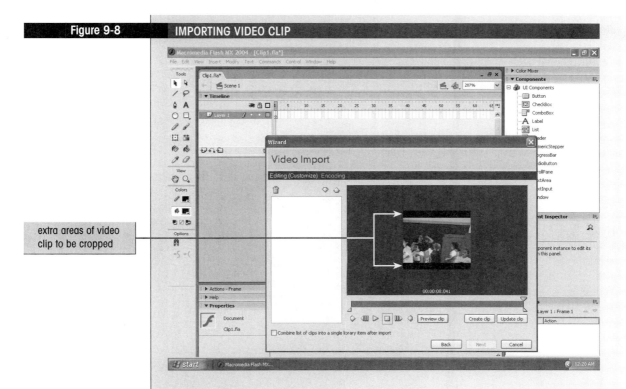

extra areas of video
clip to be cropped

5. Click the **Back** button to return to the previous dialog box in the wizard.

6. Select the **Import the entire video** option button, and then click the **Next** button. The next dialog box opens with a Compression profiles list box and an Advanced settings list box. Select **DSL/Cable 256 kbps** in the Compression profiles list box, and then click the **Edit** button to the right of the Compression profiles list box. A dialog box displaying compression settings opens.

7. Make certain the settings show Bandwidth at **225** and Keyframes at **49**. Also, if necessary, select the **High quality keyframes** check box and the **Synchronize to Macromedia Flash document frame rate** check box. Select **1:1** in the Number of video frames to encode per number of Macromedia Flash frames list box. Click the **Next** button. Then click the **Next** button again to save the settings.

8. Click the **Advanced settings** list arrow, and then click **Create new profile**. The dialog box displaying Advanced settings opens.

9. If necessary, drag the slider below the preview area to display the video. In the Dimensions section of the dialog box, enter **18** as the Crop value, as shown in Figure 9-9. The preview area displays a line indicating how the video will be cropped.

Figure 9-9   **IMPORTING VIDEO CLIP**

specify cropping value

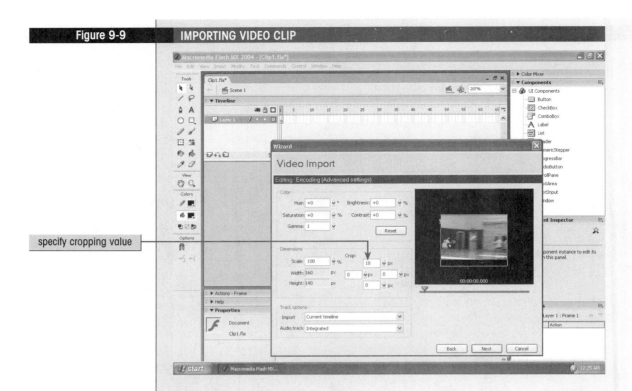

10. Drag the bottom slider for the Crop value, and also set it to **18**. Leave the Color settings and Track options unchanged. If necessary, change the options to match those shown in Figure 9-9.

11. Click the **Next** button. In the Save Settings dialog box, enter **Basketball video** in the Name text box and **Cropped 18 pixels off the top and bottom of the clip.** for the description. Click the **Next** button and then click the **Finish** button. The video is imported into the document's library.

12. Open the Library panel and click and drag an instance of the **bball 1.mpg** video clip to the center of the Stage. A dialog box opens, indicating that the Timeline span is not long enough for the number of frames in the video. Click the **Yes** button so that Flash automatically inserts the required number of frames into the Timeline. An instance of the video clip is inserted on the Stage, and Layer 1 in the Timeline extends to 95 frames.

13. Rename Layer 1 to **Video**, and insert a new layer. Name the new layer **Title**. Add a text block on the Title layer. Use the Property inspector to select **Arial** for the font, **12** for the font size, **black** for the text color, and **Align Left** for the alignment. Type **Basketball video clip #1** in the text block, and place the text block above the video clip on the Stage, as shown in Figure 9-10.

Figure 9-10 **VIDEO CLIP INSTANCE ON STAGE**

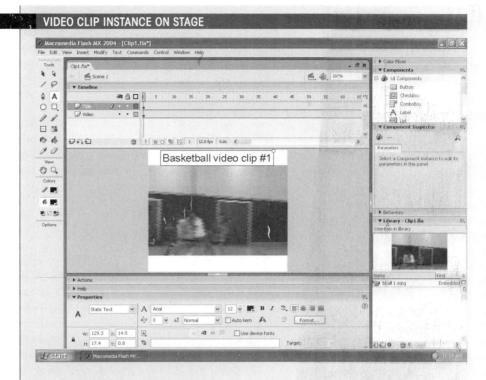

Figure 9-10   VIDEO CLIP INSTANCE ON STAGE

14. Click **File** on the menu bar, and click **Publish** to create the SWF file. Save and close the **Clip1.fla** file.

Now that you have created the Clip1.fla file, you will create another similar file with a second video clip. You will create a new document and import the second clip using the same settings as you used with the first video clip.

To create a second document with a video clip:

1. Create a new document. Set the dimensions of the document to **160 pixels** wide by **140 pixels** high. Set the frame rate to **12** and the background color to **white**. Save the document as **Clip2.fla** in the **Tutorial.09\Tutorial** folder included with your Data Files. Set the panels to their default layout.

2. Click **File** on the menu bar, point to **Import**, and click **Import to Library**. In the Import to Library dialog box, select **bball 2.mpg** from the **Tutorial.09\Tutorial** folder included with your Data Files, and then click the **Open** button. The Video Import Wizard opens.

3. Select the **Import the entire video** option button, and then click the **Next** button. Keep the Compression profile as **DSL/Cable 256 kbps**, and keep the Advanced settings as **Basketball video**. The Basketball video setting crops the video the same as the first video. Click the **Finish** button. The video is imported into the document's library.

4. If necessary, open the Library panel, and drag an instance of the video clip to the center of the Stage. A dialog box indicates that the Timeline span is not long enough for the number of frames in the video. Click the **Yes** button so that Flash automatically inserts the required number of frames, 84, into the Timeline. An instance of the video clip is inserted on the Stage, and Layer 1 in the Timeline extends to 84 frames.

5. Rename Layer 1 to **Video**, and insert a new layer. Name the new layer **Title**. Add a text block in the Title layer. Use the Property inspector to select **Arial** for the font, **12** for the font size, **black** for the text color, and **Align Left** for the alignment. Type **Basketball video clip #2** in the text block, and place the text block above the video clip on the Stage.

6. Click **File** on the menu bar, and click **Publish** to create the SWF file. Save and close the **Clip2.fla** file.

Now that the two video clips are embedded into separate Flash documents, you will modify an existing document that will be used to play the videos. The Videos.fla document created by Aly contains buttons to which you will add ActionScript code. The code will cause the buttons to load the video SWF files into a movie clip instance on the Stage of the Videos.fla file. You will also add two buttons that will be used to control the playing of the videos after they are loaded into the movie clip instance. One button will start the playing of the video, and the other button will stop the playing of the video.

To modify the Videos.fla document:

1. Open the **Videos.fla** document located in the **Tutorial.09\Tutorial** folder included with your Data Files.

2. Create a new movie clip symbol, and name it **clip_holder**. If necessary, open the symbol in symbol-editing mode. Draw a rectangle that is **160 pixels** wide by **140 pixels** high. Use the Property inspector to select **black** for the stroke and **blue (#00CCFF)** for the fill. Select both the **fill** and the **stroke** of the rectangle, and set the X and Y coordinates to **0**. Now add a text block.

3. Add a new layer and insert a fixed-width text block at the center of the rectangle. Make the text block about **125 pixels** wide. Use the Property inspector to select **Arial** for the font, **16** for the font size, **dark blue (#333399)** for the text color, and **Align Center** for the alignment. Type **Click buttons at left to view video clips.** Add an instance of the symbol next.

4. Exit symbol-editing mode and open the Library panel. Select the **Contents** layer and insert an instance of the **clip_holder symbol** in the center of the yellow rectangle on the Stage. Enter the instance name **clip_holder_mc** for the instance in the Property inspector, as shown in Figure 9-11. Add the ActionScript code to the buttons next.

Figure 9-11	MOVIE CLIP TO HOLD VIDEO

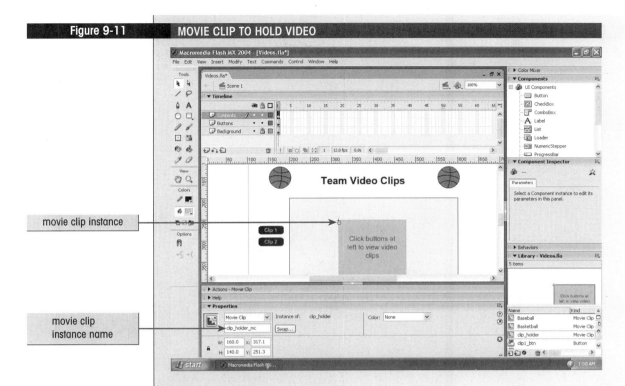

movie clip instance

movie clip
instance name

5. Select the **Clip 1** button on the Stage, and expand the Actions panel. Enter the following ActionScript code so that when the button is clicked and released, the Clip1.swf file loads into the clip_holder_mc movie clip instance on the Stage.

```
on (release) {
      clip_holder_mc.loadMovie("Clip1.swf");
}
```

6. Select the **Clip 2** button on the Stage, and then enter the following code so that clicking and releasing this button loads the Clip2.swf file into the movie clip instance.

```
on (release) {
      clip_holder_mc.loadMovie("Clip2.swf");
}
```

7. Collapse the Actions panel, click **Control** on the menu bar, and then click **Test Movie**. Click the **Clip 1** button to load the Clip1.swf file with the video clip. The video clip plays at the center of the yellow rectangle, as shown in Figure 9-12.

Figure 9-12 | VIDEO CLIP LOADED INTO MOVIE CLIP INSTANCE

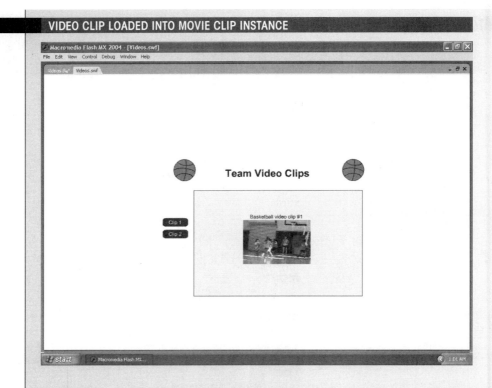

8. When you are finished testing the SWF file, click **File** on the menu bar, and click **Close** to return to the Videos.fla document.

Each video clip plays when its associated button is clicked. When a video clip plays all of its frames, it plays again from the beginning. The clip repeats continuously until another video loads into the movie clip to replace it. To allow the user to stop and play each video clip, you add new buttons. One button uses a stop() action to stop the playing of the video, and the other button uses the play() action to start the playing of the video.

To add the Stop and Play buttons:

1. Click **Window** on the menu bar, point to **Other Panels**, point to **Common Libraries**, and then click **Buttons** to open the Buttons library. Double-click the **Playback** folder icon in the Library panel to display the Playback buttons. You will add buttons from this folder of buttons to the document.

2. Select the **Buttons** layer, click and drag an instance of the **gel Stop** button from the Buttons Library panel, and place it to the left of the yellow rectangle below the Clip 2 button. Then click and drag an instance of the **gel Right** button, and place it to the right of the gel Stop instance on the Stage.

3. Select the **gel Stop** and the **gel Right** button instances on the Stage. Click **Modify** on the menu bar, point to **Align**, and then click **Top** to align the buttons horizontally.

4. Select the **gel Stop** button instance, and expand the Actions panel. Type the following code in the Actions panel. The stop() action is applied to the

Timeline of the `clip_holder_mc` instance. This causes the video clip frames to stop playing because the video clip is loaded in the movie clip instance.

```
on (release) {
        clip_holder_mc.stop();
}
```

5. Select the **gel Right** button instance, and type the following code in the Actions panel. The `play()` action causes the video clip frames to start playing.

```
on (release) {
        clip_holder_mc.play();
}
```

6. Collapse the Actions panel and test the SWF file again using the Test Movie command. This time, click the new **Stop** and **Play** buttons after a video clip has been loaded. The buttons cause the video to stop and play. Close the Flash Player window, and return to the document.

7. Save and close the **Videos.fla** file.

The Videos.fla document is now complete. You have created a Videos Web page that displays short video clips. Aly is very pleased with your work, and she tells you that this page can now be added to the Jackson's Sports Web site. She asks you to do that next.

To add the Videos page to the Jackson's Sports Web site:

1. Open the **Main.fla** document located in the **Tutorial.09\Tutorial** folder included with your Data Files.

2. If necessary, open the Library panel. Make a duplicate of the Home button, and name the duplicate **Videos button**. Edit the Videos button symbol, and change the Home text in the Text layer to **Videos**. Next, add the button to the navigation bar.

3. Open the **Navbar** symbol in symbol-editing mode. Add an instance of the **Videos** button to the bottom of the navigation bar below the Calculate button. Make certain the Videos button instance is aligned with the rest of the buttons in the navigation bar.

4. Select the **Videos** button instance, and expand the Actions panel. Enter the following code that enables the Videos button to load the Videos.swf file into level 1 of the Flash Player when it is clicked by the viewer.

```
on (release) {
        loadMovieNum("Videos.swf", 1);
}
```

5. Collapse the Actions panel and return to Scene 1.

6. Save and test the **Main.fla** document. Click the **Videos** button to load the Videos.swf file, which displays the video clips when the Clip 1 and Clip 2 buttons are clicked. Return to the **Main.fla** document and close it.

The Jackson's Sports Web site now displays video, and Aly schedules a meeting to show it to Dan Jackson.

In this session, you learned basic concepts about using video and importing it into Flash. You learned about the type of video formats you can use with Flash and about the different types of compression techniques. You also learned how to import and edit video using the Video Import Wizard in Flash. Finally, you created two Flash documents with embedded video clips and modified another document to display and control the playing of the video clips in the Jackson's Sports Web site.

Session 9.1 QUICK | CHECK

1. List three video formats that can be imported into a Flash document.

2. What is compression and what are the two types of compression techniques?

3. Which compression technique uses keyframes to compare subsequent frames in a video?

4. What is a codec?

5. Which codec is used by Flash?

6. What is the typical frame rate of video played over the Internet?

7. What are the two methods in which video can be used in Flash?

SESSION 9.2

In this session, you will learn how to use Flash components. You will create a different version of the Videos page you created in the previous session. You will use components to add a preloader for each video that is played. You will also use components to create an improved version of the Photos page for the Jackson's Sports Web site.

Using Flash Components

By now, you have seen how movie clips can make your documents more efficient. After you create a movie clip, you can make multiple instances of it and change the properties of the individual instances. You can also use ActionScript to modify a movie clip's properties when the SWF file plays in the Flash Player. Using movie clips also helps reduce the overall size of the SWF file because only one copy of the movie clip is stored with the file regardless of how many instances you create. This efficiency is taken a step further with the use of components. **Components** are prebuilt movie clips with parameters that you change using the Property inspector or the Component Inspector panel. A set of user interface components is installed with Flash. These components are actually compiled movie clips with a .swc extension, which reside in a folder where Flash is installed. You can add more components by downloading them from Web resources, such as the Flash Exchange, which is accessible from the Help menu. **Flash Exchange** is a Macromedia Web site with resources for Flash developers. You can also purchase components from other sources, such as *www.flashcomponents.com*. Downloaded components are installed using the Extension Manager, which is also accessible through the Help menu. You can even create your own components by compiling a movie clip using the menu options on the Library panel's Options menu.

The components installed with Flash can be used to create user interface elements in your documents. For example, the CheckBox component allows you to create check boxes that can be used as options from which a viewer can select on a form. When the user selects a check box, a check mark appears in the check box. This information can then be processed using ActionScript. Using a component such as the CheckBox means you do not have to create the graphics and functionality that is already built in to the component. The Flash components are located in the Components panel, as shown in Figure 9-13.

Figure 9-13	FLASH COMPONENTS

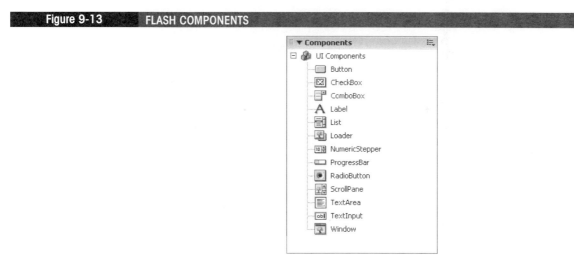

The components are described in Figure 9-14.

Figure 9-14	FLASH COMPONENTS LOCATED IN THE COMPONENTS PANEL

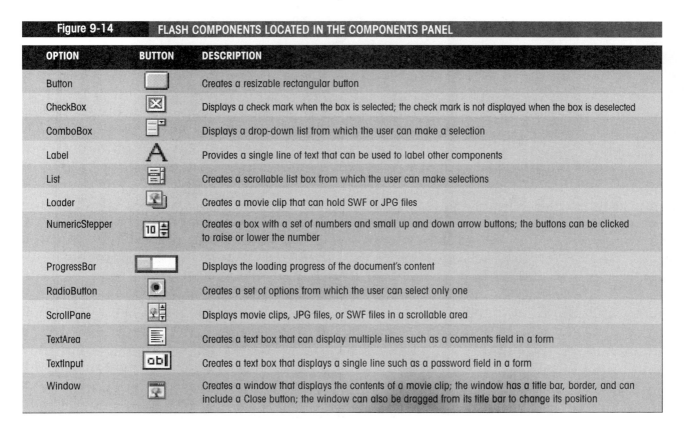

OPTION	BUTTON	DESCRIPTION
Button		Creates a resizable rectangular button
CheckBox		Displays a check mark when the box is selected; the check mark is not displayed when the box is deselected
ComboBox		Displays a drop-down list from which the user can make a selection
Label		Provides a single line of text that can be used to label other components
List		Creates a scrollable list box from which the user can make selections
Loader		Creates a movie clip that can hold SWF or JPG files
NumericStepper		Creates a box with a set of numbers and small up and down arrow buttons; the buttons can be clicked to raise or lower the number
ProgressBar		Displays the loading progress of the document's content
RadioButton		Creates a set of options from which the user can select only one
ScrollPane		Displays movie clips, JPG files, or SWF files in a scrollable area
TextArea		Creates a text box that can display multiple lines such as a comments field in a form
TextInput		Creates a text box that displays a single line such as a password field in a form
Window		Creates a window that displays the contents of a movie clip; the window has a title bar, border, and can include a Close button; the window can also be dragged from its title bar to change its position

Components are added to a document by simply dragging an instance of the component from the Components panel to the Stage. When you create an instance of a component, its compiled movie clip is automatically added to the document's library. Then, you can add additional instances of the same component by dragging them from the Library panel to the Stage. After you create an instance, you can assign it a name and view or change its parameters using either the Property inspector or the Component Inspector panel. The Component Inspector panel might contain additional parameters not shown in the Property inspector. The available parameters vary based on the particular component. For example, the ComboBox component has the parameters shown in Figure 9-15.

Figure 9-15   COMBOBOX COMPONENTS

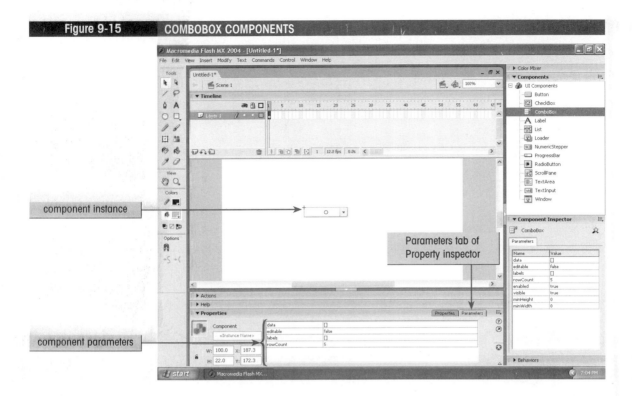

Some parameters are set by selecting from a set of options, whereas other parameters require you to enter data in a text field. Some parameters require you to enter data in a separate dialog box such as the values for the labels of a combo box, as shown in Figure 9-16.

Figure 9-16   COMBOBOX LABELS DIALOG BOX

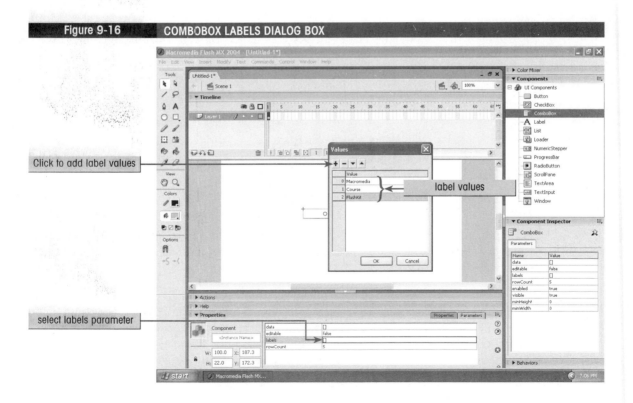

In Figure 9-16, the plus sign button is clicked to enter a new label value. The values entered in the dialog box display in the combo box, as shown in Figure 9-17.

Figure 9-17   PUBLISHED COMBOBOX WITH LABELS

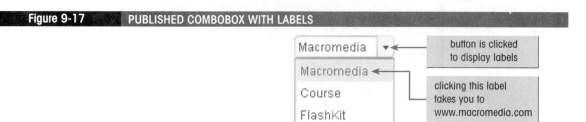

The ComboBox component also has a data parameter; the values for the data are entered in the same manner as the label values. Each data value is associated with a label value based on the order it is listed. For example, the Macromedia label in Figure 9-17 can be associated with the URL *www.macromedia.com* if it is entered as the first data value.

After you set a component's parameters, you need to write ActionScript to program how Flash responds to selections the user makes with the components, or to manipulate the properties of the components. For example, in the ComboBox instance, the user can select from one of the options listed in the label parameter. To detect when the user has made a selection, you use the on event handler just like you do to detect when a button event has occurred. In the ComboBox example, you can check for the change event, as shown in the following code.

```
on (change) {
        getURL(value);
}
```

In this case when a change occurs in the ComboBox selection, the `getURL()` function is called using the `value` property of the ComboBox. The `value` property represents the value in the data parameter that coincides with the entry in the label parameter that the user selected. If the first item, Macromedia, is selected from the combo box, the first data value, `www.macromedia.com`, is sent to the `getURL()` function, and the Macromedia Web site is opened in the Web browser window.

Now that you have learned about some of the Flash components and how they can be used, you will add two components to the Jackson's Sports site, a ProgressBar component and a Loader component.

Using the ProgressBar and Loader Components

The ProgressBar component makes it easy to create a preloader with a minimal amount of ActionScript. The ProgressBar component can receive progress information from other components, such as the Loader component, and use that information to display a progress bar animation as well as a number representing how much of the content has been loaded, as shown in Figure 9-18.

Figure 9-18   SAMPLE PROGRESSBAR COMPONENT

The ProgressBar parameters in the Property inspector are shown in Figure 9-19.

Figure 9-19   PROGRESSBAR PARAMETERS

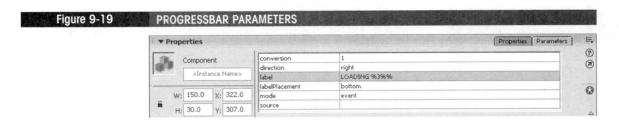

The parameters are described in Figure 9-20.

Figure 9-20   PROGRESSBAR PARAMETERS AND THEIR DESCRIPTIONS

PARAMETER	DESCRIPTION
conversion	A number that is used to divide the current bytes loaded and total bytes loaded displayed in the label parameter; the default value is 1
direction	The direction in which the progress bar fills; the default value is right
label	The text displayed in the ProgressBar instance; placeholders are used to represent the current bytes loaded (%1), the total bytes loaded (%2), and the percent of content loaded (%3)
labelPlacement	The position the label is placed in relation to the progress bar; the default value is bottom
mode	The mode of the progress bar; possible modes are event (the default), polled, and manual; the mode determines how the progress bar gets the values used to display the loading progress; in event mode, the progress bar uses the `progress` and `complete` events emitted by the source of the loading content such as another component; in polled mode, the progress bar uses the `getBytesLoaded` and `getBytesTotal` methods of the source object; in manual mode, you program the values to use with ActionScript code
source	The instance name of the source whose progress is being monitored by the progress bar

You can use the ProgressBar component together with the Loader component to display the progress of loading content, such as a SWF file, into the Loader instance. A SWF file can be loaded into the Loader instance, while the ProgressBar displays the progress of the loading. For the ProgressBar to detect the loading of the content in the Loader component, you first assign the Loader instance a name in the Property inspector. Then, you enter this name as the source parameter for the ProgressBar instance. This establishes a connection between the two components. The Loader component, which is used to load SWF and JPG files, has the parameters shown in Figure 9-21.

Figure 9-21   LOADER PARAMETERS

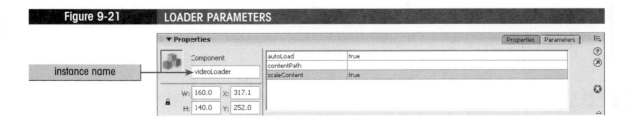

The parameters are described in Figure 9-22.

Figure 9-22	THE LOADER COMPONENT PARAMETERS

PARAMETER	DESCRIPTION
autoLoad	Indicates whether the content should load automatically (true) or should wait until the Loader's `load()` method is called (false); the default is true
contentPath	Indicates the file to load into the Loader instance
scaleContent	Indicates whether the content should scale to fit the size of the Loader instance (true) or whether the Loader instance should scale to fit the size of the content (false); the default is true

The contentPath parameter can either be set in the Property inspector or by using ActionScript. With ActionScript, you can determine which file to load into the Loader instance based on a user selection. You will use the ProgressBar and Loader components to modify the Videos page for the Jackson's Sports Web site.

Creating a Different Version of the Videos Page

Aly has met with Dan Jackson and showed him the Videos page you created in the previous session. He was pleased with the new Web page, but he expressed concern that the videos might take longer to download over a slow dial-up Internet connection, and that this might prove frustrating to site visitors. To address Dan's concerns, Aly instructs you to create a new Videos page with a preloader using the ProgressBar component, which will display the downloading progress as each video loads into the Flash Player. Because the ProgressBar component can monitor the loading of content in the Loader component, you will create an instance of the Loader component into which the videos will be displayed. The published SWF files that contain the video clips will be loaded into the Loader component based on the user's selection. The visitor will select which video to use by clicking either the Clip 1 or Clip 2 buttons. The ActionScript in the button instances needs to be changed so that when the button is clicked and released, the content of the Loader changes. To do this, you set the contentPath parameter using ActionScript code in the button instances. The code for the Clip 1 instance is as follows.

```
on (release) {
    videoLoader.contentPath ="clip1.swf";
}
```

In this code, videoLoader is the name of the Loader instance and `contentPath` is the name of the parameter that specifies which file to load into the Loader. The `clip1.swf` file contains the first video clip. When this statement is executed, the `clip1.swf` file begins to load into the `videoLoader` instance. You will create a new version of the Videos page next.

To create a new Videos page using components:

1. If you took a break after the last session, start Flash, and then open the **Videos2.fla** file located in the **Tutorial.09\Tutorial** folder included with your Data Files. Set the panels to their default layout.

2. Select the **Contents** layer, click and drag an instance of the **Loader** component from the Components panel, and place it at the center of the yellow rectangle on the Stage.

3. Click the **Parameters** tab in the Property inspector to display the available parameters for the Loader component. Enter the name **videoLoader** in the Instance
Name text box. Set the width of the Loader component to **160 pixels** and the
height to **140 pixels**. If necessary, reposition the instance so it remains centered in
the rectangle. Use the default parameters of **true** for autoLoad and scaleContent.
Leave the contentPath parameter empty. Next create the preloader.

4. Drag an instance of the **ProgressBar** component from the Components panel,
and place it below the videoLoader instance on the Stage. Note that the
videoLoader instance disappears from the Stage. The instance is still on the
Stage, but it is not visible because it is currently empty.

5. On the Parameters tab in the Property inspector, enter **videoProgress** in the
Instance Name text box. Use the default parameters for the ProgressBar
instance, and ensure that the mode is set to **event**. Then type **videoLoader** in
the source parameter text box. See Figure 9-23.

Figure 9-23	PROGRESSBAR INSTANCE AND PARAMETERS

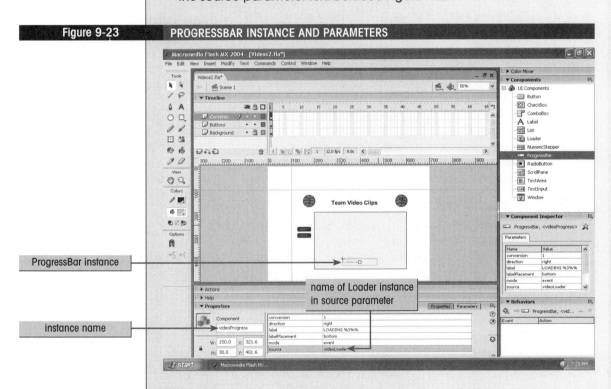

6. Select the **Clip 1** button on the Stage, and expand the Actions panel. Enter the
following code in the Actions panel. This causes the first video clip to load into
the videoLoader component when the button is clicked and released.

```
on (release) {
        videoLoader.contentPath ="Clip1.swf";
}
```

7. Collapse the Actions panel and select the **Clip 2** button on the Stage. Expand
the Actions panel and enter the following code for this button.

```
on (release) {
        videoLoader.contentPath ="Clip2.swf";
}
```

8. Collapse the Actions panel, click **Control** on the menu bar, and click **Test Movie** to test your document. In the Flash Player window, click **View** on the menu bar, point to **Download Settings**, and then click **DSL (32.6 KB/s)** to set a download speed. Click **View** again and click **Simulate Download**. When the buttons appear, click the **Clip 1** button. The progress bar fills as the percent of content loaded displays. The audio portion of the video begins playing before the video begins to play, and when the preloader reaches 100%, the video starts playing as well.

9. Test the second video clip by clicking the **Clip 2** button. The content starts to load as the preloader shows the progress of the loading. After it has loaded, the video clip starts to play.

10. Click **File** on the menu bar, and click **Close** to return to the Videos2.fla document.

Notice this new version of the Videos page does not contain Stop and Play buttons for the viewer to use to control the playing of the video. To add these buttons to the page, you will copy the Stop and Play buttons from the first Videos page you created in the previous session—the Videos.fla file.

To copy the Stop and Play buttons from the Videos.fla file:

1. Open the **Videos.fla** document located in the **Tutorial.09\Tutorial** folder included with your Data Files. Simultaneously select both the **gel Stop** and **gel Right** buttons on the Stage. Click **Edit** on the menu bar, and then click **Copy**.

2. Switch back to the Videos2.fla document, click **Edit** on the menu bar, and click **Paste in Place**. The buttons are now on the Stage in the Videos2.fla file. Now, you need to change the code for these buttons.

3. Deselect the button instances and then select the **gel Stop** button instance. Expand the Actions panel and then replace the second line of the code with `videoLoader.content.stop();`. The `stop()` action is applied to the content of the `videoLoader` component. This causes the video clip frames to stop playing. Next, change the code for the Play button.

4. Collapse the Actions panel and select the **gel Right** button instance. Expand the Actions panel and change the second line of the code to `videoLoader.content.play();`. The `play()` action causes the video clip frames to start playing.

5. Collapse the Actions panel and test the SWF file again using the Test Movie command. Click the **Clip 1** button to load the video clip. After it has loaded and started playing, click the **Stop** and **Play** buttons to see how they control the playing of the video. Close the Flash Player window, and return to the document.

The preloader is now complete. You used the ProgressBar component to show the progress of the video clips loading into the Loader component. You notice, however, that the ProgressBar stays visible on the Stage after the clips have loaded. Aly asks you to hide the ProgressBar after a clip has loaded because it might be distracting to the user viewing the video. To do this, you need to add ActionScript code to Frame 1 of the document's Timeline. You need to change the visibility of the videoProgress instance after the loading of the content in the Loader instance is complete. The videoProgress instance has a `_visible` property that can be set to `false` to hide the instance. To know when to change the `_visible` property of the videoProgress instance, you need to create a listener function and register it with the videoLoader instance. A **listener** is an object or function that can respond to an event emitted by another component.

Components emit events that can be listened to by other components. For example, an instance of the Loader component emits two events, `complete` and `progress`. When loading is taking place in the Loader instance, the `progress` event is triggered. When the loading is complete, the `complete` event is triggered. To respond to one of these events, you must register a listener object with the instance of that component. When the component emits the event, the listener object or function is notified. To register a listener with an instance of a component, you use the `addEventListener()` method. For example, the code `videoLoader.addEventListener("complete", contentLoaded);` registers the `contentLoaded` function to listen for the `complete` event of the `videoLoader` instance. You will add this code to the Videos2.fla document and create the `contentLoaded` function next.

To use the listener function to hide the ProgressBar when the video loading is complete:

1. Insert a new layer above the Contents layer, and name it **Actions**. Select **Frame 1** of the Actions layer.

2. Expand the Actions panel and type the following ActionScript code.

   ```
   videoLoader.addEventListener("complete", contentLoaded);
   ```

   The `contentLoaded` function is defined using the `function` keyword followed by the name of the function. You then place the function statements inside a pair of curly braces. In this case, you only need one statement in the function. The statement sets the `_visible` property of the `videoProgress` instance to false, which hides the progress bar.

3. Press the **Enter** key and then type the following code in the Actions panel to define the `contentLoaded` function.

   ```
   function contentLoaded() {
       videoProgress._visible = false;
   }
   ```

   The function will be executed when the `videoLoader` instance emits the `complete` event. The ActionScript should look like that in Figure 9-24.

Figure 9-24   FRAME ACTIONSCRIPT CODE

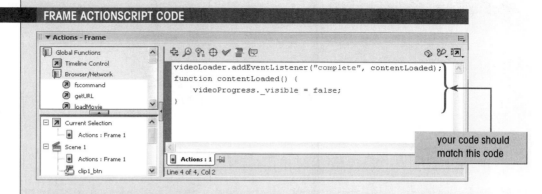

4. Collapse the Actions panel and test your file using the Test Movie command on the Control menu. Click the **Clip 1** button to load the first video clip. Notice that after a video clip is loaded, the ProgressBar instance does not display.

5. Close the SWF file and return to the document. Save and close the **Videos2.fla** file. Also, close the **Videos.fla** file.

The new version of the Videos page using components is now complete. Aly thinks Dan Jackson will be happy with this version of the Videos page, which includes a preloader animation to show the progress of the videos loading into the Loader component. Now, you will create a new version of the Photos page for the Jackson's Sports Web site using the ScrollPane component to display thumbnails of the photos available for viewing.

Using the ScrollPane Component on the Photos Page

The Photos page you created in a previous tutorial used individual buttons that the user clicks to display a picture. This worked fine for two or three pictures, but as more pictures are added, adding more buttons for the new pictures is impractical because you do not want to crowd too many buttons on one page. In addition, having buttons that all look the same does not give the user any idea of what the picture is about. As a result, Aly suggests you use the ScrollPane component to display the pictures as thumbnails. The ScrollPane component displays movie clips, SWF files, or JPG files in a scrollable area. Depending on the parameter settings, the ScrollPane can automatically display scroll bars if the content is larger than the ScrollPane. An example of a ScrollPane is shown in Figure 9-25.

| Figure 9-25 | SCROLLPANE COMPONENT EXAMPLE |

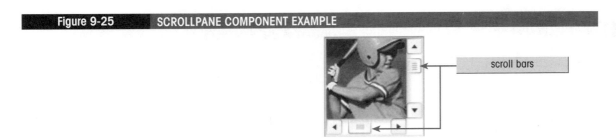

The parameters for the ScrollPane are shown in Figure 9-26.

| Figure 9-26 | SCROLLPANE PARAMETERS |

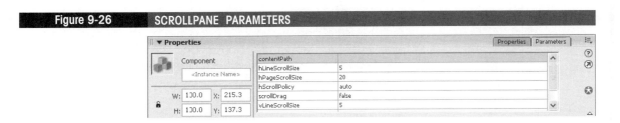

The parameters displayed in the Property inspector are described in Figure 9-27.

| Figure 9-27 | SCROLLPANE PARAMETERS AND THEIR DESCRIPTIONS |

PARAMETER	DESCRIPTION
contentPath	Indicates the content to load into the ScrollPane instance
hLineScrollSize	Indicates the number of units the horizontal scroll bar moves when you click the scroll bar arrows
hPageScrollSize	Indicates the number of units the horizontal scroll bar moves when you click the scroll bar track
hScrollPolicy	Specifies if the horizontal scroll bars will display as needed (auto), display always (on), or not display (off)
scrollDrag	If set to true, allows the content in the ScrollPane instance to be dragged by the user; the default is false
vLineScrollSize	Indicates the number of units the vertical scroll bar moves when you click the scroll bar arrows
vPageScrollSize	Indicates the number of units the vertical scroll bar moves when you click the scroll bar track
vScrollPolicy	Specifies if the vertical scroll bars will display as needed (auto), display always (on), or not display (off)

The ScrollPane component can be used to display a movie clip with thumbnails of the pictures. These thumbnails can be buttons that (when clicked) display the full-size version of the picture in a Loader component. Using these components gives you more control over how the picture is displayed, and you can easily add more pictures without having to change the size of the ScrollPane that displays the thumbnails. You will create the new Photos page next.

To add a ScrollPane component and a Loader component to the Photos page:

1. Open the **Photos.fla** file located in the **Tutorial.09\Tutorial** folder included with your Data Files. Set the panels to their default layout. You will start by creating a ScrollPane instance to hold the thumbnails.

2. Click and drag an instance of the **ScrollPane** component from the Components panel, and place it inside the yellow rectangle. Place it about 200 pixels from the top edge of the Stage with its left side even with the left edge of the yellow rectangle.

3. On the Parameters tab of the Property inspector, click **auto** in the hScrollPolicy parameter text box, and then click the list arrow and select **off** so that no horizontal scroll bars will display. Next, create a Loader instance to display the pictures.

4. Click and drag an instance of the **Loader** component from the Components panel, and place it at the center of the yellow rectangle on the Stage to the right of the ScrollPane instance. On the Parameters tab in the Property inspector, enter the name **picLoader** in the Instance Name text box. Change the width to **280** and the height to **250**. Use the default parameters of **true** for autoLoad and scaleContent. Leave the contentPath parameter empty.

5. If necessary, reposition the Loader instance so that it remains to the right of the ScrollPane and is centered in the rectangle, as shown in Figure 9-28.

Figure 9-28	SCROLLPANE AND LOADER INSTANCES

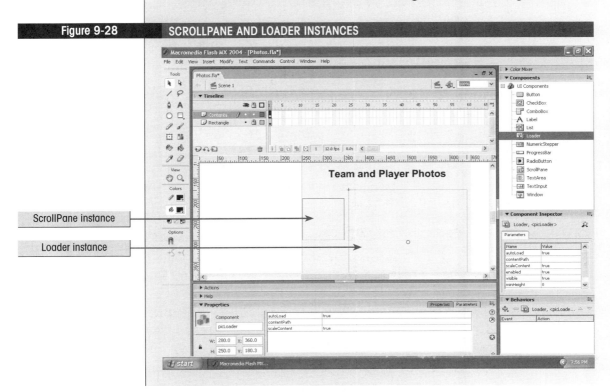

The ScrollPane and Loader components are added to the document. Next, you will create the thumbnails.

To create the thumbnails:

1. Create a new movie clip symbol, and name it **thumbnails**. In symbol-editing mode, draw a rectangle at the center of the Stage. Use the Property inspector to select **green (#00FFCC)** for the fill, and do not use a stroke. Make the rectangle **85 pixels** wide by **165 pixels** high. Enter **0** for both the X and Y coordinates. Rename Layer 1 to **Rectangle**. Next, import the images to be used for the thumbnails that Aly has provided.

2. Click **File** on the menu bar, point to **Import**, and click **Import to Library**. In the Import to Library dialog box, select **All Image Formats** from the Files of type list box. Select the **photo1_sm.jpg** and **photo2_sm.jpg** files located in the **Tutorial.09\Tutorial** folder included with your Data Files. Click the **Open** button to import the bitmaps into the document's library. Create the thumbnails.

3. Insert a new layer and name it **Thumbnails**. Open the document's Library panel, click and drag an instance of **photo1_sm.jpg**, and place it on the top part of the green rectangle, as shown in Figure 9-29.

Figure 9-29 THUMBNAIL MOVIE CLIP

4. Drag an instance of **photo2_sm.jpg**, and place it on the lower half of the rectangle. Next, convert the thumbnails into buttons.

5. Select the **top picture** and convert it to a button symbol. Name the symbol **pic1_btn**. Select the **bottom picture**, convert it to a button symbol, and name it **pic2_btn**. Next, add ActionScript to the buttons.

6. Click the **pic1_btn** instance and expand the Actions panel. Type the following ActionScript in the Actions panel.

```
on (release) {
    _root.picLoader.contentPath="Photo1.jpg";
}
```

When a thumbnail button is clicked and released, you want the thumbnail's associated picture to be loaded into the Loader instance, picLoader. To do this, you need to set the Loader's contentPath parameter. The second statement in the preceding code assigns the Photo1.jpg file name to the contentPath parameter and causes the file to be loaded into the picLoader instance. Because picLoader is in the main Timeline and not in the thumbnails movie clip Timeline, you need to include the _root keyword. The _root keyword specifies that the picLoader instance is located in the document's main Timeline.

7. Click the **pic2_btn** button instance, and type the following code in the Actions panel.

```
on (release) {
        _root.picLoader.contentPath="Photo2.jpg";
}
```

8. Collapse the Actions panel and click the **Scene 1** link in the Address bar to return to the main Timeline. Save the file.

You now have the thumbnails movie clip with buttons that load the photos into the Loader instance on the Stage. However, the ScrollPane instance does not yet have anything in its contentPath parameter. The thumbnails movie clip should display in the ScrollPane, so you could enter the name of the movie clip in the contentPath parameter. However, for the movie clip to load into the ScrollPane when the SWF file is played in the Flash Player, you need to establish a link between the ScrollPane instance and the movie clip. To establish this link, you click the Advanced button in the Symbol Properties dialog box for the movie clip, and select the Export for ActionScript check box in the Linkage section, as shown in Figure 9-30.

Figure 9-30	SYMBOL PROPERTIES ADVANCED OPTIONS

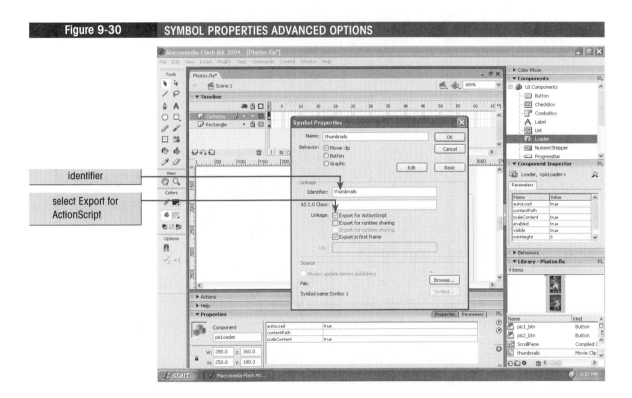

When you select this check box, the symbol name is entered into the Identifier text box. This identifier provides a link between the movie clip symbol and the ScrollPane instance when you enter it as the ScrollPane's contentPath parameter. You will add this identifier to the thumbnails movie clip.

To add the linkage identifier to the thumbnails movie clip:

1. In the document's Library panel, select the **thumbnails** movie clip. Click the **Properties** button 🔘 in the Library panel. The Symbol Properties dialog box opens.

2. Click the **Advanced** button and then click the **Export for ActionScript** check box to select it. Make certain that **thumbnails** displays in the Identifier text box. Click the **OK** button.

3. If necessary, select the **ScrollPane** component on the Stage. On the Parameters tab of the Property inspector, type **thumbnails** in the contentPath parameter text box, and press the **Enter** key. The link between the movie clip and the ScrollPane is now set. Next, test the file.

4. Use the Test Movie command to test your file. The ScrollPane displays the thumbnails. Click each of the two thumbnail pictures to see the larger photos display in the Loader component, as shown in Figure 9-31.

Figure 9-31	REVISED PHOTOS PAGE

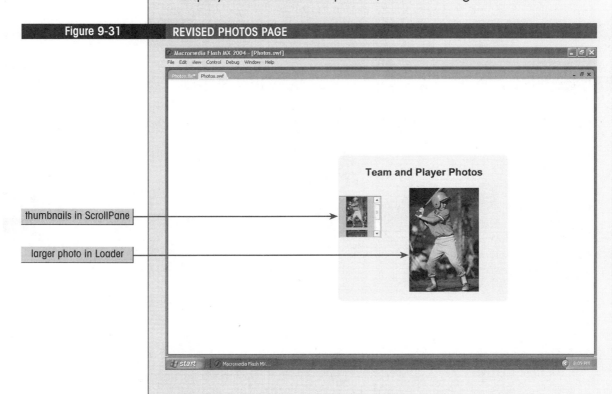

thumbnails in ScrollPane

larger photo in Loader

TROUBLE? If your computer does not have Flash Player version 7 or later, the components will not display properly. Install the most current player from the Macromedia Web site.

5. Close the Flash Player file, and return to the document.

6. Save and close the **Photos.fla** file.

You have completed and tested the new Photos page that uses components to display the player photos for the Jackson's Sports Web site.

In this session, you learned about components and how to use them in your Flash documents. You used the ProgressBar, Loader, and ScrollPane components along with ActionScript to create new versions of the Videos and Photos pages. In the next session, you will learn how to make specific content on a Flash Web site printable.

Session 9.2 QUICK CHECK

1. What is a Flash component?

2. Which component can be used to display a list of options in a drop-down list?

3. Which parameter do you set in the ProgressBar component to monitor the loading of content in a Loader component instance named `myLoader`?

4. What is the purpose of the following statement?
   `myLoader.addEventListener("complete", contentLoaded);`

5. Which parameter in the ScrollPane component is used to set whether to display the horizontal scroll bars?

SESSION 9.3

In this session, you will learn how to make content in Flash printable. You will create a Coupons page for the Jackson's Sports Web site that will contain coupons a visitor can print.

Creating **Printable Content**

The graphics and animations you create with Flash are meant to be displayed on computer screens and are usually not designed to be printed on paper. As is often the case, however, the visitor might decide to print part of the Web site. You can print the content of a Web site in two basic ways. One method is to use the Web browser's Print command; the other method is to use the Flash Player's Print command, if available. The Print command in the Flash Player can be disabled when the document is published. When the Web browser's Print command is used, the content currently displayed in the Web page prints. However, if the content of the SWF file is designed to occupy most of the width of the computer screen, it is possible that part of the content will be truncated, or cut off. This is because the layout of the computer screen is in landscape orientation, which means it is wider than it is tall. The printed page, however, is usually in portrait orientation, which means it is taller than it is wide and is meant to fit on a standard 8 ½ by 11 inch sheet of paper. Therefore, the result might be that part of the screen content will get truncated, as shown in Figure 9-32.

Figure 9-32   **PAGE CONTENT TRUNCATED WHEN PRINTED FROM BROWSER**

note area truncated on printout

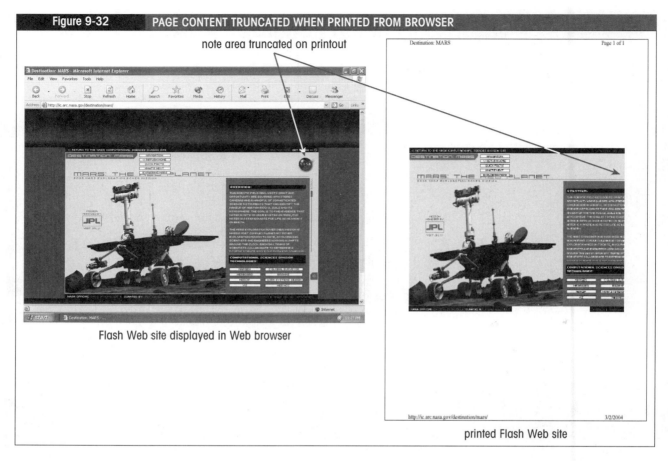

Flash Web site displayed in Web browser

printed Flash Web site

Instead of using the Web browser's Print command, the user can use the Flash Player's Print command available from a context menu. The context menu is displayed by right-clicking the SWF file content displayed on the Flash Player, as shown in Figure 9-33.

Figure 9-33   **FLASH PLAYER CONTEXT MENU**

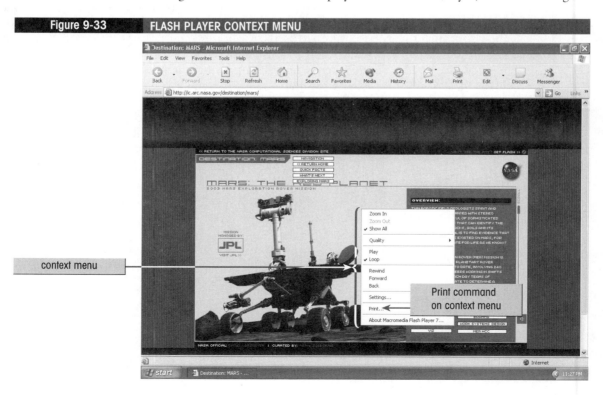

context menu

Print command on context menu

When the context menu is used to print the Flash Web site, the user can specify that only the current selection be printed. Doing so prints the currently displayed frame of the SWF file. If the user specifies that all contents be printed, then all of the frames of the SWF file print. This might not be the desired result because a SWF file might contain a long animation with many frames, such as the example shown in Figure 9-34.

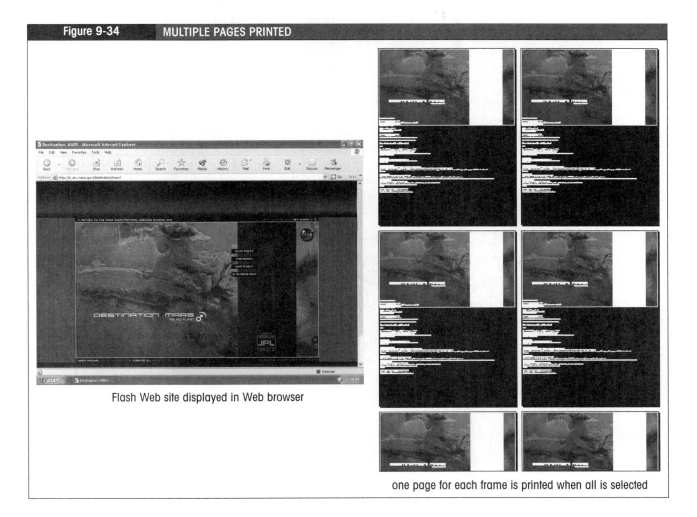

Figure 9-34   **MULTIPLE PAGES PRINTED**

Flash Web site displayed in Web browser

one page for each frame is printed when all is selected

Rather than letting the Web browser or the Flash Player control the printing of a SWF file, it is often better to design your Flash document so that specific frames are made available for printing. You can also allow the whole Stage to be printed or specify that only part of the Stage prints. You can then provide a button for the user to click to print specific elements of the Web site and, thus, keep the user from getting frustrated with undesirable print results. Depending on the site requirements. you can design certain parts of the Web site specifically for printing. For example, a store Web site might want to place a map of the store's location on the Web site. The map can be designed to print on a standard sheet of paper. Or, a store might want to include a coupon on its Web site that the user can print and redeem at the store. Making content printable involves using one of several ActionScript Print commands. You also need to decide which frames will be selected to print, and what part of the Stage area will be printed.

Controlling Printing

The ActionScript `print()` and `printAsBitmap()` functions can be used to control printing within the Flash Web site as it plays in the Flash Player. You can specify certain frames in a SWF file as printable, whereas other frames might display but not print. You can design a particular frame specifically for printing and create a button with the `print()` function that the user can click to print the frame. The `print()` function causes the user's Print dialog box to display and only the frames marked for printing to print.

The basic format of the `print()` function is `print(target, "bounding box");`, where `target` specifies the location of the frames to print. This function is designed to print frames that exist in the main Timeline or in movie clips. You can also print frames in loaded SWF files. The `bounding box` argument determines how much of the Stage area to print. By default, the size of the document's Stage determines the area to be printed. However, you can change this using one of three options for the bounding box. These include `"bmovie"`, `"bframe"`, and `"bmax"`. When you use `"bmovie"`, you designate one frame in the document to contain an object whose bounding box is used to determine the print area. The contents of this frame do not print. The bounding box of an object is a rectangular area determined by the shape of the object, as shown in Figure 9-35.

Figure 9-35	BOUNDING BOX

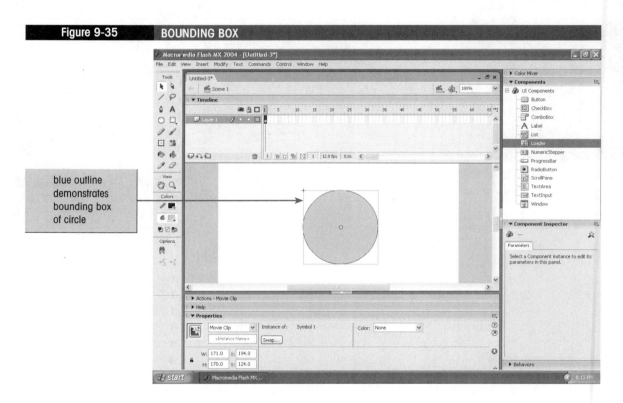

blue outline demonstrates bounding box of circle

Every frame that prints determines what area of its content to print based on the bounding box of the object in the one designated frame. When you use the `"bframe"` argument, the print area of each frame is determined by the bounding box of the frame's content. Flash determines the maximum size rectangle for each frame based on the contents of the frame.

Use the `"bframe"` setting when the content in each frame varies in size and you want the contents for each frame to fill the entire page. The third option for the bounding box is `"bmax"`. With this option, the print area is determined by comparing all of the frames to be printed and finding the maximum bounding box to fit all of the frames. When you use `"bmax"` for the bounding box, all of the frames printed are proportionally scaled to each other. The `printAsBitmap()` function works similarly to the `print()` function but is used when the contents to be printed contain transparency or color effects that require a pixel-by-pixel representation as opposed to a vector representation.

The following script shows an example of the `print()` function used to print the frames of a movie clip instance named `ball_mc`. The print area is determined by the contents in each frame of the movie clip to be printed.

```
on (release) {
      print(ball_mc, "bframe");
}
```

The next example prints the frames in the document's main Timeline, which is indicated by the 0 for the target argument. If the target argument does not refer to a movie clip instance, frames in the document's main Timeline are printed. The print area is determined by the largest bounding box based on the content of all the frames to be printed.

```
on (release) {
      print(0, "bmax");
}
```

You can also use the `printNum()` and `printAsBitmapNum()` functions to print Flash content. These functions work similarly to the `print()` and `printAsBitmap()` functions but are used to print the content of a SWF file loaded at a different level in the Flash Player. For example, the following script prints the contents of the SWF file loaded at level 1 using the "`bmovie`" bounding box option.

```
on (release) {
      printNum(1, "bmovie");
}
```

By default, all frames in a Timeline print. To avoid printing all of the frames, you can make selected frames printable by using frame labels. Add the label #p to any frame you want to print. Recall that frame labels are added to a specific frame using the Property inspector. If you add #p to one or more frames, only those specified frames print. All other frames do not print. When you issue the `print()` function, only those frames with the #p label print. You can also disable the Print command from the Flash Player context menu by adding the frame label !#p to any frame in the Timeline. Another frame label associated with printing is the #b label. You use the #b label in conjunction with the "`bmovie`" bounding box argument in the `print()` function. Recall that the "`bmovie`" argument means that one frame is designated as containing an object whose bounding box is used to determine the print area. The frame that contains this object is identified using the #b label. The frame with the #b label does not print.

Based on Aly's instructions, you are to create a Coupons page that will allow the user to print two coupons for Jackson's Sports. You will do that next.

Creating a Coupons Page for Jackson's Web Site

Recall from Aly's instructions that Dan has requested two coupons be added to the Jackson's Sports Web site. One coupon will be for 10% off any item in the store. The second coupon will be for $5 off any sale item worth more than $20. Each of the coupons will be available for anyone to print and redeem at the store. Aly has started creating the Coupons page, and she asks you to complete it by creating the printable coupons in separate documents, and then creating buttons to load the published SWF files with the coupons. She asks you to also include a button the visitor can click to print the coupons.

To create the buttons for the Coupons page:

1. If you took a break after the last session, start Flash and then open the **Coupons.fla** file located in the **Tutorial.09\Tutorial** folder included with your Data Files. Set your panels to their default layout.

2. Draw a rectangle below the text blocks. Make the rectangle **280 pixels** wide by **150 pixels** high. Use the Property inspector to select **yellow (#FFFFCC)** for the fill color, and do not include a stroke. Place the rectangle about **260 pixels** from the left edge of the Stage and about **240 pixels** from the top edge of the Stage.

3. Insert a new layer above the Contents layer, and name it **Buttons**. On this layer, draw a small rectangle with rounded corners below the second text block and to the right of the vertical guide. Make the rectangle **70 pixels** wide by **25 pixels** high, and use **10** for the corner radius points. Use the Property inspector to select **blue (#0099CC)** for the fill color and **black** for the stroke color. Place the rectangle about **150 pixels** from the left edge of the Stage and about **250 pixels** from the top edge of the Stage. Next, enter text in the rectangle.

4. Change the Stage magnification level to **100%**. Create a static text block inside the rectangle. Use the Property inspector to select **Arial** for the font, **12** for the font size, and **black** for the text color. Also, use **Align Left** for the alignment. Type **Coupon 1**. Reposition the text, if necessary, so that it is centered inside the rectangle, as shown in Figure 9-36.

Figure 9-36   **COUPON BUTTON**

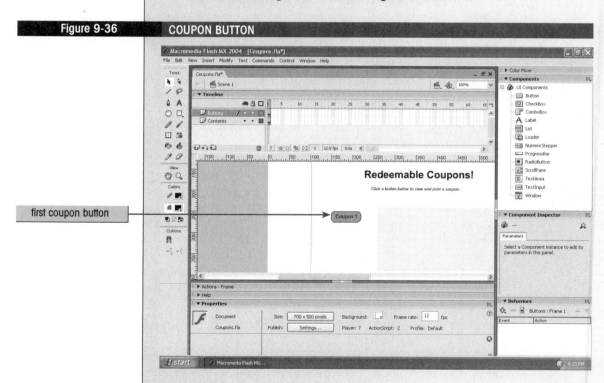

first coupon button

5. Select the **rectangle** and the **text block** inside the rectangle at the same time. Convert the selection to a button symbol, and name the symbol **Coupon1_btn**.

6. Open the Library panel and right-click the **Coupon1_btn** symbol. Click **Duplicate** to create a duplicate of the symbol. Name the duplicate **Coupon2_btn**. Modify the duplicate.

7. Place the **Coupon2_btn** symbol in symbol-editing mode, and then change the text to **Coupon 2**. Exit symbol-editing mode.

8. On the Buttons layer, add an instance of the **Coupon2_btn** symbol to the Stage and place it below the first button. Position this button instance about **150 pixels** from the left edge of the Stage and **280 pixels** from the top edge of the Stage.

9. Click **Window** on the menu bar, point to **Other Panels**, point to **Common Libraries**, and click **Buttons**. In the Buttons Library panel, double-click the **Ovals** folder. If necessary, scroll down to see the contents of the folder. Click and drag the **Oval buttons – blue** symbol and place it below the yellow rectangle. Place the button about **380 pixels** from the left edge of the Stage and **400 pixels** from the top edge of the Stage.

10. Create a static text block right below the Oval buttons – blue instance on the Stage. Use the Property inspector to select **Arial** for the font, **12** for the font size, and **black** for the text color. Also, use **Align Left** for the alignment. Type **Print Coupon** in this text block. Create a holder for the coupon files.

11. Create a new movie clip symbol, and name it **Holder**. Do not enter anything into the movie clip. Exit symbol-editing mode and place an instance of the **Holder symbol** on the Contents layer. Position the instance about **280 pixels** from the left edge of the Stage and **260 pixels** from the top edge of the Stage, as shown in Figure 9-37.

Figure 9-37	EMPTY MOVIE CLIP TO HOLD COUPON SWF FILES

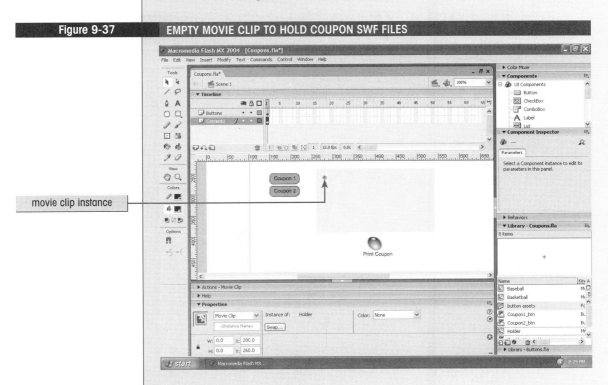

movie clip instance

12. Assign the name **Holder_mc** to the movie clip instance. Save the **Coupons.fla** file.

You have created the buttons and a Holder movie clip to display the coupons. Before you add the ActionScript code to make the buttons operational, you will create the documents with the coupons. Each coupon will be in a separate document. The published SWF files for the coupon documents will then be loaded into the Holder movie clip instance. Each coupon document will contain the coupon graphic in a separate frame, which will have the #p label. This is the frame that will be printed. There will also be a separate frame with a rectangle that will represent the bounding box to use for printing. This frame will have the #b label. Both of these frames will not be displayed. Instead, the first frame will contain a smaller version of the coupon, which will display in the Holder_mc movie clip instance of the Coupons page. You will create the individual coupon documents next.

To create the first coupon document:

1. Create a new document **300 pixels** by **300 pixels** and save it as **Coupon1.fla** in the **Tutorial.09\Tutorial** folder included with your Data Files. Change the Layer 1 name to **Labels**. Insert two more layers. Name one **Coupon** and the other **Actions**. Select the **Coupon** layer and insert a keyframe at **Frame 5**. Insert another keyframe at **Frame 6**.

2. Draw a rectangle in Frame 5 of the Coupon layer. This rectangle will serve as the outline for the coupons to be printed. Use the Property inspector to select **no fill**, **black** for the stroke color, **2** for the stroke height, and a **dashed line** for the stroke style. Be certain to use square corners for the rectangle. Make the rectangle about **560 pixels** wide by **250 pixels** high, and position it so that its upper-left corner is near the upper-left corner of the Stage. The rectangle extends beyond the Stage and into the Work Area, as shown in Figure 9-38. Create the coupon text next.

Figure 9-38	COUPON OUTLINE

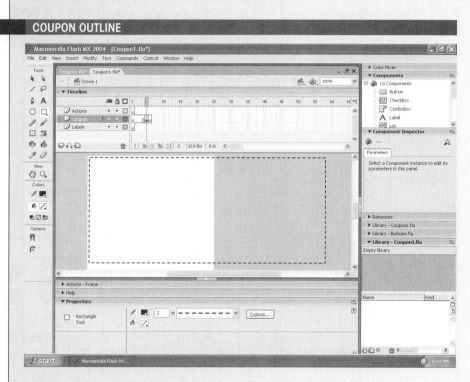

3. Create a static text block centered at the top of the rectangle. Use the Property inspector to select **Arial** for the font, **red** for the text color, and **32** for the font size. Apply the **Bold** and **Italic** styles, and use **Align Left** for the alignment. Type **Jackson's Sports Center** and center the text block at the top of the rectangle.

4. Create a static text block at the center of the rectangle. Use the Property inspector to select **Arial** for the font, **black** for the text color, and **20** for the font size. Apply the **Bold** style and use **Align Center** for the alignment. Type **This coupon is worth**, and then press the **Enter** key to create a new line. Type **10% off** and press the **Enter** key. Change the font size to **14**, type **any item in the store**, and center the text block, as shown in Figure 9-39.

Figure 9-39	COUPON TEXT

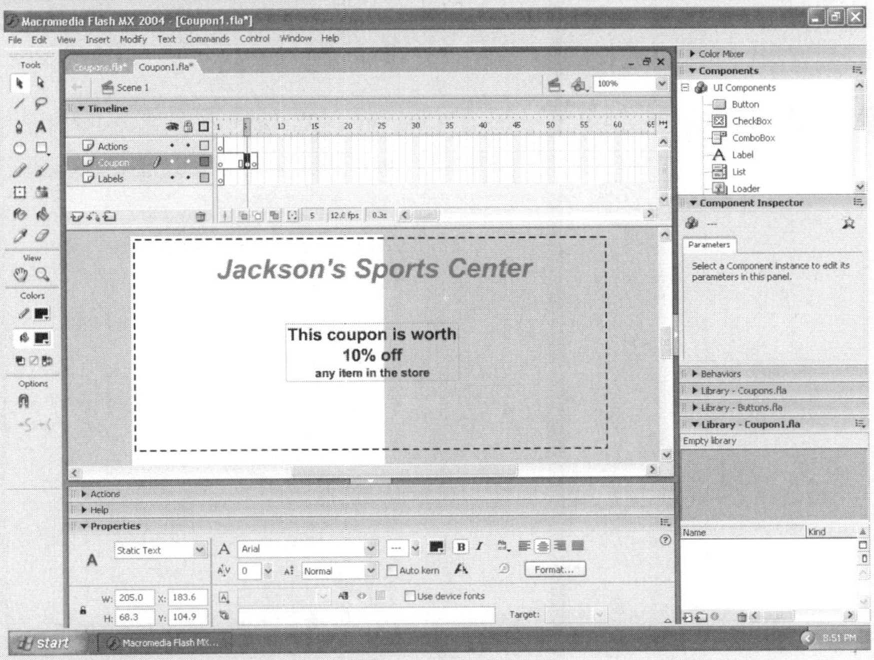

5. Create one more static text block centered at the bottom of the rectangle. Use the Property inspector to select **Arial** for the font, **black** for the text color, and **10** for the font size. Use **Align Left** for the alignment. Type **Redeem this coupon at our store**. Next, add the baseball symbol to the coupon.

6. If necessary, expand the **Library – Coupons.fla** Library panel. Click and drag an instance of the **Baseball** symbol to the left side of the Jackson's Sports Center title in the coupon. Drag another instance of the **Baseball** symbol to the right side of the title.

7. Click **Edit** on the menu bar, and click **Select All** to select the entire coupon. Click **Modify** on the menu bar, and click **Convert to Symbol**. In the Convert to Symbol dialog box, name the symbol **Coupon**, and select **Movie clip** as its behavior type. Click the **OK** button.

The coupon is now complete. Next, you need to create a rectangle in Frame 6 that the `print()` function will use as the bounding box to determine the area of the frame to print. You also need to create a small version of the coupon in Frame 1 that will display when the coupon document loads into the Coupons page.

8. Select **Frame 6** of the Coupon layer. Draw a large rectangle about **580 pixels** wide by **270 pixels** high. Use **black** for the fill, and do not include a stroke. Position the rectangle so that its upper-left corner is at the upper-left corner of the Stage. This rectangle does not display, it is only used as the bounding box for the print area. Create the displayed coupon next.

9. Select **Frame 1** of the Coupon layer. If necessary, expand the document's Library panel. Click and drag an instance of the **Coupon** symbol to the Stage. Select the **Free Transform** tool [▦], and then select the **Scale** modifier [▨]. Drag a corner handle to reduce the size of the coupon so that its width is about **200 pixels**. Reposition the coupon to the upper-left side of the Stage, as shown in Figure 9-40.

| Figure 9-40 | SMALL VERSION OF COUPON THAT WILL DISPLAY |

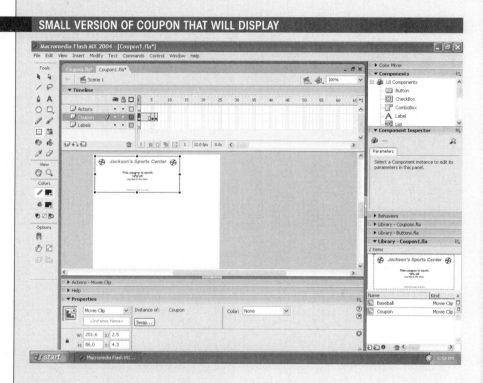

Next, create the frame labels and place a `stop()` action to prevent all of the frames from playing.

10. Insert a keyframe at **Frame 5** of the Labels layer. Enter **#p** for the frame label in the Property inspector. Insert another keyframe at **Frame 6** of the Labels layer. Enter **#b** for its frame label.

11. Select **Frame 1** of the Actions layer, and expand the Actions panel. Type `stop()` in the Actions panel, and collapse the panel. Publish the SWF file next.

12. Save the document. Click **File** on the menu bar, and click **Publish** to create the SWF file.

You have completed the first coupon file. The second coupon file will be the same as the first one except that the second coupon will be for $5 off any sale item of $20 or more. Aly suggests you copy the first coupon file to create the second coupon file. Then, all you need to do is modify the Coupon movie clip in the copied file. You will do this next.

To create a copy of the Coupon1.fla file for the second coupon:

1. Select **File** on the menu bar, and click **Save As**. Enter **Coupon2.fla** as the name of the file. Make certain the file is saved in the **Tutorial.09\Tutorial** folder included with your Data Files.

2. Open the **Coupon** movie clip in symbol-editing mode. Change the color of the title text block at the top to **blue**. Change the center text block by replacing **10%** with **$5**. Also, change the last line in this text block to **any sale item of $20 or more**.

3. Delete the two instances of the **Baseball** symbol instance from the Stage. If necessary, expand the Coupons.fla Library panel, click and drag an instance of the **Basketball** symbol, and place it to the left side of the title text. Drag another instance of the **Basketball** symbol, and place it to the right side of the title text. Exit symbol-editing mode.

4. Save the **Coupon2.fla** document, and then publish it to create the SWF file. Close the file.

The two coupon files are now complete and have both been published as SWF files. Now, you will return to the Coupons.fla file and add the ActionScript to the buttons to make them functional. The Coupon 1 and Coupon 2 buttons will load the respective SWF files into the Holder_mc movie clip instance. When a SWF file is loaded, its Frame 1 will display the smaller version of the coupon. The Print button will then print the coupon located in Frame 5 of the SWF file using the "bmovie" option that specifies the `print()` function using the frame with the #b label as the bounding box for the print area. The rectangle in Frame 6 of the SWF file has the frame with the #b label as the bounding box. You will complete the Coupons.fla file next.

To add functionality to the buttons in the Coupons.fla file:

1. In the Coupons.fla file, select the **Coupon 1** button instance on the Stage, and expand the Actions panel. Type the following code in the Actions panel.

```
on (release) {
      Holder_mc.loadMovie("Coupon1.swf");
}
```

This code loads the Coupon1.swf into the Holder_mc movie clip instance.

2. Collapse the Actions panel and select the **Coupon 2** button instance. Expand the Actions panel and enter the following ActionScript code so that the button causes the Coupon2.swf file to load into the Holder_mc movie clip instance.

```
on (release) {
      Holder_mc.loadMovie("Coupon2.swf");
}
```

The Print Coupon button will have the `print()` function to print the contents of the Holder_mc movie clip using the "bmovie" option.

3. Collapse the Actions panel and select the **Print Coupon** button on the Stage. This button contains the `print()` function. Expand the Actions panel and enter the following ActionScript code.

```
on (release) {
        print(Holder_mc, "bmovie");
}
```

Collapse the Actions panel. The buttons now have the code needed to make them functional. Test the file next.

4. Test the file using the Test Movie command. Click the **Coupon 1** button to load the first coupon. The coupon displays over the yellow rectangle. If your computer is connected to a printer, click the **Print Coupon** button. The first coupon prints on one page. Test the **Coupon 2** button to display the second coupon. Click the **Print Coupon** button to print the second coupon.

5. Close the Coupons.swf file and return to the document. Save and close the Coupons.fla file.

The Coupons.fla document is now complete. You have created a Coupons page that displays coupons and allows the site visitor to print one of two coupons. Aly is pleased with your work and instructs you to add this Coupons page to the Jackson's Sports Web site. You will do that next.

To add the Coupons page to the Jackson's Sports Web site:

1. Open the **Main.fla** document located in the **Tutorial.09\Tutorial** folder included with your Data Files.

2. If necessary, open the Library panel. Make a duplicate of the **Home** button, and name the duplicate **Coupons button**. Edit the **Coupons button** symbol, and change the Home text in the Text layer to **Coupons**. Add the button to the navigation bar next.

3. Place the **Navbar** symbol in symbol-editing mode. Add an instance of the **Coupons** button to the bottom of the navigation bar, placing it below the Videos button. Make certain the Coupons button instance is aligned with the rest of the buttons in the navigation bar. Next, add ActionScript code to the Coupons button to make it functional.

4. Select the **Coupons** button instance, and expand the Actions panel. Enter the following code so that the Coupons button loads the Coupons.swf file into level 1 of the Flash Player.

```
on (release) {
        loadMovieNum("Coupons.swf", 1);
}
```

5. Collapse the Actions panel and then click the **Scene 1** link in the Address bar. Save and test the **Main.fla** document. See Figure 9-41.

Figure 9-41   **FINAL COUPON PAGE LOADED IN MAIN WEB SITE**

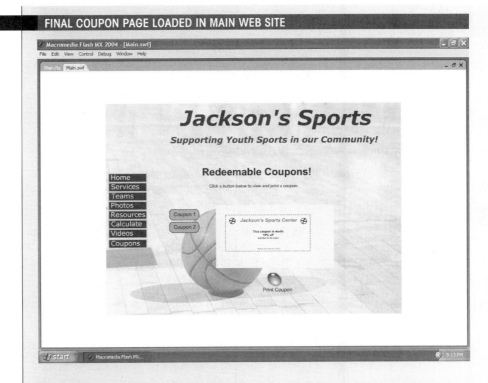

6. Click the **Coupons** button to load the Coupons.swf file, which displays the buttons for the two coupons. Click each of the two coupon buttons. The coupons display and can be printed using the Print Coupon button.

7. Return to the **Main.fla** document, and close the file.

The Coupons page for the Jackson's Sports Web site is now complete and allows site visitors to print coupons. Aly will share the completed Web site with Dan Jackson at their next meeting. She is confident he will be pleased with the finished site.

In this session, you learned about printing Flash content. You learned about the `print()` function and its options for designating the area of the Stage to be printed. You also learned how to specify which frames in the document should print. You created the Coupons page and the associated files for the coupons, and you added the Coupons page to the Jackson's Sports Web site.

Session 9.3 QUICK CHECK

1. What are two methods of printing Flash content?

2. With the `print()` function, which argument do you use when you have placed an object in a frame whose bounding box will be used to determine the print area?

3. What frame label do you use to mark a frame that is printable?

4. What frame label do you use to mark a frame containing an object whose bounding box determines the print area?

5. What frame label do you use to disable printing from the Flash Player context menu?

REVIEW ASSIGNMENTS

The Web site you have created for Jackson's Sports was well received by the staff of Admiral Web Design when it was presented at a staff meeting. Everyone was very impressed by the interactive elements of the Web site. Aly is very happy with your work, but she asks that you add a third video to the Videos page, one more photo to the Photos page, and one more coupon to the Coupons page.

If necessary, start Flash and then do the following:

1. Open the **Videos2.fla** document located in the Tutorial.09\Tutorial folder included with your Data Files. Save the file with the same name in the Tutorial.09\Review folder included with your Data Files.

2. Create a duplicate of the Clip 1 button and name it **clip3_btn**. Edit the button to change the Clip 1 text to **Clip 3**. Add an instance of the clip3_btn to the Stage on the Buttons layer. Place the button below the Clip 2 button. If necessary, move the Stop and Play buttons down.

3. Select the Clip 3 button on the Stage and add the following ActionScript code for the button:

```
on (release) {
        videoLoader.contentPath ="Clip3.swf";
}
```

4. Create a new document with the dimensions 300 pixels by 300 pixels. Save the document as **Clip3.fla** in the Tutorial.09\Review folder included with your Data Files.

5. Import the **bball3.mpg** file into the library. The file is located in the Tutorial.09\Review folder included with your Data Files. Embed the video into the document, and import the entire video. Use DSL Cable 256 kbps for the Compression profile. If necessary, select a profile for the Advanced settings. Do not change the Color settings, and do not crop this video.

6. After you import the video, create an instance of it on the Stage allowing Flash to add the number of frames needed in the Timeline. Reduce the size of the instance to 80% of its original size. Rename Layer 1 to **Video**. Insert a new layer and name it **Title**. On the Title layer, add a static text block. Use Arial for the font, 12 for the font size, and black for the text color. Type **Basketball video clip #3** in the text block. Save, publish, and close the file.

7. Test the **Videos2.fla** file to see that the basketball video displays when the Clip 3 button is clicked. Close the **Videos2.fla** file.

8. Open the **Photos.fla** file located in the Tutorial.09\Tutorial folder included with your Data Files. Save the file with the same name to the Tutorial.09\Review folder.

9. Import the **photo3_sm.jpg** file located in the Tutorial.09\Review folder included with your Data Files. Place the file in the document's library. Edit the thumbnails movie clip symbol. Change the height of the green rectangle to 250 pixels. Drag an instance of the **photo3_sm.jpg** bitmap to the Stage, and place it below the second picture and within the green rectangle.

10. Convert the **photo3_sm.jpg** instance on the Stage to a button symbol. Name the button **pic3_btn**. Add the following ActionScript code to the button instance.

```
on (release) {
        _root.picLoader.contentPath="Photo3.jpg";
}
```

11. Test the **Photos.fla** file to make certain the third photo displays. Save and close the file.

12. Open the **Coupons.fla** file located in the Tutorial.09\Tutorial folder included with your Data Files. Save the file with the same name to the Tutorial.09\Review folder.

13. Create a duplicate of the Coupon1_btn symbol and name it **Coupon3_btn**. Modify the Coupon3_btn symbol and change the text to **Coupon 3**. Add an instance of the Coupon3_btn symbol to the Stage, and place it below the Coupon 2 button.

14. Select the Coupon 3 button and add the following ActionScript code to the button instance.

```
on (release) {
        Holder_mc.loadMovie("Coupon3.swf");
}
```

15. Open the **Coupon1.fla** file located in the Tutorial.09\Tutorial folder included with your Data Files. Save it as **Coupon3.fla** in the Tutorial.09\Review folder.

16. Edit the Coupon symbol and change the title text color to dark green (#006600). Also, change the middle text block. Change its center line to **30% off** and its third line to **any clearance item in the store**.

17. Save and publish the **Coupon3.fla** file.

18. Test the **Coupons.fla** file to make certain the third coupon displays and prints. Save and close the **Coupons.fla** file.

CASE PROBLEMS

Case 1. Creating a New Cake Decoration Page for Sandy's Party Center Web Site The Flash Web site you created for Sandy's Party Center has been very well received by Sandy and her staff. In a meeting with John, Sandy mentions that they will be having a new promotion soon about their cake decorating classes. She asks if the Cake Decorating page could be changed to help in this promotion. In particular, she wants the ability to add more links to Web sites about cake decorating without cluttering the page with individual buttons. She also wants to add a coupon for $15 off the cost of one of the classes that can be printed and redeemed at her store. John tells her that the changes can be made, and he also suggests adding a picture showing a decorated cake as an example of what customers can learn by taking a cake decorating class. She likes the idea and asks John to make the changes.

John meets with you to discuss the new requests and asks you to add the new elements to the Cake Decorating page for the Web site. He instructs you to add a picture he acquired of a cake. You are to have the picture show through an oval mask. He also instructs you to use components for the links to cake decorating Web sites. Finally, you will create a coupon that the site visitor can print.

If necessary, start Flash and then do the following:

1. Open the **Cake.fla** file located in the Tutorial.09\Cases folder included with your Data Files.

2. Import the **Cake.jpg** bitmap into the document's library.

3. In Scene 1 of the document, add a new layer above the Background layer and name it **Cake**. On this layer, place an instance of the Cake.jpg bitmap on the right side of the pink rectangle. Use the Transform panel to reduce the size of the Cake.jpg instance to about 75% of its original size, making certain to reduce the size proportionally. If necessary, reposition the instance so that it is inside the pink rectangle and near the right edge of the rectangle.

4. Insert a new layer and name it **Mask**. Draw an oval on this layer of about 170 by 130 pixels. Use black for the fill color, and do not include a stroke color. Place the oval directly on top of the Cake.jpg bitmap. Convert the Mask layer into a mask layer. The Cake layer should also be converted into a masked layer. Both layers should be locked, and the cake shows through the oval mask.

Explore ▶

5. Insert a new layer and name it **Links**. Drag an instance of the ComboBox component from the Components panel to the left side of the pink rectangle. Change the width of the component to 200 pixels. Change its X coordinate to 155 and its Y coordinate to 275. Double-click the square brackets in the data parameter in the Property inspector to open the Values dialog box. Use **http://www.cakemag.com/** for the first data value and **http://www.pastrywiz.com/cakes** for the second data value for the ComboBox component.

6. Double-click the square brackets in the labels parameter, and then enter **American Cake Decorating** for the first label parameter and **Pastry Food Resource Center** for the second label parameter. Leave the editable parameter at false and the rowCount at 5. With the ComboBox instance still selected, expand the Actions panel and type the following code that will cause the selected Web site to open in a new browser window.

```
on (change) {
        getURL(value, "_blank");
}
```

Explore ▶

7. Drag an instance of the Label component from the Components panel to the Stage, and place it above the ComboBox component. Change the width of the instance to 200 pixels. Change the text parameter for the instance to **Select a cake decorating site below**.

8. Insert a new layer and name it **Button**. Draw a small rectangle with round corners, and place it in the lower-left side of the pink rectangle. Use 10 for the corner radius points, orange (#FF9900) for the fill color, and black for the stroke. Make the rectangle 60 pixels wide by 20 pixels high. Select the entire rectangle and convert it to a button symbol. Name the symbol **Coupon_btn**.

9. Edit the Coupon_btn symbol and add a keyframe in the Over frame. In this frame, change the fill color to blue (#00CCFF). Add a new layer and name it **Text**. Create a static text block in the center of the rectangle. Use Comic Sans MS for the font, 8 for the font size, and black for the text color. Use Align Left for the alignment. Type **Print Coupon** in the text block. If necessary, center the text block within the rectangle. You will add the ActionScript for the button in a later step.

10. Create a new movie clip symbol, and name it **Coupon**. In symbol-editing mode, draw a rectangle at the center of the Stage using pink (#FF99CC) for the fill color and black for the stroke color. Select a dotted line for the stroke style, and use a stroke height of 2. Select the rectangle and change its width to 500 pixels and its height to 300 pixels. If necessary, change its X and Y coordinates to 0. Rename Layer 1 to **Background**, and lock the layer.

11. Insert a new layer and name it **Graphics**. Add an instance of the confetti symbol in the upper-left corner of the rectangle. Add another instance of the confetti symbol in the upper-right corner. Add an instance of the balloon symbol in the lower-left corner of the rectangle. Add another instance of the balloon symbol in the lower-right corner. Add an instance of the Scissors symbol, and place it on the lower-left side of the rectangle so that its midpoint is over the rectangle's stroke.

12. Insert a new layer and name it **Text**. Create a static text block at the top part of the rectangle. Use Comic Sans MS for the font, 34 for the font size, and maroon (#660000) for the text color. Use Italic for the style and Align Left for the alignment. Type **Sandy's Party Center** in the text block. If necessary, center the text block in the top part of the rectangle.

13. Create a new text block in the center of the rectangle. Change the font size to 22, the text color to black, and the font style to Bold. Use Align Center for the alignment. In the first line, type **$15 off a one-day**, and then press the **Enter** key. Type **cake decorating class!** in the second line. If necessary, center the text block within the rectangle.

14. Add another text block to the bottom of the rectangle. Change the font size to 10, and do not apply the Bold or Italic styles. In the first line, type **Must be redeemed by March 31**. Press the **Enter** key and then type **Call for class availability**. If necessary, center the text block in the bottom part of the rectangle.

15. Add one more text block, and place this one below the rectangle. Change the font size to 22 and the font style to Bold. Use Align Left for the alignment. Type **Clip this coupon for great savings!** in this text block.

16. Return to Scene 1 and insert a new layer. Name the layer **Coupon** and insert keyframes at Frame 2 and at Frame 5. In Frame 2, place an instance of the Coupon symbol at the center of the Stage, and assign the instance the name **coupon_mc**.

17. At Frame 5, draw a rectangle with a black fill and no stroke. This rectangle represents the print area. Make the rectangle 550 pixels wide by 375 pixels high. Place the playhead at Frame 4, and use onion skinning to see both the coupon and the black rectangle at Frame 5 simultaneously. Make certain the rectangle completely covers the coupon. If necessary, reposition the rectangle in Frame 5 to cover the entire coupon.

18. Insert another layer and name it **Labels**. Insert keyframes at Frame 2 and Frame 5. In Frame 2, add the frame label **#p** and at Frame 5, add the frame label **#b**.

19. Select the Coupon_btn instance on the Stage, and expand the Actions panel. Type the following code for the button. The button will print the coupon_mc instance using the print area of the black rectangle in Frame 5 of the Coupon layer.

```
on (release) {
        print(coupon_mc, "bmovie");
}
```

20. Insert a new layer and name it **Actions**. Select Frame 1 and type `stop();` in the Actions panel. This prevents the extra frames in the Coupon layer from playing.

21. Save the **Cake.fla** file and test it. Check the Web site links by selecting them from the ComboBox list. (*Note:* If the Web site links do not work, check with your instructor. The URL addresses for the sites might have changed since the printing of this book.) Also, click the Print Coupon button to see how the coupon is printed on paper.

22. Close the **Cake.fla** file.

Case 2. Adding Video and a Printable Form to the River City Music Web Site Janet and Alex meet to discuss the Web site developed for the River City Music store. Janet wants to have a video clip incorporated into the Recital page to show an example of a piano recital. She thinks this will give site visitors an idea of how the recital hall might be used. She also wants a recital hall reservation request form added to the site that can be printed. She wants her customers to be able to submit their recital reservation requests using this form.

Alex asks you to help him revise the Recital page of the Web site by adding the video clip and the printable form. He instructs you to embed the video clip into the document and display it on the Recital page and to add a button to control the printing of the form.

If necessary, start Flash and then do the following:

1. Open the **Recital.fla** file located in the Tutorial.09\Cases folder included with your Data Files.

2. Import the **piano_clip.mpg** video file located in the Tutorial.09\Cases folder included with your Data Files. Embed the entire video into the document's library. Use DSL/Cable 256 kbps for the Compression profile. Create a new Advanced settings profile, and change the video's dimensions by cropping it by 100 pixels from the top, 50 pixels from the left, 40 pixels from the bottom, and 30 pixels from the right. Save these settings with the name **Piano clip** and the description **Crop the piano recital video clip**.

3. Create a new movie clip symbol, and name it **Piano_recital**. Add an instance of the **piano_clip.mpg** video clip to the Piano_recital movie clip extending the movie clip's Timeline the required number of frames. Set the X and Y coordinates of the video instance to 0.

4. Return to Scene 1, add a new layer above the Text layer, and name it **Video**. Insert an instance of the Piano_recital movie clip on the left side of the rectangle. Change the X coordinate for the instance to 60. Change the Y coordinate to 220. Also, name the instance **Piano_clip_mc**.

5. Modify the text block on the right side of the rectangle. Add a blank line below the existing paragraph, and then type **To reserve the hall for your group, click the button below to print the reservation form.** in the text block.

6. Insert a new layer above the Video layer, and name it **Buttons**. Open the Buttons Common Library. In the Buttons Library panel, open the Playback folder and drag an instance of the playback - stop symbol to the Stage. Place the instance right below the lower-left side of the video instance. Drag an instance of the playback - play symbol, and place it to the right of the playback - stop instance. Open the Circle Buttons folder, and drag an instance of the Circle with arrow symbol to the Stage. Place the instance right below the word "form" in the second paragraph of the text block.

7. Insert a new layer and name it **Form**. Insert a keyframe at Frame 5 of this layer. In this keyframe, add a static text block at the top of the Stage. Use Monotype Corsiva for the font, 54 for the font size, and black for the text color. Use Align Center for the alignment. Type **River City Music** and then press the **Enter** key for a new line. Type **Recital Hall Reservation Request** in the second line. Select the second line and change its font to Arial and its font size to 14. Reposition the text block by changing its X coordinate to 135 and its Y coordinate to 30.

8. Create a new static text block using Arial for the font and 14 for the font size. Use black for the text color, and Align Left for the alignment. Place the text block below the first text block, and type the following.

   Name:_____

   Address:_____

   _____

   Phone:_____

Explore
9. Select the entire text and click the Format button in the Property inspector. Set the Line spacing to 6 points.

10. With the text block still selected, change its X coordinate to 60 and its Y coordinate to 180.

11. Create another text block using the same properties as the previous text block. Type the following for the text block.

    Date of Recital Event:_____

    Time of Recital Event:_____

    Number of people atending:_____

12. Change the Line spacing to 6 points for the text block, and set its X coordinate to 60 and its Y coordinate to 320.

13. Create another text block with the same properties as the previous one, and type the following in the text block.

    For office use only:

    Reservation Confirmed:_____

    Date Confirmed:_____

    Reservation Fee Paid:_____

14. Change the Line spacing to 6 points for the text block, and set its X coordinate to 60 and its Y coordinate to 440. The text block is below the Stage area.

15. Draw a rectangle over the text block with the Name, Address, and Phone lines. Use light orange (#FFCC66) for the fill color and no stroke. Make the rectangle 200 pixels wide by 100 pixels high, and position it so that it acts as a background for the text block. Draw another rectangle over the text block with the Date of Recital Event line. Use the same fill color as the first rectangle. Make the rectangle 260 pixels wide by 70 pixels high, and position it as a background for the text block. Draw one more rectangle over the bottom text block. Use a light yellow (#FFFFCC) for the fill color. Make the rectangle 220 pixels wide by 90 pixels high, and position it so that it acts as a background for the text block.

16. Import the **piano.jpg** bitmap located in the Tutorial.09\Cases folder included with your Data Files. Import the image into the library, and then drag an instance of the bitmap to the Stage. Place the instance on the right side of the Stage. Change its X coordinate to 380 and its Y coordinate to 240.

17. Insert a blank keyframe at Frame 6 of the Form layer. Draw a large rectangle on the Stage. Use black for the fill color and no stroke. Make the rectangle 612 pixels wide by 800 pixels high to equal the size of an 8 ½ by 11 inch sheet of paper. Also, change the rectangle's X and Y coordinates to 0. This rectangle represents the print area.

18. Insert a new layer and name it **Labels**. Insert a keyframe at Frame 5 and another at Frame 6. Select Frame 5 and type **#p** for the frame label. Select Frame 6 and type **#b** for the frame label.

19. Select the instance of the playback – stop button on the Stage. Expand the Actions panel and type the following code. This code causes the video's movie clip playhead to stop.

```
on (release) {
        Piano_clip_mc.stop();
}
```

20. Select the instance of the playback – play button on the Stage. In the Script pane of the Actions panel, type the following code. This code causes the video's movie clip playhead to play.

```
on (release) {
        Piano_clip_mc.play();
}
```

21. Select the instance of the Circle with arrow button on the Stage. In the Script pane of the Actions panel, type the following code. This code prints the form using the rectangle in Frame 6 as the print area.

```
on (release) {
        print(0, "bmovie");
}
```

22. Insert a new layer above the Labels layer, and name it **Action**. Select Frame 1 of the Action layer, and type **stop();** in the Script pane of the Actions panel. This prevents the frames of the Form layer from playing.

23. Test the file. Click the buttons to stop and play the video clip. Also click the button to print the form. Close the SWF file. Save and close the **Recital.fla** file.

Case 3. Adding Video and Revising the Photos Page for the Sonny's Auto Center Web Site
Amanda meets with Sonny to discuss the status of the Weekly Specials Web site. Sonny tells Amanda that he wants to have a short video clip of the car lot added to the site to give potential customers an idea of the center's available inventory. He also wants to have the Photos page revised to display thumbnails of the vehicle pictures. He feels this would make it easier for potential customers to know what vehicles are on sale. Amanda agrees to make the changes.

Amanda asks you to help her change the Weekly Specials Web site. She instructs you to import the short video and to create a new Photos page that displays thumbnails of the pictures. She has prepared the small versions of the pictures to be used as thumbnails. She suggests using components to create the Photos page and to add a progress bar to display the loading of each picture as well as the video.

If necessary, start Flash and then do the following:

1. Create a new document 160 pixels wide by 140 pixels high with a white background. Save this document as **AutosVideo.fla** in the Tutorial.09\Cases folder included with your Data Files.

2. Import the **autos.mpg** video file into the document's library. Embed the entire video into the document's library. Use DSL/Cable 256 kbps for the Compression profile. Create a new Advanced settings profile, and change the video's dimensions by cropping it by 12 pixels from the top and 12 pixels from the bottom. Reduce the Scale value to 50% to reduce the size of the video, and select None for the Audio track to exclude any sound. Save these settings with the name **Autos** and the description **Reduce dimensions, crop video, and exclude audio**.

3. Drag an instance of the **autos.mpg** video to the Stage extending the Timeline the required number of frames. Set its X coordinate to 0 and its Y coordinate to 32. Add a static text block above the video clip. Use Arial for the font, 12 for the font size, black for the text color, and Align Left for the alignment. Type **Sonny's Main Car Lot** for the text. If necessary, reposition the text block so that it is centered on the Stage above the video clip.

4. Publish the **AutosVideo.fla** document to create the **AutosVideo.swf** file. Save and close the file.

5. Open the **Autos.fla** document located in the Tutorial.09\Cases folder included with your Data Files.

6. Drag an instance of the Loader component from the Components panel, and place it on the right side of the Stage. Assign the name **autoLoader** to the instance, and change its width to 160 pixels and its height to 140 pixels. Also set its X coordinate to 360 and its Y coordinate to 182.

7. Drag an instance of the ProgressBar component from the Components panel to the Stage. Place it below the autoLoader instance. Enter autoloader in the source parameter for the ProgressBar instance. Also, enter **autoProgress** as the instance name for this component instance.

8. Insert a new layer and name it **Actions**. Select Frame 1 of the Actions layer, and expand the Actions panel. Type `autoLoader.contentPath ="AutosVideo.swf";` to load the SWF file with the autos video clip into the autoLoader instance. The file loads as soon as the **Autos.fla** document starts playing.

9. To hide the ProgressBar instance from the Stage after the video has loaded, you need an event listener to check when the loading is complete. Then, a function needs to be run to hide the instance of the ProgressBar. To accomplish this, press the Enter key in the Actions panel, and type the following code.

```
autoLoader.addEventListener("complete", contentLoaded);
function contentLoaded() {
       autoProgress._visible = false;
}
```

10. Save and test the **Autos.fla** file. Use the Simulate Download command to test the ProgressBar. After the video is loaded, the ProgressBar instance is hidden, and the video starts to play. Close the **Autos.swf** and **Autos.fla** files.

11. Open the **Autophotos.fla** file located in the Tutorial.09\Cases folder included with your Data Files.

12. Import the **Auto1_sm.jpg**, **Auto2_sm.jpg**, and **Auto3_sm.jpg** files into the document's library. The files are located in the Tutorial.09\Cases folder included with your Data Files. Create a new movie clip symbol, and name it **Thumbnails**. Select Export for ActionScript in the Linkage section of the advanced section of the Create New Symbol dialog box. Make certain that Thumbnails is also entered in the Identifier text box.

13. In symbol-editing mode, create a rectangle in the center of the Stage. Use a light yellow for the fill color and no stroke. Make the rectangle 90 pixels wide by 180 pixels high. Make its X and Y coordinates 0. Add a new layer and name it **Small Photos**. On this layer, drag an instance of the **Auto1_sm.jpg** bitmap to the center of the Stage. Set its X coordinate to 4 and its Y coordinate to 12. Drag an instance of the **Auto2_sm.jpg** bitmap, and place it below the first picture on the Stage. Set its X coordinate to 12 and its Y coordinate to 60. Drag an instance of the **Auto3_sm.jpg** bitmap, and place it below the second picture on the Stage. Set its X coordinate to 12 and its Y coordinate to 120.

14. Select the top thumbnail and convert it to a button symbol. Name the symbol **pic1_btn**. Select the second thumbnail and convert it to a button symbol with the name **pic2_btn**. Then select the third picture and convert it to a button symbol with the name **pic3_btn**.

15. Select the top button instance, and expand the Actions panel. Type the following code in the Script pane. This code loads the **Auto1.jpg** photo into a Loader component instance you will add later in these steps.

```
on (release) {
        _root.autoLoader.contentPath="Auto1.jpg";
}
```

16. Select the second button instance, and type the following code in the Script pane to load the **Auto2.jpg** photo into the Loader component instance.

```
on (release) {
        _root.autoLoader.contentPath="Auto2.jpg";
}
```

17. Select the third button instance, and type the following code in the Script pane.

```
on (release) {
        _root.autoLoader.contentPath="Auto3.jpg";
}
```

18. Return to Scene 1 and drag an instance of the ScrollPane component from the Components panel to the left side of the Stage. Change the component's width to 110 pixels and its height to 80 pixels. Also, change its X coordinate to 65 and its Y coordinate 220. In the Property inspector, enter **Thumbnails** for the contentPath parameter.

19. Create a static text block above the ScrollPane instance. Use Verdana for the font, 12 for the font size, and black for the text color. Use Align Left for the alignment. Type **Click a thumbnail below**, and then press the Enter key. Then type **to see the larger picture** in the second line. Set the text block's X coordinate to 50 and its Y coordinate to 180.

20. Drag an instance of the Loader component from the Components panel to the right side of the Stage. Change the component's width to 300 pixels and its height to 225 pixels. Also, change its X coordinate to 230 and its Y coordinate to 165. Name the instance **autoLoader**.

21. The ScrollPane with the thumbnails and the Loader to show the photos is now complete. To add a progress bar that will display when each picture loads, drag an instance of the ProgressBar component from the Components panel to the right side of the Stage. Set its X coordinate to 300 and its Y coordinate to 250. Name the instance **autoProgress** and enter **autoLoader** in its source parameter.

22. Insert a new layer and name it **Actions**. Select Frame 1 of the layer and, if necessary, expand the Actions panel. Type **autoProgress._visible = false;** to hide the ProgressBar instance initially. You only want it to display when a picture is loading. You also want to hide the ProgressBar after a picture has loaded in the Loader component. Type the following code to create an event listener to check when the loading is complete and to run the function to hide the ProgressBar instance.

```
autoLoader.addEventListener("complete", contentLoaded);
function contentLoaded() {
        autoProgress._visible = false;
}
```

23. To display the ProgressBar instance when a picture is loading, you need to add a line of code to each of the thumbnail buttons to change the visibility of the ProgressBar instance. Edit the Thumbnails symbol and select the top button. Add a new line after the opening curly brace, and type `_root.autoProgress._visible = true;` to make the ProgressBar instance visible when the button is clicked. Add this same line to the code for the other two buttons so that the ProgressBar instance will be made visible each time either button is clicked.

24. Save and test the **Autophotos.fla** file. Use the Simulate Download command with a download setting of DSL (32.6 KB/s) to test the ProgressBar and click each thumbnail to see the ProgessBar display.. After a picture is loaded, the ProgressBar instance is hidden.

25. Close the **Autophotos.swf** and **Autophotos.fla** files.

Case 4. Revising the Loan Calculator and Adding Printable Content to the LAL Financial Web Site In their weekly staff meeting, Elizabeth and Michael discuss the progress you have made with the LAL Financial Web site. After reviewing the loan payment calculator, Michael asks if it is possible to limit the values that can be entered into the text fields used for the calculation. He wants to have values that the user can select instead of the user typing in a value. Michael also requests that a table of certificates of deposit rates be available for customers to print from the Rates page. If feasible, he eventually wants to have other information available for printing on this page. Elizabeth agrees to have the changes made to the loan calculator and to create a printable table of rates on the Rates page.

Elizabeth assigns you the task of revising the Loan Calculator page. She provides a draft of the file for you to complete. The draft is based on the Loan Calculator page you previously created. She also provides an Adobe Acrobat (.pdf) file with a table of the certificates of deposit rates, and she instructs you to import it into the Rates document and to create a button that will print the table.

If necessary, start Flash and then do the following:

1. Open the **PaymentCalc.fla** file located in the Tutorial.09\Cases folder included with your Data Files.

Explore 2. Drag an instance of the List component from the Components panel to the Stage, and place it right below the Loan Amount text block. Change the width of the component instance to 70 pixels and its height to 40 pixels. Enter **Principal** for the instance name. If necessary, reposition the instance so that it is centered below the Loan Amount text block. In the Property inspector, enter the values 10000 through 100000 in increments of 10000 in the data parameter text box. You will have ten values. In the labels parameter, also enter the values 10000 through 100000 in increments of 10000.

Explore 3. Drag an instance of the NumericStepper component from the Components panel to the Stage, and place it right below the No. of Months text block. Change the width of the instance to 50 pixels, and enter **Months** for the instance name. If necessary, reposition the instance so that it is centered below the No. of Months text block. In the Property inspector, enter **120** in the maximum parameter text box, **12** in the minimum parameter text box, and **12** in the stepSize parameter text box. The NumericStepper instance displays the number of months starting with 12 and ending with 120 in increments of 12.

Explore 4. Drag another instance of the NumericStepper component, and place it right below the Annual Rate text block. Change the width of the instance to 60 pixels, and enter **Rate** for the instance name. If necessary, reposition the instance so that it is centered below the Annual Rate text block. In the Property inspector, enter **8** in the maximum parameter text box, **2** in the minimum parameter text box, and **.25** in the stepSize parameter text box. The NumericStepper instance displays the rate values starting with 2 and ending with 8 in increments of .25.

5. Drag an instance of the Button component from the Components panel to the Stage, and place it right below the dynamic text field that is below the Monthly Payment text block. Enter **Calc_btn** for the instance name, and enter **Calculate** for the label parameter in the Property inspector.

Explore ▶ 6. Insert a new layer and name it **Actions**. The ActionScript code required to calculate the loan payment is in a separate file. To import the code from the file into Frame 1 of the Actions layer, select Frame 1 and expand the Actions panel. Click the options menu control in the Actions panel, and then click Import Script. Select **calcPayment.as** located in the Tutorial.09\Cases folder included with your Data Files, and then click the Open button. This code is contained within a function named `calc()`.

7. Type the following code in the blank line at the top of the code in the Script pane. This creates an event listener to check when the button instance has been clicked and to run the `calc()` function to calculate the loan payment.

```
Calc_btn.addEventListener("click", calc);
```

8. Save and test the file. Select various combinations of values for the loan amount, number of months, and annual rate. Enter **30000** for the loan amount, **48** for the number of months, and **5** for the annual rate. Click the Calculate button. A monthly payment of 691 displays. Close the **PaymentCalc.swf** and **PaymentCalc.fla** files.

9. Open the **Rates.fla** file located in the Tutorial.09\Cases folder included with your Data Files.

10. Create a static text block below the title text block. Use Garamond for the font, 12 for the font size, and black for the text color. Use Bold, Italic, and Align Left. Type **Click a button below to print a table of rates**. Set the text block's X coordinate to 140 and its Y coordinate to 150.

11. Create a static text block below the first two text blocks. Use Garamond for the font, 16 for the font size, and black for the text color. Do not use Bold or Italic. Use Align Left for the alignment. Type **Certificates of Deposit Rates**.

12. Convert the last text block to a button symbol, and name the symbol **certificate_btn**. Edit the button and add a keyframe in the Over frame. In the Over frame, change the text color to white and apply Bold formatting. Insert a new layer and name it **Background**. Move the Background layer so that it is below Layer 1.

13. Insert a keyframe in the Over frame of the Background layer. Draw a rectangle where the text is on the Stage. Use brown (#663300) for the fill color, and do not include a stroke. Make the rectangle 200 pixels wide by 25 pixels high. Set the rectangle's X and Y coordinates to 0.

14. Return to the document's main Timeline, and insert a new layer above the Action layer. Name the new layer **Print Background**. Insert a keyframe at Frame 5 of this layer. Draw a large rectangle using white for the fill color and no stroke. Make the rectangle 612 pixels wide by 800 pixels high. Set its X and Y coordinates to 0. This rectangle serves as a background for the content to be printed. Lock this layer.

Explore ▶ 15. Insert a blank keyframe at Frame 5 of the Contents layer. With Frame 5 selected, import the **LALrates.pdf** file to the Stage. The file is located in the Tutorial.09\Cases folder included with your Data Files. In the Import Options dialog box, select the Scenes, Layers, and All radio buttons. Also, ensure that the Maintain text blocks check box is selected. After clicking OK, if a Missing Font Warning alert box displays, click the Use Default button.

16. Insert a new layer and name it **Label**. Insert a keyframe at Frame 5 of this layer, and enter **#p** for the frame label.

17. Select Frame 1 of the Actions layer, and expand the Actions panel. Type **stop();** as the last line of the code in the Script pane to prevent the playhead from moving past Frame 1.

18. Select the certificate_btn instance on the Stage. Type the following code in the Actions panel. This prints the contents of Frame 5 when the button is clicked and released.

```
on (release) {
      print(0, "bframe");
}
```

19. Test the **Rates.fla** document. Click the button to print the table of rates. Close the **Rates.swf** file.

20. Save and close the **Rates.fla** file.

QUICK | CHECK ANSWERS

Session 9.1

1. Video formats that can be imported into a Flash document include .mpg, .avi, and .dv.
2. Compression is the removing of redundant data from video frames. Two types of compression techniques include temporal and spatial.
3. The compression technique that uses keyframes to compare subsequent frames in a video is temporal.
4. A codec is a compressor/decompressor program to compress video and then decompress it for playback.
5. The Sorenson Spark codec is used by Flash.
6. The typical frame rate of video played over the Internet is 10 to 15 frames per second.
7. The two methods in which video can be used in Flash are embedding and linking.

Session 9.2

1. A Flash component is a prebuilt movie clip with parameters.
2. The component that can be used to display a list of options in a drop-down list is the ComboBox.
3. The parameter you set in the ProgressBar component to monitor the loading of content in a Loader component instance is contentPath.
4. The statement registers the `contentLoaded` function with the `myLoader` instance. When the content in `myLoader` has finished loading, the `complete` event causes the `contentLoaded` function to execute.
5. The parameter in the ScrollPane component used to set whether to display the horizontal scroll bars is hScrollPolicy.

Session 9.3

1. Two methods used for printing Flash content include using the Flash Player's context menu and using the Web browser's Print command.
2. With the `print()` function, you use the "bmovie" argument when you have placed an object in a frame whose bounding box is used to determine the print area.
3. You use the #p frame label to mark a frame that is printable.
4. You use the #b frame label to mark a frame containing an object whose bounding box determines the print area.
5. You use the !#p frame label to disable printing from the Flash Player context menu.

TASK REFERENCE

TASK	PAGE #	RECOMMENDED METHOD
ActionScript, add to a button	343	See Reference Window: Adding ActionScript Code to a Button
ActionScript, add to a frame	348	Select frame, open Actions panel, double-click action from Actions toolbox
Behavior, add to a button	236	Select button instance on the Stage, click ⊞ in Behaviors panel, point to a behavior type, click the behavior, if necessary, modify values in dialog, box click OK
Behavior, add to a frame	239	Select frame, click ⊞ in Behaviors panel, point to a behavior type, click the behavior, if necessary, modify values in dialog box, click OK
Bitmap, change properties	264	Select bitmap in Library panel, click ⊙
Bitmap, convert to a vector	276	Select bitmap instance, click Modify, point to Bitmap, click Trace Bitmap, set Trace Bitmap options, click OK
Bitmap, import	260	See Reference Window: Importing a Bitmap
Button, add from common library	216	Click Window, point to Other Panels, point to Common Libraries, click Buttons, drag button from Button Library panel to the Stage
Button, create	222	See Reference Window: Creating a Button
Button, test within program window	218	Click Control, click Enable Simple Buttons, click the button on the Stage
Colors, select	36	Click Stroke color control list arrow or Fill color control list arrow to open color pop-up window, click desired color swatch
Components, create instance	433	Drag component instance from Components panel to Stage, set component parameters in Property inspector
Dynamic Text, create	389	Click Ⓐ, click Text type list arrow in the Property inspector, select Dynamic Text, click or click and drag on the Stage to create a text block, type text
External Library, open	326	Click File, point to Import, click Open External Library
Fill, apply	69	Click ⬗, select a fill color, select a Gap Size modifier, click the area to apply fill
Flash, exit program	49	Click File, click Exit
Flash document, open	9	Click File, click Open, select file, click Open
Flash document, close	49	Click File, click Close
Flash document, create from template	327	Click File, click New, click Templates tab, select category, select template, click OK
Flash document, modify	31	Click Modify, click Document
Flash document, preview	10	Click Control, click Test Movie in a Flash Player window
Flash document, preview	10	Click Control, click Play; or press Enter within program window
Flash document, preview	13	Drag playhead in Timeline header by scrubbing

TASK REFERENCE

TASK	PAGE #	RECOMMENDED METHOD
Flash document, preview	10	Click File, point to Publish Preview, click default (HTML) or click HTML in a Web page
Flash document, test animation	141	See Reference Window: Testing a Document's Animation
Flash document, test download	400	Click Control, click Test Movie, click View, click Simulate Download
Flash MX 2004, start	7	Click [start], point to All Programs, point to Macromedia, click Macromedia Flash MX 2004
Flash SWF file, display context menu	5	Right-click the Flash SWF file
Flash SWF file, publish	290	Click File, click Publish
Frame behavior or action, test	240	Click Control, click Enable Simple Frame Actions
Frame label, add	239	Select frame, type label in Frame Label text box in the Property inspector
Frames, copy	123	Select frame or frames, right-click selected frames, click Copy Frames
Gradient, create	281	Click Fill style list arrow in Color Mixer panel, select Radial or Linear, set gradient pointers and their colors
Gradient fill, apply	283	Click [fill icon], select gradient for fill color, click object on the Stage
Gradient fill, transform	285	Click [transform icon], click gradient on the Stage, adjust gradient
Grid, display	28	Click View, point to Grid, click Show Grid
Grid, edit	28	Click View, point to Grid, click Edit Grid
Grouped object, edit	35	Select object, click Edit, click Edit Selected, or double-click object
Grouped object, exit edit mode	35	Click Edit, click Edit All
Guides, create	30	Display rulers, drag guide line from a ruler to the Stage
Guides, edit	30	Click View, point to Guides, click Edit Guides
Help, display contents	47	Expand the Help panel, click the Help tab, double-click a category or click a topic
Help, display Search	47	Expand the Help panel, click [search icon], enter keyword(s), click Search, double-click a category or click a topic
Image, export	86	Click File, point to Export, click Export Image, select location, enter filename, click Save As type list arrow to select file format, click Save
Input Text, create	388	Click [A], click Text type list box in the Property inspector, select Input Text, click or click and drag on the Stage to create a text block, type text
Instance, create	97	Drag copy of symbol from the Library panel to the Stage

TASK	PAGE #	RECOMMENDED METHOD
Instance name, add	372	Select instance on Stage, enter name in Instance Name text box in Property inspector
Keyframe, insert	136	Select frame in Timeline, click Insert, point to Timeline, click Keyframe
Layer, add	120	Click Insert, point to Timeline, click Layer, or click ⊞
Layer, change properties	120	Click the layer, click Modify, point to Timeline, click Layer Properties, change layer properties, click OK
Layer, delete	119	Click the layer, click 🗑
Layer, select	119	Click the layer in Timeline
Layer folder, insert	121	Click Insert, point to Timeline, click Layer Folder
Library panel, change to Narrow (default) view	95	Click ▯ in the Library panel
Library panel, change to Wide view	94	Click ▢ in the Library panel
Library panel, open	93	Click Window, click Library
Lines, draw with Pen tool	73	Click ✒, select colors, drag pointer on the Stage, or click to create points on the Stage
Lines, draw with Pencil tool	67	Click ✏, click Pencil mode modifier, set stroke properties, draw on the Stage
Motion Guide layer, create	166	Click Insert, point to Timeline, click Motion Guide
Objects, align on the Stage	231	Select several objects at one time, open the Align panel, click the desired align button
Object, change its position on the Stage	23	Drag object with ▶, or change object's X and Y values in the Property inspector
Object, copy	75	Select object, click Edit, click Copy, click Paste
Object, flip horizontally	75	Select object, click Modify, point to Transform, click Flip Horizontal
Object, group	72	Select several objects at one time, click Modify, click Group
Object, modify anchor points	42	See Reference Window: Using the Subselection Tool
Object, modify with Selection tool	40	Click ▶, drag a line or a corner of the object to change its shape
Object, move	39	Click ▶, select the object, drag the object
Object, scale on the Stage	23	Select object with ▶, change object's W and H values in Property inspector
Object, select with Selection tool	38	Click ▶, click or double-click the object; or draw a rectangular marquee around the object

TASK	PAGE #	RECOMMENDED METHOD
Objects, select with Lasso tool	44	Click ⌕, click and drag to select objects; or click ⌕, ⚑, click points around objects
Object, transform	79	See Reference Window: Transforming an Object using the Free Transform Tool
Objects, distribute to layers	184	Select objects, click Modify, point to Timeline, click Distribute to Layers
Oval, draw	59	Click ◯, select stroke and fill colors, click and drag pointer on the Stage
Panels, collapse	19	Click ▼ on the panel's title bar
Panels, expand	19	Click ▶ on the panel's title bar
Panels, open	20	Click Window, point to Design Panels, Development Panels, or Other Panels, click desired panel
Panels, set to default layout	7	Click Window, point to Panel Sets, click Default Layout
Publish settings, change	290	Click File, click Publish Settings, select Type, click a tab, select options, click OK
Publish profile, save	291	Change publish settings, click + in Publish Settings dialog box, enter a name for publish profile, click OK
Rectangle, draw	65	Click ⬜, select stroke and fill colors, click and drag pointer on the Stage
Rectangle, specify rounded corners	65	Click ⬜, click ⌐, enter point value, click OK
Rulers, display	30	Click View, click Rulers
Scene, duplicate	128	Open Scene panel, select scene, click 🔲
Scene, rename	126	Open Scene panel, double-click scene, enter new name
Scene, select	127	Click 🎬, select Scene
Snap to Objects, select	64	Click View, point to Snapping, click Snap to Objects to toggle on and off
Sound, add to a button	244	See Reference Window: Adding a Sound to a Button
Stage, move its view	26	Click ✋, drag Stage to new position
Stage, show all	9	Click View, point to Magnification, click Show All
Stage view, change	25	See Reference Window: Changing the View of the Stage
Steps, replay	88	Open History panel, select steps in History panel, select object on Stage, and click Replay in History panel
Steps, undo	88	Click Edit, click Undo or open History panel, then move slider to previous steps in History panel
Stroke or Fill properties, copying	71	See Reference Window: Using the Eyedropper Tool
Symbol, create	96	See Reference Window: Creating a Symbol

TASK	PAGE #	RECOMMENDED METHOD
Symbol, create duplicate	97	Select symbol in Library panel, click ☰▾, click Duplicate, enter duplicate symbol's name, click OK
Symbol, edit	99	Select symbol in Library panel, click ☰▾, click Edit
Symbol, swap	150	Select instance of symbol on Stage, click Swap button in Property inspector, select symbol, click OK
Symbol, copy from external library	326	Open external library, drag symbol from Library panel to Stage
Text, create	82	Click A, set text properties in the Property inspector, click or click and drag on the Stage to create a text block, type text
Text, spell check	83	Click Text, click Check Spelling
Template, create	324	See Reference Window: Creating a Flash Template
Timeline, change its view	118	Click ⊞, click desired view
Timeline, collapse	58	Click Timeline title bar
Timeline Effect, add	131	Select object or objects, click Insert, point to Timeline Effects, point to Assistants, Effects, or Transform/Transition, click effect
Tools, select	17	See Reference Window: Selecting Tools on the Toolbar
Video, import	242	Click File, point to Import, click Import to Library, click Files of Type list arrow, select All Video Formats, select video file, click Open, follow steps in Video Import Wizard
Video, create instance	426	Drag video instance from Library to Stage, click Yes to add frames to Timeline
Web page, preview	296	Start Internet Explorer, click File, click Open, click Browse, select HTML file, click Open, click OK
Zoom level, change	26	Click 🔍, click ⊕ or ⊖, click an area of the Stage